In Dialogue with Another Gospel?

SOCIETY OF BIBLICAL LITERATURE

DISSERTATION SERIES
Saul M. Olyan, Old Testament Editor
Mark Allan Powell, New Testament Editor

Number 178
IN DIALOGUE WITH ANOTHER GOSPEL?
The Influence of the Fourth Gospel on the
Passion Narrative of the Gospel of Luke

by
Mark A. Matson

Mark A. Matson

IN DIALOGUE WITH ANOTHER GOSPEL?
The Influence of the Fourth Gospel on the Passion Narrative of the Gospel of Luke

Society of Biblical Literature
Atlanta

IN DIALOGUE WITH ANOTHER GOSPEL?
The Influence of the Fourth Gospel on the Passion Narrative of the Gospel of Luke

by
Mark A. Matson
Ph.D., Duke University, 1998
D. Moody Smith, Dissertation Advisor

Copyright © 2001 by the Society of Biblical Literature

All rights reserved. No part of this work may be reproduced or transmitted in any form or by any means, electronic or mechanical, including photocopying and recording, or by means of any information storage or retrieval system, except as may be expressly permitted by the 1976 Copyright Act or in writing from the publisher. Requests for permission should be addressed in writing to the Rights and Permissions Office, Society of Biblical Literature, 825 Houston Mill Road, Atlanta, GA 30329, USA.

Library of Congress Cataloging-in-Publication Data

Matson, Mark A., 1951–
    In dialogue with another gospel? : the influence of the Fourth Gospel on the Passion narrative of the Gospel of Luke / Mark A. Matson.
        p. cm.— (Dissertation series / Society of Biblical Literature ; no. 178)
    Includes bibliographical references.
    ISBN 1-58983-010-5 (alk. paper)
        1. Bible. N.T. Luke XXII–XXIV—Relation to John. 2. Passion narratives (Gospels—Criticism, interpretation, etc. I. Title. II. Dissertation series (Society of Biblical Literature) ; no. 178.

BS2595.52 M38 2001
226.4'06—dc21   2001020863

08 07 06 05 04 03 02 01   5 4 3 2 1

Printed in the United States of America
on acid-free paper

DEDICATION

This dissertation is dedicated to Angela Beth Matson, my first daughter, who patiently followed me to Durham in my desire to pursue this degree, but who did not see its completion, having preceded me in joining the Lord.

ὅτι αὐτὸς ὁ κύριος ἐν κελεύσματι ἐν φωνῇ ἀρχαγγέλου καὶ ἐν σάλπιγγι θεοῦ, καταβήσεται ἀπ' οὐρανοῦ καὶ οἱ νεκροὶ ἐν Χριστῷ ἀναστήσονται πρῶτον, ἔπειτα ἡμεῖς οἱ ζῶντες οἱ περλειπόμενοι ἅμα σὺν αὐτοῖς ἁρπαγησόμεθα ἐν νεφέλαις εἰς ἀπάντησιν τοῦ κυρίου εἰς ἀέρα· καὶ οὕτως πάντοτε σὺν κυρίῳ ἐσόμεθα.

1 Thessalonians 4:16-17.

TABLE OF CONTENTS

Acknowledgements xiii

Chapter 1. Introduction 1
The Issue of John and the Synoptics: Is John Dependent? 6
Problems Relative to Luke: Luke's Authorial Method 11
Reading Luke: Rhetoric and Intertextuality 14
The Shape of This Study 18

Chapter 2. The Study of the Relationship of Luke and John
   The Project in the Context of Existing Scholarship 21
Early Approaches to the Problem 22
    F. C. Baur 22
    H. J. Holtzmann 25
    P. Feine 28
    Otto Zurhellen 29
The Argument for Common Tradition 32
    Julius Schniewind 32
    F. C. Grant 38
    E. Osty 41
    Hans Klein 42
    Pierson Parker 45
    Robert Maddox 48
    Stephan Landis 51
    Matti Myllykoski 54
The Argument for John's Literary Dependence 58

J. Amedee Bailey 58
M.-É. Boismard 63
Frans Neirynck 67
The Merging of Literary and Tradition: Continuing Orality 72
Anton Dauer 72
Questioning the Relationship: New Approaches 78
Lamar Cribbs 78
Barbara Shellard 83
Summary of Approaches to the Luke-John Agreements 85

Chapter 3. The Pattern of Luke-John Relationships 91
Close Linguistic or Striking Substantive Similarities 93
Table 1 93
Discussion 97
Summary 106
Common Order 107
Table 2 107
Discussion 109
Summary 116
Common Geographical References 117
Table 3 117
Discussion 118
Summary 124
Common Individual Facts or Allusions 125
Table 4 125
Discussion 130
Summary 145
Common Omissions 145
Table 5 145
Discussion 148
Summary 152
Common Named Characters 152
Table 6 152
Discussion 153
Summary 155

Common Themes or Theology 155
    Table 7 155
    Discussion 156
    Summary 162
Conclusion 162

Chapter 4. Textual Variants:
The Western Non-Interpolations 165
Introduction 165
Method of Textual Criticism 168
External Evidence: The Documentary Attestation 170
    Luke 5:26 175
    Luke 5:39 176
    Luke 7:7 177
    Luke 9:2 177
    Luke 11:49 178
    Luke 12:19 178
    Luke 18:32 178
    Luke 19:25 179
    Summary 179
Internal Arguments 180
    Luke 22:19-20 180
    Luke 24:3 184
    Luke 24:6 186
    Luke 24:9 188
    Luke 24:12 189
    Luke 24:36 208
    Luke 24:40 211
    Luke 24:51 and 52 213
Conclusions 222
Appendix: Instances where the Western Text is Shorter 224

**Chapter 5. Luke's Editorial Method and
   the Approach of this Study** 233
  The Surgical Knife: Separating Source
   and Redaction in Luke 236
    Friedrich Rehkopf 236
    Tim Schramm 238
    Joachim Jeremias 241
    Vincent Taylor 243
    Critique and Summary 245
  Luke as Composer: Goulder and Drury 247
  Emphasizing Contents: Soards 252
  The Approach of This Study 256
    Analyze Closeness to Mark 259
    Note Similarities with Other Texts 260
    Compare Closely with John 260
    Consider the Likelihood of Luke's Compositional Practice .. 261
  What is Proof? 261

Chapter 6. Luke Chapter 22 263
  Introduction to the Passover. Luke 22:1–2 264
  Betrayal by Judas. Luke 22:3–6 266
  Preparation for the Passover. Luke 22:7–13 270
  The Last Supper. Luke 22:14–20 271
    Luke 22:14 272
    Luke 22:15–16 272
    Luke 22:17–18 273
    Luke 22:19–20 273
  Betrayal Prediction. Luke 22:21–30 274
  Peter's Denial Predicted. Luke 22:31–33 279
  The Two Swords. Luke 22:35–38 287
  Prayer on Mount of Olives. Luke 22:39–46 288
  Jesus' Arrest. Luke 22:47–53 293
    Luke 22:47a 295
    Luke 22:47b–48 296
    Luke 22:49–51 298

Luke 22:52–53 301
Peter's Denial. Luke 22:54–65 303
   Luke 22:54 307
   Luke 22:55 308
   Luke 22:56–60a 309
   Luke 22:60b–62 310
   Luke 22:63–64 310
Trial Before Jewish Leaders. Luke 22:66–71 311
   Luke 22:66 312
   Luke 22:67–68 312
   Luke 22:69 314
   Luke 22:70 315
   Luke 22:71 316
Conclusions 317

Chapter 7. Luke Chapter 23 319
   Trial Before Pilate (Pt. 1). Luke 23:1–5 319
      The Initial Accusations 322
      The Crowd 325
      Statement of Innocence 327
      The Additional Charge 330
      Summary 332
   Trial Before Herod. Luke 23:6–12 333
      Proto-Luke, Midrash, and Lukan Invention 334
      Tradition 336
      Use of Other Gospels 337
      Summary 339
   Trial Before Pilate (Pt. 2). Luke 23:13–25 339
      The Transitional Passage, vv. 13–16 342
      The Pilate Trial, Part 2 344
      Summary 360
   Road to Golgotha. Luke 23:26–32 363
   Crucifixion. Luke 23:33–38 365
   Two Criminals. Luke 23:39–43 368
   Death of Jesus. Luke 23:44–49 369

Burial of Jesus. Luke 23:50–56 373
Conclusions 376

Chapter 8. Luke Chapter 24 379
   The Empty Tomb. Luke 23:56b–24:12 381
      Luke 23:56b, 24:1–3 386
      Luke 24:4–5 392
      Luke 24:6–8 396
      Luke 24:9–11 399
      Luke 24:12 401
      Summary 409
   The Emmaus Narrative. Luke 24:13–35 410
      Lukan Style 412
      Tradition 415
      Summary 421
   Appearance before the Disciples. Luke 24:36–43 422
      Signs of Johannine Style 424
      Luke's Editing 426
      Ignatius' Testimony 429
      Summary 433
   Luke's Great Commission. Luke 24:44–49 434
   The Ascension. Luke 24:50–53 436
   Conclusions 437

Chapter 9. Conclusions 439
   Preliminary Aspects of the Study 439
   The Analysis of Texts 441
   Luke's Work as Author 445
   Future Research 446

Bibliography 449

ACKNOWLEDGEMENTS

    This dissertation would never have been possible without the continual support of my wife, Joy, and children, Emily and James. This book represents far too many evenings away from home and far too much time together sacrificed. I am also very appreciative for the emotional and spiritual support that I have received during the entire process from all the members of the Cole Mill Road Church of Christ, but particularly Dr. Paul Watson, who helped me continue to study and write after the very dark days of the death of my daughter.
    I am most grateful to my adviser, Professor D. Moody Smith, who has encouraged me, prodded me, and always been supportive of my studies. Special thanks are due to Carol Shoun, who very carefully read my work in order to hold me to a standard of writing that I too often ignore.

Chapter 1

INTRODUCTION

The relationship between John and the Synoptics has puzzled scholars for many years. A variety of general solutions has been offered; indeed, the debate over the relationship continues.[1] Within this broad relationship (or group of relationships), however, the linkage between John and Luke is unique. John's points of similarity with Luke are more extensive than those with any other of the Synoptics, and they present special difficulties that challenge the current solutions.[2] In this study I propose to re-examine the relationship between John and Luke, giving special attention to the Passion narrative, with a fresh perspective that brackets Johannine posterity.

In Luke's Passion and Resurrection narratives, the evangelist takes a significantly independent approach to the account which, in the

---

[1] A good review of the current state of the question is offered variously (from different perspectives) in D. Moody Smith, *John Among the Gospels* (Minneapolis: Fortress Press, 1992) and Frans Neirynck, "John and the Synoptics: 1975–1990," in *John and the Synoptics*, Colloguium Biblicum Lovaniense, 1990, ed. A. Denaux (Leuven: Leuven University Press, 1992), 3–62.

[2] Pierson Parker, "Luke and the Fourth Evangelist" (*NTS* 9 (1963): 331) presents a comparative list of similarities and concludes that while John and Matthew have similarities in 26 cases, and John and Mark share material 29 times, John and Luke are similar in 124 instances! Even if one disagrees on some of the particulars, the lopsided comparison is impressive.

main, he shares with Matthew and Mark.³ His approach is particularly striking since outside the Passion Luke tends to agree, at least in material common to the three Synoptics,⁴ quite closely with either Mark or Matthew.⁵ Luke's independent approach to the Passion narrative is exemplified in the opening pericopes of chapter 22.⁶

All three synoptic Gospels mark the beginning of the Passion with a reference to the nearness of the Passover feast and the simultaneous decision by the chief priests and scribes (elders) to put Jesus to death.⁷ But after that initial agreement come significant differences: Luke leaves out the story of the anointing at Bethany (Mark 14:3–9; Matt 26:6–13, but cf. Luke 7:36–50), adds the feature of Satan's entry into Judas before the common narrative of Judas' agreement to betray Jesus (Luke 22:3), reports a significantly different

---

³ The reference to "his" for the various evangelists implies no judgment about the authorship of the Gospels; it is merely a convenient convention.

⁴ Luke follows Mark quite closely in much of the gospel, but with three major exceptions: the omission of material found in Mark 6:45–8:27, and the significant addition of non-Markan material at Luke 6:20–8:3 and 9:51–18:14.

⁵ The literature on the Synoptic relationship is vast. With regard to the existence of a clear relationship between Matthew, Mark and Luke one might simply refer to some common discussions of the problem: E. P. Sanders and Margaret Davies, *Studying the Synoptic Gospels* (Philadelphia: Trinity Press, 1989); Robert Stein, *The Synoptic Problem*, (Grand Rapids: Baker Book House, 1987); Werner Kümmel, *Introduction to the New Testament* (Nashville: Abingdon Press, 1973), 38–80. The particular problems concerning Luke's relationship to the other synoptics, especially the question of the existence of other sources ("L") or a pre-Lukan gospel, are beyond the scope of this discussion. A good survey of the basic issues is contained in Joseph Fitzmyer, *The Gospel According to Luke* (I–IX), AB 28 (Garden City, NY: Doubleday, 1979), 63–106. On the variation of Luke's Passion narrative, cf. Fitzmyer, *The Gospel According to Luke* (X–XXIV), AB 28A (Garden City, NY: Doubleday, 1985), 1365–1369, and Vincent Taylor, *The Passion Narrative of St. Luke*, (Cambridge: University Press, 1972), 3–38, as well as Marion Soards, *The Passion According to Luke* (Sheffield: JSOT Press, 1987), 13–16.

⁶ A fuller exposition of these points is found in chapter 6 below.

⁷ Matt 26:1–5; Mark 14:1–2; Luke 22:1–2.

Last Supper (Luke 22:15-20, cf. Mark 14:22-25, Matt 26:26-29), and details a dispute over rank among the disciples after the dinner (Luke 22:24-30). Yet these major differences are interspersed into a narrative in which Luke generally agrees with Mark and/or Matthew: the account of Judas' dealings with the high priests, the preparations for the Passover, Jesus' prediction of Judas' betrayal at dinner, and even sections of the language in the Last Supper account are very close or virtually identical in the three synoptic Gospels.

Those examples from the short stretch of narrative in Luke 22 are illustrative of Luke's approach throughout the rest of the Passion story: in some cases material is added, missing, or quite different as compared with Mark and Matthew, while in other cases Luke seems to follow quite closely the Mark/Matthew model. It is as if Luke were weaving together more than one account, interspersing elements from various sources. In the Passion story, Luke's reliance on the Markan outline is much looser than in the rest of the Third Gospel, but it is still apparent that he knew either Mark or Matthew (or a source common with Matthew) or both.[8] There is significant variety in Luke's presentation. At times the level of correspondence is minute, following the wording of Mark and Matthew very closely. For instance, in the story of the preparation for the Passover (Luke 22:7-14) not only is the order similar between Luke and Mark, but many verses (e.g. verses 11 and 12) are almost identical. Sometimes the text seems to be close to the Mark/Matthew story, although showing editorial freedom. This is seen in the prayer on the Mount of Olives (Luke 22:39-46); the story is clearly the same, but it has been shortened and modified. And sometimes the story is very different, as Luke's account of the Last Supper (Luke 22:14-38) would suggest: not only the language

---

[8] I am assuming Markan priority and, in particular, that Mark is a primary source for Luke. Thus the dominant two-source model for synoptic relationships (i.e., Mark + Q), is generally presumed. It is possible, although in general this is not crucial to the current study, that Luke also used Matthew as a source. Cf. M. D. Goulder, *Luke: A New Paradigm* (Sheffield: JSOT Press, 1989) for a full argument of this relationship.

surrounding the bread and cup, but also the order of events is very different, and Luke reports a farewell instruction to the disciples.

A closer examination of the instances in Luke 22:1–27 named above where Luke does not follow the Mark/Matthew pattern reveals an intriguing feature: many of those instances in which Luke differs from the other synoptic accounts occur at points where the parallel Johannine narrative differs also. Often there are distinctive similarities between Luke and John at these points. Thus Luke varies from Matthew and Mark in the account of Judas' betrayal (Luke 22:3–6 and par.), primarily in the report that Satan had entered into him. But like Luke, John too has Satan entering into Judas (John 13:2, 27). A major break from the Mark/Matthew account occurs in the early verses of Luke's Passion narrative, where Luke omits the account of Jesus' anointing in Bethany. But Luke had told a different anointing story earlier, in chapter 7. And while John does report the anointing at Bethany just before the Passion (John 12:1–8), his account is in many ways closer to Luke's: Jesus' feet are anointed, and the ointment is mopped up with the woman's hair. Similarly, in Luke the conclusion of the Last Supper contains a teaching on rank and service that uses a story found in a different place in Mark/Matthew (Mark 10:41–45, Matt 20:24–28), although with significant differences. In Luke's account, the imagery of table service and Jesus' own personal example in service, bear at least some similarities to John's account of the final supper, in which Jesus washes the disciples' feet (John 13:3–20). Despite these points of similarity, though, there are relatively few uses of similar or identical language that would strongly suggest that Luke used a text in common with John. Those that do occur are found primarily in the post-Resurrection scenes in Luke 24, where, intriguingly, there is no Markan source.

Students of John have also considered the existence of a large body of material common to Luke and John to be an intriguing and yet

Introduction 5

puzzling feature.[9] It is clear that the Fourth Gospel is significantly different from all three of the synoptic Gospels, but even with the striking divergence there are nonetheless a number of general points of similarity: the broad outline of the ministry of Jesus and the order of major events; individual features in parallel accounts; and, particularly, events in the Passion narrative. In addition to the general similarities, there are many particular points of similarity between Luke and John.[10] Sometimes the similarities between these two Gospels are minor, such as the existence of the characters Mary and Martha or the references to Samaria. But sometimes the similarities are striking, such as in the anointing of Jesus' feet (Luke 7:38, John 12:3) rather than his head. And in the Passion narrative the points of similarity between Luke and John accumulate, often coinciding with Luke's departure from the Mark/Matthew account.

At the same time, certain elements of Luke and John are not part of this common relationship. And the absence itself is puzzling, should John have relied upon Luke. In the first place, material that is special in Luke (so-called L material) is rarely found in John. Of the list of sixty-four L passages in Fitzmyer, for instance, only five pericopes have significant points of contact.[11] It is difficult, therefore, to imagine

---

[9] So, for instance Raymond E. Brown, *The Gospel According to John* (I-XII), AB 29, (Garden City, NY: Doubleday, 1966), xlvi: "In many ways the possibility of cross-influence on John from Luke is the most interesting. In scenes shared by John and several synoptics, the parallels between John and Luke are usually not impressive. Rather, it is with the peculiarly Lucas material that John has the important parallels." The scholarship on the Luke-John question is extensive. An overview of the state of the question is given below in chapter 2.

[10] An extensive listing is found in F. Lamar Cribbs, "The Agreements That Exist Between Luke and John," *SBL 1979 Seminar Papers* (Missoula, MT: Scholars Press, 1979). See chapter 3 below for a summary listing of the points of contact between John and Luke.

[11] Fitzmyer, *Luke*, 83–84. The four pericopes with points of contact are 5:4–9 (the catch of fish); 10:38–42 (Martha and Mary); 22:27 (who is greater, the one who dines or the one who serves?); 23:13–16 (Pilate's judgment); and 24:13–35 (Jesus on the road to Emmaus).

John's having relied on Luke. And yet much of the material in John that is closely similar or identical to Mark is absent in Luke.[12]

One finds, then, two related issues converging. On the one hand, Lukan studies have repeatedly sought to explain the significant variation of the Third Gospel from Matthew and Mark. A major feature of this variation involves John-related material. On the other hand, Johannine studies, in grappling with the composition of John, have often addressed the frequency and nature of John's similarities to Luke. Those similarities are clearly an important feature in the composition history of the two Gospels.

How one is to explain the numerous points of contact that exist between Luke and John is a fundamental issue in understanding how Luke constructed his narratives and for what purpose he modified the Mark/Matthew passages to include the John-related material. Do the manifold similarities suggest a direct literary relationship, or can they be attributed to some common tradition behind the Gospels, either written or oral? And if a literary relationship is established, who relied on whom? These questions are not new, but given the state of current research, they are by no means settled. This study is presented in order to join this ongoing debate and to suggest a new avenue of approach.

THE ISSUE OF JOHN AND THE SYNOPTICS: IS JOHN DEPENDENT?

The discussion of the Luke-John relationships comes under the much broader rubric of the relationship between the synoptic Gospels and John.[13] For most of the last several decades, the general

---

[12] Of the list of twelve pericopes with close verbal resemblances between John and Mark cited by C. K. Barrett, *The Gospel According to St. John* (Philadelphia: Westminster, 1978), 44–45, five are not in Luke at all; a number of the similarities actually show stronger correspondence between Luke and John than between Mark and John.

[13] It is not possible here to adequately address the contours of this issue. Reviews of the state of the question can be found in D. Moody Smith, *John Among the Gospels*, which is a book-length discussion of scholarship on the John-Synoptic

consensus of scholarly opinion has tended toward the position that John and the Synoptics share traditions but that there is no literary dependence. (That is to say, most scholars have not believed that John made use of the Synoptics. Of course, the question is almost always taken to be whether John knew one or more of the Synoptics, not vice versa.) Admittedly, the consensus is no longer as stable as it once was, and a number of scholars are once again arguing that John not only was aware of but also made use of the synoptic Gospels as a source. Conclusions or presuppositions concerning this issue will certainly influence the approach taken to the more narrow question of the Luke-John relationship. But, as in many areas of New Testament study, such a large question ultimately turns on a host of far more minutely framed questions that must be answered first. A full answer to the question of John's relationship to the Synoptics must ultimately include an adequate discussion of the special relationship of Luke and John.

In fact, as Schniewind noted, the specific question of Luke's relationship to John is probably more difficult than the general question of John's relationship to the Synoptics.[14] If one is convinced that John knew the Synoptics, that view usually is based on the important role that Mark played in the formation of the Gospel genre. In particular, the overall agreement of John's Passion narrative with the outline of the synoptic Passion narrative has been adduced by some scholars as evidence of John's reliance on Mark.[15] It is certainly

---

relationship. Other helpful discussions are Frans Neirynck, "John and the Synoptics: 1975–1990," in *John and the Synoptics* (Leuven: Leuven University Press, 1992), 3–62; Neirynck, "John and the Synoptics," in *L'Évangile de Jean* (Leuven: University Press, 1976), 73–106; J. Blinzler, *Johannes und die Synoptiker. Ein Forschungsbericht* (Stuttgart: Verlag Katholisches Bibelwerk, 1965).

[14] Julius Schniewind, *Die Parallelperikopen bei Lukas und Johannes* (Hildesheim: Georg Olms Verlagsbuchhandlung, 1958), 5.

[15] See, for instance, Werner Kelber "Conclusion: From Passion Narrative to Gospel," in *The Passion in Mark*, ed. Werner H. Kelber (Philadelphia: Fortress Press, 1976), 158–59, based heavily on John R. Donahue, *Are You the Christ? The Trial Narrative in the Gospel of Mark* (Missoula, MT: SBL, 1973).

possible, however, that John knew and used Mark without having used any other of the Synoptics, including Luke. On that ground, even if John's knowledge of Mark is presupposed, a literary relationship between John and Luke need not follow, and the pattern of Luke-John similarities could stem from an entirely different source. Alternatively, if John did not know Mark or Matthew and worked from an independent source, it is likewise possible that some literary or other contact led to the specific points of similarity between Luke and John.[16] Thus a general solution to the John-Synoptic relationship does not easily resolve the matter.

There are two main facets to the question of the Luke-John relationship: (1) Is the relationship between the two Gospels a literary one? (2) What was the direction of the reliance (whether literary or tradition)?

The general direction of research in John-Synoptic relationships is heavily dependent on the relative importance that is placed on the durability of oral traditions on the one hand and the role of the individual Gospel writers as composers on the other hand. Those who privilege oral traditions usually maintain the independence of John.[17] Under this rubric, a relatively large number of verbatim or other striking similarities can be explained as having been preserved in the oral tradition. Those, however, who see much of the Gospel material as having been formed under the creative hands of the evangelists tend to argue for John's derivative status.[18]

---

[16] As, for instance, Grant has proposed extensive textual corruption as a possible source. See chapter 2 below, p. 40.

[17] So, for instance, it is not surprising that C. H. Dodd, who emphasized the durability of oral traditions (cf. his early emphasis on the oral kerygma in *The Apostolic Preaching and Its Development* [London: Hodden and Stoughton, 1936]), is a major proponent of the independence of John (*Historical Tradition in the Fourth Gospel* [Cambridge: University Press, 1963]).

[18] See the discussion of Lloyd R. Kittlaus, "The Author of John and the Gospel of Mark" (Ph.D. diss., University of Chicago, 1988), 32–113. Kittlaus maintains that with each successive methodology predominant in New Testament scholarship (i.e., source criticism, form criticism, redaction criticism), there has

The principal explanations of the Luke-John relationship have followed the outlines of the John-Synoptic research: some scholars see evidence of a literary relationship between Luke and John and hence argue for John's reliance on Luke; others understand the relationship as a product of oral tradition and hence reject John's reliance on Luke. The discussion, however, has reached an impasse; neither side seems to have developed a compelling argument for either John's use of common oral traditions with Luke, or John's literary reliance on Luke. Until now, a major feature has been missing from the discussion: the serious consideration of the possibility that Luke knew and used John.

The very way the question has generally been framed presupposes that literary reliance, if found, would be John's reliance on Luke. The question presupposes that John is a late Gospel, with the other three canonical Gospels already having been produced and available for use. There are, however, some significant reasons to doubt the facility with which the posteriority of John has been assumed.[19] The tendency to place John late and secondary to the Synoptics took place fairly early in Gospel research, indeed as early as Clement of Alexandria and the Muratorian Fragment. The assignment of John to a later date often accompanies the assumption that John writes with knowledge of the others, which he approves. Although Schleiermacher valued the Fourth Gospel as the primary source for information about Jesus, Strauss, Baur, and the main line of critical scholars were more skeptical about John. The main arguments for John's posteriority have centered in four loci: (1) John is thoroughly theological, (2) John is the product of a Hellenistic environment, (3) John is the result of

---

been a resultant reflection in the predominant view of John's relationship to Mark.

[19] For a fuller discussion of the issue of John's lateness in Gospel scholarship see Mark Matson, "The Contribution to the Temple Cleansing by the Fourth Gospel," *SBL 1992 Seminar Papers*, ed. Eugene Lovering Jr. (Atlanta: Scholars Press, 1992), 489–506. See also F. Lamar Cribbs, "A Reassessment of the Date of Origin and the Destination of the Gospel of John," *JBL* 89 (1970): 38–55 and J. A. T. Robinson, *The Priority of John* (Oak Park, IL: Meyer-Stone Books, 1987), 1–45.

extensive theological development, and (4) John is dependent on the Synoptics. Item four can be excluded from consideration here, since it is precisely the question at issue. The other three arguments for a late date of John have all been set aside, or at least called into question, in recent years. The fact that John has a distinctive theological tendency does not *a priori* speak against its independence or priority. It is clear now that all the Gospels reflect an editorial and theological shaping that is extensive.[20] Moreover, Paul demonstrates an extensive theological development well before the synoptic Gospels were written, speaking of the preexistence and descent of Christ, as well as his role in creation (Phil 2:5–11; 1 Cor 8:6).

It is not my purpose here to argue for John's temporal priority, but rather to suggest that for the purpose of the study of the Luke-John relationship (and the John-Synoptic relationship as well) it is appropriate to hold this question in suspense. If it is not certain whether John is early or late, how reasonable it is to assume that John relied on Luke? Is it more or less reasonable to consider the reverse—that Luke might have relied on John? This, in brief, is the unique approach of this study: to consider seriously the Luke-John relationship from the perspective of Luke's possible dependence instead of John's.

---

[20] Recent Gospel studies have all worked with the assumption that the evangelists are, in fact, theological shapers of tradition. Norman Perrin, *What Is Redaction Criticism?* (Philadelphia: Fortress Press, 1969) echoes this perspective when he notes that the entire range of creative authorial activities is indicative of the evangelists' theological outlook: editorial modifications of received material, choice of material, arrangement of the narrative, and new creative material added to traditions (66). Perrin's comment reflects an underlying concept that the gospels are inherently tendentious in theology and thought. But often John is viewed as *more* theological or tendentious, and thus later. This distinction is increasingly undermined as we see the full range of theological control the other gospel writers exert on their material.

PROBLEMS RELATIVE TO LUKE: LUKE'S AUTHORIAL METHOD

In some ways the question of Luke's authorial method is simpler than that of John's. It is clear that Luke functions forthrightly as both an author and an editor of previous accounts of Jesus.[21] Luke begins his narrative with an acknowledgement that he is dependent on others for the material of the Gospel.[22] It is most likely that Luke took over the basic synoptic accounts of Jesus' life, either from Mark and Q, or from Mark and Matthew,[23] and shaped them into a new account. There is little doubt that Luke makes extensive use of previous sources in his account. And given the fact that Luke does use Mark, there is at least a fixed point of comparison to see how Luke handles another source.

---

[21] Luke 1:1-4. So Fitzmyer, *Luke*, summarizes a standard view that the prologue implies at least some written sources (Mark, Q, perhaps L) and could include oral traditions (291). Goulder, *Luke*, also takes this to refer to written sources, although in this case to Mark and Matthew (198). Earl Richard suggests that Luke was following a classic Hellenistic pattern of combining sources with free composition: "Thus, Luke's practice in doing research and in composing narratives matches the theory of the period. Luke is a Hellenistic writer for whom fact and story along with literary conventions are at the service of the writer's view of things." Earl Richard, "Luke: Author and Thinker," in *New Views on Luke and Acts* (Collegeville, MN: Michael Glazier, 1990), 18.

[22] Luke 1:1-2. It is worth noting here that v. 1 implies more than one written account. Luke's use of πολλοί is vague but suggestive, and the verb ἐπιχειρέω must refer to written accounts, not just oral (see the comments of Gerd Petzke, *Das Sondergut des Evangeliums nach Lukas* [Zürich: Theologischer Verlag, 1990], 14).

[23] The main view of Luke's primary sources is that he used Mark and Q. (see for instance Fitzmyer, *Luke*, 63-65). A major alternative thesis is that originally proposed A. M. Farrer and presented in an exhaustive way by Michael Goulder in *Luke: A New Paradigm*. In this book, 46-71, Goulder presents the thesis that Luke used only Mark, Matthew, and the Old Testament. The important element at this juncture is that Farrer and Goulder argues that all of the Q elements are sufficiently explained by Luke's editorial shaping of Matthew. I will frequently use the term Mark/Matthew to point to double and triple tradition material upon which Luke relies as a source, but without making a judgment on the viability of Q as a source.

But Luke's use of the Mark/Matthew story is only the beginning point of understanding Luke's method in forming the Third Gospel. It is clear not only from Luke's references to many accounts in his prologue but also from observation about the degree of unique material in Luke that the Third Evangelist made use of additional material in shaping his story. Luke contains additional units of text, which have been inserted *en bloc*,[24] and variations even within some "synoptic" pericopes which have material not found in Mark/Matthew.[25] Just from the extensive quantity of the additional material in Luke there is a strong argument for the use of *Sondergut* alongside the Mark/Matthew material.

The big question is whether this additional material is from a written independent source, from oral sources, or from the free authorial creativity of Luke.[26] In the past, the major scholarly approach to identifying these additional sources was based on a manuscript concept of sources; thus Luke was viewed as a somewhat rote transmitter of sources. By identifying characteristics of Lukan style, one could extract "non-Lukan" units and wording from the Lukan accounts. Thus extracting the non-Lukan source, at least in portion, one was able to get behind Luke to the "original sources." In many cases this method was used to reconstruct the lost source as a coherent narrative.[27]

---

[24] This is especially true of the material from Luke 9:51–18:14 but is also argued with respect to the birth narratives. See, for instance, Fitzmyer's chart of L material, in *Luke*, 83-84.

[25] So see Tim Schramm, *Der Markus-Stoff bei Lukas* (Cambridge: University Press, 1971), and Joachim Jeremias, *Die Sprache des Lukasevangeliums* (Göttingen: Vandenhoeck & Ruprecht, 1980) for material that runs parallel with Mark; Friedrich Rehkopf, *Die lukanische Sonderquelle* (Tübingen: J. C. B. Mohr [Paul Siebeck], 1959) and Jeremias for additional material in the Passion account.

[26] For a fuller discussion of issues involving Lukan redaction see chapter 5 below.

[27] So, for instance, see Vincent Taylor, *The Passion Narrative of St. Luke*, or Friedrich Rehkopf, *Die lukanische Sonderquelle*.

But this cut-and-paste method of editing attributed to Luke has more recently been called into question, with the result that one is now less certain how to determine the boundaries of source and editing.[28] In keeping with a greater interest and appreciation for the literary ability of the New Testament authors, and Luke in particular, the question of the extent and shape of Luke's sources has become problematized. That is not to say that Luke did not use additional sources, just that Luke may have been more subtle and creative in his use of sources than previous scholarship allowed.[29]

Although it might be difficult to identify exactly the shape and limits of the sources behind Luke's account, it is still feasible to investigate what sources other than Mark or Matthew might have influenced Luke's composition of the gospel story. The possibility of additional sources becomes particularly intriguing given the existence of material in Luke that is otherwise found only in John. Is it possible that John was known by Luke? Given the probable lateness of Luke's writing and its admittedly literary approach to sources, this possibility should be seriously considered, especially if the assumption of the late dating of John is held in suspense. And while reconstruction of a *hypothetical* source other than Mark behind Luke seems to have run into a dead end, the testing of the possibility of a *still extant* source

---

[28] One might note especially here the work of Goulder, *Luke: A New Paradigm*, as well as John Drury, *Tradition and Design in Luke's Gospel* (London: Darton, Longman & Todd, 1976), both of whom would suggest instead that Luke is a *midrash*, that is a free interpretation, of the Gospel account put forward already by Mark and Matthew. In a slightly different vein, Marion Soards, *The Passion According to Luke*, while acknowledging some use of sources, takes issue with the idea that there existed a connected narrative source other than Mark. Luke has taken Mark and various pieces of tradition and creatively constructed a new version of the story. In both cases the emphasis is on Luke as a creative author, using sources with some purpose and nuance, not simply splicing together disparate sources.

[29] Even Goulder allows that there may have been sources other than Mark and Matthew, 75.

used either creatively or cautiously by Luke would add to our understanding of Luke's authorial method.

READING LUKE: RHETORIC AND INTERTEXTUALITY

The question remains why one should even attempt to extricate the sources behind Luke that might explain some of the points of contact between Luke and John. What does this profit the reader/interpreter? In defense of what may seem an outdated approach in New Testament scholarship, I offer the following rationale for the continuing effort to locate sources and explore how those sources were used, in Luke or any other text.

Beginning in the nineteenth century, early critical Gospel scholarship was sharply focused on locating the sources behind the Gospels. Hence the earliest efforts at teasing out the relationships between the synoptic Gospels were in service of an attempt to discern which Gospels or traditions were prior to, and thus sources for, the others. The major impetus for this work, of course, was the interest in the historical Jesus. The implicit assumption seemed to be that finding a source put one closer to the historical truth. The texts themselves were viewed as mere windows to the real historical situation that they describe, albeit with some distortion.

While identifying the sources might be helpful in the quest for the historical Jesus, that is not the goal I have in mind for this study. Such a procedure implicitly reduces a Gospel's primary purpose to the reporting of history; it has as its focus something that lies behind the Gospel rather than the function of the narrative itself. What it leaves out is the dynamic process by which the Gospel author used and modified sources and, perhaps more importantly, the rhetorical effect that he desired such use and misuse to have on the his audience.

But if we are not interested in discovering the historical Jesus, should we consign the study of the sources to the waste bin? Some recent sophisticated approaches to narrative literature would actually cast doubt on the too-ready disposal of sources in interpreting texts. In the works of Mikhail Bakhtin[30] and Kenneth Burke,[31] the use of sources and the intention of the author are maintained as important elements in the interpretation process. In this view of texts, which I will call rhetorical, narratives are often presented as vehicles by which authors attempt to influence an audience.[32] Such narratives (as well as reasoned arguments such as Paul's letters, or Cicero's speeches), are rhetorical in their attempt to convince readers to adopt a particular view of a situation and to act upon that view.[33] In that respect, Luke's

---

[30] Mikhail Bakhtin, *The Dialogic Imagination* (Austin: University of Texas Press, 1981) and *Rabelais and His World* (Cambridge MA: M. I. T. Press, 1968). See also T. Todorov, *Mikhail Bakhtin: The Dialogical Principle* (Minneapolis: University of Minnesota Press, 1984). On the issue of intertextuality and allusion, see also Williem Vorster, "Intertextuality and Redaktionsgeschichte," in *Intertextuality in Biblical Writings* (Kampen: Uitgeversmaatschappij J.H. Kok, 1989) and J. Hollander, *The Figure of an Echo: Modes of Allusion in Milton and After* (Berkeley: University of California Press, 1981).

[31] Kenneth Burke, *A Rhetoric of Motives* (Berkeley: University of California Press, 1969). Burke in particular examines narrative texts, such as Milton, Dante, Kafka and Diderot, to make the point that they are rhetorical.

[32] Stephen D. Moore, *Literary Criticism and the Gospels* (New Haven: Yale University Press, 1989) also notes that narratives are completely rhetorical, and as such their entire range of "presentational strategies" (plotting; characterization; the filtering of story events through theocentric, christocentric, and other perspectives; the rearrangement of chronological sequence; the use of literary patterns) are all part of the rhetorical method (61). His acknowledgement of the rhetorical role of "rearrangement of chronological sequence" suggests that even from his postmodern perspective, there is some value in examining how an author has gone about constructing his or her narrative.

[33] One might note, for instance, the way Mary Ann Tolbert, *Sowing The Gospel* (Minneapolis: Fortress Press, 1989), has shown that an opposition between the various characters in the gospel of Mark, together with viewpoint of the narrator and Jesus, function rhetorically to influence the reader to solidify a position. "These incidents and many others contribute to making the audience better than the disciples, but the effect is even greater. For portraying the disciples as failing foils to Jesus manipulates the reader to respond by becoming a better disciple" (223–23).

gospel would clearly be a rhetorical piece.[34] An important task of Lukan scholarship should be to explore more fully how the Third Gospel works as a rhetorical device, a channel of persuasive communication between author and audience.

The recognition and identification of sources used in constructing a narrative can be helpful in the explication of the narrative's rhetorical aims and effect. In the first place, the degree to which a writer (e.g., Luke) uses or modifies a source and valorizes or marginalizes that source (or parts of it) is a clear indication of how he or she is wanting to influence the audience. Recognizing how primary sources are used helps us to understand the emphases the *author* is seeking to put forward.

But recognizing sources may also help indicate the conceptual framework of the intended *audience* as well. An author often uses a source as much to embrace or augment an existing resource as to give new information. Thus an author might very well use a source even if, or particularly because, the audience already knows the source. One must assume, for instance, that Luke believed his audience knew the story of Hannah and the birth of Samuel from 1 Samuel 2:1–10. In telling the story of the annunciation of the birth of Jesus, and especially Mary's response to it, Luke draws on the earlier story of Samuel's birth to augment and interpret the new event. The story is clearly "intertextual," that is, the audience is meant to read Luke's version in light of 1 Samuel. To the degree that a source is known (or believed to be known) by an audience, it might be used to establish an intertextual web of inference and meaning.

The purpose of identifying the use of particular sources in an ancient document—in this case determining whether Luke knew and used John—is to assist in exploring how the document worked in persuading an ancient audience. I believe that Luke's audience already

---

[34] Note again the role of the prologue to the work, which has been described as having a comparative and hence argumentative tone. See Fearghus O. Fearghail, *The Introduction to Luke-Acts* (Rome: Editrice Pontifico Istituo Biblico, 1991), 110–116.

Introduction   17

had the Gospel of Mark,[35] and Luke makes specific comments that suggest he wanted to correct, though not entirely disassociate himself from, this earlier narrative.[36] Luke's use of Mark, then, is not plagiarism but a direct rhetorical use of intertextuality to supplant Mark's argument about Jesus with a competing interpretation. It is possible (though at this point only conjectural) that if Luke knew John or some Johannine tradition, then his audience did as well.[37] In that case John or Johannine tradition would have been used, and *misused*, for rhetorical effect. Locating sources and identifying redactional and compositional patterns is not simply an attempt to capture some pre-Gospel essentialist text, but is rather an attempt to understand how the texts we do have functioned historically as rhetorical units.

---

[35] A very strong case can be made that the Gospels were not meant for specific geographical communities, but for broad dissemination (cf. Richard Bauckham, "For Whom were Gospels Written," in *The Gospels for All Christians: Rethinking the Gospel Audiences* [Grand Rapids: Wm. B. Eerdmans, 1998], 1–24.) We know that Mark was available to Luke; it is likely that Mark had already circulated widely. The fact that Luke and Matthew both apparently know Mark testifies to its presence in various locations. Luke, then, would have written his Gospel, which modifies and, to a certain extent, attempts to displace Mark, knowing that the recipients of his new Gospel were aware of the previous Gospel(s).

[36] So Fearghail, "While Luke places himself alongside his predecessors in his undertaking (cf. Luke 1, 3), he gives the distinct impression through his claims for the accuracy and completeness of his investigations that his work is meant to mark an improvement on their narratives" (114). Note also Luke T. Johnson, *The Gospel of Luke* (Collegeville, MN: Michael Glazier, 1991), 11.

[37] I might note here that a number of students of the Luke-John relationship have posited as part of the solution a geographic contact. So Maddox, Parker, and even Dauer suggest that the items of commonality found in the two Gospels were because of contact between either the evangelists or their respective communities. If Luke were written for a region which was already using John or some early form of John, then we might find just this kind of intertextual reference. But if the Gospels were written for audiences not confined to a single community (see note 35 above), then the contact would have arisen from the broad dissemination of the Gospels soon after their writing.

THE SHAPE OF THIS STUDY

As stated earlier, the aim of this study will be relatively narrow: an examination of the Luke-John relationship from the perspective of Luke. Simply put, the question I want to consider is this: Is it reasonable to suppose that Luke knew and used John, either its final form or some earlier recognizable form, in the composition of the Third Gospel? In order to test that thesis, I will focus on my attention on the Passion and Resurrection narratives of Luke, which are the richest source of material for Luke-John similarities.

In chapter 2, I will undertake a survey of scholarship on the Luke-John relationship. The survey will not only highlight what has already been noted about the relationship but also reveal the assumptions that undergird those investigations. A critical analysis of the scholarship will show the need for a new investigation of the relationship from the perspective of Luke.

The major focus of this study will be on Luke's Passion and Resurrection narratives, chapters 22–24. But to deal exclusively with the Passion and Resurrection narratives is only to touch the hem of a much larger garment. It is important to see the larger scope of the Luke-John points of agreement. I will attempt in chapter 3 to capture the scope of the Luke-John relationship with a classification and discussion of the various points of contact (most of which have already been noted by previous scholars), between Luke and John. Not all the points of contact that have been previously cited have equal weight; some, in fact, may be spurious or inconsequential. Grouping the points of contact will help to provide a benchmark for later analysis. Given the focus of this study upon Luke's perspective, I will group the points of contact in the order of their appearance in Luke.

Discussion of Luke-John points of contact, especially in the Passion and Resurrection accounts, must also deal with the problem of "Western non-Interpolations." As is commonly known, Western non-

Interpolations are instances in which the usually fuller Western manuscripts are shorter than the other text forms. This group of textual variants in Luke is especially significant with respect to the matter at hand, since the large majority of them has a "Johannine" flavor. Indeed, the points of contact in the Western non-Interpolations are some of the most explicit points of contact between Luke and John. In chapter 4, then, I must examine the various arguments for and against these textual variants in order to establish the text for subsequent discussion.

The study of the possibility of Luke's use of John is really a study of Luke's compositional and redactional method. In chapter 5 I will explore how the study should be undertaken, beginning with a review of major approaches in the Lukan redaction-critical scholarship. A major tool in understanding Luke's redactional and compositional work is the analysis of his patterns of language use. But this common redaction-critical tool has limitations, especially in appreciating the use of earlier material that has been modified and become "Lukan." So what is necessary is a group of criteria beyond simple linguistic analysis that can help in comprehending Luke's redactional and compositional patterns.

The heart of this study will be chapters 6–8, a close reading of the Lukan Passion and Resurrection narrative (Luke chapters 22–24) with emphasis on those sections of Luke which have points of contact with John. The overriding question in these chapters will be whether it makes sense to see Luke using John as a source in his composition of the Third Gospel.

In a final summary, I will draw together the implications of the study, especially those concerning further study of both Luke and John.

Chapter 2

THE STUDY OF THE RELATIONSHIP OF LUKE AND JOHN

THE PROJECT IN THE CONTEXT OF EXISTING SCHOLARSHIP

The study of the relationship between Luke and John has been an important element in the study of the John-Synoptic question, but it has also developed as an item of inquiry separate from the larger issue. The solutions to the Luke-John relationship have tended to fall into one of three categories: (1) John used the Gospel of Luke, (2) John and Luke used common traditions, usually considered to be oral traditions, or (3) John's used oral traditions common to Luke, but those traditions had already been influenced by Luke's written account. To these three approaches a fourth approach, one which has only been tentatively suggested, should now be added: (4) Luke used the Gospel of John, or some Johannine narrative.

The direction of recent research on the Luke-John relationship has its roots in earlier research on the backgrounds of the Gospels. I will, therefore, begin this survey of research with an initial examination of the foundational approaches to understanding the relationship between Luke and John. This examination will demonstrate the influence of the early scholarship on the trajectory of almost all the later scholarship. I do not attempt here a survey of the broader question of the relationship between John and the Synoptics; more extensive studies of that relationship are readily available.[1] Then, beginning with the work of Julius Schniewind, the first scholar to truly focus on the Luke-John relationship, I will examine the major approaches to the question grouped by category. The organization of this study is not primarily chronological, although I examine the earliest scholars in chronological order; rather, it represents an attempt to discern the major approaches to the question and to understand the fundamental assumptions and insights that have been derived from the research thus far.

EARLY APPROACHES TO THE PROBLEM

F. C. BAUR (1847)

Perhaps the earliest critical examination of the relationship between Luke and John is found in F. C. Baur's study of the canonical Gospels.[2] In his discussion of the earliest origination of the Gospel of Luke, Baur examines a number of distinctive Luke-John similarities that differentiate Luke from the other Synoptics.[3] As part of his investigation of the background of Luke, Baur questions whether the relationship by which Luke is "distinguished" from the other Synoptics is the same as that which draws John and Luke together (annähern);[4]

---

[1] See especially D. Moody Smith, *John Among the Gospels* (Minneapolis: Fortress Press, 1992); J. Blinzler, *Johannes und die Synoptiker. Ein Forschungsbericht* (Stuttgart: Verlag Katholisches Biblewerk, 1965).

[2] F. C. Baur, *Kritische Untersuchungen über die kanonischen Evangelien* (Tübingen: Verlag und Druck von Ludw. Fr. Fues, 1847), 484–501.

[3] Baur, 427. Baur is convinced that Luke has arisen in two stages: an early version, and a subsequent later edition in which additional material was added to the early version.

[4] "...desto näher liegt die Frage, ob es nicht in demselben Verhältniss in

in other words, is there a single reason that explains both Luke's difference from Mark and Matthew and its similarity to John?

Baur summarizes the similarities between Luke and John under three headings: (1) the arena in which Jesus' actions take place, (2) the dogmatic interpretation of who Jesus is, and (3) the relatively unhistoric portrayal of Jesus.[5]

Like the other Synoptics, Luke only knows of one trip to Jerusalem within Jesus' ministry. But unlike the Synoptics, and like John, Luke does not assume that Jesus' primary locus of activity is in Galilee. Indeed, like John, Luke shows Jesus traveling through and acting within the province of Samaria. For Baur, this geographical similarity is closely linked with the interest of the Gospel writers in opposing Judaism.[6] But there is a significant difference between Luke and John in the way this opposition is portrayed: Luke's anti-Judaism is significantly less harsh than John's. Indeed, the trip to Samaria itself takes on totally different tones in the two Gospels. In John, Samaria represents a reaction against Judaism's unbelief; in Luke, Samaria, while presenting an anti-Jewish motif, suggests much more an anticipation of the church's openness to Gentiles. As a result, Baur takes Luke's compromising tone, together with the comparison of the historical likelihood of the presentations, as support of his view that Luke is the third in order of writing.[7] One can see, of course, Baur's tendentious interpretation of Luke as the synthesizing, harmonizing writer of the New Testament period.

Likewise, Baur sees a similar development in the dogmatic presentation of who Jesus is. Again, he sees Luke taking a middle or harmonizing position. In the matter of how one should interpret the term "son of God," Luke uses the term in the same "Jewish sense" as does Matthew, that is, as Messiah, but he also moves toward a fuller

---

welchem es von den beiden andern synoptischen Evangelien sich entfernt, dem johanneischen Evangelium sich annähert." (Baur, 484)

[5] Baur, 484
[6] Baur, 485.
[7] Baur, 485.

interpretation. Thus the exorcisms in Luke have a sense of coming more from Jesus' own being, than from simply his work.[8] Baur finds this relationship between Jesus' essence and his works in such pericopes as Luke's treatment of the healing of the hemorrhaging woman. He sees Luke's reporting that "power has gone from me" as analogous to John's assertion that Jesus is the resurrection and the life. What both Gospels report, in distinction from the other Synoptics, is that Jesus' healings are not just actions by him, but derive from his very essence. This explanation is related to a passage in Luke that uses a form of Logos terminology. In Luke 4:36, the crowd wonders about Jesus' *word*, which has authority and power. For Baur, this passage suggests that Luke sees in Jesus an identity of word and being similar to that seen in John's Gospel.[9]

Baur also perceives in both Luke and John a distancing from a purely historical interest. Of course, Baur completely rejects John as having any historical interest.[10] But Baur also traces the same tendency in Luke, which indicates to him that Luke was written late. Specifically, he sees in such Lukan passages as the sending of the seventy(two) and the account of Mary and Martha an idealistic reworking that is reminiscent of John.

Baur does not come to any clear ideas about the literary relationship between Luke and John. On the one hand, he thinks that John shows evidence of knowing not only the Synoptic tradition but also the Gospels of Luke and Mark.[11] And yet on the other hand, his discussion of Luke's relationship with John suggests at numerous points that he thinks Luke tends *toward* a Johannine method of

---

[8] Baur, 491.

[9] Baur, 493.

[10] Baur, 388.

[11] Baur, 280. Baur is convinced that John is late, for a number of reasons. For a summary of Baur's views on the posteriority of John, and the influence they have had on the view of the date of John's authorship see Mark Matson, "The Contribution of the Temple Cleansing by the Fourth Gospel," *SBL 1992 Seminar Papers*, ed. Eugene Lovering Jr. (Atlanta: Scholars Press, 1992), 489–494.

portraying material.[12] It is true, of course, that Baur is primarily attempting to use both Luke's and John's literary tendencies as a way of explicating the historical lateness of them both; having done so, he would have little further interest in identifying precisely which one might have influenced the other. And since Baur sees Luke as having developed in stages, he may be somewhat unclear as to what material is original and what is late.

What is important to note, though, is the way Baur frames the question initially: perhaps whatever caused Luke to vary from Matthew and Mark at key points is also behind the distinctive nature of John. Baur, of course, is primarily interested in theological development, not exegetical detail, but the same question could be posed to the greater mass of detail that binds Luke and John together in opposition to Matthew and Mark.

H. J. HOLTZMANN (1869)

Holtzmann's primary thesis, as indicated by the title of his series of articles, is that John has relied on all three of the synoptic Gospels.[13] In reaction to the Schleiermachian school[14]—particularly, Leek —

---

[12] Schniewind notes this in his brief comment on both Baur's and Wellhausen's treatment of the problem: that Baur asserts that John is literarily dependent on Luke, yet at the same time asserts that Luke's portrayal is "bent" toward the Johannine presentation. Julius Schniewind, *Die Parallelperikopen bei Lukas und Johannes* (Hildesheim: Georg Olms Verlagsbuchhandlung, 1958), 5.

[13] H. J. Holtzmann, "Die schriftstellerische Verhältniss des Johannes zu den Synoptikern." *Zeitschrift für wissenschaftliche Theologie* (Leipzig: Fues's Verlag, 1869), 62–84, 155–177, 446–456.

[14] Friedrich Schleiermacher maintained that John was the primary Gospel, having been written by John the apostle. In contrast, he believed that the Synoptics were all written independently, using written fragments of accounts instead of oral sources or one another. The Gospel of John, then, is both independent and historically superior to the synoptic Gospels. See Schleiermacher, *The Life of Jesus*, trans. S. McLean Gilmour (Philadelphia: Fortress Press, 1975), 158, and Werner Kümmel, *The New Testament: The History of the Investigation of its Problems*,

Holtzmann presents an extensive argument, looking in turn at Matthew and John, Mark and John, Luke and John, and finally all the Synoptics together and John. In the case of John and Luke, Holtzmann notes that the similarities are of particular interest—even toying with, but rejecting, the idea that John's focus on Judea comes from the Lukan source.[15] Instead, he sees Luke's "south Palestinian" orientation as occupying a "middle term" between John and Matthew and Mark.[16]

Holtzmann's method is to collect numerous points of contact, often minor, that might demonstrate John's use of the other Gospels. For instance, the fact that only Matthew and John identify Peter as "Simon, called Peter" (or Cephas in the case of John) indicates John's use of Matthew.[17] He similarly mines a host of similarities in the Gospel stories, often just snatches of words, and uses them to support his contention that John relied on the synoptics. Because Holtzmann's essay was quite influential, it is useful to examine his approaches to some Luke-John points of contact as illustrative of his method with all the Synoptics.

Holtzmann notes that only Luke and John report Jewish questioning about whether John the Baptist might be the Christ.[18] Of course, the questions arise in the two Gospels in very different contexts and on the lips of different actors (the Sanhedrin in the case of John, the people in the case of Luke). More importantly, Holtzmann notes that both Luke and John have Jesus called the son of Joseph. He concludes that John's statement οὐχὶ οὗτός ἐστιν Ἰησοῦς ὁ υἱὸς Ἰωσήφ (John 6:42) is "almost a word for word" use of Luke 4:22, without giving any consideration to the fact that the two questions occur in

---

trans. S. McLean Gilmour and Howard C. Kee (Nashville: Abingdon Press, 1972), 84–85.

[15] Holtzmann, 69, citing Köstlin.

[16] Holtzmann, 69, 70. "In Wahrheit aber stellt Lucas ... als Mittelglied zwischen die synoptische und johaneische Darstellung..."

[17] Holtzmann, 64.

[18] Holtzmann, 70.

significantly different contexts.[19] The fact that Mary and Martha appear as sisters only in these two Gospels, together with the facts that Martha "served" and they lived in a village (κώμη) are sufficient points of contact for Holtzmann to demonstrate that John refers to Luke.[20] These examples are sufficient to indicate that Holtzmann sees any and all points of similarity as transparently pointing toward John's use of Luke. The assumptions that undergird his essay are obvious: John is the later document, and any points of similarity, even if scattered about or in different contexts, must point to a literary relationship. Holtzmann here presents a common thread of scholarship on this issue: John is later, so any relationship that appears to be literary must constitute proof that John relied on Luke.

One must also note that Holtzmann's method is not systematic. He seems to select elements of commonality between Luke and John from wherever he finds them, and not on any systematic basis. There is in his study no careful sifting of the evidence, pericope by pericope, leaving the (correct) impression that in the grab bag of similarities he presents, he finds just what he is looking for. A careful analysis of the points of commonality would be more discriminating as to which similarities are adduced as bespeaking a genetic relationship.

It is intriguing, however, that Holtzmann recognizes that with the common geographical interest, Luke can at least function as a middle term. Of course, Holtzmann does not let that affect his theory. But there are observations in Holtzmann's work that cast doubt on his results.

---

[19] Holtzmann, 71.
[20] Holtzmann, 71–72.

P. FEINE (1891)

The primary subject of Feine's work on the Gospel of Luke is the variety of sources that the evangelist used in the construction of his Gospel.[21] Feine accepts the previous works that argue for Luke's use of Mark, together with a document (*Grundschrift*) that Matthew and Luke used in common. But he also suggests that Luke made use of a separate written source that contained additional material. Of course, much of the wholly unique material in Luke finds its way into the register of this *Quellenschrift*, but so does some material that might be understood as Markan or Matthean: the healing of the centurion's son; the anointing of Jesus; and, indeed, much of the Passion story. These Lukan accounts are considered by Feine to be sufficiently different that a distinct source must have been used. Feine, then, understands Luke to have woven Markan or Matthean material *together with* unique material.

In the course of this examination of Luke's special source, Feine takes up a series of contacts between Luke and John. In particular, Feine examines the special Lukan material and locates in it a number of points of commonality with the Fourth Gospel. For example, Feine identifies Luke-John similarities in the following areas, among many others: the healing of the centurion's son, the anointing of Jesus, the Samaritan stories, the sisters Mary and Martha, the parable of Lazarus, and even certain terms (e.g., son of light, the truth) in the special Lukan material. Without challenging the idea that John made use of the Synoptics (i.e., while embracing O. Holtzmann's short and flawed analysis),[22] Feine asserts that in the case of such material, there is not

---

[21] Paul Feine, *Eine vorkanonische Überlieferung des Lukas* (Gotha: Friedrich Andreas Perthes, 1891).

[22] Feine cites, approvingly, Oskar Holtzmann's discussion (*Das Johannesevangelium* [Darmstadt: Verlag von Johannes Waitz, 1887], 6). This particular study takes Johannine posterity for granted and posits that even small identities of words in similar pericopes prove literary dependence. The section of his introductory matter on John is particularly indicative of his view of literary

the stamp of a literary relationship but rather the indication that both traditions stem from the same "root."[23]

Although not primarily interested in the issue of the Luke-John relationship, Feine's study is helpful in two ways. First, he correctly distinguishes the particular issue of the Luke-John relationship from John's more general relationship with the Synoptics. That same distinction might be made within Luke-John similarities themselves: they may not all stem from the same origin. Second, he raises the question whether the relationship of common material is necessarily *schriftliche* or is the result of some common tradition. These two questions will continue to be central to the problem of how Luke and John are related.

OTTO ZURHELLEN (1909)

In an article that seeks to locate the background and origination of the Fourth Gospel, Zurhellen finds John's relationship to Luke to be a major point of interest.[24] Assuming that John knew and used Matthew and Mark, he reaches conclusions similar to Feine's about John's knowledge and use of Luke.

Zurhellen's initial task is to explore what he acknowledges are striking similarities in wording and themes. In the first place he questions whether John's *order* of the narrative betrays a knowledge of Luke's Gospel. For chapters 1–12, the answer is a very simple and straightforward "no." For chapters 13–20, the issue is a bit more

---

dependence which understands (1) John as inherently late, and (2) Luke as tending to rely on sources in a slavish cut-and-paste approach to authorship.

[23] Feine, 134.

[24] Otto Zurhellen, "Die Heimat des vierten Evangeliums," in *Theologische Arbeiten aus dem Rheinjschen Wissenschaftlichen Prediger-Verein* (Tübingen: J.C.B. Mohr [Paul Siebeck], 1909), 11: 33–92.

difficult.[25] But ultimately, the similarities in order are accounted for in ways not tied to a literary dependence.[26]

Secondly, Zurhellen examines the possibility that John shows some knowledge of Luke's *Sondergut*. In particular, he lifts up the following elements of Luke's special material that should, if John knew the Third Gospel, have left some traces in John's narrative: the virgin birth, the concern with Bethlehem as Jesus' birthplace, the relationship between John the Baptist and Jesus, the special Lukan healing stories. In all these cases, with the possible exception of some common material in the Lazarus stories, Zurhellen concludes that John shows no sign of knowing Luke.

Third, he raises the question of whether John at least follows the Lukan text in those pericopes which might be called "Synoptic." A closeness between Luke and John in synoptic-like texts is found only in the Passion narrative. But even there, where there are a number of points of similarity (e.g., the term Βασιλεύς with reference to Jesus in the triumphal entry), the overall pericopes tend to show *more* similarity with Mark or Matthew than with Luke. It is, then, highly unlikely that John followed Luke's text; but rather, he may have been influenced by some Lukan details and interests.

Finally, Zurhellen examines what he calls Lukan expansions or corrections to the Synoptic accounts. These include such striking features as Satan's involvement in Judas' betrayal and the treble declaration of innocence, as well as the absence of such details as the kiss at the betrayal, the cry of dereliction on the cross, and the flight of the disciples. Such similarities in the presence or absence of features are so striking that they cannot be accidental. But at the same time, Zurhellen is troubled that while these "Lukanisms" appear in John, other striking Lukan features (e.g., the Herod scene) are absent.

---

[25] The points at which a relationship might be suggested are as follows:
  1. Jesus' speech after the last meal.
  2. The placement of the prediction of Peter's denial.
  3. The arrest after the sword strike incident.

[26] Zurhellen, 41.

In addition to these individual points of contact, the Third and Fourth Gospels betray a number of similarities in Christology (e.g., Jesus as savior, death of Jesus as merely a passage to glorification in heaven) and other theological or geographical interests (e.g., the focus on Judea, Samaria). Such diffuse and yet pervasive similarities between Luke and John are, according to Zurhellen, indicative not of a literary dependence but rather of a close contact between the Johannine and Lukan communities in which the Gospels arose. Zurhellen finally concludes that John originated in the same region and kind of Christian community that produced Luke.[27]

The rest of Zurhellen's article is an attempt to place the origination of both Luke and John (although he focuses primarily on John) in the region of Syria—specifically Antioch.[28] He compares Antioch's thought world with that of Justin Martyr,[29] as well as with the Johannine letters and the Apocalypse. Zurhellen's primary conclusion is that the striking resemblances in thought between Luke and John argue for a common point of origin.

Zurhellen's analysis is always conducted from the standpoint of certainty that John is late and derivative: the author must have known Mark and Matthew.[30] But his article is helpful in advancing a couple of important approaches to the Luke-John relationship. First of all, Zurhellen is struck more by similarities in *content* than in *wording*.[31] For him, such issues of content are suggestive of a close relationship, albeit not a literary one. Second, he explains the relationship by

---

[27] Zurhellen, 56.

[28] An interesting aspect of his argument is the attempt to show that John 21 is from the same hand that produced the Revelation. Moreover, Zurhellen sees traces of Mark 16, Luke 5, and Luke 24 in this trailer to the Fourth Gospel, suggesting that it is a very late composition.

[29] While Zurhellen notes that Dial. 88, 316 is close to John 1:19 ff, he also comments that it has been suggested that Justin knew here a non-canonical source that is somewhere between the Lukan and Johannine presentations (66).

[30] Citing approvingly H. J. Holtzmann's work. Zurhellen, 37, n. 3.

[31] See below, chapter 5, on Marion Soards methodological approach.

THE ARGUMENT FOR COMMON TRADITION

JULIUS SCHNIEWIND

In 1914, Julius Schniewind presented the first monograph devoted solely to the relationship between Luke and John.[32] As he notes, while the question of Luke and John's relationship is related to the issue of John and the Synoptics, it is in fact a deeper and more difficult issue.[33] Schniewind acknowledges that one might find evidence for a literary relationship between John and the Synoptics that does not necessarily imply John's use of Luke. The problems are related, but certainly not synonymous.

The beginning points for Schniewind's work are the aforementioned works, especially those of H. Holtzmann and Zurhellen. The study makes full use of previous scholarship; in fact, Schniewind tends to play Holtzmann off against Zurhellen in the study, generally taking sides with Zurhellen.

What is especially significant about Schniewind's study is the careful methodical approach he takes to the question. Rather than simply comparing various points of commonality and then drawing conclusions from them, he selects as the most secure starting point those pericopes in John and Luke which are parallel, that is, those which relate essentially the same story and which have extensive points of contact, and he restricts himself to that field of inquiry. Moreover, within the group of selected passages, he is careful to discuss not only points of commonality but also differences. Schniewind's investigation focuses on the following units of scripture:

---

[32] Julius Schniewind, *Die Parallelperikopen bei Lukas und Johannes*.

[33] "Dies zweite thema [i.e., John and the Synoptics] ist nicht, wie es zuerst scheint, weiter, sondern vielmehr einfacher als unser Thema." Schniewind, 5.

α. Baptism of Jesus (Luke 3:3–20 par. John 1:19 f).
β. Peter's catch of fish (Luke 5:1–11 par. John 21:1–19).
γ. The official from Capernaum (Luke 7:1–10 par. John 4:46–54).
δ. The anointing (Luke 7:36–50 par. John 12:3–8).
ε. The entry into Jerusalem (Luke 19:28–40 par. John 12:12–19).
ζ. The prediction of denial (Luke 22:31–34 par. John 13:36–38).
η. The arrest (Luke 22:39, 47–53 par. John 18:1–11).
θ. Peter's denial and Sanhedrin trial (Luke 22:54–71 par. John 18:12–27).
ι. Pilate pericope (Luke 23:1–25 par. John 18:28–19:26).
κ. Cross and burial (Luke 23:26–56 par. John 19:16–42).
λ. Report of Resurrection (Luke 24 par. John 20).

In his examination of these pericopes, Schniewind carefully sifts the previous scholarly approaches. In contrast to earlier studies, Schniewind considers a mass of detail. It is, then, a well-reasoned and significant approach.

Schniewind concludes from his study that despite the extensiveness of the agreements between Luke and John, the relationship of the two can best be explained as one of common reliance on an oral tradition. It is clear to him that the argument that John relied on Luke is completely unproveable and is in fact contradicted by much of the evidence that presents itself in a close study.[34] Schniewind notes, for instance, the strong verbal connection between Luke and John in the prediction of Peter's denial, but he notes as well agreements between John and Matthew and Mark against Luke and between Luke and Mark against Matthew and John. More importantly, he observes that Peter's reply is completely dissimilar, thereby making a literary connection highly unlikely.[35] Likewise in his discussion of the arrest pericope, Schniewind argues that the absence of distinctly Lukan material (i.e., Jesus' word to Judas, the healing of

---

[34] Schniewind, 95.
[35] Schniewind, 31.

the ear, the final word of Jesus in Luke 22:53) works against John's literary reliance on Luke.[36]

But his conclusion is not without some subtleties. He is willing to accept as a given that John knew the Synoptics.[37] Indeed, Schniewind argues that the Fourth Gospel presupposes the synoptic Gospels, but he asserts that John did not use them as a literary source. Moreover, he admits that in at least two pericopes, the anointing pericope and Peter's catch of fish, there is evidence that reminiscences of Luke have crept into John's account in some specific and recognizable ways. In this, Schniewind anticipates to a certain extent A. Dauer's approach.[38] Still, he presents a strong counterargument to Holtzmann, who had proposed literary reliance as the sole explanation.

Given the importance of Schniewind's study to this issue, a closer examination of his work is in order. While Schniewind provides perhaps the most extensive study to date of the relationship between Luke and John, his conclusions are in large part the result of his presuppositions. For the present purpose, it is important to see what Schniewind assumes and how that leads to his conclusions.

A good place to see Schniewind's methodology is in his discussion of the anointing pericope,[39] where Schniewind notes that while the Lukan and Johannine stories are quite different, the striking similarity of the anointing of Jesus' feet and the wiping of the ointment with the woman's hair nonetheless point to a relationship that can hardly be accidental.

Previous scholars had come to contrary positions as to how this occurred: O. Holtzmann and Spitta had argued that John must have taken over the Markan or Matthean story, modifying it with an awareness of the Lukan account, while B. Weiß had argued, to the contrary, that Luke's account reflects the Johannine tradition.[40] As

---

[36] Schniewind, 37.
[37] Schniewind, 99.
[38] See below, p. 72.
[39] Schniewind, 21–26.
[40] Schniewind, 22.

Schniewind considers the various arguments, a primary issue in evaluating proposals involves the "natural sequence" of events. It appears that the deciding factor for him, then, is his perception of historical verisimilitude: the direction of literary dependence must flow from most secure historical construction to least secure. Spitta's argument is that anointing the feet and then drying them off, as found in John, makes very little sense and hence cannot be original. Thus the Johannine account must be derivative from Luke. In contrast, B. Weiβ's argument is that the remorseful tears cannot be original because the woman has already been forgiven of her sins. Between the approaches of Spitta and Weiβ, Schniewind is more convinced by Spitta; John's account must be derivative in some sense.[41]

But following questions raised by Feine, who argued against literary dependence, Schniewind takes up the question of the self-sufficiency of John's account. He argues that the Johannine account makes little sense as an anointing story (as found in Mark) that has been modified under the influence of Luke, nor does it presuppose a story that is significantly different from Luke's version. In other words, as Feine argues and Schniewind agrees, there is no evidence that John has stitched together two anointing stories; the idea of a literary reliance of John on Luke is thus discounted. The question then remains how the Lukan features made it into John's account: do they represent a "reminiscence" of Luke's account or a reliance on a common oral tradition? Although generally Schniewind argues for a common oral tradition, here he leaves the door open to the idea that John might have read Luke and included here a reminiscence of his account.[42]

It is clear, at any rate, that the "historical likelihood" is a crucial issue in ruling out Luke's reliance on a Johannine tradition. Because

---

[41] "Bei Lk. 7,38 haben wir die viel natürlicher Reihenfolge: Tränen, ἐκμάσσειν, Küβ, Salbung." B. Weiβ, *Die Quellen des Lukasevangeliums* (Stuttgart: J. G. Cotta'sche Buchhandlung Nachfolger, 1907), 23. The focus on what is most "natural" is a continual mark of Schniewind's approach.

[42] "Dabei wird sich nicht ohne weiteres entscheiden lassen, ob Joh. das uns vorliegende Lukasevangelium gelesen hat... " Schniewind, 23.

Schniewind considers the Lukan account more natural (and hence historically plausible), that account must be the more original of the two. The question then is limited to whether the usage was literary. And Schniewind is skeptical in his estimation of when to attribute material to literary reliance: mere concurrence of words is not sufficient.

In a following chapter on the announcement of Peter's denial,[43] we can see how Schniewind approaches his task of analysis: Schniewind begins the discussion by noting the agreements in order that are shared between Luke and John, contrary to Matthew and Mark. These agreements involve Luke's and John's placement of the denial prediction within the sequence of the meal/departure events.[44] The brief discussion of the construction of Luke's and John's pericopes again turns on the "natural ordering" of narratives. For Schniewind, the natural, and hence original, order of events must have linked the prediction of betrayal and the prediction of Peter's denial. The linkage is found most closely in the Fourth Gospel, assuming that 13:34–35 is a later insertion.[45] Certainly Mark and Matthew's split account, with the dinner intruding in the middle of the two events, is secondary. But so is Luke's account (albeit to a lesser extent than Matthew and Mark's), in that the dispute by the disciples over rank intrudes. For Schniewind, this early account, with a minor intrusion, suggests that Luke had access to some other source—like John—along with Q (which explains the dispute over rank), which he used in constructing the pericope.

Despite the observation of this common ordering, the primary focus of Schniewind's attention is a pair of verbal similarities between Luke and John that are different from the phraseology in Mark and Matthew: neither Luke nor John contains the phrase ταύτῃ τῇ νυκτὶ

---

[43] Schniewind, 28–32.

[44] See the chart and discussion on similarities in order, chapter 3, p. 107 below.

[45] Following Wellhausen, see Schniewind, 29.

πρὶν, found in Mark and Matthew,[46] and both Luke and John contain the wording οὐ ... ἕως, which is *not* found in Mark and Matthew.[47] The question, then, turns on whether these points of similar wording should be understood as indicating a literary dependence. Schniewind argues, based on the mass of other differences, that literary dependence is not necessary to explain such similarities. He is drawn to Zurhellen's argument that this common language could have been fixed in an oral form, but also considers the possibility that John has included in his text a reminiscence of Luke's wording.[48]

With these two examples in mind, one is in a position to better understand Schniewind's work within the framework of Schniewind's own presuppositions. In the first place, as has been noted, Schniewind operates from the belief that one can determine the most natural or most historically probable arrangement of events and that that arrangement, once determined, will point to the earliest of the accounts. Such a valuation on historical probability as a means of determining priority of Gospel material is framed on the unstated assumption that the development of gospel material has been from original (i.e., historic) to interpreted accounts and, furthermore, that the trend of those changes can be determined.[49] In an abstract sense, it might seem reasonable to assume that if the material is derived from historical reminiscence, then the most historically "sound" material must be the earliest. Of course, determining what is historically sound is a notorious crux. But even if such determination is possible, it is just as likely that an early garbled or strikingly odd account would be corrected by later handlers of the tradition as that a late account would

---

[46] Cf. Matt 26:34 and Mark 14:30.

[47] Cf. Luke 22:34 and John 13:38.

[48] Schniewind, 32.

[49] Cf. E. P. Sanders, *The Tendencies of the Synoptic Tradition* (Cambridge: University Press, 1969). Sanders examined a series of criteria (i.e., shortness, semitisms, direct speech) that has been used to distinguish early from late traditions. He found that while there are some general directions, it is really not possible to apply them to individual pericopes in order to distinguish early from

be corrupted. In other words, there is no proof that the "reasonable" account (which is often the test, for Schniewind, of historical soundness) is early nor that subsequent editors or authors would be the source of "corrupted" material. This assumption of Schniewind's —that reasonableness and historical soundness and chronological priority are somehow integrally related—simply allows him to justify whatever material he has already decided is early. It is not compelling, however, for determining the tendencies in the passing along of traditions, whether of a literary or an oral nature.

Second, there is a consistent tendency by Schniewind to assume that oral traditions contained a high degree of specificity. In other words, Schniewind shares with the early form critics the belief that the material in the Gospels reached a fair degree of fixedness that could later be expressed in common written form.

Finally, and perhaps more importantly, Schniewind works from the assumption that John must have come later than Luke and that any verbal correspondences or literary relationship could have flowed only from Luke to John. Thus when he finds material in John that is more historically plausible than corresponding material in Luke, it must be indicative of a common tradition, not Luke's having used John. That is a subtle but controlling presupposition. When instances of possible literary relationship are considered, the question that is raised is whether John might reasonably have used Luke, but not the reverse.

F. C. GRANT

In an article published in *Journal of Biblical Literature,* Grant gives a brief review of many of the often-cited parallels between Luke and John, specifically those which Grant thinks might argue for John's use of Luke rather than, or in addition to, the Gospel of Mark.[50] The

---

late.

[50] F. C. Grant, "Was the Author of John Dependent upon the Gospel of Luke?" *JBL* 56 (1937): 285–307. See also the discussion in Smith, *John Among the Gospels,* 91–93.

bulk of the article is given over to a seriatim listing of the parallels, followed by Grant's own opinion about the likely derivation of the points of similarity. His observations are not lengthy, nor do they show evidence of extensive exegetical analysis. Nonetheless, Grant provides an independent approach to the question, and one that has a number of suggestive, if not definitive, comments. In general, Grant argues that the points of similarity between the thirty-one pairs of pericopes examined should not be attributed to a literary dependence of John on Luke. Rather, the points of similarity derive from three separate and distinct sources.

1. A host of similarities is attributed to John's knowledge of a Q-like source. Thus the statements about the apostles' authority (John 5:23; 13:30; 15:23) are seen as reflecting the Q statement not only in Luke (10:16) and Matthew (10:40) but also in Mark (9:37)! It would appear that Grant understands John and Mark to have access to Q, perhaps as a written source, but more probably as an oral source.[51]

2. In a few instances, Grant seems to suggest a common oral tradition that lies behind both Luke and John. In discussing the trial before Pilate, Grant notes that although peculiarly Lukan language is missing, there is unique material present in both Luke and John that might suggest a shared tradition. That both Gospels have Pilate declaring Jesus' innocence is more than accidental. But the common material cannot be attributed to John's use of Luke, since such use would have created a closer correspondence than that actually found.[52] The explanation must be either common oral tradition, or the knowledge by John of Luke's source.

3. A number of items called points of commonality should actually be seen as simply deriving from Mark; Grant explicitly states that he thinks Mark was a source for John.[53] A number of parallels are quickly dismissed as really only Markan parallels with little or no

---

[51] Grant uses the term "echoes" in his discussion of Q, suggesting that such use of Q was more in keeping with oral recollection.

[52] Grant, 299.

[53] Grant, 285.

unique Lukan material: the naming of Peter, Jesus' real family, the feeding of the five thousand.[54] Others require a bit more explanation. For instance, Grant attributes John's anointing story (John 12:1–8) to a reworking of Mark's account: "Not a single feature of the Johannine narrative appears to be derived from Luke; on the contrary the whole is clearly rewriting of the Markan incident."[55] Of course, the only way that Grant can make that assertion is to explain away the issue of the anointing of the feet instead of the head and the drying of the feet with the woman's hair. Grant does that by attributing these features to textual glosses.

4. Perhaps the most provocative and helpful aspect of Grant's article is his concentration on the textual anomalies that pervade the Luke-John relationship. He quickly notes, for instance, the series of variants in Luke 24 (Western non-Interpolations)[56] that have a strong similarity to Johannine language. For Grant, these are clearly late additions to the Gospel of Luke. But he finds evidence of such glosses in a number of other places (anointing, triumphal entry, prediction of Peter's denial, appearance of the risen Lord) and is willing to consider the possibility of glosses even without manuscript evidence.[57] A more extensive argument for textual contamination from the John account is discussed with reference to Luke 24:37, 39–43. Grant argues that without these verses the original account flows better and that the Lucan passages make sense if we read the Johannine context alongside them.

Grant, then, independent of Schniewind and Zurhellen, rejects any Johannine dependence on Luke despite his sharing a general belief that John was late and knew Mark. He explains the points of contact

---

[54] That these were even chosen by Grant is surprising. They illustrate little or no correspondence between Luke and John, and seem to be almost straw men.

[55] Grant, 290.

[56] See chapter 4 below.

[57] Smith, 91. Grant is quite complacent about the fact that early exemplars of his reconstructed text would have simply disappeared in the early period of transmission.

partly by assuming common oral or pre-gospel sources, but primarily by attributing much of John to a free rewriting of the Gospel of Mark or to textual corruptions. Grant's article is heavily colored not only by his unargued presupposition that John knew Mark but also by his equally unargued supposition that Luke could not have used John, which he shares with other scholars and does not even think of discussing.[58]

E. OSTY

In a very short but suggestive article, E. Osty points to the striking cluster of similarities between the Lukan and Johannine Passion stories.[59] He locates forty points of contact between the Passion stories, which he breaks into four categories: theological contacts, that point to religious reverence, historical (tradition) contacts, and literary contacts (order or style issues). Some of the points are a bit vague or suggestive and there is little attempt at analysis, but in the main his is a helpful listing of similarities between the two.[60]

Of the various contacts he cites, Osty conservatively assumes the probability that most come from the use of common sources or a similar approach to oral traditions.[61] But two particular groups of similarities call for special consideration: those items of a literary

---

[58] At one point, Grant notes: "If there were any [literary dependence], it would be the wholly improbable dependence of Luke upon John, rather than John upon Luke..."(291). Moreover, the entire thrust of the text-critical argument is that obvious Johannine language in Luke must be from a textual gloss rather than any possible literary dependence.

[59] E. Osty, "Les Points de Contact Entre le Récit de la Passion dans Saint Luc et Saint Jean," *Mélanges Jules Lebreton* (Recherches de Science Religieuse 39, Paris: 1951), 146–154.

[60] See, for instance, Marion Soards' critiques of Osty's comments on "majesty," etc. Marion Soards, *The Passion According to Luke* (Sheffield: JSOT Press, 1987), 33.

[61] Osty, 153.

nature in the Fourth Gospel which might be called "Lukanisms," and those items of a theological nature in Luke which are often called "Johannine." The former items Osty is willing to ascribe to the involuntary reminiscence by an author of John—perhaps, as Boismard suggested, a late editor of John.[62]

The latter items, however, are more difficult. Osty identifies three features in Luke that suggest that the Third evangelist had contact with John: Luke has the same group of women, namely, Mary Magdalene, the mother of Jesus, and Martha and Mary; Luke shows a particular interest in John; and Luke shows John and Peter together. Osty explains these "Johannisms" by suggesting that the Fourth Gospel must have come into being over a long period of meditation and discussion, and that Luke might well have been inspired by the Johannine community in Palestine during that period.[63]

Osty's article is suggestive in a number of areas. In the first place, he allows that there might have been more than one origin for similar material; it is certainly possible that common traditions, Lukan influence on later Johannine formation, and Lucan knowledge of the developing Johannine tradition could all exist simultaneously, although that seems unduly complicated. Certainly he is open to a variety of possible impulses for the many points of commonality. Second, he points to an important issue, that is, the "Johannine" flavor of some of the similarities. Finally, he suggests a common geographical genesis as an important consideration when analyzing the points of commonality.

HANS KLEIN

Klein's article on the Luke-John material in the Passion story has its beginning point in Schniewind's book.[64] Klein wants to

---

[62] Osty, 154. Osty especially notes this is not a problem since the final version of John is later than Luke.

[63] Osty, 154.

[64] Hans Klein, "Die lukanisch-johanneische Passionstradition," *ZNW* 67 (1976): 155–186.

reexamine some of the material that Schniewind studied, but with an eye to possible written precursors to the Gospels. Especially, Klein is motivated to explain the nature of the unique Lukan material with an eye to determining its form and shape.

By assuming the existence of written *Vorlagen* behind the Gospels, Klein proposes a solution to the points of commonality between Luke, John, and Mark that relies upon interrelationships between their precursors. He suggests that behind both Luke and John there were precursor texts (LV for Luke, JV for John). These texts themselves were derived from an even earlier precursor text, G (*Grundschrift*), which was closely related to the precursor text behind Mark.[65] There is, then, no direct literary relationship between Luke and John or between John and Mark, but rather an intermediate relationship mediated by these *Vorlagen*.

Klein's approach is to study a number of specific pericopes, or even single verses, that are illustrative of a close relationship between Luke and John. He then questions whether such points found in Luke can reasonably come from Mark or from another source. Furthermore, Klein attempts to determine which is the earlier or more original version and which is derivative.[66] Such judgments, of course, are somewhat subjective but are based on Klein's awareness of the editorial tendencies of the evangelists. Two examples are illustrative of his approach.

The first example deals with the presentation of Jesus before the high priest in Luke 22:54–71 and John 18:12–24. For Klein it is noteworthy that Luke and John share some common words (συλλαμβάνειν and ἄγειν) that distinguish them from Matthew and Mark. Especially these verbal similarities,[67] together with such common points as the reference to Jesus' appearance before a high priest without mention of the Sanhedrin and the emphasis on Jesus'

---

[65] Klein, 156.

[66] A move that is very similar to Schniewind's approach.

[67] "Für die Wahl der beiden Verben in ihrer Verbindung gibt es kaum ein andere Erklärung als dei einer gemeinsamen Quelle." (Klein, 12)

majesty at the arrest (Luke 22:53), point to a common source. Indeed, Klein argues that the inclusion of the Sanhedrin at the trial in Mark is a secondary insertion by Mark into the "natural" story, hence suggesting that there is a common pre-Markan and pre-Lukan/pre-Johannine narrative behind the high priest account.[68]

The second example comes from his examination of Luke's account of the hearing before the Jewish leaders in which Jesus affirms that he is the Son of God (Luke 22:67-70). Klein, like Schniewind, notes the strong similarities of Luke's passage with John 10:24-39. In particular he is struck by the combination or ordering of the question whether Jesus is the Christ[69] together with a reference to the issue of belief. This concatenation of similarities is so striking that Klein cannot doubt a common written source over against mere tradition.[70] But if there is a common written source, it must be a document that lies behind both Luke and John. In the case of Luke, the common material has clearly been interwoven with Mark. And in the case of John, it is obvious to Klein that the material was originally from the trial scene preceding Jesus' death, and was moved by John to another location. By deduction, then, a common source, G, must be responsible for the material found in both Luke and John.[71]

---

[68] "Sie sprechen deutlich für eine gemeinsame lukanish-johanneische Passionstradition.... scheint diese Tradition älter zu sein als Markus." (Klein, 164).

[69] The question is only whether he is the Christ, not Christ, Son of God (Blessed) as in Matt/Mark. Klein, 166.

[70] Klein, 165.

[71] In a somewhat similar approach, Anton Dauer, "Spuren der (Synoptischen) Synedriumsverhandlung im 4.Evangelium," in *John and the Synoptics,* ed. A. Denaux (Leuven: University Press, 1992), 307-339 agrees that John 10:24 contains part of the missing trial before the Sanhedrin, and that John did not rely directly on the Synoptics for certain features, especially those in common with Luke. But unlike Klein, Dauer understands Luke to have relied simply on Mark and the redactional modifications to have been conflated with Mark and Matthew into an additional text (a *Verschmelzungsvorgänge*), which was the source for John.

In many ways, Klein's approach is very similar to Schniewind's in that it seeks to explain the similarities as existing prior to Luke and John. Schniewind concluded that the traditions were not so specific and extensive that they could not have been oral. Klein is far more impressed by the similarities, especially series or combinations of them, and concludes that such specificity must have come from written sources. Moreover, Klein is willing to posit a fairly precise stemma for these traditions:

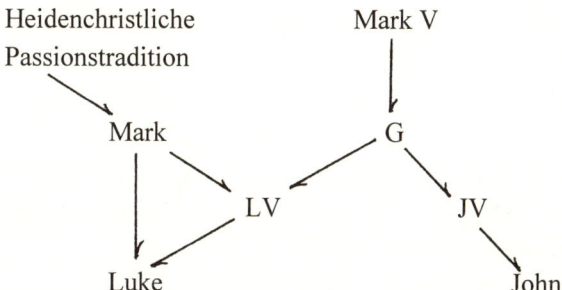

Klein focuses attention on the strength of the similarities between Luke and John in the Passion story, and in particular emphasizes some items, such as similarities in wording and order, that would point to a written rather than an oral tradition behind them. Moreover, Klein points out a number of places where Luke has clearly woven together Markan material with other material that is not Markan ("Lukas...arbeitet Markus und LV ineinander"). But while Klein considers and rejects Johannine dependence on Luke,[72] he never considers the alternative of John's possible influence on Luke.

PIERSON PARKER

In a series of articles penned over a number of years, Parker addresses in various ways the problem of the relationship between Luke and John. He calls to our attention the magnitude of the

---

[72] Klein, 167, point *a*.

relationship, but comes to the conclusion that Luke and John share a common tradition, probably oral, that arose from a relationship borne of close geographical and, perhaps, personal affinity.

The first article, "Two Editions of John,"[73] suggests that John went through a late revision in which chapters 2 (vv. 1–12), 4, 6, and 21 were added. For Parker, the compelling issues have to do with the simultaneous existence of Johannine style on the one hand, suggesting common authorship with the rest of the Gospel, and contextual disjuncture on the other hand. In other words, there must have been some disruption of an earlier narrative, but the author of the intruding elements is the same author as the rest of the Gospel. Parker especially notes at this point that there are striking contacts with the Gospel of Luke in chapters 4, 6, and 21. His conclusion is that the Fourth Gospel manifests awareness of the Lukan form of the Gospel, possibly by oral transmission, and hence this late edition must have arisen after the Third Gospel was penned.

In an important later article, "Luke and the Fourth Evangelist,"[74] Parker develops more fully the breadth of the points of contact between the Third and Fourth evangelists. The similarities have a wide range, from a similar self-consciousness toward their task as authors to common geographical, chronological, and theological concerns.[75] Moreover, Parker details a number of specific events, names, and phrases that are common to Luke and John but are absent from Mark and Matthew. The simple listing of the points of commonality is impressive. As Parker notes, quoting B. S. Easton, "In work of this sort, only bulk counts."[76] And Parker indeed provides bulk.

---

[73] Pierson Parker, "Two Editions of John," *JBL* 75 (1956): 303–14.

[74] Pierson Parker, "Luke and the Fourth Evangelist," *NTS* 9 (1963): 317–36.

[75] Parker does not use the term theological, but a number of his points of similarity reflect theological perspectives: the relative lack of interest in apocalypticism, the epiphany of Christ's glory, the depiction of Christ as a prophet like Moses, the emphasis on the role of the Holy Spirit.

[76] Parker, "Luke and the Fourth Evangelist," 326.

But the manifold points of contact do not, for Parker, suggest a literary relationship. Despite the depth and breadth of the points of contact, the divergences are significant. First, many of the similarities occur in widely different settings. Second, John's and Luke's versions of the Gospel narrative are very different. Third, the contacts that do exist are largely *allusive*, not closely similar in wording. But most important for Parker, the mind sets of the authors are completely different: John is theologically driven, while Luke misses the theological import of the events.[77] So Parker can conclude that Luke and John simply shared a common source of information and reflection on the Jesus story. But the relationship is nonetheless so close that "the Fourth Evangelist must somewhere, some time, have been associated with Luke in the Christian missionary enterprise."[78] In a later article in the Morton Smith festschrift, Parker turns again to the points of commonality between Lukan and Johannine materials.[79] In this article, which details similarities between John and Acts, similarities primarily in *concepts*, Parker still concludes, as he did earlier, that the authors of Luke-Acts and John sprang from a common early Christian community centered in Judea.

It is striking that, for Parker, proof of literary dependence would largely hinges to a great extent on the commonality of the points of view of the authors. He seemingly sweeps aside a number of close similarities, even close wording, as unimportant to the issue since Luke and John are so different in theology and purpose. The idea that literary re-working could, as Windisch noted, be employed precisely to

---

[77] This conclusion of Parker's about the primitive theological understanding of Luke would be contested by many; Luke's theology is bound up with the narrative flow of Luke and Acts.

[78] Parker, "Luke and the Fourth Evangelist," 336.

[79] Pierson Parker, "The Kinship of John and Acts," in *Christianity, Judaism and Other Greco-Roman Cults*, ed. Jacob Neusner (Leiden: E. J. Brill, 1975), 187–205.

distance one from a previous work does not seem possible to Parker.[80]

ROBERT MADDOX

As an appendix-like chapter in his study of the central theological themes in Luke-Acts, Maddox offers "Special Affinities of Luke and John,"[81] an extensive, though not exhaustive, catalogue of similarities between the Gospels of Luke and John. The similarities noted by Maddox are of a "content" nature—that is, Maddox makes no attempt to undertake a careful examination of words and phrases; rather, he makes his point by simply noting the similar concepts, order, or names[82] found in the two Gospels.

In his discussion of the anointing pericope and, in particular, of Bailey's treatment[83] of it, Maddox takes issue with both Schniewind's and Bailey's arguments that the common feature of the feet and hair in John's account could only have come about through some kind of influence from the more original Lukan story. He disagrees especially with Bailey's conclusion that the anointing of the feet and wiping with the hair is the best proof of a literary relationship between Luke and John. For Maddox, this is precisely the kind of feature that is best explained by oral tradition. One need not locate the "original" story to recognize some possible oral elements that both Gospels, independently, might have taken up.[84]

---

[80] Hans Windisch, *Johannes und die Synoptiker. Wollte der Vierte Evangelist die Älteren Evangelien Ergänzen oder Ersetzen?* (Leipzig: J. C. Hinrichs'sche Buchhandlung, 1926). Windisch rejects independence, and sees John as a deliberate displacement. The knowledge and "use" of the synoptics, in this conception, is negative—to critique and replace, not embrace.

[81] Robert Maddox, *The Purpose of Luke-Acts*, (Edinburgh: T&T Clark, 1982). See also the discussion in Smith, *John Among the Gospels*, 103–110.

[82] Maddox is particularly struck by the Mary, Martha, Lazarus connections. Maddox, 165.

[83] Maddox, 166. See also p. 59 below.

[84] Maddox, 166–67.

Perhaps Maddox's most striking observation concerning the similarities is the extent of material that shares common geographical[85] and theological[86] perspectives.

In the case of the geographical commonality, Maddox begins by noting that both John and Luke have a far greater focus on Judea than do Matthew and Mark. For the Fourth Gospel, the primary field of activity is Judea: Jesus is repeatedly in Jerusalem, for various feasts, or in the region surrounding Jerusalem. But Luke also seems to have a similar interest. From 9:51 on, Luke has Jesus heading toward Jerusalem; in other words, the bulk of the Gospel is either set in Jerusalem or traveling toward it. And while there are few specific geographical markers in the travel section, there are indications that much of it is set in Judea.[87] Specifically, both Luke and John record more frequent references to Samaria or Samaritans. Finally, Maddox notes that Luke, like John, places the locus of post-Resurrection activity in Jerusalem, not Galilee. All of that suggests a common interest in the central and southern regions of Palestine in Luke and John.

Maddox finds a number of intriguing theological similarities between the Third and Fourth Gospels. Luke, like John, has an interest in exploring the relationship of Israel to Jesus. That interest takes a number of forms. Both Gospels develop the idea that rejection of Jesus is related to a refusal by the Jews to heed the words of Moses (cf. Luke 16:29–31, John 5:46–47).[88] And both Gospels are careful to set both Jesus' ministry in the context of Judaism and to delay the Gentile mission until after the Resurrection (note the omission of Mark 6:46–8:26 from Luke and the delay of the Gentile mission until after Acts 10; cf. John 12:20–24 and 7:33–36). Both Luke and John develop, as an important feature of Jesus' teaching, the future role of the Holy Spirit (note, for instance, Luke 11:13 and John 14:16–26).

---

[85] Maddox, 168–170.
[86] Maddox, 170–174.
[87] Maddox, 169.
[88] Maddox, 171.

Finally, Maddox argues that both Luke and John in their respective eschatologies have reduced the importance of the future consummation in favor of a belief that at least parts of the eschatological promises are already fulfilled (e.g. see Luke 4:21, 10:17–20; Acts 2:17–21; John 3:15, 3:36; 4:23; 5:25).

What explanation is made of the series of common themes and items of content between these Gospels? For Maddox, the geographical commonalities are particularly telling. Like Zurhellen and Parker, Maddox believes they must point to a common region for the communities from which the Gospels or their traditions originated: southern Palestine.[89] By virtue of geographical proximity, these communities would have some common material not contained in Matthew or Mark. In other words, Maddox argues that the two Gospels contain unique oral traditions that stem from their close geographical proximity.

Maddox, even more than Schniewind, sees the development of oral traditions behind the common material in John and Luke. That is perhaps because he gives more importance to the thematic similarities that are difficult to discuss in narrow exegetical studies of the common passages. But it is also clear that Maddox is more open to the form-critical model that valorizes oral traditions.[90] There is no assumption in Maddox that John is necessarily later than Luke. Indeed, given the emphasis on oral transmission, the question of literary order becomes simply unimportant in Maddox's study.

---

[89] Maddox, 175. Maddox does not assume the gospels were necessarily written in southern Palestine, but rather that the traditions arose there. The actual composition could have been done anywhere; moreover it involved a relatively complex process of revision over time.

[90] It is important to note Maddox's explicit acceptance of Gardner-Smith's arguments, which Maddox places in opposition to Blinzler. See Maddox, 158–162, in which the entire discussion is framed at the outset by this consideration of the form-critical perspective.

STEPHAN LANDIS

In a recent study, Stephen Landis examines the relationships between the various versions of the healing of the centurion's servant/royal official's son in Matthew, Luke and John.[91] He concludes that the relationships that exist stem from developments in the pre-Gospel traditions, that are assumed to have been summarized into written documents early on rather than to have remained as oral traditions.

Landis begins his study with an effort to determine the sources behind the Gospels (Q, *Sondergut* [Sg] used by Luke, Semeia [SQ] source in John) and then the extent of the evangelists' editorial modifications. With respect to Luke, Landis finds that, aside from the Q material in Luke 7:6c–9, most of this account was derived from the *Sondergut*;[92] Luke's editorial modification is confined to a few clauses that seam together the Sg and Q materials.[93] Similarly, Landis distinguishes between Johannine redaction and tradition in John 4:46–54, concluding that the Fourth evangelist as well was a conservative redactor of material. John modifies source(s) primarily to adapt to the geographical setting of the narrative and to introduce a critique of faith based on signs (v. 48). Landis finds that the bulk of the account stems from the Semeia source.[94] The main focus of the book, contained in the fourth chapter, is Landis' comparison of the redactional elements in the Gospels with the sources in order to determine whether any possible overlap occurs: (1) John with indications of redaction in Matthew and Luke, (2) Johannine redaction

---

[91] Stephan Landis, *Das Verhaltnis des Johannesevangeliums zu den Synoptikern: Am Beispiel von Mt 8,5–13; Lk 7,1–10; Joh 4,46–54*, BZNT 74 (Berlin: Walter de Gruyter, 1994).

[92] Landis, 10–17, 18–27.

[93] Landis presents a very sparse summary of Luke redactional language in 7:2–10. A mere forty-five words are presented as Luke's editorial contribution to the passage. (Landis, 10).

[94] Landis, 28–37.

with Q, (3) SQ with Q, (4) Johannine redaction with Sg, (5) SQ with Sg. Based on his analysis, Landis reaches the following conclusions.

1. Not a single indication of Matthean or Lukan redaction is found in John. John did not use Matthew or Luke in their final forms.[95]

2. The one agreement between John and Q (the word κύριε) is accidental: John did not know Q.[96]

3. The agreements between SQ and Q are tradition-history contacts: there is no literary relationship between SQ and Q.[97]

4. No agreements at all exist between John's redaction and Sg: there is no literary relationship between John and Sg.[98]

5. Despite finding a series of agreements between SQ and Sg, the agreements between SQ and Sg employ significantly different terminology (descriptions of the illness and, especially, use of δοῦλος instead of υἱός): there is no literary relationship between SQ and Sg.[99]

Thus, according to Landis, no literary relationship exists between any of the accounts other than Matthew and Luke's common use of Q. Landis interprets his data to suggest that all three accounts stem originally from an early *oral* miracle story. This miracle story was taken up in three separate literary forms: SQ, a miracle story; Luke-Sg, a miracle story used in support of an evangelistic commission; and Q, a sayings story.[100] What Landis has done, then, is to assert in a slightly modified way Schniewind's thesis that the relationship between Luke and John exists at the level of tradition, although in this case Landis would posit written tradition(s) rather than an oral one.

One might question the ease with which Landis presupposes both written forms of Q and the Lukan *Sondergut*, as well as the apparent transparency of the text that allows Landis' separation of source and editorial work. Landis' claims to be able to separate source

---

[95] Landis, 42.
[96] Landis, 44–45.
[97] Landis, 45–46.
[98] Landis, 46.
[99] Landis, 46–47.
[100] Landis, 53–56.

and redaction are often not supported with detailed arguments and are often contrary to others' determinations of source and redaction.[101] While such differences between scholars as to precise limits of source and redaction are common, what makes the issue crucial is that this separation determines the final results: if, for instance ἔμελλεν τελευτᾶν in Luke 7:2 is from Sg rather than Luke's hand (contra Dauer's analysis), then its similarity to John's ἔμελλεν ἀποθῄσκειν (4:47) could not be an indication of some literary relationship between the two evangelists.[102] Since such key determinations are not carefully argued, but often simply posited, Landis' argument loses much of its power.

In his approach to analysis as well as in his final results, Landis—though never citing him—is very similar to Schniewind. For Landis, literary relationships require a strong standard of proof. Similar language, even when it is part of an extensive pattern, can be attributed to oral development rather than literary reliance unless there exists a near identity in the language. This is, in part, a hesitancy to attribute much creativity in the use of sources to any of the evangelists. It appears, for instance, that the similarities found between the SQ and Sg materials are very suggestive of some form of literary relationship.[103] Yet Landis, by not sufficiently allowing for creative modification by authors has ruled out that possibility in advance. A literary relationship, under this standard, could only be considered if there were extensive examples of verbatim similarity.

Landis' methodology, like that of Dauer, has some sophistication that is helpful. He is correct in focusing on the distinction between source and redaction as a way of determining

---

[101] Cf. Dauer's analysis of the same pericope, *Johannes und Lukas: Untersuchungen zu den johanneish-lukanischen Parallelperikopen Joh 4,46–54/ Lk 7,1–10—Joh 12,1–8/ Lk 7,36–50; 10,38–42—Joh 20,19–29/ Lk 24,36–49*, Forschung zur Bibel 50 (Würzburg: Echter Verlag, 1984), 51–75 (John) and 110–16 (Luke).

[102] Landis, 20. Compare Dauer, *Johannes und Lukas*, 111-12.

[103] Landis, 47.

where the relationship took place. But it is questionable whether Landis is successful in this, in view of the completely different results reached by Dauer. Also of benefit, Landis examines the possibility that Johannine redaction could have been taken up in Luke and Matthew rather than simply assuming synoptic priority.

MATTI MYLLYKOSKI

In a recent article from Finland dealing with issues of Luke and Acts, Myllykoski turns his attention also to the special similarities between Luke and John.[104] The central question in Myllykoski's inquiry is whether it is likely that John relied on Luke as a source.

Myllykoski begins by significantly narrowing the field of similarities that should be considered. He considers and rejects "vague and general similarities" in four major areas: (1) theological similarities, (2) shared motif circles or similar theme construction, (3) similarities in the order of pericopes, and (4) shared missing details that do not appear in Mark. The first of these, theological similarities, would include common theological outlooks between the two Gospels that are not represented in Mark or Matthew.[105] The shared motif circles are such issues as common geographical concerns (e.g., Samaria) or common people (e.g., Mary and Martha) where the actual stories are not the same. Similarly, Myllykoski is aware that common absence of material is often striking between Luke and John, but that silence is a very difficult basis from which to make an argument. Myllykoski rejects these categories because, while they are suggestive of some link, it is not possible to definitively analyze them for literary relationships. More surprising than his rejection of the similarities (1), (2), and (4) is his rejection of the similarities in the order of pericopes. He considers these to be quite few in number: only one similarity in

---

[104] Matti Myllykoski, "The Material Common to Luke and John," in *Luke-Acts: Scandinavian Perspectives* (Göttingen: Vandenhoeck & Ruprecht, 1991), 115–56.

[105] See the Table 7, Chapter 3 below, p. 155.

Jesus' last supper and one in the conclusion of the Pilate trial. But he also tends to see them as only accidents, with few of the marks of either literary reliance or common tradition.[106]

After that radical winnowing, Myllykoski turns his attention to two major areas of similarity between Luke and John: those pericopes in which there are "concrete" minor agreements, and those in which Luke and John have parallel accounts.

The first major group of similarities he determines to have arisen entirely from common oral traditions that found their way into Luke and John independently. The compelling argument in each case is that the point of similarity has no contextual relationship with the other Gospel. One such example of Myllykoski's analysis is found in the accounts of Jesus' predictions of betrayal and Peter's denial, in Luke 22 and John 13. With respect to the prediction of Judas' betrayal, Myllykoski agrees that the common feature of Satan's entering into Judas could hardly occur in both accidentally.[107] But because John and Luke frame it so differently, it must not be the result of a literary usage. At one point Myllykoski allows that it is possible that John found this idea in Luke and modified it,[108] but he concludes that it is unlikely because of the widely different contexts in which the feature is found in the two Gospels.

Likewise, Myllykoski notes that Jesus' predictions of Peter's denial are strikingly similar. While he is able to explain much of the language in Luke as based on Mark, he admits that the οὐ..ἕως construction, which is virtually identical with John and markedly different from Mark and Matthew, is very difficult to account for as Lukan redaction. John, on the other hand, while having a kernel of similarity with the Synoptics has a different take on the stories, which would contradict a literary usage.

---

[106] Myllykoski, 122–23.

[107] Myllykoski, 128.

[108] Note that he never considers the possibility that Luke found the idea in John.

Myllykoski, then, sees literary usage of Gospels as always maintaining the original context of a saying or an idea. Specifically, for Myllykoski, it is not credible that John would use items from Luke, significantly changing the context or thrust of the material so used. Instead, striking similarities in widely different contexts must suggest a common oral (or perhaps written?)[109] tradition, not a literary reliance of John on Luke.

There is a stronger case to be made in those instances of parallel pericopes: Peter's draught of fish (Luke 5:1–11 par. John 21:1–14), the healing at Capernaum (Luke 7:1–10 par. John 4:46–54), Jesus' anointing (Luke 7:36–50 par. John 12:1–11), "If you are the Christ, tell us" (Luke 22:67–68 par. John 10:24–25), and the empty tomb and Jesus' appearance to the disciples (Luke 24:12 par. John 20:3–10 and Luke 24:36-43 par. John 20:19–23). In these cases the similarities are strong enough to warrant consideration of a literary relationship—especially so because Myllykoski finds many of the similarities to be situated in the redactional material of Luke (and John!). So, for instance, the common material in the healing at Capernaum belongs to the "last redactional phase of the text," which suggests that there was a possible use by one evangelist of the other.[110] But Myllykoski ultimately cannot bring himself to see John as having relied on Luke; the explanation must still be reliance on common oral tradition since the contexts are so radically different.

In the case of the empty tomb and appearance stories, however, Myllykoski becomes more open to a literary relationship: "The similarity of Lk 24:36–43 and Jn 20:19–23 is also obvious. One can hardly avoid the conclusion that either John knew the Lucan pericope and used it as his source or that both evangelists used a common tradition."[111] He rejects the idea that the textual variants are glosses and then struggles to understand the close relationship between the

---

[109] Myllykoski at a few points, such as the οὐ μὴ .. ἕως construction in John 13:38, suggests that John found them in his "literary source" (130).

[110] Myllykoski, 138.

[111] Myllykoski, 144.

two. A major factor in his conclusion is the "problematical" fit of certain features in the Lukan account. Luke was, according to him, struggling to fit disparate ideas together—namely the motifs of doubt and joy—in Luke 24:41. These "problematical" features suggest that Luke was fitting a traditional account similar to John's together with another account subject to his own redactional effort. Similarly, he finds that John has some of the same tensions. In analyzing the pre-Lukan and pre-Johannine traditions, he finds a strong similarity as well.[112] His conclusion in these cases is that Luke and John relied on a common tradition, possibly a written source.

Myllykoski provides a fresh look at much of the material common to Luke and John, but there are some presuppositions behind his analysis that bear examination. In the first place, as we have already seen so frequently, Myllykoski thinks a literary relationship can only be John's use of Luke; he never considers the reverse.

Perhaps more problematic are two assumptions Myllykoski makes about the nature of literary reliance on a source. In the first place, he assumes that an author (John, in his case) would rather slavishly follow a source; if material is freely selected, modified, and shaped to fit a different theological or narratological purpose, there cannot be a literary reliance. This, I believe, is the substance behind his protest that if material is in widely different contexts, there cannot be a literary dependence. But surely authors can use material in widely different ways. They can variously copy, slightly modify, radically reshape, and perhaps only allude to documents that they have "used."[113] Because of this assumption, Myllykoski has too quickly removed from consideration of a literary relationship much of the common material. Second, he is very vague about the nature of the "traditions" being used separately by John and Luke. At times it appears these are oral.

---

[112] Myllykoski, 149.

[113] So, for instance, it is very possible that Windisch's suggestion that John used the Synoptics for the purpose of refuting them is the best overall solution to the John-Synoptic question. If so, then John has a literary relationship with the Synoptics that is out of context precisely in order to overturn that context.

But at other times they are a highly ordered series of similarities (as in the empty tomb and appearance stories) that can only be textual in form. In this case Myllykoski has come close to positing a primary source similar to Klein's.

THE ARGUMENT FOR JOHN'S LITERARY DEPENDENCE

J. AMEDEE BAILEY

In 1962, J. Amedee Bailey examined the issue of Luke-John relationships in a small monograph.[114] Like Schniewind, Bailey framed the question in terms of the value of the Fourth Gospel as an independent historical witness to Jesus; that is, he pursues the question because of its impact on providing early historical information about Jesus. And since Luke was written late (in the eighties), the dating of John is dependent, in part, on whether John used Luke. Unlike Schniewind, Bailey offers a generally positive assessment concerning the literary relationship: John can be shown to have known and used Luke at a number of points:

> We have seen that John knew Luke's Gospel, and that he drew on Luke for elements in his account of the anointing of Jesus, of the last supper and last discourse, of the high-priestly prayer, of the arrest, of the trial before Pilate, of the crucifixion, death and burial, and of the appearances of Jesus in Jerusalem.[115]

Bailey's study covers much of the same ground as Schniewind's; in addition, it addresses some passages in which the verbal similarities are absent but thematic or theological connections exist, as in the

---

[114] J. Amedee Bailey, *The Traditions Common to the Gospels of Luke and John*, Novum Testamentum Supplements 7 (Leiden: E. J. Brill, 1963).

[115] Bailey, 115.

matter of Jesus' activity in Samaria.[116] In general, however, Bailey's study focuses on the same groups of passages that Schniewind's did: the anointing, John the Baptist, the miraculous catch of fish, and the Passion. It serves, then, as a counter statement to Schniewind's study on some of the same material.

Two assumptions appear to guide Bailey throughout his work. The first assumption is that John knew and used the Gospel of Mark. This assumption appears initially in the first chapter, where Bailey examines the close similarity between Mark and John in the pericope about Jesus' anointing (John 12:1–8 par. Mark 14:3–9). The points of similarity include: the three hundred *denarii*, the location of the event in Bethany, the reproach about extravagance, Jesus' statement about the poor, the reference to anointing of Jesus before his death, and the use of the word πιστικός.[117] For Bailey, this concurrence of points of similarity "make it absolutely certain" that John knew Mark.[118] The issue is never argued, however, only postulated. Similarly, Bailey begins his examination of the Johannine version of the account, both conceptually and literally, with the sweeping statement that, in reference to John 12:12, "the majority critical verdict is that John is here using Mark as his source."[119] In support of his statement he cites only Barrett, Hoskyns, and Klostermann, and appears to ignore Dodd and others who have taken the position of Johannine independence.[120] Bailey never argues the question of John's use of Mark but rather

---

[116] Bailey suggests in his preface that his work is larger in scope than Schniewind's, but outside of the issue of Jesus' activity in Samaria, he touches on few of the parallels in content that do not also have strong literary parallels.

[117] It appears that the words πιστικός and three hundred denarii are the crucial issues here.

[118] Bailey, 2.

[119] Bailey, 25.

[120] Indeed, Bailey does not even include Dodd's works in his bibliography. Gardner-Smith is included, but never cited. Bultmann is often cited in the book in other contexts, which suggests that rather than wishing to examine the issue, Bailey is simply glossing over the deep divisions on it with his reference to "the majority."

assumes that it is self-evident and already sufficiently treated in the scholarly literature.

The second assumption is a basic tenet of Bailey's methodology. For Bailey, as with Holtzmann before him, verbal similarities are "proof" that a literary relationship exists; absence of such similarities tends to "prove" that there is no literary relationship. Thus, as we have seen, the linkage of six similarities between John and Mark in the anointing pericope is sufficient evidence for John's use of Mark. The reverse is also true. In his discussion of the entry to Jerusalem, Bailey notes a number of verbal similarities between John and Luke, but the deciding factor appears to be that the wording of the acclamation by the crowd is sufficiently different to preclude, in this pericope at least, reliance of John on Luke.[121] For Bailey, knowledge and usage of a source is conceived as a cut-and-paste affair; evidence for the cutting and pasting is the sole determinant of literary dependence.

The key passage for Bailey's study of the relationship of Luke and John is the anointing pericope, and he opens his book with a discussion of this passage. He begins by noting the striking similarity in wording: both have a woman dry Jesus' feet with her hair (Luke: ταῖς θριξὶν τῆς κεφαλῆς αὐτῆς ἐξέμασσεν; John: ἐξέμαξεν ταῖς θριξὶν αὐτῆς). The common elements of anointing the feet and drying with the hair can only be explained, according to Bailey, by John's use of Luke.[122] As noted earlier, verbal similarities are for Bailey "proof" of a literary relationship, thus this striking similarity is de facto sufficient to show John's dependence.[123]

---

[121] Bailey, 26.

[122] Bailey, 3.

[123] A similar, though more brief, approach to the anointing pericope is found in E. P. Sanders, *The Historical Figure of Jesus* (London: Penguin, 1993), 126–7. He sees the Johannine account as a composite account, drawn from three separate stories in the Synoptics: Luke 7:36–50, Luke 10:39–42, and Matthew 26:6–13 par. Mark 14:3–9. While Sanders suggests that John drew on Luke for his anointing account, in part because it is a simpler solution, he allows that a common source is also possible (303, n.5).

A similar instance in which Bailey argues for Johannine reliance on Luke is in the prediction of denial following the Lord's Supper (Luke 22:31–34 par. John 13:36–38). This latter example offers a good perspective on Bailey's methodology. In the prediction of denial passage, Bailey is particularly struck by two facets of the account: (1) that it took place during the last supper (contra Matthew and Mark), and (2) that both Luke and John use a construction of οὐ ...ἕως plus the subjunctive, as opposed to Matthew and Mark's πρίν (Matt 26:34 par. Mark 14:30). Moreover, Luke and John lack the phrase ταύτῃ τῇ νυκτί. These two features are compelling evidence for Bailey that there is literary dependence. But what kind of literary dependence? Dependence on whom? In the case of the common order of events, Bailey suggests that Luke and John are derived from a source that predated Luke, John, and even Mark.[124] On the other hand, Bailey argues that John must have used a written source in 13:38, since οὐ...ἕως plus the subjunctive occurs only here in John.[125] But it could not have been the same source that Luke used (a written source, per Bailey), since then John and Luke would be more similar; Bailey instead argues that John used Luke directly while freely retelling the story! The logic is hardly compelling. Finally, Bailey thinks the common pattern of a discourse after the meal, although very different in content, must be explained by John's patterning his story after Luke.[126] It is not clear why, for Bailey, the placement of the denial in the Last Supper is derived from a pre-Lukan source, while the placement of the discourse after the supper derives from Luke's own hand.

But a number of similarities found between John and Luke are not judged to have resulted from John's use of Luke. The speculation that John the Baptist was the Christ, for example, is a similarity that is

---

[124] The reason here is that Mark's pattern is "secondary." Luke and John must contain the more original pattern; hence it is part of the early tradition underlying both.

[125] Bailey, 39.

[126] Bailey, 45.

adjudged to have come from common oral tradition, not Johannine use of the Third Gospel.[127] The reason is that there is little verbal correspondence. Perhaps more striking is his assessment of the miraculous catch of fish. Here Bailey finds strong similarities between John and Luke and yet does not argue for John's reliance on Luke. Instead, he recognizes that the similarities are better accounted for by Luke's using a tradition that could be called "Johannine."[128]

Thus Bailey's criteria for judging literary reliance, which heavily weigh the discovery of some exact similarity in language and which assume the lateness of John, lead him to suggest a rather curious relationship between the Third and Fourth Gospels. On the one hand, Bailey argues, there are places where John has clearly used Luke (as well as Mark).[129] On the other hand, there are places where Luke has close similarities to John that must have derived from a common or related tradition(s).[130] John, then, has used Luke occasionally but has also used common traditions that only Luke and John knew, and it is not clear that Bailey can cogently distinguish between them. Bailey is forced by his cut-and-paste concept of source usage to develop a very convoluted mixture of sources for both John and Luke.

---

[127] Bailey, 10–11.

[128] Bailey, 17. The use of Σίμων Πέτρος is particularly seen as Johannine. And the emphases on Peter and Peter's confession of sin do not cohere easily with the call setting. He concludes that Luke must have converted this Johannine type of story into a call story with the use of some Markan features. What that might suggest in terms of the composition process of the Fourth Gospel is never developed.

[129] In addition to those already discussed above, Bailey argues for Johannine use of Luke's Gospel in (1) John's use of σατανᾶς in 13:27 (29–31); (2) a series of items in the arrest (51–53); (3) trial before Pilate (71–77) (4) the crucifixion, death and burial (82–84); and (5) appearances in Jerusalem (92–96).

[130] In the case of the approach to Jerusalem (21–28), Bailey suggests that the commonalities between John and Luke came not from a common source, but from two distinct sources that shared some common points!

M. -É. BOISMARD

A frequent commentator on the relationship of John to the Synoptics who has focused attention on the striking similarities between John and Luke is M.-É. Boismard. In a series of articles, and most exhaustively in his commentary on the synopsis of the four Gospels, the similarities between John and Luke have become a central factor in his conception of Synoptic and Synoptic-Johannine relationships.[131] At a fundamental level, Boismard's theory of the relationship between Luke and John is one which posits a literary relationship; John is clearly reliant on a written form of Luke, as well as other Synoptic documents. But the literary relationship proposed by Boismard is not a straightforward one of John's using our Third Gospel; it is far more complex.

The relationship between John and Luke is a continuing theme in Boismard's study of the Gospel relationships. In an earlier article, Boismard studied John 4:46–54 (the healing of the royal official's son), as well as John 20:24–31 (the presentation of the crucifixion wounds to Thomas) and John 1:1–18 (the prologue to the Gospel of John, which represents a point of contact with Paul as well), and came to the conclusion that the elements of similarity strongly point to Lukan redaction of the Johannine account.[132] Thus verse 47 of John chapter 4 parallels closely Luke 7:3. Moreover, some puzzling aspects of John's account (the negative view of signs in v. 48) are attributable not to the original Johannine form but to Lucan reformulation in the

---

[131] M.-É. Boismard and P. Benoit, *Synopse des Quatre Évangiles*, Tome 2 (Paris: Les Éditions du Cerf, 1972) and M.-É. Boismard and A. Lamouille, *L'Évangile de Jean*, Synopse des Quatre Évangiles en Français, Tome 3 (Paris: Les Éditions du Cerf, 1977). See also the discussion in D. Moody Smith, *John Among the Gospels,* 140–47, as well as the extended critique of Boismard's position in Frans Neirynck, *Jean et les Synoptiques* (Leuven: University Press, 1979).

[132] M.-É. Boismard, "Saint Luc et las Rédaction du Quatrième Évangile," *Review Biblique* 69 (1962): 185–211.

final edition. Although Boismard does utilize some linguistic analysis of similarities between the Gospels, the primary thrust of his analysis is based on *theological* tensions in the Gospel (e.g., the signs in 4:48; cf. the tension Luke creates between the apparent demands for signs in Luke 1:18 and 1:38).

In the first version of his synopsis, Boismard has discarded the earlier idea of Luke's final redaction of John, but he still sees a complex literary relationship between John and Luke (and the other Gospels). Boismard's new theory has four source documents: A (primary source for Matthew), B (primary source for Mark), C (John's primary source), and Q. These sources were variously used by the early versions of Matthew (A plus Q), Mark (B plus A plus C), Luke (Q plus B plus C), and John (C plus A plus Proto Luke). These early versions (called intermediary by Boismard) were further redacted, being influenced along the way by one another: Matthew was influenced by Mark Intermediate, Mark was influenced by Matt Intermediate and Proto Luke, Luke was influenced by Mark Intermediate, and John was influenced at a late stage by final Matthew. In Boismard's conception then, John certainly had a literary influence from the Synoptics, but it took its shape first from early source documents, which also had their influence on the other Gospels. And the key source document C stands behind John and Luke.

Boismard's Gospel Interrelationship

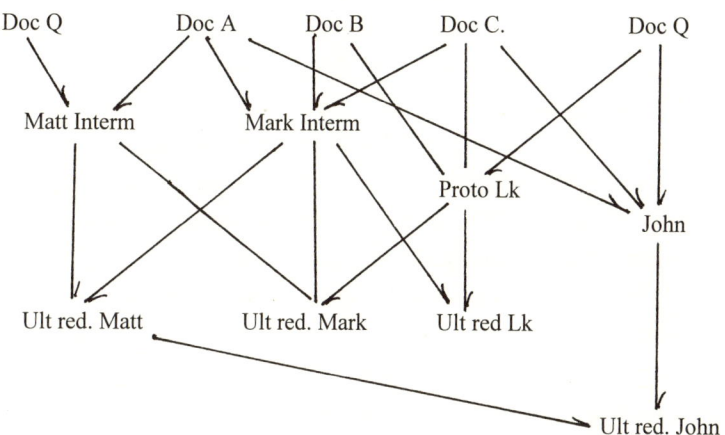

In the final volume of Boismard's synopsis, the commentary on John, this scheme has been expanded to see John with an additional step in the redactional process before its final form, a redaction that was influenced by knowledge of all the other final forms of the Synoptics.[133]

While a study of linguistic patterns is an important part of Boismard's approach,[134] it is clear that the driving issue in conceiving of the layers of redaction is the conception of developing theological and narrative patterns.[135] Thus he admits that the primary reason for positing a difference between his Proto-Luke and the final edited form is to allow for some differences in the way the material that appears to

---

[133] See the chart in Smith, *John Among the Gospels*, 143.

[134] A compilation of Johannine stylistic features compared to the rest of the New Testament is found in the appendix to Boismard and Lamouille, *L'Évangile de Jean*.

[135] Although using the linguistic patterns, Boismard clearly feels that they are of less importance in determining the relationships of the Gospels' theological issues.

have a literary relationship in the two Gospels is finally displayed.[136] This is related to his view of the Gospel writing procedure, somewhat of a cut-and-paste procedure in which variation in material is often best explained by some use or slight modification of sources. For example, Boismard notes extensive contacts between Luke and John in the appearance before Pilate and the death sentence as found in Luke 23:2–5, 13–25 and John 18:29–19:16. But in Luke the scene is broken up by the Herod trial, which Boismard sees as a later editorial development. Thus while John must have drawn on Luke for the points of similarity (not on common sources!), it could not have been the final form of Luke but must have been, rather, an early form.[137] Boismard, then, sees John's use of Luke as following fairly closely his source, although allowing for some editorial modification.

Boismard appreciates the mixed character of linguistic evidence. He sees its value as one indicator of source material, especially when a word or grammatical usage stands out as unusual or out of place in a Gospel. But he is also wary of placing too much weight on such evidence. Ultimately, it is the mixture of traditions, ideas, and theological currents that is more telling about the use of sources. Certainly, an evangelist combining sources might very well make modifications of the language. But having said that, Boismard nonetheless has a cut-and-paste view of Gospel writing. Each piece of material seems to have to traced to a documentary source, rather than to the creative impulse of the evangelists. It is this need to locate documentary sources all along the way that produces the plethora of documents that make up Boismard's schema. And while Boismard is willing to posit an early form of John that predates, or at least is dated to the same time as the Synoptics, the final form is nonetheless

---

[136] Boismard notes that "cette distinction entre un proto-Lc et une ultime rédaction lucanienne apparaît nettement quand on étudie les rapports entre Lc et Jn, spécialement dans les récits de la passion et de la résurrection." (Boismard and Benoit, Tome 2, 40)

[137] Boismard and Benoit, 40.

understood de facto as being later than and hence derivative from the Synoptics.[138]

Boismard's approach is, at one level, unassailable. By modifying the number of levels of redaction (as he has done between vols. 2 and 3 of his synopsis), Boismard is able to explain almost any series of similarities between the Gospels. Ultimately, they all seem to be literarily related, either directly or indirectly. But, as Neirynck has also argued, such a complex development seems to try to explain too much with too little evidence. At some point Occam's razor must be called upon to judge such a conception.

FRANS NEIRYNCK

With a prodigious output of articles, Frans Neirynck has been an indefatigable proponent of the two-document theory for the synoptic relationship and of Johannine dependence for the John-Synoptic relationship. For Neirynck, it has been clear: Mark and Q represent the two primary documents from which the vast majority of the Gospel narratives are drawn. In the case of John and the Synoptics, Neirynck has waged a steady campaign to explain the similarities as the result of John's dependence on the Synoptics: "not the traditions behind the Synoptic Gospels but the Synoptic Gospels themselves are the sources of the Fourth Evangelist."[139] For Neirynck, the issue of simplicity becomes a crucial one. Although he allows that there might be some

---

[138] In this respect he appears to be arguing for both independence and dependence of John on the Synoptics.

[139] Frans Neirynck, "John and the Synoptics: 1975–1990," in *John and the Synoptics*, Colloguium Biblicum Lovaniense, 1990, ed. A. Denaux (Leuven: Leuven University Press, 1992), 3. This article is a follow-up to a previous discussion, "John and the Synoptics," in *L'Évangile de Jean*, ed. M. de Jonge (Leuven: Leuven University Press, 1977), 74–106, as well as "John and the Synoptics. Response to P. Borgen," in *Interrelations of the Gospels* (Leuven: Leuven University Press, 1990), 438–450, and Peter Borgen's reply, 451–458. See also for a general discussion of Neirynck's position on the issue of John and the Synoptics, Smith, *John Among the Gospels*, 147–58.

other sources for John, the simplest solution to most points of similarity between John and the Synoptics is that he knew and used them, albeit modified under the influence of his own authorial design. As with most scholars studying the relationship, Neirynck begins with an assumption that John is late.

It is noteworthy that Neirynck has maintained a vigorous debate with Boismard, whose approach was outlined above. In particular, he produced an entire monograph to critique Boismard's theory and, in the process, support his own simpler view that John simply used the Third Gospel.[140] For Neirynck, Boismard, having admitted a literary relationship between Luke and John, should have simply acknowledged that the differences are due to John's redaction of Luke and the other Synoptics. While these two approaches can be similarly grouped under the rubric "John's Literary Dependence," they are vastly different approaches.

Some of the special relationships between John and Luke have been the object of Neirynck's study, especially since they present a bit of a problem for Neirynck's approach.[141] In particular, he has focused on a series of points of contact between Luke and John found in Luke 24.[142] Based on the strength of the papyri, Neirynck, along with many

---

[140] Frans Neirynck, with Joël Delobel et. al., *Jean et les synoptiques: Examen critique de l'exégèse de M.-É. Boismard* (Louvain: Louvain University Press, 1979).

[141] See especially Neirynck, "The Uncorrected Historic Present in Lk xxiv.12," *ETL* 48 (1972): 548–55; "ΠΑΡΑΚΥΨΑΣ ΒΛΕΠΕΙ. Lc 24:12 et Jn 20.5," *ETL* 53 (1977): 113–52; "ΑΠΗΛΘΕΝ ΠΡΟΣ ΕΑΥΤΟΝ. Lk 24.12 et Jn 20.10," *ETL* 54 (1978): 104-118.; "John and the Synoptics," in *Evangelica* (Leuven: University Press, 1982), 365-400; "Lc 24,36-43 et la Rédaction Lucanienne," in *A Cause de L'Évangile,* Mélanges offerts à Dom Jacques Dupont (Cerf: Publications de Saint-André, 1985), 665–79; "John and the Synoptics: The Empty Tomb Stories," *NTS* 30 (1984): 161–87.

[142] Neirynck, "ΑΠΗΛΘΟΝ ΠΡΟΣ ΕΑΥΤΟΝ. Lc 24,12 et Jn 20,5"; "ΠΑΡΑΚΥΨΑΣ ΒΛΕΠΕΙ. Lc 24,12 et Jn 20,5,"; "Uncorrected Present in Lk. xxxiv.12"; and "Lc. 24,36-43. Un récit lucanien."

modern scholars, accepts 24:12 and 24:36 and 24:40 as authentic.[143] In these verses, however, are points of contact between Luke and John that do not readily appear to fit well with Lukan authorship. The problem for Neirynck is to show that non-Lukan features can be explained within Luke's compositional style. If he can do that, then these passages are particularly rich for his argument that John has relied on Luke. The main problems found in Luke 24 are:

1. Luke 24:12 has the uncorrected present βλέπει,[144]
2. παρακύψας, ὀθόνια, and ἀπῆλθε πρὸς ἑαυτόν in Luke 24:12 are "Johannine words,"[145]
3. The reference of a plurality of disciples in 24:24 who go to the tomb(καὶ ἀπῆλθόν τινες τῶν σὺν ἡμῖν)suggests another tradition known to Luke, a tradition that is given full expression in John with the visit of Peter and the "other disciple,"[146]
4. Luke 24:36 εἰρήνη ὑμῖν is Johannine,
5. Luke 24:40 produces a Johannine picture of Jesus showing his crucifixion wounds.

For Neirynck, the solution to these problems despite their significant number, is to assert that the various words are not Johannine, but instead arose from Luke's own editorial tendencies. The points of commonality, then, simply add weight to Neirynck's general proposition that John is wholly dependent on the Synoptics. In other words, if Luke created these features himself, then their existence in John is due to John's reliance on Luke.

It would be worthwhile to briefly summarize the arguments used to show that Luke 24:12 is wholly a Lukan composition.

---

[143] See chapter 4 below.

[144] See especially Neirynck "The Uncorrected Historic Present in Lk xxiv.12."

[145] See Neirynck, "ΑΠΗΛΘΕΝ ΠΡΟΣ ΕΑΥΤΟΝ," 116; already noted by B. Weiss, *Markus und Lukas*, 589.

[146] Neirynck, "John and the Synoptics: the Empty Tomb Stories," 589.

1. Neirynck readily agrees that, in general, the historic present is rare in Luke, as Jeremias suggests.[147] But Neirynck is unwilling to accept that the historic present is "distinctively Johannine"; the possibility of a pre-Lukan tradition as the source for this historic present does not preclude John's dependence on Luke. Neirynck produces one possible parallel in Luke 16:23, where Luke uses a historic present with a *verbum videndi*. But more importantly, Neirynck is primarily arguing that ἀναστὰς βλέπει corresponds very closely with Mark's announcement in 16:4, ἀναβλέψασαι θεωροῦσιν, and therefore should be seen as a Lucan editorial modification of Mark.[148]

2. It is important for Neirynck that παρακύψας does not necessarily mean "to stoop over" or "peer in" (pencher), but can simply mean "to pay attention to" (regarder). Thus, the Lukan form could represent reformulation of Mark 16:4.[149] In Luke's use, it does not necessarily suggest looking in from outside, and indeed Luke might have understood that Peter did indeed enter the tomb. In that case John took up the word but misunderstood Luke's sense. John used the more literal "peered in" to set up the dramatic anticipation (he did not go in, οὐ μέντοι εἰσῆλθεν) of the other disciple's arrival. In other words, John and Luke do not use the term in the same way, but Luke's use corresponds more closely with Mark 16, and John's use, it can be argued, displays John's later redactional interest.

3. Neirynck does not discuss extensively the use of ὀθόνια by Luke. The word is used four times by John but only once in Luke. He does suggest, though, that the phrase ὀθόνια μόνα is important. He argues that the term is used in a simple sense by Luke to refer to the absence of Jesus' body from the tomb, that is, the grave clothes only with no body. In contrast, he sees John's double use of ὀθόνια in

---

[147] Luke has modified the historic present found in Mark ninety-two times; it is found in Luke only seven times. See Joachim Jeremias, *Die Sprache des Lukasevangeliums* (Göttingen: Vandenhoeck & Ruprecht, 1980), 313 and 169.
[148] Neirynck, "Uncorrected Historic Present," 551.
[149] Cf. Neirynck, "ΠΑΡΑΚΥΨΑΣ ΒΛΕΠΕΙ," especially 144–48.

20:5–6 as a development of an interpretation of μόνα. That is, John understood μόνα to mean apart from other clothes, and so expanded the story to make that idea explicit.[150]

4. The similarity between Luke's ἀπῆλθεν πρὸς ἑαυτὸν θαυμάζων τὸ γεγονός and John's ἀπῆλθον οὖν πάλιν πρὸς (ἑ)αυτούς (20:10) is denied by Neirynck. The primary thrust of his argument is that John is employing a very semitic use of the *dativus ethicus* with the verb to depart to one's house.[151] In this case, Neirynck sees the Johannine version as a modification of Luke's ὑπεστρέψασαι ἀπὸ τοῦ μνεμείου (24:9), to return to their house. Luke instead uses πρὸς ἑαυτόν to form a reflexive complement of the participle θαυμάζων, which is not a semitism, has very little similarity with the Johannine version.

5. Neirynck finds no cause to see an implicit tradition behind Luke of more than one disciple visiting the tomb. Agreeing with Muddiman, Neirynck prefers to see the plural reference in 24:24 simply as a "generalizing plural."[152]

In short, by a careful analysis of each potential point of contact Neirynck has called into question each item. He maintains that in every case the contact is best explained by Luke's use and modification of an original Markan story and John's reuse, and perhaps misunderstanding, of Luke. Neirynck's individual assessments appear to be very cogent, although each of them can be argued in opposite fashion. More importantly is whether this kind of micro-analysis ultimately does justice to the compelling accumulation of similarities. Each one might be explained away exegetically, but can they all be explained away *together*? It would appear that Neirynck makes a forceful case on individual points, but it is hard to imagine such an accumulation of separate explanations as accounting for the close relationship between Luke and John.

---

[150] Neirynck, "The Empty Tomb Stories," 593.

[151] And so argues from Josephus' use that this was common. Neirynck, "ΑΠΗΛΘΟΝ ΠΡΟΣ ΕΑΥΤΟΝ," 110.

[152] Neirynck, "The Empty Tomb Stories," 589.

THE MERGING OF LITERARY AND TRADITION: CONTINUING ORALITY

ANTON DAUER

In a couple of very detailed examinations of Johannine passages that contain strong similarities to the Synoptics, and particularly in his study of three pericopes in which Luke and John have strong similarities, Dauer has suggested an explanation of the relationship between the two Gospels that avoids the simple dichotomy "literary relationship" or "common source."[153] Dauer concludes that the Gospel of John shows an awareness of and use of Luke (as well as Matthew and Mark). But John's use of Luke was not direct literary reliance; rather, the *Vorlage* to John was influenced by Luke, and the author of John then edited that source without direct reliance on Luke.[154]

In his dissertation, Dauer develops the thesis of Noack, Dahl, and Borgen that the relationship of John and the Synoptics is one of an oral influence, not literary reliance.[155] In his study of John 18, Dauer develops this argument in two stages. First, he attempts to show that a series of similarities that exist between John and various synoptics arose at the hand of the synoptic evangelists, not some common source. So, for instance, in the arrest account (John 18:1–11 and Luke 22:39–53) he notes the following similarities between John and Luke:[156]

1. John 18:1 par. Luke 22:39 specifically mentions the disciples as following Jesus.

---

[153] Anton Dauer, *Johannes und Lukas*, and Anton Dauer, *Die Passiongeschichte im Johannesevangelium. Eine traditionsgeschichtliche und theologische Untersuchung zu Joh 18,1–19, 30*, Studien zum Alten und Neuen Testament 30 (München: Kösel-Verlag, 1972).

[154] See further discussion in Smith, *John Among the Gospels*, 122–127.

[155] Cf. Neirynck's discussion in "John and the Synoptics" in *L'Evangile de Jean*, ed. M. De Jonge (Leuven: University Press, 1976), 93.

[156] Dauer, *Passiongeschichte*, 53–60.

2. John 18:1 par. Luke 22:40 has the name "Gethsemane" absent.
3. John 18:2 par. Luke 22:39 notes that Jesus goes to a place that he frequented often.
4. John 18:3 par. Luke 22:47 portrays Judas as leading those who would arrest Jesus.
5. John 18:10 par. Luke 22:50 has the right ear of the servant cut off.
6. John 18:11 par. Luke 22:50 has the sword fight occur before the arrest rather than after.

In every one of these instances, Dauer concludes that the similarity, as well as its point of difference from the Mark/Matthew pattern, stems from Luke's redactional interest, not from a *Sondergut* source.[157] As a result, it is clear to Dauer that since these redactional items are found in John, John has somehow become aware of the Gospel of Luke, not just a common source.

The second aspect of Dauer's study is his examination of the Johannine material for source and redactional levels. He concludes that the verses in which the similarities occur can be traced to John's source(s), not to Johannine redaction.[158] Thus it is not that the Fourth evangelist used Luke directly, but rather that the source upon which John relied knew and used it. But the similarities between Luke and John's source do not frequently extend to common phraseology; instead, the points of contact are more casual and sporadic. This suggests to Dauer that the relationship cannot be literary but, rather, oral.[159] Moreover, Dauer finds that the variants from both Matthew and

---

[157] Dauer, *Passiongeschichte*, 60: "Die Untersuchung der lk Parallelen zum joh Traditionsbericht (und Unterschiede zu Mk) hat ergeben, daß sie nicht durch einen Sonderbericht des Lukas, sondern durch seine Redaktionstätigkeit und der Mk-Vorlage bedingt sind."

[158] Dauer, *Passiongeschichte*, 22–29, 44–48.

[159] Dauer, *Passiongeschichte*, 60.

Luke are intermixed, thus betraying a period of oral assimilation into the Johannine tradition.

A major issue concerning Dauer's approach is his acceptance of a Johannine source theory and, indeed, whether the separation of such a source from the evangelist is a viable undertaking. Thus Sabbe and Neirynck have both pointed to the source theory for John as the major weakness in his approach: "It is superfluous to separate redactional parts of the text of John and to ascribe the other parts to a pre-Johannine source, influenced by the Synoptic Gospels."[160] If, in fact, there were no intervening pre-Johannine source, then one could claim that Dauer has made a case for direct Johannine use of the Synoptics.

In *Johannes und Lukas*, Dauer focuses more closely on the Luke-John relationship and comes to some conclusions that are slightly more nuanced, although generally still in the same vein as those in his previous work. Dauer finds that the nature of Luke's relationship to John's *Vorlage* varies slightly in the three pericopes studied. In the case of the captain from Capernaum (Luke 7:1–10 par. John 4:46–54), he sees John's source as a free rendition (*freie Wiedergabe*) of the Matthean story (Matt 8:5–13), which had been influenced in some particulars by the Lukan account.[161] Here, elements of Luke's account are present, but they perhaps only crept into a strongly Matthean version. In the case of the anointing story (Luke 7:36–50 par. John 12:1–8), John's source is seen to be an admixture of the Markan and Lukan accounts, perhaps the result of continued oral telling of the story in which the Markan account was expanded with some Lukan details.[162] Finally, in the case of the appearance account (Luke 24:36–49 par. John 20:19–29), Dauer proposes that the John's source

---

[160] M. Sabbe, "The Arrest of Jesus in Jn 18,1–11 and its Relation to the Synoptic Gospels" in *L'Evangile de Jean* (Leuven: University Press, 1976), ed. M. de Jonge, 233. Cf also F. Neirynck "John and the Synoptics" in *L'Evangile de Jean* (Leuven: University Press, 1976), ed. M. de Jonge, especially 93–95.

[161] Dauer, *Johannes und Lukas*, 120–21. Cf. the discussion on Landis, above p. 51.

[162] Dauer, *Johannes und Lukas*, 204–6.

knew the Lukan account, which was then shortened and mixed with some other oral traditions.[163] These modifications, Dauer maintains, took place before the author of John edited his source(s).

Dauer's methodology in *Johannes und Lukas* is very much like that in *Passiongeschichte*. Here Dauer's approach is, after establishing the verbal and substantive parallels, to engage in a detailed examination of the Lukan and Johannine passages to determine which parts of the passages are traditional and which are redactional. If Lukan redactional material occurs primarily in the Johannine traditional material, that would suggest that Luke had influenced John's source(s). Some examples are necessary to fully appreciate Dauer's method of study.

Among a number of elements of Luke 24:36–49 which were determined likely to be from Luke's hand are:

1) Luke 24:36 ἔστη ἐν μέσῳ αὐτῶν,[164]
2) Luke 24:40 καὶ τοῦτο εἰπὼν ἔδειξεν αὐτοῖς τας χεῖρας,[165]
3) Luke 24:41 the theme of the disciples' "joy,"[166]
4) Luke 24:49 the theme of the sending of the Spirit.[167]

Moreover, there are a number of similar themes between Luke and John which have nonetheless distinctive differences. But since the differences are usually attributable by Dauer to the editorial pattern of John, these themes as well can be seen as examples of Lukan material in John.[168] The existence of these Lukan elements and themes in John, together with the explainable differences, clearly indicates to Dauer that John presumes the Gospel of Luke, not just a common source.[169]

---

[163] Dauer, *Johannes und Lukas*, 283–88.
[164] Dauer, *Johannes und Lukas*, 261, 284.
[165] Dauer, *Johannes und Lukas*, 268, 284.
[166] Dauer, *Johannes und Lukas*, 272, 284.
[167] Dauer, *Johannes und Lukas*, 279, 284.
[168] So, for example, the idea that the disciples are afraid of Jesus (Lk 24:37) is modified in John to their being afraid of the Jews (Jn 20:19). But this difference is seen to be John's later editorial modification. Dauer, *Johannes und Lukas*, 220.
[169] Dauer, *Johannes und Lukas*, 285.

But there are important differences that call into question the probability that John used Luke directly. The closed-door setting of John's account, John's pattern "hand and side" as opposed to Luke's "hand and foot," and the phrasing of Jesus' words about forgiveness of sins—all of which Dauer finds to be traditional, not redactional, elements in John—suggest a separate tradition, independent of Luke that was intertwined with Lukan material *before* John took it up in the final redaction.

Dauer's study, which is very careful and well argued, is based upon three foundations that might be questioned:

1. Dauer's conclusions are based fundamentally on his identification of specific layers of tradition and redaction in Luke and John. However, these layers are not self-apparent, and errors in identification could substantially modify the results. Other scholars of the Lukan tradition, for instance, have come to different conclusions about what is redaction and what is tradition in Luke.[170] While Dauer finds that Luke 24:36 (ταῦτα δὲ αὐτῶν - ἔστη ἐν μέσῳ αὐτῶν) and 24:40 (the entire verse) are the redactional work of the author, Jeremias finds no examples of Lukan redaction in either case, and specifically cites 24:40 as having come from tradition.[171] The determination of what stems from Luke's editorial hand is not a precise process, and Dauer's results are heavily dependent on that determination. Similar difficulties can be adduced for the identification of tradition and redaction in the Fourth Gospel.[172] The problem for Dauer is the importance that he places on such identification.

---

[170] In addition to the examples cited below, see Stephan Landis, who uses a similar methodology but, based on very different identification of tradition and redaction, comes to very different conclusions about the relationship between Luke and John in the pericope about the captain from Capernaum.

[171] Jeremias, *Sprache*, 320–1.

[172] E. Schweizer, *Ego Eimi* (Göttingen: Vandenhoek & Ruprecht, 1939) and E. Ruckstuhl, *Die literarische Einheit des Johannesevangeliums*, (Freiburg: Paulusverlag, 1951) have raised serious questions about the ability to separate source and redaction in the Fourth Gospel.

2. A major point for Dauer, and the major point that separates him from Neirynck, is that the influence on John took place at the level of his *Vorlage*, not his writing. The major argument for this is the existence of some non-synoptic traditions intermixed with the synoptic-like material. Dauer cannot trace this material easily to the hand of the Fourth evangelist, and he therefore concludes that it was pre-Johannine: "Neben den auffallenden Gemeinsamkeiten bestehen nämlich nicht unbeträchtliche Unterschiede zwischen den jeweiligen Perikopen, die sich nicht aus joh Redaktionstätigkeit erklären ließen und die deshalb vor-joh sein müssen."[173] Dauer assumes that the evangelists, and John in particular, were very conservative users of tradition, not free composers. If John were shown to be willing to mix and modify sources in a more creative fashion, then Dauer's point would be significantly weakened.

3. Perhaps the most limiting assumption of Dauer's study is that which excludes the possibility that Luke might have known or relied upon John or Johannine traditions. Although extensive in his consideration of possible explanations for the various similarities and differences between John and Luke, all of his options have John as either independent of or dependent upon Luke.[174] The one time he seems to actually entertain the idea that Luke might have used John (when discussing the common wording καὶ λέγει αὐτοῖς· εἰρήνη ὑμῖν),

---

[173] Dauer, *Johannes und Lukas*, p. 297.

[174] So, for instance, Dauer lists six possible explanations for the similarities and differences in the appearance narrative:
 1. John used Luke as a literary source, making extensive modifications.
 2. John relied upon a memory of Luke, not Luke as a literary source.
 3. John and Luke relied on the same literary source.
 4. John and Luke relied on a common oral tradition.
 5. John 20:19–29 is an insertion by later redactors.
 6. Jn used a tradition which was based upon Luke's account.

Nowhere does Dauer seriously entertain the idea that Luke might have used some form of John (either written or somehow influencing Luke's sources). *Johannes und Lukas*, 218–19.

he dismisses the possibility without discussion: "Das Abhängigkeit des Lukas vom 4. Evangelium nicht wahrscheinlich ist..."[175]

QUESTIONING THE RELATIONSHIP: NEW APPROACHES

LAMAR CRIBBS

Lamar Cribbs has added significantly to the literature about the Luke-John relationship with a series of articles beginning in 1971. The lengthiest of his treatments, found in the SBL Seminar papers of 1973, is an article that is primarily an extensive catalogue of various Luke-John similarities.[176] Despite the encyclopedic nature of this article, it is not as useful as it might be because Cribbs finds and lists trivial similarities along with the striking and substantial ones.

In a subsequent article in the SBL Seminar papers of 1979,[177] Cribbs summarizes and lists much of the material discussed in the 1973 article. Some very helpful summaries of similarities are presented:

1. Luke-John close verbal parallels[178]
2. Luke-John verbal resemblances[179]
3. Factual agreements between Luke and John[180]
4. Luke-John omissions of Mark/Matthew material[181]

But perhaps the most suggestive of Cribbs' articles is the first one, written in 1971.[182] In this initial article, Cribbs makes some very important observations about the nature of the agreements between Luke and John.

---

[175] Dauer, *Johannes und Lukas*, 224.

[176] F. Lamar Cribbs, "A Study of the Contacts That Exist Between St. Luke and St. John," *SBL 1973 Seminar Papers* (Cambridge: SBL, 1973), 1–93.

[177] F. Lamar Cribbs, "The Agreements that Exist Between Luke and John," *SBL 1979 Seminar Papers* (Missoula, MT: Scholars Press, 1979), pp. 215–251.

[178] Cribbs, *SBL 1979*, 220.

[179] Cribbs, *SBL 1979*, 227.

[180] Cribbs, *SBL 1979*, 231.

[181] Cribbs, *SBL 1979*, 233.

[182] "St. Luke and the Johannine Tradition," *JBL* 90(1971): 422–50.

1. The agreements between John and the Synoptics (including Luke) are rarely of close verbal parallels,[183] but there are more such verbal parallels between John and Luke than between John and any other of the synoptics.[184]

2. The agreements tend to be limited to the entry, Passion and Resurrection stories, together with the baptism and feeding of the five thousand stories, elements of the basic kerygmatic story of Jesus.[185]

3. There is little similarity between John and Luke in the blocks of peculiarly Lukan material (e.g. 1:1–2:52 and 9:51–18:14).[186]

4. John contains passages that would tend to raise doubt that he knew the Synoptics. For instance, John's inference that the Son of Man was an unfamiliar term (John 12:34) can hardly reflect a knowledge of the Synoptics, where the term is frequent.[187]

These points raise doubts about John's dependence on the synoptics, even Luke. Based on these doubts, Cribbs examines a number of the similarities and arrives at the following conclusions about the nature of the agreements:

1. Luke agrees with John frequently at those sections in John's narrative which contain material similar to the synoptics. And it is precisely here that Luke departs from a normal close agreement with Mark/Matthew to present a variation in the "Synoptic" narrative.[188] Despite the fact that Luke generally makes few major alterations in material that he shares with *only* Mark and Matthew, of the twenty pericopes that Luke shares with *all three* evangelists, he departs significantly from the Mark/Matthew narrative in nineteen.

Luke makes major alterations of his Matthean/Markan source in every one of the other nineteen pericopes that he shares with John as well as with Matthew and Mark in ways that are substantially different

---

[183] Cribbs, *JBL*, 425.
[184] Cribbs, *JBL*, 448.
[185] Cribbs, *JBL*, 425.
[186] Cribbs, *JBL*, 425.
[187] Cribbs, *JBL*, 426.
[188] Cribbs, *JBL*, 447; *SBL 1973*, 16.

from any of the modifications which Luke elsewhere makes of the Matthean/Markan traditions.[189]

For instance, all four Gospels contain a story of the anointing of Jesus.[190] But John's account, while set in Bethany before the Passion, has Mary anointing Jesus' feet and then wipe up the excess with her hair. Luke's account is very different from all of the others, being set far earlier in the narrative. Moreover, one feature of Luke's account is the anointing Jesus' feet (with tears, not oil) and wiping off the excess with hair. What is rather surprising about this passage is that Luke has been following rather closely the order and general features of Mark's and Matthew's material in the section leading up to the Passion. Luke's departure from the Mark/Matthew pattern is striking and surprising; the fact that it occurs precisely where John has a similar and yet distinctive account, Cribbs argues, is important.

2. Luke frequently omits material found in Mark/Matthew at those points where John's narrative has material that disagrees with Mark/Matthew.[191] There are a number of common omissions of Mark/Matthew material as well. While any argument based on what is missing is tentative, these common omissions of material are suggestive of a more extensive pattern of similarities. And since John is often at variance with the Synoptics, the absences in Luke at these points are more noteworthy than the absences in John.

For example, Cribbs notes Luke's omission of the place names Caesarea Philippi (Luke 9:18) and Gethsemane (Luke 22:39) at the comparable points in the narrative. John also omits these place names. Similarly, Luke refrains from any mention of the high priest's rage upon hearing Jesus' response to the question whether he is the Christ (Luke 22:71). John, likewise, has no such mention.

3. Luke's narrative often seems to represent a "middle position" between John and the Synoptics.[192] There are, of course, sentences in

---

[189] Cribbs, *JBL*, 428.
[190] Cf. Cribbs, *JBL*, 437–41.
[191] Cribbs, *JBL*, 429–431, 447; *SBL 1973*, 18.
[192] Cribbs, *JBL*, 429, 447; *SBL 1973*, 17.

Luke which contain very close verbal similarities to John, or factual information that is simply closer to John than to similar material in Mark or Matthew (e.g., the wording of Jesus' prediction of Peter's denial in Luke 22:34). But more commonly Luke appears to follow Mark/Matthew and yet modify that account in a number of places where John is also shows a difference. When compared to John, the alterations to the Mark/Matthew account have the appearance of a middle term, as if Luke were attempting to carefully navigate between two opposing positions without denying either of them.

For instance, in the account of the arrest of Jesus, Mark and Matthew record that Judas and the arresting officers had arranged ahead of time for a kiss to be a sign of identification for the arrest. In the arrest scene itself, Judas does step forward and kiss Jesus, which triggers the arrest. In contrast, John has no mention at all of a kiss at the arrest. Luke's account is somewhere in the middle. Unlike Mark and Matthew, Luke does not mention a prior arrangement for a kiss. At the arrest there is an allusion to a kiss (He approached Jesus to kiss him, but Jesus said to him, "Judas is it with a kiss that you are betraying the Son of Man?" [Luke 22:48]) but no kiss itself. Luke's account appears to cohere with Mark and Matthew in the reference to the kiss but with John in the absence of reference to arrangements for a kiss and the kiss itself.

4. The agreements between Luke and John exist almost entirely in the narrative sections of John, not the dialogues.[193] It is striking that, if John were relying on Luke, no common material seems to creep into the dialogues, which are so important in the development of Johannine themes.

5. Cribbs notes in a few instances in which, although Luke follows quite closely Mark's order of events, the order is modified in some pericopes where John portrays a different order.[194] The most explicit example is that of Luke 22:7–34. Here, in the account of the Last Supper and the predictions of betrayal and Peter's denial, Luke

---

[193] Cribbs, *JBL*, 449.
[194] Cribbs, *SBL 1973*, pp. 10, 50.

deviates from Mark's order in a number of places. The prediction of Judas' betrayal takes place in Luke after the Supper instead of before. In addition, the prediction of Peter's denial takes place at the dinner setting, before the departure to the Mount of Olives instead of after. Finally, Luke inserts a discourse with the disciples in the supper setting, a feature not found in Mark or Matthew. In each of these modifications in the order or structure of the narrative, Luke's account has a parallel, although often not an exact one, in John's Gospel.

This pattern of relationships, Cribbs finds, challenges both the idea that John knew and relied on Luke and the notion that John is entirely independent of Luke. Had John known Luke, there should be more points of commonality than simply where Mark and Matthew also have similar material. Why would John have acted this way in culling material from Luke to use in his own account? At the same time, the extensive pattern of similarities seems to suggest something more than just accidental agreement based on some oral traditions. Rather than choosing between these two unattractive options, Cribbs offers a very tentative suggestion that Luke instead may have been influenced by the Johannine tradition or an early version of John.

A major weakness of Cribbs' articles is their failure to adequately differentiate between minor and major points of commonality. In Cribbs' later essays, the profusion of facts without analysis is at times disorienting.

Nevertheless, Cribbs has made a major advance in turning attention to the Lukan side of the Luke-John relationship. Instead of seeing the patterns and problems from the side of John, he asks the question, What would explain Luke's compositional pattern? In particular, Cribbs is very perceptive in discerning two major features of the Luke-John similarities: the strong similarities between Luke and John coincide with Luke's departures from Mark and Matthew and, conversely, Luke's modifications of the Mark/Matthew account appear to be influenced by the tradition found in John. These observations have not been adequately addressed in subsequent literature.

BARBARA SHELLARD

In a recent provocative article, Shellard briefly surveys the shared omissions and common material of Luke and John and concludes that there is indeed a strong case for some form of literary dependence.[195] It is difficult to explain the amount and detail of the agreements between Luke and John solely on the basis common use of tradition. But she rightly points out that other scholars (with the exception of Lamar Cribbs) who have concluded that there was literary dependence have all assumed Lukan priority to John.[196] The assumption of Lukan priority has not been based on verifiable reasons (e.g., firm dating of the Gospels or a clear theological development); without it, many passages that have served most strongly to support John's use of Luke (as, for instance, Bailey's discussion of Luke 22:3–34) would be more easily explained by Luke's use of John. Shellard's argument, then, reinforces Cribbs' suggestion that Luke may have known and used John.[197]

Shellard examines a small sample of passages: John the Baptist (Luke 3 *par.* John 1), the anointing (Luke 7 *par.* John 12), Jesus' appearance before the Jewish authorities and Peter's denial (Luke 22 *par.* John 18), and the post-Resurrection narratives (Luke 24 *par.* John 20–21). In these passages, Shellard consistently finds that Luke takes a mediating approach between material found in Matthew and Mark and that found in John. In the John the Baptist sequence, for instance, while Matthew and Mark clearly identify John the Baptist with Elijah, and while John denies that identification, Luke softens the Markan material to reduce, if not totally erase, it.[198] In this passage, as in the other

---

[195] Barbara Shellard, "The Relationship of Luke and John: A Fresh Look at an Old Problem," *JTS* 46 (1995): 71–98.

[196] Shellard, *JTS*, 75.

[197] Shellard, *JTS*, 82.

[198] Shellard, *JTS*, 82. Note that Luke omits the description of John the Baptist in Mark 1:6, omits the Elijah pericope in the transfiguration scene, has no parallel to Matt 11:14, and omits the word ὀπίσω μου in the parallel to Matt 3:11

pericopes examined, Shellard concludes that Luke "seems ... to be conflating the two traditions [Mark and John] and seeking to mediate between them when they disagree."[199] Indeed, the appearance that Luke is often mediating between two widely varying accounts suggests a literary relationship in which Luke is working with two existing texts.

Shellard's thesis, which is really only sketched and not developed, is best seen in her development of the trial and denial stories in Luke and John. Shellard finds small points of agreement to be highly telling. For instance, the common downplaying of Peter's denials and, particularly, the absence of the Peter's self-curse are significant. Shellard, like Cribbs, is strongly impressed with common absences (or omissions, to make the point more explicit) of material.

Certain terms in Luke are seen to be Johannine (e.g., οὐκ εἰμί in Luke 22:58) and thus can hardly be explained by John's use of Luke.[200]

So also, Shellard sees in Luke 22:59 the combination of disparate traditions: specifically the identification of Peter as Galilean (from Mark 14:70) *and* as having been seen with Jesus (from John 18:26). This reliance on John for actual wording is most explicit in Luke 22:67, which Shellard sees as very close to John 10:24–25. It is hard to see from what place in Mark Luke would be deriving this account, but if he is drawing on John as well, then it would appear that Luke 22:67–71 is the interweaving of the Markan account with the closest thing to a trial in John.

Late in the writing of this dissertation I was able to secure Shellard's more extensive dissertation in which she argues that Luke is the fourth Gospel and presupposes the other three.[201] As far as John

---

and Mark 1:7.

[199] Shellard, *JTS*, 84.

[200] Shellard, *JTS*, 88.

[201] Barbara Shellard, "Luke as the Fourth Gospel: Its Purpose, Sources and Literary Context," (M. Phil. diss., Oxford University, 1997). The scope of the dissertation is large, attempting to show that Luke used Mark, Matthew and John, thus being the last of the four gospels. Much effort is spent showing why Matthew

and Luke are concerned, however, there are no fundamental advances beyond the previously discussed article. Shellard examines in some detail a number of passages with strong Luke-John points of commonality. She often offers strong considerations for conceiving of Luke as subsequent to John. In particular certain verbal similarities, and the frequent observation that Luke seems to serve as middle term, are offered as evidence. Her study does underscore Cribbs' points, but because she does not engage in a systematic study of the problem, she unfortunately does not advance the case.[202] Because she does not engage in extensive exegesis of the passages, however, her argument is based more on the assertion that commonalities point to Luke's use of John. What is missing from Shellard's study, and which this study attempts, is a careful examination of the relationship from the perspective of Luke's editorial patterns.

Shellard, like Cribbs, links these phenomena together to suggest a new way of thinking about the Luke-John relationship: it is literary, and the difficulty of conceiving John's reliance on Luke means that Luke must have used John, not just Johannine traditions.

SUMMARY OF APPROACHES TO THE LUKE-JOHN AGREEMENTS

From this survey of studies that directly or indirectly deal with the points of contact between Luke and John one can see certain patterns that have dominated the discussion, as well as a place for a new examination of the issue.

In the first place, there is a large group of similarities between Luke and John that suggests a substantial relationship between the two Gospels. Beginning in earnest with Schniewind's work in 1914, these points of contact have been identified, first in the obvious parallel

---

was used instead of Q.

[202] In her conclusion to the Luke-John relationship, she concedes that proof of priority in such a literary relationship is difficult—which it is—but argues that in almost every case Luke's use of John makes better sense. Shellard, "Luke as Fourth Gospel," chapter 5, § 5.

pericopes. More recently, Cribbs has catalogued the similarities extensively. There has not been a particularly convenient way to categorize the similarities, Cribbs' attempt in 1979 being perhaps the best, and often the attempt to find similarities has extended to meaningless and trivial points of contact. But despite all these problems, research has defined the basic outlines of the points of contact:[203]

1. Points of contact are primarily confined to pericopes of events that Luke and John share in common with the other Synoptics.

2. There are some, but not a great many, striking similarities in phraseology.

3. A number of similarities in names and geographical interest exist in pericopes that are not otherwise marked by common themes or language.

4. In a number of places, the Lukan and Johannine order of events is different from that of Mark/Matthew.

5. Both the Third and Fourth Gospels leave out a number of items that are prominent in the First and Second Gospels.

6. Notwithstanding the points of contact, the tone of the Gospels is still very different: Luke is still "synoptic" in tone, while John is not.

7. In many instances it is hard to see why John, if based upon Luke, would have chosen to include some items and not others.

These basic elements of the problem have, over the years, led to a variety of studies whose observations and concerns are grouped below. In many cases the presumptions that supported the studies have limited their usefulness or cast doubt on their results. But a critique of the previous studies suggests some revised approaches that any new study of the problem should include.

1. An overriding assumption has been that John was written later than Luke. Except in the case of Cribbs and of Shellard, it is clear that that assumption not only helped some (i.e., Bailey, Neirynck) conclude that John knew and used Luke, but it prevented others (i.e.,

---

[203] The clearest and most important points of contact will be outlined and categorized in chapter 3.

Schniewind, Dauer, Landis) from extending their inquiry into possible "Johannine" material in Luke. A primary thrust of this study is to re-examine the material with that assumption specifically set aside.

2. Many scholars, notably Schniewind and Klein, but also Bailey, have worked with an assumption that by determining historically "sound" material, one could discover the earliest form of the tradition, and thereby could determine the direction and flow of literary or oral traditions. This approach is not viable. There is no way to neatly determine what is historically "sound" material. And even if that determination were possible, it would in no way identify the earliest form; early forms could contain errors and later forms corrections.

3. There has been a tendency by some to argue for "proof" of a literary relationship from a few instances of close verbal resemblances (so Holtzmann, Klein, Landis, Myllykoski and Bailey all worked from the position that if they only could identify some "clear" verbal similarities, they would have compelling proof of a literary relationship). Others, on the other hand, have argued that the lack of extensive verbal correspondence proves that the relationship is not literary but, rather, oral (so such scholars as Feine, Zurhellen, Schniewind, Grant, Parker, and Maddox have suggested that the fact that most similarities are not verbatim similarities was proof that the relationship was not literary). It would appear that the reigning paradigm of Gospel research has been the influential matter in this debate.[204]

---

[204] See Lloyd Kittlaus, "The Author of John and the Gospel of Mark" (Ph.D. diss., University of Chicago, 1988). Kittlaus suggests that the issue of the relationship perceived between John and the synoptics (here the gospel of Mark) has been dependent on the reigning paradigm: when source criticism was the primary paradigm, scholars saw the points of contact as demonstrating literary dependence. When form criticism became ascendant, scholars were inclined to find common oral, not literary, traditions. Cf., also, D. M. Smith, "John and the Synoptics and the Question of Gospel Genre," in *The Four Gospels 1992* (Leuven: University Press, 1992), 1783–98. See also chapter 1, note 18, above.

In light of the strikingly different conclusions reached by scholars as to the existence of a literary relationship between Luke and John, one must conclude that the process of discerning between literary relationship, oral tradition, or some combination thereof is much more difficult than has been assumed. On the one hand, a small number of verbal correspondences does not "prove" literary dependence. It is indeed possible for notable quotations or catchwords to circulate orally. On the other hand, the lack of verbatim similarities does not deny such a relationship. To affirm the latter is to assume that literary relationships between the Gospels are always cut-and-paste procedures. One can certainly conceive of deft use of literary sources that is based in allusion rather than direct quotation. It must be acknowledged that the "proof" in these issues will never be clear-cut. What is necessary is to assess the accumulation of evidence, both literal and allusive.

4. A striking series of observations about the relationship between Luke and John has noted the common interest in geography. Beginning with Zurhellen and reiterated by Osty, Parker and Maddox, the interest in geography, has remained at the center of inquiry. The geographical commonalities are not in the category of close verbal similarities, yet are highly suggestive of some common interest. But it may be going beyond the evidence to try to locate the composers of the two Gospels in the same region. At best this aspect of the relationship between Luke and John is highly suggestive and potentially important.

5. A number of scholars have rightly pointed out the vital role that the order of events must play in determining the relationship of these two Gospels. Zurhellen, Schniewind, Klein, Cribbs, and Maddox have all focused attention on order. Order is particularly important in the Passion narrative where the longest sustained series of contacts is found. In particular, if the order of pericopes is a major element in the creative work of an evangelist, then the possible influence of one evangelist's order on another would be a compelling aspect of the

issue.²⁰⁵ Any analysis of the relationship between Luke and John must pay attention to the issues of order.

6. Both Baur and Osty have made important observations about the possible existence of Johannine features in Luke. The assumption that John was written last has tended to push this issue to the margin. A full investigation of the relationship should take into account distinctive factual or theological features, either Lukan or Johannine, that might appear in the other Gospel. A pattern of use of such features might be as important as verbatim or close verbal similarities.

7. Grant raised the matter of correspondences that might have a text-critical dimension. Grant's proposals, which explain almost any Johannine material in Luke as a textual gloss, are perhaps an extreme solution. But the number of close correspondences in the series of textual variations in Luke 24 should at least alert one to the possibility of a relationship emerging after the initial composition of the Gospels.

8. The approach begun by Dauer and Landis is, I think, very helpful. These two scholars take seriously the need to understand the common material in terms of the evangelists' editorial programs. This analysis has been done for John, but it has not been done adequately for Luke. At the very least, there is a need to try to assess what might be the use of traditional material and what is the pattern of Luke's arrangement, modification and composition with respect to his sources. A part of this study should take cognizance of the evangelist's use of language, but it must be acknowledged that any author's language is a mixture of words and styles, so an overly precise distinction between tradition and redaction might reflect overconfidence on the part of the interpreter. Fully as important as language study is the awareness of the evangelist's theological or tendential purpose.²⁰⁶

---

²⁰⁵ So see for instance K. L. Schmidt, *Der Rahmen der Geschichte Jesu* (Berlin: Trowitsch & Sohn, 1919) argues that the ordering of pericopes in Mark is Mark's work.

²⁰⁶ Soards has examined Luke 22 with a partial eye on the Johannine relationship. This will be important. See the discussion in chapter 5 below.

9. Finally, Neirynck's reasoning that complex solutions are inherently suspect is sound. Given a choice between a viable complex solution to the relationship between Luke and John and a viable simple one, one must be drawn to the simpler one. But while Neirynck's solution is simple, it is nonetheless not viable because it does not satisfactorily account for the various points of similarity, not even in the pericopes he examines. As an alternative, the simple solution of Luke's having used John should be examined more closely.

Chapter 3

THE PATTERN OF LUKE-JOHN RELATIONSHIPS

As has been shown in the preceding chapter, numerous scholars have explored, in one fashion or another, the relationship between John and Luke. The elements of commonality that make up this seemingly close relationship are of a variety of kinds. There are some close similarities in language, some agreements in order of events, and some common interest in geographical points and even theological themes.

Although many scholars have made listings of similar features in Luke and John, some more extensive than others, few have examined the commonalities with an eye to discerning patterns among the points. As a backdrop to the more detailed work of exploring the relationship in the Passion narrative, a review and analysis of all the points of similarity is in order.

In this chapter I have summarized the significant points of similarity that have been documented between Luke and John.[1] In an effort to gain some perspective on the variety of the points of similarity, I have arranged them into a series of tables based upon the

---

[1] I have not listed all points put forward by others. Some, I have determined, are not valid; others are not unique to Luke and John. Only those which are distinctly points of contact between Luke and John, that is, which are different from Mark and/or Matthew, are listed. I have attempted to list the major references in the secondary literature for the points I have included.

different areas of commonalities. I have used the following classification groups:
different areas of commonalities. I have used the following classification groups:

    1. Close linguistic or striking substantive similarities
    2. Common order
    3. Common geographical references
    4. Common individual facts or allusions
    5. Common omissions
    6. Common named characters
    7. Common themes or theology

There is some overlapping of areas of commonality; in order to represent fully the similarities within the classification system, some duplication has been allowed. For instance, the absence of the cry of dereliction on the cross is an important common omission. But it may stem from, and at least reflects, a common interest in depicting Jesus as being in control of his death.[2] As a result, this point of similarity is listed under both common omissions and common themes or theology.

In addition to arranging the various points of similarity by areas of commonality, the lists are arranged in order of their appearance (or absence) in the Lukan narrative. This is done in order to identify where the most similarities occur and to see if there is any pattern in the points of similarity that might correspond with Luke's tendencies in using his literary sources.[3]

The purpose of this list is to gather together and group observed points of similarity between Luke and John; I do not presuppose or here attempt to prove that all of the points of similarity constitute or participate in a literary relationship, although the later analyses will

---

[2] See pp. 152 and 158 below.

[3] It is well known that Luke tends to use Mark and Q material, derived from whatever source, in blocks. Of interest will be whether Luke uses his *Sondergut* material in a like fashion and whether the pattern of usage helps point to the source of the material. Cf. Henry J. Cadbury, *Style and Literary Method of Luke* (Cambridge: Harvard University Press, 1920), 76, and Joseph Fitzmyer, *The Gospel*

argue that a literary relationship does exist. At this point in the study, it is important simply to place all the significant points of similarity on the table in order to see where and what kind of similarities are involved. The discussion after each grouping is meant to elucidate the kind of commonality that has been observed in the literature, not to argue for its validity. The analysis of this material will await chapters 6–8, below.

CLOSE LINGUISTIC OR STRIKING SUBSTANTIVE SIMILARITIES

Table 1

Lk 3:15	Jn 1:19,25	Is John the Baptist the Christ?[4]
cf. Acts 13:25	Jn 1:20	(οὐκ εἰμὶ ἐγώ)
Lk 3:16	Jn 1:26	John the Baptist's speech begins with ἀποκρίνεται[5]
Lk 3:16	Jn 1:27	"Thong of whom I am not worthy (fit) to untie."[6]
Lk 4:22	Jn 6:42	οὐχὶ υἱός ἐστιν Ἰωσὴφ οὗτος.[7]
Lk 6:13	Jn 6:70	ἐκλέγομεν + δώδεκα is used for selection of the disciples.[8]

According to Luke (I-IX) (Garden City: Doubleday, 1981), 67.

[4]Julius Schniewind, *Die Parallelperikopen bei Lukas und Johannes* (Hildesheim: Georg Olms Verlagsbuchhandlung, 1958), 8; Robert Maddox, *The Purpose of Luke-Acts* (Edinburgh: T&T Clark, 1982), 165; Lamar Cribbs, "Study of the Contacts that Exist Between St. Luke and St. John," *SBL 1973 Seminar Papers* (Cambridge, MA: SBL, 1973), 3, 25; Cribbs, "St. Luke and the Johannine Tradition," *JBL* 90 (1971):422–450, 423; Cribbs, "The Agreements That Exist Between Luke and John," *SBL 1979 Seminar Papers* (Missoula Montana: Scholars Press, 1979), 231; Pierson Parker, "Luke and the Fourth Evangelist" *NTS* 9 (1963): 317–36), 320; John A. Bailey, *The Traditions Common to the Gospels of Luke and John* (Leiden: E. J. Brill, 1963), 9; Matti Myllykoski, "The Material Common to Luke and John: A Sketch" in *Luke-Acts: Scandinavian Perspectives* (Göttingen: Vandenhoek and Ruprecht, 1991), 126.

[5] Cribbs, *SBL 1973*, 27; *JBL*, 432; *SBL 1979*, 220.
[6] Cribbs, *SBL 1973*, 27; *JBL*, 431; *SBL 1979*, 220.
[7] Cribbs, *SBL 1979*, 220.
[8] Cribbs, *SBL 1973*, 88.

Table 1 - Continued

Lk 7:2	Jn 4:47	ἔμελλεν is used with a verb of dying.[9]
Lk 7:3	Jn 4:47	Centurion "heard" (ἀκούσας) of Jesus (or his arrival).[10]
Lk 7:3	Jn 4:47	ἐρωτάω is used (uncommon outside of Lk/Jn)[11]
Lk 7:3	various	Elders of the "Jews" (Johannine phrase).[12]
Lk 7:3	Jn 4:47	Bearers of request go πρὸς αὐτόν.[13]
Lk 7:6	Jn 4:50, 51	πορεύεσθαι, ἤδη δέ αὐτοῦ + gen. abs.[14]
Lk 7:38	Jn 12:3	Jesus is anointed on his feet.[15]
Lk 7:38	Jn 12:3	Woman wipes Jesus' feet with her hair.[16]
Lk 19:38	Jn 12:13	Acclamation by crowd includes Jesus being called ὁ Βασιλευς.[17]
Lk 22:3	Jn 13:27 (2)	Satan enters Judas' heart (to explain betrayal).[18]

---

[9] Schniewind, 16; Robert Fortna, *The Gospel of Signs* (Cambridge: University Press, 1970), 46; M.-É. Boismard, "Saint Luc et la rédaction du quatrième évangile (Jn. 4.46–54)," *Revue Biblique* 69 (1962): 198; Stephan Landis, *Das Verhältnis des Johannesevangeliums zu den Synoptikern. Am Beispiel von Mt 8,5–13; Lk 7,1–10; Joh 4,46–54*, BZNT 74 (Berlin: Walter de Gruyter, 1994), 46; Myllykoski, 137.

[10] Myllykoski, 137.

[11] Schniewind, 18; Landis, 46.

[12] Schniewind, 18.

[13] Fortna, 46. Boismard, 198; Landis, 46.

[14] Landis, 47; for πορεύεσθαι, Schniewind, 17.

[15] Schniewind, 22; Maddox, 165; Bailey, 2; Cribbs, *SBL 1979*, 231; Myllykoski, 140.

[16] Schniewind, 22–23; Maddox, 166; Cribbs, *SBL 1973*, 35–38; Cribbs, *SBL 1979*, 231; Bailey, 1 ff.; Myllykoski, 140.

[17] Schniewind, 26; Cribbs, *SBL 1973*, 45; Cribbs, *JBL*, 442; Cribbs, *SBL 1979*, 231; Parker, 326; Bailey, 23.

[18] Hans Klein, "Die Lukanisch-johanneische Passiontradition," *ZNW* 67 (1976): 164; Cribbs, *SBL 1973*, 4, 48; *JBL*, 443; *SBL 1979*, 231; Parker, 321; Bailey, 29; Marion Soards, *The Passion According to Luke* (Sheffield: JSOT, 1987), 26, 32; E. Osty, "Les Points de Contact Entre le Récit de la Passion dans Saint Luc et dans Saint Jean," *Mélanges Jules Lebreton I*, (Récherches de Science

Pattern of Luke-John Relationships 95

Table 1 - Continued

Lk 22:14	Jn 13:1	"When the hour came" introduces final meal.[19]
Lk 22:33	Jn 13:37	Peter addresses Jesus as κύριε.[20]
Lk 22:34	Jn 13:38	οὐ φωνήςει + ἕως (vs. φώνησαι + πρίν in Mk/Mt).[21]
Lk 22:37	various, & Jn 19:28–30	τοῦτο τὸ γεγράμμενον is used for scripture, and τελέω.[22]
Lk 22:39	Jn 18:1	Jesus ἐξῆλθεν alone, with his disciples following.[23]
Lk 22:50	Jn 18:10	*Right* ear is cut off.[24]
Lk 22:54	Jn 18:12	συλλαμβάνειν + ἤγαγον.[25]
Lk 22:67	Jn 10:24	εἰ σὺ εἶ ὁ Χριστός, εἶπον ἡμῖν.[26]
Lk 22:67	Jn 10:25; 3:12,8:45	Εἶπον + ὑμῖν, οὐ + πιστεύειν.[27]

Religiuse 39. Paris, 1951), 146; Myllykoski, 129.

[19] Cribbs, *SBL 1973*, 51; Soards, 33. Note also the use of "hour" in a uniquely Johannine sense in Luke 22:53b (cf. Cribbs, *SBL 1973*, 58). Klein sees wholly different usage here, 171.

[20] Soards, 37; Klein, 172.

[21] Schniewind 30; Klein, 172; Cribbs, *SBL 1973*, 53; Cribbs, *JBL*, 443; Bailey, 37; Osty, 147; Myllykoski, 129.

[22] Osty, 147–48.

[23] Anton Dauer, *Die Passiongeschichte im Johannesevangelium: eine traditions-geschichtliche und theologische Untersuchung zu Joh. 18,1-19,30* (Munich: Kosel, 1972), 22, 53.

[24] Schniewind, 35; Klein, 180; Maddox, 164; Cribbs, *SBL 1973*, 4; *JBL*, 444; *SBL 1979*, 231; Parker, 322; Bailey, 47; Osty, 149; Dauer, *Passionsgeschichte*, 46, 57; F. Rehkopf, *Die lukanische Sonderquelle* (Tübingen: J. C. B. Mohr [Paul Siebeck], 1959), 65; Soards, 74.

[25] Klein, 162; Osty, 149; Rehkopf, 66; Dauer, *Passionsgeschichte*, 97.

[26] Klein, 165; Cribbs, *SBL 1973*, 63; *JBL*, 444; Soards, 80–81; Myllykoski, 142.

[27] Schniewind, 43–44; Klein, 165; Cribbs, *SBL 1973*, 89; *JBL*, 444; Soards, 80–81; Myllykoski, 142.

Table 1 - Continued

Lk 23:4,14,22	Jn 18:38, 19:4,6	Pilate declares, "I find no crime in him."[28]
Lk 23:16,20,22	Jn 19:12	Pilate wishes (seeks) to ἀπολῦσαι Jesus.[29]
Lk 23:18	Jn 19:15	αἴρειν is used for Jesus' destruction.[30]
Lk 23:20–23	Jn 19:4–6	Crucify him, crucify him (doubled).[31]
Lk 23:49	Jn 19:24	Women and friends stand (ἐστήκεισαν) by cross.[32]
Lk 23:53	Jn 19:41	The tomb is one in which "no one had yet been laid."[33]
Lk 24:12	Jn 20:4 ff	Peter runs to tomb, stoops (παρακύψας) in.[34]
Lk 24:12	Jn 20:5,6,7	Burial clothes called ὀθόνια.[35]
Lk 24:36	Jn 20:19	Jesus ἔστη ἐν μέσῳ αὐτῶν (εἰς τὸ μεσόν).[36]
Lk 24:36	Jn 20:19	εἰρήνη ὑμῖν.[37]

---

[28] Schniewind, 69; Cribbs, *SBL 1973*, 58, 68; Cribbs, *JBL*, 423, 445; Osty, 150 (he notes difference between use of αἴτιον and αἰτία); Bailey, 64. Note common use of εὑρίσκειν; Dauer, *Passionsgeschichte*, 156; Myllykoski, 133.

[29] Klein, 161–2; Cribbs, *SBL 1973*, 73; *SBL 1979*, 232; Osty, 151; Dauer, *Passionsgeschichte*, 162.

[30] Schniewind, 72; Klein, 177; Bailey, 65, 77; Dauer, *Passionsgeschichte*, 163; Cribbs, *SBL 1979*, 232.

[31] Klein, 180; Cribbs, *SBL 1973*, 4, 73; *JBL*, 423; *SBL 1979*, 232; Osty, 151; Dauer, *Passionsgeschichte*, 160; Parker, 326; Bailey, 65.

[32] Osty, 152; Bailey, 79.

[33] Cribbs, *SBL 1973*, 4, 80; Cribbs, *SBL 1979*, 232; Bailey, 78; Myllykoski, 135.

[34] Textual variant see chapter 4 below; Schniewind, 88 ff.; Myllykoski, 143.

[35] Osty, 152.

[36] Schniewind, 91; Maddox, 165; Cribbs, *SBL 1973* 4, 85; Bailey, 85; Anton Dauer, *Johannes und Lukas: Untersuchungen zu den johanneisch-lukanischen Parallelperikopen Joh 4,46–54/Lk 7,1–10—Joh 12,1–8/Lk 7,36–50; 10,38–42—Joh 20,19–29/Lk 24,36–49* (Würzburg: Echter Verlag, 1984), 207; Myllykoski, 144.

[37] Schniewind, 91; Cribbs, *SBL 1973*, 85; Dauer, *Johannes und Lukas*, 209; Myllykoski, 144.

Pattern of Luke-John Relationships 97

Table 1 - Continued

Lk 24:39 (40)   Jn 20:20   Jesus shows his hands and feet (side).[38]
Lk 24:40   Jn 20:27   Jesus invites disciples to touch his hands.[39]

DISCUSSION

This category is, perhaps, the most important group of similarities because it deals with one of the strongest indicators of a literary connection. In this group are those similarities between Luke and John in which a common word or phrase is found in both Gospels. In addition, I have included some striking substantive similarities which, although lacking the common word or phrase, nonetheless suggest literary sharing or a very close common tradition.

It is clear that the closest similarities are found in clusters in the Lukan narrative. In particular, the following groupings stand out: the account of John the Baptist (Luke 3:15–20), the healing of the centurion's servant (Luke 7:1–10), the anointing of Jesus (Luke 7:36–50), the prediction of Peter's denial (22:31–34), the arrest and denial of Jesus (Luke 22:47–62), the trial before the council (Luke 22:66–71) and before Pilate (Luke 23:1–5, 13–25), the crucifixion and burial (Luke 23:26–56), and the Resurrection (Luke 24). That there is no broad distribution of similarities, but rather small clusters, is an indication that Luke is following a pattern of using sources similar to that found in the rest of the Third Gospel. In particular, the preponderance of similarities in the Passion and Resurrection narratives suggests that a focused study of these passages in Luke is in order.[40]

---

[38] Textual variant: see below, chapter 4. Schniewind, 91; Maddox, 165; Cribbs, *SBL 1973*, 85; Cribbs, *SBL 1979*, 232; Bailey, 86; Dauer, *Johannes und Lukas*, 207.

[39] Cribbs, *SBL 1973*, 4, 85.

[40] See chapters 6 through 8 below.

Luke 3. The three similarities in Luke surrounding the reaction to John the Baptist show Luke to be very close in subject matter to John. Although the way the issue is presented is somewhat different, it is striking that both Luke and John portray the crowds as questioning whether John the Baptist is the Christ. Luke puts the issue into a summarizing statement of the narrator: "All men questioned in their hearts concerning John, whether perhaps he were the Christ, (Luke 3:15)." In contrast, the Fourth Gospel presents the matter in direct dialogue both from the mouth of John and in a question raised by a delegation of priests and Levites. In the first instance, John, responds to the Jews' asking him who he is with the assertion "I am not the Christ" (John 1:20), clearly interpreting the question to mean "Are you the Christ?" In the second instance, the Jewish delegation acknowledges that this indeed is the key issue, when they ask why John is baptizing "if you are neither the Christ nor Elijah nor a prophet" (John 1:25).

There is an intriguing point of similarity in this matter of whether John was understood to be the Christ in the greater body of Lukan texts. Acts 13:25 includes in Paul's sermon at Pisidian Antioch a recapitulation of the questioning of John. Paul has John responding to a supposed question of whether he is the Christ with the same language found in John 1:20, οὐκ εἰμὶ ἐγώ. Moreover, the balance of the passage strongly echoes John's language predicting the coming one, ἀλλ᾽ ἰδοὺ ἔρχεται μετ᾽ ἐμὲ οὗ οὐκ εἰμὶ ἄξιος τὸ ὑπόδημα τῶν ποδῶν λῦσαι. Luke, in this version put in Paul's mouth, appears to be drawing on the same tradition that John uses and perhaps even to show knowledge of the Johannine version.

The second and third similarities are closer in wording, though perhaps not in content. John responds to the people's questioning by "answering" (ἀποκρίνεται). Mark and Matthew have neither the crowd's questioning, nor, as a result, John's answering. That is not, in and of itself, a significant similarity. But it is coupled with a strong similarity in the statement that follows: οὗ οὐκ εἰμὶ [ἐγὼ] ἱκανὸς (ἄξιος) λῦσαι (ἵνα λύσω αὐτοῦ) τὸν ἱμάντα τῶν ὑποδημάτοων αὐτοῦ.[41] The pattern of the sentence is very similar, except that where the Fourth Gospel has John proclaiming he is not ἄξιος to untie Jesus' sandal, Luke has John not being ἱκανός. And John uses ἵνα plus the subjunctive to express the purposive construction, while Luke uses the infinitive. Indeed, Luke's language on these points is identical to Mark's, while sharing with John the absence of the participle κύψας. Luke's version, then, shares important features with John, and yet is strikingly similar to Mark; it would appear to be midway between John's and Mark's constructions.

Luke 4:22. Jesus' preaching in the synagogue is a programmatic passage for the Third Gospel. The setting resembles Matthew and Mark, but Luke presents an extensive sermon, while the first two Gospels relate only that teaching took place. At the close of sermon, the crowds in the synoptic Gospels discuss Jesus' family origin. Unlike Mark and Matthew, who have the crowd discuss mother and brothers and sisters, Luke has the crowd simply ask if Jesus is Joseph's son. This comment by the crowd is very similar to the comment by the people in the feeding passage of John (6:42), where his parentage is tied to Joseph by name. The Luke and John passages are very close in actual wording, but the context is quite different.

Luke 6:13. A minor point of common language, and one that is probably unimportant, is the use of the term ἐκλέγομαι by Luke and John (John 6:70) to refer to the calling of the twelve disciples. In contrast, both Mark and Matthew instead use the term προσκαλοῦμαι. But too much can be made of this point of similarity. Indeed, all four of the gospels deal at some point with the calling of the twelve (δώδεκα). Luke's version follows, in many respects, the pattern of Mark—that is, the setting on the mountain, the call, and then the listing of the disciples, which itself more or less agrees with Mark (with some points

---

[41] Johannine variants from the Lukan version are shown in parentheses; square brackets show a Johannine textual variant.

of commonality with Matthew). In contrast, John's version is a remark made on the occasion of Peter's confession of faith, and it bears virtually no other marks of similarity to Luke.

Luke 7:2–6. A cluster of remarkable similarities between Luke and John is found in the story of the centurion from Capernaum (cf. John 4:43–54). Both Luke and John relate that the centurion's[42] son was at the point of death, and both use the construction of ἤμελλεν plus an infinitive. John uses the term ἤμελλεν ἀποθνήσκειν, while Luke uses ἤμελλεν τελευτᾶν. John and Luke, contrary to Matthew, introduce the embassy to Jesus by noting that the centurion had "heard" of Jesus. Luke's centurion "heard" about Jesus (presumably, his power) to explain why he was interested in Jesus; John's ruler "heard" about Jesus (that he had come from Judea to Galilee) to explain that an embassy was practical. Moreover, Luke and John both have the embassy to Jesus use the phrase πρὸς αὐτόν, as well as the direct inquiry with a form of ἐρωτάω. This cluster of similarities, all found in Luke 7:3, is in material in which Luke is quite dissimilar from Matthew.[43]

Luke and John have substantially different endings to this story, in that Jesus sets out for the house in Luke, while the man departs for home alone in John. But in both instances the announcement of the healing is reported immediately after the petitioner sets out toward the house. In each case this report has the return toward the house indicated by πορεύομαι and the proximity to the house by the phrase ἤδη δέ αὐτοῦ plus a verb expressing closeness (οὐ μακρὰν ἀπέχοντος in Luke, καταβαίνοντος in John) in the genitive participle.

Luke 7:38. The anointing of Jesus' feet in Luke is both quite similar to the anointing stories in Matthew and Mark and yet at the same time quite different. In Luke the anointing takes place seemingly in Galilee,

---

[42] Βασιλικός in John.

[43] And Mark does not have the story of the healing of the centurion's son at all.

while in Mark/Matthew, as well as in John, it is at Bethany near Jerusalem (John 12:1); in Luke the account takes place chronologically early in the ministry of Jesus, while in the other Gospels it is just before the Passion; in Luke the story drives home the issue of love and forgiveness, while in the other Gospels the story serves to anticipate the burial of Jesus; and in Luke the main characters are a sinful woman and a Pharisee named Simon, while in the other Gospels they are simply a woman (Mary in the Fourth Gospel) and the disciples. In one feature, though, Luke is very close to John. The woman anoints Jesus' feet (ἤλειφεν, ἤλειψεν), not his head, and she wipes his feet with her hair (ἐκμασσω + θριξίς). These features are quite at variance with the Mark/Matthew version, in which Jesus is anointed on his head. Since this feature is so striking, it stands out as an important point of similarity between Luke and John.

Luke 19:38. In the triumphal entry into Jerusalem, all four Gospels have similar acclamations by the crowd: variations of "blessed is the one coming in the name of the Lord." A striking similarity is found in the Luke and John accounts. Only in these two Gospels is Jesus called a "king" (βασιλεύς). John has it as an appositive, "even the King of Israel"[44] (John 12:13) while Luke simply modifies the coming one with the term "king."

Luke 22:3. In connection with the last dinner scene, both Luke and John have the unique and vivid imagery of Satan's entering into Judas as a way of explaining why Judas would betray Jesus. There are differences, but the very importance of this scene suggests that it is more than just a passing allusion. In Luke, Satan is said to enter into Judas *before* the dinner, prompting Judas to arrange in advance the arrest with the chief priests and officers; a pre-arranged arrest is also a part of the Mark/Matthew version. In John, the reference to Satan's entering into Judas is found twice. First at the beginning of the meal (John 13:2), John relates that the "devil" (τοῦ διαβόλου) had already

---

[44] Reading the NA²⁷, καὶ ὁ Βασιλεὺς τοῦ Ἰσραήλ.

placed the idea of betrayal into Judas' heart. But then in the midst of the meal, John relates that "Satan" entered into Judas, who then goes out to betray Jesus.

Luke 22:14. The very beginning of the Last Dinner scene in both Luke and John begins with a form of the phrase "the hour has come." However, there is some real question as to whether the phrase is used the same way. In John, Jesus' hour clearly is highly charged with meaning. "His hour" is the foreordained focus of the Gospel, the departure from life and return to the spiritual existence (John 13:1). In Luke, however, the word seems to refer to the beginning of the Passover. Still, given the sacramental importance of the meal in Luke, it is possible that Luke intends as well some of the telic meaning that is carried in John.

Luke 22:33. In the dialogue leading up to Jesus' prediction of Peter's denial, both Luke and John relate a very similar statement by Peter. In both instances Peter addresses Jesus as "Lord" (κύριε). Moreover, in both Luke and John Peter claims to be ready to die for Jesus, although the actual wording is different (John 13:37). In contrast, Mark and Matthew are almost identical in reporting that Peter simply claims he will never fall away; in neither case does Mark or Matthew address Jesus as Lord.

Luke 22:34. With respect to in actual language used, this is one of the most striking similarities between Luke and John (cf. John 13:38). Both Gospels use a construction of ἀλέκτωρ (in nominative) +φωνέω + ἕως..(ἀπ)αρνήσῃ. Around this basic construction there are some differences: Luke uses the indicative future form of the verb φωνέω with the negative οὐ, while John uses an aorist subjunctive with the emphatic οὐ μὴ; Luke has the explanatory εἰδέναι with the denial, while John simply has ἀρνήσῃ. In contrast, both Mark and Matthew use an infinitive construction of πρὶν ἀλέκτορα φωνῆσαι ἀπαρνήσῃ.

Luke 22:37. In this uniquely Lukan verse, Luke uses two terms that are strikingly Johannine in flavor: τὸ γεγράμμενον as a term for scripture (versus, for instance, ἡ γραφή), which is not used otherwise by the Synoptics, and τελέω for the Passion (cf. John 19:28–30).

Luke 22:39. At the conclusion of the Last Supper, both Luke and John report that Jesus and his disciples "went out" to a place located on the Mount of Olives (although John phrases this as being across the Kidron). It is interesting that, as will be discussed later, Luke and John both avoid at this point the place name Gethsemane. And it is also interesting that in both instances an allusion is made that the place on the Mount of Olives was a customary place of assembly for Jesus and the disciples (cf. Luke 22:39 and John 18:2). But at this point, striking verbal similarity is with the wording that Jesus "went out," suggesting a common conception that they left the formal boundaries of Jerusalem, a conception perhaps lacking in Mark/Matthew.

Luke 22:50. The striking issue here is the notation that the ear that was cut off was the *right* ear (John 18:10). In other features, the Lukan verse has some notable variations not only from the Johannine version but from the synoptic version as well: the word for ear is οὖς, not ὠτίον (Matthew) or ὠτάριον (Mark and John); and the verb used is πατάσσω, not παίω. In one instance, the use of the ἀφαιρέω instead of ἀποκόπτω for cutting off the ear, Luke stands closer to the other Synoptics than to John. Still, despite these differences, Luke's similarity to John here is very much worthy of note.

Luke 22:54. We find in the arrest of Jesus a combination of words that link Luke and John in a similar construction (cf. John 18:12). Both report Jesus' being first seized and then led to the high priest. Each uses a form of the verb συλλαμβάνω plus the verb ἤγαγον. Luke's use of συλλαμβάνω is in a genitive absolute clause, while John's use is as a separate finite verb. But in contrast to Luke and John, Mark has no seizure, and Matthew uses κρατέω. And both Matthew and Mark use the compound verb ἀπήγαγον rather than simply ἤγαγον.

Luke 22:67. This verse at Jesus' trial has two striking similarities with the gospel of John. The first is a request by the elders of the Jewish people that Jesus openly identify himself as the Christ: εἰ σὺ εἶ ὁ χριστός, εἰπὸν ἡμῖν. This phrase is almost identical with the phrase in what appears to be John's version of a trial in John 10:24, where the Jews ask the same question.

Second, the same exchange between Jesus and his accusers in John is followed immediately by Jesus' response that he had said so and they did not believe (εἶπον ὑμῖν καὶ οὐ πιστεύετε). This is strikingly similar to Luke's conditional statement: ἐαν ὑμῖν εἴπω, οὐ μὴ πιστεύσητε. While the verb's mood is different, the linkage of the request for self-identification with the idea that it was not/would not be believed is clearly a strong similarity.

Luke 23:4–23. There are a number of similarities in Pilate's trial that can be taken together here, especially since they include a recurring theme spread over a number of verses:

1. Pilate announces openly in Luke 23:4 οὐδὲν εὑρίσκω αἴτιον ἐν τῷ ἀνθρώπῳ τούτῳ. This is essentially repeated in verse 22 and echoed (use of αἰτίον) in verse 14. Luke's language here is very similar to John 18:38 and 19:4 and 6, which have almost identical language to Luke 23:4 (ἐγὼ οὐδεμίαν εὑρίσκω ἐν αὐτῷ αἰτίαν). Mark and Matthew have no similar statement at all.

2. Both Gospels have the crowd respond to Pilate's attempt to free Jesus with the cry "Crucify, crucify" (doubled). In Luke the cry is in the present imperative, while John has the aorist imperative. Nevertheless, the effect of the double imperative is very striking.

3. Both Luke and John use the verb αἴρω in similar contexts to refer to Jesus' death.

4. Both Luke and John refer to Pilate wishing to release Jesus, a motive not ascribed to him in the other Gospels.

Luke 23:49. In the crucifixion scene itself is a rather striking similarity. While all the Gospels have the women observing the crucifixion, Mark and Matthew do so with a simple statement that the women ἀπὸ μακρόθεν θεωροῦσαι. While Luke's version is similar,but he adds that the women "stood" at a distance in order to observe the scene. This note about the women "standing" is similar to John 19:25, although he has the women standing nearby (παρὰ), not at a distance.

Luke 23:53. All of the Gospels record that Jesus was buried in the tomb of Joseph of Arimathea. Three of the Gospels (Matt, Luke, John) report that the tomb was "new"; Luke and John, by use of the phrase "in which no one had yet been laid." But while the substance of this phrase is very similar, it should be noted that the actual language used is quite different, both in construction and in word choice. Luke says ἔθηκεν αὐτὸν ἐν μνήματι λαξευτῷ οὗ οὐκ ἦν οὐδεὶς οὔπω κείμενος. In contrast, John reports ἦν ... ἐν τῷ κήπῳ μνημεῖον καινὸν ἐν ᾧ οὐδέπω οὐδεὶς ἦν τεθειμένος (John 19:41).

Luke 24:12. Both Luke and John detail the story of Peter's racing to the tomb and stooping in to glimpse the empty grave and burial clothes (cf. John 20:4–10). The reports are striking: Peter ἔδραμεν to the μνημεῖον. At the tomb, the language becomes almost identical: παρακύψας βλέπει [κείμενα] τὰ ὀθόνια [μόνα].[45] And the striking thing here, at least for Luke, is the use of the present tense verb βλέπει in a historic sense. Moreover, here Luke, like John, uses the term ὀθονία to refer to the burial clothes; previously in 23:53, in contrast to John, he had used language similar to the other Synoptics (σινδόνι) to refer to those clothes.

Luke 24:36. In the Resurrection appearances, Luke and John report very similar experiences in which Jesus appears and shows his wounds. The accounts are strikingly similar in two phrases: First, both

---

[45] Note that this is a major textual variant that will be discussed in detail, chapter 4 below.

accounts have Jesus appear "in the midst of them." The language is not exactly the same: both use the aorist ἔστη and the adjective μέσος, but while Luke uses the dative ἐν μέσῳ αὐτῶν, John uses the accusative substantive εἰς τὸ μέσον (John 20:19). Still, the phrasing is very similar. Second, in both accounts Jesus immediately speaks to them, saying, "peace to you." It is worth noting once again the use of the historic present (λέγει) in Luke.[46]

Luke 24:39–40. Following the similarities of Jesus' sudden appearance in their midst, both Gospels report that Jesus shows them his hands and feet/side. With the exception of the difference where either the feet or side (John 20:20) is shown, the language of the two accounts is almost identical: καὶ τοῦτο εἰπὼν ἔδειχεν [αὐτοῖς] τὰς χεῖρας καὶ τοὺς πόδας/ τὴν πλευρὰν [αὐτοῖς].

SUMMARY

There are, then, a large number of very significant parallels between Luke and John. As the preceding table and discussion have shown, the level of similarity is often so precise that it is hard not to infer some kind of literary relationship between the two Gospels at those points.[47] At other times, however, the similarities, though striking, could be just as easily explained by a common use of tradition.

It is, I think, very important that the parallels are not evenly distributed over the entire corpus of the Gospels. Rather, they are focused in a small handful of stories in addition to the Passion: the story of John the Baptist, the healing of the centurion's son, the anointing of Jesus, as well as a couple of scattered references. It is, I

---

[46] Note that this is a major textual variant that will be discussed in detail, chapter 4 below.

[47] Although such an inference is tempting on the basis of occasionally similar language, the demonstration of a literary relationship requires more evidence, generally the concurence of numerous kinds of similarity. See the

think, particularly noteworthy that in these narratives Luke is especially divergent from the Markan narrative pattern. What this suggests is that Luke periodically drew on a source or sources similar to John, which he used along with Mark in certain selected narratives and did not use in others.

The largest group of strong similarities is found in the Passion narrative. Here the similarities are numerous and often very close in wording. The pattern of strong similarities suggests that, at least in the Passion narrative, there is some kind of literary relationship between Luke and John.

COMMON ORDER[48]

Table 2

Lk 3:19–20	Jn 3:24	Jesus' ministry takes place while John the Baptist is alive?[49]
		cf. Lk 3:18 as an outworking of this?
Lk 9:10–22	Jn 6:1–71	Peter's confession is immediately after feeding.[50]
Lk 22:1–34	Jn 13:1–38	The order of Last Supper events is common in Lk/Jn:
vv 1–2	v 1	*a.* Frame of story (Passover, Passion anticipation).
vv 3–6	v 2	*b.* Satan's entering Judas.
vv 7–13		*c.* Preparation of meal.
vv 7–20	vv 3–20	*d.* Meal itself + sacrament/memorial.
vv 21–23	vv 21–30	*e.* Prediction of betrayal.[51]
vv 24–30	vv 31–35	*f.* Intervening dispute/teaching.[52]

---

discussion below, chapter 5, p. 262.

[48] Here, as in the following tables, the "common" elements are ones common to Luke and John in distinction from Matthew and Mark.

[49] Schniewind, 8.

[50] Maddox, 163; Parker, 319.

[51] Schniewind, 45; Maddox, 163; Cribbs, *SBL 1973*, 4; Rehkopf, 30; Soards, 35.

[52] Soards, 35–36.

Table 2 - Continued

vv 31–34	vv 36–38	g. Prediction of denial.[53]
		N.B.: Meal intervenes *after* (*e*) in Mk/Mt.[54]
Lk 22:54	Jn 18:12	Arrest is immediately after sword incident (vs. before).[55]
Lk 22:56–62	Jn 18:13–27	Peter's denial is interlaced with trial (vs. after trial in Mk/Mt).[56]
Lk 22:56 f	Jn 18:19–24	The order of trials and decisions seems to be consistent. The decisive session is in the morning. There is no night trial.[57]
Lk 23:2–4	Jn 18:29–38	Order of Pilate pericope is common:
v 2	vv 29–30	*a.* Accusation
v 3	vv 33–37	*b.* Question about "king"
v 4	vv 38	*c.* Declaration of innocence
		d. (vs. Mk/Mt:question about king, accusation, silence of Jesus)[58]
Lk 23:13–18	Jn 18:38–19:1	Order of trial events is common:[59]
		a. People (or Jews) as Pilate's audience
		b. Statement of innocence
		c. Desire to set Jesus free
		d. Scourging (or statement about scourging)
Lk 23:16,22	Jn 19:1	Scourging is discussed before death sentence.[60]
Lk 23:18–19	Jn 18:39–40	Barabbas demanded by crowd before explanation of who he is.[61]

---

[53] Schniewind, 28; Maddox, 163; Cribbs, *SBL 1973*, 53; Cribbs, *JBL*, 423; Bailey, 42; Soards, 37. Peter's denial is predicted at supper vs. on the way to Jesus' final prayer.

[54] Schniewind, 29; so see chart also in Cribbs, *SBL 1973*, 50; Myllykoski, 122.

[55] Cribbs, *SBL 1973*, 58; *JBL*, 444; Bailey, 47; Dauer, *Passionsgeschichte*, 58; Soards, 74.

[56] Schniewind, 44.

[57] Schniewind, 39.

[58] Schniewind, 62–3, 66.

[59] Klein, 162.

[60] Cribbs, *JBL*, 424; Osty, 150–51; Myllykoski, 122.

[61] Osty, 151; Dauer, *Passionsgeschichte*, 157.

Table 2 - Continued

Lk 23:33	Jn 19:18	Initial description of crucifixion refers to the two evildoers crucified with Jesus. Mk/Mt report this later as a separate item.[62]
Lk 23:54	Jn 18:42	Day of Preparation is mentioned right after description of tomb.[63]
Lk 24:36–49	Jn 20:19–22	Order of Resurrection appearances is common:
v 36	v 19	*a.* Appearance by Jesus
v 36	v 19	*b.* "Peace to you"
vv 39–40	v 20	*c.* Showing of feet and hands (or side)
vv 45–48	v 21	*d.* Sending of disciples to witness,
v 49	v 22	to be aided by Holy Spirit[64]

DISCUSSION

Luke and John agree at a number of points in the common ordering of material. The number of contacts here, spread over a number of chapters, would seem to preclude an accidental coincidence of retelling individual oral units. If oral tradition alone were responsible for the common ordering, it would suggest that large units of material circulated in connected fashion.[65] This common ordering of material suggests some contact between Luke and John—large common oral units or a literary connection.

Luke 3:19–20. In Matthew and Mark, Jesus' public ministry begins with the arrest of John the Baptist. The temptation in the desert is immediately followed by the arrest of John, an event which drives Jesus to Galilee and the beginning of his public ministry. Both John and Luke, in different ways, seem to have a different sense of how Jesus' ministry relates chronologically to John's. In the case of the

---

[62] Schniewind, 78; Osty, 152; Dauer, *Passionsgeschichte*, 222.

[63] Myllykoski, 135.

[64] Schniewind, 91.

[65] Cf. K.L. Schmidt, *Der Rahmen der Geschichte Jesu* (Berlin: Trowitzsch & Sohn, 1919), v.

Fourth Gospel, it is clear that Jesus and John have simultaneous ministries. Jesus and his disciples (the call of disciples takes place before John is arrested) have a baptizing ministry in the Judean countryside while John is still baptizing at Aenon (John 3:22–24). Indeed, this concurrent ministry provides the opportunity for "Jews" to sow the seeds of conflict between John's and Jesus' ministries (John 3:25–30, and 4:1–2).

In Luke, the issue is less clear. It is true that in the Third Gospel Jesus inaugurates his public ministry after John's arrest is related: the preaching at Nazareth begins in 4:16, after the temptation in the desert, while John the Baptist's arrest occurs in 3:19. But Luke's narrative technique has removed any direct chronological sequence; precisely how John the Baptist's arrest and Jesus' ministry relate is ambiguous. The ambiguity is achieved in two ways. First, the arrest of John the Baptist is related as a conclusion of his ministry; it serves to close one aspect of the narrative and open the next.[66] Thus the baptism of Jesus (3:21–22) actually follows John's arrest, indicating that Luke's way of dividing up the narrative is schematic, not chronological. It is as if to say that at 3:20 the story of John ends, and at 3:21 the story of Jesus begins in earnest.

The second way Luke has made the chronology ambiguous is by beginning the story of Jesus anew with the genealogy in 3:23. That effectively starts a whole new story, with no chronological ties back to 3:1–22. In Luke, then, it is quite possible to see Jesus' and John's ministries functioning at the same time, although Jesus' clearly supersedes John's in importance. But it is also possible to see Jesus' ministry becoming active after John's imprisonment. In all, Luke's chronology is not that of Mark and Matthew, but neither is it that of the Fourth Gospel.

Luke 9:10–22. Although Luke follows the Markan order in most cases, a striking departure takes place right after the account of the feeding of the five thousand. The material in Mark 6:45–8:26 is the Third

---

[66] So see Fitzmyer, *Luke*, (I–IX), 476.

Gospel's "big omission" of Markan material, material that includes, among other things, the feeding of the four thousand and the walking on the water. Luke jumps directly from the feeding of the five thousand to the confession of Peter, both of which are recorded in all four Gospels.

In John, too, the confession of Peter closely follows the feeding of the five thousand. In between the two in John are the walking on the water (John 6:16–21) and the discourses on bread (6:25–66). The discourse material in John is, of course, not present in the Synoptics, and indeed it seems to set up the circumstance for Peter's confession. Moreover, Peter's confession in John is markedly different than in the Synoptics. Nonetheless, the close proximity of the accounts of the feeding of the five thousand and the confession of Peter in both John and Luke links these Gospels in contrast to Mark and Matthew.

Luke 22:1–34. The agreement in the order of events between Luke and John in the final Passover meal is striking. The two Gospels have in a common order the fundamental features of the story: (*a*) an initial statement that sets the meal in the Passover period and refers to the upcoming Passion, (*b*) the statement that Satan enters Judas' heart to effect the betrayal, (*c*) the meal preparation is mentioned in Luke, but is the one item missing in John, (*d*) the meal itself, a meal in which Jesus establishes a ritual that is to be repeated ("Do this in remembrance of me" in Luke 22:19; "For I have set you an example, that you also should do as I have done to you" in John 13:15)[67], (*e*) the prediction of betrayal, (*f*) an opportunity for teaching, *(g)* the prediction of Peter's denial.

The agreement in the order of events is perhaps more striking, however, when we see that the Mark/Matthew pattern is significantly different. Mark and Matthew present the following order: (a) a setting statement linking the Passover with the Passion, (b) the anointing of Jesus at Bethany, (c) Judas' betrayal of Jesus to the ruling authorities,

---

[67] This item is valid only if the longer reading of Luke 22:19–20 is considered original.

(d) the Passover arrangement, (e) the prediction of betrayal, (f) the meal, with no ritual focus for remembrance, (g) the departure from the room, (h) the prediction of abandonment by the disciples, and (i) the prediction of Peter's denial.

Luke shares with the Mark/Matthew versions two features that set Luke apart from John. The preparation for the Passover (Luke 22:7–13), a feature absent in John, is described in Luke very much as it is in Mark and Matthew. And Luke, like Mark and Matthew, has Judas actually making the arrangements for the betrayal before the dinner occurs (Luke 22:4–6); the announcement by Jesus of Judas' betrayal thus comes as no surprise to the reader. But despite these two similarities between Luke and the other Synoptics, it is clear that his narrative stands far closer to John's. Five major differences distinguish Luke and John from Mark and Matthew:

1. In Luke and John, the prediction of betrayal is after the meal proper.

2. In Luke and John, the meal has a far more sacramental focus if one accepts the longer reading in Luke 22:19–20.[68]

3. In Luke and John, there is a teaching or dispute after the meal before the prediction of denial. But, it must be noted, that this intervening story is quite different between the two Gospels.

4. In Luke and John, the denial account is focused entirely on Peter, while in Mark and Matthew it is addressed initially to all the disciples and then specifically to Peter. And indeed in Mark and Matthew, the disciples still understand Peter's proclamation of his intention to stay with Jesus to be their own proclamation as well.

5. In Luke and John, the prediction of Peter's denial takes place in the same setting as the meal, while in Matthew and Mark it takes place after they have left for the Mount of Olives.

It appears that Luke has deliberately modified his account of the Last Supper, and has done so in ways that do not at first glance have importance to themes he usually emphasizes: he has the reordered the meal and betrayal segments, as well as the denial and exit to the Mount

---

[68] The longer reading is rejected in the analysis in chapter 4 below.

Pattern of Luke-John Relationships   113

of Olives segments. It is hard to see what these reorderings do for Luke, other than to conform Luke to an alternative sequence that he might have known from some source or tradition.

Luke 22:54. In the account of the arrest of Jesus, Luke varies from Mark and Matthew in the order of the actual arrest. In Mark and Matthew, Judas arrives with the predetermined plan to kiss Jesus, which would signal the arrest. The crowd of people then arrest Jesus; they "laid hands onus" (ἐπέβαλον τὰς χεῖρας). Subsequent to the actual arrest is the sword strike and Jesus' remark about how they approached him as a robber.

In Luke, however, while the account in many instances is very similar to Mark and Matthew (see the striking similarity of Luke 22:49–52 with Mark 14:47–49), the actual arrest happens only *after* the sword strike and the ensuing address by Jesus to the crowd. In John, too, the seizure (συλλαβόντες in Luke, συνέλαβον in John) occurs after the sword strike and after a remark by Jesus.

Luke 22:56–62. In Mark and Matthew, the account following the arrest scene occurs in two blocks of action that follow one another: first the trial of Jesus with the priests, and then Peter's denial. It is not clear if these are meant to be seen as coordinate in time or as following one another, but they are clearly separate narrated events.

Luke's account initially parallels the other Synoptics, with Peter following the arrested Jesus at a distance to the high priest's home. But then Luke tells a quite different story. There is, of course, no night trial before the council of elders in Luke; it awaits the daylight (Luke 22:66–71). The retold story, then, has Peter's denial occurring immediately after the arrest in the general presence of Jesus (Luke 22:61). Next is the mocking of Jesus by the men holding him. Then follows the trial and subsequent dispatch to Pilate.

John's version, in 18:13–27, is significantly different, but the structure and order of events agrees in many ways with Luke. As in

Luke, the arrest leads directly to a scene in the courtyard of the high priest. In John, there is a hearing before the high priest but not a trial before a council,[69] and the various events of the denial are intertwined with this hearing: first the setting in courtyard, then the first denial, next the interrogation of Jesus by the high priest, and then two more denials. It appears that Jesus' interrogation is in the courtyard where Peter is denying Jesus. And at least the first denial—indeed, the whole intercalated scene—takes place immediately following the arrest.

Luke 23:2–4. Mark and Matthew are striking in the abrupt way they begin the trial before Pilate, with no preceding word of accusation by the Jewish leaders; Pilate simply asks, "Are you the King of the Jews?" Only after Jesus' vague answer do the Jewish leaders accuse him of "many things." In the face of these charges, Jesus remains completely silent.

In contrast, Luke introduces the trial with a specific bill of indictment by the Jewish leaders, one charge of which is that Jesus claims to be a king. Based on that charge Pilate asks the direct question whether Jesus was King of the Jews, followed by Jesus' vague answer, "You have said so." Then, in Luke's version, Pilate immediately finds Jesus innocent of the charges.

John also introduces the scene with a discussion of the bill of accusation, although here the leaders are quite vague, suggesting only that Jesus is an evildoer (John 18:30) and that his crime is worthy of death (John 18:31). It is this veiled reference to insurrection that gives rise to Pilate's asking (as in the synoptics) whether Jesus was, in fact, the King of the Jews. After an exchange with Jesus that leads to Pilate's ironic question "What is truth?", he pronounces Jesus innocent of any crime.

John and Luke, then, share a basic order of events that distinguishes them from Mark and Matthew: the scene is preceded by an accusation of crime, reference to the accusation is then absent after

---

[69] It appears that the formal trial has already taken place in John 10.

Jesus affirms that Pilate has called him king, and after that exchange, Pilate announces that Jesus is innocent.

Luke 23:13–22. In Luke's version of the sentencing of Jesus, one finds a number of agreements in the order of events with John that are distinctive:

1. In both Luke and John, after the declaration of innocence, Pilate takes the positive step of seeking to release Jesus (Luke 23:16, John 18:39). In neither Mark nor Matthew does Pilate find Jesus innocent, and no direct move to release Jesus follows.

2. In both Luke and John, the crowd immediately requests that Barabbas be released instead of Jesus. Only after their request do John and Luke describe who Barabbas is. In Mark and Matthew, the sentencing narrative begins with a description of the governor's custom of releasing a prisoner and then introduces Barabbas, all of this well before Pilate brings up the issue of Jesus. And in both Mark and Matthew, the issue that follows is not simply whether to release Jesus, but rather a choice offered to the crowd: Jesus or Barabbas?

3. In both Luke and John, the issue of scourging Jesus (chastising in Luke) is introduced not as part of the crucifixion sentence but as distinct from the crucifixion. In Luke, Pilate desires to chastise Jesus *instead* of crucifixion. In John, Jesus is scourged, but only before Pilate attempts once more to release Jesus and wash his hands of the matter; the scourging appears to be an alternative punishment given when there is still hope for release.

Luke 23:33. Luke and John both initially describe the two criminals as an integral part of the crucifixion scene. In each case the term "they crucified him" is followed by a comment about the two criminals, one on the right and one on the left. After this, they record the inscription place above Jesus.

In Mark and Matthew, the criminals are described only after the dividing of Jesus' garments and the inscription on the cross are described.

Luke 23:54. At the end of the crucifixion scene, as they are preparing to place Jesus into a burial tomb, Luke comments that it was the Day of Preparation (for the sabbath). John includes a very similar comment at precisely the same point in the narrative. Mark also says that Jesus died on the Day of Preparation, but his point is made at the beginning of the pericope, when Joseph of Arimathea is identified. The common language at the same place in the narrative is an important connection between Luke and John.

Luke 24:36–49. There is a series of important similarities in the order of events in the post-resurrection narratives. Jesus appears in the midst of the disciples rather suddenly. His initial greeting is a pronouncement of peace. He shows the disciples his body to demonstrate that he is truly the risen Lord and not an apparition. Then, in both accounts Jesus implicitly or explicitly charges to the disciples to go announce the good news. In Luke, the charge is implicit in his announcement that repentance will be preached in his name to all nations; in John, it is perhaps more explicit, but also more brief—"As the Father has sent me, even so I send you." Finally, both Gospels end the epiphany with the promise or the reception of the Holy Spirit.

Mark, of course, has no post-Resurrection narratives; the women run away afraid. Matthew's account records the great commission received by the disciples in Galilee. While it contains references to the apostolic ministry the disciples were being given, it lacks the other features common to Luke and John.

SUMMARY

It is clear that in a number of important narrative units, the Gospels of Luke and John have strong similarities in the order of events. These generally occur where Luke has major deviations from the Mark/Matthew account. Virtually all of the agreements in order occur in the Passion narrative, beginning with the Last Supper. The

Last Supper unit is particularly striking in the number of similarities in order of events. The Resurrection narrative demonstrates strong similarities in order as well. The agreement in order in these narrative units is highly suggestive of a literary relationship.

COMMON GEOGRAPHICAL REFERENCES

Table 3

Lk 3:3	Jn 1:28	John the Baptist operates in the area around the Jordan (vs. desert).[70]
Lk 4:14–16	Jn 2:1–11	Jesus begins his ministry in the hill country near Nazareth (vs. Sea of Galilee).[71]
Lk 4:44	Jn 3:22–24, 4:1–3	Jesus has an early ministry in Judea prior to the Passion.
Lk 9:10	Jn 6:1,5	Feeding occurs at Northwestern corner of Galilee.[72]
Lk 9:10 ff	Jn 6:1–7:9	There is no clear reference to Galilean ministry after feeding of 5000.[73]
Lk 9:51 ff, 10:29–37, 17:11–19.	Jn 4:4–43	Interest is shown in Samaria or Samaritans.[74]
Lk 22:39	Jn 18:2	Mount of Olives was frequently visited.[75]
Lk 22:40	Jn 18:2	Gethsemane is called "the place."[76]
Lk 24:36–41	Jn 20:11–31	Post-Resurrection appearances are in Jerusalem, not Galilee.[77]

---

[70] Schniewind, 9; Maddox, 165; Cribbs, *SBL 1973*, 21. Cribbs also notes the passages and suggests the similarity is in the extensive ministry of John the Baptist (not his geographical location), *SBL 1973*, 3.

[71] Cribbs, *SBL 1973*, 3; *JBL*, 423.

[72] Cribbs, *SBL 1973*, 40; *JBL*, 437; Parker, 319.

[73] Parker, 319.

[74] Parker, 318.

[75] Schniewind, 32; Maddox, 164; Klein, 173; Bailey, 47; Cribbs, *SBL 1973*, 55; *JBL*, 443; *SBL 1979*, 231; Parker, 318; Dauer, *Passionsgeschichte*, 26, 55.

[76] Cribbs, *SBL 1973*, 19, 55; Cribbs, *SBL 1979*, 231; Soards, 71.

[77] Cribbs, *SBL 1973*, 4, 84; *JBL*, 424; Maddox, 169.

Table 3 - Continued

Lk 2:41,4:44, 7:17,7:36–51 10:29–37, 10:38–42, 19:1–10	numerous	Judea is more central to narrative than in Mk/Mt.[78]

DISCUSSION

It has often been noted that Luke's sense of geography is markedly different from Mark's and Matthew's, and that his geographical presentation is an important part of his story of Jesus.[79] Luke's geographical references show some striking similarities with John, such that it has been suggested at least that they both arise from the same provenance.[80]

Unlike many other points of comparison, geographical references are often more diffuse or topical. It is difficult to obtain a clean verse-to-verse point of contact. For that reason, in the following discussion I have tried to organize the common geographical references into narrative and regional groupings.

Jordan Region. Mark and Matthew appear to locate John the Baptist's activity relatively close to Jerusalem in the "wilderness" region near the Jordan. The geographical note is that the people of Jerusalem and Judea went out to him to be baptized in the Jordan. In contrast, the account in John is less clear about John's locus of activity. On the one hand, John's Gospel gives more precise locations,[81] yet the account of John's activity suggests an itinerancy in the general region of the

---

[78] Parker, 318; Cribbs, *JBL*, 429; Maddox, 168–70.

[79] See Hans Conzelmann's important entry point to his discussion of Luke, Part one "Geographical Elements in the Composition of Luke's Gospel" in *Theology of St. Luke* (London: Faber and Faber, 1960), 18–94.

[80] Maddox's suggestion (Maddox, 174–76). See chapter 2 above, p. 50.

[81] In 1:28, variously Bethany or Bethabara near the Jordan; in 3:23 at Aenon

Jordan, both in Judea and farther north. This account of John's ministry accords more closely with Luke's note at Luke 3:3 that John "went into all the region about the Jordan." Thus Luke knows of an itinerant ministry in the Jordan region, which must have had an extensive reach beyond just the Jerusalem region.

Galilee. In Luke, Jesus begins his ministry in Nazareth (Luke 4:16) and then proceeds to the region around the Sea of Galilee, specifically, staying in Capernaum directly after Nazareth. In John, Jesus begins his public ministry in Galilee at Cana and then proceeds to Capernaum. Both Cana and Nazareth are west of Galilee in the foothills. In contrast, while Matthew agrees that Jesus resided in Nazareth, the beginning of his public ministry begins in Capernaum, and only then does he proceed to Nazareth.

In the introduction to the feeding of the five thousand at Luke 9:10, Luke has the specific geographical notation that Jesus took the disciples to the city of Bethsaida, which is on the northeast tip of the Sea of Galilee. Mark and Matthew have no specific geographical reference to this event—only that it was a lonely place alongside the sea—but it appears to be on the west side of Galilee: the preceding geographical reference was to Jesus' "own country" which would suggest the region of Nazareth-Capernaum (Mark 6:1, 4; Matt 13:54). Furthermore, immediately after the feeding, Mark has the disciples cross over the sea to Bethsaida ("other side" in Matthew), suggesting that it was on the other side of Galilee.

John's account of the feeding places it at the Sea of Galilee, as do all the others. His reference is simply to the "other side" of the sea, but it appears that this should be understood to be near Bethsaida. The chapter just prior (John chapter 5) takes place in Jerusalem, not Galilee. But it appears that this chapter may be out of place in the Gospel, since especially the geographical references here witness abrupt shifts: chapter 4 ends in Capernaum, chapter 5 is in Jerusalem, and chapter 6 begins suddenly at the Sea of Galilee. Thus many

---

near Salim; and in 10:40, "across the Jordan."

scholars have argued that chapter 5 was moved here in a later stage of composition.[82] If so, then the preceding geographical reference would be to Capernaum (4:46), and the "other side" would, as with Luke, be around Bethsaida or some region nearby.

Samaria. Luke and John alone have an interest in this region between Galilee and Judea. Mark and Matthew focus the early part of their narratives almost exclusively in Galilee or the region around it (Mark's "Gentile" tour). And then they have a rather abrupt shift of scene from Galilee to Jerusalem (Mark 10:1; Matt 19:1), leaving no place for, or interest in, the region in between.

In contrast, the Fourth Gospel situates in Samaria a major narrative unit, the exchange with the Samaritan woman and the conversion of Samaritans (John 4:4–42). Samaria is not simply noted as a region through which one must pass between Galilee and Judea; Samaria's people become a focus of attention.

Unlike John, Luke does not have a unit in which Jesus evangelizes or interacts extensively with the Samaritans. Nonetheless, he does refer to Samaria or Samaritans in ways that suggest a lively interest in the region:

1. In Luke 9:51, Luke introduces the beginning of Jesus' long journey from Galilee to Judea with a reference to a certain village of the Samaritans. The people there would not receive Jesus because he was going to Jerusalem. After this, Luke has virtually no geographical references in the narrative until Jesus arrives, close to Jerusalem, at the town of Jericho (18:35)! In reading the narrative, it is certainly

---

[82] Rudolf Bultmann, *The Gospel of John: A Commentary* (Oxford: Basil Blackwell, 1971), 209; C. K. Barrett, *The Gospel According to St. John*, 2nd Edition (Philadelphia: Westminster, 1978) 23. Cf. Raymond Brown, *The Gospel According to John* (I–XII), AB 29 (Garden City, NY: Doubleday, 1966), 235. Fortna, is surely sympathetic to displacement, resolving the issue differently by bringing John 21 forward so that it is just before the feeding (96, 104).

possible to see that the events in the long intervening unit of material as taking place in either Samaria or Judea.[83]

2. Late in the long Lukan narrative, one finds a vague reference to the region between Samaria and Galilee; the casual nature of the reference may mean that Luke understands much of the narrative to take place in this region, even though he does not explicitly say so. In Luke 17:11–19, Jesus meets a group of ten lepers, whom he heals. Only one healed leper comes back to praise God, and he is a Samaritan. The Samaritan, then, is cast in a positive light in this story.

3. In Luke 10:29–37, Jesus tells the parable of the Good Samaritan in which the one who acted appropriately with respect to the Law was a Samaritan. The parable is set on the road between Jerusalem and Jericho, and clearly envisages Samaritans freely moving about in the region.

It is difficult to assess what this common interest in Samaria might mean. Clearly, it does not demand or represent a direct literary relationship. At the very least, it suggests a common interest in, and awareness of, Samaria as a region in which Jesus spent some time.

Judea. As to Samaria, so also to Judea does Luke pay greater attention than do the other Synoptics. Tellingly, the entire journey that begins in Luke 9:51 is undertaken with Judea and Jerusalem in mind. And from a point just after the feeding miracle (9:10 has a reference to Bethsaida), Luke makes no specific reference to the ministry in Galilee. Instead, at 9:51, the narrative is proleptically focused on Judea: "When the days drew near for him to be taken up, he set his face to go to Jerusalem." The emphasis on Judea is all the more remarkable since from this point until the arrival in Jericho (18:35), no firm topographical references are given, leading to the ambiguous sense that Jesus is moving toward, and perhaps in the region of, Jerusalem/Judea.[84] Luke's general interest in

---

[83] Cf. Maddox, 168.

[84] Helmuth Egelkraut, *Jesus' Mission to Jerusalem: A Redaction Critical Study of the Travel Narrative in the Gospel of Luke, Lk 9:51–19:48*, (Frankfurt: Peter Lang, 1976), 11.

Judea is similar to John, who has Jesus working in Judea and Jerusalem much of the time, alternating between Galilee and Judea. Thus John 2:13–4:3 (note especially 3:22), 5:1–47; and 7:10 through the Passion, all have Jesus in Judea, with narratives set in Galilee sandwiched in between.

And, as with Luke 9:10 forward, John places virtually no action in Galilee after the feeding; Jesus is said to be remaining in Galilee because the Jews are trying to kill him (John 7:1–9), but he departs right away to Judea anyway (7:10), apparently never to return to Galilee.

In a more specific series of references, however, it is clear that Judea is the backdrop for much of the narrative world with which Luke deals. There is, for instance:

Luke 2:41. As a child, Jesus was a regular pilgrim to Jerusalem and engaged the teachers in the temple in debate.

Luke 4:44. Here Jesus, after his inaugural sermon, is said to have preached in the synagogues of Judea.[85]

Luke 7:17. After the healing at Nain (unique to Luke, and in southern Galilee), the account of John the Baptist's disciples follows a general note that "this report concerning him (Jesus) spread through the whole of Judea and the surrounding country." That seems to place the this exchange in Judea, especially since John the Baptist's ministry is around the Jordan.

Luke 7:36–50. If, as the geographical note in Luke 7:17 seems to suggest, Jesus was working and was well known in Judea, then Luke 7:36–50 would also take place in that region. In the other Synoptics, as

---

[85] This is a major textual variant adopted by NA[27] and UBS[4]. Other variants have synagogues of Galilee, or simply of "them." These other readings tend to be Western or Byzantine and are probably explained as harmonization with Matthew and Mark.

well as in John, the anointing story takes place at Bethany, which is near Jerusalem. So, despite the displacement in the chronology of the anointing story, Luke may still understand it to take place in Judea.

Luke 10:29–37. Luke tells the story of the Good Samaritan, which has as a setting the road from Jericho to Jerusalem. This may simply be the "story world" of the parable; on the other hand it might suggest that Luke thinks, or wants the reader to think, that Jesus told this parable in the vicinity of Jerusalem.

Luke 10:38–42. Luke immediately follows the story of the Good Samaritan with the story of Mary and Martha, who welcome Jesus into their home. This account, of course, is absent in the other Synoptics. It is intriguing that in the Gospel of John, Mary and Martha live with Lazarus in Bethany, along the Jerusalem to Jericho road. In other words, Luke might well conceive of the Mary and Martha story as taking place in Judea, linked with the setting of story of the Good Samaritan.

Luke 19:1–10. When Jesus' journey reaches the region around Jerusalem, Luke adds to the Synoptic narrative an additional story set in Jericho. Zacchaeus, the tax collector, is unique to Luke. His story adds to the sense that Luke knows more than the other (synoptic) writers about Judea that he wants to emphasize the region.

Passion Story. In the Passion narrative, there are two striking similarities between Luke and John in geographical references. Cohering with the previous discussion on Judea and with the amount of time Jesus is said to have spent in the region is the statement about the place where Jesus is arrested. All of the synoptics have a reference to Jesus' going to the region of the Mount of Olives after the Last Supper (Matt 26:30, Mark 14:26, Luke 22:39). In contrast, John has Jesus crossing the Valley of Kidron, which would also place him on the Mount of Olives. But Luke agrees with John, over against the other Synoptics, that the place to which Jesus retires after the Supper is one that is known and frequented often. For John, this place is well known to Judas, because Jesus often went there with his disciples (πολλάκις συνήχθη ἐκεῖ μετὰ τῶν μαθητῶν). For Luke, the journey to the Mount of Olives is κατὰ τὸ ἔθος. Moreover, neither John nor Luke call the area where Jesus prays "Gethsemane," and the area where Jesus is arrested is known simply as "the place" (Luke 22:40; John 18:2).

Resurrection Story. In the post-Resurrection accounts, both Luke and John have a theologically significant agreement in the location of the appearance of Jesus. While Matthew locates the appearance in Galilee, and Mark suggests that such an appearance might take place there, Luke and John locate the epiphanies in Jerusalem or the region around it. Thus Luke 24:28–43 has Jesus near Jerusalem, within a day's journey. And the subsequent appearance is clearly in Jerusalem proper (cf. 24:33). This location becomes important to Luke as the center of the new movement ("Repentance and forgiveness should be preached in his name to all nations, *beginning from Jerusalem*" [Luke 24:47]; emphasized again in Acts [Acts 1:4–19]). John also locates the appearances in Jerusalem. The disciples are still close to the area of the cross (John 20:1–10), and the appearance takes place in the house where the disciples are staying (20:19–29).

SUMMARY

The geographical similarities between Luke and John are not striking similarities that can easily be attributed to literary usage. Indeed, the primary points of commonality involve an awareness of and appreciation for the Judean and Samarian locus of some of Jesus' ministry. How the two Gospels work that out is quite different. But the common references to location in the Passion and Resurrection story are significant and suggest both a literary and theological affinity that is worked out in the geography of the story.

COMMON INDIVIDUAL FACTS OR ALLUSIONS

Table 4

Lk	Jn	
Lk 1:5–25	Jn 1:6, 33	John the Baptist is divinely sent.[86]
Lk 2:11	Jn 4:42	Jesus is called Σωτήρ.[87]
Lk 3:22	Jn 1:32	Descent of dove is objective event, not experience of Jesus.[88]
Lk 3:20; 9:9	Jn 3:24	Only passing comment is made on John the Baptist's imprisonment and death.[89]
Lk 4:30	Jn 10:39	Jesus slips through the crowd.[90]
Lk 5:1–11	Jn 21:1–19	Miraculous catch of fish:[91]
v. 1	v. 1	* Settings shifts suddenly from Judea to Galilee.[92]
v. 8	v. 2 f	* Double name is used for Simon Peter.[93]
v. 4	v. 6	* Jesus commands the net be thrown out.[94]
v. 6	v. 11	* Net is about to break.[95]
v. 5	v. 3	* Men toil all night.[96]
v. 5	v. 3	* *Nothing* is caught all night.[97]
v. 10	v. 2	* Sons of Zebedee are mentioned.[98]
Lk 7:3	Jn 4:47	Jesus receives a direct request to come.[99]
Lk 7:6	Jn 4:50–51	Two embassies are sent. Middlemen appear.[100]

---

[86] Parker, 320.
[87] Parker, 323.
[88] Cribbs, *SBL 1973*, 28; Myllykoski, 127.
[89] Parker, 320.
[90] Parker, 324.
[91] Maddox, 163; Cribbs, *SBL 1973*, 3.
[92] Parker, 322.
[93] Cribbs, *SBL 1973*, 29; *JBL*, 433; Bailey, 17.
[94] Parker, 322.
[95] Schniewind, 11.
[96] Parker, 322.
[97] Cribbs, *SBL 1979*, 231.
[98] Parker, 322.
[99] Schniewind, 16; Myllykoski, 137.
[100] Schniewind, 17.

Table 4 - Continued

Lk 7:10	Jn 4:51	Healing is verified by eyewitnesses.[101]
Lk 9:11	Jn 6:2	Crowds *follow* Jesus to site of 5000 feeding.[102]
Lk 9:32	Jn 1:14	Followers see Jesus' "glory."[103]
Lk 10:40	Jn 12:2	Martha serves. (though in a different setting).[104]
Lk 12:37	Jn 13:4	Master girds himself, serves his slaves.[105]
Lk 19:37	Jn 12:17, 18	In triumphal entry, crowd's reaction is because of the wonders (sign, Lazarus) Jesus has done.[106]
Lk 19:39	Jn 12:19	Pharisees react negatively upon crowd's reaction to Jesus' entry.[107]
Lk 19:47;21:37	Jn 7:37; 10:22	Jesus has taught frequently in the temple.[108]
Lk 22:23	Jn 13:22	Response to Jesus' prediction of betrayal is a *reflexive* discussion among disciples.[109]
Lk 22:31f	Jn 21:15–17	Jesus charges Peter with restoration & care for the disciples. Peter is called Simon.[110]
Lk 22:33–34	Jn 13:36–38	Peter does not protest prediction of denial, but Jesus responds to Peter's prior word of constancy (I will die for you).[111]
Lk 22:45	Jn 16:6, 20 f	Disciples' grief is discussed.[112]
Lk 22:47	Jn 18:3	Judas is seen "leading" the arrest.[113]
Lk 22:49 f	Jn 18:8 f	Disciples try to prevent arrest.[114]

---

[101] Schniewind, 16.

[102] Cribbs, *SBL 1973*, 41; Cribbs, *JBL*, 437; Cribbs, *SBL 1979*, 231.

[103] Parker, 324; Cribbs, *SBL 1973*, 88.

[104] Maddox, 165.

[105] Maddox, 162.

[106] Schniewind, 27; Maddox, 164; Cribbs, *SBL 1973*, 45.

[107] Schniewind, 27; Cribbs, *SBL 1973*, 46; Cribbs, *JBL*, 442; *SBL 1979*, 231; Parker, 322; Myllykoski, 128.

[108] Parker, 319.

[109] Klein, 169; Cribbs, *SBL 1973*, 52; Osty, 147; Rehkopf, 27.

[110] Maddox, 167; Parker, 321; Soards, 37.

[111] Klein, 172; Parker, 321.

[112] Maddox, 162.

[113] Osty, 148; Dauer, *Passionsgeschichte,* 56; Rehkopf, 49.

[114] Maddox, 163; Bailey, 47; Rehkopf, 65 (sword strike is defensive).

Pattern of Luke-John Relationships

Table 4 - Continued

Lk 22:51	Jn 18:11	Jesus specifically tells his disciples to cease resisting.[115]
Lk 22:52	Jn 18:3	Arresting group includes some officials of the high priests (although different depictions), not just crowd.[116]
Lk 22:53	Jn 13:1, 5:27,	Johannine terms: ὑμῶν ἡ ὥρα, ἐξουσία, σκοτία.[117]
Lk 22:54 & 63-71	Jn 18:13 & 19-24	Hearing before High Priest is informal, not formal.[118]
Lk 22:55,56	Jn 18:18, 25	Fire is lit in courtyard to warm them.[119]
Lk 22:55-60	Jn 18:17, 25-27	Only one woman interrogator is at denial scene.[120]
Lk 22:58	Jn 18:25	Peter's second denial: "I am not."[121]
Lk 22:63	Jn 18:19-23	The beating in Lk seems to presuppose an exchange as in Jn,[122] since it does not follow the Sanhedrin's judgement (not a due punishment) as in Mk/Mt.[123]
Lk 22:67	Jn 18:20 f	Jesus is not silent at hearing.[124]
Lk 23:2	Jn 19:12-15	Charge of sedition is brought by Jewish authorities.[125]

---

[115] Rehkopf, 63.

[116] Schniewind, 35–36; cf. Osty, 148–49.

[117] Osty, 149; regarding ὥρα, Rehkopf, 81. See also Joseph Fitzmyer, *The Gospel According to Luke* (X-XXIV), AB 28A (Garden City, NY: Doubleday, 1985), 1452.

[118] Schniewind, 40–41; Maddox, 164; Bailey, 55.

[119] Schniewind, 56; Cribbs, *SBL 1973*, 59; Dauer, *Passionsgeschichte*, 98; Soards, 77; Myllykoski, 132.

[120] Cribbs, *JBL*, 444; Cribbs, *SBL 1979*, 231 (second accuser a man); Dauer, *Passionsgeschichte*, 98; Soards, 77; cf. Osty, 150.

[121] Klein, 167; Cribbs, *SBL 1973*, 60; *JBL*, 444; *SBL 1979*, 231; Myllykoski, 132.

[122] Schniewind, 40, 42.

[123] Cribbs, *SBL 1973*, 74.

[124] Schniewind, 41; Soards, 79.

[125] Charged with being king: Maddox, 164; Schniewind, 65; Parker, 322; Bailey, 64; Cribbs, *SBL 1979*, 232.

Table 4 - Continued

Lk 23:4	Jn 18:35	Jesus is taken to Pilate by "high priests *and crowd*." [126]
Lk 23:4 & 14, 22	Jn 18:38 & 19:4, 6	Pilate declares Jesus innocent 3 times.[127]
Lk 23:16	Jn 19:1–12	Scourging offered as alternative to death.[128]
Lk 23:17ff	Jn 18:39	Cry for Barabbas arises without explanation.[129]
Lk 23:25	Jn 19:16	Jews do the crucifying? Jesus is delivered to them?[130]
Lk 23:33	Jn 19:18	Those crucified with Jesus are not called λῃσται.
Lk 23:35	Jn 19:20	Crowds of Jews are at crucifixion.[131]
Lk 23:44	Jn 19:14	Luke's time reference seems to agree with John's that the entire crucifixion begins at 6th hour (not 3rd).[132]
Lk 23:56	Jn 19:39 f	Anointing spices are prepared the night of death.[133]
Lk 24:1	Jn 20:1	Women go very early.[134]
Lk 24:4, 23 (cf Acts 1:10)	Jn 20:12	*Two* angels (men) at tomb.[135]

---

[126] Schniewind, 64; Bailey, 64; Dauer, *Passionsgeschichte*, 156.

[127] Maddox, 164; Schniewind, 66; Klein, 161, 178; Cribbs, *SBL 1973*, 4; Cribbs, *JBL*, 445; Cribbs, *SBL 1979*, 232; Osty, 150; Parker, 322; Bailey, 64; Dauer, *Passionsgeschichte*, 158–60; Myllykoski, 133.

[128] Maddox, 164; Parker, 322; Osty, 150–51; Klein, 162, "Geisselung als »Züchtigung«"; Dauer, *Passionsgeschichte*, 160–61; Cribbs, *SBL 1973*, 4 argues that the signficance is on the scourging coming before death sentence.

[129] Schniewind, 65; Cribbs, *SBL 1979*, 234: "chief priests did not persuade crowd;" Myllykoski, 134.

[130] Parker, 322.

[131] Schniewind, 78.

[132] Schniewind, 81; Klein, 180.

[133] Schniewind, 81.

[134] Schniewind, 86; Bailey, 85.

[135] Schniewind, 86; Parker, 323; Cribbs, *SBL 1973*, 4, 80; *JBL*, 424; *SBL 1979*, 232.

Table 4 - Continued

Lk 24:5	Jn 20:13	Angelic comments are in form of question, not announcement.[136]
Lk 24:9–11	Jn 20:1–12	Mary returns to disciples with account of what heard and seen.[137]
Lk 24:16	Jn 20:14	Resurrected Jesus is not recognized.[138]
Lk 24:15, 31	Jn 20:19, 26	Jesus comes and goes mysteriously.[139]
Lk 24:22 f	Jn 20:1–10	Summary of Resurrection account is similar.[140]
Lk 24:24	Jn 20:3–10	Disciples rush to tomb on report of Mary.[141]
Lk 24:26	Jn 12:28 f	Christ must suffer to enter his glory/be glorified.[142]
Lk 24:36–41	Jn 20:19 f	Christ appears in Jerusalem.[143]
Lk 24:36	Jn 20:19	Jesus appears in Jerusalem in the evening of Resurrection.[144]
Lk 24:41	Jn 20:20	Disciples' reaction to Jesus is joy.[145]
Lk 24:41	Jn 20:25, 27	Unbelief is disciples' reaction.[146]
Lk 24:41–43	Jn 21:12 f	Jesus after Resurrection eats "broiled" fish with his disciples.[147]
Lk 24:47–49	Jn 20:21–23	Jesus discusses reception of Holy Spirit & preaching of forgiveness of sins.[148]

---

[136] Schniewind, 86.
[137] Schniewind, 87; Parker, 323; Cribbs, *SBL 1973*, 83; Bailey, 85.
[138] Schniewind, 94.
[139] Schniewind, 95.
[140] Maddox, 164; Myllykoski, 145.
[141] Parker, 323; Bailey, 85.
[142] Maddox, 164.
[143] Schniewind, 28, 87–88; Maddox, 164–65; Parker, 323.
[144] Cribbs, *SBL 1979*, 233; Maddox, 165.
[145] Schniewind, 91; Dauer, *Johannes und Lukas*, 208; Cribbs, *SBL 1979*, 232; Maddox, 165.
[146] Dauer, *Johannes und Lukas*, 208.
[147] Maddox, 167; Parker, 323.
[148] Maddox, 165.

Table 4 - Continued

Lk 24:49	Jn 14:16, 15:26, 16:7	Jesus has previously promised Holy Spirit.[149]
Lk 24:51, 9:51	Jn 20:17, 6:62	Reference is made to Jesus' ascension.[150]

DISCUSSION

In addition to the very close similarities in wording listed in table 1, there are many additional agreements between Luke and John that often do not share precisely the same wording, and yet still suggest a connection between the two Gospels. Many of these agreements are items of single words, facts, or interpretation of the events recounted. The list is quite large, and rather than discuss each agreement extensively, it will be necessary to simply point out the more striking ones and to note the accumulation of them in some narrative units.

Chapter 1. Only one minor item of agreement between Luke and John is found in chapter 1 of Luke: the recognition, absent in Mark and Matthew, that John the Baptist was himself sent by God. In Luke, this point is made by the narrative of the prediction and reception of the birth of John the Baptist (Luke 1:5–25), a narrative that is told in parallel with the narrative of Jesus' birth. John's ministry is even described prophetically in terms of scripture, put in the mouths of God's angels. In John, the point is made more explicitly: John is said specifically to be sent from God (1:6, 33).

Chapter 2. A small point of similarity is found in Luke chapter 2: both Luke (Luke 2:11) and John (John 4:42) refer to Jesus as the "savior," a term that Mark and Matthew do not use. The settings, however, are in no way similar.

---

[149] Schniewind, 95. And also the similar theme that such things are spoken of "while with you on earth" see John 14:25; 15:11; 16:25. Maddox, 165

[150] Parker, 324.

Chapter 3. All four Gospels recount the baptism of Jesus, but the event is told from very different perspectives. In Mark and Matthew, when Jesus is baptized, the descent of the dove is told from the perspective of Jesus: "He saw the Spirit descending." One is not sure if this is a vision or simply a shift of the narrative perspective. In contrast, John tells the story from John the Baptist's viewpoint in indirect narrative. John reports that John the Baptist saw the Spirit descend as a dove. Luke's account (Luke 3:22) is very much like Mark and Matthew's in that it is a third person narrative. But the descent of the Holy Spirit is told in the same fashion as John's—as an event that was observable. And indeed the dove had a "bodily form," emphasizing the external observable nature of the event. Thus Luke and John both seem to think of it as an event that was observable and reportable, not just something seen from Jesus' perspective.

In close proximity to this, Luke chooses to relate very sparsely the imprisonment of John the Baptist (Luke 3:19–20), and later remarks only briefly on his execution (Luke 9:9). This is in contrast to Mark and Matthew's extensive narrative about the imprisonment and execution. The Fourth Gospel as well shows little interest in John's imprisonment and death, with only a passing comment on John's imprisonment (John 3:24).

Chapter 4. The conclusion of Jesus' preaching in Nazareth, Luke 4:28–30, has a narrative feature that is absent in Mark and Matthew but reminiscent of John: the miraculous escape from the crowd. Luke relates that the crowd was trying to kill him by throwing him down a hill, but he passed away out of their midst (διελθὼν διὰ μέσου αὐτῶν ἐπορεύετο). This theme of slipping out of the grasp of the crowd when faced with a violent end is also found in John 10:31–39. Here also the crowd is wishing to kill Jesus, but he escapes from their grasp.

Chapter 5. Luke's call narrative in Luke 5:1–11 is completely different from Mark and Matthew's call, while it has a series of striking similarities with John's post-Resurrection narrative at the sea.[151] In both accounts Jesus is passing alongside the sea and addresses the disciples, who are fishing offshore. (Luke 5:4; John 21:6). In both accounts Simon and the sons of Zebedee are part of the group, although in John the list also includes Thomas and Nathanael (Luke 5:10; John 21:2). In both accounts the disciples have been fishing all night with no success (Luke 5:5; John 21:3). In both accounts Jesus tells the disciples to cast out again, which they do (Luke 5:4; John 21:6). In both accounts the catch is extremely large: in Luke the nets were about the break (5:6); in John they were unable to haul in the catch because of its size (21:6). And in both accounts Simon is called "Simon Peter" (Luke 5:8; John 21:3, 7). This last name is consistent in John's account; indeed it is John's normal term for Peter (only John 1:42 and 43 being exceptions, and this right after 1:41, which uses Simon Peter). In Luke, the double term Simon Peter is used only here.

This pericope nicely illustrates the fact that when John differs sharply from Mark/Matthew, Luke either follows John or, as in this case, presents an alternative episode. Moreover, the series of points in this area if commonality in many ways typifies the way that Luke-John similarities of this classification occur. Such similarities are marked by common themes or facts that are generally absent in Mark and Matthew and whose actual wording is rarely even close. In this instance, only Σίμων Πέτρος might be called "verbatim." But the combination of many items has a cumulative force that is nonetheless compelling.

Chapter 7. A cluster of striking similarities to John has already been noted in the account of the healing of the centurion's slave (Luke 7:1–10).[152] But in addition to the close wording noted above, there are

---

[151] John's chapter 21 is frequently thought to be a later addition to the gospel (cf. Raymond Brown, *The Gospel According to John* [XIII–XXI], AB 29A [Garden City, NY: Doubleday, 1970], 1077–82), or a transposition of earlier material (Fortna, 87).

[152] See p. 100 above.

a number of additional points that should be listed. Luke differs from both Matthew and John in that the centurion sends people (elders of the Jews) to Jesus to request healing rather than going himself. But Luke (7:3) and John (4:47) agree that Jesus is specifically requested to come and heal the boy; in Matthew, by contrast, Jesus responds spontaneously to the report of the boy's illness without any request at all. Moreover, in both Luke (7:6) and John (4:51), when Jesus arrives near the home, he is met by emissaries who mediate between the young man and Jesus. Luke's form of this encounter is quite close to Matthew's, but in Luke's narrative sequence it happens when Jesus has nearly reached the centurion's house and so is close to the Johannine structure. Finally, in both Luke and John the healing is confirmed by a report within the narrative world that indeed the boy was found to be well.

Chapter 9. This chapter has a few minor agreements between Luke and John. In the setting of the feeding of the five thousand, Luke (9:11) and John (6:2) both report that the crowds followed Jesus to the site of the feeding miracle. This contrasts with Mark and Matthew's account, which has Jesus putting out to sea in a boat, and then upon landing, finding the crowd waiting for him. An echo of John's interests is found later in the chapter (Luke 9:32), when Luke's transfiguration scene reports that Peter saw Jesus' "glory," a term which only John uses for Jesus (cf. John 1:14).

Chapter 10. A possible echo of John (12:2) is found in Luke 10:40. In both Gospels, Martha is depicted as "serving," while her sister Mary takes on a more public role with respect to Jesus. But Luke's and John's stories are completely different. While John's Mary appears in his anointing scene (an account which is told very differently in Luke), in Luke, Mary and Martha appear in a unique story meant to exemplify the difference between serving and listening to Jesus.

Chapter 12. A passage in the Lukan *Sondergut* has some similarity to John's final supper. In Luke (12:37), Jesus teaches about the need to be watchful. The servants, he says, who are faithful to the end will be served by their master (κύριος). The master will gird himself (περιζώσεται) and serve (διακονήσει) them at the table. At the final supper (John 13:4), John has Jesus girding himself (διέζωσεν) and washing the disciples' feet. And following that action he points to himself as an example: as their teacher and Lord (κύριος), he had served them by washing their feet (although the verb διακονέω is not used).

Chapter 19. In Luke's triumphal entry (19:37), the crowds react strongly to Jesus because they are aware of the mighty works (wonders) he has done. It is not clear which miracles are being discussed. Mark and Matthew are silent on the reason for the acclamation by the crowds. But John (12:17–18) has a comment very similar to Luke's, that the crowd went out to meet him because of the miracle (sign) of the raising of Lazarus.

Moreover, both Luke (19:39) and John (12:19) agree in their accounts by having the Pharisees react negatively to the entry and the crowd's reaction. Mark and Matthew are silent on this as well.

At the close of the temple cleansing pericope (Luke 19:47), Luke adds a note not found in Mark and Matthew to the effect that Jesus had been teaching daily (καθ' ἡμέραν) in the temple; a similar note is added at Luke 21:37. In the short time span of the Passion, this comment seems a bit out of place, but in fact reflects a tradition that Jesus did teach in the temple often, a perspective actually found in John, where Jesus is frequently placed in Jerusalem teaching in the temple precincts.

Chapter 22. The Passion narrative finds the number of points of similarity increasing. Aside from the Lord's Supper passage, chapter 22 has extensive points of contact between Luke and John.

Prediction of Betrayal. As has already been noted, there are some striking similarities between Luke and John in actual wording and order in the sequences dealing with the prediction of betrayal and arrest.[153] In addition to those points of commonality, there are a number of additional agreements that are suggestive of some common influence. For instance, only in Luke and John is the disciples' reaction to the prediction of betrayal one of reflexive questioning as to who the betrayer might be. Luke (22:23) says the disciples questioned one another; in John (13:22), they merely look at one another. But in both the issue is clearly one of questioning and wondering about who among the others the betrayer might be. In contrast, Mark and Matthew have the disciples asking Jesus individually whether they might be the one: "Is it I, Lord?"

Prediction of Peter's Denial. At the prediction of Peter's denial, Luke has two features that are suggestive of John. In the first place, although Jesus predicts that Peter will deny him, he immediately follows up with a command (prediction) for Peter to nonetheless return and help the other disciples (Luke 22:32). This is reminiscent of Jesus' admonition in John 21 to Peter to "feed my sheep." Moreover, both accounts have Peter being addressed as Σίμων, a term not regularly used by Luke but found in a number of pericopes that have strong similarities to John (Luke 5; 22:31).

In another way, Luke's prediction of Peter's denial echoes John's version. Both Luke and John do not have Peter initially responding to Jesus' prediction of abandonment and denial, but rather find Jesus predicting the denial only *after* Peter himself first rashly offers to go even as far as death in support of Jesus. So Luke (22:33) reports that Peter volunteers to go to prison and even death to remain with Jesus. And John (13:37) has Peter similarly asserting, "I will lay down my life for you." Only after those statements does Jesus predict Peter's denial. In basic structure and tone, though not in wording, John's and Luke's accounts are quite similar.

---

[153] See above, p. 101 and 111.

Sorrow. In a minor, and possibly coincidental, difference from Mark and Matthew, Luke (22:45) has the disciples sleeping because of sorrow (λύπη). John (16:6) also suggests that the disciples are filled with sorrow, but there is little other similarity between the passages.

Arrest. The arrest scene has a number of commonalities that are not strikingly similar in wording yet suggest some contact in tradition or source. In both Gospels Judas is actively leading the arrest group (Luke 22:47 and John 18:3). When he approaches Jesus, he does not kiss him. In Luke, he attempts to kiss him, but Jesus stops the kiss with a question. In John, no mention is made of a kiss. It appears that Luke is midway between Mark/Matthew and John. In the same scene, Mark and Matthew have Jesus immediately arrested. In Luke (22:49–50) and John (18:10–11), the disciples appear to attempt to stop the arrest by attacking with swords; in Matthew and Mark, the sword strike is merely a futile gesture after the arrest has taken place. Luke's enigmatic command ἐᾶτε ἕως τούτου (Luke 22:51) appears to be an attempt to stop the disciples' resistance, which is similar to John's words (John 18:11) to return the sword to its sheath. But this similarity is not unique to Luke and John; Matthew has a command similar to John's.

Luke's arresting party is a bit different from Mark and Matthew's in that it has chief priests and officers of the temple among the members (Luke 22:52). Schniewind and Osty see a close connection with John in this fact, since John has officers (ὑπηρέτας) of the chief priests in the party. But Mark and Matthew also have their "crowd" come from the high priests; it is not clear that this is a strong connection.

Finally, Luke concludes the arrest at 22:53 with a statement by Jesus that this is the priests' "hour" and the "power of darkness." Those terms, especially the latter, are strikingly Johannine, although John's Gospel does not use them in this context.

Hearing. Luke 22, as John, has no night trial; that awaits the daylight hour before the assembly. The hearing (Luke 22:54, 63–71) that is held is informal: no witnesses are called and no specific charge filed. Moreover, the formal verdict by the Jewish council is never made; instead, they simply rush Jesus to Pilate for trial. This agrees with John, inasmuch as John has only an informal hearing between Annas and Jesus, from which Jesus is sent on to Caiaphas and then immediately to Pilate. In addition, Luke has an expanded version of Mark's account of Jesus' response to the priest. While Mark has Jesus initially quiet (Mark 14:61), Luke has Jesus respond immediately to the questioning, with a statement that is almost sarcastic: "If I tell you, will not believe..." (Luke 22:67). But he then goes on to predict the coming Son of Man seated in glory in language that is very similar to Mark's second response. And finally, upon a repeated question from the priest, Jesus gives the almost Synoptic answer: "You say that I am" (Luke 22:70). John has a cynical or sarcastic response (John 18:20–21), but none of the rest. In a way, Luke appears to be a middle term between Mark and John.

Within the trial pericope, Luke also reports the beating of Jesus in a way that evokes the Johannine account more than the Mark/Matthew version. In Luke 22:63–65, the guards taunt Jesus and beat him despite the fact that he has not yet received a hearing, let alone a judgment, from the priests. The beating appears to be unofficial brutality. John also reports a similar unofficial attack, when the guards strike Jesus after his sarcastic response to the high priest's questioning (John 18:22). In contrast, Mark and Matthew present a scene very similar to Luke's about the striking and taunting of Jesus, but their scene comes after Jesus is condemned to death as a response to the guilty verdict.

Peter's Denial. John's denial scene opens with Peter and another disciple gaining entrance to the court of the high priest (John 18:15). As they enter, the maid who allows them in asks Peter if he too is a disciple of Jesus, which he denies (οὐκ εἰμί). Thereafter a group of servants and officers ask him the same thing, which he again denies (οὐκ εἰμί). Finally, a specific servant asks him, and the narrator says he denies it again. Two features in this narrative are quite similar to Luke and dissimilar to Mark and Matthew. The first is the questioners: as does John, Luke has only one question from a woman (Luke 22:56), while Mark and Matthew have two. The second similarity is the direct discourse of Peter in responding: οὐκ εἰμί (Luke 22:58, cf. John 18:25). Mark and Matthew have instead the direct discourse οὐκ οἶδα (as does Luke to the first questioner). The phrase οὐκ εἰμί sounds Johannine, and if its use in John 18 is indeed meant to be a direct contrast to Jesus' frequent phrase ἐγώ εἰμι, then it is very suggestive for the relationship between Luke and John.[154]

Both John and Luke set the scene for the denial account with a story of the lighting of the fire (Luke 22:55–6, John 18:18). In John, this account is fuller, with the purpose (to warm themselves) being added. In contrast, Matthew has no mention of the fire at all, and Mark has a fire, with Peter warming himself, but no reference to the lighting of the fire. A curious item is that Mark calls the fire a φῶς, and while Luke initially calls the fire a πῦρ, he later on refers to Peter's being seen sitting in the light (φῶς). Luke seems to have some items in agreement with John (lighting the fire), and yet other features from Mark.

Chapter 23. As with chapter 22, chapter 23 in the Passion narrative of Luke is at some points quite different from the other Synoptics yet quite similar to the Johannine version.

Pilate Trial. The trial before Pilate begins in Luke 23:2 with the Jewish leaders bringing formal charges against Jesus. Specifically, they say that Jesus is guilty of treason by claiming to be king and interfering with the peaceful administration of Roman rule. Of this formal indictment the other Synoptics know nothing; Mark and Matthew

---

[154] Cf. Brown, *John*, (XIII–XXI), 824.

begin the scene *in media res* with Pilate examining Jesus on the question whether he is the king of the Jews, a question asked by Pilate in all four Gospels. John's account is similar to Luke's in that the Jewish leaders present a formal indictment, but the substance of that indictment is not stated, only implied.

The understanding of the nature of the group that has presented Jesus to Pilate may also be quite similar in Luke and John, although it is not absolutely clear. In Mark and Matthew, the group turning Jesus over to Pilate is the chief priests (and elders in Matthew). In the latter part of the scene, where Barabbas is requested to be freed, there are crowds, but the focus remains on the chief priests, who incite the crowds to demand Barabbas' release. In contrast, the delegation in Luke 23:4 that hands Jesus over to Pilate and accuses him is made up of the chief priests and the multitudes (ὄχλους). The latter remain essential to the story throughout, and they always act together with the leaders: the chief priests and rulers and people (τὸν λαὸν) are mentioned again in 23:13 after the Herod episode, and the assembled group together (παμπληθεί) cries out for Barabbas instead of Jesus. John's account seems to be in agreement with Luke's in that the chief priests are not the only antagonists of Jesus before Pilate, although that is more implied than clearly stated. Pilate tells Jesus that his nation (τὸ ἔθνος) and the chief priests have accused him. The crowd that cries out for Barabbas is simply a communal "they." Still, the construction of the opponents in John is very vague; too much should not be made of this similarity.

As was previously noted (table 1), in the latter section of the Pilate trial are some literal similarities between Luke and John: Pilate found "no crime" in Jesus and the cry to crucify Jesus is doubled (σταύρου σταύρου). But there are some other close similarities that, while not literal agreements, certainly are striking. In both Luke and John, Pilate declares Jesus innocent three times. In Luke, this occurs in *three* different instances with almost the same wording — οὐδὲν εὑρίσκω αἴτιον (Luke 23:4, 14, 22). In the same way, John has three declarations with almost identical wording, all of which are similar to Luke. In both Luke and John, the crowd calls for Barabbas to be released without any previous discussion of Barabbas or indeed any offer by Pilate to release anyone (Luke 23:17; John 18:39). In Mark and Matthew, Pilate presents the people with a choice between Jesus and Barabbas; the crowd's cry is thus understandable in the narrative. Finally, Luke and John seem to present the scourging as an alternative to the crucifixion, not a part of it. In Luke (23:16), Pilate proposes to chastise Jesus and release him, but the crowd prevails, calling for crucifixion instead. In John (19:1), Pilate has Jesus scourged, but he then presents Jesus again to the crowd with a final unsuccessful attempt to release him. In both Mark and Matthew, the scourging takes place only after the sentence is imposed, and it thus appears to be part of the crucifixion sentence.

Luke and John agree that Pilate hands Jesus over to the *Jews* to be crucified; that is, that the onus of the crucifixion is especially on the Jewish leaders and people. Thus in John, Pilate says that the Jews should deal with Jesus (19:6), and at the end of the scene he turns Jesus over to them (the Jews) (19:16). In Luke, the final wording, "he delivered Jesus to *their* will" (Luke 23:25), perhaps suggests that he turned him over to the Jewish authorities. In Mark and Matthew, it is clear that the Roman authorities keep control of the process: Pilate simply hands Jesus over to be crucified, and the soldiers retreat into the Praetorium to mock him and prepare him for crucifixion.

Crucifixion. With respect to the crucifixion itself, there are some similarities between Luke and John, although not striking ones. In Mark and Matthew, the two who are crucified with Jesus are λησται, perhaps to emphasize that Jesus was considered to be an insurrectionist.[155] Luke and John studiously avoid this term, Luke (23:33) preferring the term κακούργους and John (19:18) simply saying that there were two "others" crucified with Jesus. Luke and John also portray a scene in which there are crowds watching the crucifixion. In Luke, the people (λαός) watch (Luke 23:35), and then the multitudes (ὄχλοι) depart after his death (Luke 23:48). In John the title over the cross is read by "many Jews" (John 19:20). This seems to cohere with the idea that the Jews took control of the crucifixion.

Mark states that the crucifixion actually began at the third hour and that at the sixth hour darkness settled over the area until the ninth hour. John reports instead that the actual crucifixion began later, a little after the sixth hour (John 19:14). Luke's account can be seen as agreeing perhaps with John, but perhaps with Mark. Luke's first time comment occurs after the announcement that Jesus was crucified with the criminals. He says, "It was now about the sixth hour, and there was darkness over the whole land until the ninth hour, while the sun's light faded" (Luke 23:44). It would appear that Luke has the crucifixion *begin* at the sixth hour and go until dark, the ninth hour. This agrees with John, who also has the death just before dark, because the Jews wanted to be sure it took place before the Sabbath began. But while the hours seem to agree between Luke and John, the actual wording is very close between Luke and Mark.

Both Luke and John report that some preparation or action relative to Jesus' being anointed with spices and ointments took place that very evening after he was taken from the cross. In Luke (23:56) the women prepare spices for the upcoming anointing of Jesus, and it explicitly says they rested on the sabbath to emphasize that this was done that evening (Luke 23:56). In John (19:39) the anointing actually takes place by Joseph of Arimathea and Nicodemus, but here again a

---

[155] The term λῃστης was commonly used for political criminals, not for common thieves. Josephus uses this term for the zealots. (cf. K. H. Rengstorff, "λῃστης" in *Theological Dictionary of the New Testament* [Grand Rapids, MI: Eerdmans, 1967], 4: 257–262, especially 258). Barabbas, for instance, was termed a λῃστης by John.

reference to the coming Sabbath makes the time reference important. Mark has all efforts regarding the anointing await the post-Sabbath Sunday, while Matthew makes no mention of anointing the body of Jesus.

Chapter 24. In the Resurrection and Ascension accounts, John and Luke continue to share a large number of similarities that do not arise from common wording, yet do suggest a close contact of sources.

At the Tomb. All four of the Gospels agree that the women went to the tomb early on the first day of the week, as soon as the Sabbath was over. John in particular emphasizes the earliness of their visit, it's being still dark (πρωι σκοτίας ἔτι, John 20:1). In that respect Luke 24:1 perhaps bears some relationship, although minor, to John in that his descriptive phrase ὄρθρου βαθέως also emphasizes the very early quality of that visit.

At the tomb the women in Luke and John meet not one but two messengers who announce Jesus' Resurrection. Luke 24:4 reports that these are two *men*, although they are clothed in dazzling apparel and make prophetic announcements about the Resurrection. In a later recapitulation of this story, (24:23), these two are said to be angels. In John (20:12) the two are said to be angels in white. In contrast, both Matthew and Mark have a *single* messenger (an angel in Matthew, a young man in Mark).

In both Mark and Matthew the angel makes an announcement that Jesus is risen. In contrast, although in very different ways, Luke and John have the angels engaging the women with a question, which allows for a bit more development of the narrative (Luke 24:5, John 20:13).

In Mark, of course, the women run away afraid, and that is the end of the second Gospel's story. Matthew, although reporting that the women do return to the disciples, has only a very brief report. In Luke 24:9 and John 20:2, however, the women return to the disciples; the initial report of the Resurrection is based entirely on the women's report. Moreover, in both Luke and John, Mary Magdelene is explicitly mentioned as one of the ones who made this report to the disciples, a feature that is absent in Matthew.

Emmaus Story. Only Luke contains the account of Jesus' appearance to the disciples on the way to Emmaus. The story does contain some similarities to John's Gospel, albeit in a very different context.

In the Lukan account, Jesus appears to the disciples, but they at first do not recognize him: "their eyes were kept from recognizing him" (24:16). Jesus then talks with the disciples, and it is only at the breaking of bread (24:31) that they recognize him. A similar motif occurs in John with Jesus' appearance to Mary. She does not recognize Jesus, but rather mistakes him for a gardener (20:14–17). Only when Jesus calls her "Mary" does she appear to realize who he is.

In the Emmaus story, Jesus rather suddenly arrives on the scene with the disciples, despite its being a distance from Jerusalem. And more strikingly, at the end of the story after he is recognized, he suddenly disappears. The overall effect is to emphasize some discontinuity between the risen Jesus and the normal confines of the physical world. Again this seems to resemble, at least in its general motif, Jesus' sudden arrival among the disciples in John. Here (John 20:19, 26) Jesus arrives despite locked doors. It is also interesting that in both Luke and John, Jesus shows his hands and feet (or side) to demonstrate his physical Resurrection, and yet in both he moves about rather unnaturally. What Luke and John have in common is a sense of continuity and yet discontinuity between Jesus and the physical world, although that sense is manifested in very different ways.

An interesting note, perhaps a shared theological perspective, is the comment in Luke 24:26 that Jesus must suffer to enter into his glory. The emphasis on glory, and indeed the relationship between the cross and Jesus' glorification, is very reminiscent of John, especially John 12:28, where the two concepts are coupled.

Perhaps most striking in the Emmaus account is the secondary narrative by the disciples of the events that have recently transpired (Luke 24:19–24, especially 22–24). Their account agrees with John 20:1–12 in its major points: (a) the women went to the tomb early, (b) angels appear where Jesus' body had been, (c) the women go back to tell the other disciples, and (d) the disciples do not see Jesus there. The Emmaus account also agrees with the earlier straightforward account in Luke 24:1–12. This is important, as we shall see, since 24:12 has striking similarities with John (see above table 1) but is a major textual variant.

Appearance in Jerusalem. Of course only Luke and John have Jesus appearing to the disciples in Jerusalem. This focus on Jerusalem as opposed to Galilee has already been noted above (table 3). In the Jerusalem appearances, though, there are also some similarities that are noteworthy. In both accounts, the disciples respond with joy. (In Luke 24:41 they disbelieve ἀπὸ τῆς χαρᾶς; in John 20:20 they respond joyfully, i.e., ἐχάρησαν.) And in both cases, one response to the risen Jesus is disbelief (Luke 24:41; John 20:25, 27). Moreover, Luke's account ends with Jesus eating broiled fish (Luke 24:41–43), a feature suggested in the post-Resurrection narrative of John 21.

Ascension. Luke and John alone of the four Gospels have specific references to Jesus' ascension to God after the Resurrection, although they do it in very different ways and use different words (Luke =ἀναθέρω, John=ἀναβαίνω). In both of these Gospels, the Ascension is coupled with references to the Holy Spirit and the preaching of forgiveness: in John, after breathing on them Jesus specifically links the reception of the Holy Spirit with the request to forgive sins; in Luke, the preaching of forgiveness of sins is commanded, but the disciples are to wait for the power of the Holy Spirit. Furthermore, Luke contains a specific reference that this gift of the Holy Spirit was promised, a promise also made in various places in John.

SUMMARY

This group of similarities is particularly marked by its size and distribution. Although the individual commonalities are not in and of themselves striking or suggestive of a literary relationship, the large number of them does have a cumulative impact. One cannot help but notice the large number of Luke-John similarities whose relationship is not based on the use of common words or phrases.

Perhaps most striking here, though, is the distribution of the similarities. They are found in clusters in Luke, very much as if Luke uses Mark or Q/Matthew material but interspersing at certain points with other material. The clusters of these particular Luke-John similarities are found in Luke chapters 3, 5, 7, 9, 19, 22–24. Most importantly, the largest clusters are those in chapters 22–24.

COMMON OMISSIONS

Table 5

Approximate Location		
In Luke	In John	
Lk 3:1–6	Jn 1:21	John the Baptist is <u>not</u> Elijah, contra Mk/Mt.[156]
Lk 3:3–10	Jn 1:19–28	No description is given of baptist's clothing or diet.[157]
Lk 3:18–21	Jn 1:29–34	Jesus is not said to be baptized by John.[158]
Lk 4:22–23	Jn 6:42–44	Jesus' brothers' names are not mentioned.[159]
Lk 9:11	Jn 6:2	At feeding, Jesus and disciples do not go to place by boat.[160]
Lk 9:18–21	Jn 7:	Second feeding miracle is absent.[161]

---

[156] Parker, 320; Cribbs, *JBL*, 429.
[157] Schniewind, 8.
[158] Parker, 320; Cribbs, *JBL*, 429.
[159] Cribbs, *JBL*, 430; *SBL 1979*, 233.
[160] Cribbs, *SBL 1973*, 41.
[161] Cribbs, *SBL 1973*, 3; *JBL*, 423; *SBL 1979*, 231; Parker, 319.

Table 5 - Continued

Lk 19:37–38	Jn 12:13–15	At triumphal entrance, no mention is made of David.[162]
Lk 22:31–34	Jn 13:36–38	No promise is made of going before into Galilee.[163]
Lk 22:31–34	Jn 13:36–38	Peter's assertion "while all may fall away, I will not" is absent.[164]
Lk 22:31–34	Jn 13:36–38	Peter's vehement protest to Jesus' prophecy is also lacking.[165]
Lk 22:31–34	Jn 13:36–38	No quotation of Zech 13:7 is included.[166]
Lk 22:31–34	Jn 13:36–38	No reference is made to other disciples' pledge of loyalty.[167]
Lk 22:31–34	Jn 13:36–38	No response is made by Peter after prediction of denial.[168]
Lk 22:40	Jn 17:1	No request is made to Peter, James, and John to stay awake.[169]
Lk 22:40	Jn 18:1	Name Gethsemane is absent.[170]
Lk 22:47–49	Jn 18:3–7	At arrest, no mention is made of Judas arranging a kiss as a sign nor of the kiss actually taking place.[171]
Lk 22:53	Jn 18:11–12	Flight of disciples after arrest is missing.[172]

[162] Cribbs, *JBL*, 430; *SBL 1979*, 233.
[163] Cribbs, *SBL 1979*, 233.
[164] Cribbs, *SBL 1973*, 53; *SBL 1979*, 233.
[165] Cribbs, *SBL 1973*, 53; *JBL*, 443; *SBL 1979*, 233.
[166] Barbara Shellard, "The Relationship of Luke and John: A Fresh Look at an Old Problem," *JTS*, n.s. 46 (1995): 72; Cribbs, *SBL 1979*, 233, *JBL*, 443; Schniewind, 28.
[167] Cribbs, *SBL 1979*, 233.
[168] Cribbs, *SBL 1973*, 20.
[169] Shellard, 72.
[170] Schniewind, 32; Cribbs, *SBL 1973*, 55; Cribbs, *JBL*, 430; Cribbs, *SBL 1979*, 233; Osty, 148; Dauer, *Passionsgeschichte*, 54.
[171] Schniewind, 33; Bailey, 47; Dauer, *Passionsgeschichte*, 29; Soards, 73; Shellard, 72.
[172] Schniewind, 35; Cribbs, *SBL 1973*, 58; *JBL*, 444; *SBL 1979*, 233; Bailey, 47; Soards, 76; Shellard, 72.

Table 5 - Continued

Lk 22:60	Jn 18:27	At third denial, Peter does not curse himself and swear.[173]
Lk 22:66–71	Jn 18:19–24	Jesus is not said to have blasphemed.[174]
Lk 22:66–71	Jn 18:19–24	Jesus is not condemned by council.[175]
Lk 22:66–71	Jn 18:19–24	No witnesses are called in trial.[176]
Lk 22:66–71	Jn 18:19–24	High priests' rage over Jesus' response to "Are you the Christ?"is missing.[177]
Lk 23:10–12	Jn 19:1–3	Soldiers do not spit on Jesus or hit him with reed.[178]
Lk 23:19–21	Jn 19:3–6	Pilate does not ask what he should do with Jesus.[179]
Lk 23:35–38	Jn 19:18–27	No comment is made by onlookers to Jesus about his destroying the temple."[180]
Lk 23:35–38	Jn 19:18–27	No offer of wine with myrrh or gall is made to Jesus on cross.[181]
Lk 23:44–45	Jn 19:23–30	No cry of dereliction (Eli, Eli) on cross is reported.[182]
Lk 23:44–45	Jn 19:23–30	No reference by crowd to "Elijah" is made.[183]
Lk 23:53–54	Jn 19:41–42	No mention of a stone closing the grave is made.[184]

---

[173] Cribbs, *SBL 1973*, 20; Dauer, *Passionsgeschichte*, 98; Soards, 77; Shellard, 72.

[174] Cribbs, *SBL 1979*, 234.

[175] Cribbs, *SBL 1979*, 234.

[176] Schniewind, 41; Cribbs, *SBL 1973*, 19; Cribbs, *JBL*, 431; *SBL 1979*, 233 (no false witnesses); Shellard, 72.

[177] Cribbs, *SBL 1973*, 19; *JBL*, 431.

[178] Cribbs, *SBL 1979*, 234.

[179] Cribbs, *SBL 1979*, 234.

[180] Schniewind, 78; Cribbs, *SBL 1973*, 75.

[181] Schniewind, 78; Dauer, *Passionsgeschichte*, 223; Cribbs, *SBL 1973*, 75, *SBL 1979*, 234.

[182] Maddox, 164; Schniewind, 78; Cribbs, *SBL 1979*, 234.

[183] Cribbs, *SBL 1979*, 234.

[184] Schniewind, 82; Cribbs, *SBL 1979*, 234.

Table 5 - Continued

Lk 24:6–11   Jn 20:11–18   Women are not told that Jesus will go before them to Galilee.[185]

DISCUSSION

The common omission of material from the Mark/Matthew narrative is difficult to evaluate. The mere common absence of material is, by itself, hardly indicative of a literary relationship. In particular with Luke and John, the difficulty is intensified in that much of John's Gospel is widely different from the Synoptics; therefore, any omission in Luke might simply be coincident with the absence of similar material in John.

However, having said that, there are some common omissions that might be suggestive of a relationship, especially when omissions occur in units of material in which John's presentation is quite similar to that of the Synoptics (e.g., John the Baptist material, the hearing before Pilate, etc.).

Luke 3. John the Baptist and his ministry, as has been noted, appears in Luke 3 in some ways that are similar to John's depiction.[186] In part, this similarity is made more striking by the absence of some material that is found in Mark and Matthew. For instance, John the Baptist is introduced in Luke with none of the descriptive phrases that would identify John with Elijah,[187] nor is this picture of John given in the Fourth Gospel. But Luke and John also appear to agree as well in their rejection or omission of the possibility that John might be Elijah. While Mark suggests and Matthew affirms just such an identity (Mark

---

[185] Cribbs, *SBL 1979*, 234.

[186] See p. 98 above.

[187] It would appear that the reference to John's wearing camel hair and having a leather belt around his waist is meant to conjure up the image of Elijah as found in 2 Kings 1:8.

9:11–13; Matt 11:14, 17:11–13), that identification is absent from Luke and John, and John even explicitly denies it (John 1:21).

Further, neither John nor Luke reports that Jesus was baptized by John. John leaves out Jesus' baptism altogether; while the descent of the Holy Spirit in John is similar to that in the Synoptics, it is only familiarity with the Synoptics which suggests a baptism also takes place. Luke certainly has Jesus baptized (3:21), but it is in a passive construction that leaves the identity of the agent unclear, if indeed Jesus was baptized by someone else. Luke's omission of the agent of baptism appears to agree with John's own perspective of the event.

Luke 4. All the Gospels contain a point at which the crowd asks in wonderment or alarm "is this Joseph's (or Mary's) son?" In Matthew and Mark it occurs in the synagogue teaching well into Jesus' ministry; in Luke, at his opening sermon in Nazareth; in John, at the feeding of the five thousand. In Mark and Matthew, the question refers to Mary and is expanded to include reference to his brothers, who are named, and his sisters. In contrast, Luke and John both refer to Joseph by name[188] and omit any reference to brothers or sisters.

Luke 9. The feeding miracles exhibit two Luke-John omissions of material—one minor, one major. The minor omission deals with the setting for the feeding of the five thousand. Mark and Matthew introduce the pericope with a boat journey to a lonely place—a place to which the crowd nonetheless follows on foot. Luke, although seeming to draw most of the pericope from the Markan version, alters the setting so that Jesus and the disciples merely withdraw to a city called Bethsaida, to which the crowds also go. John has a different location, the other side of the Sea of Galilee.[189] Neither Luke nor John note a boat journey, or the people's following on foot.

The major omission is the absence in both Luke and John of a second feeding miracle, the feeding of the four thousand.

---

[188] See below, p. 153.
[189] See above, p. 119.

Luke 19. In what might be a minor issue, neither Luke nor John in the triumphal entry have the crowds refer to Jesus as the son of David. Interestingly, both Luke and John *do* refer to Jesus as the "king," but without reference to David. Does this represent a common theology that seeks to distance Jesus from David? That seems unlikely, since both John and Luke take pains to connect Jesus with the Davidic rule: Luke, in the angelic announcement to Mary (Luke 1:32) and John by means of the question of Jesus' origin (John 7:42).

Luke 22. Luke and John differ significantly in their accounts of the prediction of Peter's denial, yet they are closer to each other than to the other Synoptics, in part by their common failure to report distinctive features that are found in Mark and Matthew. The entire introduction to the prediction is absent: the prediction that all the disciples will fall away, the supporting reference to Zech 13:7, the promise of restoration in Galilee. This common omission is in agreement with some major narrative features of the two Gospels: neither has all the disciples falling away, even for a time (contra Mark/Matthew), neither has the restoration taking place in Galilee (contra Mark/Matthew). Moreover, Peter's response to Jesus' words is strikingly different: neither Luke and John includes a comparative reference to the other disciples' failures; instead, Peter simply responds with a brash confidence in his steadfastness (although in different ways in the two Gospels).

At the final prayer, neither Luke nor John focuses on the disciples' sleeping. Neither has Jesus going after the dinner to a place called "Gethsemane," although both have him going to a place at the Mount of Olives known to the disciples.

At the arrest scene, Luke and John are absent a number of features that seem to drive the narrative in Mark and Matthew. Judas does not kiss Jesus, nor is such a kiss arranged ahead of time as a sign. Once Jesus is arrested, the disciples are not said to flee, perhaps in agreement with the omission of such a prediction.

At the end of the account of Peter's denials while in the courtyard of the high priest, Mark and Matthew both underscore emphatically the significance of Peter's failure when they show Peter invoking a curse on himself and swearing the final denial (ἀναθεματίζειν καὶ ὀμνύναι). While Luke and John report the three denials, there is no curse formula nor swearing at the final denial.

In the trial narrative, again, some significant features are absent in Luke and John that seem to be mainstays in Mark and Matthew. Jesus is never accused of having blasphemed, nor is he explicitly condemned by a council. There are no witnesses called in Luke or John. Nor does the high priest fly into a rage over Jesus' remarks.

Luke 23. At the trial before Pilate, John and Luke do not make mention of Jesus being spat upon or hit with a reed by the soldiers as do Mark and Matthew. In Luke the soldiers do mock Jesus and treat him scornfully, and in John they strike him with their hands. But the other specific features of disrespect are absent. Nor does Pilate ask the crowd what he should do with Jesus, a question that, in Matthew and Mark, elicits the cry from the crowd to crucify him. Indeed, it is striking that in Luke and John, the crowd needs no urging to call for the release of Barabbas and the destruction of Jesus.

Luke and John also agree in the omission of material concerning the crucifixion. No one from the crowd mentions the charge of destroying the temple, and Jesus is not offered wine with myrrh or gall. Nor do Luke or John record the crowd mocking Jesus on the cross, although Luke has the rulers' taunts. Of course, neither Luke nor John has the cry of dereliction or the crowds' misunderstanding of that cry as a call for Elijah; both Luke and John have Jesus stoically anticipating the death and controlling its time.

Luke 24. Again, in agreement with the Jerusalem focus of Luke and John, the women at the tomb are not told by the angelic visitors to go to Galilee nor that Jesus will go before them.

152   In Dialogue with Another Gospel?

SUMMARY

Omissions are a dangerous thing to use as a basis for common literary sources; it is hard to prove anything from absence. But the large number of common omissions and the striking absence of some of the Mark/Matthew material from Luke certainly demand some explanation. As with the common facts and allusions (table 4), the sheer frequency of the common omissions between Luke and John is impressive.

Once again a crucial feature of the omitted material is its distribution. By far the greatest clustering of common omissions with respect to Luke is in chapters 3, 9, and 22–24. These are some of the very same chapters that have the greatest clustering of common facts and allusions. And again, the omissions tend to coincide with Johannine differences from Mark and Matthew.

Many of the common omissions seem to cohere with a common interest in geography or an agreement of theology, which might suggest an underlying relationship between Luke and John.

COMMON NAMED CHARACTERS

Table 6

Lk 1:26	Jn 2:1–12; 19:25–27.	Special interest is shown in the mother of Jesus.[190]
Lk 2:33, 41, 48; 4:22	Jn 1:45; 6:42	Joseph is Jesus' "father." [191]
Lk 3:2, Acts 4:6	Jn 11:49, 18:13, 24	Both Annas and Caiaphas are high priests?[192]
Lk 6:16, Acts 1:13	Jn 14:22	Another Judas is mentioned besides Iscariot.[193]

---

[190] Parker, 320.

[191] Parker, 320.

[192] Maddox, 164, Schniewind, 38, 57; Cribbs, *SBL 1973*, 20; Cribbs, *SBL 1979*, 231; Bailey, 55; Osty, 150.

[193] Parker, 321.

Table 6 - Continued

Lk 10:38–42	Jn 12:2; 11:1	Mary and Martha are mentioned.[194]
Lk 10:39	Jn 12:3	Martha is characterized as serving.[195]
Lk 16:19–31	Jn 11:1	Lazarus is mentioned (raised v. dinner party).[196]

DISCUSSION

One might argue that this group of similarities should have been included under table 4 (Common facts or allusions). But the common use of names or similar interest in key figures is distinctive enough to warrant a special category.

Jesus' Parents. Luke and John both seem to have a special interest in Jesus' parents, although that interest is worked out in slightly different ways. Jesus' mother especially receives major emphasis in Luke at the beginning of the Third Gospel, with the annunciation and Mary's own song of response. While Matthew records the birth of Jesus also, Mary's character is not developed and certainly is not given special attention. And in Mark and Matthew (and, modified, in Luke) the attempt of Mary and Jesus' brothers to see Jesus is characterized as a negative event (Mark 3:31, Matt 12:46; cf. Luke 8:19–21). In John, Jesus' mother (never called Mary) is a major character in the wedding at Cana (John 2). And perhaps more importantly, John gives special attention to her at the close of his Gospel. There Jesus looks at his mother from the cross and entrusts her special care to the "beloved disciple." Both Luke and John, although in very different ways, amplify the mother of Jesus as an important and positive figure in the narrative.

There is an even stronger similarity in the two Gospels' treatment of Joseph. In distinction from Mark and Matthew, both Luke and John refer to Joseph as Jesus' father. Indeed, this reference is used

---

[194] Maddox, 165; Bailey, 1.
[195] Parker, 320; Bailey, 1.
[196] Maddox, 165; Parker, 320; Bailey, 6.

in both Gospels to discredit his teaching (Luke 4:22 and John 6:42). In contrast, in Matthew Joseph is only the husband of Mary, never the father of Jesus. And Mark never refers to Joseph at all.

Annas and Caiaphas. Caiaphas is mentioned not only in Luke and John but also in Matthew, who knows him simply as the high priest. In Luke, as in Acts, the high priest is apparently Annas, but at each mention Caiaphas is linked immediately with him. In a seeming agreement with Matthew, John identifies Caiaphas as high priest (John 11:49, 18:24). In the narrative sandwiched into the denial sequence, Jesus is *first* taken to Annas, who was the father-in-law of Caiaphas, the high priest that year (John 18:13). But Annas also is identified as the high priest (18:19). Annas sends Jesus to Caiaphas (18:24), who is again called the high priest. Thus John and Luke include both Annas and Caiaphas under the rubric of high priest, with very little explanation as to how this could be.

Judas. Both Luke and John make reference to a disciple named Judas besides the one (Iscariot) who betrayed Jesus. In Luke, he is explicitly named Judas the son of James; in John, he is simply referred to as "Judas (not Iscariot).."

Mary and Martha. Only Luke and John have the sisters Mary and Martha appear as characters. In John, the sisters are related to Lazarus; they appear in the narrative about Lazarus' raising, as well as in the subsequent narrative of the anointing. John's anointing story is very close to that of Mark and Matthew, but the figures of Mary and Martha are absent in those two synoptic Gospels. One feature of John's dinner scene in which Jesus is anointed by Mary is the remark that Martha "served" (διηκόνει).

Luke's mention of Mary and Martha is in a completely different context, immediately after the sending of the seventy (two) and the telling of the parable of the Good Samaritan. In the Third Gospel, Jesus is received into the house of Mary and Martha. Mary sits at Jesus' feet and listens to his teaching, while Martha is distracted by much serving (διακονίαν).

Lazarus. Both Luke and John refer to a Lazarus, but in very different ways. In John, the figure is the brother of Mary and Martha who is raised from the dead. In Luke, the figure is a character in a parable (The Rich Man and Lazarus, Lk 16:19–31). There is little similarity between the figures, other than the fact that both die, and some discussion in both (one actual, one proposed) of returning to life.

SUMMARY

The common references to people in Luke and John are not so clear or striking that they demand a literary connection. Indeed some of the commonalities seem to be only faintly connected. Nevertheless, the number of commonalities make a strong and compelling implication that there exists some close relationship between these two Gospels. While the Judas reference might be coincidental, the linkage of Caiaphas *and* Annas as high priests, the linkage of Mary and Martha with Martha serving, and the clear references to Joseph as Jesus' father, (indeed offered as a criticism of Jesus' authority), suggest some common material and can be most easily explained in terms of a literary relationship between the Gospels.

COMMON THEMES OR THEOLOGY

Table 7

Mk 7:24 omitted	Jn 12:20–24	Jesus' ministry is restricted to Jews until after Resurrection.[197]
Lk 1-2; Acts 3:24–25	Jn 4:22; 1:49	"Israel" is closely related to Christology.[198]

---

[197] Maddox, 171.
[198] Maddox, 171, 32.

Table 7 - Continued

Lk 16:29	Jn 5:46	Jews fail to heed Moses.[199]
Lk 10:18; 22:53; 22:31	Jn 1:5; 12:35; 17:15	Darkness/Dualism (Satan/ruler of this world) a significant feature.[200]
Lk 22:53	Jn 16:1–4, 32; 17:1	"The Hour" as predetermination of Jesus death.[201]
Lk 23:43–46	Jn 19:11, 30	Jesus exhibits serenity, confidence at cross.[202]
Lk 9:31–32; 24:26	Jn 7:39; 12:16 13:31–32.	Death is entry into Jesus' glory.[203]
Lk 4:21; Acts 2	Jn 4:23; 5:25; 12:23–28	Eschatology is future, but also fulfilled.[204]
Lk 11:13	Jn 14:16	Holy Spirit to be given to those who follow Him.[205]
Lk 2:25; Acts 9:31	Jn 14:16,26 16:7–14	Holy Spirit is a παρακλητος/παρακλησις.[206]
Lk 24:50–51 Acts 1:9	Jn 3:13; 12:32; 20:17	The Ascension is prominent.[207]

DISCUSSION

Israel. John and Luke locate Jesus' ministry exclusively within the geographical and cultural boundaries of Judaism. The Fourth Gospel is limited entirely to Jesus' interaction within the confines of Judaism (the Samaritans being viewed as "Jewish"[208]). The one case of contact with non-Jews is in the passage in John 12:20, in which some Greeks ask to see Jesus. Jesus responds to this request not with an agreement

---

[199] Maddox, 171.
[200] Klein, 175.
[201] Klein, 175.
[202] Osty, 151.
[203] Maddox, 172.
[204] Maddox, 173.
[205] Maddox, 172.
[206] Maddox, 173.
[207] Maddox, 172.
[208] As Maddox, 172, notes.

to meet the Greeks but with a prediction of his impending "glorification." Indeed, the "Jewishness" of Jesus' ministry is underlined by his comment that salvation comes from the Jews (John 4:22).

Similarly, Luke restricts Jesus' ministry during his lifetime to Jews. The trips outside of Galilee found in Mark, for instance, are conspicuously absent in Luke (the "great omission"). It appears that the delay of preaching to Gentiles until after the death and Resurrection is an important theological feature of the Third Gospel.[209] By conceiving the church as the successor to Israel, Luke is in effect also suggesting that salvation for Gentiles comes "from the Jews."

The limitation of Jesus' ministry to Israel is linked, however, with a strong acknowledgement that the his life and death have universal implications. In Luke that acknowledgement is played out in the subsequent narrative of Acts. In John, it is the conclusion to be drawn from the passage in which the Greeks seek Jesus: after he has died, then he will "draw all people to [him]self" (John 12:32). The universal impact of Jesus is anticipated in John's prologue (John 1:4, 9) and reiterated throughout his Gospel (3:16 ff, 12:44 ff, 17:20 ff), but that impact is clearly seen from the standpoint of Jesus' risen glory.

One feature of John's and Luke's location of Jesus within Judaism, which also coheres with the idea that the true Israel will be formed in the church after His death, is the view common to Luke and John that the Jews have in fact rejected Moses and the Law. Indeed, the rejection of Jesus is merely a symptom of this rejection of the Law and the Prophets. So Jesus' statement in Luke 16:29 is very similar in thought to that in John 5:46, in its suggestion that failure to believe Moses precludes belief in Jesus.

---

[209] So Conzelmann, *Theology of St. Luke* argues that Jesus' ministry stands at the center of history, poised between Israel on the one hand and the period of the Church and the Spirit on the other hand. (cf. 149 ff). Jesus' ministry is still located within the period of Israel; it awaits the coming of the Spirit and the arrival of the church to replace Israel as a vehicle of salvation for all humanity (209).

Dualism. Although a dualistic viewpoint is present in all four Gospels, at least to the extent that Jesus is seen as representing God and being opposed by demons or the devil, the aspect of opposition is heightened in John, but also in Luke.

The opposition is a pervasive feature of John's presentation of the Gospel. The world and darkness are closely related concepts; Jesus comes to a world which *is* darkness, He is the light, and those who follow him are sons of light (John 12:36) and are called to overcome the world. This darkness/light motif is developed in terms of a specific spiritual entity that opposes the light and the sons light: the "evil one" (17:15). This evil one (or devil or Satan), is behind the plot to kill Jesus (13:2, 27). So, for John, the conflict between darkness and light is cosmic and is represented by the opposition between Jesus and the leaders of humanity. It is this darkness that leads to Jesus' death. Nonetheless, even death cannot overcome the light: "the light shines in the darkness, and the darkness has not overcome it" (1:5).

Luke places a similar emphasis on the cosmic scope of the opposition to Jesus and his victory over it despite his death.[210] Luke alone reports the fall of Satan, and the disciples' authority to overcome the spirits and the power of the "enemy" (Luke 10:18–20). As in John, the enemy is Satan, who causes Judas to betray Jesus (22:3) and who seeks to capture Peter also (22:31). Indeed, as in John, this power that brings Jesus to his arrest and execution is the power of "darkness" (22:53).

Predetermination and Jesus' Death. Along with the cosmic nature of the opposition to Jesus, there is in John and Luke a certain predetermination and givenness to this final conflict. In Luke, the beginning of the conflict is called "your hour" (Luke 22:53), and the context seems to suggest that "your" embraces not only the Jewish leaders but also Satan. Jesus anticipates this conflict, of course, and faces the outcome with confidence (Luke 23:43–46).

---

[210] Cf. Susan Garrett, *The Demise of the Devil: Magic and the Demonic in Luke's Writings* (Minneapolis: Fortress Press, 1989), 37.

Pattern of Luke-John Relationships 159

The theme of predetermination, which is found in echo form in Luke (cf. also Acts 2:23), is particularly strong in John. Here the time of Jesus' glorification by death is his "hour" (John 2:4; 7:30; 12:23; 12:27). More broadly, this "hour" is also the term for Jesus' revelation, and it is already upon humanity with his incarnation (John 5:25; 4:23). But Jesus is aware of the arrival of the "hour" of death (13:1; 17:1), and is resolute and confident in facing it (19:11, 30), knowing that the death and Resurrection are already predetermined. Therefore, in neither Luke nor John does Jesus cry out "My God, My God, why have you forsaken me."

In addition to their common approach to Jesus' death as a predetermined hour that can be faced with confidence (Luke 23:43–46, cf. John 19:11, 30), both Gospels also understand it as the arrival of Jesus' glory. In the case of John, this theme is strong and recurring. Jesus will be glorified at his death (John 7:39); indeed, that glorification in John begins at the earliest stage of the Passion (13:1, cf. 13:31), when Jesus' "hour" has arrived. This same theme is suggested in Luke's version of the Transfiguration, in which Jesus is seen in "glory." In Luke's version, Moses and Elijah, who also appear "in glory," specifically refer to Jesus' departure and the coming Passion in Jerusalem. In Luke, the vision of glory is intimately connected with Jesus' Passion and his "departure" (ἔξοδος). The theme is reiterated by Jesus himself to the disciples at Emmaus when he refers to the Passion as the "entrance into his glory."

Eschatology. John's Gospel has an eschatology that anticipates a future fulfillment of the kingdom but that, in a paradoxical way, is already fulfilled in Jesus. Thus Jesus can speak of a time (ὥρα!) that is coming when worship will be in the spirit, and when the dead will hear and respond to the voice of the Son of God. He looks forward to a last day when all will be raised from the dead. But while these appear to be future events, they in fact are fulfilled in the present ("The hour is coming, and now is..." cf. John 4:23; 5:25–28). And thus while Jesus anticipates his glorification in the future (12:23), God responds that he has already glorified his name. The present and yet telic understanding of the kingdom is manifested by statements that link present belief with present inheritance of life (3:18; 5:24). There is then the constant understanding that the coming salvation (future) has already taken place in Jesus (present).

It has become a commonplace to note that Luke has "delayed" the parousia from Mark's imminent anticipation.[211] The eschaton has been removed, it would seem, until the far future. But this is undoubtedly an overstatement of the Lukan position.[212] Luke clearly does look forward to the future coming of the kingdom, as in Mark (Luke 17:22–37; 21:5–36). Moreover, it would appear that he expects the eschatological event to be coming in the near future, before the disciples' death (cf. 21:32; 9:27). In the preaching of the early church presented by Luke, the anticipation of the coming end is clearly future oriented, although not with a precise or distant horizon (Acts 17:30). At the same time, however, Luke (as does Matthew) emphasizes the present nature of the kingdom (Luke 7:18–28; 11:20!). Moreover, as will be discussed below, Luke sees the coming of the Holy Spirit as inaugurating in a special way the arrival of the last days. Thus the command to stay in Jerusalem until the Holy Spirit has come (Luke 24:45–59; Acts 1:8) is framed in terms of its being the arrival of the "promise" of God, which has been just sketched in eschatological terms. Moreover, in Acts, upon the manifestation of the Spirit among the disciples, Peter quotes Joel in an eschatological reference with the clear implication that that scripture has now been fulfilled. Luke, then, appears to be presenting the eschaton as future and present, in a way with which John might well agree, although with perhaps less emphasis on the future.

---

[211] Especially since Conzelmann, *The Theology of St. Luke*; cf. especially 97 ff. See the further treatment of this in John T. Carroll, *Response to the End of History* (Atlanta: Scholars Press, 1988).

[212] Cf. Maddox, 100.

Holy Spirit. Both Luke and John place a strong emphasis on the giving of the Holy Spirit following the death of Jesus and in that common emphasis are some similar features. Of course, the Holy Spirit in John is the παράκλητος, the counselor/advocate. The term is a major feature of the Fourth Gospel; it suggests a broad view of the function of the Spirit in the church. The παράκλητος, it would seem, not only serves as an advocate before the heavenly judgment but also serves to comfort, to bring recollection, and to advise (John 14:26–27). A variation of the term also appears in Luke, although perhaps not as a major element in Luke's conception of the Spirit. In Luke 2:25, Simeon expects the παράκλησις of Israel, and the Holy Spirit comes to rest upon him. Similarly, Acts 9:31 reports that the church was filled with the παράκλησις of the Holy Spirit.

In both Luke and John, the giving of the Holy Spirit follows closely the ascension of Jesus. In John, Jesus tells Mary not to touch him because he has not yet ascended, but instead sends her to the disciples saying "I am ascending to my Father and your Father, to my God and your God," (John 20:17). In the subsequent scene, presumably having already ascended, Jesus appears amongst the disciples and breathes on them, thus giving them the Holy Spirit (John 20:21–22). Luke also links the Ascension with the giving of the Spirit. Thus in Acts 1, Jesus' final words as he is preparing to ascend are to remain in Jerusalem until the Holy Spirit comes. And Peter's speech in Acts 2:33 makes clear that Jesus bestowed the Spirit after having himself received it following his ascension.

Ascension. As indicated above with respect to the Holy Spirit, both Luke and John emphasize Jesus' physical ascension to heaven. The Ascension is anticipated in John with statements about Jesus' descent and ascent (John 3:12–13), the rich image of his being "lifted up" (12:31–33), and the reference to "going to the Father" (14:1–4). For John, a two-storied world of heaven and earth is a major element in explaining Jesus' origination and destination. Luke also frames Jesus' death and Resurrection of Jesus in terms of such an ascension. Luke 9:51 (cf. Mark 10:1 and Matt 19:1) frames the Passion in terms of being "taken up" (ἀναλήψεως). Moreover, Luke both concludes his Gospel and begins Acts with the Ascension, underscoring the importance of this concept in his theology.[213]

SUMMARY

There are some striking similarities in the theological themes developed in Luke and John. Some are natural extensions of common material already developed in the discussions above. (For example, the interest in the Holy Spirit, discussed here as a theological affinity, is derived from commonalities discussed previously in table 4.) And yet these thematic similarities, like the geographical similarities, are more powerful because of their pattern and number. Moreover, since these thematic issues are part of the basic thought and structure of the two Gospels, it is hard to see their common occurrences as having arisen simply from common use of a source or sources. It would appear that one of the writers has had a deep influence on the other.

CONCLUSION

Looking at the whole array of similarities discussed above, the extensive nature of the points of contact between Luke and John is apparent. Indeed, not only are there many points of contact, but they are found in many forms. The wide-ranging variety of the similarities, as well as their sheer number, suggests a literary relationship, not just the use of a common source or sources.

Traditionally, the existence of verbatim or near-verbatim similarities has been the hallmark of acknowledged literary reliance. Certainly there are some close wordings between the two Gospels, but not of a sufficient number to establish a compelling case. But when one adds the common order, especially where Luke has varied from

---

[213] See Maddox, 10.

Mark, the myriad small facts or allusions, and the omissions, the case for a literary relationship begins to appear quite strong.

But of equal importance to the sheer number of similarities cited above is the pattern that they present in Luke. It is striking that the vast majority of the similarities, regardless of classification, are found in a few sections of Luke: chapter 3 (John the Baptist), chapter 5 (the miraculous catch of fish), chapter 7 (the healing of the centurion's slave), and chapters 22, 23, and 24 (the Passion and Resurrection).[214] Luke tends to use other, known, sources (Mark; Q or Matthew) in blocks;[215] it is significant that the pattern of Luke-John agreements occur in Luke only in certain blocks, which are reflective of the narrative portions of John. In particular, the pattern of the Luke-John relationship in Luke makes it clear that, in the Passion story at least, Johannine elements are extensive and manifold.

---

[214] There are some points of commonality found in a few other sections (i.e., chapters 4, 6, 9, 19), but they are more scattered and could derive simply from the use of a common (oral) source. However, with the striking pattern noted above, it is probable that they, too, are attributable to a literary reliance.

[215] Cadbury, 75.

Chapter 4

TEXTUAL VARIANTS:
THE WESTERN NON-INTERPOLATIONS

INTRODUCTION

In their landmark study published in 1882, Westcott and Hort cast serious doubt on the authenticity of a significant number of commonly accepted readings in the New Testament; indeed, the Received Text (*Textus Receptus*) was shown in many instances to be the end result of a long process of conflation and addition.[1] In their exposition, a strong case was made for a common tendency in the transmission of texts to include material from variant traditions, material that often expanded and explained the original text. In their examination they found that the textual tradition best represented by the Codex Vaticanus (B) and Codex Sinaiticus (א) was in most instances closer to the earliest form of the text. This reconstructed text they called the "Neutral Text."[2]

But in a very few instances, Westcott and Hort believed, the textual tradition represented in Codex Vaticanus was not the purest. Specifically, they found a number of places where the text in Codex Vaticanus was longer and more expansionistic than that found in other

---

[1] B. F. Westcott and F. J. A. Hort, *Introduction to the New Testament in the Original Greek*, 2 vols. (New York: Harper and Brothers, 1882).

[2] Westcott and Hort, 169–71.

textual traditions, notably the Western text family represented by Codex Bezae (D) and certain early Latin and Syriac versions.[3] Although the Western text was considered to be inferior, its antiquity—and therefore its possibility of containing an original reading—was acknowledged.[4] The Western text was normally longer and more expansionistic than the Neutral Text, but in the specific instances identified by Westcott and Hort, it was shorter. In part because the readings in this group ran contrary to the normal expansionistic tendency of the Western text,[5] they were believed to have retained the original form of the text, and Codex Vaticanus (and Sinaiticus), to have incorporated additions, generally due to harmonizations. Westcott and Hort grouped these texts under the rubric "Western non-interpolations,"[6] a term that at once conveys their estimation of the shorter text as more original and their avoidance of an overt suggestion that their Neutral Text had expanded or interpolated material into the text.[7]

A significant number of Western non-interpolations are found in the resurrection narrative of Luke. Moreover, in many cases these tex-

---

[3] Westcott and Hort, 175–77. The terminology referring to this text type has frequently been challenged; the fact that the old Syriac text is a major witness to the text type should raise questions about the geographical nature of the designation. However, since the designation is so widespread and well known, it will be readily accepted here.

[4] The existence of a coherent Western text, as identified especially with Codex Bezae, in the second century has been questioned. But J. Neville Birdsall, "The Western Text in the Second Century," in *Gospel Traditions in the Second Century* (Notre Dame: University of Notre Dame Press, 1989), 3–18) is willing to say that Western readings can be traced to the second century.

[5] It might be more appropriate to call the Western text "free" in that it is marked by expansion but also by omission and substitution. See the sketch of the Western text's tendency in W. H. P. Hatch, *The "Western" Text of the Gospels* (Evanston, Illinois: Seabury-Western Theological Seminary, 1937).

[6] Westcott and Hort, 175–77.

[7] Joseph Fitzmyer, *The Gospel According to Luke* (I–IX), AB 28 (Garden City, NY: Doubleday, 1981), 130.

tual variants contain material strongly similar to the Gospel of John and are therefore particularly germane to our study of the Luke-John relationship in the Passion narrative. One cannot, then, avoid the question of the originality of these Western non-interpolations.

Westcott and Hort considered twenty-seven texts as possible Western non-interpolations.[8] Of these, they positively identified only nine as non-interpolations, displaying them in double brackets, which signified a rejected reading. The nine texts are: Matt 27:49; Luke 22:19–20; Luke 24:3; Luke 24:6; Luke 24:12; Luke 24:36; Luke 24:40; Luke 24:51; and Luke 24:52. The first cited, Matt 27:49, is not a Western non-interpolation by narrow definition, since the witnesses excluding the reading are not truly Western but rather a mixed text that has been called since then Caesarean.[9] While Codex Bezae excludes the reading, the Itala and Syriac texts do not.[10] Since it is not in Luke, our field of investigation, this verse will be excluded from further consideration.

The preponderance of Western non-interpolations, then, are found in the Passion and Resurrection narratives of Luke. Moreover, it is striking that the long texts of Luke 24:12, 24:36, and 24:40 share significant points of commonality with John. Two others, Luke 24:6 and 24:52, show similarities to the Gospel of Matthew. It would appear that the textual variants in Luke chapters 22 and 24 may, in many cases, be a manifestation of either (1) harmonistic, and possibly theologically expansive, tendencies of an early copyist of Luke or (2) a

---

[8] A convenient list can be found in K. Snodgrass, "Western Non-Interpolations," *JBL* 91 (1972): 370–71, See also Bruce Metzger, *A Textual Commentary on the Greek New Testament* (Second Edition. Stuttgart: United Bible Societies, 1994), 165, nn. 2, 3.

[9] The question whether this is a text type has been properly raised. However, there often does seem to be a pattern of common readings found in θ, f¹, f¹³. See Bruce Metzger, *Text of the New Testament*, 3rd ed. (Oxford: Oxford University Press, 1992), 214–15.

[10] Snodgrass, 377. Westcott and Hort ([ii], *Appendix*, 21-22) never actually call it a Western non-interpolation but rather say it "resembles" a Western non-interpolation.

strong influence on the composition of Luke at these points by the Gospels of John and Matthew, an influence whose resulting similarities were removed by a later copyist.

METHOD OF TEXTUAL CRITICISM

Despite the handy term "Western non-interpolations" for this class of textual variants, one cannot argue for or against the inclusion of the readings as a group. Each variant potentially has its own history and origination, either as the original text or as a modification of the text. So despite the fact that there is a common set of features in various readings, any of the variants theoretically could be either original or a corruption, and each must be argued on its own merit.[11]

Having said that, though, this study will chart a course between two extremes in textual criticism. On the one hand, it will resist the tendency to emphasize too readily the value of certain manuscript types. As was noted above, Westcott and Hort were convinced that the text type which they called "Neutral" was extremely valuable as an early witness to the original text of the New Testament. Even so, they were acutely aware that this text type, found most clearly in Codex Vaticanus and frequently in Sinaiticus, was not inherently pure or original. With the discovery of early papyri, however, the emphasis on the value of certain manuscripts has increased. K. Aland has argued extensively, both abstractly[12] and with reference to the Western non-

---

[11] This, of course, is what Westcott and Hort were actually recommending. The point of the study of genealogy of the texts is to note that a preponderance of manuscript evidence is, in fact, not definitive to the question of originality. A single variant that can be seen to have arisen at an early point in the manuscript transmission may just as possibly have been original, despite an overwhelming number of witnesses to an alternative reading. Once the early date of a variant has been established, its originality must then be argued primarily on the basis of internal criteria.

[12] K. Aland and B. Aland, *The Text of the New Testament* (Grand Rapids: Eerdmans, 1989), posits a set of rules for textual criticism that include "3. Criticism of the text must always begin from the evidence of the manuscript tradition and

interpolations, that the early dates of the papyri, together with the fact that they often agree with Codex Vaticanus, make them qualitatively superior as witnesses to the original text and that this is sufficient to establish the original text against other internal grounds.[13] But simply offering another early example of the Alexandrian text type does not invalidate the possible strength of an alternate early reading.

On the other hand, the use of internal evidence alone, what has been called "radical" or "rigorous eclecticism" perhaps understates the value that a study of manuscript tendencies can offer. While it may be theoretically appropriate to argue that any variant in a manuscript is potentially the original reading, the nature of the manuscripts certainly can be a compelling indication of the *probability* that such a variant is original. Just as courtroom witnesses are assessed as to their reliability, so also manuscripts must be assessed as to their reliability. In particular, it will be necessary to inquire into tendencies of textual witnesses.

What is proposed, then, is the use of "reasoned eclecticism" in this study of the textual variants in Luke.[14] In particular the study will involve the following:

---

only afterward turn to a consideration of internal criteria," and "4. Internal criteria ... can never be the sole basis for a critical decision, especially in opposition to external evidence" (280). These rules are combined with the *qualitative* categorization of manuscripts, in which early papyri (along with B and ℵ) are given pride of place as Category I documents (335 f.).

[13] K. Aland, "Die Bedeutung des P[75] für den Text des Neuen Testaments," in *Arbeitung zur Neutestamentlichen Text Forschung*, 2 (Berlin: Walter de Gruyter, 1967); cf. especially the discussion at 156.

[14] See Gordon Fee, "Rigorous or Reasoned Eclecticism—Which?" in *Studies in New Testament Language and Text* (Leiden: E. J. Brill, 1976), 174–97. This is ostensibly the approach taken by the editors of the United Bible Societies in the production of the Greek New Testament — that is, the combination of internal and external criteria in evaluating readings. But, as even a casual review of Metzger's *Textual Commentary* shows, and as J. K. Elliott argues in "The United Bible Societies' Textual Commentary Evaluated" [*NT* 17 (1975): 130–50], the actual criteria are heavily weighted toward manuscript attestation. For a historical

1. The external evidence of the manuscripts will be reviewed, evaluating any tendencies in the Western textual tradition that might be germane to the specific variants at hand.

2. The internal criteria of style and transcriptional probability will be evaluated for each variant, considering why a variant has come into being.

Then, using internal and external criteria together, the study will attempt to establish for each significant variant what is most likely the original text.

EXTERNAL EVIDENCE: THE DOCUMENTARY ATTESTATION

In each of the cases cited above, the preponderance of the textual evidence favors inclusion of text that is lacking in the Western versions. The vast majority of codices, both uncial and minuscule, as well as significant witnesses in the early versions, favor the longer text. From the weight of this documentary evidence, a majority of scholars now argues for the longer texts. Indeed, it appears that this evidence was the compelling issue in most of the decisions to include the longer texts in the UBS text.[15]

---

overview of the problem, as well as a further assessment of the tendency toward external criteria in the UBS text and a plea for reasoned eclecticism, see Eldon Epp, "Eclectic Method in New Testament Textual Criticism: Solution or Symptom?" *HTR* 69 (1976): 211-57.

[15] So see comments in Metzger, *Textual Commentary* (156) on Luke 24:3. In each of the other cases, the documentary evidence was not the only criterion, yet it appears to have been the deciding factor. cf. Richard Dillon, *From Eye-Witnesses to Ministers of the Word* (Rome: Biblical Institute Press, 1978), 59, n. 172.

Western Non-Interpolations 171

The documentary evidence for and against the Western non-interpolations in Luke is outlined below:[16]

1. **Luke 22:19b-20.** τὸ ὑπὲρ ὑμῶν διδόμενον· τοῦτο ποιεῖτε εἰς τὴν ἐμὴν ἀνάμνησιν. καὶ τὸ ποτήριον ὡσαύτως μετὰ τὸ δειπνῆσαι λέγων· τοῦτο τὸ ποτήριον ἡ καινὴ διαθήκη ἐν τῷ αἵματί μου τὸ ὑπὲρ ὑμῶν ἐκχυννόμενον. Includes: P^{75} ℵ A B C K L T W X Δ Θ Π Ψ 063 f^1 f^{13} aur e f q r^1 vg $syr^{h,pal}$ $cop^{sa,bo}$ arm geo. Excludes: D a d ff^2 i l

2. **Luke 24:3.** τοῦ κυρίου Ἰησοῦ. Includes: P^{75} ℵ A B C K L W X Δ Θ Π Ψ 0124 f^1 f^{13} aur c f q vg $syr^{h,pal}$ $cop^{sa,bo}$ arm eth geo Eusebius. Excludes: D a b d e ff^2 l r^1.

3. **Luke 24:6.** οὐκ ἔστιν ὧδε ἀλλὰ ἠγέρθη. Includes: P^{75} ℵ A B C^3 K L W X Δ Θ Π Ψ 063 0124 f^1 f^{13} aur c f q vg $syr^{c,s,h,pal}$ $cop^{sa,bo}$ arm (eth) geo. variants of inclusion: C^*, syr^p $cop^{bo\,mss}$ Diatesseron, Epiphanius; Marcion; c. Excludes: D a b d e ff^2 l r^1 geo^b.

4. **Luke 24:12.** Ὁ δὲ Πέτρος ἀναστὰς ἔδραμεν ἐπὶ τὸ μνημεῖον καὶ παρακύψας βλέπει τὰ ὀθόνια μόνα, καὶ ἀπῆλθεν πρὸς ἑαυτὸν θαυμάζων τὸ γεγονός. Includes: P^{75} ℵ A B K L W X Δ Θ Π Ψ 063 079 0124 f^1 f^{13} aur c f ff^2 vg $syr^{c,s,p,h,pal.mss}$ $cop^{sa,bo}$ arm eth geo Eusebius Cyril. Excludes: D a b d e l r^1 $syr^{pal.mss}$ Marcion Diatesseron.

5. **Luke 24:36.** καὶ λέγει αὐτοῖς Εἰρήνη ὑμῖν. Includes: P^{75} ℵ A B K L X Δ Θ Π Ψ f^1 f^{13} $syr^{c,s}$ $cop^{sa,bo}$ Eusebius Chrysostom Augustine Cyril; variants P aur c f vg $syr^{p,h,pal}$ $cop^{bo.mss}$ arm eth geo Diatesseron Ambrose Augustine; W. Excludes: D a b d e ff^2 l r^1.

---

[16] Manuscript citations are following the conventions outlined Nestle Aland 27, 57-76.

6. **Luke 24:40.** καὶ τοῦτο εἰπὼν ἔδειξεν αὐτοῖς τὰς χεῖρας καὶ τοὺς πόδας. Includes: **P**⁷⁵ ℵ A B K L W Δ Θ Π Ψ f¹ f¹³ aur c f q vg syr^(p,h,pal) cop^(sa,bo) arm geo Eusebius Athanasius Chrysostom Cyril John-Damascus. Excludes: D a b d e ff² l r¹ syr^(c,s).

7. **Luke 24:51.** καὶ ἀνεφέρετο εἰς τὸν οὐρανόν. Includes: **P**⁷⁵ ℵ^c A B C K L W X Δ Θ Π Ψ 063 f¹ f¹³ aur c f q (r¹) vg syr^(p,h,pal) cop^(sa,bo) arm geo² Diatesseron Augustine^(2/3) Cyril Cosmas. Excludes: ℵ* D a b d e ff² l (syr^s) Augustine.

8. **Luke 24:52.** προσκυνήσαντες αὐτόν. Includes: **P**⁷⁵ ℵ A B C K L W X Δ Θ Π Ψ063 f¹f¹³ aur f q syr^(p,h,pal) cop^(sa,bo) arm geo. Excludes: D a b d e ff² l syr^s Augustine.

However, to be complete, the list should include Luke 24:9, which was included by Hort as a possible Western non-interpolation.[17]

9. **Luke 24:9.** ἀπὸ τοῦ μνημείου. Includes: **P**⁷⁵ ℵ A B C K L W X Δ Θ Π Ψ 0124 f¹ f¹³ aur c f q vg syr^(h,pal) sa bo arm aeth geo Eus, Cyr, Marcion. Excludes: D a b c d e ff² l r¹ Diatesseron.

In every case the longer reading is found in Vaticanus, Bodmer Papyrus, and Sinaiticus, as well as a number of other Greek and versional witnesses. On the other hand, the shorter reading is found in Bezae, together with some Old Latin and, occasionally, Syriac manuscripts. Except for Luke 24:51 and 24:52 with Augustine, or 24:12 with Marcion, there is no patristic support for the shorter readings. There is, then, an overwhelming manuscript evidence for the

---

[17] Westcott and Hort, 176. They enclose 24:9 in parentheses, but no explanation of the parentheses is given.

longer readings; still, the shorter readings are found in an important strain of early manuscripts.

The documentary evidence, in particular the value of the Bodmer Papyrus (**P**[75]), has been especially stressed by Kurt Aland. In essence, Aland's argument is that the papyri in general offer such early and valuable evidence that all other arguments become secondary.[18] The extent to which this argument has been persuasive is seen, for instance, in the ready acceptance of the longer text by Fitzmyer with little extensive analysis of the arguments from internal evidence:

The reasons for the new trend are the realization of the importance of the Papyrus text P[75], a codex that was only published in 1961 and hence was unknown to Westcott and Hort, and an even greater awareness of the rather arbitrary decisions made by those editors. P[75] contains all the eight Lucan passages and joins the witnesses of the Alexandrian text-tradition that were always cited in favor of the inclusion of these passages.... What is puzzling is the grade of reading that has been assigned to these texts in the third edition of the UBS text; in my opinion most of them merit at least a B reading (i.e., texts that have only some degree of doubt).[19]

Aland focuses almost exclusively on the strength of the documentary evidence in building his argument for the priority of the longer text form in Luke 24. Although touching on various internal arguments (e.g., the stylistic similarities between Luke 24:12 and John 20, or the possibility that Marcion might have had reason for deleting such a story), the argument that he puts forward is actually very simple: the Greek witnesses, especially confirmed by **P**[75], predominately display the longer text type, while the shorter form is only found in D and a few Latin (and, occasionally, Syriac) texts. This, for Aland and others who follow him, is the primary and sufficient argument in favor of the longer text in each of the instances of Western non-interpolation cited above.

---

[18] See K. Aland, "Bedeutung des **P**[75] für den Text des Neuen Testaments," 166–72.

[19] Fitzmyer, *Luke* (I–IX), 131.

While the external evidence is significant, it is nonetheless not sufficient as the sole argument for the priority of the long text form. Since a textual corruption might have crept into the texts at any point in the process of transmission, even a single witness might be correct. It would seem that from this standpoint, each reading must always stand not only on the basis of documentary evidence but also on internal criteria.[20]

On external grounds, the high estimation by Hort of the Western text *in these readings* was based on the fact that it ran contrary to known scribal tendencies in this text type. The tendency, Hort noted, was toward a paraphrastic text that often ran to additions in the text. Hort noted especially the tendency toward interpolation in his specific examples of the Western scribal tendency: the interpolation of καὶ τῆς νύμφης at Matt 24:1, γεννῶνται καὶ γεννῶσιν at Luke 20:34, and Σὺ εἶ ὁ υἱός μου ὁ ἀγαπητός ἐν σοὶ εὐδόκησα at Luke 3:22, as well as the reference to the long interpolation at Matt 20:28.[21] Of course the Western text of Acts contributes especially to the impression that it is an expansive text type. Hort noted this tendency to expansion; he also cited the "static" of accidental corruptions and the harmonistic tendency of the Western text.[22]

But Hort's description of the text as paraphrastic included as well the tendency to change or omit verses with "astonishing freedom,"

---

[20] Kurt and Barbara Aland, in *The Text of the New Testament*, 280, list twelve rules of textual criticism which also include the need for internal criteria: "2. Only the reading which best satisfies the requirements of both external and internal criteria can be original." However, the impact that the internal criteria have in their model is severely curtailed by many of their other rules: "3. Criticism of the text *must always begin from evidence of the manuscript tradition* and only afterward turn to a consideration of internal criteria," "4. Internal criteria...can never be the sole basis of a critical decision, *especially in opposition to external evidence*," and "5. The primary authority for a critical textual tradition lies with the Greek manuscript tradition, with versions and Fathers serving no more than a supplementary and corroborative function...." (emphases mine).

[21] Westcott and Hort, 122–23.

[22] Westcott and Hort, 122–25.

Western Non-Interpolations 175

a tendency often overlooked, since Hort gave only concrete examples of the expansionistic tendency. These additional features were noted by Hatch in his study of the Western text. In particular, the tendency of the Western text to omit text, sometimes as part of a harmonistic tendency, should be noted. Hatch cites three examples of omissions found in Bezae, to which more could be added.[23]

In a review of the Western text's tendency toward omission, I counted seventy-seven instances in Luke alone where the Western text had a shorter reading than NA[27] shows as the text of Luke.[24] A similar extensive pattern of shorter Western readings is found in the other Gospels. The majority of these shorter readings appear to be scribal omissions, some clearly deliberate.[25] A number of extensive "omissions" in Luke are worth briefly considering to gauge the tendencies in the Western shorter readings:

LUKE 5:26

At the conclusion of the healing of the paralytic, most of the manuscripts read καὶ ἔκστασις ἔλαβεν ἅπαντας, καὶ ἐδόξαζον τὸν θεὸν at the beginning of the verse. These two clauses are absent in a wide variety of textual evidence, including Bezae and the Latin manuscript Palatinus (e); it would appear to be a Western variant. This variant is made more difficult by the existence of the omission in a number of other Greek witnesses, some of which have Alexandrian or Byzantine tendencies (i.e., W, which tends toward Alexandrian in this section of Luke; M, X, ψ, Ω), as well as f[13]. Unfortunately, the text is deficient in P[75] at this verse. The shorter reading, then, has wide attestation. It

---

[23] Hatch, 22-24.

[24] The list is printed as Appendix, p. 224. A Western reading in this count is one in which Codex Bezae (or Sinaiticus, in the first eight chapters of John) finds support from at least one additional Old Latin or Syriac text.

[25] A similar list of harmonizing omissions is found in Jeremias, *The Eucharistic Words of Jesus* (Philadelphia: Trinity Press, 1990), 148. He includes: Lk 5:39; 7:7; 7:33; 10:41 f.; 11:35 f.; 12:19; 12:21; 12:39; 19:25; 21:30 and many

seems likely in this instance that the longer text is an insertion to harmonize Luke's text with Mark.[26]

LUKE 5:39

The entire verse is absent in Bezae and almost all the Old Latin manuscripts (e a b c d ff² l r¹). It is also absent in Marcion, Irenaeus, and Eusebius. But the verse is present in most other manuscripts of Luke, including **P**[75] in fragments. This is a clear Western short reading, which Hort includes in his list of possible Western non-interpolations. It is possible that the verse about drinking old wine is a midrashic expansion of the preceding verses, which have contrasted the old and the new by questioning whether new wine would be put in old wineskins. But if so, it is an odd expansion since it turns upside down the example of old and new. The occurrence of a proverb similar to this in Gospel Thomas 47 suggests a traditional origination of the text; it would not be surprising for Luke to have drawn on a parallel tradition in his composition.[27] It is hard to imagine why a scribe would have inserted this here. But the difficulty of the verse and its absence in Mark and Matthew would certainly have given good reason for its deletion. It has been supposed that the omission derives from Marcion, who saw it as supporting the Old Testament.[28] Or it could be a harmonizing omission by a Western scribe.

---

of the Western non-interpolations studied below.

[26] It is surprising that this text is not discussed in Metzger's *Textual Commentary*.

[27] Fitzmyer, *Luke* (I–IX), 596.

[28] Metzger, *Textual Commentary*, 139. Marcion's text excision is cited in A. von Harnack, *Marcion: Das Evangelium vom fremden Gott* (Leipzig: J. C. Heinrichs'sche Buchhandlung, 1924), 53. The explanation of the omission, that it was unacceptable because it referred to the Old Testament, is found also in E. C. Blackman, *Marcion and His Influence* (London: SPCK, 1948), 46.

LUKE 7:7

Most of the Greek manuscripts contain the entire verse, including the introductory clause διὸ οὐδὲ ἐμαυτὸν ἠξίωσα πρός σε ἐλθεῖν. This clause is absent, however, in D and most of the Itala manuscripts (e a b c d ff² gat l r¹), as well as the Sinaitic Syriac version. It is difficult to see why it would have been added by a scribe; it does not clarify or modify the preceding verse. But it could have been omitted by a scribe attempting to bring it in line with the Matthean version of the story. It appears to be a harmonistic deletion.

LUKE 9:2

In most of the witnesses to Luke 9:23, Jesus' words exhorting his followers to take up their crosses and follow him include the modifier "daily" (καθ' ἡμέραν). The entire phrase καὶ ἀράτω τὸν σταυρὸν αὐτοῦ καθ' ἡμέραν is absent in D and some Old Latin (a d l), while modifier καθ' ἡμέραν is absent as well in a large number of witnesses, mostly Byzantine, as well as additional Old Latin texts: e b c ff² q r¹, Sinaitic Syriac, and a number of patristic citations. The omission of the καθ' ἡμέραν would appear to be a harmonistic deletion.[29] But what is to be made of the longer omission represented in Bezae? It is not likely that it is a harmonization; the first part of the line is found exactly in Mark and Matthew. It is possible that Bezae represents the original text and that 9:23b is a harmonization to Mark and Matthew. But given that Luke relies on Mark and that there is little redactional reason to have modified the Markan form, it seems more likely that Luke has taken over Mark and strengthened it with καθ' ἡμέραν; thus the short form is a corruption. The most likely explanation is that this omission arose from mechanical error, possibly homoeoarcton.[30]

---

[29] So Metzger, *Textual Commentary*, 147–48.
[30] Metzger, *Textual Commentary*, 147.

LUKE 11:49

Codex Bezae and some of the Old Latin manuscripts are absent the reading at the beginning of 11:49, καὶ ἡ σοφία τοῦ θεοῦ εἶπεν. The text is absent from b and d, as well as from the patristic witness Lucifer. In addition, Marcion omits the entire first part of the verse from δία through προφήτας.[31] In Marcion, the deletion appears to be an attempt to avoid reference to the role of Old Testament prophets. But the shorter deletion in the Western witnesses appears rather to be a harmonization to Matthew 23:34, which is very close to Luke but without the omitted phrase.

LUKE 12:19

Most of the second half of the verse, the clause κείμενα εἰς ἔτη πολλά· ἀναπαύου, φάγε, πίε, is missing in D and a large portion of Old Latin (e a b c d ff²). It is difficult to see why this clause would have been added; it offers little to the story. Since this parable does not occur in other Gospels, it cannot have been omitted for the purpose of harmonization. Nor does a theological rationale for its omission seem to be likely. It appears that the verse was omitted by accidental mechanical transmission.

LUKE 18:32

The word ὑβρισθήσεται is missing in D, the majority of Old Latin manuscripts (e a b c d ff² i l q r¹), and the Peshitta and Harklean forms of the Syriac versions. It is present in almost all other witnesses. It is possible that this is simply a mechanical omission arising from parablepsis: the eye could easily have skipped over one of the εται endings in the chain καὶ ἐμπαιχθήσει καὶ ὑβρισθήσεται καὶ ἐμπτυσθήσεται. But it is more likely that the omission is a deliberate harmonization. Luke 18:32 follows Mark 10:34 quite closely here

---

[31] von Harnack, *Marcion*, 54.

except for the addition of ὑβρισθήσεται. Moreover, although Matthew is quite different, Matthew also omits any mention of ὑβρίζειν. The omission in Luke is likely a scribal move toward agreement with Mark and Matthew.

LUKE 19:25

The entire verse is missing in D, W and a few other Greek codices, a number of Old Latin manuscripts (e b d ff²), some Syriac (s c), cop^bo, and in Lucifer; the verse is present in all other manuscripts. It is possible that the longer version was an insertion from a marginal comment,[32] but that is hardly likely since the verse appears intrusive and does not explain the text. It seems more likely that the verse was deleted by a scribe attempting to reconcile it with the Matthew version (Matt 25:28-29).

SUMMARY

The evidence from this sample is mixed. At least one of the examples (Luke 5:26) appears to be an interpolation in the Alexandrian text (a non-Western interpolation!). Others, though, appear to be deletions that have arisen from mechanical errors (Luke. 9:23) or efforts to harmonize with the other Gospels (Luke 5:39; 7:7; 11:49; 18:32; 19:25). From this review of a few examples, it is apparent that Western readings found in Bezae and Old Latin manuscripts not infrequently omit text, and often to harmonize with other Gospels.[33] Thus Hort's broad statement that the Western text is paraphrastic and given to omissions as well as additions must be kept in mind when the

---

[32] Metzger, *Textual Commentary*, 169.

[33] See further on the harmonizing tendencies of the Western text, Heinrich Joseph Vogels, *Die Harmonistik im Evangelientext des Codex Cantabrigiensis* (Leipzig: J. C. Hinrichs'sche Buchhandlung, 1910); confirmed in D. C. Parker, *Codex Bezae. An Early Christian Manuscript and its Text* (Cambridge: University Press, 1992), pp. 192–193, 258.

strength of the Western textual tradition is assessed. This tendency in the Western text undermines the strength of Westcott and Hort's assertions about the originality of the Western non-interpolations. It is, in fact, a characteristic of the Western text that its witnesses do omit material from the Gospel texts for various reasons.

INTERNAL ARGUMENTS

LUKE 22:19–20

Intrinsic Probability Based on Style. The difficult structure of Luke's Last Supper in 22:15–20 raises questions about the integrity of the long form of the verse. The cup-bread-cup sequence of the long text, not found in other versions of the Lord's Supper, begs for some explanation. The final cup saying and the second half of the bread saying are missing in the shorter text. Was the longer saying added later, drawing on parallel versions, in order to enhance some feature or remove some perceived deficiency? Or did the difficulty in the cup-bread-cup prompt a scribe to delete what appeared to be duplicative text?[34] Efforts to explain the difficult structure of the long form have not been totally convincing.[35] Of course, the abrupt ending of the supper at 19a in the shorter text calls for explanation as well. But the difficulty of the short ending is more imagined than real; an alternative structural reading of the short text that focuses on the contrastive

---

[34] Metzger, *Textual Commentary*, 148.

[35] J. H. Petzer, "Luke 22:19b–20 and the Structure of the Passage." *NovT* 26 (1984): 249–252. Petzer argues that there is a parallel structure of eat-kingdom/drink-kingdom in vv. 15–16 and 17–18b on the one hand, and a second parallel structure of bread-body/cup-blood in vv. 19–20 on the other hand. Thus the cup-bread-cup portrayal is false; it is really eat-drink-bread-cup. But the stronger structure begins with Jesus' command in v. 17: "Take this (cup)...." Petzer's solution, while interesting, seems to be a pattern forced on the text.

elements at the close of the supper seems equally convincing.³⁶ The difficulty of the structure must be considered together with the observation that the longer form of the text in 22:19b–20 contains features that suggest harmonization with Mark and Paul. Specifically, the language of Jesus' blood "poured out" (ἐκχυννόμενον) is reminiscent of Mark; that is not surprising, though, if Mark is the source for Luke. More importantly are the Pauline features, which have no parallels in Mark or Matthew: the cup "which is given for you," "in my blood," and "in the same way also the cup." Indeed, most of the longer text is almost identical with the Pauline form found in 1 Corinthians 11, as the following parallel shows:

Luke 22:19–20	1 Corinthians 11:23c–25
καὶ λαβὼν ἄρτον	ἔλαβεν ἄρτον καὶ
εὐχαριστήσας ἔκλασεν καὶ	εὐχαριστήσας ἔκλασεν καὶ
ἔδωκεν αὐτοῖς λέγων·	εἶπεν·
τοῦτό ἐστιν τὸ σῶμά μου	τοῦτο μού ἐστιν τὸ σῶμα
τὸ ὑπὲρ ὑμῶν διδόμενον·	τὸ ὑπὲρ ὑμῶν
τοῦτο ποιεῖτε εἰς τὴν ἐμὴν	τοῦτο ποιεῖτε εἰς τὴν ἐμὴν
ἀνάμνησιν	ἀνάμνησιν
καὶ τὸ ποτήριον ὡσαύτως	ὡσαύτως καὶ τὸ ποτήριον
μετὰ τὸ δειπνῆσαι λέγων·	μετὰ τὸ δειπνῆσαι λέγων·
τοῦτο τὸ ποτήριον ἡ καινὴ	τοῦτο τὸ ποτήριον ἡ καινὴ
διαθήκη ἐν τῷ αἵματί μου	διαθήκη ἐν τῷ ἐμῷ αἵματι
τὸ ὑπὲρ ὑμῶν ἐκχυννόμενον.	τοῦτο ποιεῖτε ὁσάκις ἐὰν
	πίνητε εἰς τὴν ἐμὴν ἀνάμνησιν

The comparison is striking, and it shows that except for a few minor word order or tense changes, or the final clause in each, the two

---

[36] Bart Ehrman, *The Orthodox Corruption of Scripture* (New York: Oxford University Press, 1993), 206. Ehrman's recent book provides the most significant arguments for the shorter Western text in these instances of the Western non-Interpolations, based on internal grounds. It will, then, serve as a major conversation partner throughout the subsequent discussion. In addition to the specific arguments, a good discussion of the problem of the Western non-

are the same. There is clearly some form of relationship, either literary or oral, between the long text of Luke and Paul.

The striking similarity between Luke and Paul in these verses does not automatically indict the long form of the Lukan text as inauthentic, but other stylistic features add more doubt to their inclusion. In addition to their strong similarity to Paul's version of the Lord's Supper, certain important phrases in the longer text are found in Luke-Acts only here:[37] ἀνάμνησις (used here twice), ὑπὲρ ὑμῶν,[38] καινὴ διαθήκη.[39] Their absence in the rest of Luke-Acts raises some questions about whether the long form of the text is a later scribal intrusion into Luke's account. The question of a stylistic critique of material in the institution of the Lord's Supper is made more difficult because it is a liturgical text. Jeremias makes a good point that precisely such texts would have been transmitted with little variation, and that Paul himself has taken over his wording from a previous source.[40] Thus simply finding non-Lukan language here is not surprising or convincing with respect to the authenticity of the long text. Yet some of the wording tends to run contrary to Luke's thought, especially the doubled phrase τὸ ὑπὲρ ὑμῶν [διδόμενον/ἐκχυννόμενον]. As has frequently been pointed out, Luke never refers to Jesus' death as an atonement for sins.[41] Indeed, at points where one might do so, as

---

Interpolations is found in his excursus on the subject (223–27).

[37] See Kobus Petzer, "Style and Text in the Lucan Narrative of the Institution of the Lord's Supper (Luke 22:19b–20)," *NTS* 37 (1991): 113–29.

[38] Except in 9:50, in a proverbial saying of Jesus (par. Mark 9:40).

[39] Luke uses διαθήκη only to refer to the Mosaic covenant! (Luke 1:72; Acts 3:25; 7:8).

[40] Jeremias, *Eucharistic Words*, 155.

[41] Hans Conzelmann, *Theology of St. Luke* (London: Faber and Faber, 1960), p. 201; Richard Zehnle, "The Salvific Character of Jesus' Death in Lucan Soteriology," *TS* 30 (1969): 438; cf. Ehrman, 199. The sole possibility is Acts 20:28 which, as Zehnle points out, needs not be read as indicating a theology of atonement or satisfaction (cf. also Ehrman, 202). Jesus' salvific character Luke derives from the fact that he is Lord; because of his life and his obedience, including death, he pours out his Spirit on the church.

when he cites from the Servant songs of Isaiah 53, Luke clearly avoids any use of the atonement motif (e.g. "wounded for our transgressions" in the Servant songs).[42] So also in his redaction of Mark 10:45, he clearly avoids the atonement motif. This theological difference between Luke and the longer text is very significant, raising serious questions about the text's authenticity on intrinsic grounds.

Transcriptional Probability. When one considers the relative probability that the longer text was either added by scribes or deleted by them, the clear choice is in favor of a secondary interpolation. One can readily imagine that a scribe, surprised at the order of sacramental elements, cup-bread, and at the absence of much of the expiatory language used in the church liturgy, might have added to the text to make clear what "should be there." The evidence that the longer text is almost identical with Paul's language makes the probability of such an addition even more compelling. Thus, the stark difference between Luke's short text and the expected language of the church's eucharistic liturgy would certainly be enough reason to supplement the text.[43]

In addition, Ehrman points out that the atonement quality of the eucharist was frequently used against docetic interpretations of Christ. The addition of precisely those features from Paul which emphasize the atoning quality of the flesh and blood would have been particularly useful as a reaction against Docetists. Moreover, the absence of precisely those features in Luke may well have raised suspicions that Luke's text had been tampered with by the Docetists.[44] There are, then, compelling reasons that can be adduced as to why scribes would have added the long text to Luke's short version.

---

[42] That is, in Acts 8 or Acts 3, where he makes use of the fourth Servant song, but does not mention Isaiah 53:4–5. Cf. Ehrman, 200.

[43] John Creed, *The Gospel According to St. Luke* (London: Macmillan, 1930), 264.

[44] That Luke would be suspected of this is not surprising, given Marcion's excision of elements of the Third Gospel. Because of Marcion's willingness to modify the text of Luke, it might well have been examined with some care by

It is more difficult to conceive of a viable rationale for the omission of verses 19b–20. If a scribe had been attempting to harmonize the text to Paul or the other Gospels, it would have made more sense to delete verses 17–18 (the reference to the first cup) rather than verses 19b–20; this omission can hardly be seen as a harmonization. The alternative offered by Jeremias, that the sacral language was deleted so that it would not be read by an outsider who wouldn't understand, is hardly convincing.[45] The fact that verse 19a was not deleted seems by itself to cripple that theory fatally.

On transcriptional grounds, then, the evidence is overwhelmingly in favor of the originality of the short form of the text.

Summary. Although the external attestation is strongly in favor of the longer text of Luke's Lord's Supper, internal probabilities make it almost certain that the short text is, in fact, original. The extremely close similarity of the variant text to Paul's language, the dissimilarity of the theology of atonement found in those verses to Luke's theology, the probability that the interpolation of these verses served both to harmonize the text to other accounts of the Lord's Supper as well as to aid in anti-docetic arguments, and the absence of any reasonable explanation why the long text might have been deleted all argue convincingly for the short text.

LUKE 24:3

Intrinsic Probability Based on Style. The question whether the variant τοῦ κυρίου Ἰησοῦ is original is often based largely on whether it represents Lukan style. As has been noted, the term never occurs elsewhere in Luke or in the other three Gospels.[46] On the other hand, it is a common feature in Acts, occurring fourteen times. The question, then, is whether the variant is an intrusion into Luke from Acts or

---

scholars in the church for deletions or additions.

[45] Jeremias, *Eucharistic Words,* 158.
[46] Ehrman, 219.

simply a common feature of the same author. Given that usage in Acts is normally a strong sign of Luke's own redactional hand in Luke, it is hard to conceive of this variant as non-Lukan. Of course, Luke in his Gospel uses the term κύριος a number of times to refer to Jesus, and these appear to be narrative "retrojections" of Jesus' status as risen Lord onto the earthly existence.[47] But still, until this verse Luke does not use the precise linked term "Lord Jesus" in his Gospel. Of course, the use of κυρίου Ἰησοῦ at this point in the narrative might well be deliberate: because Jesus is now risen, he can appropriately be called "Lord." That the term is not a confession, as are the later uses in Acts, is unimportant; Luke frequently imposes on the text his own understanding of reality (as noted above with respect to narrative retrojections of the term Lord), which does not always fit the narrative. It appears that for Luke, the significance of the Resurrection can be shown through a change in terminology regarding Jesus. In other words, the use of the term here does not seem to be a violation of Luke's style.

Transcriptional Probability. Ehrman suggests that one reason for the interpolation of the phrase at 24:3 could be to underline the bodily resurrection of Jesus. Admitting that this is not a clear-cut example, Ehrman does argue that the phrase would "heighten" the emphasis that Jesus' body was actually missing, so reducing the possibility of a docetic interpretation of the Resurrection.[48] He argued, then, that a scribe who was concerned about docetic tendencies might have thus strengthened Luke's Resurrection accounts to confound the heretics.

That is certainly possible. And Ehrman's query why a scribe would have deleted the phrase does not have a ready answer. The only realistic explanation for its omission would be mechanical error, not intentional deletion. But Ehrman's proposal, while possible, falls short of being compelling. The addition of τοῦ κυρίου Ἰησοῦ only slightly

---

[47] Fitzmyer, *Luke* (I–IX), 203.
[48] Ehrman, 219.

strengthens the sense of the missing body; that the body mentioned is that of Jesus seems obvious.

There is no compelling explanation that tilts the transcriptional probability toward interpolation or omission.

Summary. The intrinsic probability of the verse appears to favor the longer text, but the transcriptional tendency is unclear. There is, then, no clear answer provided by internal arguments. Based on both the tendency of the Western text to be free and its pattern of omissions, there is a slight probability that the longer reading is original.

LUKE 24:6

Intrinsic Probability Based on Style. There is little in the longer text that would betray either non-Lukan usage or any particular Lukan patterns. Jeremias has suggested that the term ὧδε is non-Lukan,[49] but he errs in that judgment.[50] Luke does not use the passive ἠγέρθη frequently; more frequently, Luke speaks of God's raising Jesus in an active construction. But those stylistic observations are not sufficient grounds to refute the longer reading. There is a bit of a lexical tension between the angels' words "he is risen" (ἠγέρθη) in 24:6 and Jesus' prediction to rise (ἀναστῆναι) in 24:7, but that is well within Luke's tendency toward variation.

It has been argued that the recapitulation of events in 24:23 (in which some women went to the tomb and not finding the body they report a vision of angels who announced that Jesus was alive) requires the disputed text in 24:6 as a basis.[51] But Ehrman disagrees and notes that there is a significant difference between 24:6, which has the angels repeat Jesus' prediction that said that he will rise, and 24:23, which

---

[49] Joachim Jeremias, *Die Sprache des Lukasevangeliums,* (Göttingen: Vandenhoeck & Ruprecht, 1980), 311.

[50] See chapter 7, on Luke 23:5, below.

[51] Snodgrass, 375.

reports that the angels said that he was alive.[52] Henry Cadbury has noted, though, that one feature of Lukan style is the tendency toward repetition and variation.[53] That is especially true of Acts, where entire episodes are told and then recited again, often in a retrospective speech.[54] The pattern, then, of a statement that Jesus was raised from the dead (24:6) with a confirmation from Jesus' prediction (24:7) and a subsequent recapitulation of the story (24:23), would clearly agree with Luke's style. The variation of language seen here (raised, v. 6; alive, v. 23) would be not be inconsistent with Luke's compositional procedure. But it is also true that 24:23 could still function as a backward glance to 24:5–7 without the phrase in question.[55] The absence of the phrase would also fit with the pattern of variation, in which 24:23 could simply refer to the angels' question "Why seek the living among the dead?", and their subsequent citation of Jesus' prediction.

Transcriptional Probability. Once again, Ehrman suggests that the inclusion of the language served to heighten the emphasis on the physical Resurrection of Jesus.[56] Without the disputed text, the words of the angels are less emphatic. The angels do point to the Resurrection by means of a reference to Jesus' own promise that he would rise (ἀναστῆναι) on the third day (Luke 24:7). But that this prediction is actually fulfilled is only clearly made if the text at 24:6 is included. It is, then, a very reasonable reconstruction to imagine that a scribe added the phrase οὐκ ἔστιν ὧδε, ἀλλὰ ἠγέρθη in order to clarify and strengthen the reality of the Resurrection. On the other hand, it is difficult to see why a scribe would have deleted the phrase.[57]

---

[52] Ehrman, 219.

[53] Henry J. Cadbury, "Four Features of Lucan Style," in *Studies in Luke-Acts* (Philadelphia: Fortress Press, 1980), 88. See also p. 195 below.

[54] Examples would include Luke 24:36–49 retold in Acts 1:2–12; Acts 9 retold in Acts 22 and 26; Acts 10 retold in Acts 11 and 15:7–9.

[55] Ehrman, 220.

[56] Ehrman, 219–20.

[57] Ehrman, 219.

Snodgrass speculates that the phrase would have seemed superfluous given the subsequent answer by the angels in 24:7, but this seems to be a strained attempt at a reason.[58] The likelihood that the text is an interpolation is especially strong given the scribal tendencies toward harmonization, especially toward Matthew, in the Gospels. The text under consideration is very close to Mark's version of the empty tomb and almost identical with Matthew's words: οὐκ ἔστιν ὧδε, ἠγέρθη γάρ. Given the rhetorical power of the verse and its likely use in the church's liturgy and proclamation, its absence in Luke might well have been deemed an oversight or deletion that needed correcting.

Summary. While stylistic features are not decisive for this variant, the transcriptional probability weighs more heavily against its originality. It is probably an interpolation.

LUKE 24:9

Intrinsic Probability Based on Style. There is no stylistic problem with ἀπὸ τοῦ μνημείου. The word for tomb used here is common enough in Luke: uses μνημεῖον eight other times (seven in Luke, one in Acts), and uses μνῆμα five times (three in Luke, two in Acts). Moreover, the use of the prepositional phrase after ὑποστρέφειν is quite normal in Luke; though most uses are with εἰς, not ἀπό, Luke also uses ὑποστρέφειν without any prepositional phrase.

Transcriptional Probability. It is difficult to see why the longer text would have been deliberately added or deleted. It adds little to the meaning of the verse to include it; after verses 1–2 the returning women would clearly have been coming from the tomb. But its deletion does not help the verse either. Snodgrass' suggestion that it was deleted because it was superfluous makes little sense as a scribal

---

[58] Snodgrass, 375.

reason.⁵⁹ It is probable that the text was omitted as a scribal accident.⁶⁰ The pattern απ... απ at the beginning and end of the omitted text only makes this explanation more reasonable.

Summary. There is little internal evidence that would constitute a reason for adding the text, and the only explanation for omission is an error in copying. The longer text appears to be original.

LUKE 24:12

Intrinsic Probability Based on Style. The question of style in Luke 24:12 can be argued both ways. On the one hand it has been suggested that the language of 24:12 is not representative of Luke's general usage and is therefore an intrusion into the text;⁶¹ on the other hand, there are clear examples of Lukan style in the verse that would point to its coming from Luke's hand. Three features in 24:12 have consistently been identified with Lukan language style: the pleonastic use of ἀναστάς,⁶² the word θαυμάζειν, and the words τὸ γεγονός.⁶³ While the usage of ἀναστάς is not exactly like that seen elsewhere in Luke-Acts,⁶⁴ it must be said that the uses of these three words do accord well

---

⁵⁹ Snodgrass, 375.

⁶⁰ Metzger, *Textual Commentary*, 157.

⁶¹ Especially note K. Peter G. Curtis, "Luke xxiv.12 and John xx.3–10," *JTS*, (ns), 22 (1971): 512–515. Cf. also Ehrman, 212.

⁶² Jeremias, *Sprache*, 55, 312; John Hawkins, *Horae Synopticae* (Oxford: Clarendon Press, 1909), 35.

⁶³ Jeremias, *Eucharistic Words*, 150; Hawkins, 36.

⁶⁴ Ehrman, 213. When Luke uses ἀναστάς, he always has it precede the named subject of the participial phrase if one is cited (e.g., in Acts 1:15, ἀναστὰς Πέτρος ἐν μέσῳ). But this can be overemphasized, since the vast majority of the pleonastic uses of ἀνιστήμι have no stated subject. Moreover, a similar paradigm can be seen with the pleonastic use of ἀποκρίνομαι, where the same word order pattern occurs. But in Luke 9:20, despite using Mark, he alters the order to give the form Πέτρος δὲ ἀποκριθεὶς εἶπεν, the precise word order found in our present passage. (Cf. J. Muddiman, "A Note on Reading Luke xxiv.12," *ETL* 48 [1972]:

with Lukan style, even if not strikingly so.⁶⁵ And to this list of Lukan words one might add μνημεῖον.⁶⁶ There are signs, then, that whoever composed the verse used features that could be termed Lukan.

A strong case can be made, however, for the non-Lukan character of other words in the verse. In particular, the uncorrected historical present, βλέπει, strikes one as an intrusive element.⁶⁷ In virtually every other case where Luke has utilized an uncorrected present from his main source, Mark, he has corrected the grammatical form to an aorist.⁶⁸ This uncorrected present does not fit with Luke's general editorial approach.⁶⁹ And the Johannine-sounding terms ὀθόνια,⁷⁰ παρακύψας, and ἀπῆλθον πρὸς ἑαυτὸν are also unusual for Luke, never occurring elsewhere in the Lukan lexicon.⁷¹

We have, then, a split situation on the stylistic evaluation of Luke 24:12. On the one hand, one finds a number of stylistic features that might be taken to be Lukan, but are not compelling enough by themselves to warrant the verse as part of the original text of Luke.⁷² On the other hand, one also finds a number of intrusive stylistic

---

545). So the perceived Lukan stylistic pattern in this case is not absolute.

⁶⁵ Jeremias, *Sprache*, 312.

⁶⁶ Jeremias, *Sprache*, 312; Muddiman, 543. See p. 188 above on 24:9.

⁶⁷ Jeremias, *Sprache*, 313. See also Frans Neirynck, "The Uncorrected Historic Present in Lk xxiv.12," *ETL* 48 [1972]: 548–553. But Luke does have three instances of the historical present outside of use with verbs of saying (ten instances of these), one of which occurs in L material (16:23). Cf. Muddiman, 545; William L. Craig, "The Disciples' Inspection of the Empty Tomb" in *John and the Synoptics* (Leuven: University Press, 1992), 615.

⁶⁸ Curtis, 514.

⁶⁹ Contra Neirynck, who unconvincingly seeks to explain it as Luke's attempt to modify Mark's term θεωρέω from Mark 14:4.

⁷⁰ But it is hardly more Johannine. As Snodgrass points out, three of the four occurrences in John are in precisely this context of 20:3–10. Furthermore, Luke alone uses a related term, ὀθόνη, in Acts. Cf. Muddiman, 543.

⁷¹ Curtis, 512–515; Jeremias, *Sprache*, 150; Ehrman, 214. But note, with reference to πρὸς ἑαυτόν that this term could be the complement to the participle θαυμαζων, in which case it would be fairly Lukan. J. Muddiman, 543.

⁷² As does Snodgrass, 373.

features in the passage, many of which suggest a connection to the Fourth Gospel. And it is not convincing to simply assert that these features are demanded by the material and are thus not specifically Johannine.[73] Although it is by no means a clear-cut situation, it nonetheless would appear that the various features of Johannine style encountered in this verse point to some sort of direct reliance on John's text—specifically John 20:3-10.[74] And it is not simply a matter of common words between Luke and John; the *order* of similarities between Luke and John suggest a literary connection between the two passages.[75] The following portrayal illustrates the close connection between Luke 24:12 and John 20:3-10:

---

[73] Jeremias, *Eucharistic Words*, 150. See also Snodgrass, 379.

[74] Ehrman, 214. Note here the highly unlikely thesis of Neirynck that Luke is drawing upon Mark for this, based on his use of Βλέπει. Further discussion of the stylistic issue is contained in Dillon, 59, n. 173.

[75] Of course, it has often been proposed that the close connection displayed below is due to John's use of Luke. (So Frans Neirynck in "John and the Synoptics: Empty Tomb Stories," *NTS* 30 (1984) 161-87, as well as "ΑΠΗΛΘΕΝ ΠΡΟΣ ΕΑΥΤΟΝ," *ETL* 54 (1978): 104-18, and "Uncorrected Present.") But this position has some real problems. Besides attempting to explain away what are clearly Johannine features — generally by attributing them, with difficulty, to Mark — it leaves unexplained why none of the particularly Lukan features appears then in John! It seems to me that the double difficulty of this position simply makes it too improbable. From the standpoint of this chapter, however, our concern is only to focus on the authenticity of Luke's text — and the Johannine features raise difficult concerns.

In Dialogue with Another Gospel?

Lk	----------- ὁ δὲ Πέτρος---------------------- ἀναστὰς ἔδραμεν ἐπὶ τὸ μνημεῖον
Jn 20:3	Ἐξῆλθεν οὖν ὁ -- Πέτρος καὶ ὁ ἄλλος μαθητὴς καὶ ἤρχοντο εἰς τὸ μνημεῖον

Lk	---
Jn 20:4	ἔτρεχον δὲ οἱ δύο ὁμοῦ. καὶ ὁ ἄλλος μαθητὴς προέδραμεν τάχιον τοῦ ετροῦ καὶ ἦλθεν πρῶτος εἰς τὸ μνημεῖον,

Lk	καὶ παρακύψας βλέπει ---------- τὰ ὀθόνια μόνα,
Jn 20:5	καὶ παρακυψας βλέπει κείμενα τὰ ὀθόνια οὐ μέντοι εἰσῆλθεν.

Jn: 20:6–9	additional development.

Lk	καὶ ἀπῆλθεν ------------πρὸς ἑαυτὸν θαυμάζων τὸ γεγονός.
Jn 20:10	ἀπῆλθον οὖν πάλιν πρὸς αὐτους οἱ μαθηταί.

It is striking that the general order of ideas is similar between the two and that, even within the sentence structure, the presentation is very much alike. Either John is a major expansion of the Lukan verse, or Luke 24:12 is a condensation of the Johannine account. But if Luke or a scribe has used John as a base, it is not a simple shortening and echoing of John's story, but a thoroughgoing modification:

> Lk 24,12 entspricht nicht Joh 20,3–10. Wohl werden in V. 12 eine Reihe von Wörten und Wendungen gebraucht, die auch Joh 20,3–10 vorkommen, aber Lk V. 12 kann keine abkürzende Reproduction des joh Berichtes sein; denn: bei Lk fehlt der ander Jünger; die Reaktion des Jüngers wird jeweils anders beschrieben: Joh: Glaube — Lk: Erstaunen; Lk 24,12 ist zu unbeholfen für eine Zusammenfassung von Joh Vv. 3–10; Lk 24,12 verfehlt gerade das Eigentliche von Joh 20,3–10.[76]

---

[76] Anton Dauer, "Lukas 24,12 — ein Produckt lukanischer Redaktion?" in *The Four Gospels* (Leuven: University Press, 1992), 1699.

The pattern and order of similar features, together with stylistic difficulties that point away from purely Lukan composition, suggests some sort of literary linkage between Luke 24:12 and John 20:3–10, with Luke's reliance on the Johannine text most probable. But the question remains whether this epitomizing was the work of a scribe who modified the text of Luke or of the author of Luke himself.

At this point it is well to reintroduce the central concern of this dissertation: the extensiveness of the points of contact between Luke and John. That there are Johannisms in the Luke account is not, in itself, surprising given the pattern of relationship we have seen from chapter 3.[77] That is to say, similarities between Luke and John would be, to a certain extent, a sign of Lukan style.[78] But the extensive nature of the verbatim similarities and, especially, the order of the similarities, are particularly striking here, even given the larger pattern of Luke-John points of contact. Aside from textual interpolation, Luke's use of John as a source would well explain the strong similarity here. This issue will be taken up later in chapter 8.[79] For now, it is important to take careful note of the Johannine features, but in themselves they do not mandate a conclusion of scribal interpolation.

Other stylistic questions relate to how well Luke 24:12 fits into the larger context of Luke 24:1–35. Specifically, the concerns have been framed as follows:[80] (1) Luke 24:12 is not necessary to the flow of the narrative; it could be removed without affecting the sense of the text; (2) there is a "roughness" between Luke 24:11 and 24:12 that suggests an insertion; (3) Luke 24:12 does not fit well with the outline of events in 24:24; and (4) the mention of Peter in Luke 24:34 implies that, for Luke's sources, he was primarily known for being the first to

---

[77] See chapter 3 above.

[78] So also K. Aland "Neue Testamentliche Papyri II," *NTS* 12 (1965–66): 206. Aland especially notes the fact that in the Passion narrative the relationship between Luke and John is particularly strong.

[79] See chapter 8 below.

[80] Conveniently listed in Robert Mahoney, *The Two Disciples at the Tomb*, (Bern: Herbert Lang, 1974), 58–59.

see Jesus alive, not for running to an empty tomb, and the intrusion of this "secondary" story is unlikely except by interpolation. These concerns will be addressed directly in turn, then more generally with a discussion of stylistic variation.

1. In one respect, it is true that the absence of Luke 24:12 would still allow for a cohesive story. But this feature in itself, without an accompanying sense of *intrusiveness*, is little help in arguing against the authenticity of the text. In fact, as Mahoney himself notes, this observation really cuts the other way as well. Because the text can be read coherently without 24:12, a scribe might not have noticed its absence if it were accidently omitted.[81]

2. The argument that the transition from Luke 24:11 to 24:12 is "rough" and thus suggests an interpolation seems hardly convincing. According to Mahoney, the disciples' dash to the tomb does not cohere with the statement in 24:11 that they "disbelieved." But why is that rough? If we read 24:12 after 24:11, Peter rushes to verify their story precisely because the women are doubted. Rather than being rough, the disciples' disbelief of the women establishes the basis for the subsequent narrative.

3. To argue that Luke 24:12 is an interpolation because it does not "fit" with 24:24 is also difficult, since that reason could just as easily give a valid basis for deleting it.[82] Mahoney's actual argument is that, given the report in 24:24, 24:12 is superfluous. But, as will be discussed more below, such repetition, especially in speeches, is quite common for Luke. In other words, superfluousness is Lukan! It is true that 24:24 reports that more than one disciple ran to the tomb (as in John!), while 24:12 only recounts one disciple, Peter, running to the tomb. That is precisely the kind of discontinuity that one might expect within a narrative, and certainly Lukan narratives, especially when part of the narrative is told as reminiscence.[83] The distinction between the

---

[81] Mahoney, 58.
[82] Mahoney, 58; cf. Dillon, 59.
[83] Dillon, 62.

number of disciples in 24:12 and 24:24 ultimately does not help us in this matter.

4. Mahoney's final argument rests on two assumptions. First is the improbability that two Resurrection stories involving Peter exist in the tradition simultaneously. For Mahoney, the primary story is that Peter was the first to see Jesus alive, and that story would tend to suppress any other secondary account, such as the empty grave visit. Why only one story could be recalled, especially given Luke's tendency to use multiple sources, is not clear. The second assumption is that Luke could not have received his information about the empty grave visit from the Fourth Gospel unless it was an interpolation. Clearly, the second assumption is the issue at hand in this study; it will have to be bracketed for now as "what is to be demonstrated."

As Mahoney has pointed out, observations about style are not always limited to the study of lexical patterns. We noted previously that a subtle aspect of Lukan style is his tendency toward repetition and variation.[84] This stylistic feature raises the question of whether the combination of Luke 24:12 and Luke 24:24 accords with Lukan style or not. In other words, does the existence of 24:24 add some credibility, based on compositional style, to the authenticity of 24:12? On the one hand, the fact that 24:24 refers to a trip by certain of the disciples to the tomb after the women had reported the angelic appearance appears to confirm that Luke knew of the 24:12 account. On the other hand, there are tensions between 24:12 and 24:24: in the first instance, Peter alone runs to the tomb; in the later account, "certain ones" (τινες) go, indicating that more than one disciple ran to the tomb. There is no mention in the later story of finding only the burial clothes—there is instead reference only to finding things just as the women reported. For many, this disjuncture between 24:12 and 24:24 is a clear indication that 24:12 is secondary or later.[85]

---

[84] Cadbury; see the discussion p. 187 above.

[85] E.g., Raymond E. Brown, *The Gospel According to John* (XIII–XXI), AB 29A (Garden City, NY: Doubleday, 1970), 1000.

In a study of Luke's tendencies in speeches, Dauer comes to the conclusion that Luke is open both to significant variation as well as to "recalling" events that have not previously been reported.[86] His use of speeches or recapitulation of events often introduces tensions or disagreements with previous reports. So, for instance, in Luke 7:24, Jesus refers to John's locus of activity as "the wilderness," while in a previous reference (Luke 3:2) Luke suggests that John worked "around the Jordan," and that Jesus, after his baptism, went "from the Jordan region" out "to the wilderness" (Luke 4:1), clearly distinguishing between John's locus of activity and the wilderness. This tension between a speech and a previous narrative is also seen in Acts 9:27. Here Barnabas describes how Paul at his conversion "saw the Lord" and heard him speak. This description appears to refer to Acts 9:7, 8–9; however, in those verses, while Paul hears the voice, it would *appear* that he does not see Jesus: a bright light flashes, Paul is left blind, and his companions, though hearing sound, see nothing. Acts 9:27 thus expands and corrects the previous narrative.[87] Similarly, Paul's sermon in Acts 19:4 says that John told people to believe in the one who was coming after him, that is, Jesus. Such a preaching of *belief* in Jesus is never found in Luke.[88] So one can certainly say, as Cadbury notes with other examples, that Luke is quite willing in retelling an account to introduce often significant variations.[89]

But Dauer also notes that Luke frequently introduces material, especially in speeches, that has never been reported previously. One can see this clearly in Acts, where Peter addresses the believers in

---

[86] Anton Dauer, *Beobachtungen zur literarischen Arbeitstechnik des Lukas* (Frankfurt am Main: Anton Hain, 1990). See also "'Ergänzungen' und 'Variationen' in den Reden der Apostelgeschichte gegenüber vorausgegangenen Erzählungen," in *Vom Urchristendum zu Jesus* (Freiburg: Herder, 1989).

[87] Dauer, *Beobachtungen*, 79–80.

[88] Dauer, *Beobachtungen*, 101–2.

[89] Cadbury, 89. Cf. also Joachim Wahnke, *Die Emmauserzählung* (Leipzig: St. Benno-Verlag, 1973), 76–83, especially 82–83 dealing with 24:21–24 as a "schriftstellerischer Nachtrag."

1:16–17 and urges them to choose a replacement for Judas, who has killed himself.⁹⁰ Unlike Matthew, Luke has not previously reported Judas' death. Perhaps a more apt example comes in Luke 24:34, following the Emmaus pericope. Here the disciples from Emmaus return to Jerusalem and are told that Jesus appeared to Simon, an appearance that has not been related in the text.⁹¹ Dauer concludes from his study that any attempt to base the reliability of Luke 24:12 on the subsequent report of 24:24 is misplaced, since Luke frequently introduces new material that has not been previously mentioned. He does not further observe, however, that the variations he notes in Luke's recapitulations would also support the existence of Luke 24:24 as a subsequent variation and corrective of 24:12. Dauer clarifies Luke's compositional tendencies, but he does not resolve the problem of Luke 24:12.

In summary, then, the stylistic arguments are not clear. The lexical arguments offer a split testimony. There are clearly Johannine features present, but there are also signs of Lukan editorial shaping and modification. When the larger issues of context and narrative style are considered, the evidence tends to be more supportive of the authenticity of Luke 24:12. The arguments that 24:12 is intrusive and that it clashes with 24:11 or 24:24 are not persuasive. Indeed, Luke's style of repetition and variation appear to allow for precisely the pattern of 24:12 and 24:24. Yet it must be said that Luke also tends to introduce new information, especially in summary speeches, thus allowing for the absence of 24:12 within Luke's compositional style as well. The stylistic argument does not offer a solution here.

Transcriptional Probability. Along with matters of style, the argument from internal evidence must consider whether expansion or truncation is more likely as a transcriptional likelihood. In general, the reasons for a scribe to have introduced an expansion of the text would be to harmonize with another gospel account or to resolve a narrative or

---

⁹⁰ Dauer, *Beobachtungen,* 69.

⁹¹ Dauer, *Beobachtungen,* 63.

theological difficulty. The reasons to have deleted a text would be the same, with the added possibility of accidental omission. In the case of Luke 24:12, the addition of verse 12 could have been an effort to harmonize with John, as well as to develop theological concerns. An omission here is unlikely to have been an accident or to have arisen from the mechanics of transcription; an omission would either have been to harmonize Luke toward Mark/Matthew or to resolve a theological problem.

Bart Ehrman has presented the most convincing argument against the authenticity of 24:12 based on theological tendencies. In summary, Ehrman argues that 24:12 shows signs of interpolation from the Johannine post-Resurrection account in order to quash a docetic reading of the Gospel.[92] In his view, Luke's account without verse 12 is potentially ambiguous as to the nature of the Resurrection, allowing for a spiritual rather than physical interpretation: the women who see the tomb are unreliable witnesses, and Jesus' resurrected appearances are disconnected from the natural world. Because of the ambiguity of this verse, an early scribe would have undergirded the women's report by adding the account of Peter, the lead apostle, seeing the empty tomb as well. In that way, the testimony concerning the empty tomb would have been strengthened to emphasize the physical Resurrection.

Although this argument is attractive because it gives a plausible reason for the interpolation, a closer examination of Luke's Resurrection accounts suggests that it is not as strong as Ehrman proposes. Ehrman's argument depends on reading Luke 24 as ambiguous without the passage. But the appearance to the women in 24:2–7 is hardly ambiguous: two men in dazzling apparel (ἐσθῆτι ἀστραπτούσῃ), clearly meant to be angels (cf. Luke 17:24), ask why they seek the living among the dead. The question is then interpreted by a reference to Jesus' own prediction that he would die and rise again (24:7). In other words, by means of the question and the reference to Jesus' words, the men/angels indicate that Jesus is alive having been raised on the third day after death. Then, following 24:12,

---

[92] Ehrman, 216.

Jesus is portrayed talking with certain disciples and, finally, breaking bread with them (24:30). In the midst of this episode, on the road to Emmaus, the disciples themselves refer to the account of 24:2–12: the two "men," interpreted as angels, have said that Jesus is alive and some of the disciples have returned to the grave to authenticate it (Luke 24:24). Thus, even with 24:12 absent, the account is quite clear: Jesus has been raised, this Resurrection is announced by angels, and the report of the women is disbelieved at first but is confirmed by subsequent examination.

Moreover, 24:12 is in general agreement with 24:24.[93] The argument that the main reason to insert this passage was to make up for a supposed lack in the account does not take seriously enough the force of the developing narrative and the intertextual links between 24:1–12 and 24:13–27, links that in a narrative reading produce a powerful cohesive portrayal of the Resurrection. While 24:24 is stronger with 24:12 as a previous reference, 24:12 is not necessary to provide a strong picture of an empty tomb, empty because of a resurrected Jesus.[94]

But is there a reason that a scribe in the second or third century would have deleted Luke 24:12? Those who have argued for long text have recognized that this is a weak point in their argument. Few reasons have been proposed for why a scribe might have deleted the verse, and none of them have been very convincing. Generally, it has been suggested that the deletion might have been a scribal accident or an attempt to do away with a divergence from the Johannine text, where there are two disciples that run to the tomb.[95] The pattern of harmonizing omissions in the Western text could also help us view the

---

[93] Contra Mahoney, 58. See the discussion, p. 194 above.

[94] So in this sense Mahoney's argument that 24:12 can be removed from the text with no effect on its surroundings (58) is partially correct. Luke 24:12 is not necessary to clear understanding, but it does enhance and strengthen the vividness of the portrayal.

[95] Snodgrass, 373; Dillon, 60, n. 173; Julius Schniewind, *Die Parallelperikopen bei Lukas und Johannes* (Hildesheim: Georg Olms Verlags-

omission as part of a *pattern* in the Western text, but it does not adequately explain the *reason*.[96] It is because of this difficulty that proponents of the longer text generally emphasize the strength of the manuscript evidence.

But the controversies of the second and third centuries, one of which Ehrman has put forward as a reason for the insertion of the disputed text, also provide an explanation of the omissions. There was in the late second century and early third century significant opposition from within the orthodox church to the Johannine literature, especially the Fourth Gospel and the Apocalypse.[97] This opposition arose probably in response to the use of John by the Montanists, although the use of John by Gnostics could also have encouraged such resistance in certain quarters. The strong echo of John 20 in Luke 24:12 would have been a compelling reason for these individuals to suspect an interpolation by heretics and to move toward a deliberate deletion of the offending passage.

There is strong evidence that the Gospel of John met with significant resistance *within* the orthodox church beginning in the second century and continuing well into the third century.[98] Irenaeus is

---

buchhandlung, 1958), 88.

[96] See discussion above, p. 175, and Appendix, p. 224.

[97] We can approximately date the beginning of this controversy around the rise of Montanism, ca. 170 C.E.; Irenaeus (*Against Heresies* 3.11.9) refers to opponents of John's Gospel, and Hippolytus responded against the continued opposition to the Gospel of John and the Apocalypse in the early third century with a treatise defending them (see Dionysius bar Salibi commentaries on John and Revelation for fragments; Hippolytus' essay is the basis for Epiphanius' comment in *Panarion* 51.3).

[98] The following studies lay out the basic contours of the controversy over the Fourth Gospel: A. von Harnack, *History of Dogma* (New York: Dover, 1961) 3:14; Ned Stonehouse, *The Apocalypse in the Ancient Church* (Goes: Oosterbaan & Le Cointre, 1929), 59–71 and 92–109; August Bludau, *Die ersten Gegner der Johannesschriften* (Freiburg: Herder and Co., 1925); Hans von Campenhausen, *The Formation of the Christian Bible* (Philadelphia: Fortress Press, 1973); Joseph D. Smith, "Gaius and the Controversy over the Johannine Literature" (Ph.D. diss.,

the first to refer to this opposition to the Fourth Gospel:

> And since this is the case, all those are futile, ignorant and presumptuous who set aside the form of the gospel and introduce either more or fewer faces than the Gospels of which we have been speaking.... But others, in order that they might set aside the gift of the Spirit, which was poured out in the last times upon the human race by the good pleasure of the Father, do not accept that form (of the Gospel according to John) in which the Lord promised to send the Paraclete, but reject at the same time both the Gospel and the Prophetic Spirit. These are truly wretched persons who indeed choose to be false prophets but in fact reject the prophetic grace from the church, acting exactly like those who because of those who come in hypocrisy and even (furthermore) separate themselves from the communion of the brethren.[99]

Irenaeus, in the course of his opposition to Valentinus, is making a general case for a fourfold gospel. And in the process of that argument, he refers to a different group (*alii*) than either Marcion (who only accepted a pared-down version of Luke) or the Gnostics (who had more than Irenaeus' four Gospels). This "other group" rejects the Gospel of John because it contains the promise of the Paraclete. It is generally surmised that the rejection of the Paraclete stemmed from an anti-Montanist agenda.[100] While the group is criticized by Irenaeus for its rejection of the Gospel of John (and probably also the Apocalypse), its members are nonetheless apparently within the bounds of orthodoxy, since they have not "separated themselves from the communion of the brethren."[101] Indeed, it is likely that the anonymity

---

Yale University, 1979); Theodore Zahn, *Geschichte des ntl. Kanons* (Erlangen: Verlag von Andreas Deichert, 1888) I:220; II:967.

[99] Irenaeus, 1.27.2–4, as translated in Joseph Smith, 141–42.

[100] Joseph Smith, 159; Stonehouse, 59–60; von Harnack, *History of Dogma*, 3:17.

[101] As Joseph Smith paraphrases Irenaeus to make more clear the argument from within orthodoxy: "Because you yourselves condemn and reject the gift of prophecy as it is derived from John's Gospel—the Paraclete—, then, consequently,

of these "others" indicates that they could be ranking members of the church.[102] Irenaeus' arguments are very pointed and specific; that is, they deal only with the rejection of the Gospel of John as a part of scripture. No attempt is made to criticize them generally or to consider them cut off from the catholic church. It is quite likely that the group Irenaeus is opposing was situated in Asia Minor, since that was the point of origination of Montanism (and probably its early opposition), as well as the location of both Irenaeus' and the Church in Gaul's special concern regarding the Montanist controversy.[103]

We learn of a similar rejection of the Johannine writings in Epiphanius,[104] who refers to a group he calls the ἀλόγοι because of the rejection of the Gospel of John:

> The Alogoi — for that is the name I have given them ... reject the books of John. Since therefore they do not accept the Word preached by John, let them be called Alogoi. They accept neither the Gospel of John nor his Revelation. Now if they accepted the gospel but rejected the Revelation, we might perhaps say ... But as it is, they do not accept John's books at all.... The excuse they make is that they are not from John, but from Cerinthus, and are not worthy to be read in Church.[105]

---

consequently, you would have to reject all prophecy and prophetic charisma; in effect you yourselves are thereby attempting to play the role of prophets, yea even false prophets, so that you convict yourselves of that very same gross error for which you condemn your adversaries and like them become hypocrites who separate themselves from the Church." (151). And see the discussion regarding the catholicity of these "others" (151–68).

[102] Joseph Smith, 163–64.

[103] Stonehouse, 67–69.

[104] Epiphanius writes 374–76 C.E., but that does not suggest that the controversy over the Gospel of John continued until then; he is relying on earlier sources and referring to previous controversies.

[105] Epiphanius, *Panarion*, 51.3, as translated by Philip R. Amidon, *The Panarion of St. Epiphanius, Bishop of Salamis* (Oxford: University Press, 1990), 177.

In Epiphanius' discussion objecting to this group's rejection of John's Gospel, he gives some indication of the basis for their suspicion of John, that is that John does not agree with the Synoptic presentation of the life of Jesus. The specific issues surround the early elements of the Gospel narratives: the order and timing of the early period of Jesus' life (51.11) and the number of years of his ministry (51.22). Their objections, then, rest on critical evaluation of the Gospels, in which the synoptic Gospels are given priority.

It would appear at first glance that Epiphanius' Alogoi and Irenaeus' "others" are unrelated; the former oppose John because of its disagreement with the other Gospels, the latter because it gave quarter to the Montanists. But Epiphanius was dependent for his information on the writings of Hippolytus, who wrote a treatise against Gaius of Rome.[106] Gaius of Rome, we know from Eusebius, wrote a treatise of his own, *Dialogue with Proclus*, which opposed Proclus the Montanist.[107] Fragments of Hippolytus' treatise against Gaius, found in Dionysius bar Salibi's "Commentary on the Apocalypse of John" and "Commentary on the Gospel of John,"[108] cite arguments against the Gospel of John and the Apocalypse that are very similar to those cited by Epiphanius in connection with his Alogoi.[109] Thus the rejection of John based on its stark difference from the synoptic Gospels appears to

---

[106] There is some question whether Hippolytus wrote more than one treatise against Gaius. I accept here Joseph Smith's conclusion that there was one treatise, variously called *Heads against Gaius* or *Defense of the Gospel of John and Revelation*. (cf. his discussion on Hippolytus' treatises, p. 202). See also Stonehouse, p. 67.

[107] On the identification of Proclus as a Montanist, see Barbara Aland, "Proclus" in *Encyclopedia of the Early Church* (New York: Oxford University Press, 1992), 713. Eusebius (*E.H.* 2.25.6, cf. 6.20.3) refers to him as "Proclus, leader of the Phrygian heresy," which would certainly point to his being a Montanist.

[108] See Joseph Smith, 196.

[109] Joseph Smith argues, convincingly, that the Alogoi of Epiphanius are to be identified with Gaius of Rome. Compare his summary of the evidence regarding Epiphanius at 257–62.

have been used as part of an anti-Montanist argument; both Irenaeus and Epiphanius are referring to criticisms of the Gospel of John in the midst of opposition to the Montanists.[110]

The figure of Gaius presents us with more evidence on the standing of the opposition to John within the church. Although Eusebius is strongly in favor of the Fourth Gospel, he nonetheless refers to Gaius as a "churchman" (ἐκκλησιαστικός *E.H.* 2.25.6) and a "scholar" (λόγιος *E.H.* 6.20.3). The first person to designate Gaius a heretic—clearly based on his opposition to the Johannine writings—is Dionysius bar Salibi.[111] So not only was the opposition to the Fourth Gospel found within the church, it was proffered by a leading member. Moreover, the designation of Gaius as a "scholar" and the nature of his criticism of the Fourth Gospel, based in part on its disagreements with the synoptic Gospels, should alert us to the critical study of the Gospels in the early third century and the negative evaluation of significant differences.

One of the criticisms of the Fourth Gospel contained in Gaius' *Dialogue* is confusing as criticism of Montanism. It is said that Gaius attributed the authorship of the Fourth Gospel to Cerinthus, and indeed it appears that at least a significant portion of Hippolytus' response to Gaius is concerned with showing that such could not be the case since Cerinthus and the Fourth Gospel are in opposition. Since Gaius' *Dialogue* is missing except in fragments of Hippolytus contained in Epiphanius and Dionysius bar Salibi, it is difficult to say too much. But it is possible that Gaius was engaging in a many-headed argument: in addition to opposing the Fourth Gospel because of its use by the

---

[110] Joseph Smith wants to take the argument further and identify Irenaeus' "others" with Gaius as well. That seems to go too far in consolidating the opposition to John. It is more probable (as Stonehouse, 67, argues) that there was opposition in Rome, most notably in the person of Gaius, to which Hippolytus and, subsequently, Epiphanius refer, as well as opposition in Asia Minor before this, to which Irenaeus refers.

[111] Dionysius bar Salibi wrote ca. 1170 C.E. Others who considered Gaius to be orthodox include Jerome and Photius.

Montanists, Gaius might have been doing the same against its use by Gnostics.[112] It is intriguing that the name Cerinthus keeps being connected with John, not only by Gaius' attribution to Cerinthus of authorship of the Fourth Gospel, but also by Irenaeus' implication that John wrote in part to refute Cerinthus[113] and by the story retained in Eusebius and Irenaeus that John the Apostle fled a bathhouse for fear of being seen with Cerinthus.[114] Cerinthus maintained views that would be called Gnostic, views that certainly would be in agreement with much of Valentinus' theology.[115] Thus it is possible that Gaius' arguments against the Fourth Gospel were in response to Gnostic use as well as to Montanist use of the Fourth Gospel.

We can conclude, then, that (1) there was a significant opposition to the Fourth Gospel at the end of the second century and

---

[112] The Fourth Gospel was used extensively by the early Gnostics and for that reason was viewed cautiously by others. J. N. Sanders, *The Fourth Gospel in the Early Church* (Cambridge: University Press, 1943), 66, even argues that Irenaeus was the first catholic writer to *overcome the prejudice that was felt against the Fourth Gospel*, thus suggesting that the earliest reception of the Gospel of John was by non-catholic segments of the church. Cf. J. N. Sanders, 47, and Elaine Pagels, *The Johannine Gospel in Gnostic Exegesis* (Nashville: Abingdon Press, 1973).

[113] Irenaeus, 3.11.1: "John, the disciple of the Lord, preaches this faith, and seeks, by the proclamation of the Gospel, to remove that error which by Cerinthus had been disseminated among men, and a long time previously by those termed Nicolaitans, who are an offset of that 'knowledge' false so called."

[114] Irenaeus, 3.3.4; Eusebius, *E.H.* 3.28.6.

[115] Irenaeus goes on here, and in 1.26.1, to describe Cerinthus in terms of Gnostic theology. "[John sought to] persuade them that there is but one God, who made all things by His Word; and not, as they allege, that the Creator was one, but the Father of the Lord another; and that the Son of the Creator was, forsooth, one, but the Christ from above another, who also continued impassable, descending upon Jesus, the Son of the Creator, and flew back again to His Pleroma, and that the Monogenes was the beginning, but Logos was the true son of the Monogenes; and that this creation to which we belong was not made by the primary God, but by some power lying far below Him, and shut off from communion with the things invisible and ineffable." Cf. also Hippolytus, *Against all Heresies*, 7.33.1.

the beginning of the third century; (2) the opposition was certainly found in Rome, but quite possible also in Asia Minor; (3) the opposition to the Fourth Gospel was in response, certainly, to the Montanists but perhaps also to certain Gnostic groups who were using the Gospel to their advantage; (4) the basis for objection to John was, in part, the result of critical study and comparison of the Fourth Gospel with the Synoptics; and (5) the opposition to the Fourth Gospel was from within the orthodox church and, very possibly, from well-respected individuals.

With this general framework in mind, then, it is possible to assess the probability that the text in Luke 24:12 might have been deleted. A striking feature of Luke 24:12, as has been noted so frequently by modern scholars wanting to strike the verse from the text of Luke, is that it is very much like John 20:4–10. Had this striking similarity been noticed by scribes who were suspicious of the Fourth Gospel, or perhaps by Gaius himself in his critical comparison of John with the Synoptic Gospels, it would indeed have raised questions as to whether the verse in question had been interpolated by the Montanists or the gnostics. And in response to such a perceived corruption of the text of Luke, those scribes might have stricken the verse from their texts as suspect. Given the suspicion that the Fourth Gospel engendered in certain circles—possibly even most of the church—at the turn of the third century, such a critical perspective seems likely.

The transcriptional probability that 24:12 would be deleted by orthodox scribes suspicious of its "johannisms" is very high.

Summary. With respect to the internal evidence of the reading, the stylistic evidence does not prove interpolation, but it does suggest a strong link with John. Evaluations of Luke 24:12 that downplay the literary relationship with John, especially in light of the order of common material in question, are quite unsatisfactory. But despite the Johannine similarities, the passage has both Lukan and Johannine features, which would argue against a rather blind *pastiche* of John 20 into Luke's account. The marks of Lukan editing of the material tilt the stylistic argument, in my opinion, in favor of its authenticity.

The transcriptional evidence is also of a mixed nature, but one which ultimately inclines toward inclusion of the verse. The rationales offered for the interpolation are less than convincing. While verse 12 would help strengthen a case for the physical Resurrection of Jesus, it is hardly required. Indeed, one is left wondering how a supposed scribe would have proceeded in this interpolation. The scribe must have

1. turned to a copy of John 20:3–10, or known it fairly closely by heart,

2. modified the account by deleting the reference to the other disciple (despite the presence of a reference to another disciple in 24:24),

3. added the Lukan stylistic form of a pleonastic ἀναστάς,

4. modified the term προέδραμον, in which the προ- must clearly refer to the race between Peter and the other disciple, to ἔδραμεν, yet

5. left the term βλέπει uncorrected, and

6. added the Lukan terms θαυμάζω and τό γεγονός.

In other words, the interpolation would not have been a simple harmonization to a variant version in John. What is necessary to this reconstruction is a fairly sophisticated editor of texts or traditions with an eye to Lukan style. Interpolation in this case, while possible, does appear to represent a more deliberate and thoughtful attempt to alter the text than simple scribal insertion.

On the other hand, it is quite easy to imagine a scribe reading Luke 24 and noting the similarity of the account with John, together with the absence of the same account in the other synoptic Gospels. Faced with this discrepancy in the Synoptics—and harboring suspicion about the Gospel of John—a scribe would simply have deleted the verse.

LUKE 24:36

Intrinsic Probability Based on Style. There is little that stands out in the textual variant in Luke 24:36 to establish it as either Lukan or intrusive to Luke. None of the vocabulary is particularly Lukan or non-Lukan. This verse does present another instance of the use of a historical present (λέγει). But while this grammatical form is not common in Luke (seven times in the Gospel, fourteen times in Acts), it is not completely excluded. In particular, the most common use of the historical present in Luke-Acts is with words of saying (φησίν, λέγει).[116]

The salutation Εἰρήνη ὑμῖν is best known from John, where the precise formula occurs three times (John 20:19, 21, 26) and a pair of variations occur in 14:27. Of course, the concept of a greeting of peace is not unknown in Luke.[117] But it is especially intriguing that the wording of the whole passage, in which the variant, καὶ λέγει αὐτοῖς Εἰρήνη ὑμῖν stands, is strongly similar to John 20:19 and 26 even outside the disputed textual variant.

Lk 24:36 Ταῦτα δὲ αὐτῶν λαλούντων --------------αὐτὸς ἔστη ἐν μέσῳ αὐτῶν
Jn 20:19 ἦλθεν ὁ Ἰησοῦς καὶ ---------------------- ἔστη εἰς τὸ μέσον
Jn 20:26 ἔρχεται ὁ Ἰησοῦς τῶν θυρῶν κεκλεισμένων καὶ ἔστη εἰς τὸ μέσον

Lk 24:36 καὶ λέγει αὐτοῖς, Εἰρήνη ὑμῖν.
Jn 20:19 καὶ λέγει αυτοῖς, Εἰρήνη ὑμῖν.
Jn 20:26 καὶ εἶπεν,------ Εἰρήνη ὑμῖν.

The similarity to John has suggested to many that verse 36b is an interpolation from John; however, the strong similarities between

---
[116] Jeremias, *Sprache*, 169.
[117] Dillon, 187. Note especially the command to greet the household upon entering it in Luke 10:5 (not found in the parallel Matthew text): λέγετε Εἰρήνη τῷ οἴκῳ τούτῳ. A similar interest in peace salutations is found in Luke 7:50 and 8:48: πορεύου εἰς εἰρήνην.

Luke and John by themselves are hardly sufficient basis for such an assessment.[118] In addition is the complicating issue that the setting in this verse is also very close to John: in both Luke and John, Jesus stands in the disciples' midst. But that part of the verse, ἔστη ἐν μέσῳ αὐτῶν, is not part of the textual variant; the Johannine style here points directly to a secure part of the verse. As has been shown in Chapter 3 and will examined more closely in Chapters 6–8, the similarities between Luke and John are part of the fundamental nature of the Third Gospel and thus would suggest, if anything, that Johannine features are stylistically original, not a corruption.

Transcriptional Probability. Ehrman has again suggested that a significant reason for the interpolation of this text can be found in its perceived uncertainty.[119] According to Ehrman, with the suspect words absent, the appearance of Jesus might have been perceived as a ghost and hence have produced the reaction of fear found in verse 37. Thus the original text, according to Ehrman, is probably the shorter text. A subsequent scribe, wishing to remove any possible doubt about Jesus' physical Resurrection, would have added the words "Peace to you" to remove any further misconception.

But, as Ehrman himself notes, the passage immediately does go on to show Jesus speaking again and then pointing to his hands and feet as evidence of the physicality of the Resurrection; indeed, Jesus offers to have the disciples touch his hands and feet. It is hard to imagine why in such a close context, one in which any possible ambiguity is immediately resolved, a scribe would have felt the need to insert an additional word from Jesus.

An intriguing aspect of this textual variant is found in some additional minor variations. In some manuscripts (G P it^c vg syr^{p,h,pal} cop^{bo} arm eth geo Diatesseron^{a,i,n}), following the disputed words of

---

[118] So Fitzmyer, *The Gospel According to Luke* (X–XXIV), AB 28A (Garden City, NY: Doubleday, 1985), 1575. As argued above, p. 193, with respect to Luke 24:12.

[119] Ehrman, 220.

Jesus is a further expansion: εἰρήνη ὑμῖν· ἐγώ εἰμι, μὴ φοβεῖσθε. And in some other manuscripts (W 579), the additional words come before the peace greeting: ἐγώ εἰμι, μὴ φοβεῖσθε· εἰρήνη ὑμῖν. These additional variants all appear to stem from the text found in B and P[75]; they all require the introduction of καὶ λέγει αὐτοῖς, found only in this variant. What we have, then, is a constellation of four variants: no text, UBS[4]/NA[27] text, a longer form found in some Latin and Syriac versions, and another longer text found in a very few Greek manuscripts. Can all of the variants be explained from one of these forms? The only form that could explain all of the variants is the long form now in UBS[4]/NA[27]. The variants containing ἐγώ εἰμι, μὴ φοβεῖσθε are also suggestive, because they seem to be drawn from John 6:20. It appears that a scribe heard εἰρήνη ὑμῖν, perhaps through its use in the church, with John-attuned ears and connected it with another Johannine assurance. Such variants indicate the scribal alertness to the relationship between this text form and the Gospel of John.

It is possible that a scribe might have deleted this part of verse 36 by mere error, but there is no obvious parablepsis or other mechanical reason that would encourage such an error. But, as in the discussion regarding Luke 24:12, the very fact that this text is so Johannine sounding would have encouraged a scribe to delete it as a corruption.[120] Without rehearsing the argument detailed above, suffice it to say that the Gospel of John was suspect in some quarters of the church in the latter part of the second and early third centuries. The suspicion about John did lead to a treatise calling for its disuse in the catholic church because of its use by Montanist and Gnostic segments of the church. And that same suspicion, I argued, would have been sufficient cause to delete Johannine-sounding texts from Luke as probable interpolations. A likely reason for omission of 24:36b can be found in the early disputes over the canon of Scripture.

---

[120] See p. 199 above.

Summary. There is little compelling evidence in terms of stylistic quality or theological purpose that would strongly support either inserting or deleting Luke 36b. The most compelling issues here are two. First, it is hard to see how the other textual variations could have arisen without the long form of verse 36b as the textual exemplar. Second, the stylistic similarities to John extend beyond the textual variant. The Johannine-sounding features are apparently integral to the verse!

On the side of transcriptional probability, the argument for interpolation in order to counter docetic interpretation seems strained. It is possible, however, that opponents of the Gospel of John might have deleted the verse because it sounded Johannine, hence rendering them suspicious of a heretical interpolation. The longer form of the text is most likely original.

LUKE 24:40

Intrinsic Probability Based on Style. There are again no stylistic features which would, *per se*, suggest that this verse is either Lukan or non-Lukan. Every word and usage is well attested in Luke. The only unusual feature is that the verse is almost word for word identical with John :

Lk 24:40 καὶ τοῦτο εἰπὼν ἔδειξεν αὐτοῖς τὰς χεῖρας καὶ τοὺς πόδας.
Jn 20:20 καὶ τοῦτο εἰπὼν ἔδειχεν ---- τὰς χεῖρας καὶ τὴν πλευρὰν αὐτοῖς.

This remarkable similarity, with differences only in the substitution of feet for side and the placement of the indirect object, αὐτοῖς, surely suggests a literary connection. It is not sufficient to note this similarity and simply attribute it to oral tradition.[121] But such literary connection need not suggest the secondary textual nature of the verse.

---

[121] Jeremias, *Sprache*, 321: "Lukas folgt in v. 40 also der (wohl mündlichen) Tradition"; cf. Fitzmyer, *Luke* (X–XXIV), 1576.

Transcriptional Probability. Given the possibility of this text's having come from John, what is the probability that a scribe might, indeed, have inserted it for some purpose? Ehrman again argues that the final emphasis of showing his hands and feet in Luke 24:40 strengthens an attempt to remove any doubt about the physical nature of Jesus' Resurrection.[122]

But once again, it is hard to imagine why a scribe would have inserted such a strengthening passage in the midst of what is already one of the strongest anti-docetic passages in Luke:

1. Following the reference to the fear of the disciples at his appearance, Jesus invites his disciples to *look* and to *touch him* to verify that it is really he: ἴδετε τὰς χεῖράς μου καὶ τοὺς πόδας μου... ψηλαπφήσατέ με καὶ ἴδετε (24:39a,b). The implication of the narrative is that the disciples do so, with or without the inclusion of verse 40.

2. The whole point of Jesus' invitation cited above is to verify that he is not a ghost or spirit but is indeed really human, ὅτι πνεῦμα σάρκα καὶ ὀστέα οὐκ ἔχει (24:39c). Thus the anti-docetic quality of the invitation is highlighted as its stated purpose.

3. The invitation is followed, in verse 42, with Jesus' taking broiled fish and eating it before his disciples. His eating would seem to confirm that he actually has a physical body; it appears to be a further reaction to the disciples' disbelief.

Within this narrative construction, in which Jesus offers two proofs specifically to combat disbelief in his physical Resurrection, Jesus' second offering of his hands and feet for inspection (24:40) seems almost anti-climactic and certainly unnecessary. It would hardly have helped to advance, to any significant degree, an anti-docetic concern of a scribe at a later point. Is it likely, then, that a scribe would have taken the Johannine text and inserted it here, with appropriate modifications to adjust it to the Lukan features of verse 39, in order to strengthen the anti-docetic import of the narrative? It seems an unusual place to add emphasis if the reason for the insertion is concern over docetic misreadings of scripture.

---

[122] Ehrman, 218.

It is possible, however, to imagine a scribe deleting the text because of its close similarity to John. Even despite the substitution of feet for side, its striking Johannine flavor might well have given a scribe pause. As has been shown above,[123] the Gospel of John was suspect in some quarters, and any extreme similarity to John might have been viewed as a "heretical" corruption of the text. Thinking that it was an intrusion, a scribe might have deleted the verse.

Summary. Once again, the evidence does not establish a clear case for inclusion or exclusion of 24:40. Intrinsic issues such as style do not help in this case. While one might argue, as Ehrman does, that the only realistic prospect is that of a scribe's interpolating the verse rather than deleting it, the reason for such interpolation remains somewhat obscure. Granted that the verse is somewhat anti-docetic, it is nevertheless hard to imagine why a scribe would have gone to the trouble at precisely this point, in the midst of a passage that is filled with language affirming the physical Resurrection. However, its obvious similarity to John would have raised concerns by scribes who were suspicious of John and might have prompted its deletion. The internal arguments favor inclusion of 24:40.

LUKE 24:51 AND 52

Intrinsic Probability Based on Style. The intrinsic probability that the textual variant καὶ ἀνεφέρετο εἰς τὸν οὐρανόν is original to Luke is complicated by two significant issues: (1) the word used for Jesus' ascension here in 24:51 is not used elsewhere in Luke, and (2) that there is another ascension in Acts 1:3–11.[124]

The first issue raises questions as to whether the reading matches Lukan style. Not only does Luke not use ἀναφέρω elsewhere in Luke or Acts, but in the one instance where Mark uses the word, Luke

---

[123] See p. 199 above.

[124] Metzger, *Textual Commentary* (162), also suggests that the rhythm of the sentence requires the final clause, but that seems too vague a standard to use.

changes it: Luke's modification of Mark's account of Jesus' leading Peter, James, and John to the mountain of transfiguration (Mark 9:2 par. Luke 9:28) prefers ἀνέβη to ανάφερει. But too much can be made of this word in an analysis of Luke 24:51. First of all, the word is also quite rare in the other Gospels, occurring only in the transfiguration scene in Mark and Matthew and not at all in John. Thus its singular use at Luke 24:51 does not stand out as unusual. And second, Luke's avoidance of the word at 9:28 could be based in part on Mark's historical present, which necessitated a change anyway, as well as on a preference for βαίνω cognates when the narrative indicates a move in location. It has been noted that the word has a primary meaning in the New Testament of offering up (a sacrifice),[125] but its meaning here in the passive of being taken up to "heaven" is good traditional usage.[126] While the word is unusual for Luke, it fits well here and could easily be Lukan.

Luke, in the first chapter of Acts, also speaks of Jesus' ascension in a number of other references:

> Acts 1:1–2 In the first book, Theophilus, I wrote about all that Jesus did and taught from the beginning until the day when he was taken up (ἀνελήφθη) ...

> Acts 1:9 When he had said this, as they were watching, he was lifted up (ἐπήρθη), and a cloud took him (ὑπέλαβεν) out of their sight.

> Acts 1:11 This Jesus, who has been taken up (ἀναλημφθείς) from you [into heaven] will come in the same way as you saw him go (πορευόμενον)into heaven.

---

[125] Metzger, *Textual Commentary*, 163.

[126] William Arndt and F. Wilbur Gingrich, *A Greek-English Lexicon of the New Testament* [*BAGD*], 2nd ed. (Chicago: University Press, 1957), 63; Henry G. Liddell and Robert Scott, *A Greek-English Lexicon*, 9th ed. (Oxford: Clarendon Press, 1968), 125. See additionally Dillon, 176 and Gerhard Lohfink, *Die Himmelfahrt Jesu* (München: Kösel-Verlag, 1971), 42.

Acts 1:22 ... beginning from the baptism of John until the day when he was taken up from us (ἀνελήμφθη)...

The difficulties of these references in Acts are numerous, and they do not allow easy solution in any case. First, Luke's general usage for the Ascension appears to be ἀναλαμβάνω, which raises specific questions about the likelihood that he would have used ἀναφέρω in Luke 24:51. Second, the reference in Acts 1:2 seems to be a recapitulation of Luke, which concludes with an ascension. And third, it appears that there is a conflict in chronology between Luke and Acts: Luke appears to relate the Ascension soon after his Resurrection, while Acts suggests that it took place forty days later (Acts 1:3). Is it likely that Luke wrote about two separate ascensions, or was he confused?

The fact that Luke tends to use a different word in Acts might be an indication that Luke's text is an interpolation. But the argument is not clear-cut. If Luke is an interpolation, it is likely a harmonizing interpolation based on Acts. In that case, one would expect a scribe to have used the Acts verb, that is ἀναλαμβάνω, not a wholly different verb. So the very uniqueness of the word in Luke might speak for its originality.[127] Furthermore, even Acts seems to testify to a variety of words used for the Ascension, again pointing to Luke's tendency toward stylistic variation.

A major question is whether Acts 1:2 is a backward glance to Luke. It has generally been taken that way; that understanding then tends to locate the chronology problem squarely within Acts, even if the variant in Luke 24:51 is not there.[128] More importantly, if Acts 1:2 is referring to the Ascension, then it seems to strongly imply that Luke 24:51 is authentic, since Acts 1:2 refers back to something. Ehrman raises questions as to whether Acts 1:2 is, in fact, a backward glance to

---

[127] Metzger, *Textual Commentary*, 162–63.

[128] On the understanding that this backward glance includes the resurrection, see Ernst Haenchen, *The Acts of the Apostles* (Philadelphia: Westminster, 1971), 137–39. On the internal conflict within Acts if this is a backward glance of the Ascension, see Ehrman, 229.

24:51. The term ἄχρι ἧς ἡμέρας ... ἀνελήμφθη, in Ehrman's argument, suggests a backward glance of events up to, but not including, the Ascension.[129] The improbability of Luke's internal contradiction of an ascension immediately following the Resurrection (Luke 24:51 if authentic and Acts 1:2 if it embraces the Ascension in Luke) and an ascension forty days later (Acts 1:9) leads Ehrman to understand Luke 24:51 as a later interpolation.

But is there a contradiction between Acts 1:2, when read as a backward glance to Luke *up through* the Ascension, and Acts 1:9? The assumption has been that Luke's narrative recounts an ascension immediately following the Resurrection. But the textual unit from 24:44 to 24:53 need not, and indeed should not, be read as immediately following 24:43. The final verses of Luke appear to be recapitulative and anticipatory: preaching of forgiveness is to begin in Jerusalem (24:47), the disciples are to wait until they receive power (24:49), Jesus is taken up (24:51), and the disciples spend their time in the temple continually praising God (24:53). Within the narrative time frame of Acts, the preaching of forgiveness, the reception of power, and the activity in the temple take place *after* Jesus' ascension.[130] Luke concludes his Gospel, then, with a schematic conclusion to the life of Jesus which makes no attempt at chronological verisimilitude but rather anticipates the major features of the continuation of the story.[131]

While there are apparent stylistic problems with Luke 24:51, upon closer examination they are not compelling. The use of ἀναφέρω and the repetition of the Ascension in Luke 24 and Acts 1 are both well accommodated by Luke's compositional style and strategy.[132]

---

[129] Ehrman, 229.

[130] Preaching begins at Acts 1:15. Reception of power from the Holy Spirit awaits Pentecost at Acts 2:1, and the reference to their activity in the temple takes place as a continuing activity beginning in Acts 2:46.

[131] So also see Dillon, 180.

[132] As before, see the discussions pp. 187 and 195 above.

There are few stylistic problems with Luke 24:52;[133] the short reading that the disciples worshipped Jesus when he ascended offers little for a stylistic critique: the reading could be Luke, but it also could easily be seen as an intrusion. The verb προσκυνέω occurs only two other times in Luke's Gospel, neither time with reference to Jesus. However, it is used (although sparingly) in Acts. In Luke, it is clearly linked to the text of 24:51. If Jesus ascended in Luke 24:51, it makes sense that the disciples worshipped him;[134] if he did not, then the variant in 24:52 seems out of place.

Transcriptional Probability. Once again we must inquire into the probability that a scribe would have either inserted text or deleted text from a known exemplar. The following proposals have been offered as reasons for why a scribe's having deleted the text:

1. Mechanical error, probably arising from homoeoarcton.[135]
2. To resolve the apparent contradiction between Luke and Acts.[136]
3. To advance a theological distinction between the time of Jesus and the Church Age, (e.g. between Luke and Acts).[137]
4. To downplay the representation of Jesus being taken up physically (a general tendency of the Western text scribe).[138]

---

[133] Despite the caution earlier that each variant should stand on its own, the variants in 24:51 and 52 are clearly linked together. The worship of Jesus in 24:52 is the consequence of his being raised up into heaven. This linkage also tends to reduce the impact of Codex Sinaiticus' omission of 24:51, since it does contain the long text in 24:52; the existence of the long text in 24:52 suggests the prior existence of the long text in 24:51. See further on the need for linking these two variants, A. W. Zwiep, "The Text of the Ascension Narratives," *NTS* 42 (1996): 225–26.

[134] Lohfink, 171–74.

[135] Metzger, *Textual Commentary*, 163.

[136] B. H. Streeter, *The Four Gospels* (London: MacMillan and Co., 1951), 142; cf. Metzger, *Textual Commentary*, 163.

[137] Metzger, *Textual Commentary*, 163.

[138] Eldon Epp, "Ascension in the Textual Tradition of Luke-Acts," in *New*

Of these arguments in favor of the longer text (and the reason for the Western text's shorter reading), the strongest is that a scribe deleted 24:51 in order to reduce the difficulties with Acts 1 (item 2). I will return to this shortly. The other arguments have what appear to be significant difficulties. In the first place, while a mechanical error is always possible, it would appear that text in 24:51 must be taken together with 24:52; the long text of προσκυνήσαντες αὐτόν in 24:52 fits only with the long text in 24:51, while the shorter text in 24:51 coheres only with the shorter text in 24:52. While the similar beginnings και α ... και α might explain the omission of the phrase in 24:51, they hardly explain the omission of προσκυνήσαντες αὐτόν in 24:52. And while a similar explanation can be offered for 24:52, the probability that both omissions arose from different mechanical errors is very low. The proposal that a scribe would have attempted to emphasize a distinction between the age of Jesus and the age of the Church by deleting the Ascension and worship of Jesus in Luke implies a sophistication for which there is little evidence.

Eldon Epp's study of the Western textual tradition of the Ascension does raise significant questions about the tendencies in the Western text. He studies Western variants in five texts: Luke 24:51; Acts 1:2, 9, 11 and 22. He finds a tendency in those readings to eliminate or diminish the impact of a physical ascension. The variants are as follows:

In Luke 24:51:[139]   omit ἀνεφέρετο εἰς τὸ οὐρανόν
                       read ἀπέστη ἀπ' αὐτῶν instead of διέστη ἀπ' αὐτῶν

In Acts 1:2:[140]   omit ἀνελήμφθη
                       modify the participle clause ἐντειλάμενος to a finite

---

Testament Textual Criticism (Oxford: Clarendon Press, 1981), 131–45.

[139] In ℵ* D it sy^s.

[140] Omit ἀναλήμφθη in gig t* Augustine Vigilius Ephraem, move to after ἡμέρας in D d sy^{p,hmg} co. Add ἐκέλευσε in D d sy^{hmg} Aug. Vig. Eph. Add κηρύσσειν τὸ εὐαγγέλιον in D d ar gig t lux vg^{codd} sy^{hmg} cop and Fathers.

| | verb clause ἐκέλευσε
add κηρύσσειν τὸ εὐαγγέλιον |
| --------------- | ---------------------- |
| In Acts 1:9:[141] | omit αὐτῶν βλεπόντων ἐπήρθη καὶ
modify to ἀπήρθη ἀπὸ ὀφθαλμῶν αὐτῶν |
| In Acts 1:11:[142] | omit εἰς τὸν οὐρανόν
modify the strength of ἀναλημφθείς with receptus or acceptus instead of assumptus |
| In Acts 1:22:[143] | read assumptus for ἀναλημφθείς |

The patterns of omission in Luke 24:51; Acts 1:2; and Acts 1:11 are especially noteworthy, suggesting an extensive pattern of either omission or expansion.[144] But Epp's argument is weakened by the lack of consistency in witnesses to the Western text that he offers. While Luke 24:51; Acts 1:2; and Acts 1:11 share at least Codex Bezae along with some Old Latin witnesses, the other examples are missing either in Bezae, or the Latin. Epp has constructed a Western "type" without a single coherent example of a text that can be traced to a scribe.[145]

Ehrman argues that such harmonization between different books, though a common solution to the problem, cannot be shown to be a

---

[141] In D.

[142] For the omission of εις τον ουρανον, D d gig t* vg[codd] cop[bo]. For the modification of ἀναλήμφθεις, e gig p for receptus, Augustine for acceptus.

[143] In gig p.

[144] Surprisingly, Mikael Parsons (*The Departure of Jesus in Luke-Acts* [Sheffield: JSOT Press, 1987]) consistently maintains the originality of the shorter text in Luke — arguing that P^{75} engaged in a thoroughgoing textual tendency, including interpolation in Luke and John — and yet in Acts, he argues for the longer text — that the Western text has omitted text as part of a harmonization with the short reading in Luke. He is aware of the tension in his approach, but does not, in my opinion, adequately address it.

[145] Ehrman, 231.

pattern of scribal activity.[146] But are his negative examples of unresolved conflict between accounts similar in nature to the Ascension accounts? Only Luke and Acts, both commonly acknowledged to be by the same author and connected by the linking prefaces, contain accounts of the physical ascension of Jesus. That these lone references to the Ascension would be compared is not surprising; they would seem as likely to be harmonized as the Gospel accounts, instances of which are readily accepted. It is easy to understand why a scribe would have worried about harmonizing Luke and Acts, given the importance of the Ascension in the proclamation of the early church:[147] such an event, addressed in narrative only by Luke and Acts, should be consistently related; inconsistencies could be attributed to previous corruption. Although Epp's study is not convincing, in itself, as an explanation of the textual variant in Luke 24:51, it does illustrate a feature that is significant: in some versions of Acts 1:2, the reference to the Ascension is also eliminated. In other words, some scribes of the Western text tradition, upon deleting the text in Luke 24:51, also felt compelled to omit the text in Acts 1:2, thus eliminating entirely the seeming contradiction between Luke 24:51 and Acts 1. What is particularly noteworthy is that one portion of the Western textual tradition in the Ascension accounts of Luke and Acts specifically supports this harmonizing tendency: deletions were made to either Luke 24:51 or Acts 1:2 or 1:11 in various attempts to resolve the seeming problem of two separate ascensions.

Turning to arguments for the shorter text, the following proposals have been offered why a scribe would interpolate the text:

1. To reconcile Luke with Acts 1:2.[148]

---

[146] Ehrman, 230 and 259, n. 192.

[147] This importance, aside from its inclusion in the early creeds, can be seen in non-narrative references to the Ascension in the New Testament, i.e. John 6:62; 20:17; Eph 4:8–10; 1 Tim 3:16; 1 Pet 3:21–2; Heb 9:24; 4:14.

[148] Creed, 301; Alfred Plummer, *The Gospel According to St. Luke*, ICC (New York: Charles Scribner's Sons, 1902), xx.

2. To strengthen the physical Resurrection of Jesus.[149]

The proposal that a scribe added the reference καὶ ἀνεφέρετο εἰς τὸν οὐρανόν in order to provide the prior reference suggested by Acts 1:2 falls on two grounds. First, if a scribe had intended to harmonize the two texts by interpolations, it seems more probable that he would have added one of the words used in Acts (e.g., ἀναλαμβάνω or ἐπαίρω or πορεύομαι). Second, it is difficult to imagine that a scribe, adding text to Luke in order to minimize difficulties, would not have realized that the addition created other problems of coherence.

As he does with other Western non-interpolations, Ehrman finds the solution in a scribal interpolation for theological reasons. He explains a scribe's addition of the Ascension narrative at Luke 24:51 (and 24:52) as an attempt to strengthen the anti-docetic focus of the text. With the interpolations added, the text is even clearer that Jesus was *bodily* raised and that he *bodily* ascended to heaven. This is a possible explanation, but as with 24:12, the interpolations would have been added to narrative units that already make clear the bodily Resurrection and ascension of Jesus. While the text is strengthened by the interpolation, it is already clear at least in Acts that Jesus was bodily raised.

Summary. The intrinsic arguments from style and internal coherence are not decisive, but they would appear to tilt toward authenticity of the longer text in both 24:51 and 52. The very fact that Luke 24:51 uses slightly different vocabulary is more an argument for originality than for interpolation. But the seeming contradiction between Luke and Acts might have led some scribes to attempt emendation. It is likely that Western scribes, in an effort to reduce the conflict, deleted text in Luke 24:51 and 52, as well as in some instances in Acts 1.

---

[149] Ehrman, 231.

CONCLUSIONS

The external evidence from the manuscripts is very heavily in favor of the longer texts in this group of textual variants. Notwithstanding the well-noted tendency of the Western text toward expansion and variation, there is also a noted pattern of omission. The pattern of Western omission, often harmonizing omission, adds some support to the probability that Western scribes did delete text. But despite the overwhelming external evidence, it is nonetheless clear that the shorter text is very early and thus cannot be completely disregarded, especially if there are no compelling internal arguments that would explain the deletion of the textual variants by a Western scribe.

As the language of this chapter has repeatedly indicated, textual arguments are by their very nature arguments from probability. Since there are here (at least) two competing textual traditions that date from a very early period in the text's transmission, the focus of the argument is necessarily on the internal arguments from intrinsic probability (style) and transcriptional probability. But despite the tentative nature of the arguments, the following conclusions about the original form of the text in Luke 22 and 24 can be offered with some confidence.

1. Luke 22:19b–20. The internal arguments from intrinsic probability, both style and theological content, and from transcriptional probability strongly support the short text. The longer form of the text was an interpolation to bring it in line with other versions of the Lord's Supper and to add atoning features to Luke's account.

2. Luke 24:3. The internal arguments are not decisive. The strength of the external evidence argues for the longer form of the text as most likely original.

3. Luke 24:6. The transcriptional probability suggests that the longer text is probably a harmonizing interpolation from Matthew. The shorter text is probably original.

4. Luke 24:9. Based on stylistic features, the longer text is considered original. The omission was likely caused by mechanical error.

5. Luke 24:12. The internal argument from style is not decisive, but signs of Luke's editorial hand and of Johannine similarity point to the authenticity of the longer text. The longer text's deletion by scribes as part of an effort to rid the church of the Johannine literature seems more likely than its inclusion as an anti-docetic move. The text was likely omitted because it sounded too Johannine. The longer text is considered original.

6. Luke 24:36. Based on transcriptional probability, the longer text is considered original. The text was likely omitted because it sounded too Johannine.

7. Luke 24:40. Based on transcriptional probability, the longer text is considered original. The text was likely omitted because it sounded too Johannine.

8. Luke 24:51. The stylistic arguments against the longer text are not compelling. Instead, it appears that the text was omitted by scribes in an effort to avoid a seeming conflict with the Ascension in Acts 1.

9. Luke 24:52. This textual variant is linked with 24:51. With the ascension deleted in 24:51, the account of worship of Jesus is likewise considered suspect. Both were deleted as part of a move to avoid conflict with Acts 1.

APPENDIX:
INSTANCES WHERE THE WESTERN TEXT IS SHORTER

The following list of textual variants was culled from the NA[27]. The criterion for inclusion was simply an omission's being cited in the Gospels represented by a combination of Codex Bezae (D) and at least one Old Latin or Old Syriac manuscript.[1] The simplistic assumption used was that the published Greek text is more or less correct and that variations are, indeed, omissions. The assumption was merely a working one used to provide a snapshot of a tendency. Clearly, many of the variants are the result of oversights or mechanical errors. But an interesting pattern of Western omissions does appear that tends to comment on the widely stated tendency that the Western text is expansionist.

LUKE	MISSING TEXT	DOCUMENTS
1:56	ὡς	D *pc* it sa bo[pt]
2:9	κυρίου	D *pc* it
2:37	ἕως / ὡς	D it
4:34	ἔα	p) D 33 *pc* it sy[s] co
4:40	αὐτῶν	D 565 *pc* lat
5:12	ἐδεήθη αὐτοῦ	D e r[1]
5:26	καὶ ἔκστασις ἔλαβεν ἅπαντες καὶ ἐδόξαζον τὸν θεὸν	D W Ψ 1241 al e
5:39	καὶ οὐδεὶς πιὼν παλιὸν θέλει νέον· λέγει γὰρ ὁ παλαιὸς χρηστός ἐστιν	p) D it Mcion Ir Eus
6:34	τὰ ἴσα	D it sy[s]
6:45	γὰρ	D W *pc*
6:49	εὐθὺς	D a c
7:3	πρὸς αὐτὸν	D f[13] 700 *pc* it bo[ms]
7:4	πρὸς τὸν Ἰησοῦν	D it

---

[1] In the case of the first eight chapters of John, Sinaiticus was also included since it is a witness to the Western text in this portion of John; Gordon Fee, "Codex Sinaiticus in the Gospel of John: A Contribution to Methodology in Establishing Textual Relationships," *NTS* 15 (1968–69): 23–44.

Western Non-Interpolations 225

7:7	διὸ οὐδὲ ἐμαυτὸν ἠξίωσα πρὸς σὲ ἐλθεῖν	D 700* it sy^s
7:30	εἰς ἑαυτούς	ℵ *pc* sa
7:46	τοὺς πόδας μου	D W 079 it
7:47	ὅτι ἠγάπησεν πολύ· ᾧ δὲ ὀλίγον ἀφίεται ὀλίγον ἀγαπᾷ	D (e)
8:13	τῆς πέτρας	D e
8:15	καλῇ καὶ	D it
8:32	ἱκανῶν	D c r bo^{pt}
8:44	τοῦ κρασπέδου	p) D it
9:8	τις	D *pc* a e
9:15	καὶ κατέκλιναν ἅπαντας	D *pc*
9:16	καὶ κατέκλασεν	D q
9:23	καὶ ἀράτω τὸν σταυρὸν αὐτοῦ	D a l
9:23	καθ' ἡμέραν	p) ℵ C D M it sy^{s,hmg} sa^{ma}
9:48	αὐτοῦς	P45 D it sy^{s,c}
10:19	οὐ μὴ	ℵ* D, Did
10:22	μου	D a c l vg sy^s; Mcion
10:23	κατ' ἰδίαν	D 1424 *pc* lat sy$^{s.c}$
10:24	καὶ βασιλεῖς	p) D it; Mcion
10:42	γὰρ	D *pc* lat sy$^{s.c}$
11:26	τότε	D sy^c bo^{ms}
11:26	ἐκεῖ	D 33 it
11:46	τοῖς φορτίοις	D (a) b^{vid} q sy$^{s.c}$
11:49	καὶ ἡ σοφία τοῦ θεοῦ εἶπεν	p) D b; Lcf
12:19	κείμενα εἰς ἔτη πολλά ἀναπαύου, φάγε, πίε	D it
12:21	οὕτως ὁ θησαυρίζων ἑαυτῷ καὶ μὴ εἰς θεὸν πλουτῶν	D a b
13:17	ταῦτα λέγοντος αὐτοῦ	D e
13:17	πάντες	P45 D it
14:2	τις	D f^1 *pc*
14:10	πάντων	D W Ψ M lat sy^s
14:22	κύριε	D c e
14:25	πολλοί	D Θ it sy^c
16:6	καθίσας ταχέως	D bo^{ms}
16:18	ἀπὸ ἀνδρὸς	D 28 *pc* sy$^{s.p}$ bo^{ms}

16:19	δὲ	D Δ Θ *pc* lat sy[s]
17:24	εἰς τὴν ὑπ' οὐρανὸν	D 700 *pc* it
18:2	λέγων	P75 B D it sa
18:9	τὴν παραβολὴν ταύτην	D f[1] *pc* sy[s.c.p]
18:29	ὅτι	ℵ* D Δ lat
18:32	καὶ ὑβρισθήσεται	p) D L 700 1241 *pc* it
18:34	τοῦτο	D f[1] *pc* it sy[s.c]
18:39	πολλῷ	D c sa
18:40	πρὸς αὐτόν	D f[1] *pc* it sy[s.c]
19:2	καὶ αὐτός	D e sa
19:7	λέγοντες	D it sy[c]
19:24	τὴν μνᾶν	D a e s
19:25	vs) καὶ εἶπαν αὐτῷ· κύριε, ἔχει δέκα μνᾶς	p) D W 69 *pc* b e ff[2] sy[s.c] bo[ms]
19:31	διὰ τί λύετε	p) D it
19:43	ἐπὶ σὲ	D sy[s.c]
20:16	τούτους	D e sy[s] co
20:36	καὶ υἱοί εἰσιν	D *pc* it sy[s]
22:11	σοι	D N 063 1241 *pc* q sy[s.c.p]
22:19–20	τὸ ὑπὲρ ὑμῶν διδόμενον· τοῦτο ποιεῖτε εἰς τὴν ἐμὴν ἀνάμνησιν. καὶ τὸ ποτήριον ὡσαύτως μετὰ τὸ δειπνῆσαι λέγων· τοῦτο τὸ ποτήριον ἡ καινὴ διαθήκη ἐν τῷ αἵματί μου τὸ ὑπὲρ ὑμῶν ἐκχυννόμενον.	D it
22:22	τῷ ἀνθρώπῳ	D e sy[s.c]
22:37	γὰρ	D 1423 it sy[s.c]
22:52	Ἰησοῦς	D f[1] *pc* e i l sy[s].
23:39	οὐχὶ σὺ εἶ ὁ χριστός; σῶσον σεαυτὸν καὶ ἡμᾶς	D e
24:1	ἀρώματα	D it sy[s.c]
24:9	ἀπὸ τοῦ μνημείου	D it
24:12	ὁ δὲ Πέτρος ἀναστὰς ἔδραμεν ἐπὶ τὸ μνημεῖον καὶ παρακύψα· βλέπει τὸ ὀθόνια μόνα καὶ ἀπῆλθεν πρὸς ἑαυτὸν θαυμάζων τὸ γεγονός.	D it

Western Non-Interpolations 227

24:30	μετ' αὐτῶν	D e sy$^{s.c}$
24:36	καὶ λέγει αὐτοῖς· εἰρήνη ὑμῖν	D it
24:40	καὶ τοῦτο εἰπὼν ἔδειξεν αὐτοῖς τὰς χεῖρας καὶ τοὺς πόδας.	D it sy$^{s.c}$
24:49	τοῦ πατρός	D e
24:51	καὶ ἀναφέρετο	ℵ* D it sy^s
24:52	προσκυνήσαντες αὐτὸν	D it sy^s

MARK	MISSING TEXT	DOCUMENTS
1:6	καὶ ζώνην δερματίνην περὶ τὴν ὀσφὺν αὐτοῦ	D it
1:45	πολλὰ	D W latt
2:22	ἀλλὰ οἶνον νέον εἰς ἀσκοὺς καινούς	D it bo^{ms}
2:26	ἐπὶ Ἀβιαθὰρ ἀρχιερέως	p) D W pc it sy^s
3:5	συλλυπούμενος	W b c d
3:8	καὶ ἀπὸ τῆς Ἰδουμαίας	p) ℵ* W Θ f1 pc c sy^s
3:29	εἰς τὸν αἰῶνα	D W Θ 1.28.565.700 pc it (sy^s); Cyp
4:3	σπεῖραι	D sa^{ms} bo^{pt}
4:19	καὶ αἱ περὶ τὰ λοιπὰ ἐπιθυμίαι	D (Θ) W f^1 28. (565.700) it
4:24	καὶ προστεθήσεται ὑμῖν	p) D W 565 pc b e l sa^{ms} vg^{mss}
5:22	ὀνόματι Ἰάϊρος	D it
5:43	πολλὰ	D 1424 pc it
6:48	πρὸς αὐτοὺς	D W Θ 565 it
6:53	καὶ προσωρμίσθησαν	D W Θ f^{1,13} 28.565. 700 it sy$^{s.p}$
7:30	αὐτῆς	P45 D W f^1 28 it bo^{ms}
9:35	καὶ λέγει αὐτοῖς· εἴ τις θέλει πρῶτος εἶναι, ἔσται πάντων ἔσχατος καὶ πάντων διάκονος	D k
10:30	νῦν	D pc a q sy^s
10:32	οἱ δὲ ἀκολουθοῦντες ἐφοβοῦντο	D K f^{13} 28.700.1010 al a b

228   In Dialogue with Another Gospel?

10:34	μαστιγώσουσιν αὐτὸν καὶ ἀποκτενοῦσιν	D pc ff² (k)
11:9	ὡσαννά	D W it
11:28	ἤ τίς σοι ἔδωκεν τὴν ἐχουσίαν ταύτην ἵνα ταῦτα ποιῇς;	D pc k
12:13	πρὸς αὐτόν	D it sa^{ms}
12:14	δῶμεν ἤ μὴ δῶμεν;	D it (sy^s)
12:30	καὶ ἐξ ὅλης τῆς διανοίας σου	D pc c
12:42	πτωχὴ	D Θ 565 it
13:9	βλέπετε δὲ ὑμεῖς ἑαυτούς	D W Θ f¹ 28.565.700 it sy^s
13:19	ἥν ἔκτισεν ὁ θεὸς	D Θ 565 pc it
13:22	ψευδόχριστοι καὶ	D pc i k
14:1	καὶ τὰ ἄζυμα	D a ff²
14:1	ἐν δόλῳ	D a i r¹
14:21	ὁ υἱὸς τοῦ ἀνθρώπου	D 700 a
14:39	τὸν αὐτὸν λόγον εἰπών	D it
14:45	ἐλθὼν εὐθὺς	D Θ (f¹) 565.700 pc it (sy^{s.p})
14:61	πάλιν ὁ ἀρχιερεὺς ἐπηρώτα αὐτὸν	D a ff²
14:65	καὶ περικαλύπτειν αὐτοῦ τὸ πρόσωπον	D a sy^s bo^{mss}
14:65	οἱ ὑπηρέται	D c k
14:70	τῷ Πέτρῳ	D a
14:72	ὅτι πρὶν ἀλέκτορα φωνῆσαι δὶς τρίς με ἀπαρνήσῃ	D a
15:19	καὶ τιθέντες τὰ γόνατα προσεκύνουν αὐτῷ	p) D pc k
15:24	τίς τί ἄρῃ	D pc it sy^s
15:34	ὁ Ἰησοῦς	D Θ pc i k sy^s bo^{pt}
15:41	καὶ διηκόνουν αὐτῷ	C D Δ pc n
16:1	διαγενομένου	D (k) n

MATTHEW MISSING TEXT   **DOCUMENTS**

3:6	ποταμῷ	C³ D L f¹³ M lat mae
4:4	ἐκπορευομένῳ διὰ στόματος	D a b g¹
5:11	ψευδόμενοι	D it sy^s; Tert
5:13	ἔτι	D W it sy^{s.c.p}; Cyp

Western Non-Interpolations 229

5:30	καὶ εἰ ἡ δεξιά σου χεὶρ σκανδαλίζει σε, ἔκκοψον αὐτὴν καὶ βάλε ἀπὸ σου· συμφέρει γὰρ σοι ἵνα ἀπόληται ἕν τῶν μελῶν σου καὶ μὴ ὅλον τὸ σῶμά σου εἰς γέενναν ἀπέλθῃ	D pc vg^{ms} sy^s bo^{ms}
5:32	καὶ ὅς ἐὰν ἀπολελυμένην γαμήσῃ μοιχᾶται	D pc a b k; Or?
5:38	καὶ	D f^{13} it mae
6:10	ὡς	D* a b c k bo^{mss}
9:22	Ἰησοῦς	ℵ* D pc it sy^s
9:34	οἱ δὲ Φαρισαῖοι ἔλεγον· ἐν τῷ ἄρχοντι τῶν δαιμονίων ἐκβάλλει τὰ δαιμόνια.	D a k sy^s; Hil
10:17	δὲ	D 28 pc it sy^s sa^{mss} mae
12:11	ἐὰν	D f^{13} 700* pc b ff^2 sy$^{s.c}$ sa bo
12:11	τοῦτο	D it sy$^{s.c.p}$
12:49	αὐτοῦ	ℵ* D al lat; Epiph
13:1	τῆς οἰκίας	D it sy^s
13:26	καὶ	D W Θ f^{13} 1010.1424 pc it sy$^{s.c}$ sa mae bo^{ms}
13:46	ἕνα	D Θ pc sy^c
14:3	Φιλίππου	D lat
14:22	αὐτόν	D it
14:24	ἤδη	D 28 pc lat sy$^{c.p}$ co
15:28	ὁ Ἰησοῦς	D Γ pc (sy$^{s.c}$) sa^{mss}
16:4	καὶ μοιχαλὶς	p) D it
16:12	τῶν ἄρτων	D Θ f^{13} 565 pc a b ff^2 sy^s
16:14	οἱ μὲν	D W it
18:18	ἔσται δεδεμένα ἐν οὐρανῷ, καὶ ὅσα ἐὰν λύσητε ἐπὶ τῆς γῆς	D* n
18:34	πᾶν	D pc sy^s
21:32	οὐδὲ	D (c) e ff^{1*} sy^s

21:44	καὶ ὁ πεσὼν ἐπὶ τὸν λίθον τοῦτον συνθλασθήσεται· ἐφ' ὃν δ' ἂν πέσῃ λικμήσει αὐτόν.	D 33 it sy^s; Eus
22:17	εἰπὲ οὖν ἡμῖν	D *pc* it sy^s
23:34	καὶ ἐξ αὐτῶν μαστιγώσετε ἐν ταῖς συναγωγαῖς ὑμῶν	D a; Lcf
25:24	σε	D Θ *pc* lat sa mae
25:29	παντὶ	D W *pc* sy^p
26:22	αὐτῷ	P37^{vid}.45 D Θ f^{13} 700.1424 *pc* latt sy^s mae bo; Eus
26:34	ἐν	P37 D it
26:44	ἐκ τρίτου	P37 A D K f^1 565. 1424 al it
26:73	καὶ σὺ	p) D Θ f^1 *pc* sy^s sa^{ms}
28:7	ἀπὸ τῶν νεκρῶν	D 565 *pc* lat sy^s; arm

JOHN	MISSING TEXT	DOCUMENTS
1:25	καὶ ἠρώτησαν αὐτόν	ℵ a e sy^c
1:46	καὶ	ℵ *pc* a b e sy$^{s.p}$
2:6	κείμεναι	ℵ* *pc* a e
3:28	ὅτι	ℵ A D L Ws Θ Ψ 086 f^1 33 Koine lat
3:28	ἐγὼ	D Ws 086 a aur ff^2 j l sy^c
3:31	ἐπάνω πάντων ἐστίν	P75 ℵ* D f^1 565 *pc* it sy^c sa Hipp Or Eus
4:9	οὐ γὰρ συγχρῶνται Ἰουδαῖοι Σαμαρίταις	ℵ* D a b e j
4:11	οὖν	ℵ D Ws *pc* it sy$^{s.c.p}$ sa^{mss} bo^{mss}
4:17	αὐτῷ	ℵ(*) A D K L Ws Γ Δ Θ Ψ 1.13 565 579 ...lat sy^h ^{amss}
4:24	αὐτόν	ℵ* D* ff^2 (j)
4:38	ὃ	D* L Ws (*pc*) e
4:39	εἰς αὐτόν	ℵ* *pc* a e

Western Non-Interpolations   231

4:51	αὐτοῦ	ℵ D L Ψ f¹ 565 892 1241 *pc* lat
5:9	ἐν ἐκείνῃ τῇ ἡμέρᾳ	D e
5:18	οὖν	ℵ D *pc* it sy^p pbo bo^m
5:25	καὶ νῦν ἐστιν	ℵ* a b Tert
6:36	ἔξω	ℵ* D ^pc a b e sy^s.c
6:42	καὶ τὴν μητέρα	ℵ* W b sy^s.c
7:6	οὖν	ℵ* D W *pc* e sy^s.c.p pbo bo^bt
7:9	δὲ	ℵ D K Θ 070 f¹ 33 565 1424 al lat pbo bo^ms
7:10	ὡς	ℵ D 1424 *pc* it sy^s.c ac² mf pbo
7:33	με	ℵ D *pc* lat pbo bo^bt
7:36	με	P66 ℵ D L W Θ Ψ 0105 f¹³ 33 koine lat
7:47	οὖν	ℵ D f¹ 33 579 1424 al it sy^s.c.p co
8:16	πατήρ	ℵ* D sy^s.c
8:34	τῆς ἁμαρτίας	D b sy^s
8:53	πατρὸς ἡμῶν	D W it sy^s pbo
8:58	γενέσθαι	D it
9:2	αὐ᾿οῦ λέγον᾿ε᾿	D e
9:28	δὲ	D it
10:18	ἀλλ᾽ ἐγὼ τίθημι αὐτὴν ἀπ᾽ ἐμαυτου	D l
10:38	καὶ γινώσκητε	D 1424 (it) sy^s
10:41	ὅτι	ℵ D *pc* c e
11:18	ὡς	D W sy^s
12:8	v) τοὺς πτωχοὺς γὰρ πάντοτε ἔχετε μεθ᾽ ἑαυτῶν, ἐμὲ δὲ οὐ πάντοτε ἔχετε	D sy^s
12:9	μόνον	D *pc* be sy^s
12:31	τούτου	P66* D W pc lat sy^s ac² pbo bo^ms
13:25	οὕτως	ℵ A D W Θ Ψ f¹ 565 579 700 892 1241 lat sy sa pbo bo
13:27	μετὰ τὸ ψωμίον	
15:17	ἵνα	D e bo^ms
15:24	καὶ	ℵ* D 579 844 ^pc it bo

16:18	ἔλεγον οὖν	P66 D it vg^{mss}
16:28	ἐξῆλθον παρὰ τοῦ πατρὸς	D* it sy^s
17:8	καὶ ἔγνωσαν	D W b ff² sy^s ac² pbo
		ℵ* A D W *pc* a e q
		ac² pbo
17:14	καθὼς ἐγὼ οὐκ εἰμὶ ἐκ τοῦ κόσμου	P66* D f¹³ *pc* it sy^s
20:21	ὁ Ἰησοῦς	ℵ D L W Ψ 050 844
		pc lat sy^s co

Chapter 5

LUKE'S EDITORIAL METHOD AND THE APPROACH OF THIS STUDY

Important to this investigation is the question of how Luke went about constructing his Gospel. The general consensus on Luke's method of composition follows the classic solution to the synoptic problem. The center of the majority view of the synoptic question is the two-source theory, which sees Matthew and Luke as primarily dependent on Mark and an additional common source, "Q."[1] While this basic paradigm has some significant problems[2] and, indeed, has been challenged recently, especially by scholars who argue for Mat-

---

[1] See recent summaries of the argument in E. P. Sanders and Margaret Davies, *Studying the Synoptic Gospels* (Valley Forge: Trinity Press International, 1989), 51–66, and Robert Stein, *The Synoptic Problem* (Grand Rapids: Baker Book House, 1987), 45–112. A good review of the major issues and argument for the majority approach, is also found in Werner Kümmel, *Introduction to the New Testament* (Nashville: Abingdon Press, 1975), 42–80, as well as Joseph Fitzmyer, *The Gospel According to Luke* (I-IX) (Garden City, NY: Doubleday & Co., 1981), 63–97.

[2] As, for instance, the difficulty of the minor agreements between Matthew and Luke against Mark. See the problems raised in Sanders and Davies, 67–73.

thean priority[3] or those who are not convinced of the viability of Q,[4] it is held as the working approach by the majority of Gospel students.

Whether one follows the two source theory or Farrer/Drury/Goulder's alternate theory of Markan priority without Q, much of Luke can be explained; still there remain a number of much of Luke can be explained; still there remain a number of questions concerning its composition. A comparison of Luke with Mark and Matthew reveals unique Lukan material—material that either is additional or is significantly different in presentation from Mark and Matthew. That unique material needs an explanation.

The additional material is manifest in Luke primarily in narrative blocks that bear no relation to Mark or Matthew. A quick glance at some of that material will underline how significant it is to Luke:[5]

* The Infancy Narrative, 1:5–2:52
* Jesus' visit to Nazareth, 4:17–30[6]
* The Raising of the widow of Nain's son, 7:12–17
* The Parable of lost coin, 15:8–10
* The Parable of prodigal son, 15:11–32
* The Parable of dishonest manager, 16:1–8
* The Parable of the rich man and Lazarus, 16:19–31
* The Cleansing of ten lepers, 17:12–19
* The Zacchaeus story, 19:1–10
* Jesus' trial before Herod, 23:6–12
* Jesus' appearance on road to Emmaus, 24:13–35

---

[3] Cf. William R. Farmer, *The Synoptic Problem: A Critical Analysis* (New York: Macmillan, 1964).

[4] A. M. Farrer, "On Dispensing with Q," in *Studies in the Gospels: Essays in Memory of R. H. Lightfoot* (Oxford: Blackwell, 1955), 55-88; M. D. Goulder, *Luke: A New Paradigm* (Sheffield: JSOT Press, 1989); John Drury, *Tradition and Design in Luke's Gospel* (London: Darton, Longman & Todd, 1976).

[5] See Fitzmyer, *Luke* (I–IX), 83–84 for a more inclusive list of unique material, as well as B. H. Streeter, *The Four Gospels* (London: Macmillan, 1951), 198.

[6] The feature of a preaching in the Synagogue is similar to Mark 6:1–6, but the contents of the sermon in Luke, which are significant, are unique.

* Jesus' appearance to disciples in Jerusalem, 24:36–43

Indeed, much of the section from 9:51–18:14 (the so-called Great Interpolation) is unique to Luke. In these instances, where there appears to be no parallel with other Gospels, one can conclude either that Luke drew on a special source or sources or that he freely composed the material.

The second type of unique Lukan material—seen in the Passion narrative—is presented in a very different way than in the "L" passages discussed above. Instead of such material being found in blocks, Luke often seems to follow Mark, at least in a general way, and yet presents significant variations from the Second Gospel.[7] The variations are characterized by the addition of new material, a significant freedom from the Markan source, and a frequent tendency toward transposition of order. While Mark appears to have been the primary source for Luke in these passages, it is possible, and frequently suggested, that an independent narrative, which is somewhat similar to Mark, was used instead.[8]

Luke's Gospel, especially in the Passion narrative, presents an interesting question about his use of sources and his editorial or compositional approach. In general, there have been three different approaches to understanding Luke's use of sources:

1. A careful analysis of Luke's language and style to discriminate, on a word-by-word basis, between sources and redaction;

2. An emphasis primarily on Luke's own creative efforts in working with sources and composing narrative material;

3. An attempt to detect sources, based on content, while allowing Luke's considerable flexibility as an editor/composer.

These three approaches will be examined in more detail below.

---

[7] John Hawkins, "Three Limitations to St. Luke's Use of St. Mark's Gospel," in *Studies in the Synoptic Problem*, ed. W. Sanday (Oxford: Clarendon Press, 1911), 76–94.

[8] The theory of a connected narrative that was used in preference to Mark in Luke's Passion narrative is detailed, for instance, in Vincent Taylor, *Behind the Third Gospel* (Oxford: Clarendon Press, 1926), 33–75, and in a revised form in *The*

THE SURGICAL KNIFE:
SEPARATING SOURCE AND REDACTION IN LUKE

Given the strong probability that Luke has used other sources besides Mark and merged them skillfully into his Gospel, several analyses of Luke have sought to distinguish between Luke's own editorial work and his use of sources. The method used is a very careful linguistic analysis of the text. Four scholars in particular best exemplify this approach in Lukan studies.

FRIEDRICH REHKOPF

As a first step in evaluating the probability that Luke used sources other than Mark in the Passion narrative, Friedrich Rehkopf focuses his attention on two pericopes of Luke 22: verses 21–23 (the announcement of betrayal) and verses 47–53 (the arrest of Jesus).[9] He finds that Luke in these pericopes contains (a) several variations in the order of material from Mark; (b) some additional material not found in Mark; (c) a scarcity of agreement in wording with Mark, and (d) seven specific agreements with John.[10] The combination of these features leads Rehkopf to argue that Luke used a separate source alongside Mark in the construction of the passages—indeed, that Luke used that source as the chief source for his Passion narrative, expanding it through occasional use of Mark.[11]

Rehkopf's approach is to analyze the text, asking whether individual words or phrases in Luke's version can be attributed to Mark or to Luke's editorial changes, or whether it must come from another source. Initially, Rehkopf ascertains roughly the degree of

---

Passion Narrative of St. Luke (Cambridge: University Press, 1972).

[9] F. Rehkopf, *Die lukanische Sonderquelle* (Tübingen: J. C. B. Mohr [Paul Siebeck], 1959).

[10] Rehkopf, 83. Note in particular the agreements with John in Luke 22:15–23 (cf. John 13:22, the disciples looked at each other); 22:23; 22:47a; 22:50; 22:51a; 22:53b; 22:54a.

[11] Rehkopf, 84.

Markan material in a pericope. He then uses five criteria to distinguish between Lukan redaction and pre-Lukan material. A word or phrase is deemed pre-Lukan in the following cases:

1. It was rarely or never used by Luke himself.
2. It is a term that Luke regularly changed when he modified Mark.
3. It is a close substitute for a more regularly used Lukan word.
4. It occurs with some frequency in non-Markan material.
5. It is rarely or never found in the Acts speeches or "we" material.[12]

Employing these criteria, Rehkopf works through the text and distinguishes word by word between Luke's own editorial work and Luke's other sources. For instance, in Luke 22:22 he discerns the following:[13]

1. ὅτι is from Mark.
2. The placement of μέν (and absence of a corresponding δέ)is a variation from Mark, but it is not consistent with Luke's customary good classical Greek. This is a sign of a distinct non-Markan source.
3. The use of πορεύεται instead of ὑπάγει is attributable to Luke's stylistic tendencies.
4. κατὰ τὸ ὡρισμένον instead of Mark's καθὼς γέγραπται περὶ αὐτοῦ is not Lukan, and, with Luke 22:53 (this is your ὥρα), points to a pre-Lukan source.
5. The use of πλὴν οὐαί, instead of Mark's οὐαὶ δέ, points to a variant translation of a common Aramaic original, as the use of πλὴν ἰδοὺ in 22:21 even more strongly suggests.

---
[12] Rehkopf, 87.
[13] Rehkopf, 14-22.

6. The shortening of the final clause by the deletion of a repetitive ὁ υἱὸς τοῦ ἀνθρώπου is understood as good Lukan editorial practice.
7. The omission of the Markan phrase that it would be better for the betrayer never to have been born is ambiguous. It could be Lukan editorial practice, or it could be missing in another source.

Rehkopf's analysis certainly highlights some of the interesting features of Luke's use of the Markan source. It is clear that Mark 14:18–21 lies behind Luke 22:21–23. But the variations raise questions: is Luke using editorial license, or is another source or tradition having an impact on the Lukan version? Rehkopf claims to be able to define Luke's editorial style so that anything adjudged neither Lukan nor Markan, must necessarily be attributable to another source that Luke used alongside Mark.

TIM SCHRAMM

Tim Schramm's project is on a much larger scale than Rehkopf's. He attempts to explain the unique elements in Luke's units of narrative of that are based on Markan material, the so-called *Markus-Stoff*.[14] The initial impetus for Schramm's study came from two features of the Third Gospel: (1) the occasional occurrence of doublets, in which one is clearly reliant on Mark and the other is not, and in which the pericope derived from Mark shows influence from the non-Markan text;[15] and (2) the existence of Markan style or material in essentially non-Markan pericopes.[16] These two features in Luke's Gospel led

---

[14] Tim Schramm, *Der Markus-Stoff bei Lukas* (Cambridge: University Press, 1971).

[15] The doublets handled by Schramm: (1) Luke 8:16 *par*. Mark 4:21; Luke 11:33 *par.* Matt 5:15; (2) Luke 9:1 f *par*. Mark 6:6 f; Luke 10:1 f *par*. Matt 9:35 f; 3) Luke 11:43 and Luke 20:46, *par*. Mark 12:38 and Matt 23:6 f. Schramm, 23–31.

[16] The non-Markan blocks studied are: Luke 3:3b f; 3:16; 4:1 f; 7:1–10; 7:36–50; 8:4–9:50; 12:10; 11:15 f; 17–23; 10:25–28.

Schramm to believe that Luke was not simply alternating blocks of material between Mark and other source(s), but often was interweaving material from Mark and other source(s).

The doublets in Luke are remarkable because often one of the pericopes shows a strong similarity to Mark and the other, a similarity to Matthew. This suggests that Luke used another source in addition to Mark, a source with accounts very similar to Mark—in this case, Q. Mark and Q, then, are shown to be distinct sources that are yet very similar. What is most important, however, is that Schramm finds that the non-Markan material influenced the Mark-derived accounts.[17] Luke's compositional style, then, seems to have been one that intertwined features of Mark and another parallel source.

This pattern of influence of one source on another can also be found in non-Markan blocks of material in Luke. Markan features find their way into this material, suggesting again Luke's tendency to intertwine sources. Of interest as an example of this inquiry is Schramm's examination of Luke 7:36–50, the pericope of the anointing in Simon's house. Schramm finds this pericope to be closer in many details to John 12:1–8. Yet there are a number of details that could only have been derived from Mark: ἀλάβαστρον μύρου in Luke 7:37; Σίμων in Luke 7:40, 43, 44; and the words of forgiveness in Luke 7:48–50, which echo Mark 2:5 and Mark 5:35.[18] What Schramm proposes, here as in other places, is that Luke used another source (a *Nebenquelle*), but that source was significantly influenced by a similar story in Mark.

From this background understanding of the influence of Mark upon non-Markan material, and the influence of non-Markan doublets upon Markan material, Schramm shifts his focus to the larger issue of the possible influence of other source(s) on blocks of primarily Markan material in Luke, that is, blocks of text in Luke that are clearly based on Mark. Such influences would be indicated by (a) minor agreements of Matthew and Luke against Mark,[19] (b) unique elements that would

---

[17] Schramm, 32.

[18] Schramm, 43–44.

[19] Schramm, 72–77. Schramm sees the minor agreements of Matthew and

point to a Lukan special source (*Sondergut*),[20] and (c) semitisms that are different from those found in Mark.[21] Schramm concludes from his study of the Markan blocks of material that in a number of instances there is evidence that another tradition has influenced Luke's redaction of Markan material.[22]

One can see how this approach works out in Schramm's treatment of Luke 5:12–16.[23] In this pericope, Schramm finds examples of (a) minor agreements, (b) unique material, and (c) semitisms. The minor agreements are the presence of καὶ ἰδού (also a semitism) and κύριε in Luke 5:12 (cf. Matt 8:2, contra Mark 1:40). Along with the minor agreements, Schramm finds unique material: the final section of the pericope, Luke 5:15–16, has a report both of people coming to be healed and of Jesus going out to the wilderness to pray that is not found in the other parallels. And, finally, the pericope contains the following semitisms that are not simply taken over from Mark: καὶ ἐγένετο (v. 12, also a sign of paratactic style), ἐν τῷ εἶναι (v. 12), ἐν μιᾷ τῶν πόλεων (v. 12), καὶ ἰδού (v. 12), καὶ αὐτός (v. 14), ἦν ὑποχωρῶν (v. 16 — a periphrastic construction). For Schramm, these features combined are strong evidence that Luke used an alternative source along with Mark. In addition to the use of Mark (1:40–45) and this other parallel source, Schramm sees Luke's redactional hand as well, as for instance in the phrase ἀνὴρ πλήρης λέπρας (5:12), in ἐδεήθη (5:12), and in παρήγγειλεν (5:14). The result is that Schramm sees a fairly complex mixing of Mark, another source that is very much

---

Luke against Mark as a sign of a source that is parallel with Mark.

[20] Schramm, 77–78.

[21] Schramm, 79–85. Specifically, he lists the following indications of such semitic usage that are indicative of a non-Lukan source: (1) paratactic construction, (2) periphrastic conjunction, (3) construction with ἐγένετο, (4) ἐν μιᾷ τῶν..., (5) ἐν τῷ with infinitive, (6) καὶ ἰδού, and (7) καὶ αὐτός.

[22] The pericopes that show influence of another source or tradition are 5:12–16, 17–26, 33–39; 6:12–19; 8:4–8, (9f.), 16–18, 22–25; 9:1–6, 10–17, 18–22, (23–27), 28–36; 9:37–43a, 43b–45; 18:31–34, (35a); 19:28–38; 20:(1a), 9–19, 27–40, (46); 21:5–36; (22:3). Schramm, 186.

[23] Schramm, 91–99.

like Mark, and Luke's own editorial modifications. And his careful analysis can confidently discriminate between Mark, another source, and Luke's own redactional touches.

JOACHIM JEREMIAS

Jeremias takes an approach similar to Schramm's, but he focuses on the non-Markan material in Luke.[24] For Jeremias, the issue is to distinguish the "Lukan" material from the traditional material in Luke. Obviously, since he deals with non-Markan material, Jeremias does not attempt to locate Markan style, and because that control text is not present, the task is necessarily more speculative. His approach works on a seemingly straightforward methodology of identifying the Lukan lexicon and style, similar to Hawkins and Rehkopf before him.[25]

For each verse that is not in a Mark-derived pericope, Jeremias identifies various elements under the rubrics "Tradition" and "Redaction." Tradition is indicated by style markers that point to a special source; redaction is indicated by use of specifically Lukan language or constructions. Jeremias has set out the following criteria for identifying traditional material:[26]

1. A word, word group, or syntactical construction rarely or never occurs elsewhere in Luke.
2. The word or construction is found in Markan material and generally avoided by Luke.
3. The word or construction has an alternative word in the Lukan lexicon whose use by Luke would be expected.
4. Construction is clearly semitic.

---

[24] J. Jeremias, *Die Sprache des Lukasevangeliums* (Göttingen: Vandenhoeck & Ruprecht, 1980). Non-Markan material, for Jeremias, is found in the following blocks: 1:5–4:30; 5:1–11; 6:20–8:3; 9:51–18:14; 19:1–27, 39–44; 21:34–38; 22:14–24:53.

[25] John Hawkins, *Horae Synopticae* (Oxford: Clarendon Press, 1909).

[26] Jeremias, *Sprache*, 8.

5. The word or construction is clearly limited to non-Markan material.
6. The material can be attested by the rest of the New Testament as traditional material of the church.

As Jeremias develops his study, it appears that Luke took over traditional material and modified it throughout with his own, often extensive, revisions. In the opening verses of the anointing story, for example, Jeremias finds traditional material in the following verses: 7:36, the construction ἠρώτα ... ἵνα; 7:37, and elsewhere, the term ἁμαρτωλός; 7:38, the use of ἄρχομαι plus an infinitive (a semitism that was normally changed when Luke used Mark); 7:39, the term προφήτης; 7:40, the construction καὶ ἀποκριθεὶς ... εἶπεν and the use of the historical present in φησίν. At the same time Jeremias finds clear signs of specifically Lukan language: κατακλίθη in 7:36, evincing Luke's tendency to use κατα-prefixed words; καί ἰδοὺ γυνὴ ... καὶ ἐπιγνοῦσα, the use of ἥτις, and κατάκειται in 7:37; the term παρὰ τοὺς πόδας, along with the term καταπιλέωin 7:38; the constructins ἰδὼν δὲ, and εἶπεν ...λέγων in 7:39; and εἶπεν with πρός, as well as ἔχω with an infinitive, to indicate intention.[27]

One can certainly argue with specific judgments as to whether some word or phrase is tradition or redaction.[28] Jeremias, perhaps, demonstrates a tendency to consider material as traditional without sufficient grounding. But he does offer compelling evidence that Luke has

---

[27] Jeremias, *Sprache*, 167–69.

[28] That is, is he really convincing that the term ἁμαρτωλός in 7:37 and elsewhere is from tradition (as he argues on p. 135)? Jeremias is on relatively safe ground in saying that the term τελωνῶν καὶ ἁμαρτωλῶν in 5:30 and 7:34 is from tradition (in this case, Matthew or Q; cf. Matt 9:11 and 11:19). But he also sees the use of ἁμαρτωλός in Luke 15:7, 10 as a paronomasia on the Hebrew or Aramaic words חדוה (joy=χαρά) and חטא (sinner=ἁμαρτωλός). While this is possible, it is not at all certain. From these two examples, he also decides that the use in 7:37 is by attraction to 7:34, and thus traditional (once removed?). Based on these examples, Jeremias concludes that all uses of the word in non-Markan texts must be Luke's use of tradition, not his redaction. Jeremias' tendency is heavily weighted toward finding material from tradition.

often used material from another source(s), and adapting it somewhat to his own writing and narrative style.

VINCENT TAYLOR

Following Streeter, Vincent Taylor also proposes an early pre-Lukan Gospel on which Luke drew as a primary source, especially in the Passion story. With some slight development upon his earlier work,[29] Taylor proposes that the Passion and Resurrection accounts in Luke were primarily drawn from an earlier, non-Markan connected narrative. With few exceptions, according to Taylor, the Markan material in Luke chapters 22–24 is primarily found in the form of insertions and additions.[30] At some points, the Markan material is assimilated or intertwined with the non-Markan material, but it also occurs in blocks, as in 22:1–13 and 22:54b–61.

Taylor uses a number of criteria to distinguish between Lukan material and the various sources: statistical patterns of "Markan" words, Lukan style, Lukan theology, and the order of events.[31] No single criterion is decisive, but a combination of criteria can be strongly suggestive. In order to find that a verse was based on Mark instead of an alternate source, *the* key factor is usually the existence of a mathematical preponderance of Markan words in the verse; usually this would require more than 50% of the verse being very close to Mark's language. Again, some examples will help to clarify Taylor's approach.

In his consideration of Luke 22:1–2, he first calculates the percentage of words in common with Mark: 62.5 percent. This high percentage suggests to him that Luke relied on Mark. In addition, his examination of the non-Markan words in the unit points to Luke's

---

[29] Taylor, *Behind the Third Gospel*.

[30] Taylor, *Passion*, 119.

[31] It is clear that, especially in the later book, Taylor relied on the works of Rehkopf and Hawkins to delineate Lukan style and indicators of pre-Lukan style, as his comments on Rehkopf's book indicate. *Passion*, 24–27.

editorial hand, not a separate source. He concludes, then, that the verse is drawn from Mark, with Lukan redactional modifications.[32]

The next unit to be considered, Luke 22:3–6, falls below the 50 percent mark of Markan words; the calculated percentage in 45.4. But despite this lower number, Taylor still finds that most of Mark's account is represented in Luke. The additions and modifications can, for the most part, be attributed to Luke's stylistic changes. The only place where Taylor does not find either Markan tradition or Lukan redaction is in 22:3, where Satan enters into Judas. Since this feature also appears in John 13:2, Taylor admits that it could come from another tradition. In sum, however, he concludes that this unit is Luke's redaction of Mark.[33]

The situation is changed, however, after Luke 22:14, where there is much less evidence of Luke's use of Mark. In Luke 22:39–46, for instance, only 26 percent of the words are Markan. While several instances of Lukan words and style are found in the text, Taylor understands their significance to be minor. He perceives, therefore, Luke's reworking of a pre-Lukan source.[34]

This statistical analysis leads Taylor to conclude that Luke in many cases primarily followed a source other than Mark, but he adapted that source with Markan material, especially in periodic insertions. Thus, according to Taylor's analysis, the crucifixion of Christ in Luke 23:33–49 is, with a few minor insertions of Markan material (Luke 23:26, 23:34b, 23:38, 23:44, 23:49), based on a non-Markan source. And the entire passage of the women's reaction after the death (Luke 23:55–56a) is non-Markan. But in between these units of text, Taylor finds a block of Markan material, the burial of Jesus (Luke 23:50–54), which has only a small admixture of Johannine tradition. So while Luke primarily followed another source, he occasionally did add Markan material into the narrative. Furthermore, Taylor is willing to discern in both the Markan blocks and the non-Markan material

---

[32] Taylor, *Passion*, 42.

[33] Taylor, *Passion*, 42–44.

[34] Taylor, *Passion*, 69–72.

Luke's editorial revisions and modifications. While primarily following the guidance of the statistical method he embraces, he too is able to discern with some specificity the distinction between sources and redaction in Luke's final narrative.

CRITIQUE AND SUMMARY

These four scholars' conclusions are similar in that they all perceive a parallel source, in most instances a connected narrative, that was used along with Mark or even in preference to Mark. But the similarity goes beyond their common conclusion of the connected Proto-Luke narrative; these scholars operate from a similar approach. For each scholar, either very close or verbatim agreement is necessary to argue for reliance on a source, especially Mark. And a similar "conservative" stance is taken with respect to Luke's redaction: only well-attested Lukan tendencies will stand as evidence for Luke's editorial modification, and certain features, such as semitisms, are ruled non-Lukan at the outset. A corollary to these approaches is that material that cannot be identified with a known source or redaction is often attributed to the unknown source or tradition that is being reconstructed. The careful attention to verbatim agreements, as well as the construction of a lexicon of Luke's style, allows them (especially Jeremias and Rehkopf) to construct a complementary lexicon of the pre-Lukan source.

These studies have added significantly to the understanding of Luke's Passion narrative. In each case, they have correctly noticed that Luke, in a number of pericopes, seems to have been combining Mark with some other tradition that strongly influenced the resultant narrative. At a number of junctures, the careful analysis of language seems to have detected traces of this other source or tradition that Luke used along with Mark. Moreover, the studies have helped define with much greater rigor many of the features of Luke's style.

There are, however, difficulties with these approaches. One wonders how reasonable their assumptions ultimately are, given the following:

1. After the identification of Markan material, non-Markan material, and Lukan redaction, one is often left with what seems to be a patchwork-quilt narrative that appears as the result of a cut-and-paste editorial process. How likely is it that Luke, with Mark at one side, a pre-Lukan source at the other, and the "glue" of his editorial efforts pasted together such a collage—first with a word from Mark, then a word from the other source, and so on? Even if one allows for the identification of traces of non-Markan material in the pericopes (which I do), how likely is it that one can precisely delineate between Mark and tradition in mid-sentence? Is it not more likely that Luke, if he were melding together multiple sources, would have often modified both Mark and the other source, so that precise delineations would be even more difficult?

2. As suggested above, the approaches are heavily tilted toward finding non-Markan tradition in Luke's Passion narrative. This is attributable to (a) the careful restriction of what is called "Markan" to very close or verbatim similarities, and (b) the use of negative criteria to define traditional material. The latter issue is particularly important, as Schürmann pointed out.[35] So, for instance, in material that is deemed non-Markan, the pre-Lukan source is identified whenever there is either a stylistic feature not often used by Luke or a semitism. That is to say, if it is not Mark, and it does not seem to fit a careful outline of Luke's style, then it must be pre-Lukan. This use of negative criteria to define pre-Lukan material is inherently tilted toward its identification. But if Luke's editorial or compositional strategies were understood to be more flexible, then less material could be attributed to a pre-Lukan source. The degree of flexibility in Luke's own style

---

[35] H. Schürmann, "Protolukanische Spracheigentümlichkeiten?" in *Traditionsgeschichtliche Untersuchungen zu den synoptischen Evangelien* (Düsseldorf: Patmos-Verlag, 1968), 211.

becomes a critical issue in this analysis.[36] My own conclusion is that Luke may well have been more adaptive and flexible as a writer than these studies credit, which undermines their results.

3. The tendency in almost all the studies, with the possible exception of Taylor's, is to focus narrowly on individual words and phrases. This emphasis on the micro-texture of Luke's narrative overlooks what may be the far more compelling evidence of Luke's use and modification of sources, the change in order and emphasis of the narrative units. In retelling the story, Luke exercised significant control over Mark (and possibly other sources) in his changing of the order and even deleting of certain segments of a story. Scholars, by emphasizing the study of individual words in discerning Luke's editorial practice, have overlooked these elements of his work.

LUKE AS COMPOSER: GOULDER AND DRURY

A very different approach to Luke's compositional work is taken by John Drury. Casting a skeptical eye on traditional source criticism and on previous efforts to find a hypothetical Proto-Luke source upon which Luke relied, Drury argues for a Lukan authorship modeled on the Jewish *midrashim*.[37] Drawing in part on Michael Goulder's early work with Matthew, which argued that Matthew was a *midrash* on Mark, Drury argues for such a view of Luke as well.[38] But the situation is a bit more complicated with Luke. Drury believes that Luke, while basing his story on Mark, was also influenced by the Old Testament and Matthew as he created a new *midrash* of Jesus.

Drury argues that much that is unique to Luke stemmed from Luke's own reading of Old Testament scripture and his reapplication

---

[36] A key issue is the use of semitisms. Many think that Luke was quite able to adopt a Septuagintal style, which is very semitic, as a narrative and rhetorical device. (cf. Fitzmyer, *Luke* (I–IX), 113–25; also, the discussion in Raymond E. Brown, *The Birth of the Messiah* [Garden City, NY: Image Books, 1979], 244–47).

[37] Drury, 39–45.

[38] Drury's debt to Goulder is indicated on p. xi. Cf. M. D. Goulder, *Midrash and Lection in Matthew* (London: S. P. C. K., 1974).

of those stories to Jesus' life. So not only the infancy stories, but also such units as the Zacchaeus story and the parable of the prodigal son are due to the influence of the Old Testament on Luke's composition.[39] While he drew the basic narrative, especially the order of events, from Mark,[40] Luke has interwoven material, as well as having gained a historical awareness, from Matthew.[41] And Luke has corrected Mark, and to this added his own free interpretation to create the Third Gospel.

Where Drury fires the opening shot, Goulder leads the ground forces. Following Drury, and his own previous work on Matthew, Michael Goulder provides the detailed argument for Luke as a *midrash* on Mark in his two-volume work, *Luke: A New Paradigm*.[42] Goulder's thesis is essentially that of Drury: the text of Luke can be best explained in almost every instance by understanding Luke to be an author who worked with his Markan and Matthean sources in a free fashion, shaped by a deep knowledge and interest in the Septuagint. To Drury's thesis, Goulder adds his interest in the calendar and the lectionary as the organizing influence, but these are not as central to his thesis as the rejection of hypothetical sources.[43] As a result of this view of Luke as a creative author, there is no need to posit any major additional sources: not a disconnected saying source such as Q,[44] and

---

[39] Drury, 71–79.

[40] Drury, 84.

[41] Drury, 164–67.

[42] Cf. also M. D. Goulder, "On Putting Q to the Test," *NTS* 24 (1978): 218–24, and "Farrer on Q," *Theology* 83 (1980): 190–95.

[43] Mark Goodacre, *Goulder and the Gospels* (Sheffield: Sheffield Academic Press, 1996) suggests, correctly I think, that Goulder has three central concerns: (1) Luke's knowledge of Matthew, thus dispensing with Q; (2) the creativity of the evangelists, thus dispensing with special sources (M, L, Proto-Luke), and (3) the lectionary theory. The lectionary theory becomes less important in his treatment of Luke than it is in his treatment of Matthew (38).

[44] Goulder, *Luke*, 27–71.

certainly not a hypothetical pre-Lukan Gospel.[45] In general, if one could imagine a text as arising from Luke's creative adaptation of known sources, this is the preferred option. It is clear that Occam's razor is a major interpretative tool for Goulder in his reconstruction of Luke's sources.

But what is striking in theory is not ultimately convincing in the detailed analysis. Although Goulder's work is quite extensive and thought provoking, and thus quite impossible to adequately treat here, some of the main features can be addressed as illustrative of his approach. In order to explain Luke's unique presentations, Goulder suggests a number of elements of Luke's style that he believes explain the resultant Third Gospel based on Mark and Matthew alone. These elements include, in addition to such frequently observed features as Luke's pleonastic use of ἀναστάς and ἤρξατο under the rubric of promptitude and alacrity,[46] a number of compositional strategies that support Goulder's thesis.[47]

1. Inference of setting. Luke tended to infer certain features from the setting of the accounts he took over. For instance, Luke's reading of the call narrative in Matthew, according to Goulder, seems to have presupposed both Jesus' teaching and a significant event that defined the perception of Jesus by the disciples, with the result that they left their nets to follow him (Mark 1:16; Matt 4:18). Luke combined the presumption that Jesus taught the disciples before the call, so that the preaching of repentance must have implied teaching (hence Jesus' teaching from the boat); the assumption that fishing was done from boats, so Peter must have also been in a boat (hence two boats in

---

[45] Goulder, *Luke*, 73–88. Goulder is actually willing to accept that Luke had some traditions. What he most objects to is the construction of a hypothetical document in preference to known sources. Hence his comment: "We have to choose between two further possibilities. It could be a source unknown to us, about which we know nothing; or it could be Mark or Matthew. We certainly ought to consider the devil we know before opting for the devil we don't know." (88). Unfortunately, John is never seriously considered as one of his known devils.

[46] Goulder, *Luke*, 92–93.

[47] Goulder, *Luke*, 105–7.

Luke's story); and especially, the inference that a defining event, such as a miracle, occurred (hence the miraculous catch of fish). These departures from and expansions upon the Mark/Matthew account are explained as Luke's natural inference from the previous Gospels.[48]

2. Combination of sources. Luke frequently combined two or more sources into a single story. Thus, for instance, at the tomb Luke combined Mark's story of the young man inside the tomb (Mark 16:5–7) and Matthew's story of the angel outside the tomb (Matt 28:2–7), and produced two men standing by the women (Luke 24:4–7).

3. Splitting of sources. In precisely the opposite tendency, Luke sometimes split one story into two. Thus, for example, in the trial of Jesus, which he took over from Mark as a whole unit, Luke but divided features between Pilate's trial (tried, condemned) and a trial before Herod (transfer of splendid robe, Jesus' silence, and soldiers' mockery).

4. Transfer of elements. Goulder sees Luke having taken elements from one story and transferred those elements into another story. Thus the feature of Jesus' teaching from the boat, which leads into Luke's call narrative (Luke 5:2–11), was transferred from Mark (4:1–2, the beginning of the parable discourse), and deleted in Luke's own treatment of the parable of the sower (Luke 8:4–8).

One can see Goulder's method clearly in his treatment of Luke 7:36–50, the story of the anointing woman. Goulder argues that Luke *combined* two pericopes from Matthew that occur quite close together: Matt 9:9–17, the story of Jesus eating with tax collectors and sinners, and Matt 9:20–22, the story of the woman with the hemorrhage. Luke combined these so that the repentant woman is one of the "sinners" present at the dinner party. To this combination, Luke also *transfers elements* from Mark's story of the anointing at Bethany (Mark 14:1–9: the setting at Simon's house, reclining at table, a woman bringing an alabaster of myrrh). And finally, Luke *infers* certain actions *from the setting*, namely that a sinful woman might stand behind Jesus at the dinner, weep, kiss his feet, and wipe his feet with her hair. So the story

---
[48] Goulder, *Luke*, 316–21.

in Luke can be explained by virtue of three of the stylistic or editorial approaches that Goulder has defined as Lukan.[49]

This particular passage is a good illustration of Goulder's approach to the question of Luke's compositional method. It is clear that Goulder sees Luke as a very creative re-teller of stories, although those stories are, in his view, limited to Mark and Matthew and the Old Testament. But how likely is this scenario? In the first place, Goulder would have Luke combine into a new, unique passage two pericopes from Matthew that are also presented in their "normal" forms by Luke (the dinner with sinners, Luke 5:27–32; the woman with the hemorrhage, 8:43–48). So Luke not only combined these passages but also duplicated them. And with the transfer of elements from the anointing story, Luke was, in effect, weaving three stories together. Furthermore, the elements that Luke added, based on certain inferences about the customary action of a sinner woman, would make Luke a highly creative author. On the one hand, Goulder presents Luke as relying on sources, but doing so in a very contrived and complicated way. One wonders how Luke would have thought to combine these three stories to form Luke 7:36–50. On the other hand, Goulder denies the possibility that any other sources might be the explanation for unique elements in Luke. While he very aptly demonstrates that Luke wrote creatively, he perhaps goes too far in denying the possibility that some other sources might lie behind some of the creative work. In the anointing pericope, the close similarities to John's Gospel might suggest that some of the features derived from either a common tradition or Luke's knowledge of John. But these are never seriously considered, since John is written off as a "muddle," and John's posterity is affirmed almost axiomatically.[50]

Goulder's work does very helpfully stress Luke's own creative work as an author in shaping and fashioning his Gospel. Rather than allowing Luke to be seen as a mere collector of stories from Mark and elsewhere, Goulder forces one to consider the possibility that Luke, as

---

[49] Goulder, *Luke*, 397–405.
[50] Goulder, *Luke*, 403.

composer, was a major force behind the Third Gospel. But his limitation of the sources to just Matthew, Mark, and the Old Testament seems forced and unproven.

EMPHASIZING CONTENT: SOARDS

Soards' primary focus is to locate and explain the material in Luke 22 that varies from the Markan narrative.[51] It is, of course, Luke's substantial deviation from the Markan Passion story that drives the study. In particular, Soards notes first that Luke's order follows Mark generally, but in the Passion narrative, deviates significantly.[52] And second, he observes that in terms of content, Luke at times relates a similar incident as Mark, but tells it very differently, omits elements that are in Mark, and adds totally unique material that is not present in Mark.[53] Did Luke use other sources, or was he simply being creative in his version of the story? Behind the study is a continual dialogue (both spoken and unspoken), with Vincent Taylor's proposal that in the Passion narrative, Luke's source was a single non-Markan source, Proto-Luke.[54] Soards' stated desire is to reexamine the question with an eye to ferreting out Luke's method and sources.

A major advantage of Soards' study is his critique of earlier methods of examining the material, especially Taylor's. The concerns are summarized under three heads.

1. The use of word statistics[55] to isolate Markan from non-Markan material does not adequately identify all the literary depend-

---

[51] Marion Soards, *The Passion According to Luke*. (Sheffield: JSOT Press, 1987).

[52] Soards, 13.

[53] Soards, 13–16.

[54] Soards, 17, referring primarily to Taylor's *The Passion Narrative of St. Luke*.

[55] Not only is this approach used by Taylor, it is, either with statistics or simply references to other word usage patterns, the primary approach used by Hawkins, Schramm, and Jeremias as well.

ence between Luke and Mark.[56] It is possible—indeed, frequently does happen—that Luke reflects the Markan story even when the actual literary reliance is low. In other words, Luke's use and redaction of his primary source, Mark, need not have been simplistic or stilted.

2. Taylor, along with other students of Luke's use of sources, seems to assume with respect to each verse that it either came from Mark or from another source. Soards correctly argues that this produces an artificial either/or.[57] Luke might instead have been blending various sources, freely redacting—and even composing—using multiple sources.

3. Soards notes that often the image of Luke's compositional technique is that of a cut-and-paste approach. The use of such language as "inserting" a Markan phrase into a generally non-Markan narrative suggests just such a conception.

For Soards, these earlier methods tend to reduce the amount of Markan material seen in Luke 22 and expand the "additional" non-Lukan material. As an alternative, Soards reexamines Luke with a more critical eye toward such "additional" material. He sets out five criteria for establishing "special Lukan material":

1. Sentences that are entirely without parallel in Mark
2. Sentences that represent an agreement of Luke with Matthew or John against Mark
3. Sentences that form a story sequence different from that of Mark
4. Sentences that have a low level of verbal correspondence between Luke and Mark
5. Sentences that contain so-called telltale Lukan language

The first two criteria are sufficient to define special material. Soards requires a combination of more than one from among the latter three criteria to establish a text as special Lukan material.[58] Based on his delineation of the scope of that "additional" material, he tries to

---

[56] Soards, 18.
[57] Soards, 18.
[58] Soards, 20.

reframe Luke's compositional technique. In addition, Soards is very emphatic that his focus is less on stylistic and statistical analysis than on thought and content. This caveat is due in part to the fact that stylistic and statistical analysis have not produced broad agreement. But more importantly, it is because he believes that the focus on words (as opposed to thoughts) unduly restricts the analysis of Luke's editorial work.[59] In other words, Soards credits Luke with more flexibility and creativity as an author. Given such creativity, one must look beyond the simple surface pattern of words and inquire whether Luke shows evidence of the influence in thought and content from another source. Perhaps Soards' awareness of this is best seen in his recognition of the third criterion, in which a changed story sequence might be an indication of another source. Similarly, agreement with Matthew or John *in content* (criterion 2) might also point to non-Markan material upon which Luke has relied.

One can observe Soards' method in his analysis of Luke 22:15–23, the story of the Last Supper and Jesus' prediction of betrayal. Although he finds the Lukan Last Supper account to be quite different from Mark's narrative, he is unwilling to say that it is entirely without parallel in Mark. Instead, he finds it to be probably Markan material that has been influenced by a non-Markan tradition.[60] In the betrayal sequence that follows, there is also material quite extraneous to the Markan story: (a) the use of "hand" in verse 21, (b) the common use of πορεύεσθαι for death in Luke and John in verse 22, (c) the order of events common to Luke and John, and (d) an interaction between the disciples after the announcement in both Luke and John. In evaluating the betrayal material, items a, b, and d are deemed coincidences or artificial parallels.[61] The order of the narrative is considered significant, but is seen as an indication of Luke's pattern of reworking the Markan material in order to emphasize a Lukan pur-

---

[59] Soards, 19.

[60] Soards, 30, 50. He sees Luke as having worked together Mark and a tradition similar to 1 Cor 11:23–25.

[61] Soards, 34–36, 38–39.

pose—in this case a desire to portray the Last Supper as a testamentary banquet.[62]

It should be no surprise, in light of his approach, that Soards finds more of Luke 22 derived from Mark than do other scholars. He examines the Lukan Passion narrative from the perspective of Mark; by refocusing attention on Luke's creative use of Mark, he has enhanced the understanding of Luke's work as an author. But while the focus is on demonstrating Luke's extensive and primary use of Mark even outside of clearly "Markan" language, Soards nonetheless identifies a significant amount of Luke 22 that cannot be accounted for simply by Luke's redaction of Mark. And much of that non-Markan material represents an agreement with John. Soards' conclusion is that these similarities come from Luke's use of oral traditions that were also used by John.[63]

Soards' study is significant for its emphasis on the importance of "ideas" and "content" as indicators of source material. But if Taylor and others, by focusing on word usage only, tended to understate the basic underlying Markan narrative in Luke's Passion, Soards may tend to understate other sources that might have complemented the Markan narrative. In his attempt to question the Proto-Luke hypothesis, he understates the various points of contact with John and Matthew. One way this understatement takes place is that he rarely connects the criterion of changed sequence with the criterion of common material with John or Matthew. Nor does he seriously consider Luke's omission of material that is in common with others, which then becomes a form of changed sequence.

Given the acknowledged contacts with John, perhaps other elements in the study that are dismissed as coincidences[64] might be

---

[62] Soards, 55.

[63] Soards, 119. "Luke had recourse to oral tradition that went beyond Mark, and he included some of that information in ch. 22 by smoothly blending with the basic Markan narrative."

[64] Soards, 74, 77–78. See, for instance, his easy dismissal of contacts in Luke 22:50b; 22:55a–60b.

reexamined on the basis of idea and content, not just exact wording, to see if there is evidence for more than simply common tradition. In particular, Soards' treatment of Johannine and Matthean similarities individually, in isolation from one another, tends to discount any possible influence by John or Matthew on Luke. Soards' critique of the tendency to dismiss Markan material when the differences are, perhaps more simply, due to Luke's editorial interest is equally valid for his own analysis of material common to Luke in John in the same narratives.

These weaknesses in Soards' study are primarily the result of its narrow focus, which was to reexamine Luke's use of Mark, not to examine Luke with respect to another Gospel or narrative. Soards' basic approach toward studying the matter of Luke's sources and his criteria for evaluation are fundamentally sound. The method used in this study will be very close to that advocated by Soards, but it will be extended to focus on the comparison of the non-Markan elements with John's account.

THE APPROACH OF THIS STUDY

The purpose of this study is to explore the possibility that Luke knew and used John in the composition of the Third Gospel. If Luke did, in fact, know John, then there should be strong evidence of John's influence in Luke's redaction of known sources.

The starting point for any analysis of Luke's composition must be the identification of Luke's known source That identification is essentially what all of the studies cited above have undertaken; the primary source for the Gospel of Luke is clearly the Gospel of Mark. Accordingly, the Lukan texts under consideration in this study will first be examined with respect to Mark.

When Luke's Passion narrative is examined, pericope by pericope, for its relationship with Mark, two extreme possibilities immediately arise for each unit of text.

1. Luke and Mark are closely related. In this case, Luke may contain minor modifications of grammar or presentation, but the basic presentation is still very close to Mark. Much of the triple tradition material in the Third Gospel presents itself in this way (e.g., Luke 4:40–41 par. Mark 1:32–34). Because of the extensive pattern of relationship throughout much of Luke, if the text in the Passion story is very close to Mark, one can begin with a fundamental assumption that Mark is *the* source for the narrative unit in question. In such a case, an explanation for the variations from Mark will be of primary interest.

2. Luke is not at all parallel with Mark. In this case, Luke contains material that is totally different from that in Mark. This is the case especially with either double tradition material (e.g., Luke 6:20–23 par. Matt 5:3–12) or special Lukan material (e.g., Luke 11:5–8). If the material is found to be without parallel in Mark, it must, initially at least, be compared with other known narratives for possible similarities. In particular, such material will be compared with the Gospels of Matthew and John.

But such clear options of "all Mark" or "no Mark" will not often present themselves in this study of Luke. Especially in the Passion narratives, Luke often seems to have relied on Mark for much of the material, and yet shows significant differences from the Second Gospel. This presents, then, a third option.

3. Luke seems to follow Mark, and yet contains significant modifications, arising either from Luke's own creative impulse or the influence of another narrative. Such a mixed narrative might well contain important features from Mark but, in either content or order, might nonetheless be quite different. This kind of narrative unit, very common in Luke, requires holding open the possibility that Luke was mixing together various elements to create a new compound story. In these instances, then, it will be necessary to explore further the various influences that have helped create Luke's narrative.

In this examination of Luke's use of Mark and other sources, a fitting point of departure is the affirmation of important elements of

Soards' approach to the question.[65] In particular, the following observations are, I think, important features in the study of Luke's editorial method in the Passion narrative.

Thought content, over against exact agreements in wording, will often be more important for identifying Luke's use of Mark, as well as for identifying other sources upon which Luke might have relied. Luke, as an editor and composer drawing upon various sources and working under the impulse of a theological and historiographical program, may well have taken over ideas from another source without having followed exactly its language.

Modifications of order of a story are important indicators of an influence from another source. The order of a narrative is as much an indication of thought content as are other bits of information. Departures from Mark's order will be a strong sign that another source has been used. Moreover, the presence of a common order in another source will be a strong argument for a literary influence.[66]

Omissions from Mark's narrative can be significant signs of possible influence. However, the simple absence of material from Luke

---

[65] Soards, 16–21. See especially the emphasis on thought content, as well as the criteria for locating special Lukan material.

[66] In addition to Soards, others working with Luke's compositional process have noted the importance of order as a criterion for locating special Lukan (=non-Markan) material. Special note has been made of this by J. Jeremias, *The Eucharistic Words of Jesus* (Philadelphia: Trinity Press, 1990 [1960], 98–99. Jeremias argues that whenever Luke followed Mark's narrative, he followed painstakingly Mark's order. Indeed, up until the Passion narrative, there are only two small deviations from Mark's order. "Deviations in the order of the material must therefore be regarded as indications that Luke is not following Mark" (98). Such a wholesale conclusion is perhaps overstating the case, but I think this observation is on the right track. In the same vein, note the comments by Hawkins in his article in *Studies in the Synoptic Problem*, (80–82) on the significance of inversions or transpositions in Luke's Passion account. Rehkopf finds changes in order are significant indications of Luke's use of another source (1–4). And Taylor, *Passion* (126), finds a fundamental confirmation of his Proto-Luke source in the fact that the order of narratives in his reconstructed source agrees with John.

and another source cannot, by itself, be a strong indication of a literary relationship.

Telltale Lukan language may be particularly present where Luke melded various sources; in other words, it may indicate the presence of multiple sources, not just Lukan creativity.

With an awareness of possible complex combinations of reliance on Mark and on other sources that Luke may have used, the analysis should begin by identifying the known—in this case Mark—and move toward identifying the unknown. In general, the process outlined below will be followed, either explicitly or implicitly for each pericope.

ANALYZE CLOSENESS TO MARK

The analysis will begin by comparing a unit of text[67] with Mark to see whether, or to what degree, Luke relied on Mark for that unit. The comparison will involve at least the qualitative evaluation of the degree of closeness of Luke's text to Mark. Although not being restricted by the linguistic analysis, such study of word usage will still be an important part of the evaluation of Luke's closeness to Mark. At the beginning of each unit of text, the close linguistic similarities that Luke shares with Mark will be highlighted. Taylor's statistical analysis of the textual units will be helpful, especially in cases where Luke was clearly following Mark. But a negative finding by Taylor will not be definitive. At a basic level, the question will be "Is it the same story?" If indeed it is, the examination will note with respect to Mark, the following features:

1. Similarities in wording.
2. Similarities in content, including omissions.
3. Similarities in order.

The necessary complement to the comparison is an examination of Luke's *differences* from Mark. That examination will seek indications

---

[67] Generally a fairly large sense unit, since, according to the discussion above, the emphasis will be more on thought content than on linguistic similarities. The use of longer sense units will accommodate the flow of the thought in the unit.

that Luke modified or distanced himself from Mark. Such indications might point to non-Markan material that influenced Luke in his composition. Specifically, as above, the examination of Luke will note, with reference to Mark, the following features:
1. Differences in wording.
2. Differences in content, including omissions.
3 Differences in order.

NOTE SIMILARITIES TO OTHER TEXTS

As differences are noted, a comparison with other known texts will become necessary. In particular, the Lukan text will be compared with the other Gospels and with the rest of Luke.
1. Matthew. A few minor agreements with Matthew need to be noted and evaluated.
2. Luke. A constant effort is necessary to consider whether non-Markan language might result from Luke's editorial work, betrayed by his own style and theological tendencies. The presence of Luke's style might indicate an attempt to clean up Mark's language, his own creative composition, or his editorial interweaving of two or more sources. In this effort, the works of Hawkins, Jeremias, Rehkopf, and Schramm will be particularly helpful.
3. John. Of course, the Luke-John relationship is the focus of this study. The comparison of Luke and John will be extensive whenever Luke shows significant deviations from Mark.

COMPARE CLOSELY WITH JOHN

In the comparison with John, special attention will be paid to the following features:
1. Verbatim or very close similarities in wording. Strong similarities in wording will be important. In such instances, the question of the origination of such wording needs to be considered: does it seem more Lukan or more Johannine?

2. Common order of events or elements in the pericopes. When John departs from Mark's order, it will be particularly important to compare John's order with Luke's order.

3. Similar thought content. Important elements in the flow of the narrative, such as common narrational features, timing, and emphasis, might be important, especially when Luke departs from the Markan pattern.

4. Common omissions in a narrative. Common omissions might show some relationship, but such evidence, by nature, is weak.

CONSIDER THE LIKELIHOOD OF LUKE'S COMPOSITIONAL PRACTICE

The mere listing of similarities is ultimately not compelling. Some attempt needs to be made to understand what Luke was doing as he departed from the Markan pattern. Specifically, having located departures from Mark's narrative, one must offer a reasonable explanation of Luke's method that coheres with what is known of Luke's theology, redactional practice elsewhere, and overall interests. In other words, a compelling explanation will ultimately be one that narratively *explains* Luke as a composer with respect to his various sources.

WHAT IS PROOF?

As many studies have shown, Luke in the Passion narrative is quite different from Mark and Matthew. And at the same time, this study has noted significant similarities in the same Passion narrative between Luke and John. Proof of a literary relationship is probably impossible even in the best of circumstances, but what evidence might tend to suggest that Luke was relying on John? I consider the following elements, especially when taken together, to be strongly suggestive of a literary relationship in which Luke's account has been influenced by John's.

1. Verbatim or other striking linguistic similarities. Such similarities are strong indications of a literary relationship. Similarities that contain Johannine language are important evidence of Luke's having been influenced by John.

2. Luke's departure from Mark's order of events at a place where John's order is similar. The concurrence of a departure in order from Mark and a similarity in order to John at the same place is especially suggestive of John's influence on Luke. In addition, common omissions between Luke and John should become probative when Luke's omission involves a departure from the Markan order of events.

3. The presence of Johannine features in the Lukan narrative. Even if relatively small units of content, such features would indicate a possible relationship, with Luke's having been influenced by John.

4. Non-Markan material that is common to Luke and John that is difficult to place within Luke's theological program.

5. A cumulative weight of these elements. No one feature is, by itself, compelling. But if a significant number of them occur, the weight of the evidence becomes much stronger.

Chapter 6

LUKE CHAPTER 22

In the next three chapters, I will examine Luke's Passion narrative with an eye to his use of sources. In particular, I will ask whether it is a reasonable hypothesis that Luke used John as one of his sources. My examination will be structured according to the following procedure.

1. I will cite the Greek text of Luke in narrative units, highlighting what appear to be close links with the other Gospels. Material that is very close to Mark will be <u>underlined</u>. Material that is similar to Matthew, and therefore could represent use of Matthew (or possible a source common with Matthew), will be set in **bold** font. And material that is strongly similar to John will be marked by ***bold italics***.

2. I will attempt to clarify the elements of the Lukan story that are derived from Mark, either directly or with some modification, and those derived from Matthew. From that analysis, it will become possible to identify unique material that cannot be traced back to Mark or Matthew. This unique material could have come from Luke's creative hand, from a special written source (L), from some oral traditions—or from the influence of the Gospel of John. It is, of course, the last possibility that is the focus of this study.

3. Finally, I will attempt to read that unique material as if Luke knew John, testing the plausibility of the hypothesis that Luke was

influenced by the Fourth Gospel or an early version of John. Throughout the discussion I will generally refer to Luke's relationship to John, though always holding open the possibility that the literary relationship I am testing is to an earlier version of John.[1] Would such a pattern of usage and modification fit with the finished product of Luke? Could such a pattern of usage and modification be fit into Luke's known editorial tendencies?

Introduction To The Passover. Luke 22:1–2

[1] Ἤγγιζεν δὲ ἡ ἑορτὴ τῶν ἀζύμων ἡ λεγομένη πάσχα. [2] καὶ ἐζήτουν οἱ ἀρχιερεῖς καὶ οἱ γραμματεῖς τὸ πῶς ἀνέλωσιν αὐτόν, ἐφοβοῦντο γὰρ τὸν λαόν.

Luke begins his account of the events that lead up to the Passion by drawing closely on Mark's account.[2] There are no indications that another source contributed to this introduction; Soards, for instance, finds no special Luke material in these two verses.[3]

Luke, like Mark, begins by noting the closeness of the Passover. But while drawing on Mark's introduction to the final days, Luke replaces the precise chronological marker of "two days" with a more general ἤγγιζεν. That modification is understandable given the Luke's relocation of the anointing story to 7:36. In Mark, the anointing story comes immediately after the introduction to the Passion and appears to fill at least one of his "two days." In contrast, since Luke has no

---

[1] Such an earlier version, for instance, has been proposed by Robert Fortna in *The Gospel of Signs* (Cambridge: University Press, 1970) and *The Fourth Gospel and its Predecessor* (Philadelphia: Fortress Press, 1988).

[2] Joachim Jeremias, *Die Sprache des Lukasevangeliums* (Göttingen: Vandenhoeck & Ruprecht, 1980), 285, simply notes that Luke 22:1–13 is a "*Markusblock*"; Vincent Taylor, *The Passion Narrative of St. Luke* (Cambridge: University Press, 1972), 42; Joseph Fitzmyer, *The Gospel According to Luke*, (X-XXIV), AB 28A (Garden City, NY: Doubleday, 1985), 1368.

[3] Marion Soards, *The Passion According to Luke* (Sheffield: JSOT Press, 1987), 26, 32, 38, 40.

anointing at this point,[4] his chronology is a bit more vague, as reflected in his language: Mark's "two days before Passover" (Mark 14:1) becomes "the feast of the Passover drew near" (Luke 22:1). Luke also combines the two feasts, that of the Unleavened Bread and the Passover, and counts them as one feast. While this combination is not technically correct, it was practically so.[5] These differences represent the minor modifications that Luke was quite willing to make to his source.

Two items contribute to the strong sense that Luke is highly reliant on Mark. First, the vocabulary is very similar. Taylor notes that 62.5 percent of the words in these two verses of Luke agree with Mark. While not conclusive, such agreement is suggestive of a close relationship.[6] Second, the ordering of the pericope in the context of the rest of the Passion narrative is common—a strong sign of reliance.

But perhaps most important, the main content of Luke's portrayal of the beginning of the Passion is very close to Mark's. Like Mark, Luke notes at the outset that the chief priests and scribes were seeking to kill Jesus. Luke modifies the ἀποκτείνωσιν only slightly to a more sinister ἀνέλωσιν. Moreover, the sense that the Jewish leaders were worried about arresting Jesus during Passover because of the people (λαός) is maintained in Luke's "they feared the people (λαός)." While Luke has made certain modifications to Mark's account, it is nonetheless apparent that he was drawing on the Second Gospel. There is no reason to suggest that another source lay behind Luke's editorial changes to Mark.

---

[4] As has often been noted, Luke's anointing story, whose move has produced this dislocation in the text, shows significant common elements with John's anointing story. It is possible that the move was prompted by the differences Luke found between the Markan and Johannine accounts. In this discussion only the fact that it has been moved from its Markan position will be considered.

[5] Fitzmyer, *Luke* vol. 1, 439–40.

[6] Taylor, 42.

BETRAYAL BY JUDAS. LUKE 22:3–6

³*Εἰσῆλθεν* δὲ *Σατανᾶς εἰς* Ἰούδας τὸν καλούμενον *Ἰσκαριώτην*, ὄντα ἐκ τοῦ ἀριθμοῦ τῶν δώδεκα· ⁴ καὶ ἀπελθὼν συνελάλησεν τοῖς ἀρχιερεῦσιν καὶ στρατηγοῖς τὸ πῶς αὐτοῖς παραδῷ αὐτόν. ⁵ καὶ ἐχάρησαν καὶ συνέθεντο αὐτῷ ἀργύριον δοῦναι. ⁶ καὶ ἐξωμολόγησεν, καὶ ἐζήτει εὐκαιρίαν τοῦ παραδοῦναι αὐτὸν ἄτερ ὄχλου αὐτοῖς.

Following the anointing pericope (which is absent in Luke), Mark and Matthew turn immediately to Judas' arrangement with the high priests to betray Jesus, the event that Luke records next as well. In the general narrative order, and in much of the language, Luke appears to draw on the Markan account:

1. Judas departs from Jesus' group and goes to the high priests.
2. Judas' intent is to betray (παραδίδωμι) Jesus to the high priests.[7]
3. The high priests rejoice (ἐχάρησαν) and promise Judas money (ἀργυριον).
4. Judas seeks an appropriate time to betray Jesus.

This linkage of ideas, with significant similarity in words at key places, makes it very clear that Luke was essentially following Mark in his story. While the percentage of common vocabulary is not extremely high, the common content, as well as the order of that content, makes Luke's reliance on Mark virtually certain. Of course Luke was willing to modify the Markan account. He added guards (στρατηγοῖς) to the group to whom Judas goes, perhaps anticipating their participation at the arrest (Luke 22:52). Other changes, such as the term καλούμενον to describe Judas or the use of the term ἀριθμός to describe his participa-

---
[7] Or possibly to "hand over" Jesus. Cf. the discussion on παραδίδωμι in Raymond Brown, *The Death of the Messiah* (Garden City, NY: Doubleday, 1994), 210–11.

tion in the Twelve, are stylistic variations.⁸ Luke used his source, but made some modifications.

The opening line of Luke's account, however, is quite at variance with Mark's.⁹ In Luke's story, the betrayal does not arise simply from some unknown rejection of Jesus (as in Mark's account), or from greed (as in Matthew's telling modification of the story); in Luke's story, the betrayal is attributed to Satan. Luke says, as does John (John 13:27), that Satan "entered into" Judas.¹⁰

The later Gospels tend to reconstruct the disciples over against Mark's generally negative characterization. Thus Matthew has the disciples hear and respond to Jesus after the resurrection (Matt 28:16) despite their absence at the cross; more tellingly, Luke and John have some of the disciples remain at the cross. That trajectory, moving from Mark to Matthew and then Luke, might be discerned, then, in the Judas story. Thus even Judas is recast as acting not out of simple betrayal but, first in Matthew, out of greed from which he ultimately repents (Matt 27:3), and then, in Luke, under the influence a hostile force, Satan, who has entered into him.¹¹ Alternatively, the addition by Luke

---

⁸ Taylor, *Passion*, 43; M. D. Goulder, *Luke: A New Paradigm* (Sheffield: JSOT Press, 1989), 725, 805: καλούμενον is a Lukan word. While ἀριθμός is a *hapax legomenon*, there are signs of Lukan style in the way Mark's εἷς τῶν δώδεκα is modified with ὄντα ἐκ τοῦ ἀριθμοῦ.

⁹ And so it is quite surprising to find that Jeremias, *Sprache*, (285) simply locates the entirety of Luke 22:1–13 as a block of Markan material. T. Schramm, *Der Markus-Stoff Bei Lukas*, (Cambridge: University Press, 1971), 182–84 is a bit more careful in his assessment: while accounting for 22:1–13 as being drawn from Mark, he acknowledges that at least v. 3 cannot be so attributed. For Schramm, this verse was drawn from a special source from which John drew as well.

¹⁰ Soards concludes that the best explanation for the similarity is neither literary reliance nor simply theological development, but an independent tradition upon which both Luke and John relied (49).

¹¹ R. H. Lightfoot, *History and Interpretation in the Gospels* (London: Hodden and Stoughton, 1935), 172. See also William Klassen, *Judas: Betrayer or Friend of Jesus?* (Minneapolis: Fortress Press, 1996), 117.

might be his way of explaining how one of Jesus' chosen Twelve fell away.[12]

It is also very possible that Luke was drawing upon an independent tradition to which John also had access.[13] The question, then, is whether that tradition was a written source[14] or an oral tradition.[15] In either case, such an explanation sees Luke as one who was willing to modify the basic Markan story in order to "fit in" other disparate material. The difficulty with the explanation, based as it is on unknown sources, is that it can be made to conveniently account for any features that intrude into a clearly explainable Lukan redaction of Mark. Unless a coherent source or tradition can be clearly extracted from the Lukan Passion story, this explanation seems unconvincing.

There is, however, a written document that does contain a reference to Satan's entering into Judas: the Gospel of John. In John 13:2 and 13:27 John reports Satan's influence on Judas. In the first instance, as part of his introduction to the Passion, he records that "the devil had already put into the heart of Judas, son of Simon Iscariot, to betray him." The context of this reference is the anticipation of the final supper with Jesus. Unlike Luke, John here uses διαβόλος, not σατανᾶς, but the figure is the same and the theme a similar theme. In the second reference, at the dinner itself, John records that when Jesus gave Judas bread, "Satan entered into him." While the setting is different, the wording in this instance is very similar to Luke. There are, then, two accounts in John, somewhat at odds, that refer to Satan's entrance into Judas.

---

[12] Goulder considers all of Luke 22:1–13 to follow Mark as the core source. Any variances, as in the reference to Satan, are simply examples of Luke's own creativity with his basic source (720).

[13] Soards, 49.

[14] That is, a part of a pre-Luke Passion narrative. Cf. Taylor, 65–66; F. Rehkopf, *Die lukanische Sonderquelle* (Tübingen: J. C. B. Mohr [Paul Siebeck], 1959), 96.

[15] Heinz Schürmann, "Jesu Abschiedsrede. Lk 22, 19–20," in *Neutestamentliche Abhandlungen*, 20 Band, 4 Heft (Münster: Aschendorffsche Verlagsbuchhandlung, 1955), 99–116.

Another explanation, then, for Luke's reference to Satan's entering Judas, more likely than the theory that he was drawing entirely on an unknown source, is that Luke was weaving together two known disparate accounts—Mark's and John's.[16] Both Mark and Matthew describe Judas as going to the priests and agreeing upon money as reward for betrayal; John, on the other hand, explains the betrayal simply as the work of Satan. John does refer to the money box, not as a factor in the betrayal, but rather to explain a misunderstanding about Judas' departure from the dinner scene. Instead of choosing between these two contrasting descriptions of Judas' betrayal, Luke appears to have combined the two accounts. From Mark, he relates the exchange of money between Judas and the chief priests; from John, he adopts the explanation that the whole situation has been prompted by Satan's entrance into Judas. Luke, then, is the middle and conciliatory term between two competing explanations.

Of course the relationship between the Third and Fourth Gospels on this point has been explained by John's use of Luke, not the other way around. This has been proposed by Bailey, who sees John 13:27 as stemming from a direct reliance on Luke and John 13:2 as a later summary written to anticipate the subsequent betrayal.[17] But it is hard to see why John would have used Luke at 13:27, modifying the placement within the narrative order. Why would he have moved Satan's entrance into Judas from the beginning of the Passion story to the middle of the dinner scene itself? And then, having made the decision to place it at the dinner, why would either John or a later editor then subsequently also make an additional reference, that time changing the name from σατανᾶς to διαβολός, at the beginning of the dinner, thus agreeing with Luke once again? If John was influenced by Luke's chronological placement, why did he not simply place the reference at the beginning

---

[16] As Taylor, *Passion*, notes: "In attributing the action of Judas to Satanic influence he appears to reflect Johannine tradition (Jn. xiii.2), and this allusion may be his attempt to reconcile two different views" (44).

[17] J. A. Bailey, *The Traditions Common to the Gospels of Luke and John* (Leiden: E. J. Brill, 1963), 30.

of the dinner scene, where it is in Luke, instead of creating a confusion? Bailey's observation that the similarities between Luke and John point strongly to a literary relationship is correct. But given the extant texts, it is far more reasonable to imagine that Luke knew the two statements in John and melded them together, choosing the 13:2 location (before the dinner) as more fitting for his story.

PREPARATION FOR THE PASSOVER. LUKE 22:7–13

⁷ ῏Ηλθεν δὲ ἡ ἡμέρα τῶν ἀζύμων, ἐν ᾗ ἔδει θύεσθαι τὸ πάσχα· ⁸ καὶ ἀπέστειλεν Πέτρον καὶ Ἰωάννην εἰπών, Πορευθέντες ἑτοιμάσατε ἡμῖν τὸ πάσχα ἵνα φάγωμεν, ⁹ οἱ δὲ εἶπαν αὐτῷ, Ποῦ θέλεις ἑτοιμάσωμεν; ¹⁰ ὁ δὲ εἶπεν αὐτοῖς Ἰδοὺ εἰσελθόντων ὑμῶν εἰς τὴν πόλιν συν αντήσει ὑμῖν ἄνθρωπος κεράμιον ὕδατος βαστάζων· ἀκολουθήσατε αὐτῷ εἰς τὴν οἰκίαν εἰς ἣν εἰσπορεύεται, ¹¹ καὶ ἐρεῖτε τῷ οἰκοδεσπότῃ τῆς οἰκίας, Λέγει σοι ὁ διδάσκαλος, Ποῦ ἐστιν τὸ κατάλυμα ὅπου τὸ πάσχα μετὰ τῶν μαθητῶν μου φάγω; ¹² κἀκεῖνος ὑμῖν δείξει ἀνάγαιον μέγα ἐστρωμένον· ἐκεῖ ἑτοιμάσατε. ¹³ ἀπελθόντες δὲ εὗρον καθὼς εἰρήκει αὐτοῖς καὶ ἡτοίμασας τὸ πάσχα.

The preparation for the Passover meal in Luke is drawn from Mark with very little in the way of major modifications. Jeremias is surely correct in this instance that this is purely Markan material.[18] Unlike Matthew, who reduces Mark's version to a summary account, Luke maintains not only the basic narrative pattern but also such details as the jar of water that the householder carries (Lk 22:10, cf. Mark 14:13). As both Taylor and Schürmann have shown in their thorough studies, the level of reliance is extremely high, with only minor modifications in style.[19] Luke's modifications to the story are

---

[18] Jeremias, *Sprache*, 285.
[19] Heinz Schürmann, "Der Paschalmahlbericht. Lk 22,(7–14)15–18." *Neutestamentliche Abhandlungen*, vol. 19 part 5, (Münster: Aschendorffsche Verlagsbuchhandlung, 1953), 77–104; Taylor, 44; Fitzmyer, 1377. Taylor computes the agreement with Mark to be 65.2 percent.

minor, appearing to place more emphasis on Jesus' own prior planning and deliberation. For instance, in Mark, the disciples initiate the action of preparing the Passover; in Luke, Jesus initiates the action. There are no similarities between Luke and Matthew against Mark, nor are there any similarities to John.

THE LAST SUPPER. LUKE 22:14–20

¹⁴ Καὶ ὅτε ἐγένετο ἡ ὥρα, ἀνέπεσεν καὶ οἱ ἀπόστολοι σὺν αὐτῷ. ¹⁵ καὶ εἶπεν πρὸς αὐτούς, Ἐπιθυμίᾳ ἐπεθύμησα τοῦτο τὸ πάσχα φαγεῖν μεθ' ὑμῶν πρὸ τοῦ με παθεῖν· ¹⁶ λέγω γὰρ ὑμῖν ὅτι οὐ μὴ φάγω αὐτὸ ἕως ὅτου πληρωθῇ ἐν τῇ βασιλείᾳ τοῦ θεοῦ. ¹⁷ καὶ δεξάμενος ποτήριον εὐχαριστήσας εἶπεν, Λάβετε τοῦτο καὶ διαμερίσατε εἰς ἑαυτούς· ¹⁸ λέγω γὰρ ὑμῖν ὅτι οὐ μὴ πίω ἀπὸ τοῦ νῦν ἀπὸ τοῦ γενήματος τῆς ἀμπέλου ἕως οὗ ἡ βασιλεία τοῦ θεοῦ ἔλθῃ. ¹⁹ καὶ λαβὼν ἄρτον εὐχαριστήσας ἔκλασεν καὶ ἔδωκεν αὐτοῖς λέγων, Τοῦτο ἐστιν τὸ σῶμά μου τὸ ὑπὲρ ὑμῶν διδόμενον· τοῦτο ποίειτε εἰς τὴν ἐμὴν ἀνάμνησιν. ²⁰ καὶ τὸ ποτήριον ὡσαύτως μετὰ τὸ δειπνῆσαι, λέγων, Τοῦτο τὸ ποτήριον ἡ καινὴ διαθήκη ἐν τῷ αἵματί μου τὸ ὑπὲρ ὑμῶν ἐκχυννόμενον.

Luke's Last Supper is, of course, significantly different from the Mark/Matthew account. Luke's account is made more difficult by the textual difficulties.[20] If we accept the long form of the text, then it

---

[20] There are two variant texts, a long form and a short. The contested verses are vv. 19-20: τὸ ὑπὲρ ὑμῶν διδόμενον· τοῦτο ποιεῖτε εἰς τὴν ἐμὴν ἀνάμνησιν. καὶ τὸ ποτήριον ὡσαύτως μετὰ τὸ δειπνῆσαι, λέγων· τοῦτο τὸ ποτήριον ἡ καινὴ διαθήκη ἐν τῷ αἵματί μου τὸ ὑπὲρ ὑμῶν ἐκχυννόμενον. The long form is attested by all Greek mss except D, and by most of the versions and church fathers. But the short form, ending at 19a, is found in D,a,d,ff$_2$,i,l,b,e and Old Syriac. An excellent discussion of the textual issues is found in Jeremias, *Eucharistic Words of Jesus*, 139, as well as B. Ehrman, *The Orthodox Corruptions of Scripture* (New York: Oxford University Press, 1993), 197. It is my conclusion that the short form is more original — see the discussion in chapter 4 above, p. 180. Cf. also Bruce Metzger, *A Textual Commentary on the Greek New Testament*, 2d ed. (Stuttgart: United Bible

appears that Luke was drawing on another tradition in addition to Mark. If we accept the short form, however, it seems that either Luke extensively modified Mark (most likely), or drew on another supper tradition instead of Mark (less likely). It is tempting to adopt the long form of the text, in which case Luke appears to be interweaving Mark with the other (Pauline) form of the tradition, but as argued in chapter 4 above, the short form is most probably original.

An analysis of the text of Luke 22:14-20 yields the following comparisons.

LUKE 22:14.

While it does not have many words common with Mark, this verse nonetheless follows Mark's content and thought closely (cf. Mark 14:17). In both instances, the three major elements are featured: a temporal reference, the beginning of the dinner, and a reference to Jesus' companions.[21] The differences are attributable to Lukan redaction of the Markan account.[22]

LUKE 22:15–16.

Verse 15 has no parallel in Mark at all. It appears to be primarily a Lukan creation to introduce the dinner teaching. Verse 16 should probably be seen also as having no formal parallel in Mark, although it does have echoes of Mark 14:25.[23] But since Mark 14:25 is more closely paralleled in Luke's verse 18, perhaps something more complex is taking place. Luke seems to have been freely working with the basic Markan text, here expanding the first bread saying to make it parallel with the cup saying in verse 18.

Societies, 1994), 173.
    [21] Soards, 27.
    [22] Jeremias, *Sprache*, 286.
    [23] Soards, 27.

LUKE 22:17-18.

Verse 17 has some strong similarity to Mark 14:22, primarily in the command λάβετε (τοῦτο). But again, this verse in Mark is much more strongly paralleled in Luke verse 19. The command λάβετε, though, appears to have been derived from Mark. Verse 18, on the other hand, is very close to Mark 14:25. Again, it appears that Luke was drawing on Mark here, despite the rather loose connections.[24]

LUKE 22:19-20.

In these verses, Luke's connection with Mark is even more tenuous. On the one hand, Luke's τοῦτο ἐστιν τὸ σῶμα μου is identical with Mark 14:22. On the other hand, what follows (τὸ ὑπὲρ ὑμῶν διδόμενον τοῦτο ποιεῖτε εἰς τὴν ἐμήν ἀνάμνησιν) is not found in Mark, but is exactly the wording found in 1 Cor 11:24. And while verse 20 has some parallel with Mark 14:23-24, it is closer to the 1 Corinthians version. It appears that a later scribe, transcribing Luke's Gospel, preferred the Pauline form of the eucharistic words and inserted them in verses 19-20, but without entirely leaving the Markan form: the final clause in Luke, τὸ ὑπὲρ ὑμῶν ἐκχυννόμενον, shows that Mark's version of the supper also influenced the long form of the text.

Overall, Jeremias comes to the conclusion that the Lukan text (long form) is heavily Pauline, so much that he tends to use the shorthand Luke/Pauline together with Mark/Matthew in discussing the two major forms of tradition extant. Similarly, Goulder has argued that Luke was accommodating the Markan story to the tradition of 1 Corinthians. While Mark provides the narrative structure and the basic

---

[24] Soards concludes, "... it seems best to say that the unit *as a whole* is without an exact match in Mark; but it is necessary to recognize that within the unit, 17a-18c have rough parallels in Mark 14.23,25" (2). Perhaps Soards' conclusion is still too cautious, however. Goulder seems to be closer to the mark when he concludes "Dependence — one way or the other — is plain..." Despite Schürmann, straightforward dependence of Luke on Mark seems the easier" (725).

content, there is a strong influence from 1 Corinthians where Paul's form is different from Mark's. But, of course, such considerations assume that the long form of the text is original, which we have concluded it is not. There are no similarities with John in this unit of text. Luke has made substantial modifications to Mark in creating his form of the supper account.

BETRAYAL PREDICTION. LUKE 22:21–30

²¹ πλὴν ἰδοὺ ἡ χεὶρ τοῦ παραδιδόντος με μετ' ἐμοῦ ἐπὶ τῆς τραπέζης. ²² ὅτι ὁ υἱὸς μὲν τοῦ ἀνθρώπου κατὰ τὸ ὡρισμένον πορεύεται, πλὴν οὐαὶ τῷ ἀνθρώπῳ ἐκείνῳ δι' οὗ παραδίδοται. ²³ καὶ αὐτοὶ ἤρχαντο συζητεῖν πρὸς ἑαυτοὺς τὸ τίς ἄρα εἴη ἐξ αὐτῶν ὁ τοῦτο μέλλων πράσσειν. ²⁴ Ἐγένετο δὲ καὶ φιλονεικία ἐν αὐτοῖς, τὸ τίς αὐτῶν δοκεῖ εἶναι μείζων. ²⁵ ὁ δὲ εἶπεν αὐτοῖς· οἱ βασιλεῖς τῶν ἐθνῶν κυριεύουσιν αὐτῶν καὶ οἱ ἐξουσιάζοντες αὐτῶν εὐεργέται καλοῦνται. ²⁶ ὑμεῖς δὲ οὐχ οὕτως, ἀλλ' ὁ μείζων ἐν ὑμῖν γινέσθω ὡς ὁ νεώτερος καὶ ὁ ἡγούμενος ὡς ὁ δαικονῶν. ²⁷ τίς γὰρ μείζων, ὁ ἀνακείμενος ἢ ὁ διακονῶν; οὐχὶ ὁ ἀνακείμενος; ἐγὼ δὲ ἐν μέσῳ ὑμῶν εἰμι ὡς ὁ διακονῶν. ²⁸ Ὑμεῖς δέ ἐστε οἱ διαμεμενηκότες μετ' ἐμοῦ ἐν τοῖς πειρασμοῖς μου· ²⁹ κἀγὼ διατίθεμαι ὑμῖν καθὼς διέθετό μοι ὁ πατήρ μου βασιλείαν, ³⁰ ἵνα ἔσθητε καὶ πίνητε ἐπὶ τῆς τραπέζης μου ἐν τῇ βασιλείᾳ μου, καὶ καθήσεσθε ἐπὶ θρόνων τὰς δώδεκα φυλὰς κρίνοντες τοῦ Ἰσραήλ.

In Jesus' prediction of betrayal (22:21–22), it is clear that Luke was working with Mark even though most of the wording is not closely related.[25] First of all, in Luke Jesus indicates after the eucharistic words that the one who is betraying him (παραδιδόντες) is eating with him at the table. The language that is used is quite different from Mark's, where Jesus at the onset of the dinner predicted specifically that one of the ones eating with him will betray him (παραδώσει, future tense). Each of the disciples in Mark reacts to Jesus' prediction by

---

[25] Soards, for instance, sees no "non-Markan" features in these verses.

asking if it is he that will betray; Jesus' specific identification that the betrayer is dipping into the dish with him is cast as a response to the disciples' self-questioning. Luke, in contrast, has the betrayal not as a prediction, but as a suggestive descriptive comment about one of the Twelve; it serves more to heighten the sense of sacrifice and kenosis attached to the Lord's Supper than to predict a future act. But despite the differences, the basic story is clearly the same; Luke has simply shortened the story to its bare minimum.

That Luke was using Mark becomes clearer in the following verse (v. 22), where much of the language is in fact clearly dependent: thirteen out of the eighteen words are identical and in the same order. Luke added some of his normal editorial modifications; the use of κατὰ τὸ ὡρισμένον instead of γέγραπται and such particles as πλὴν show Luke's hand.[26] The dependence in verse 22 is shown in the following comparison:

Luke: ὅτι ὁ υἱὸς μὲν τοῦ ἀνθρώπου κατὰ τὸ ὡρισμένον πορεύεται
Mark: ὅτι ὁ μὲν υἱὸς τοῦ ἀνθρώπου ὑπάγει καθὼς γέγραπται περὶ αὐτοῦ

Luke: πλὴν οὐαὶ τῷ ἀνθρώπῳ ἐκείνῳ δι' οὗ   παραδίδοται
Mark: οὐαὶ δὲ τῷ ἀνθρωπῳ ἐκείνῳ δι' οὗ ὁ υἱὸς τοῦ ἀνθρώπου παραδίδοται

Indeed, Luke's obvious use of Mark in verse 22, together with his freedom from Mark in verses 21 and 23 demonstrates Luke's editorial procedure. He was quite willing to shorten, delete, and reformulate Mark to serve his purpose. Thus the introduction to the story found in Mark 14:18-19 is deleted, both because stating the setting at the table is unnecessary (the dinner scene having already been established at the Lord's Supper beginning in v. 14), and because Luke transforms the nature of the disciples' questions; instead of initially asking, "is it I?" the disciples in Luke respond to Jesus' prediction of betrayal by questioning one another. Then the statement about the one

---

[26] Jeremias, *Sprache* (288) notes Luke's use of ὁρίζω; cf. Goulder, 730. Goulder is clearly more correct than Jeremias in listing πλὴν as a Lukan editorial word than one drawn from tradition.

dipping bread (Mark 14:20) is modified, but still retains much of the force of Mark. This is followed, as noted above, by an almost word-for-word reliance in the prediction of Jesus' departure and the pronouncement of woe for the betrayer. Finally, Luke creates a new conclusion that emphasizes the disciples' response as he knows it. It is thus clear that Luke drew on Mark, but was willing to depart from Mark's version to reinterpret the story as needed.

Despite the clear reliance on Mark, however, Luke has some features that raise questions about the influence of other traditions.

1. In Mark (and Matthew), the disciples response to Jesus' prediction is a self-directed questioning, perhaps reflecting the existential purpose of the Second Gospel.[27] In contrast, in Luke has disciples question one another, which sets up the conflict scene that follows: the dispute over who among them is the greatest. The interrogation is reciprocal, not private and internal.

2. Luke's narrative of what happens next appears to be drawn from material reported previously in Mark (Luke 22:24–27 par. Mark 10:41–45), as well as from Q or Matthew material (Luke 22:28–30 par. Matt 19:28). Such departure from Mark's order is a fairly unusual pattern for Luke; usually where Luke draws from Mark, his account follows Mark's order quite closely.[28] Why at this point did Luke choose to modify the basic Markan outline? Aside from using the material from Mark 10 and from Q/Matthew, Luke makes other significant modifications, particularly in emphasizing Jesus' statements about service.

    a. Luke's statement that the leader must be one who serves (vs. the first must be slave of all), strengthens the climax statement in

---

[27] I interpret the purpose of the Second Gospel to be to persuade readers to critique their own response to Jesus based on the narratives' portrayal of the disciples' response to Jesus and the gospel. See Mary Ann Tolbert, *Sowing the Gospel* (Minneapolis: Fortress Press, 1989), 301 ff. and Robert Tannehill, "The Disciples in Mark: The Function of a Narrative Role," *JR* 57 (1977): 386–405.

[28] Henry J. Cadbury, *The Style and Literary Method of Luke*, Harvard Theological Studies 6 (Cambridge: Harvard University Press, 1919), 77.

verse 27 ("I am among you as one who serves"), suggesting that the central issue is Jesus' own service as an example.

b. Luke's teaching about service is focused around the setting of the dinner table rather than an unrelated gnomic or possibly eschatological statement about the Son of Man. So not only does Luke use the word διακονέω to refer to his personal service, which might be taken in its narrow sense of table-service, but he also uses an image drawn from the table setting: "For which is the greater, the one who sits at table, or one who serves? Is it not the one who sits at table? But I am among you as one serving (διακονῶν)." This example serves to focus attention back on the setting of dialogue: the farewell supper.

c. Luke's conclusion of the matter personalizes the issue of service: "I am among you as one who serves." Service is not just an idea in abstract or something done by the "Son of Man;" Jesus himself at that point is the one who serves.

3. In Mark and Matthew, the prediction of betrayal takes place before the formal eucharistic sayings over the meal; in Luke, the prediction takes place after the meal itself.

These three basic changes from the Markan pattern here suggest that Luke was either very independent in his use of Mark (and Matthew or Q) or that he had another source that cast an influence on his use of primary sources.

What is interesting is that John contains, in one form or another, some of the same aspects of Jesus' discourse at the final meal:

1. As in Luke, so also in John the disciples respond to the revelation of the betrayal not with a self-examination but rather with a reciprocal questioning in the disciples' looking and thinking (cf. Luke's "asking") about one another. In John 13:25, the disciples look at one another, uncertain of who Jesus is speaking of, and finally ask Jesus "who is it?"

2. In John, the meal is dominated by Jesus' own footwashing, which is an example of humility and service. The climax of this ritual act is Jesus' statement "If I then, your Lord and Teacher, have washed

your feet, you also should do as I have done to you" (John 13:14). John, as Luke, clearly emphasizes Jesus' serving as a personal example of service to others.[29] Moreover, John as well closely links this personal service to the dinner table.

3. In John, the prediction of betrayal also takes place *after* the meal proper, not before. The ritual focus takes place first, and only after this does the suggestion that one of them will betray him occur.

Thus while it is apparent that Luke has drawn primarily on Mark, the places where Luke departs from Mark show strong similarity to features of John's account of the Last Supper. Once again it appears that Luke knew John and found some features of his account to be particularly creditable or influential.

It is not difficult to imagine that Luke was following the Markan outline of the preparation for the supper and the supper itself but also trying to reconcile it with John's account. In John, the supper itself is integrally connected with Jesus' footwashing and the related teaching on service. And in John, the betrayal is announced after the dinner is eaten. Luke was faced with two opposing accounts of what appears to be the same event. But he did not simply choose one or the other. The dinner scene and the Lord's Supper he drew from Mark. But the order of the betrayal, the reaction of the disciples to the betrayal, and the focus of the teaching on service he incorporated from John.

Finally, that the influence on Luke's use of Mark might have come from another (non-Markan) source is strengthened by the fact that these changes in Luke cannot be adequately accounted for by Luke's theological tendencies.[30] It appears that Luke made changes in

---

[29] As another example of Luke's connection to this passage in John, cf. Luke 12:37.

[30] Soards argues that Luke here was interpreting Mark 10:42–44 under the influence of Luke 9:46, not some outside influence. But Soards does not explain why Luke has returned to a theme he already dealt with in 9:46 (an argument of who is greatest), given his tendency to avoid doublets. Moreover, it is not at all apparent that 9:46 is an apt parallel to Luke's modifications here.

Mark, his preferred source, not to make a major point, but rather to reflect a variant understanding of events.

Peter's Denial Predicted. Luke 22:31-33

³¹ Σίμων Σίμων, ἰδοὺ ὁ σατανᾶς ἐξῃτήσατο ὑμᾶς τοῦ σινιάσαι ὡς τὸν σῖτον· ³² ἐγὼ δὲ ἐδεήθην περὶ σοῦ ἵνα μὴ ἐκλίπῃ ἡ πίστις σου· καὶ σύ ποτε ἐπιστρέψας στήρισον τοὺς ἀδελφούς σου. ὁ δὲ εἶπεν αὐτῷ· κύριε, μετὰ σοῦ ἕτοιμός εἰμι καὶ εἰς φυλακὴν καὶ εἰς θάνατον πορεύεσθαι. ³³ ὁ δὲ εἶπεν· λέγω σοι, Πέτρε, *οὐ φωνήσει* σήμερον *ἀλέκτωρ ἕως* τρίς με ἀπαρνήσῃ εἰδέναι.

Luke continues the dinner scene after the discussion of who will betray Jesus with a prediction of Peter's denial. All four of the Gospels contain the account of the prediction of Peter's denial, and at casual glance they all appear to be relatively similar. Is Luke's account, as in most circumstances, close to the Mark/Matthew version? A close comparison of Luke with the other Synoptics shows some significant differences in content, such that it is hard to establish definitively that Luke was drawing upon Mark's account.

1. Luke reports the prediction of Peter's denial within the setting of the dinner scene, not on the Mount of Olives.[31]

2. Luke does not report a prediction of general falling away (σκανδαλίζειν) drawing on Zechariah 13:7, which introduces the subject in the other Synoptics.[32]

---

[31] Julius Schniewind, *Die Parallelperikopen bei Lukas und Johannes* (Hildesheim: Georg Olms Verlagsbuchhandlung, 1958), 28, notes that this setting within the dinner scene is a major point of similarity with John. This change in order is also noted by Goulder, who argues that this change was introduced for liturgical reasons (739). The argument for a liturgical structure in Luke I find the most unpersuasive aspect of Goulder's book.

[32] Schniewind, 28; Soards, 52.

3. Luke alone reports Jesus' statement that Satan was seeking to sift the disciples like wheat and that Peter after the denial will have some special function with the disciples.

4. Luke disagrees on the substance of Peter's protest. Instead of recording Peter's protest that he will not fall away like the rest of the disciples, which follows the prediction from Zechariah in the other Synoptics, Luke reports Peter's assertion that he is ready to go to prison and even death. Thus Peter in Luke is positively predicting his courage and loyalty, not protesting against his weakness.

5. Luke's wording of the final prediction by Jesus varies substantially from Mark/Matthew, although it appears to be saying the same thing as in Mark 14:30.[33]

The first half of this text unit (22:31–32) is really without parallel in Mark. Not only does the Lukan language not follow Mark, but Luke in fact omits a major unit of the Markan tradition, namely the prediction, using Zechariah 13:7, that the disciples will flee. One major suggestion for the derivation of verses 31–32 is use of an independent tradition (L material).[34] But there is little in outstanding non-Lukan style that would compel such a conclusion without some evidence of another text that also contains this tradition.[35]

---

[33] Taylor, 65: eight out of fifteen words are common to Luke and Mark.

[34] Cf. Fitzmyer, *Luke* (X–XXIV), 1421. Those who hold to the use of a tradition source are, not surprisingly, Schürmann, Taylor, and Rehkopf, as well as Hans Klein "Die Verleugnung des Petrus: Eine traditionsgeschichtliche Untersuchung," *ZTK* 58 (1961): 285-328.

[35] Although Jeremias, *Sprache*, (291, 61) lists such non-Lukan style as the doubling Σίμων Σίμων and the word σατανᾶς, as well as antithetical parallelism and certain qualities like the failure to include the addressee in a prayer (ἐδεήθην περὶ σοῦ and the use of ἐκλείπω), others, notably Goulder (734), find more convincingly that these style markers are in fact Lukan. So here Σίμων Σίμων reflects Luke's use of Martha, Martha; Master, Master; Saul, Saul. And Satan, of course, has already appeared in Luke 22:3. So, similarly, Goulder notes that the use of δέεσθαι is uniquely Lukan in the NT and such words as περί and ἐκλείπω are frequent in Luke's vocabulary. It is clear that Jeremias' analysis is at times suspect and needs to be double-checked.

It is likely however, as Soards and Goulder suggest, that Luke omitted the Markan account and composed a replacement account that sets the scene for the prediction of Peter's denial.[36] Luke's tendency is to downplay Mark's depiction of the disciples as absent and afraid at the death of Jesus. In other words, Luke's account rehabilitates the disciples; and that appears to be a common theme running throughout the Third Gospel. Since Luke does record the disciples present at the cross, and indeed has them remaining together in Jerusalem even after the death of Jesus, the prediction contained in Mark was simply untenable. Moreover, certain stylistic features in Luke's account actually cohere with Luke's writing style: the doubling of the address to Simon,[37] the use of the person Satan,[38] and certain language traits.[39] There is, then, a strong case to be made that Luke has actively reworked traditions taken over from other sources.

The initial verse, in which Jesus says that Satan has desired to sift the disciples (plural ὑμᾶς), appears to be continuing the theme, already developed by Luke (and John), that Satan is at work in the testing of the disciples. The theme was introduced in 22:3 with Satan's entering into Judas (cf. John 13:2, 27). But Luke here broadens the role of Satan to include weakening the disciples at least temporarily: Peter after returning is to strengthen the others. In this feature, Luke is echoing slightly the Markan theme of the disciples' flight and fear. It is possible that Luke took over a traditional saying of Satan's sifting and fit

---

[36] Soards, 52, Goulder, 734. Goulder actually claims that Luke was redacting the Markan account, but if so, he was doing such a radical re-writing that it in effect was the same as a composition. I take it, then, that Soards and Goulder are really saying the same thing.

[37] See, for instance Goulder: Master, Master; Martha, Martha; and Saul, Saul (734); but Rehkopf (98), and Jeremias (*Sprache*, 291), see this as sign of pre-Lukan tradition.

[38] Soards, 52; Rehkopf sees this as tradition, not redaction (96).

[39] e.g. Exclamation ἰδού, infinitive plus τοῦ, and the words ἐπιστρέφειν, στηρίζειν, ἀδελφούς, πειρασμός. See Fitzmyer, *Luke* (X–XXIV), 1421; Soards, 53; John Hawkins, *Horae Synopticae* (Oxford: Clarenden Press, 1909), 48; Taylor, 65; Goulder, 734–36; cf. Rehkopf, 97; Jeremias, *Sprache*, 291.

it into the Markan narrative, leaving telltale signs of the seam. Hence the shift from plural ὑμᾶς to singular σοῦ could be a sign of the shift from tradition to Lukan editing with little modification in the former. But such clumsy "cut and paste" editing seems unlikely. The story has a smooth movement from the general concern for the disciples to the mediation of that concern by Peter as a leader.[40] Thus it appears that Luke was weaving together the Markan theme of a certain defection of the disciples with another theme, contained also in John, that the disciples did indeed remain faithful. The actual language shows strong signs of Luke's compositional impress: Luke thoroughly reworked his sources.

The second half of the pericope, 22:33–34, is much closer to Mark's account. Peter responds to Jesus with a claim of readiness, which sets the scene for Jesus' final blunt prediction of the denial. Furthermore, Jesus' prediction of denial contains the same reference to the cock crowing and a three-time denial. As a result, the latter half of the passage is frequently seen as a modification of the Markan account made to fit the alternate setting created by verses 31–32.

But there are two major divergences from the Markan account, and in both of them Luke manifests agreement with John. First of all, it is striking that in both Luke and John, Peter rather suddenly announces, before there has been any prediction of a falling away, that he is ready to follow Jesus, even to death. The reference to willingness to follow even in death does occur in the final iteration of the exchange in Mark and Matthew, after the prediction of denial. But it is striking that in both Luke and John the statement is made before the prediction of denial, and not in a grudging, concessive way. It is, in both, a positive, almost enthusiastic, claim by Peter before any doubt has been created about his loyalty. There is, then, a basic agreement between Luke and John in the structure and sense of the exchange between Jesus and Peter:

---

[40] Compare a similar theme in John 21:15–19.

Luke Chapter 22

Mark and Matthew	Luke and John
Jesus predicts the disciples will fall away. Mk 14:26-28; Mt 26:30-32.	**No such prediction**
No such discourse.	Jesus and Peter have a discourse in which Peter is predicted to have a future leadership role. Lk 22:31-32; Jn 13:36.
Peter objects: I won't fall away. Mk 14:29; Mt 26:33.	Peter voluntarily offers to follow even to death. Lk 22:33; Jn 13:37.
Jesus predicts Peter's denial. Mk 14:30; Mt 26:34.	Jesus predicts Peter's denial. Lk 22:34; Jn 13:38.
Peter responds vehemently: I will not deny you, even if I must die. Mk 14:31; Mt 26:35.	**No such response.**

Second, Luke and John agree in important features in the wording of Jesus' prediction of Peter's denial. So while Luke and Mark are clearly reporting the same event, it is nonetheless apparent that Luke radically modified Mark. These modifications are indeed quite surprising if Luke was relying only on Mark as a source.[41] Observe also the following basic points of agreement between these two primary approaches to Jesus' prediction of the denial:

---

[41] Thus it is a bit surprising that Fitzmyer, *Luke* (X–XXIV) can so confidently conclude that "There can be little doubt about v. 34, where 'half its words (8/15) are common to Luke and Mark'" (1421). While the words are similar, the construction is not, and Luke is *more* similar to John!

Mark 14:30 and Matt 26:34	Luke 22:34	John 13:38
ἀμὴν λέγω σοι ὅτι	λέγω σοι	ἀμὴν ἀμὴν λέγω σοι
ἐν ταύτῃ τῇ νυκτὶ	οὐ	οὐ μὴ
πρὶν	—	—
ἀλέκτορα φωνῆσαι	φωνήσει σήμερον ἀλέκτωρ	ἀλέκτωρ φωνήσῃ
—	ἕως	ἕως οὗ
τρὶς ἀπαρνήσῃ με	τρίς με (ἀπ)αρνήσῃ	ἀρνήσῃ με τρίς

In Mark and Matthew, the direct address is introduced by ὅτι, while Luke and John move directly into the words of Jesus. More importantly, Mark and Matthew use the temporal term "in this night" (ἐν ταύτῃ τῇ νυκτί) plus the adverb "before" (πρίν) to set up the prediction in a positive sense. That is, Peter *will* deny Jesus three times before the cock crows. The basic construction is very different in Luke and John. They share the alternate approach of a negative statement; the cock will *not* (οὐ or οὐ μὴ) crow *until* (ἕως) Peter denies Jesus three times. True, Luke and John disagree on the emphatic nature of the negative (John uses the emphatic οὐ μὴ; Luke does not) and on the mood of the verb (Luke is in the future indicative; John in the aorist subjunctive), but the basic pattern is strikingly similar.

Can Luke's reliance on John explain the cluster of similarities between Luke and John and likewise the departure of Luke's account from his Markan source? Once again, I think Luke's knowledge of John as a parallel source to Mark explains very well the final version of the passage.

One can certainly understand Luke's reluctance to repeat the prophecy from Zechariah. Given Luke's understanding of the role of the disciples, especially at and immediately after the crucifixion, this prophecy does not cohere with his portrayal of the final events: the disciples do not all flee. Luke's editorial tendency is even more reasonable if he had before him an alternate version that left out the Zechariah prophecy and which also had some disciples present to the end of the story. In an alternate account such as the Fourth Gospel, Luke would note an exchange between Peter and Jesus that could serve as the germ for a more emphatic and Lukan interpretation—one in which Peter would be tested but would return to strengthen the brethren. The key elements of this exchange between Jesus and Peter are very Lukan, but they are not far removed from John's version, in which Peter is denied the immediate opportunity to follow but assured of an ultimate one (John 13:36). Following Jesus, in Luke's editorial modification, is seen as ministering to the disciples; this is undoubtedly an expansion and interpretation based on Luke's immediately preceding dialogue on service. One can imagine, then, that Luke, was modifying and expanding John's introduction to the denial prediction, interpreting John's version in light of Luke's previous narration about service.

Luke then follows quite closely the Johannine version of Peter's response, even to Peter's claim that he will follow even to death. Although Luke knew Mark's version, it did not fit his understanding of Peter and Peter's response to the events of the Passion. Since John reports a variant account, Luke was able to draw on this alternative interpretation of the prediction of Peter's denial, choosing John's account over Mark's. In the final verse of the prediction, Luke even follows fairly closely John's wording of the exclamation rather than Mark's. It appears that Luke was strongly influenced by the Johannine account; while paying some attention to Mark, he tended to follow John instead. This is seen as well in Luke's deletion of Peter's final counter statement, also absent in John's version.

Even more important than the agreement in such matters as the absence of the prediction of falling away or Peter's vehement response or the inclusion of a discourse on Peter's future role is the fact that these occur in Luke and John in the same order. And perhaps even more important than that is the common shift of the denial story from after the Supper to the Supper setting itself. The striking similarity in the structure of the narrative is often overlooked or downplayed in analyses of the Lukan account. So, for instance, Goulder explains the change in setting (from Gethsemane to the dinner setting) as a liturgical arrangement.[42] But such reliance on a liturgy seems foreign to Luke and still does not explain why Luke and John have this common structure.

The positioning of the denial prediction in Luke's narrative is very significant and suggests the influence of another source or tradition. While there are strong indications that Luke was working with Mark's narrative, if Luke was using only Mark, it is unclear why he would have modified Mark's ordering of the prediction of Peter's denial. There is no strong Lukan theme that is developed by such a move. Granted that Luke tends toward redeeming Peter and the disciples from Mark's more pessimistic assessment, the placement of the prediction of denial *per se* does not appreciably advance that cause. Precisely the absence of a compelling Lukan motive for the change in order suggests the influence of a competing tradition or source. Brown, in a footnote, acknowledges precisely this fact, that there is another tradition (which he calls pre-Johannine) that has the prediction of denial situated in the Last Supper setting.[43] This order is found in John. Brown argues that Luke came to know this order only from a pre-Gospel contact between Luke and the Johannine tradition! That is possible. But since the Johannine tradition only is presently known only through the Fourth Gospel, one can safely say that Luke appears to have been influenced by another order of events seen now in John, and that this other order of events apparently displaced the Markan order.

In this section, Luke does not follow Mark closely at all. But one need not look to an unknown source (L) to explain the divergences of Luke from Mark.[44] Luke agrees with John's broad ordering of the narrative. And indeed at frequent points in the text, Luke appears again to be the middle term between Mark and John, having woven together the two accounts, with the priority given to John's.

---

[42] Goulder, 739.

[43] Brown, *Death*, 143, n. 42.

[44] As in Taylor, *Passion*, 65.

THE TWO SWORDS. LUKE 22:35–38

³⁵ Καὶ εἶπεν αὐτοῖς· ὅτε ἀπέστειλα ὑμᾶς ἄτερ βαλλαντίου καὶ πήρας καὶ ὑποδημάτων, μή τινος ὑστερήσατε; οἱ δὲ εἶπαν· οὐθενός. ³⁶ εἶπεν δὲ αὐτοῖς· ἀλλὰ νῦν ὁ ἔχων βαλλάντιον ἀράτω, ὁμοίως καὶ πήραν, καὶ ὁ μὴ ἔχων πωλησάτω τὸ ἱμάτιον αὐτοῦ καὶ ἀγορασάτω μάχαιραν. ³⁷ λέγω γὰρ ὑμῖν ὅτι τοῦτο τὸ γεγραμμένον δεῖ τελεσθῆναι ἐν ἐμοί, τό καὶ μετὰ ἀνόμων ἐλογίσθη· καὶ γὰρ τὸ περὶ ἐμοῦ τέλος ἔχει. ³⁸ οἱ δὲ εἶπαν· κύριε, ἰδοὺ μάχαιραι ὧδε δύο. ὁ δὲ εἶπεν αὐτοῖς· ἱκανόν ἐστιν.

This section of Luke is unique, without parallel in either the other Synoptics or John. It is possible that Luke drew upon an independent source.[45] It is also possible that Luke composed this statement, drawing upon themes from the Old Testament (Isa 53:12) and from within his own Gospel (Luke 13:32 and 18:31) in order to set the scene for 22:49–50 and 23:32 ff. But with no specific similarity to a text apparent, it is hard to decide between these possibilities. It is clear, however, that Luke felt free to depart from Mark and to anticipate the subsequent events in his narrative.

Whether the source of this unit of text is primarily a pre-Lukan tradition[46] or is the free composition of Luke,[47] it is clear that Luke used it in narrative coordination with the sword-strike incident that occurs in 22:49–51. Luke, like Matthew and John, describes the one who wields the sword in that pericope as one of the followers of Jesus, a matter that is unclear in Mark. Luke's reference here back to the sending of the twelve and the seventy (Luke 9:1–6, 10:1–12) reinforces the connection between the followers of Jesus and the use of the

---

[45] So Soards, 54.

[46] See also Taylor, *Passion,* 67–68; Schürmann, "Jesu Abschiedsrede," 116–142. Jeremias, *Sprache* (292–93), also identifies much of the material as traditional.

[47] Goulder, 736-39.

sword. And Jesus' enigmatic recasting of the previous sending events[48] creates the narrative context that explains why his followers had swords to cut off the ear at the arrest. Luke, then, appears to have interwoven a reference back to his own story together, possibly, with an independent tradition or source, resulting in a version of the arrest that is slightly at odds with Mark's version.

PRAYER ON MOUNT OF OLIVES. LUKE 22:39-46

³⁹ Καὶ ἐξελθὼν ἐπορεύθη κατὰ τὸ ἔθος <u>εἰς τὸ ὄρος τῶν ἐλαιῶν</u>, ἠκολούθησαν δὲ αὐτῷ καὶ οἱ μαθηταί. ⁴⁰ γενόμενος δὲ ἐπὶ τοῦ τόπου εἶπεν αὐτοῖς· <u>προσεύχεσθε μὴ εἰσελθεῖν εἰς πειρασμόν</u>. ⁴¹ καὶ αὐτὸς ἀπεσπάσθη ἀπ' αὐτῶν ὡσεὶ λίθου βολὴν καὶ θεὶς τὰ γόνατα <u>προσεύχετο</u> ⁴² λέγων· **πάτερ**, εἰ βούλει <u>παρένεγκε τοῦτο τὸ ποτήριον ἀπ' ἐμοῦ</u>· πλὴν μὴ τὸ θέλημά μου ἀλλὰ τὸ σὸν γινέσθω. ⁴⁵ καὶ ἀναστὰς ἀπὸ τῆς προσευχῆς ἐλθὼν πρὸς τοὺς μαθητὰς εὗρεν κοιμωμένους αὐτοὺς ἀπὸ τῆς λύπης, ⁴⁶ καὶ εἶπεν αὐτοῖς· τί <u>καθεύδετε; ἀναστάντες πρσεύχεσθε, ἵνα μὴ εἰσέλθητε εἰς πειρασμόν</u>.

In broad terms, Luke's account of Jesus' departure after the meal follows Mark's narrative development: Jesus and his disciples go out to a place some distance away, to the Mount of Olives; at that place, Jesus engages in private prayer in which he anguishes over his role in the events to come but ultimately asks for God's will to be done; upon returning from prayer, Jesus finds his disciples sleeping. But aside from these basic structural similarities, Luke's account is significantly different from Mark and Matthew.

---

[48] Is the scene ironic, or does it simply contain highly suggestive language about the crisis of Jesus' impending death? Cf. Fitzmyer, *Luke* (X-XXIV), 1430. Taylor, suggests that v. 36 is ironic, but that the disciples misunderstood the irony and took him seriously (*Passion*, 67). Likewise, the final words of Jesus, "It is enough," are considered to be an ironic reflection on the coming arrest and crucifixion.

1. Luke reports the journey to the Mount of Olives after the prediction of Peter's denial, not before as do Mark and Matthew.[49]

2. Luke does not name the place of prayer as Gethsemane.

3. Luke reports Jesus' instruction to the disciples as an admonition to pray for themselves in order to resist temptation. Mark and Matthew report the instruction as primarily one of watching Jesus during his prayer. But Mark does refer to the disciples' need to pray in order to resist temptation (ἵνα μὴ ἔλθητε εἰς πειρασμόν) after they fail to remain awake, perhaps to suggest that they will indeed fail because they do not pray.

4. Mark and Matthew focus on Peter, James and John, who are selected from the rest to be closer and who alone are said to fall asleep. Luke treats all the disciples as a common group.

5. Luke records that Jesus only prays once, and admonishes the disciples once; Mark and Matthew report a three-fold pattern of request and failure by the disciples.

6. Luke's shortening of the episode removes the references to Jesus' anguish over the coming Passion. It appears, then, in Luke that Jesus is more resolute in his facing death.[50]

7. Luke's conclusion is more positive regarding the disciples. Their sleep is from sorrow, not from weakness. And the shortened version leaves little impression that the disciples were unfaithful.

8. Luke does not report that Jesus was sorrowful or distressed.

Aside from the different geographical setting and the altered order of the departure to the Mount of Olives, modifications can easily be seen as Lukan redaction of a Markan source. It appears that Luke simply shortened the story. The initial instruction to the disciples

---

[49] See the discussion p. 286 above.

[50] It should be noted that this understanding of the text is only valid if the textual variant of 22:43–44 is not read. Cf. Bart Ehrman and Mark Plunkett, "The Angel and the Agony: The Textual Problem of Luke 22:43–44," *CBQ* 45 (1983): 401–16, and alternatively, Brown, *Death*, 180–190.

(Luke 22:40) is indeed found in Mark, in the second admonition.[51] The wording (προςεύχεσθε μὴ εἰσελθεῖν εἰς πειρασμόν in v. 40; προσεύχεσθε ἵνα μὴ εἰσέλθητε εἰς πειρασμόν in v. 46) is very close to Mark's phrasing in 14:38. Luke thus retained this element from Mark's version, removed the focus on watchfulness, and collapsed the episode to one prayer. Moreover, Jesus' prayer itself is quite close in wording to Mark, with the opening phrase being almost identical: παράνεγκε (τοῦτο) τὸ ποτήριον ἀπ᾽ ἐμοῦ αλλ᾽ (πλὴν).... The second half of the prayer retains the general sense of Mark's prayer, though Luke's sense is more careful.

A sign of Luke's theological reworking of the Markan account can be seen most clearly in the deletion of Mark and Matthew's statement that Jesus was distressed and sorrowful. But Luke demonstrates a general tendency to suppress Jesus' emotions. As Brown notes, Luke's depiction of Jesus and Paul is often for the purpose of providing a model for Christians to follow.[52] Removing the doubt of pain and fear is consistent with Luke's tendency.

The major changes cohere with Luke's general tendency to avoid painting the disciples in a totally negative light. The disciples remain together as a group instead of splintering. The focus on prayer is expanded to include both disciples and Jesus, thus including the disciples still in the work of Jesus. Indeed, it appears that Jesus' admonition to pray in order to avoid temptation or trial is meant as much for himself as for his disciples.[53] By only having one time of prayer, the disciples fail only once, not three times. And finally, the disciples' sleep is specifically due to grief rather than their weakness. In all, the modifications made in this unit affirm the role of the disciples and

---

[51] Although the wording in 22:40 is different from that in 22:46, the meaning is the same. The infinitive clause must surely have a purposive meaning. So both 22:40 and 46 are drawing on Mark 14:38 (contra Soards, 63).

[52] Brown, *Death*, 157.

[53] So Fitzmyer, *Luke* (X–XXIV), calls the two admonitions an *inclusio* that embraces both the disciples failure and Jesus' successful prayer (1436).

emphasize the role of prayer, both of which are common themes in Luke.[54]

Luke's different reference to the geographical setting, however, and the order of the event relative to the denial and the arrest suggest that he knew of some other tradition about these events. While the absence of the term "Gethsemane" is intriguing in light of its common absence in John, it does not offer a strong link to John or to other possible sources behind Luke. The reference to going to a place κατὰ τὸ ἔθος, however, at this juncture in Luke's narrative is more suggestive of a link to another tradition. It is possible that Luke was looking back to references in Mark and Matthew that Jesus went out of the city a number of times (Mark 11:2, 11–12; 13:3; Matt 21:1, 17; 24:3; 26:6; Luke 19:29, 37). But only two of the references in each Gospel refer to the Mount of Olives. The first instance connects it with the road from Bethany and Bethphage;[55] the second, simply to the site of Jesus' eschatological teaching, which is more importantly located "opposite the temple." In neither instance is there a suggestion of importance regarding this site or of a regular pattern of going there. Thus it does not appear that Luke was trying to connect to Mark's and Matthew's previous geographical references. It is more likely that Luke was making reference to an earlier geographical note in the Third Gospel (Luke 21:37), a reference that is also reminiscent of one in John (John 18:1-2). So Luke seems to have been familiar with a tradition in which Jesus regularly went to the Mount of Olives, contrary to Mark and Matthew.

But Luke's specific reference in 22:39 to Jesus' custom of going to the Mount of Olives may have been inserted there for two reasons.

---

[54] For the role of the disciples, see Joseph Fitzmyer, *Luke the Theologian* (New York: Paulist Press, 1989), 123-28. On the importance of prayer in Luke, see Fitzmyer, *Luke* (I–IX), 244-47, and Allison Trites, "The Prayer Motif in Luke-Acts," in *Perspectives in Luke-Acts*, ed. Charles Talbert (Danville: Association of Baptist Professors of Religion, 1978), 168–86.

[55] See Jack Finegan, *The Archaeology of the New Testament* (Princeton: University Press, 1969), 88-89.

First of all, John's Gospel also makes reference to the frequency of Jesus' meeting there with his disciples[56] at precisely this point in the narrative, just after the transition from the dinner scene to the arrest scene (John 18:1–2).[57] Second, Luke may have made reference to the custom of meeting there regularly for the same reason that the reference seems to be required in John's account. In the Fourth Gospel, the reference is important because Judas has left the disciples before the conclusion of the dinner scene. How else, in the Johannine narrative, would Judas know where to go with the arresting party? Mark, Matthew, and Luke never say when Judas departs, but the reader would assume from the narrative in Mark and Matthew that he leaves around the time of the prediction of Peter's denial ("You will all fall away...." Mark 14:27). This prediction of Peter's denial in Mark and Matthew is, of course, *after* Jesus and the disciples have arrived in Gethsemane. In Luke, Judas' departure, as in John, appears to come at the scene of the dinner (i.e., at the prediction of Peter's denial). If so, then Luke has the same problem as John of explaining how Judas knows where to find Jesus. The casual reference to κατὰ τὸ ἔθος appears to link Luke to John both in the actual reference and in the basic understanding of the order of events.

One can discern, then, Luke's general use of Mark, modified to fit Luke's own interpretation of the importance of prayer and Jesus' use of prayer in the final hours, and modified to recast the disciples' character from Mark's rather negative view. But aside from these ideologically driven themes, one can discern as well possible desire to fit the narrative structure to that seen in John.

---

[56] In John, the term is "across the Kidron," but the reference is to the same place.

[57] Schniewind, 33; Zahn, *Das Evangelium des Lucas,* (Leipzig: A. Deichertsche Verlagsbuchhandlung, 1920), 687.

Jesus' Arrest. Luke 22:47-53

⁴⁷ Ἔτι αὐτοῦ λαλοῦντος ἰδοὺ ὄχλος, καὶ ὁ λεγόμενος Ἰούδας εἷς τῶν δώδεκα προήρχετο αὐτοὺς καὶ ἤγγισεν τῷ Ἰησοῦ φιλῆσαι αὐτόν. ⁴⁸ Ἰησοῦς δὲ εἶπεν αὐτῷ, Ἰούδα, φιλήματι τὸν υἱὸν τοῦ ἀνθρώπου παραδίδως; ⁴⁹ ἰδόντες δὲ οἱ περὶ αὐτὸν τὸ ἐσόμενον εἶπαν, Κύριε, εἰ πατάξομεν ἐν μαχαίρῃ; ⁵⁰ καὶ *ἐπάταξεν* εἷς τις ἐξ αὐτῶν τοῦ ἀρχιερέως τὸν δοῦλον καὶ ἀφεῖλεν τὸ οὖς αὐτοῦ *τὸ δεξιόν*. ⁵¹ ἀποκριθεὶς δὲ ὁ Ἰησοῦς εἶπεν, Ἐᾶτε ἕως τούτου· καὶ ἁψάμενος τοῦ ὠτίου ἰάσατο αὐτόν. ⁵² εἶπεν δὲ Ἰησοῦς πρὸς τοὺς παραγενομένους ἐπ' αὐτὸν ἀρχιερεῖς καὶ στρατηγοὺς τοῦ ἱεροῦ καὶ πρεσβυτέρους, Ὡς ἐπὶ λῃστὴν ἐξήλθατε μετὰ μαχαιρῶν καὶ ξύλων; ⁵³ καθ' ἡμέραν ὄντος μου μεθ' ὑμῶν ἐν τῷ ἱερῷ οὐκ ἐξετείνατε τὰς χεῖρας ἐπ' ἐμέ· ἀλλ' αὕτη ἐστὶν ὑμῶν ἡ ὥρα καὶ ἡ ἐξουσία τοῦ σκότους.

Luke begins the arrest narrative with almost word-for-word reliance on Mark. With only minor modifications, Luke has Jesus still speaking when Judas, who is specifically identified as "one of the twelve," arrives with a crowd. Luke's reliance on Mark is strong in a number of places throughout the pericope, but especially in the opening verses and Jesus' address to the crowd.

But despite the strong similarities, there are a number of ways in which Luke differs from his Markan source.

1. Luke appears to have Judas in a position of greater leadership within the crowd than do Mark or Matthew. Judas leads the arresting party (προήρχετο αὐτοὺς vs. παραγίνεται ... μετ' αὐτοῦ ὄχλος) rather than just being a member of it.

2. Luke makes no mention of weapons in the hands of the crowd.

3. Luke does not seem to acknowledge the use of the kiss as a sign. Indeed, while Judas attempts to kiss Jesus, it appears that Jesus does not let him, stopping the action with an accusatory question.

4. Luke places the sword strike by the disciples between the kiss and the arrest; Mark and Matthew follow the kiss immediately with the arrest.

5. Luke identifies the ear cut off as the right one, and Jesus heals it.

6. Luke has Jesus stop the fighting with a curt command.

7. Luke includes in the crowd gathered to arrest Jesus the chief priests, officers, and elders. Mark and Matthew's crowd is *from* this group but is in no way identified as being composed of such officials of the Jewish people.

8. Luke's unit concludes with a statement about "your hour, the power of darkness."

9. Luke does not have the disciples flee at the conclusion of the arrest.

These major changes once again raise the question of how Luke went about modifying his major source (Mark) and whether he was drawing on any sources to supplement the Markan account. Despite the use of Mark as the structure for the narrative, it appears that Luke was working with another understanding of the arrest which saw (*a*) Jesus as more assertive at the arrest, (*b*) the disciples as more assertive with the officials, and (*c*) Jesus as more in control of his own fate and willingly being arrested.

Once again, some of the distinctive features in Luke's version can also be found in John:

1. Judas is the leader of the arresting party.

2. Jesus initiates the exchange between the arresting group and himself.

3. There is no kiss.

4. The sword strike occurs before the arrest and thus takes the form of a defense of Jesus rather than an attempt to free him.[58]

5. The ear cut off is identified as the right one.

6. Temple officials are present at the arrest.

7. The disciples do not flee.

---

[58] Rehkopf, 65–66.

Most of Luke's points of divergence from Mark are found also in John. But despite this list of intriguing similarities, there are virtually no linguistic similarities between Luke and John that would point to a direct literary relationship.[59] Indeed, some of the similarities share the same content, but none of the distinctive language.[60] How closely linked are Luke and Mark and, alternatively, Luke and John in the arrest unit? A closer look, broken down by subject matter, will help the analysis.

LUKE 22:47a.

Luke follows Mark very closely in the opening verse. The introductory participial phrase is identical, setting the scene in close conjunction with the prayer scene that precedes it. The introductory phrase is followed by the arrival of Judas, who is called one of the twelve, and the crowd (ὄχλος). Taylor notes that ten of fourteen words in the initial sentence are common to Mark and Luke, a strong suggestion that Luke used Mark here.[61]

But why does Luke have Judas "leading" the crowd?[62] There is little suggestion in Mark or Matthew that Judas was initiating the activity, only that he was looking for a means to betray Jesus at the right moment. The introductory phrase in John, though, does contain a similar idea—that Judas had initiated the action and led the soldiers to the place. Here Judas procures the arresting party (λαβὼν τὴν σπεῖρα...) and procedes to the arresting site. The singular verb used by John, ἔρχεται, shows that the focus is on Judas. If Luke knew John or some version of John's tradition, then one can imagine Luke having used the Markan account but having modified it to fit this additional feature of

---

[59] The exception is the common use of συλλαμβάνω in the final account of the arrest. But this is only one word, and little else is alike.

[60] So Schniewind, because of this lack of linguistic similarities, rejects any literary relationship (37).

[61] Taylor, 74.

[62] Cf. also Acts 1:16.

Judas the leader. This is especially true if, following the similarities already noted previously, Judas' defection was in Luke's eyes really due to Satan's entering into him. Judas with Satan thus in him would have been the initiator of the action against Jesus, and Luke would have made room in his narrative for precisely that information.

Luke does not, however, have any notice of the crowd's coming with weapons. This is an omission from the Mark and Matthew narratives,[63] as well as the Johannine version. In each of those cases the crowd is said to have weapons (in Mark/Matthew: μετὰ μαχαιρῶν καὶ ξύλων; in John: μετὰ φανῶν καὶ λαμπάδων καὶ ὅπλων). Luke knew of the weapons (cf. 22:52). But it appears that Luke preferred to emphasize, by its abruptness, the sword strike by the disciples, and he thus deleted the descriptive material that would perhaps explain or anticipate the violence of the sword strike.

LUKE 22:47b–48.

In the Markan story (Mark 14:45), the identification of Jesus by a kiss is anticipated by the prior discussion of such identification between Judas and the chief priests. That discussion is absent in Luke, perhaps as an unnecessary detail. More probably, Luke felt that the focus on the agreement with the Jewish guards detracted from Judas' own leading role in the betrayal. Instead, he has Judas step forward with an attempt to kiss Jesus but apparently not actually kissing him. In Luke, Jesus' response that the kiss would be an act of betrayal shows Jesus' awareness of the purpose of the kiss, and reveals that purpose to the reader as well. But the combination of the attempted kiss and Jesus' words about its being a betrayal make it fairly certain that Luke had the Markan account in his mind as the background for his revised version. Indeed, Judas' attempted kiss in Luke, without the reader's prior knowledge of Mark, would be a bit inexplicable at this point. Luke

---

[63] Rehkopf's assertion that the simple ὄχλος is original in an early tradition common to Luke and Mark, to which Mark inserted the modifiers. There is no evidence that Luke and Mark worked with a common source.

echoes Mark's kiss sign, but he weakened its power and significance in order to enhance and strengthen Jesus' persona.

In addition to the absence of a clear kiss as a sign of betrayal, there is a major difference in the narrative order at this point of the episode. In the Markan and Matthean accounts, when Judas kisses Jesus, the crowd (they) comes forward and arrests Jesus immediately. The sense is of a rabble that is bent on doing violence to Jesus; against its energy Jesus is unable to offer any resistance. But that is not the case in Luke. The actual arrest takes place only after the ear is cut off the servant, and only after Jesus' exchange with the arresting party. A coy question by Jesus addressed to Judas serves to show Jesus' control of the situation. And the sword strike, and Jesus' stopping of the violence, as well as the healing of the ear, further serve to show Jesus' power over the situation. In Mark and Matthew, then, the arrest is almost the initial action of the scene, with the sword strike and Jesus' comments to the crowds as postscripts, whereas in Luke, the arrest is the culminating event.

A narrative construction similar to Luke's is found in John: Jesus' verbal exchange with the arresting party, followed by Simon Peter's sword strike and Jesus' calm resignation to the arrest ("Shall I not drink from the cup which the Father has given me?"). Only at the conclusion of this series of events is Jesus taken into custody. John, then, shows the same pattern and order as Luke. John likewise shares Luke's emphasis on Jesus' control over the events, as well as Jesus' power which comes into play as the arresting party falls backward to the ground when he identifies himself.

While it is clear that Luke drew on Mark, the differences, that Judas does not kiss Jesus and Jesus is not arrested right away, are remarkable. Why would Luke have removed the kiss if he knew about it from his source (Mark)? And why would he have moved the arrest to the end of the narrative? These two issues are linked, in that the kiss is the sign to arrest Jesus. It is striking that John reports no kiss at all, and that the arrest is at the end of the narrative as well. It is not unreasonable to imagine that Luke drew primarily on Mark for the account of the arrest but, knowing an alternate account in John that mentions no kiss and reports the arrest as the culmination of the exchange, modified Mark's account under that influence. Luke does keep the kiss, however, in a modified way: the kiss is only attempted, it is referred to only obliquely as a sign of betrayal.

LUKE 22:49-51.

The Lukan account of the sword strike itself is dependent on the Markan version, but it is a free rendition. As does Mark, Luke has a group of followers around Jesus at the time (οἱ περὶ αὐτόν, which is probably Lukan redaction[64]). One follower strikes the slave of the high priest, cutting off his ear; Jesus responds with an admonition to stop. In particular, there are some strong similarities in the language that point to Luke's reliance on Mark: the assailant is identified as εἷς of the group; the person struck is the slave of the high priest (τὸν δοῦλον τοῦ ἀρχιερέως in Mark, τοῦ ἀρχιερέως τὸν δοῦλον in Luke); and the ear is cut off (ἀφεῖλεν). Moreover, these events all happen in the same order.

But Luke's version, again, has a number of features that are distinctive:

1. The sword strike is preceded by the followers asking Jesus whether they should strike.

2. There is no mention of the assailant's drawing his sword.

3. The ear cut off is the slave's "right ear."

4. Jesus responds with ἐᾶτε ἕως τούτου, which should probably be taken to mean "no more of this" or "this is enough."

5. Jesus heals the ear of the slave.

The first difference, the question posed to Jesus about the use of the sword, is unique to Luke and appears to be his own attempt to bring the arrest into agreement with 22:35-38. Thus Luke was making intertextual references to his own Gospel, and perhaps to another

---

[64] Fitzmyer, *Luke* (X-XXIV), 1448 citing Acts 21:8 for the term.

source or tradition that lies behind verses 35–38. There is some evidence that points to another source or tradition about the use of swords to which Luke might have been referring.⁶⁵ But that evidence is not overwhelming; it must thus be concluded that the question to Jesus could originate either from Lukan composition or a special tradition.

Unlike all the other Gospels, Luke does not report anyone drawing his sword as a prelude to the actual sword strike. The question posed to Jesus seems to serve the purpose of an introduction to the sword strike itself, and perhaps Luke felt that any other description before the sword strike would be superfluous. This difference, therefore, seems to be attributable to Luke's own editorial tendencies.

An unusual feature in Luke's account is the identification of the ear that is cut off as the "right" ear. This feature is intriguing because it is a specific point of agreement with the Gospel of John. But the evidence for a clear literary reliance is not extremely strong. Most importantly, Luke uses a different word for ear than any of the other Gospels, including John. We have, then, the following differences:

Mark	Matthew	Luke	John
ἀφεῖλεν αὐτοῦ	ἀφεῖλεν αὐτοῦ	ἀφεῖλεν	ἀπέκοψεν αὐτοῦ
τὸ ὠτάριον	τὸ ὠτίον	τὸ οὖς αὐτοῦ	τό ὠτάριον
		τὸ δεξιόν	τὸ δεξιόν

Luke follows Mark in the use of the verb ἀφεῖλεν, is unique in the use of the noun οὖς, and aligns with John in the use of the adjective τὸ δεξιόν. Luke's use of the word οὖς, though, is probably attributable to his own editorial tendency. Of the words for ear, Luke clearly favors οὖς: he only once uses ὠτίον, in Luke 22:51,⁶⁶ and never uses ὠταρίον. Moreover, while Luke takes over Mark's use of οὖς in one place (Mark

---

⁶⁵ Jeremias, *Sprache*, argues that κύριε here points to the use of a non-Lukan tradition (295). Cf. also Rehkopf, 67, and Taylor, *Passion*, 74. Indeed, Rehkopf suggests that Mark 14:47 is itself an insertion of the same non-Markan source!

⁶⁶ The term here in 22:51 is the healing of the ear and is thus a backward reference to 22:50. So Luke uses both terms in one passage, possibly to avoid repetition. Luke clearly avoids the Markan term ὠτάριον.

4:9), and follows Q/Matthew in another (Matt 10:27), he also adds the word in clearly redactional phrases.[67] Furthermore, the word οὖς is used in two uniquely Lukan passages, 1:44 and 4:21, which might be Lukan compositions. Is it possible or likely that Luke drew from the Johannine account the notice of the "right" ear? It is difficult to say with any certainty, but it does not appear that Luke was relying here on a *Sondergut* account. Other than τὸ δεξιόν, Luke appears to have used Mark with his own editorial modifications. And it is possible that Luke might simply have been following a tendency to add specificity.[68] But given Luke's tendency to interweave various versions, it is not unlikely that he was influenced by John's specific identification of the right ear and thus modified a basically Markan account.

Jesus' response to the sword strike, however, cannot have been drawn from Mark, since the Second Gospel does not have any verbal response by Jesus. John and Matthew do record a response: Jesus instructs the individual to put the sword back in its place, then alludes to the necessity of the arrest and/or Passion. In contrast to these similar (though verbally dissimilar) statements, Luke only has Jesus cry out ἐᾶτε ἕως τούτου. The general import is probably the same ("No more of this!"[69]), although it could be positive (That is sufficient!). The use of ἐάω suggests Luke's compositional hand here, not the use of a source.[70] But there is a similarity in tone between Jesus' command and John's own version of the response to the sword strike: βάλε τὴν

---

[67] Luke 9:44; 14:35.

[68] cf. Lk 6:6, where Luke seems to have added δεξιά to specify the hand in a Markan parallel.

[69] Fitzmyer, *Luke* (X–XXIV) 1451; cf. Bauer-Arndt-Gingrich-Driver, 212.

[70] Note especially the extensive use of ἐάω in purely Lukan usage: of nine times in the Gospels (one time in Matthew) Luke uses it in 4:41 as a redaction of Mark 1:34 and seven times in Acts! cf. Jeremias, *Sprache*, 295. But Taylor, *Passion*, argues that the cry "... is of a kind that Luke often sets aside, but that is frequent in his special source" (74). Unfortunately, Taylor offers no evidence for this assertion. See Brown, *Death*, 280.

μάχαιραν εἰς τὴν θήκην.[71] So it is not impossible, although not a strong likelihood, that Luke knew of a summary response to the sword strike from John or Matthew and created his own wording for it that better fit the Lukan context.

The healing of the ear of the high priest's servant is unknown in the other Gospel accounts. It is possible that Luke knew of another tradition[72] or source,[73] which he introduced at this point. But the passage has some marks of Lukan redaction, such as the use of ἰάομαι, which might point to Luke's having composed the phrase.[74] It is just as likely that Luke added this feature as a way of painting Jesus in a more humane and merciful light.[75]

LUKE 22:52-53.

Only here, at the close of the pericope, does Luke introduce the fact that the crowd that accompanied Judas included chief priests, officers of the temple (στρατηγοί), and elders. This depiction is a departure from the Markan account, which merely has individuals sent *from* the chief priests, scribes, and elders. Only John's account is in this respect somewhat similar to Luke's: the arresting party was made up of soldiers (σπεῖρα καὶ ὁ χιλίαρζος) and officers (ὑπηρέτας) from the chief priests. The official nature of Luke's delegation is strengthened in that only here does Luke introduce the fact that they have swords and clubs. Since this fact is in close conjunction with the description of officers, one gets the impression of an armed temple guard. In other words, Luke's account, with armed officials of the temple court, is a middle term between Mark's unofficial crowd and

---

[71] Rehkopf, 63. Although Rehkopf suggests that all rely on the "S" source. Note, though, that John's command is to Peter alone, while Luke addresses the command to Jesus' followers generally (note the plural verb).

[72] Taylor, *Passion*, 75.

[73] Rehkopf, 63-65.

[74] Jeremias, *Sprache*, 295.

[75] Fitzmyer, *Luke* (X-XXIV), 1448, cf. also Fitzmyer, *Luke* (I-IX), 257-58.

John's soldiers and officers.[76] It is reasonable, given Luke's editorial procedure, to see him modifying the Markan text (even to the point of retaining the term chief priests and elders) under the influence of John's understanding of the participants in the arresting party.

Luke concludes his account of the arrest with a saying that seems to be a composite of Mark and some other source. Jesus' responce in verse 53a about the time he spent in the temple without being arrested is very close to Mark 14:49. Fully seven out of fifteen words in the clause are the same and are in more or less the same order. But verse 53b is not found in any of the other Gospels. However, Jesus' comments about "the hour" and the "authority of darkness" in verse 53b sound very Johannine. The term "hour" used here by Luke is not so much a temporal term as a philosophical one denoting the period in which the powers of darkness are ascendant and Jesus is crucified. In such a use, the term is strongly linked to the Gospel of John (cf. John 7:30; 8:20; 12:23; 12:27; 13:1; 17:1),[77] where "the hour" is a term for the Passion of Jesus, not a specific moment in time. In contrast, the synoptic use appears to be temporal (cf. especially Mark 14:41, Matt 26:45 and Luke 22:14). There are significant differences, though, between Luke's usage here and John's. Luke calls it "your hour," while John tends to term the same time frame "my hour"; each is referring to Jesus' arrest and death, but the point of view is different. Despite this difference, one must conclude that Luke was relying on some conception other than Mark's, and that John's theological perspective is echoed here.[78] Similarly, the use of darkness as a motif to describe evil,

---

[76] So Brown, *Death*, (248): "In a certain sense Luke's account, which has a crowd consisting in part of Temple captains, forms a bridge between Mark/Matt's account of a crowd and John's account which has no crowd but soldiers and police-like attendants."

[77] Rehkopf, 81; Jeremias suggests that ὑμῶν ἡ ὥρα is not Lukan but is based on tradition.

[78] It is scarcely possible that Luke picked up the negative idea of the "hour" from Mark 14:35 and 41 (contra Soards, 100). The former is possibly eschatological; the latter does not appear to be. While Mark's reference is negative,

especially the evil of the crucifixion, is suggestive of John's own use of the terminology to describe the battle between Jesus and the world.[79] Verse 53, then, draws on Mark for Jesus' initial response to the arresting party but then interprets the party's action in an eschatological sense which appears to draw on some tradition closely linked to John. Still, there is no evidence of a literary linkage with John; the Fourth Gospel has no parallel wording in the arrest sequence.

Finally, it is important to note that Luke, like John, does *not* contain the final references in Mark and Matthew that the disciples all flee. As we shall see below, the basic plot outline of the disciples' presence in Jerusalem and at the tomb is somewhat similar as between Luke and John. To argue from an omission is dangerous, but one does see a common interest and perspective.

PETER'S DENIAL. LUKE 22:54–65

⁵⁴*Συλλαβόντες* δὲ αὐτὸν *ἤγαγον* καὶ εἰσήγαγον εἰς τὴν οἰκίαν τοῦ ἀρχιερέως· ὁ δὲ Πέτρος ἠκολούθει μακρόθεν.⁵⁵ περιαψάντων δὲ πῦρ ἐν μέσῳ τῆς αὐλῆς καὶ συγκαθισάντων **ἐκάθητο** ὁ Πέτρος μέσος αὐτῶν. ⁵⁶ ἰδοῦσα δὲ αὐτὸν παιδίσκη τις καθήμενον πρὸς τὸ φῶς καὶ ἀτενίσασα αὐτῷ εἶπεν, Καὶ οὗτος σὺν αὐτῷ ἦν· ⁵⁷ ὁ δὲ ἠρνήσατο λέγων, Οὐκ οἶδα αὐτόν, γύναι.⁵⁸ καὶ μετὰ βραχὺ ἕτερος ἰδὼν αὐτὸν ἔφη, Καὶ σὺ ἐξ αὐτῶν εἶ. ὁ δὲ Πέτρος ἔφη, Ἄνθρωπε, *οὐκ εἰμί*. ⁵⁹καὶ διαστάσης ὡσεὶ ὥρας μιᾶς ἄλλος τις διϊσχυρίζετο λέγων, Ἐπ᾽ ἀληθείας καὶ οὗτος μετ᾽ αὐτοῦ ἦν, καὶ γὰρ Γαλιλαῖός ἐστιν· ⁶⁰εἶπεν δὲ ὁ Πέτρος, Ἄνθρωπε, οὐκ οἶδα ὃ λέγεις. καὶ παραχρῆμα ἔτι λαλοῦντος αὐτοῦ ἐφώνησεν ἀλέκτωρ.⁶¹καὶ στραφεὶς ὁ κύριος ἐνέβλεψεν τῷ Πέτρῳ, καὶ ὑπεμνήσθη ὁ Πέτρος τοῦ ῥήματος τοῦ κυρίου ὡς εἶπεν αὐτῷ ὅτι Πρὶν ἀλέκτορα φωνῆσαι σήμερον ἀπαρνήσῃ με τρίς. ⁶² καὶ ἐξελθὼν ἔξω ἔκλαυσεν πικρῶς. ⁶³ Καὶ οἱ ἄνδρες οἱ συνέχοντες αὐτὸν ἐνέπαιζον αὐτῷ

---

it has little of the focus on the passion as a battle between good and evil that is implicit in John's and Luke's references. Better is Taylor's simple summation: This concept [of the hour] is Johannine" (p. 76).

[79] So John 1:5; 6:17; 12:35, 46. Cf. Fitzmyer, *Luke* (X–XXIV), 1452.

δέροντες, ⁶⁴ καὶ <u>περικαλύψαντες αὐτον</u> ἐπηρώτων, <u>Προφητευσον</u>, **τίς ἐστιν ὁ παίσας σε**; ⁶⁵καὶ ἕτερα πολλὰ βλασφημοῦντες ἔλεγον εἰς αὐτόν.

In the main, Luke's story of the denial of Peter follows the Markan account. The setting and much of the wording is reminiscent of Mark, although there are many differences. In particular, the phrases Πέτρος ἠκολούθει μακρόθεν, πρὸς τὸ φῶς, and γὰρ Γαλιλαῖός ἐστιν and Peter's memory of Jesus' words at the cock crow are strong indications of Luke's basic reliance on Mark.⁸⁰ It is not difficult to see the Markan story as the underlying framework throughout Luke's account, although there has clearly been strong editing by Luke.⁸¹

The story of Peter's denial in Luke is especially distinguished from both the Synoptic account and John by the order of events and its relationship to the trial before the Jewish authorities. Although it begins by following Mark's outline, Luke's account immediately deals with Peter's denial before any hearing with the Sanhedrin or high priest. Mark, in contrast, has the main trial first, then the beating of Jesus, then the denial story. It will be helpful to outline the major features of the denial and trial accounts in order to see how they differ:

---

⁸⁰ Taylor, *Passion,* 77. David Catchpole, *The Trial of Jesus* (Leiden: E. J. Brill, 1971) notes these similarities with Mark and discounts them, although certainly allowing for Luke's possible use of Mark. Catchpole notes that a number of similarities in even these points show some connection with John: the μετ' αὐτοῦ in Luke 22:59 corresponds with John 18:26, and the imperfect of ἠκολούθει in Luke 22:54 is a point of contact with John 18:15 (162–63). Catchpole argues, however, that Luke is relying on an independent tradition that has strong points of contact with John.

⁸¹ Goulder would argue that the influence of Matthew accounts for much of the difference between Luke and Mark (747). But aside from two remarkable agreements in wording (the question, "Prophesy....Who is it that struck you?" in Matt 26:68 and Luke 22:64, and the final comment that Peter "went out and wept bitterly" in Matt 26:75 and Luke 22:62), Matthew does little to explain the major deviations of Luke from the Mark and Matthew account.

Luke Chapter 22

Mark and Matthew (Mk 14:53–54, 66–72; Mt 26:57–58, 69–75)	Luke (Lk 22:54–62)	John (Jn 18:13–27)
Jesus to high priest. Peter follows.	Jesus to high priest's house Peter follows.	Jesus to Annas Simon Peter and another disciple follow
Peter Sits with guards warming himself.	Peter sits with "them" when they have lit a fire.	Maid questions Peter. answer: "I am not."
Trial: false witnesses and inquisition by High Priest.	Maid identifies Peter. Answer: "I don't know him."	Fire made by servants, Peter sits with them.
All condemn Jesus to death.	Someone else identifies Peter. Answer: "Man, I am not."	High Priest interrogates Jesus.
Jesus spit on, struck. Crowds jeer: "Prophecy!" Guards beat Jesus.	Still another identifies Peter as Galilean. Answer: "I don't know what you are saying."	Jesus struck by officer. Sent to Caiaphas.
A maid identifies him. Answer: "I don't know what you mean."	Cock crows. Answer: "I am not."	"They" question Peter.
Another maid identifies. answer: "I don't know him." Peter denies it.	Peter remembers. Goes out and weeps bitterly.	Servant of high priest questions Peter.
A bystander identifies as Galilean. Answer: "I don't know the man."	Crowd mocks and beats crowd cries "Prophecy!"	Cock crows.
Cock crows (twice)	Jesus is led to council.	

Peter remembers prediction	Jesus questioned by	Jesus sent to
Goes out and weeps	Sanhedrin.	Praetorium.
(bitterly)		

At first glance, it appears that Luke and Mark have merely switched the places of the denial and trial scenes. But it is not that simple. For Luke, the story is primarily one of Peter's denial, since what is left of a trial is reduced to a relatively innocuous exchange about whether Jesus is truly the Christ. The "trial" in Luke (Luke 22:67–71) does not result in a formal condemnation and thus serves mostly to introduce the trials before Pilate and Herod. Peter, and his response to questioning, remains the central focus throughout Luke's version. In Mark, by contrast, the central focus is on the trial, with Jesus tried by means of false witnesses, condemned to death, and mocked and beaten as a result of the condemnation by the high priests. It is intriguing that John presents a scene that has the two features woven together. By alternating between denial and "trial," John presents a story that more integrally links the two but can be termed primarily a denial story. The central focus of the story is the basis of the argument by many scholars that Luke is closer to John than to Mark, an argument that Soards finds confusing.[82] By introducing the first denial early on in the story, before the questioning by the high priest, John set the scene for the subsequent denials. The questioning in between comes as an interruption, thus focusing attention on the denials. Luke, by rearranging the order of events and deleting the trial has significantly altered the essential thrust of the scene in the high priest's court and turned it also into a denial story, even though the language is heavily Markan.[83] In terms of individual words, Luke is closer to Mark, but in terms of the overall sense of the passage, Luke is closer to John.

The question that must be posed is how Luke's account of the denial arose. Was it the result of an extensive rewriting of Mark, or

---

[82] Soards, 77.

[83] Cf. Schniewind, 58.

was Luke influenced by other sources as well? The scholarly consensus is that the bulk of Luke's scene is a heavily redacted Mark, but with some possible influence from some separate (possibly L) source or sources.[84] Here we must account especially for Luke's very different focus. How did he come to change a trial story into a denial story?

In addition to the change in central focus, there are features in Luke that are hard to explain if he was relying on Mark:
 1. The lighting of the fire.
 2. The identification of the servants.
 3. The purpose and placement of the mocking and beating of Jesus.

LUKE 22:54.

The initial sentence of Luke's denial scene, while superficially similar to Mark's in that Jesus is brought to the house of the high priest, appears to be a deliberate modification of the Markan account. Unlike Mark and Matthew, Luke does not record an assembly of priests and elders. For Mark, of course, this scene is a formal trial scene in which Jesus is charged and condemned to death for blasphemy. As noted above, there is no such scene in Luke. The fact that Jesus is led to the high priest's house, as opposed to the high priest, is an indication that for Luke Jesus is never brought before the high priest himself before daybreak.

Like Mark, and unlike Matthew and John, Luke does not record the name of the high priest to whose house Jesus is taken. Indeed, Luke appears to have understood both Annas and Caiaphas to be high priests, with Annas perhaps having preeminence.[85] While avoiding any direct interrogation by the high priest(s), Luke appears to have understood a situation in which the "house of the high priest" could

---

[84] Fitzmyer, *Luke* (X–XXIV), 1456.
[85] So the two references by Luke to high priests by name, Luke 3:2 and Acts 4:6, list Annas and Caiaphas together, and Annas is always listed first. Cf. Brown, *Death*, 404.

allow for the double interrogation found in John. But Luke, nonetheless, prescinded from any discussion of an interrogation.

Jeremias argues that the verb συλλαμβάνω in verse 54 is an indication that Luke was drawing on a tradition.[86] In the Johannine account, the successive scenes of the officers seizing Jesus (συλλαμβάνω) and leading (ἄγω) him to Annas, are a combination very similar to Luke's συλλαβόντες δὲ αὐτὸν ἤγαγον καὶ εἰσήγαγον, in which the final εἰσήγαγον has been noted as a sign of Lukan redaction.[87] Although, as Soards notes, one should not place too much weight on this combination, it is perhaps an echo of another narrative of which Luke was aware and that left some impress in his account.[88] And it is noteworthy that Taylor connects verse 54a with verses 52–53 which he finds, as does this analysis, to be replete with non-Markan material,[89] material we have identified as influenced by John.

The second half of verse 54, Peter's following, is found in all four Gospels. Luke's use of the modifier μακρόθεν makes certain that Luke was following Mark.

LUKE 22:55.

Luke introduces the setting around the fire by first describing its being lit. That feature is not found in Mark and Matthew but is found in John. However, the account in John is strikingly different: the wording is entirely different (ἀνθρακιὰν πεποιηκότες instead of περιαψάντων πῦρ), Peter is standing rather than sitting, and the order of events is different. So while there is a faint resemblance, it is hard to see more than possible factual items that would have influenced Luke in his composition of the account. Instead, it appears that Luke has

---

[86] Jeremias, 296.
[87] Jeremias, *Sprache*, 296.
[88] Soards, 76.
[89] Taylor, *Passion*, 76. See p. 301 above.

worked with and modified Mark's basic setting, even including Peter's sitting with the guards.[90]

LUKE 22:56–60a.

Luke's first denial is strikingly similar to Mark's account. A number of words are identical or show evidence of having been based on Mark (thus Luke may have simply substituted the more intensive ἀτενίσασα for ἐμβλέψασα, or the aorist εἶπεν for λέγει). Luke's second denial account strays from the Markan version more extensively. Instead of the παιδίσκη, the questioner is a man (ἕτερος), although the substance of his question is very similar: Peter is ἐξ αὐτῶν. But Peter's response is quite different: "I am not." In that response, Luke is very similar to the responses given in John, although in both cases it is a natural response to the question. The similarity in wording gives little reason to think that Luke was drawing on John. The third question to Peter in Luke is again very similar to Mark's third question, although the questioner in Luke is one person, while in Mark it is a group. Most strikingly, the reason given for the third question in Luke, that Peter is also a Galilean, confirms that Luke was drawing on Mark.

Throughout the denial story there are strong indications of Luke's compositional shaping. The frequent use of vocatives seems to be an attempt at narrative immediacy. The words used are part of Luke's vocabulary, such as διΐστημι and διισχυρίζετο.[91] So while Luke drew upon the Markan account as his basic structure, he also made editorial modifications that might be expected of him. There is no indication of a source other than Mark.

One striking difference in Luke's account is the absence of Peter's cursing at the final denial. In this omission, Luke is similar to John, although it is difficult to rely too much on an isolated omission. And particularly in this instance, the absence of the curse would more

---

[90] So συγκαθισάντων appears to be drawn from Mark, not a sign of Lukan redaction (contra Jeremias, *Sprache*, 296).

[91] Jeremias, *Sprache*, 297.

naturally be attributable to Luke's tendency to paint the disciples in a better light, and so is quite understandable as a Lukan editorial effort.

LUKE 22:60b-62.

All four Gospels record the cock's crow after the third denial, and there is little difference in the accounts other than Mark's note that this was the second crow. It would appear that Luke followed a tradition or text (John? Matthew?) that knew only one cock crow. Only Luke has Jesus looking at Peter at precisely this moment, which seems to be a Lukan composition to heighten the effect of the moment.[92] But the conclusion of denial sequence shows again Luke's strong reliance on Mark. Peter's recollection of Jesus' prediction is closely drawn from Mark's account, with only minor modifications. And Peter's final response, that of weeping, is also similar to Mark, albeit with close links to Matthew in the adverb πικρῶς.[93]

LUKE 22:63-64.

At the conclusion of the denial story, Luke recounts the beating of Jesus. Luke's account is very similar to the account in Mark and Matthew, although it is in a very different position in the narrative. Thus in Mark and Matthew it comes as a response to the high priests' verdict, while in Luke it is a rather surprising event that arises without reason. Otherwise, with one exception, it appears that Luke was closely relying on Mark. The exception is the wording of the taunt: προφήτευσον, τίς ἐστιν ὁ παίσας σε;. The latter part of the taunt is identical with Matthew, again suggesting reliance on Matthew, Q, or a common tradition.[94]

---

[92] Gerhard Schneider, *Verleugnung, Verspottung und Verhör Jesu* (München: Kösel-Verlag, 1969), 91–93.

[93] Goulder argues for Luke's reliance on Matthew (750); Soards suggests a common oral tradition (102).

[94] See the note on v. 62 above.

The placement of Jesus' mistreatment pericope in Luke is a problem. Why did Luke choose to place it here in the narrative rather than after the hearing in verses 67–71? It is possible that he simply wanted to emphasize the cruelty of the arresting party, having them beat Jesus before any formal hearing was held.[95] But perhaps Schniewind's perspective has more substance. Schniewind sees behind Luke originally two hearings, one of which "dropped out" in the editorial process of shortening the story.[96] In other words, Luke knew of a narrative construction, similar to John's, where there were hearings before both Annas and Caiaphas. Only the hearing before Annas has been deleted, and the hearing before Caiaphas finds its expression primarily through the use of Mark. In this scenario, Luke maintained the placement of Jesus' mistreatment after the Annas trial in spite of having deleted that trial. And he maintained the placement of the Caiaphas trial in the early morning, (which is in agreement with John). While this reconstruction is possible, it is difficult to imagine that Luke's account resulted from his use of John as we now have it; it seems more likely to have been the result of a common tradition or an different version (earlier?) of John.[97] The problem of the placement of the mistreatment story is difficult, and probably has no satisfactory solution other than attributing it to Luke's creative hand. It is not likely that John's Gospel was an influence on Luke's departure from Mark's presentation in this verse.

- **TRIAL BEFORE JEWISH LEADERS. LUKE 22:66–71**

⁶⁶ Καὶ ὡς ἐγένετο ἡμέρα, συνήχθη τὸ **πρεσβυτέριον τοῦ λαοῦ**, ἀρχιερεῖς τε καὶ γραμματεῖς, καὶ ἀπήγαγον αὐτὸν εἰς τὸ συνέδριον αὐτῶν,⁶⁷λέγοντες, *Εἰ σὺ εἶ ὁ Χριστός, εἰπὸν ἡμῖν*. εἶπεν δὲ αὐτοῖς, Ἐὰν ὑμῖν *εἴπω* οὐ μὴ *πιστεύσητε*·⁶⁸ἐὰν δὲ ἐρωτήσω οὐ μὴ ἀποκριθῆτε. ⁶⁹

---

[95] But Catchpole (167) argues there is not theological or circumstantial reason for Luke to change the order.
[96] Schniewind, 60.
[97] So also Fitzmyer, *Luke* (X–XXIV) with a similar proposal (1456).

ἀπὸ τοῦ <u>νῦν δὲ ἔσται ὁ υἱὸς τοῦ ἀνθρώπου καθήμενος ἐκ δεξιῶν τῆς δυνάμεως τοῦ θεοῦ</u>.⁷⁰εἶπαν δὲ πάντες, Σὺ οὖν εἶ <u>ὁ υἱὸς τοῦ θεοῦ;</u> ὁ δὲ πρὸς αὐτοὺς ἔφη, Ὑμεῖς λέγετε ὅτι <u>ἐγώ εἰμι</u>. ⁷¹ οἱ δὲ εἶπαν, <u>Τί ἔτι ἔχομεν μαρτυρίας χρείαν;</u> αὐτοὶ γὰρ <u>ἠκούσαμεν</u> ἀπὸ τοῦ στόματος αὐτοῦ.

LUKE 22:66.

Luke begins the hearing before the Jewish leaders with a summary statement that seems to have behind it Mark 15:1. The συμβούλιον of Mark becomes a πρεσβυτέριον τοῦ λαοῦ, a Lukan preference.⁹⁸ So also the imprecise term πρωί becomes ἐγένετο ἡμέρα. These are generally Lukan stylistic features, which suggests Lukan editing. But the broad similarity of the opening verse suggests that Luke was following Mark 15:1 in its description of a formal hearing.

LUKE 22:67–68.

At first glance, Luke's request posed to Jesus, Εἰ σὺ εἶ ὁ Χριστός εἰπὸν ἡμῖν, is similar to Mark's σὺ εἶ ὁ Χριστός; But Mark's question is a straightforward request, while Luke's is a conditional sentence. Moreover, in Mark the answer to the question is a simple "I am." Luke, on the other hand, has Jesus countering with a statement of his own that throws the burden back on the Jewish leaders. Luke's question/answer session is, then, more confrontational. In addition, Luke separates the question of whether Jesus is the Christ from his identity as the Son of God. The terms are not necessarily identical for Luke, and the double question allows Luke to emphasize that in Jesus is found both Christ *and* Son of God.⁹⁹

---

⁹⁸Jeremias, *Sprache*, 299.

⁹⁹See, for instance, a similar effort to emphasize the double nature of Jesus' identity in Peter's speech in Acts 2:36: "Therefore let the entire house of Israel know with certainty that God has made him both Lord and Messiah, this Jesus whom you have crucified." Cf. Fitzmyer, *Luke* (X–XXIV), 1462. I do not find

In both the actual phrasing of the question, as well as the general tone of the response, Luke is remarkably similar to John 10:24–26. John 10 is perhaps the closest narrative there is to an actual trial before the Jewish leadership in the Gospel of John, so despite its different placement in the Fourth Gospel, one should consider whether it influenced Luke.[100] An examination of the context in John 10 shows that it has numerous similarities with the Sanhedrin trial: the participants are Jesus and the "Jews," John's term for the leadership of Israel; Jesus is condemned to death; and the reason for the sentence is blasphemy, which is linked to the identification of Jesus as God's Son. It is, then, very likely that John 10 was associated with the trial(s) of Jesus.

A comparison of Mark, Luke, and John shows the striking similarities between Luke and John in the language and structure of the exchange between Jesus and the Jewish leaders:

Mark (14:61–62)	Luke (22:67)	John (10:24–25)
σὺ εἶ ὁ χριστὸς ὁ υἱὸς τοῦ εὐλογητοῦ;	εἰ σὺ εἶ ὁ χριστός	εἰ σὺ εἶ ὁ Χριστός
	εἰπὸν ἡμῖν.	εἰπὲ ἡμῖν παρρησίᾳ
ὁ δὲ Ἰησοῦς εἶπεν· ἐγώ εἰμι.	εἶπεν δὲ αὐτοῖς ἐάν ὑμῖν εἴπω, οὐ μὴ πιστεύσητε·	ἀπεκρίθη αὐτοῖς ὁ Ἰησοῦς εἶπον ὑμῖν καὶ οὐ πιστεύετε·

---

persuasive Goulder's argument that Luke found the combination of the two terms uncomfortable (753).

[100] Robert Fortna, *The Fourth Gospel and its Predecessor*, 155, 158, considers 10:24–26 to be a displaced section which originally was part of the chapter 18 trial. Similarly Anton Dauer, "Spuren der (synoptischen) Synedriumsverhandlung im 4. Evangelium — Das Verhältnis zu den Synoptikern," in *John and the Synoptics*, 307–40 (Leuven: University Press, 1992), argues, as does Klein (see above chapter 2) that here in John 10 we have traces of the trial before the Sanhedrin. Alternatively, Raymond Brown, *The Gospel According to John* (X–XXI), AB 29A (Garden City, NY: Doubleday, 1970), 405, suggests that

As noted above, the initial question by the authorities is identical in both Luke and John. But the similarities continue. In Luke and John, but not in Mark, the authorities seek a specific verbal answer: "tell us." Jesus' answer is not a clear answer, as in Mark, but rather an elusive sparring with the priests that turns the issue back on their own failure to understand. Luke's answer, with its emphasis on believing, is difficult to imagine as a Lukan insertion or composition. While Luke at times added the word πιστεύω when working over a Markan text, he far more often avoided or deleted it.[101] Believing appears to be less important in Luke than it is in Mark or John. So instead of Luke's having modified Mark on his own initiative, it appears likelier that Luke was influenced by another source in which this idea was already present.[102] Again, it seems quite likely that some form of John found its way into Luke's account of the interrogation.

LUKE 22:69.

Luke now appears to have turned to Mark for a continuation of Jesus' response to the priests' questions. Jesus' response in Luke is very close to Mark, although some important modifications are found. First of all, the future sense of the visible return of the Son of Man, drawn from Daniel 7, is changed to an existential reality that begins at once. So ὄψεσθε is changed to ἀπὸ τὸ νῦν...ἔσται, which seems to be

---

John's portrayal of trials and disputes preceding the final week is more accurate, and the synoptic portrayal of one trial is an artificial composition. Either way, the current Gospel of John seems to portray in a number of scattered pericopes what is concentrated only in the Passion week in the Synoptics.

[101] Luke added the term in 8:12 and 13, but deleted it in reworking Mark at 9:23, 24, 42; 15:32. Moreover, a number of Markan passages with believing as a significant feature have no parallel in Luke: Mark 1:15; 11:23, 24; 13:21.

[102] Catchpole (194–95) suggests that there is strong evidence for a literary connection between Luke and John at this point, and that John cannot be using Luke at this point. He concludes that John and Luke are relying on a common source in this feature.

more in line with Luke's eschatology.[103] Second, and in line with the changes outlined above, Luke drops the direct reference to the visible manifestations of coming on the clouds. These changes, though, are explicable as ways of bringing the Markan image in line with Luke's conception of the present and coming Kingdom of God.

LUKE 22:70.

In Mark's version, the high priest has, of course, already asked Jesus whether he is the Son of God (Son of the Blessed in Mark, Son of God in Matthew). Luke now also turns to this question, in a way that emphasizes the dual nature of Jesus' person, both Christ and Son of God. The obvious parallelism of the two questions in verse 67 ("If you are the Christ") and verse 70 ("Are you the Son of God?") is a means of emphasis. The question whether Jesus is the Son of God, though, is based directly on Mark. Yet Luke has Jesus' answer to the question remain enigmatic and somewhat confrontational, as with the previous question. The answer, "You say that I am," appears to affirm the question put by the high priest but does not truly have Jesus answer directly as Mark does. This evasive answer is also found in a slightly modified form later, in Jesus' response to Pilate (Luke 23:3). It is, in concept, very similar to Matthew's σὺ εἶπας, and it is possible that Luke was combining the two traditions by using Mark's simple ἐγώ εἰμι and expanding it to ὑμεῖς λέγετε ὅτι ἐγώ εἰμι.

---

[103] So see Hans Conzelmann, *The Theology of Luke* (London: Faber and Faber, 1960), 95. But while Conzelmann thinks Luke's modifications of the Markan eschatological statements point to a temporal delay of the parousia, it is probably more correct to say that Luke thought the eschaton in some very real way had already come, and with Jesus' death and resurrection, and especially the coming of the Spirit, the new plan of God had already been instituted. See Robert Maddox, *The Purpose of Luke-Acts* (Edinburgh: T&T Clark, 1982), 137–145.

LUKE 22:71.

Luke follows Mark fairly closely in the Jewish leaders' response to Jesus' words: Luke's τί ἔτι ἔχομεν μαρτυρίας χρείαν is remarkably close to the Markan form and is a bit surprising in that no trial or witnesses have yet been mentioned in Luke. Similarly, while not using the term "blasphemy," Luke's reference to what was heard from Jesus' mouth is suggestive of Mark's substance.

Thus, in general this analysis has shown that the hearing before the Jewish authorities in Luke has drawn primarily from Mark, despite the rearrangement of Mark's trial with respect to the denial of Peter and the mistreatment of Jesus. But in the matter of rearrangement, as well as in the content of a few specific passages, Luke's use of Mark appears to have been modified under the influence of a Passion story with features like those found in John.

The net effect of these modifications of Mark's trial narrative is to produce a hearing of a surprisingly different tenor. In Mark and Matthew, the Jewish leaders conduct a formal trial with witnesses and a final condemnation—even if flawed by the false testimony and night timing. The focus in Mark and Matthew appears to be on the Jewish leaders; they have caused Jesus' death, and Jesus' mistreatment is shown almost as an anticipation of his death. In contrast, in Luke and John, the Jewish action in the trials is seen as only preparatory to Roman judgment, where the actual witnesses, accusation, and judgment (of innocence) are found. The absence of witnesses, of a formal condemnation of guilt, and of the high priest's outrage, as well as the timing of the mistreatment of Jesus, all contribute to the sense that Luke's and John's trials are more forms of harassment than trials proper. Thus in tone as well as in particular features, Luke's trial narrative has striking similarities to John's. One might well wonder, then, why Luke has departed so significantly from the Mark/Matthew account of the nocturnal trial, unless he was influenced by another narrative which itself was also absent such trial.

CONCLUSIONS

My analysis of Luke chapter 22 suggests that there is indeed an interweaving of Luke's primary source, Mark, with a narrative strongly similar to John, as well as some other traditions. In most instances it is clear that Luke has drawn on Mark, with modifications that can be attributed to his editorial or theological tendencies. But in certain sections it is difficult to discern any clear theological purposes in Luke's departure from the Markan account. In many of those instances, I have noted commonalities with John or some other source; in those sections, it appears that Luke was influenced by either the Fourth Gospel, or a tradition behind it, in addition to Mark. Besides using and editing his major sources, it appears that Luke occasionally composed freely to produce a new Passion narrative with its own tendencies. My results can be summarized as follows:

22:1–2.	Close reliance on Mark.
22:3–6.	Lukan redaction of Mark, influenced by John.
22:7–13.	Close reliance on Mark.
22:14–20.	Lukan redaction of Mark.
22:21–30.	Lukan redaction of Mark and Q or Matthew, influenced, especially in the matter of order, by John.
22:31–32.	Lukan composition.
22:33–34.	Lukan composition based loosely on both Mark and John.
22:35–38.	Lukan composition.
22:39–46.	Lukan redaction of Mark, heavily influenced by John.
22:47–53.	Lukan redaction of Mark, heavily influenced by John.
22:54–65.	Lukan redaction of Mark, perhaps somewhat influenced by John in verse 54a.
22:66–71.	Lukan redaction of Mark, influenced by John, especially in verses 67–68.

Chapter 7

LUKE CHAPTER 23

TRIAL BEFORE PILATE (PT. 1). LUKE 23:1–5

¹ Καὶ ἀναστὰν ἅπαν τὸ πλῆθος αὐτῶν **ἤγαγον αὐτὸν** ἐπὶ τὸν Πιλᾶτον. ² ἤρξαντο δὲ κατηγορεῖν αὐτοῦ λέγοντες, Τοῦτον εὕραμεν διαστρέφοντα τὸ ἔθνος ἡμῶν καὶ κωλύοντα φόρους Καίσαρι διδόναι καὶ λέγοντα ἑαυτὸν Χριστὸν βασιλέα εἶναι. ³ ὁ δὲ Πιλᾶτος ἠρώτησεν αὐτὸν **λέγων**, Σὺ εἶ ὁ βασιλεὺς τῶν Ἰουδαίων; ὁ δὲ ἀποκριθεὶς αὐτῷ **ἔφη**, Σὺ λέγεις. ⁴ ὁ δὲ Πιλᾶτος εἶπεν πρὸς τοὺς ἀρχιερεῖς καὶ τοὺς ὄχλους, *Οὐδὲν εὑρίσκω αἴτιον* ἐν τῷ ἀνθρώπῳ τούτῳ. ⁵ οἱ δὲ ἐπίσχυον λέγοντες ὅτι Ἀνασείει τὸν λαὸν διδάσκων καθ᾽ ὅλης τῆς Ἰουδαίας, καὶ ἀρξάμενος ἀπὸ τῆς Γαλιλαίας ἕως ὧδε.

While Luke's initial scene of Jesus' trial before Pilate bears some broad similarity to Mark, a number of significant divergences from the Second Gospel's account exist. Only verse 3 bears any close verbal similarity to Mark; in the rest of the pericope, only six words are shared by Luke and Mark: ὁ, δέ, Πιλᾶτος, κατηγορέω, ἀρχιερεύς and αὐτός. Moreover, in terms of content, Luke has a number of features that are simply absent from Mark, for example, the presentation of three charges against Jesus before Pilate speaks, the presence of a crowd, and the declaration of Jesus' innocence. These differences have frequently led scholars to conclude that another source (or sources) in addition to Mark was used by Luke.¹

Luke's introduction to the Pilate trial bears all the marks of his style. The pleonastic use of ἀναστάς and the phrase ἅπαν τὸ πλῆθος are both Lukan features and suggest Luke's composition or forceful redaction.² But the existence of such Lukan features is probably best explained as Luke's free adaptation of the Markan account.³ In Mark, as in Luke, the hearing before the council of chief priests and scribes concludes with the delivery of Jesus to Pilate. It appears that Luke simply freely edited Mark to create his own transition from the Jewish council to the Pilate trial. The whole company referred to by Luke appears to mean the chief priests and scribes also described by Mark and Matthew; Luke has merely strengthened the sense of unanimity of action by his language.

Despite the strong probability that Luke was using Mark in verse 1, it is curious that he did not use the term παρέδωκαν for the handing over to Pilate. This term is used elsewhere extensively by Luke to refer to precisely such an action of handing over, and would appear to fit his narrative plan admirably.⁴ Moreover, Luke drops any reference to Jesus' being bound, a feature found at this location in Mark and Matthew, and also in John, albeit there it takes place before Jesus is sent to

---

¹ Vincent Taylor, *The Passion Narrative of St. Luke* (Cambridge: University Press, 1972) 86–87, A. Büchele, *Der Tod Jesu im Lukasevangelium* (Frankfurt am Main: Joseph Knecht, 1978), 27–28.

² J. Jeremias, *Die Sprache des Lukasevangeliums* (Göttingen: Vandenhoeck & Ruprecht, 1980), 300; Joseph A. Fitzmyer, *The Gospel According to Luke* (X-XXIV), AB 28A (Garden City, NY: Doubleday, 1985), 1472.

³ So also Joel Green, *The Death of Jesus* (Tübingen: J. C. B. Mohr [Paul Siebeck], 1988), 79, suggests v. 1 is based loosely on Mark, despite finding vv. 2, 4 and 5 to be based on a non-Markan source. The differences in wording notwithstanding, Luke and Mark do have in common the transfer from the Jewish priests to Pilate. So the common *content* becomes a key factor in identifying this passage as based on Mark.

⁴ Cf. especially Luke 18:32; 20:20 and elsewhere. Green, *Death*, 77.

Caiaphas (John 18:24). But perhaps these absences are indicative of Luke's freedom from Mark at this point, despite his following Mark's basic outline. At the very least, they show Luke's active editing of material. It is possible that there are here signs of Luke's knowledge of John—the use of ἄγειν and the lack of παρέδωκεν reflect similar features in John's version. But ἄγω is a common Lukan word, and its use might simply indicate Luke's editorial work.[5] Moreover, as Goulder has pointed out, Luke shares this word (in a cognate form, ἀπάγω) also with Matthew.[6] It is more likely that Luke simply modified Mark according to his interpretation of the event than that he directly relied on another source.

That Luke was relying on Mark's account of the Pilate trial becomes very clear in verse 3, which is almost verbatim from Mark. Pilate's question whether Jesus is the king of the Jews and Jesus' deflecting response, "You say so," show very few signs of modification Luke has changed the verb ἐπερωτάω to the simple form ἐρωτάω, which, while not a strongly Lukan feature, is not unusual for his editorial practice.[7] At the very least, one can see Luke's reliance on Mark in this verse.[8]

In addition to the agreements with Mark, there are a few minor

---

[5] Joseph A. Fitzmyer, *The Gospel According to Luke* (I–IX), AB 28 (Garden City, NY: Doubleday, 1981), 113; John Hawkins, *Horae Synopticae* (Oxford: Clarenden Press, 1909), 27.

[6] M. D. Goulder, *Luke: A New Paradigm* (Sheffield: JSOT Press, 1989) 756.

[7] Jeremias, *Sprache* (130, 300), argues that Luke (and John) prefers ἐρωτάω, a sign of Lukan style. But Jeremias is a bit hasty in arguing for clear Lukan preference here. He notes that Luke inserts ἐρωτάω three times where Mark has a word for asking and replaces ἐπερωτάω three times with ἐρωτάω. More often, Luke accepts Mark's form of ἐπερωτάω; he also accepts it in a number of L passages. But Luke also adds ἐπερωτάω three times when no word for asking is found in parallel Mark passages (i.e., changes "said" to "asked," clearly an editorial choice) and changes ἐρωτάω to ἐπερωτάω one time! So while it is within Lukan editorial practice to modify the word, he appears to have no clear preference.

[8] Taylor, *Passion* (86–87), while arguing for a non-Markan source for vv. 1–5, sees v. 3 as an "insertion" of Markan material.

agreements with Matthew in this pericope: both Luke and Matthew use a form of ἄγω to refer to the movement from the Jewish council to Pilate, both have a pleonastic λέγων referring to Pilate's questioning of Jesus, and both have Jesus responding with the verb ἔφη. Goulder suggests that these are signs of Luke's use of Matthew.[9] What is striking for this study is that these narrow grammatical similarities with Matthew are minor compared to the broad substantive agreements with John, as shall be shown below.

Despite the obvious use of Mark in selected portions of the pericope, Luke in verses 1–5 has added features that significantly alter the sense of the Markan narrative:

1. The presentation of a formal set of accusations *before* Pilate's examination.

2. The existence of a crowd at the hearing.

3. Pilate's statement of Jesus' innocence.

4. An additional accusation of sedition after Pilate's declaration of innocence.

These will now be considered in turn.

THE INITIAL ACCUSATIONS

In Mark and Matthew, Pilate's question put to Jesus, "Are you the king of the Jews?" comes as a surprise since there has been no dialogue between the Jewish leaders and Pilate that has communicated such a charge. Luke's account in verse 2 is more logical and orderly, in that the leaders present their bill of particulars before the examination begins.[10] It is interesting that Luke presents two specific charges leveled against Jesus: that he forbade tributes to Caesar and that he claimed to be Christ, a king. These two charges are supporting accusa-

---

[9] Goulder, 756–57.

[10] See Paul Walasky, "Trial and Death of Jesus in Luke," *JBL* 94 (1975): 83, who notes that Luke has created a stark difference between the disordered Sanhedrin trial (contra Mark) and a well-ordered Pilate trial, in which charges are brought and an extensive hearing is held.

tions to the overarching claim that Jesus was leading the people astray (διαστρέφειν).[11] Both of these specific charges are untrue according to the Lukan narrative; Jesus has specifically allowed for the payment of taxes to Caesar (Luke 20:20–26),[12] and he avoids directly claiming to be the Christ (Luke 22:67–71). But the two charges do develop issues that have been previously raised in the context of attempts to publicly entrap Jesus: the payment of taxes question was brought up in an effort to trap Jesus (Luke 20:20), and the question whether he was the Christ was formally put to him in his appearance before the chief priests and scribes.

A crucial question is whether Luke was relying on a source for his presentation of the formal accusation or, alternatively, whether he was attempting to smooth out Mark's narrative difficulty at this point. The language in verse 2 contains a number of Lukan stylistic features: the emphatic use of τοῦτο and the verb διαστρέφω appear to be signs of Luke's hand,[13] and the use of εὑρίσκειν and κωλύειν, as well as τὸ ἔθνος ἡμῶν, might also be Lukan.[14] Jeremias argues that the use of ἄρχομαι with the infinitive is non-Lukan[15] and therefore a sign of a source, but the almost identical phrase ἤρξαντο κατηγορεῖν αὐτοῦ λέγοντες in Acts 24:2 suggests that Luke may well have chosen this language as well. The parallelism of Luke 20:25 and 23:2, and the common use of φόρος (contra Mark's and Matthew's κῆνσος) are also indications of Luke's editorial hand.[16] Based on this pattern of

---

[11] Raymond E. Brown, *The Death of the Messiah* (Garden City, NY: Doubleday, 1994), 738.

[12] Hans Conzelmann, *The Theology of Luke* (London: Faber and Faber, 1960), 140, notes that Luke makes it explicit that this is a deliberate lie; the same people (priests, etc.) are involved in both scenes.

[13] Jeremias, *Sprache*, 300.

[14] Goulder, 757; cf. J. Amadee Bailey, *The Traditions Common to the Gospels of Luke and John* (Leiden: E. J. Brill, 1963), 66. But notice that John also refers to "your people" (τὸ ἔθνος τὸ σόν in Pilate's recapitulation of the charge, (John 18:33).

[15] Jeremias, *Sprache*, 300.

[16] Bailey, 66; cf. also Martin Dibelius, "Herodes und Pilatus," *ZNW* 16

extensive Lukan style, Goulder thinks that Luke created this verse in order to correct Mark's oversight of an accusation before the hearing.[17] Certainly Goulder is correct in countering the argument that there is little of Luke in the verse and that it therefore stems from a pre-Lukan source.[18] The fact that Luke 23:2 and Luke 20:25 have a contradiction is certainly not an indication of an external source, but rather it shows Luke's ability to use irony in his construction of the specifics of the accusation.[19]

But it is more probable that Luke did not just create out of whole cloth the idea of an accusation before the beginning of Pilate's question. John also presents an accusation before Pilate begins his examination of Jesus. In the Fourth Gospel, the need for an accusation is raised by Pilate himself; before he will proceed with the hearing, he wants to know the formal accusation against Jesus. The accusation offered by the Jews is sketchy at best: Jesus is an evil-doer, and when pressed, the Jews allow that the crime is one that is worthy of the death penalty (John 18:29-32). Having read John, Luke would likely have been struck by the need for a specific accusation in order for Pilate to hear the case; Pilate's demand for a formal accusation in John is a striking feature in its framing of the hearing. Luke has the Jewish leaders anticipate what is specifically requested by Pilate in John. While it is likely that Luke has fashioned the specific accusations found in Luke 23 in an effort to quash any political explanation of Jesus' death,[20] it is also likely that the idea of an accusation preceding the Pilate hearing

---

(1915): 119.

[17] Goulder, p. 756. Similarly Bailey argues that the accusation was included as a "necessary prelude to Pilate's question to Jesus in v.3," (66). But, of course, it was not necessary for Mark or Matthew. cf. also Fitzmyer, *Luke* (X–XXIV), 1473.

[18] As Taylor, *Passion* (89) argues for a pre-Luke Passion story.

[19] B. Weiß, *Die Quellen des Lukasevangeliums* (Stuttgart und Berlin: J.G. Cotta'sche Buchhandlung Nachfolger, 1907), 224-25.

[20] Gerhard Sloyan, *Jesus on Trial* (Philadelphia: Fortress Press, 1973), 100. Note especially that these political charges presented at Jesus' trial are found immediately and repeatedly to be insubstantial.

was derived from the Johannine account.[21] From both Mark and John, Luke knew that Pilate's question to Jesus would be whether he is king of the Jews; Luke therefore framed the accusation more clearly around that very issue.

THE CROWD

In Mark and Matthew, the group that accompanies Jesus to Pilate is a delegation of the chief priests and elders (Mark 15:3; Matt 27:12). Only at the introduction to the Barabbas scene that follows (Mark 15:6) does a crowd appear, and its entrance onto the scene is specifically noted (καὶ ἀναβὰς ὄχλος ἤρξατο αἰτεῖσθαι...). So Luke's reference at the first scene of the Pilate hearing to a crowd in addition to the chief priests (τοὺς ὄχλους, Luke 23:4) is a bit surprising if it is based on Mark. The crowd addressed by Pilate in Luke 23:4 remains there during all the subsequent controversies, insisting first on Jesus' prosecution (23:5), then calling for Barabbas' freedom instead of Jesus, (23:18), and finally calling for Jesus' crucifixion (23:21). This could simply be part of the Lukan pattern of introducing crowds where none exist in other synoptic passages.[22] But this particular instance seems surprising, even given Luke's tendency to use crowds. It is also possible that Luke was merely anticipating the feature of a crowd that is introduced at a later point in the narrative by Mark (15:8), the suggestion Goulder presents.[23] But even Goulder admits that this is a "forceful manipulation." Similarly, Bailey argues that Mark's presentation has a problem: the sudden appearance of the crowd in 15:11 with

---

[21] The very nature of the charge, that Jesus was leading the people astray, may also have found its origination in John. In John 7, certainly the first formulation of the Jewish leaders' opposition, Jesus is thought to be deceiving people (πλανάω, 7:12 and 7:47), a closely related term to Luke's διαστρέφω. Compare the importance of this term in John's Gospel and, as a rationale for Jesus' prosecution and death, in J. Louis Martyn, *History and Theology of the Fourth Gospel* (Nashville: Abingdon Press, 1979), 74–81, 158–60.

[22] See, for instance, Luke 18:36; 22:47. Cf. Fitzmyer *Luke* (I–IX), 467.

[23] Goulder, 756.

no explanation as to how they got there. He sees Luke solving the problem by including the crowds at the very beginning; this feature, according to Bailey, is a Lukan invention.[24] But as noted above, Mark does introduce the crowd as arriving in 15:8. It appears that Luke deliberately inserted the crowd early in response to another source, not to the internal dynamics of Mark's story.

The Johannine account of the Pilate hearing, however, includes other people in addition to the chief priests and officers. And Luke, having read John, would have been prompted to bring the crowds to Pilate's hearing earlier, rather than later, in the narrative. The question in John, of course, is who "they" are in 18:28: "Then they led Jesus from the house of Caiaphas to the Praetorium." Looking backward, the possible antecedents for "they" could be the high priest Annas (18:19), one of the officers of the high priest (18:22), or possibly Caiaphas (18:24). But if one of those is suggested, why the plural "they?" As the narrative unfolds, it becomes apparent that the "they" of verse 28 refers to "the Jews," so designated in verses 31 and 38. Indeed, this group called "the Jews" acts very much like a crowd in its unified and strident call for Jesus to be crucified instead of Barabbas (18:40; 19:6, 7). And in contrast to Mark and Matthew, John never introduces the arrival of a crowd; rather, the same group that has brought Jesus to Pilate engages in the series of exchanges with him.

Could "the Jews" of John's Gospel be interpreted as an angry crowd that calls for aggressive prosecution of Jesus and insists on Barabbas' freedom instead of Jesus'? It has been argued that the term "the Jews" is a technical term for the Jewish leaders, i.e., the chief priests and Pharisees.[25] But as the Pilate trial in John shows, the term is often broader than that. Here it appears to be distinguished from the Jewish leaders, and identifies the opposition to Jesus with the Jewish

---

[24] Bailey, 74.

[25] U. C. van Wahlde, "The Johannine Jews: A Critical Survey," *NTS* 28 (1982): 33–60.

nation.²⁶ In this broader sense of "the Jews," the term is remarkably similar in function to the crowds in Luke: both appear with the chief priests at the trial, and both respond with increasing passion to Pilate's attempts to release Jesus, demanding instead his crucifixion. Moreover, a more precise allusion to the "crowds" can also be seen in John. Pilate, in his first interview of Jesus, refers to the fact that Jesus was handed over to him by the τὸ ἔθνος τὸ σὸν καὶ οἱ ἀρχιερεῖς (John 18:35).²⁷ "Your nation" in 18:35 suggests a group of people larger than just the priests who had presented charges against Jesus. So John, in more than one way, establishes the scene so that the Jewish leaders are supported and accompanied by a group that represents the Jewish people.

There is, then, a strong similarity to John in the way that Luke presents the group who brought Jesus to Pilate. Luke, following only Mark, would have had no basis for this feature. But with John as an additional source, Luke's modifications become understandable. It appears that Luke used John in the construction of the crowd's petitioning Pilate for Jesus' death.

STATEMENT OF INNOCENCE

A major difference between Luke and Mark is found in Pilate's reaction to Jesus after the initial exchange. In Luke, Pilate concludes immediately that Jesus is innocent: οὐδέν εὑρίσκω αἴτιον ἐν τῷ ἀνθρώπῳ τούτῳ. This is a significant element in Luke's understanding

---

²⁶ John Ashton, *Understanding the Fourth Gospel* (Oxford: Clarendon Press, 1991), 132. See also his earlier article "The Identity and Function of the Ἰουδαῖοι in the Fourth Gospel," *NT* 27 (1985): 40–75. Also cf. Brown, *Death*, 744; and Raymond E. Brown, *The Gospel According to John* (X–XXI), AB 29A (Garden City, NY: Doubleday, 1970), 844.

²⁷ Julius Schniewind, *Die Parallelperikopen bei Lukas und Johannes* (Hildesheim: Georg Olms Verlagsbuchhandlung, 1958), 64; as Bailey notes, this term τὸ ἔθνος τὸ σὸν is surely synonymous with "the Jews" (75). This passage in John also has a striking similarity to Luke's note at 23:13: "Pilate called the priests and the rulers *and the people* (λάον) and said to them, 'You brought me this man.'"

of Pilate, evidenced by the fact that it is but the first of three such declarations of innocence (Luke 23:4; 23:14; 23:22). Such a declaration of innocence is never found in Mark or Matthew. In addition, this declaration comes as a bit of a surprise within the narrative, being a rather abrupt response to Jesus' noncommittal answer in verse 3. One might expect more of an exchange, perhaps a follow-up question, before such a sweeping declaration of innocence.[28] The abruptness of the declaration is confusing at best. Regardless of whether Jesus' answer to Pilate's question in verse 3 is understood as "yes" or "no," Pilate's response here seems out of place. A further discussion between Jesus and Pilate seems to be implied, although it is not related by Luke.

The impression one gets from verse 4 is that, in addition to understanding that there were participants other than just the chief priests as outlined above, Luke was aware of another narrative in which (a) the response to the charges presented against Jesus was an acquittal, and (b) there was perhaps more of an exchange before the declaration of innocence.[29]

Precisely those features in which Luke diverges from Mark are found in John. The Fourth Gospel also has Pilate declare Jesus innocent in words that are very similar to Luke: ἐγὼ οὐδεμίαν εὑρίσκω ἐν αὐτῷ αἰτίαν (John 18:38; cf. 19:4, 6). As shall be discussed more below, this declaration of innocence is given three times in John, as in Luke; thus the similarity extends beyond simply this scene.[30] In addition to this threefold pattern, John does have a longer exchange between Jesus and Pilate that makes the declaration of innocence less abrupt. John 18:34–38 records a very Johannine dialogue between Jesus and Pilate in which Jesus again reiterates his origination as "not from this world" and introduces the major Johannine themes of coming

---

[28] See also Green, *Death*, p. 79.

[29] Green also notes the abruptness of the declaration of innocence, but proposes that another source was used in which there was *no* further exchange, hence explaining Luke's abruptness here. I think it more likely that the abruptness signals something left out in the editing process. Cf. also Dibelius, "Herodes und Pilatus," 119.

[30] See p. 353 below.

into the world and testifying to truth. The dialogue finally concludes with Pilate's question, "What is truth?" In John, the examination of Jesus by Pilate, the dialogue that ensues, and the declaration of innocence are all integrally related and appear to be part of John's fundamental presentation of the trial.[31] It is for this reason that Schniewind concludes that Luke has in mind the exchange that actually takes place in John: "die joh. Tradition das deutlich macht, was bei Lk. undeutlich bleibt."[32] It is hard to imagine John's having relied on Luke's abrupt trial scene; the Fourth Gospel presents a well structured unity that shows no signs of reliance on another tradition.[33]

With these features in mind, then, it appears that Luke heavily modified his Markan source under the influence of a source similar to John. From Mark, Luke knew of a simple hearing before Pilate in which Jesus answers Pilate obliquely as to whether he is the king of the Jews. In Mark, of course, an accusation is not offered until after the questioning of Jesus, a feature that must have appeared out of order to Luke. But if Luke also knew of John's version, in which formal charges are leveled first and in which Pilate declares Jesus innocent immediately, then he quite reasonably might have combined the two sources, especially since John's version accords with Luke's own political agenda of emphasizing Jesus' innocence as a part of establishing Christianity as a *religio licita*.[34] In such a scenario, Luke, following John's structure, developed with some specificity charges that fit the circumstance, particularly the charge of being king. Having sub-

---

[31] Brown, *John*, 861-62; cf. Rudolf Bultmann, *The Gospel of John. A Commentary.* (Oxford: Basil Blackwell, 1971), 648: "18.28-19.16a is an organic unity."

[32] Schniewind, 64.

[33] Although in direct opposition to this, R. Baum-Bodenbender, *Hoheit in Niedrigkeit* (Würzburg: Echter Verlag, 1984) argues that the Johannine narrative is not unified and that it shows signs of later adaptation to the synoptic, and in this case Lukan, presentation. For Baum-Bodenbender, John's original coherent account is to be found in 18:33, 36-38; the rest is later modification (110 f. and see especially 128–139).

[34] Henry J. Cadbury, *The Making of Luke-Acts* (London: SPCK, 1968), 306.

sequently relied on Mark's version of the questioning of Jesus, with Jesus' striking and enigmatic answer σὺ λέγεις, Luke turns to John for the declaration of innocence, but was unwilling to follow John in the extensive dialogue which led up to that declaration. Luke's unwillingness to expand the dialogue might have come, in part, from a desire to retain the essential element of Mark—Jesus' basic silence in the proceedings. Such a conception of Luke's compositional process, using both Mark and John, helps to explain the account's impression of abruptness.

THE ADDITIONAL CHARGE

In Luke, after Pilate's declaration of innocence, the Jewish opposition renews its accusation, this time broadening it to the charge that Jesus is stirring up the people: ἀνασείει τὸν λαὸν διδάσκων καθ' ὅλης τῆς Ἰουδαίας (Luke 23:5). This charge of political sedition cuts more to the heart of why Jesus' being labeled king was so dangerous. Instability was particularly feared by the Roman governors of regions, so this development of the accusation against Jesus was especially dangerous. In Mark and Matthew, the charge that is presented after Pilate's examination of Jesus is vague: "they accused him of many things (πολλά)," though no specifics are stated. So, while it is possible that Luke has added an additional charge after the first examination of Jesus in order to agree with Mark, it is hard to see any real connection between the two Gospels. Nor is there any suggestion of an additional accusation lodged against Jesus in John either. It appears that Luke has composed this second accusation to reiterate the polemical motives and false nature of the Jewish opposition.

Goulder suggests that Luke forcefully rewrote Mark in this verse. The persistence of the chief priests and the term ἀνασείειν Goulder sees in Mark 15:11 and 14b,[35] although the sense there is far different. If Luke was relying on Mark, he was doing so with considerable freedom.

---

[35]Goulder, p. 756.

It is only slightly possible that Luke was relying solely on a unique source for this verse. Although the verse contains *hapax legomena* (ἐπισχύειν and, for Luke, ἀνασείειν), the evidence of Lukan style is nevertheless very strong. Jeremias can claim only ἕως ὧδε as pre-Lukan, evidence that is rather weak.[36] A strong indication of the Lukan origination of the verse is the phrase καθ' ὅλης τῆς Ἰουδαίας καὶ ἀρξάμενος ἀπὸ τῆς Γαλιλαίας, which is identical with Acts 10:37 (cf. also Acts 9:31). Since this verse introduces Galilee into the hearing, it was possibly constructed by Luke as a seam to provide the opening for the Herod trial, which follows in Luke 23:6–12.[37]

While the marks of Lukan redaction are apparent, there is an echo of John in the charge as well. As noted in chapter 6 above, the equivalent to the Jewish "trials" in John seem to occur in John 10:22–39 and 11:45–53. In John 11:48, just before the Sanhedrin's formal conclusion that Jesus should die, the concern is raised that Jesus is stirring up the people such that the Romans will perceive there is an insurrection. Thus the expression of the concern that Jesus was creating an insurrection, placed on the lips of the Jewish leaders as an accusation before Pilate in Luke 23:5, is also voiced by the leaders of the Sanhedrin in John 11:48. It certainly possible that the accusation, absent in Mark and Matthew, is a reflection of John's narrative.

Although the verse does serve as a seam leading into the Herod pericope, it is also likely that Luke wrote this verse in order to emphasize a fundamental programmatic concern of his Gospel: to portray Jesus' ministry as one of travel from the outer reaches, especially Galilee, through Judea and up to Jerusalem itself. Thus the verse emphasizes the centrality of Jerusalem and the purposeful journey toward Jerusalem, a theme that is seen throughout the Gospel. And, more particularly in the context of the trial narratives, it emphasizes Jesus' direct challenge of the Jewish leadership in bringing his mini-

---

[36] Jeremias, *Sprache*, 301. Cf. Fitzmyer, *Luke* (X–XXIV), 1472, who notes that both ἕως and ὧδε are used frequently by Luke. The former is used thirteen times, the latter sixteen times, although together only here (1472).

[37] Green, *Death*, 79; Brown, *Death*, 762.

stry to Jerusalem. This geographic summary interpretation of the charge against Jesus appears to be a Lukan construction and interpretation.[38] In addition, the very charge of sedition appears to ironically convict the Jewish authorities; in Luke 23:18–19, they choose a known insurrectionist for release over Jesus.[39] Not only does Luke construct this verse to reflect on the geographical purpose of Jesus, as well as to provide a seam for the Herod pericope, but also to condemn the Jewish leadership in their call for Barabbas' release.

SUMMARY

Luke's introductory pericope for the Pilate trial, Luke 23:1–5, is significantly different from Mark's similar passage. While some scholars have argued that Luke was relying on Mark for the entire section,[40] others have believed that he knew some other source that would account for the differences between Luke and Mark. One feature of the passage is Luke's extensive editing the unit: Luke's language and style are pervasive. Nonetheless, key elements of *content* point to an outside influence in the setting, the cast of characters and the thrust of the Pilate trial, which is introduced here.

My examination has shown that many of the major features in content of the passage have a strong similarity to John's Gospel. Specifically, the existence of a crowd along with the chief priests, the fact that charges are lodged against Jesus before Pilate examines him, the declaration of innocence by Pilate, and the accusation that Jesus was instigating an insurrection, all suggest a common view of the trial before Pilate.

---

[38] See William Robinson Jr., *Der Weg des Herrn* (Hamburg: Herbert Reich, 1964), 30 ff., and Joseph Tyson, *The Death of Jesus in Luke-Acts* (Columbia: University of South Carolina, 1986), 130–31.

[39] Conzelmann, 140.

[40] Goulder, 755–56. See also Gerhard Schneider, "The Political Charge against Jesus" in *Jesus and the Politics of His Day*, (Cambridge: University Press, 1984), 403–14.

More important than the mere existence of similarities, however, is the pattern of interweaving of Markan elements with other features, a pattern that we have already seen in Luke's use of a parallel narrative along with Mark. In this case, the crowds and the first statement of innocence in this introductory passage link with coordinate features in the subsequent Pilate trial, indicating a pervasive alternate narrative. Luke appears to have used features from this alternative narrative—which has a substantial similarity to John's Gospel—along with the Gospel of Mark to produce a distinctive Passion story.

TRIAL BEFORE HEROD. LUKE 23:6-12

⁶ Πιλᾶτος δὲ ἀκούσας ἐπηρώτησεν εἰ ὁ ἄνθρωπος Γαλιλαῖός ἐστιν· ⁷ καὶ ἐπιγνοὺς ὅτι ἐκ τῆς ἐξουσίας Ἡρῴδου ἐστὶν ἀνέπεμψεν αὐτὸν πρὸς Ἡρῴδην, ὄντα καὶ αὐτὸν ἐν Ἱεροσολύμοις ἐν ταύταις ταῖς ἡμέραις. ⁸ ὁ δὲ Ἡρῴδης ἰδὼν τὸν Ἰησοῦν ἐχάρη λίαν, ἦν γὰρ ἐξ ἱκανῶν χρόνων θέλων ἰδεῖν αὐτὸν διὰ τὸ ἀκούειν περὶ αὐτοῦ, καὶ ἤλπιζέν τι σημεῖον ἰδεῖν ὑπ᾽ αὐτοῦ γινόμενον. ⁹ ἐπηρώτα δὲ αὐτὸν ἐν λόγοις ἱκανοῖς· αὐτὸς δὲ οὐδὲν ἀπεκρίνατο αὐτῷ. ¹⁰ εἱστήκεισαν δὲ οἱ ἀρχιερεῖς καὶ οἱ γραμματεῖς εὐτόνως κατηγοροῦντες αὐτοῦ. ¹¹ ἐξουθενήσας δὲ αὐτὸν καὶ ὁ Ἡρῴδης σὺν τοῖς στρατεύμασιν αὐτοῦ καὶ ἐμπαίξας περιβαλὼν ἐσθῆτα λαμπρὰν ἀνέπεμψεν αὐτὸν τῷ Πιλάτῳ. ¹² ἐγένοντο δὲ φίλοι ὅ τε Ἡρῴδης καὶ ὁ Πιλᾶτος ἐν αὐτῇ τῇ ἡμέρᾳ μετ᾽ ἀλλήλων· προϋπῆρχον γὰρ ἐν ἔχθρᾳ ὄντες πρὸς αὐτούς.

Luke's story of the hearing before Herod is unique in the four Gospels. Did Luke compose the story himself, or did he rely on a source? Those who argue that Luke relied on a source, usually the proto-Luke Gospel, note that the Herod scene merges almost seamlessly with the Pilate hearing before and after it. Thus Perry, for instance, marks the pericope as including all of 23:1–16, with only verse 3 showing any reliance on Mark.[41] Others see the scene as free Lukan composition, especially given its predominately Lukan style of the passage.[42] One such view sees Luke composing the scene as a midrash of Psalm 2, the scripture for which Herod's involvement in Acts 4:27 is cited as a fulfillment.[43] A more conservative assessment, one that also acknowledges the passage's extensive Lukan style, sees it as a Lukan redaction of a pre-Lukan (oral) tradition, especially since evidence of that tradition is found in Acts 4:25–27.[44] Goulder understands that heavily reworked tradition to be Matthew.[45] Soards, more convincingly, argues that the passage is a Lukan composition based in part on Mark and in part on a historical tradition about contacts with Herod, which are referenced elsewhere in Luke and in Acts.[46]

PROTO-LUKE, MIDRASH, AND LUKAN INVENTION

One can, with some confidence, rule out some of these solutions to the origination of the Herod trial. This analysis has not yet found

---

[41] Perry, *Sources of Luke's Passion Narrative* (Chicago: University of Chicago Press, 1920), 45. Others who follow him in locating a source for most of the account are Joseph Tyson, "The Lukan Version of the Trial of Jesus," *NovT* 3 (1959): 249–258; Winter, Winter, P. *On the Trial of Jesus* (Berlin: de Gruyter, 1974); Harold Hoehner, *Herod Antipas* (Cambridge: University Press, 1972), 224–50. See also Brown, *Death*, 760–61.

[42] This position of Lukan composition is held by John Creed, *The Gospel According to St. Luke* (London: MacMillan, 1920), 280 ; Sloyan, 96. See also Erwin Buck, "The Pericope 'Jesus Before Herod,'" *Wort in Der Zeit* (Leiden: E. J. Brill, 1980), 165–78. Buck holds that Luke has constructed this story to serve as an anticipation of Peter's hearings before Pilate and Herod in Acts 4 and 12; thus, it has a paraenetic purpose for the early church.

[43] See Bailey, 66, n. 3; Cadbury, *The Making of Luke-Acts*, 231; Dibelius, "Herodes und Pilatus," 113–26.

[44] So Taylor, *Passion* 87.

[45] Goulder, 758.

[46] Marion Soards, "Tradition, Composition and Theology in Luke's Account of Jesus Before Herod Antipas," *Bib* 66 (1985): 344–63.

Luke Chapter 23 335

any evidence of a proto-Luke Gospel that Luke used instead of Mark.[47] Indeed, this study has found that Luke thus far has generally followed Mark, interweaving with Mark material from John and occasionally other sources. Without evidence of a distinct unified source at this point, one should look for other possibilities.

Jeremias finds only few indications in these verses of non-Lukan material: Ἱεροσολύμοις (Luke in the Gospel prefers Ἱερουραλήμ), λίαν, ἀπεκρίνατο, ἐμπαίξας, and πρὸς αὐτούς with a reciprocal sense.[48] The existence of so few signs of non-Lukan material in this relatively large unit of text is surprising, suggesting more than anything that the story is primarily a Lukan composition.[49] While stylistic evidence of non-Lukan material is scant, signs of Luke's composition or redaction are extensive; the use of ἐν ταύταις ταῖς ἡμέραις, χαίρειν, ἱκανός, χρόνοι, ἐπερωτάω, σύν, αὐτὴ ἡ ἡμέρα, φίλος, καὶ αὐτός and τέ are all strong indications of Luke's style.[50] The lack of a clear sign of an extensive source and the prevalent pattern of Lukan style cast doubt on the Proto-Luke source for this story. But it is also difficult to see how Luke would have composed this passage based only on Psalm 2. Luke's interpretation of Psalm 2 in Acts 4 is that Jesus was killed by the collusion of the kings and rulers of the earth. In contrast, Luke 23 shows Herod *not* plotting against Jesus; indeed Herod sends Jesus back with the assessment that he is not guilty (cf. 23:15). Thus if Luke com-

---

[47] For further discussion of the viability of the proto-Luke hypothesis, with a negative conclusion, see Allen F. Page, "Proto-Luke Reconsidered: A Study of Literary Method and Theology in the Gospel of Luke," Ph.D. Diss., Duke University, 1968.

[48] These are not clearly non-Lukan in every case. The Greek form of Jerusalem, while uncommon in the Gospel, is almost ubiquitous in Acts, suggesting that it is indeed Lukan. It is not clear that πρὸς αὐτούσ is a unique idiom, despite its reciprocal sense in English. Both the existence of λίαν and the middle form of ἀποκρίνομαι are unusual for Luke and may reflect tradition or some echo of another source.

[49] Brown, *Death*, 779.

[50] Goulder, 759; Taylor, *Passion*, 87; Büchele, 32. See also Hawkins, 15–53; Fitzmyer, *Luke* (X–XXIV), 1479; Brown, *Death*, 761, 768, 773–76.

posed this passage as a midrash of Psalm 2, he did so in opposition to his own later interpretation of the Psalm in Acts.[51]

TRADITION

It is hard to deny the possibility of an independent tradition (p. 335 above) of a Herod hearing upon which Luke has fashioned the account in 23:6–12.[52] The divergent tradition in Acts 4, in which Herod is seen as an opponent of Jesus, is certainly suggestive of this. Furthermore, the Gospel of Peter also contains a tradition in which Jesus appears before Herod.[53] The question, of course, is whether that independent tradition was written or oral. Taylor finds little evidence in this pericope for his Proto-Luke source, but he too sees a tradition behind verses 6–16 that has a connection with the Gospel of John. He cites two points that connect verses 6–16 with the Gospel of John: the declaration of innocence in verse 15, which is outside of the purview of this discussion, and Jesus' silence before Herod, which Taylor links with John 19:9.[54] Does this connection point to (oral) tradition, or to an echo of the Fourth Gospel?

---

[51] Fitzmyer, 1479; Brown, *Death*, 780.

[52] Gerhard Schneider, *Die Passion Jesu nach den drei älteren Evangelien* (München: Kösel-Verlag, 1973), 91, suggests that at least here there is an independent tradition. Other than the Herod pericope, he sees Luke's passion story to be based entirely on Mark and understands all the differences arising from Luke's redactional emphases.

[53] Gos. Pet. 1:1–4:9. For a discussion on the dating and relationship of Gospel of Peter to the canonical gospels, see John Dominic Crossan, *The Cross that Spoke* (San Francisco: Harper & Row, 1988) and Jerry Walter McCant, "The Gospel of Peter: The Docetic Question Re-Examined," (Ph.D. diss., Emory University, 1978). Opposing Crossan on the dating, and yet finding some reason for an independent basis for this tradition about Herod, see Raymond E. Brown, "The Gospel of Peter and Canonical Gospel Priority," *NTS* 33 (1987): 337. Brown, *Death*, 781, also notes a tradition found in Ignatius (*Smyrneans* 1.2) that he takes to be independent of Luke as well.

[54] Taylor, *Passion*, 87.

USE OF OTHER GOSPELS

One must finally consider the possibility that Luke used existing Gospels, heavily modifying them to fit his scheme. Goulder's thesis that Matthew was the source seems hardly credible, being based almost entirely on two words, λίαν in 23:8 and the middle voice of ἀποκρίνομαι in 23:9. There is scant else that would suggest a literary connection with Matthew. Even Goulder considers this interpretation a "tour de force."[55] While it is possible that the two terms Goulder identifies are echoes of Matthew (assuming that Luke knew Matthew), it is nevertheless hard to see Luke's having based the Herod story simply on Matthew's account.

The final approach, one that appears to be more reasonable, is Soards' argument that Luke used a combination of Mark, a core tradition about Herod, and his own creativity to fashion the account.[56] Soards notes that there must have been some core Herod tradition, but, as discussed above, only a basic knowledge that Jesus appeared before Herod would have been necessary to account for the Herod material in Luke's story. In addition, Luke may well have interjected here two features from Mark that he omitted elsewhere in his more direct use of Mark: Jesus' silence at the trial (Luke 23:9), and the mocking of Jesus (Luke 23:11). For some reason, Luke chose not to include Jesus' silence before Pilate (Mark 15:4–5) in his account of the Pilate trial; he did include the silence motif in the Herod scene. Perhaps if Luke was modifying the Pilate trial scene under the influence of John, then σὺ λέγεις was as close to silence as such a conflation would allow. The silence motif, then, might have been transferred to the construction of the Herod trial. More strikingly, Luke has Herod's soldiers mock Jesus and then clothe him in splendid apparel. Luke does not record a mocking or robing of Jesus in his parallel to Mark's account (Mark 15:16–20); in Luke, after Pilate accedes to the demands for Jesus' crucifixion, Jesus is immediately led away to the place of the Skull. It

---
[55] Goulder, 759.
[56] Soards, "Tradition...Herod," 347.

appears, then, according to Soards, that Luke transferred the mocking and robing of Jesus from the close of the Pilate trial to the Herod trial. Such a transfer could serve to protect Pilate's image in the Third Gospel, certainly a Lukan motif: in Luke, it is not Pilate who allows the mocking, but the Jewish king Herod.

There are, however, difficulties in seeing Mark as the source for Luke's presentation. As Soards himself notes, Mark presents the robing and mocking as somehow integrally related; indeed, the robe is removed after the mocking, as if to emphasize the robe's being related only to the mocking. In contrast, Luke has the robing take place *after* the mocking, and the robe is not removed.[57] Furthermore, Mark presents the mocking, as well as the flogging, as apparently part of the death sentence itself.[58] Again in contrast, Luke has the mocking (and later, in verses 16 and 22, the suggestion of flogging) as part of a warning to a troublemaker, not a punishment.

While one can see the similarity to Mark, the same points of similarity can be found to John—and with a greater sense of connection between the various elements. Like Mark, John has a point in the Pilate scene at which Jesus is silent (John 19:8–9).[59] Mark has the mocking and clothing take place well after the silence of Jesus; in between occur the Barabbas incident, the verdict, and the handing over of Jesus for punishment. But more similar to Luke, John has the silence closely connected with the mocking and robing of Jesus (John 19:2–5); it is one continuous scene. And, also in contrast to Mark but similar to Luke, the Fourth Gospel presents the mocking as part of the inquisition, not part of the punishment. Furthermore, like Luke, John does not have Jesus stripped of his clothes after the mocking. These features are not decisive, but they do cast doubt on Soards' tendency to find Mark behind all the features in the Herod scene; there may well be echoes of John in some of the elements Soards calls Markan.

---

[57] Cf. Brown, *John* (XIII–XXI), 887, chart.

[58] Walaskay, 91.

[59] As noted above, Taylor, *Passion* (87), sees this as a point of similarity between Luke and John.

SUMMARY

The Herod scene is a difficult conundrum in the analysis of Luke's use of sources. It is clear that Luke actively and forcefully reshaped whatever material he used to form this account. There is strong evidence that some tradition of a hearing before Herod lies at the core of the account, but it is difficult to locate the contours of that tradition, well integrated as it is into Luke's composition. Attempts to connect the passage with Psalm 2 or with Matthew are unconvincing. Soards' argument that much of the account could still be explained by Luke's use of Mark is attractive. However, at precisely those points where Soards finds the strongest link to Mark—Jesus' silence in questioning and the mocking and robing accounts—there are difficulties that are better explained by Luke's knowledge of John.

TRIAL BEFORE PILATE (PT. 2). LUKE 23:13–25

¹³ Πιλᾶτος δὲ συγκαλεσάμενος τοὺς ἀρχιερεῖς καὶ τοὺς ἄρχοντας καὶ τὸν λαὸν ¹⁴ εἶπεν πρὸς αὐτούς, Προσηνέγκατέ μοι τὸν ἄνθρωπον τοῦτον ὡς ἀποστρέφοντα τὸν λαόν, καὶ ἰδοὺ ἐγὼ ἐνώπιον ὑμῶν ἀνακρίνας *οὐθὲν εὗρον* ἐν τῷ ἀνθρώπῳ τούτῳ *αἴτιον* ὧν κατηγορεῖτε κατ᾽ αὐτοῦ, ¹⁵ ἀλλ᾽ οὐδὲ Ἡρῴδης· ἀνέπεμψεν γὰρ αὐτὸν πρὸς ἡμᾶς· καὶ ἰδοὺ οὐδὲν ἄξιον θανάτου ἐστὶν πεπραγμένον αὐτῷ. παιδεύσας οὖν αὐτὸν ἀπολύσω. ¹⁸ ἀνέκραγον δὲ παμπληθεὶ λέγοντες, Αἶρε τοῦτον, <u>ἀπόλυσον</u> δὲ ἡμῖν <u>τὸν Βαραββᾶν</u>· ¹⁹ ὅστις ἦν διὰ <u>στάσιν</u> τινὰ γενομένην ἐν τῇ πόλει καὶ <u>φόνον</u> βληθεὶς ἐν τῇ φυλακῇ. ²⁰ πάλιν δὲ ὁ Πιλᾶτος προσεφώνησεν αὐτοῖς, θέλων ἀπολῦσαι τὸν Ἰησοῦν· ²¹ οἱ δὲ ἐπεφώνουν λέγοντες, Σταύρου, *σταύρου* αὐτόν. ²² ὁ δὲ τρίτον εἶπεν πρὸς <u>αὐτούς</u>, Τί γὰρ κακὸν <u>ἐποίησεν</u> οὗτος; *οὐδὲν αἴτιον* θανάτου *εὗρον ἐν αὐτῷ·* παιδεύσας οὖν αὐτὸν ἀπολύσω. ²³ <u>οἱ δὲ</u> ἐπέκειντο φωναῖς μεγάλαις αἰτούμενοι αὐτὸν <u>σταυρωθῆναι</u>, καὶ κατίσχυον αἱ φωναὶ αὐτῶν. ²⁴ καὶ <u>Πιλᾶτος</u> ἐπέκρινεν γενέσθαι τὸ αἴτημα αὐτῶν· ²⁵

ἀπέλυσεν δὲ τὸν διὰ στάσιν καὶ φόνον βεβλημένον εἰς φυλακὴν ὃν ᾐτοῦντο, τὸν δὲ Ἰησοῦν παρέδωκεν τῷ θελήματι αὐτῶν.

After the hearing before Herod, Luke again picks up the story of the trial before Pilate. The basic sequence of (a) the choice between releasing Jesus or Barabbas, (b) the crowd's cry to crucify Jesus, and (c) the handing over of Jesus for crucifixion is common to Mark and Luke—and, indeed, John. But around this basic sequence, there are notable differences. The following chart illustrates the organization of the basic elements of the final trial narrative in Mark, Luke, and John.

Mark 15:5–15	Luke 23:13–25	John 18:39–19:16
	1. Not guilty.	
	2. Offer to chastise and release.	
3. Explanation of custom of release		3. Explanation of custom of release
4. Explanation of Barabbas		
5. Arrival of crowd		
6. Pilate: release King of Jews?		6. Pilate: Release king of Jews?
7. Chief priests incitement of crowd to request Barabbas' release	7. Crowd: No; release Barabbas	7. Crowd: No; release Barabbas
	(4). Explanation of Barabbas	(4). Explanation of Barabbas
	8. Desire to release	
9. Crowd: Crucify him.	9. Crowd: Crucify, crucify	
		10. Jesus scourged and mocked
		(1). Not guilty
		(9). Crowd: Crucify, crucify
11. What evil has he done?	11. What evil has he done?	
	12. Not guilty.	12. Not guilty

		13. Interview with Jesus
	14 (2). Chastise and release	14. Desire to release
15. Crowd: Crucify him (2nd time)	15. They were urgent	15. Crowd: Crucify him (2nd time)
16. Release of Barabbas	16. Release of Barabbas	
17. Delivered to be crucified	17. Delivered to their will	17. Delivered him to be crucified.

There is not an identity in the sequence of events between Luke and Mark; nevertheless, there are sufficient links to lead one to the conclusion that Luke followed Mark in the basic outline, making modifications in light of another narrative.[60] In particular, it is notable that Mark and Luke have a common order in certain key features of the narrative: the crowd's call to release Barabbas (item 7); the call to crucify Jesus (item 9); Pilate's asking, "What evil has he done?" (item 11); the second request to crucify Jesus (item 15); the release of Barabbas (item 16); and the handing over of Jesus for crucifixion (item 17). This common order of key events is undoubtedly attributable to Luke's following Mark in the basic framework of the story.

There are also scattered instances in which the language of Luke clearly reflects Mark. The most significant deal with the description of Barabbas as an insurrectionist and murderer (διὰ στάσιν καὶ φόνον, Luke 23:19, which echoes ἐν τῇ στάσει φόνον πεποιήκεισαν, Mark 15:7) and the question Pilate puts to the crowd after they call for Jesus' crucifixion (τί γὰρ κακὸν ἐποίησεν οὗτος, Luke 23:22, cf. Mark 15:14). These explicit agreements, though few, do suggest a link to Mark.

Despite the existence of links between Mark and Luke that suggest Luke's use of Mark, there are again a number of major differences between the two Gospels as well. As the table above shows, Luke deviates significantly from Mark in a number of points. These differences will be examined in detail in the following discussion.

---

[60] Cf. Green, *Death*, 83.

THE TRANSITIONAL PASSAGE, VV. 13–16

Verses 13–16 in this passage are unique to the Third Gospel. It appears that Luke composed these verses for the purpose of both constructing a bridge between the Herod hearing and the Barabbas scene that follows and creating a link between the two Pilate hearings and the Herod trial. The language is strongly Lukan. Jeremias finds only two features that would suggest a pre-Lukan source: προσφέρω in 23:14[61] and ἀλλ' οὐδέ in 23:15;[62] these are not, however, compelling indications of another source. Indeed, the elements of Lukan style are extensive, indicating that Luke fashioned this himself.[63]

More telling than the style, however, are the substantive issues in verses 13–16 that connect the passage with Luke's previous and subsequent narratives.

1. The audience addressed consists of the high priests, rulers, and people. Notable is the reference to the people, which suggests Luke's previous group before Pilate of "the high priests and the crowds."[64] The use of the word "people" here as a substitute for the previous word "crowd" appears to underline the representation of the Jewish people as the participants in prosecuting Jesus.[65] In other words, the "Jews," not just the leaders, are responsible for Jesus'

---

[61] Jeremias, *Sprache*, 303. But cf. Green, *Death*, 83. There is clear Lukan usage in 23:36; Acts 8:18; 21:26.

[62] Jeremias, *Sprache*, 303. But this is used by Luke in Acts 19:2 as well. Goulder considers this term to be a Lukan expression (761)!

[63] For example, Lukan vocabulary συνκαλέω, ἄρχοντες, λαός, εἶπεν πρός..., ἐνώπιον, οὐδὲν ἄξιον θανάτου, and εἶναι + perfect participle (πράσσω) are relatively secure examples of Lukan style. See Jeremias, *Sprache*, 303; Green, *Death*, 83–84; Goulder, 761.

[64] See the discussion p. 325 above on the introduction of the crowds in Luke's narrative.

[65] Schneider, *Passion* (102) notes that λαός here clearly indicates the "Bundesvolk Israel." Cf. also Brown, *Death*, 790–91.

death.⁶⁶ It is interesting that Luke varied the titles of the audience each time: the entire body in 23:1, high priests and crowds in 23:4, chief priests and scribes before Herod in 23:10, "all of them" in 23:18. It appears that Luke understood Jesus' audience consisted of religious leaders and a large group of followers and that he varied his language to express that composition in different ways.

2. The specific charge that Jesus is leading the people astray is reiterated. In this case, the term is ἀποστρέφοντα τὸν λαόν, which ties to the previous charge against Jesus in 23:2 that he was διαστρέφοντα τὸ ἔθνος. The slight difference in terminology (ἀποστρέθειν vs. διαστρέφειν, λαός vs. ἔθνος) is merely an indication of Luke's desire to have some variety in language. Despite the difference, the resonance between these two accusations against Jesus is clear and deliberate.

3. Pilate again declares that Jesus is not guilty—a theme, already introduced in 23:4, that appears a third times in 23:22.

4. In declaring Jesus not guilty, Pilate refers back to Jesus' appearance before Herod, claiming that Herod as well found no cause deserving of death in Jesus. There is, then, a link back to the Herod trial, a trial that is unique to Luke.

5. Pilate announces that he wants to chastise (παιδεύω) Jesus and release him. That announcement is repeated later in Luke 23:22, and in a modified form in 23:20.⁶⁷

These features of Luke 23:13–16, which echo themes that have been previously mentioned or are subsequently developed, only underline the function of this pericope as a bridge between the Herod trial and the two parts of the Pilate trial. Having incorporated the independent tradition of a hearing before Herod, Luke must reconnect it with the Pilate account as developed in his major source, Mark. But Luke, in this composition, displays the importance of an account other than Mark. The fact that significant non-Markan features occur in a

---

⁶⁶ As is well argued by John T. Carroll, "Luke's Crucifixion Scene," in *Reimaging the Death of the Lukan Jesus*, ed. Dennis D. Sylva (Frankfurt am Main: Anton Hain, 1990), 108–13.

⁶⁷ See further discussion of this feature p. 354 below.

clearly Lukan composition indicates that they are features Luke considers to be important. The repeated declarations of innocence, together with the statement of desire to chastise and release Jesus, are indications that Luke was very much influenced by another tradition, as shall be discussed further in the consideration of the subsequent references.

THE PILATE TRIAL, PART 2

Once again, Luke's presentation of the balance of the Pilate trial is significantly different from Mark's version. Luke's variance from the Markan pattern raises real questions concerning the degree to which he followed Mark. The significant differences can be summarized as follows.

1. The issue of whether Jesus or Barabbas should be released is presented in a completely different manner. In Mark and Matthew, the narrator first presents the background information that at the Passover it was a custom to release one prisoner. He next identifies the character Barabbas. Then, after the introduction these salient facts, Pilate asks the people whether he should release Barabbas or the king of the Jews. Finally, the chief priests incite the crowd to request Barabbas instead of Jesus. None of these features are present in Luke. Instead, Luke jumps directly from Pilate's desire to chastise and release Jesus (without reference to Barabbas) to the crowd's call for Barabbas' release instead. Only after the crowd calls for Barabbas' release does Luke explain to the reader who Barabbas is.

2. In Luke, the crowd, in direct address, specifically calls for Barabbas instead of Jesus. In Mark, that request is also found, but in a note by the narrator, not in direct address. Matthew has a bit of both: the narrator first relates that the people ask that Jesus be destroyed; then, in a response to a follow-up question, the people cry out for Barabbas in direct address.

3. In Luke, Pilate is said to desire to release Jesus twice more (the first instance having occurred in the transitional passage, 23:16), in verses 20 and 22. In Mark and Matthew, Pilate asks for direction from the crowd but never indicates his desire to release Jesus.

4. The crowd in Luke cries out emphatically with the double call "crucify, crucify." In Mark, the crowd calls only once, "crucify him," and Matthew's modification of that call softens it to a passive imperative, "Let him be crucified." Luke's doubled imperative is striking in its intensity.

5. Luke again indicates that Pilate cannot find in Jesus sufficient cause to warrant a death sentence. Mark knows nothing of a finding of innocence, only a vague question by Pilate (Mark 15:14).

6. The final sentence of Luke's Pilate account finds Jesus being delivered to "their will," which suggests that Pilate turned Jesus over to the Jewish crowd.

7. In Luke, there is no scourging at the conclusion of the trial, contrary to Mark and Matthew, where Jesus is scourged before being handed over for crucifixion.

In addition to the significant differences in the details of the account, there are very few literary connections that would indicate that Luke had relied extensively on Mark. Overall, the number of common words is at most 30 percent, and the verbatim similarities are confined to verses 22 and 25.[68] The balance of similarities are scattered words. Taylor notes that of the 26 words in vv. 18–25, only six are common to Luke and Mark.[69] It appears that Luke's direct reliance on Mark was slight, and yet the overall structure of his account, as shown in the outline above,[70] is essentially Markan.

As with 23:13–16, an analysis of the style of this passage does not indicate extensive use of another source. Jeremias can locate only one term, πάλιν (Luke 23:20), that might indicate Luke's use of a tradi-

---

[68] Green, *Death*, 83.
[69] Taylor, *Passion*, 88.
[70] See p. 340 above.

tion,⁷¹ and this is surely Luke's modification of Mark 15:12. On the other hand, Lukan terms and patterns of usage are ubiquitous in this unit of text.⁷² If Luke knew and used another source here, which is highly likely, he thoroughly assimilated it to his style of language.⁷³

While it appears that Luke very consciously constructed the scene using his own phraseology, there are consistent echoes of John's account throughout. In fact, each of the seven distinctive differences from Mark outlined above has a relationship with the Fourth Gospel. It is appropriate, at this point, to consider carefully Luke's account of the Pilate trial with an eye to understanding his redaction of sources.

A. Luke 23:[17]–19. There can be little doubt that verse 17 was a secondary addition to the text of Luke, made in an effort to assimilate it to the story line of Mark/Matthew, and perhaps even John.⁷⁴ Verse 17 says that Pilate was obliged to release one prisoner at the time of the feast, which mitigates the abruptness and narrative surprise of the crowd's calling for Barabbas' release.⁷⁵ All the other Gospels have a description of the practice of releasing a prisoner at Passover; thus, it is easy to see a scribe inserting a similar qualifier here.

Beginning in verse 18, however, Luke resumes the basic story line of Mark, and the resemblance is clear, despite the differences.

---

⁷¹ Jeremias, *Sprache*, 304.

⁷² Jeremias, *Sprache*, 303–5.

⁷³ Green, *Death* (86), regarding this passage, states, "We conclude on the basis of this inquiry that Luke did know another account of the Roman trial of Jesus which overlapped with the Markan, and that in relating this phase of Jesus' trial he has conflated his two sources while including a few phrases of his own invention."

⁷⁴ Bruce Metzger, *A Textual Commentary on the Greek New Testament* (Stuttgart: United Bible Societies, 1994), 179. While the text is found in some old Greek codices and Latin and Syriac texts (ℵ, W, Θ, Ψ, $f^{1,13}$; placed after v. 19 in D and sy^{s,c}), it is absent from P^{75}, B, A, K, L, T, and 070. The strongest witnesses are absent the text, but the most compelling argument is that it is easy to see how it could have been added, but difficult to see why it would have been deleted.

⁷⁵ Schniewind notes, "Also der Lk.-Bericht scheint in sich unverständlich; kein Wunder, daß sekundäre handschriften v.17 hinzugefügt haben, der die Sitte der

Luke has a call by the crowd for Barabbas' release followed by another appeal from Pilate, then a call for Jesus' crucifixion. In the basic outline of the story, Mark appears to provide a framework.[76] Moreover, the description of Barabbas in verse 19, although in a different location than in Mark, strongly reflects Mark's description. Luke uses language from Mark, calling Barabbas one involved in στάσις and φόνον.[77]

But while aware of Mark's story, and using it as a basic outline, Luke portrays a very different scene than does Mark. Without verse 17, verse 18 provides a stark contrast between Pilate and the crowd. Pilate has just found Jesus not guilty and that he wants to release him. Note that, in contrast to Mark, Matthew, and John, Pilate here does not ask the crowd if he should release Jesus; the desire to release him is simply stated as a judgment. The crowd (indefinite "they"), without being offered any choice, requests instead Barabbas' release and calls (ἀνέκραγον) for Jesus' death in direct address: "away with him" (αἶρε τοῦτον). By not relating any information about Barabbas or the custom of release, Luke has made the crowd's call more deliberate, more opposed to Jesus, and, compared to Pilate, certainly more unjust. The contrast between Pilate and the Jewish crowd is made more emphatic by the use of the word παμπληθεί, which casts a negative light on all the Jewish people present, with priests and people acting in complete concord.[78]

As noted above, all three of the other Gospels present at least the question whether Pilate should release Jesus. Moreover, in stark contrast to Luke, Mark and Matthew both present a description of who Barabbas is, after which his name is put before the crowd as an alternative to Jesus' release. In Mark (15:11), the chief priests bring up the name, while in Matthew (27:17), Pilate first offers the choice between Barabbas and Jesus, and the chief priests then encourage the choice of the former. And in each of those instances, the crowd's request is

---

Freigabe erzählt" (65).

[76] Schneider, *Passion*, 102.
[77] Taylor, *Passion*, 88.
[78] Brown, *Death*, 807. A hapax legomenon.

recounted in indirect speech. But in the Fourth Gospel (18:40), Barabbas is not presented as an option, yet the crowd cries out κραύγασαν and requests in direct speech that Pilate release not Jesus but Barabbas. And this is then followed by a summary note that Barabbas was a λῃστης.[79]

Once again, Luke's version of the beginning scene of the Barabbas episode becomes more understandable when seen as a modification of the Markan account in light of a conflicting, Johannine, version. Luke thus constructed the episode to more closely follow the pattern found in John, in which the crowd's call for Barabbas is an abrupt and surprising occurrence. Only after the request for Barabbas' release does Luke explain who Barabbas is. The abruptness, as noted before, certainly explains the later scribal emendation of verse 17. Schniewind has pointed out that it is hard to imagine Luke's having modified Mark's narrative, which is relatively clear in its presentation, to such an abrupt and less clear pattern unless there was another source exerting some influence:

> Warum das klare künstlich unklar machen? Es läßt sich keinerlei Motiv entdecken, weshalb etwa Lk. die Erwähnung und Kennzeichnung des Barabbas unnatürlicherweise und den Schluß der Episode hätte rücken sollen, wenn ihm die natürliche Anordnung schon vorlag. Es gibt nur eine Erklärung; gerade bei mündlicher Erzählung läßt sich begreifen, wie der Name Barabbas unvorbereitet, gleichsam Spannung erregend, im Mund des Volkes auftritt, und erst nachträglich wird dann kurz erklärt, wer dieser Barabbas war.[80]

For Schniewind, such a change clearly indicates an oral tradition, common to John, that is at odds with Mark. Schniewind's sense

---

[79] This term is probably meant to have the same import as being involved in an insurrection (στάσις), since it often refers to the Zealots. See K. H. Rengstorf, "λῃστης," *TDNT*, Vol. IV (Grand Rapids, MI: Wm. Eerdmans, 1967), 257–62, especially 258, regarding Josephus' use of the term, and 261–62, on the term with respect to Barabbas.

[80] Schniewind, 65.

about the importance of the order of this pericope is correct, but it is more likely that Luke simply found this pattern in the Fourth Gospel itself. Finding John's presentation, that the crowd instigated the release, to be more dramatic and, possibly, more credible, he followed its basic outline, leaving out Pilate's question to the crowd whether he should release the king of the Jews. This question did not fit well with the blanket statement of innocence and desire to release Jesus that Luke had already narrated; in Luke, then, Pilate attempts to release Jesus without reference to the crowd's desires. It thus appears that Luke followed John's pattern of the crowd's unsolicited request for Barabbas, the direct speech, and the subsequent identification of Barabbas.

Luke's reliance in 23:18 on the Johannine version is also indicated at the lexical level by the use of the word ἀνακράζω, which is a Lukan form of the Johannine word κραυγάζω.[81] In contrast, Mark and Matthew do not describe in the first instance the crowd crying out. Perhaps also reflecting John's account, Luke has the crowd ask for Jesus' death with the words αἶρε, echoing the crowd's later response in John 19:15: ἆρον, ἆρον.[82] Schniewind notes that not only is the wording similar (although as Taylor notes, in a different location in the story), but the particular use of the word αἴρω is unique to Luke and John. The imperatival use of αἴρω for "away" is found only in John 19:15, here, and in Acts 21:36 and 22:22, which are also Lukan, out of 102 occurrences in the New Testament.[83] This similar usage of αἴρω, more than the simple existence of a common word, indicates a literary connection.

The lexical evidence aside, the construction and order of the episode indicate that Luke was deliberately moving away from the

---

[81] Cf. W. Grundmann, "κράζω, κτλ." in *TDNT* vol. III (Grand Rapids, MI: Wm. B. Eerdmans, 1965), 898–903. κραυγάζω is used by John six times, and in Luke perhaps once (in a textual variant, Luke 4:41) and in Acts once. Luke often prefers ανα- prefixes; he certainly uses ἀνακράζω three times.

[82] This similarity has also been noted by Green, *Death*, 84; Taylor, 88.

[83] Schniewind, 72.

Mark/Matthew construction and toward the Johannine form of the narrative.

B. Luke 23:20–21. In verse 20, Luke follows Mark 15:12 in having Pilate address the crowd again (πάλιν).[84] In Mark and Matthew, this subsequent address has Pilate ask the crowd what he should do with Jesus, to which the crowd responds in direct address, "Crucify him." In keeping with his pattern of emphasizing Pilate's verdict of innocence, Luke instead has Pilate once again indicate his desire to release Jesus, a theme seen previously at 23:16. Against that backdrop, the crowd's demand to crucify Jesus is, once again, a strong contrast to Pilate's judgment of innocence. The doubling of the cry to σταύρου, σταύρου only amplifies what is already a stark contrast.

The two basic departures from the Markan pattern are again in features that Luke shares with John: the desire to release Jesus and the strengthened doubling of the cry to crucify him. Again, an examination of Luke's affinities with John suggests that Luke departed from the primary Markan source because of the pattern already found in John.

Luke 23:20 is Luke's second report that Pilate wished to release Jesus; a third one is found at 23:22, with almost exactly the same language as in 23:16, a desire to chastise Jesus and release him. It appears that Luke expanded the feature of Pilate's desire to release Jesus into a threefold pattern in order to drive home the theme of innocence. But Pilate's desire to release Jesus is found in John as well, in a form that is perhaps more original.

In John 19:12, at the conclusion of the trial, Pilate finally concludes that Jesus should be released, and only upon the crowd's repeated cries and their intimation of Pilate's own complicity in sedition does he turn Jesus over for crucifixion. Preceding this (19:1), John reports that Jesus was scourged (μαστιγάω) and humiliated, not as a judgment, but rather as part of the trial procedure, perhaps in an effort to satisfy the crowd short of death.[85] John's version, which presents

---

[84] Green, *Death*, 84.
[85] See Brown, *John* (XIII–XXI), 886.

first the scourging, then the desire to let the Jews crucify him, and finally the desire to release him, seems a natural combination of Roman cruelty with the increasing realization that Jesus was not a real political threat. John does not make a lot out of the desire to release Jesus; it is part of the progression of final events. If John had known of Luke's threefold pattern of attempting to release Jesus, linked with his possible chastisement, it is hard to imagine that he would have collapsed Luke's stylized statements into this sequence of events.[86]

The linkage of the scourging with the release is presented in Luke in a more consistent, repetitive, and stylized form: Pilate's wish to chastise and release Jesus is, repeated three times (Luke 23:16, 23:20, 23:22). Had Luke known John's narrative, it is understandable that he would have fixed on the scourging as an alternative to death and the desire to release Jesus and would have emphasized them together as he did. The threefold attempt to release Jesus, based perhaps on the pattern of the threefold judgment of innocence, and the close linkage of the release with the chastisement, suggests development of a theme found in embryonic form in John. John's version is muddled, while Luke's appears to be well thought out and rhetorical.

It is perhaps natural that Luke would have emphasized the crowd's demand that Jesus be crucified by doubling the word; Luke has already shown a pattern of doubling words.[87] But in the other instances, the doubled words are vocatives, not imperative verbs. The doubled cry of "crucify" cannot, then, be easily explained as Lukan style. But, again, a similar feature is found in John. In John's second exchange of Pilate with the Jews (John 19:6), corresponding to Luke's "Pilate addressed them once more" (Luke 22:20), the chief priests and officers cry out σταύρωσον σταύρωσον, in a double imperative similar

---

[86] Contra Bailey, who thinks that John would have done this as an expansion of the Lukan suggestion that chastisement was an alternative to death (73). But the actual effect of John's version is a confusion and understatement of the link between the desire to release Jesus and the chastisement. It is hard to see John's logic if he had been expanding Luke.

[87] Cf. Luke 10:41; 13:34; 22:31.

to Luke's. As elsewhere, the correspondence is not exact—here the tense is different—yet the similarity is striking. This doubling of an imperative appears to be part of John's style; a similar feature is found in 19:15 with ἆρον ἆρον. It is very likely that Luke was adapting his Markan account to certain features found in John.

C. Luke 23:22–23. After the call of the crowd for crucifixion, Luke reaches a crescendo in his series of comments about the difference in attitude toward Jesus between Pilate and the Jewish crowds. That Luke intended to highlight the difference is clearly indicated by his counting the number of times that Pilate appealed to the crowd. Following Mark almost word for word at this point, Luke has Pilate ask what wrong Jesus has committed to warrant crucifixion. But unlike Mark, Luke has Pilate go on to affirm Jesus' innocence and his desire to release him. Luke's explicit statement that Pilate was speaking to them a third time concludes two separate series of three. Pilate has declared Jesus innocent three times (23:4; 23:14; 23:22) and sought to release him three times (23:16; 23:20; 23:22). That each of these features occurs here for the third time, undoubtedly no accident, is an indication of Luke's literary construction of the episode.

At various points in the foregoing discussion of Jesus' trial before Pilate, the points of commonality between Luke and John in the declaration of innocence and desire to release Jesus have been noted. While the individual points of contact are impressive, the pattern of repeated declarations of innocence and desire to release is even more vital for this analysis. The existence of a common pattern—one that is woven into the very fabric of the narratives—is strong evidence of a literary relationship.

Both Luke and John have repeated statements about Pilate's declaration of Jesus' innocence. These can be summarized as follows:

Luke	John
1. οὐδὲν εὑρίσκω αἴτιον ἐν τῷ ἀνθρώπῳ (Lk 23:4)	ἐγὼ οὐδεμίαν εὑρίσκω ἐν αὐτῷ αἰτίαν. (Jn 18:38)
2. οὐθὲν εὗρον ἐν τῷ ἀνθρώπῳ τουτῷ αἴτιον ὧν κατηγορεῖτε κατ' αὐτοῦ (Lk 23:14)	οὐδεμίαν αἰτιαν εὑρίσκω ἐν αὐτῷ (Jn 19:4)
3. ὁ δὲ τρίτον εἶπεν πρὸς αὐτούς·... οὐδὲν αἴτιον θανάτου εὗρον ἐν αὐτῷ. (Lk 23:22)	ἐγὼ γὰρ οὐχ εὑρίσκω ἐν αὐτῷ αἰτίαν (Jn 19:6)

The threefold pattern in the two Gospels is very striking. But Luke and John used the declaration of innocence in very different ways and places in their narratives. John has the first declaration of innocence immediately after the first interview with Jesus in the Praetorium (John 18:33–38). Pilate goes back out to the Jews and declares him innocent. The second and third declarations occur after Pilate has Jesus flogged and robed (John 19:1–3). They are functionally part of the same scene, but they are separated by Pilate's presentation of Jesus to the Jews as a spectacle (the Ecce Homo scene, John 19:5–7).[88]

Luke, on the other hand, has a carefully delineated sequence of Pilate's declarations of innocence. The first occurs near the conclusion of the first interview before Pilate (Luke 23:1–5). The second occurs after the hearing before Herod (Luke 23:6–12), in the transitional passage (Luke 23:13–16) before Pilate resumes his hearing. And the third occurs at the conclusion of the Barabbas scene (Luke 23:17-23). There is, then, a statement of innocence summarizing each of the three major scenes in the trial.[89]

It is difficult to pair up the three declarations of innocence between Luke and John. As Schniewind notes, the first declaration of innocence (John 18:38) is roughly parallel to the first declaration in Luke (23:4); both occur after Pilate's first question, "Are you the king

---

[88] Schniewind, 66.
[89] Schniewind, 66.

of the Jews?" The second and third declarations in John (19:4, 6) are roughly equivalent to the third declaration in Luke (Luke 23:22), at the end of the Barabbas scene. What is missing in John, of course, is the Herod scene and the resulting declaration at that point.[90]

But if the declarations do not correspond exactly, what can one say? The striking nature of the similar pattern suggests some relationship, as the frequent mention of the similarity in the literature attests. Bailey argues, "This is one of the very few instances in John where in composing a discourse on the basis of a passage from one of the synoptic Gospels the fourth evangelist remained so close to his source that we can discern with certainty the tradition as he found it and the material which he added to it."[91] But how does one explain John's having used a clear and ordered threefold declaration of innocence in a way that confuses the sense of it? It is hard to imagine John's having chosen to use three declarations of innocence, one of which occurs in the Herod trial, but to double up one of the declarations and to omit the Herod trial. As Schniewind notes, Luke's presentation is a clear arrangement while John's is not: "Diese deutliche Disposition des Lk., die durch den entscheidenden Gesichtspunkt bestimmt ist, läßt sich nun nicht unmittelbar by Joh. wiederfunden."[92] A more reasonable explanation is that Luke took over John's pattern, which is a bit inchoate, and ordered it around his tripartite scheme of hearings: Pilate, Part 1; Herod; Pilate, Part 2. Luke used the triple declarations in his mature and highly schematized construction of the hearings. Not only did the declaration of innocence suit his political message, its repetition perhaps inspired him to divide the trial into three parts. It is reasonable to see Luke's having used John's pattern to better effect; it is difficult to see John's having confused Luke's clear pattern.

Both Luke and John, as noted, also have Pilate specifically stating that he wishes to release Jesus. In John, this occurs only at the very

---

[90] Schniewind, 66.
[91] Bailey, 71.
[92] Schniewind, 66.

conclusion of the Barabbas scene, John. 19:12.⁹³ In Luke, there is a threefold pattern of this as well, but it is not as well structured as that of the declarations of innocence: the first statement occurs at the conclusion of Herod's trial, connected to the second declaration of innocence; the second, in the middle of the Barabbas scene, after the crowd requests Barabbas instead of Jesus; and the third, at the conclusion of the Barabbas scene along with the third declaration of innocence. Schniewind argues that in John this desire to release is the true third member of Pilate's efforts to release Jesus: that is, (1) Jesus is innocent, John 18:38; (2) Jesus is innocent, John 19:4, 6; and (3) desire to release Jesus, John 19:12. Perhaps that is so. But again, Luke appears to have recognized the value of the threefold repetition of the desire to release Jesus as well as that of the declaration of innocence.⁹⁴ These features, which are not exploited rhetorically in John, are expanded and emphasized in Luke.

Following the declaration of innocence, Luke again follows Mark's narrative outline, having the crowd continue to cry out for Jesus' crucifixion. Luke's final comment, καὶ κατίσχυον αἱ φωναὶ αὐτῶν, is a postscript that the crowd was at odds with Pilate, who remained in opposition to the decision to crucify Jesus. There is little

---

⁹³ F. C. Grant, "Was the Author of John Dependent upon the Gospel of Luke?" *JBL* 56 (1937): 299, tries to argue that John sought to release Jesus five times (John 18:31, 33; 19:4, 6, 12). But he counts as declarations of innocence a desire to release (19:12), and an initial effort to refuse to hear the case (18:31) as well.

⁹⁴ It is worth noting here that Luke's penchant for threefold patterns has been seen elsewhere in chapter 23. Büchele, indeed, sees threefold patterns everywhere! In addition to the examples already cited, he sees three groups of people with Jesus going to the crucifixion (Simon, women, evildoers), three groups who mock Jesus (leaders, soldiers, an evildoer), three groups who acknowledge his death (centurion, crowds, acquaintances and women), and a threefold inclusio at the burial (Joseph, preparation day, women) (67–68 and 112–14). This seems excessive, but does give some hint of the way that Luke used traditional material in Mark and elsewhere to amplify patterns that are more strongly seen in the Third Gospel.

that would point to Mark, and the language is comfortably Lukan. In this, the final comment is clearly Luke's editorial addition.[95]

D. Luke 23:24–25. The main elements of these verses follow Mark in content; there can be little doubt that Luke was using the Second Gospel here. Luke, like Mark, indicates that Pilate judged Jesus in accordance with the desires of the crowd. The language is very different, but the sense is the same. Luke avoids saying in this section that Pilate judged Jesus guilty or that he passed the sentence of crucifixion; such a statement would stand in direct opposition to the Lukan pattern of portraying Pilate as believing Jesus is innocent. But he does have Pilate accede to the crowd, as does Mark. This is followed by the common theme that he released Barabbas. Luke reiterates the description of Barabbas' crimes (στάσιν καὶ φόνον), highlighting the contrast between Jesus, who is held and the criminal, who is released. The language referring to Barabbas is a near verbatim repetition of Luke's previous description, in 23:19.

When we compare Luke with Mark at the conclusion of the Pilate trial, it is striking that Luke omits the scourging and mocking of Jesus at the hands of the Roman soldiers. Mark and Matthew record common elements in a common sequence: (a) the scourging of Jesus, followed by (b) clothing of Jesus in a robe, (c) crowning him with thorns, (d) mocking him as King of the Jews, (e) striking and spitting on him, and (f) stripping off the cloak and putting back on Jesus own clothes. That the robing and mocking of Jesus is reported by Luke in the Herod trial has already been discussed; it is perhaps not surprising that Luke as well includes no record of a scourging. But the matter of scourging seems to have independent importance to Luke. Two of the times that Pilate indicates his desire to release Jesus, he also offers to chastise (παιδεύω). Thus in Luke, the scourging/chastisement seems to be clearly offered as an alternative punishment to crucifixion.

This feature of scourging as an alternative to crucifixion, in an unusual way, is found also in John. John, like Matthew and Mark,

---

[95] Taylor, 89; Green, *Death*, 85; Fitzmyer, *Luke* (X–XXIV), 1492.

combines Jesus' scourging with the crown of thorns, the robing, the calling him king of the Jews, and the striking of Jesus. But John, unlike Mark and Matthew, does not place the scourging at the conclusion of the trial, but during it. After the scourging Pilate presents Jesus to the crowd, declares him innocent, and subsequently seeks to release him. Despite the similarity of the scourging itself to Mark and Matthew, John is following a pattern of presenting chastisement as an alternative to crucifixion. The question, of course, is whether Luke is derivative of John, or John derivative of Luke. Previously, in the discussion of Luke 23:20–21, John's description has been characterized as unself-consciously original.[96] John appears to have made little rhetorical advantage out of the chastisement; he does not directly link the scourging with the desire to free Jesus.[97] It is difficult to imagine John's having developing this scene as an effort to expand on Luke's "I will chastise him and release him." But it is reasonable that Luke would have seen a logical link between John's scourging during the trial, which has quite a different sense from Mark's scene after the verdict, and his subsequent presentation of Jesus before the Jews with Pilate's desire to release him. The schematization of this event into a threefold pattern is, then, understandable as Luke's development of a theme. And avoiding the actual scourging would fit with Luke's agenda of reducing the negative portrayal of Pilate and the Romans. Luke's omission of the scourging is an intentional redaction of Mark, a redaction that finds its germ in the Johannine presentation and is anticipated in Pilate's threefold declaration that he desires to release Jesus.

In all four Gospels, the conclusion to the trial has Pilate delivering Jesus up (παρέδωκεν) to be crucified. In Mark, Matthew, and John, the result of the handing over—that is crucifixion—is clearly stated. In Luke, it is not clearly stated, but it is implied. Beyond these similarities, however, Luke has two striking differences with respect to Mark. First, as has already been discussed, Mark and Matthew both have Jesus being scourged (φραγελλώσας) in anticipation of the

---

[96] See p. 350 above.
[97] Cf. Schniewind, 69.

crucifixion; Luke does not. Second, Mark and Matthew have the Roman soldiers carry out the sentence (clearly so in Matthew: στρατιῶται τοῦ ἡγεμόνος; just soldiers in Mark). In Luke it is not absolutely clear who is in charge of the crucifixion, but the most natural reading is that it is the Jewish people: Pilate delivers Jesus to their will (τῷ θελήματι αὐτῶν), and in 23:26 "they" lead him away.[98] The natural antecedent to these plural pronouns (including those in 23:18; 23:20; 23:21; and 23:23) is "the chief priests, the rulers and the people" in 23:13. Granted, there are soldiers at the crucifixion; notwithstanding this, the main thrust of Luke's narrative is that the Jewish people direct the crucifixion. Brown argues that Luke did not mean to imply that the Jews took Jesus for crucifixion, but rather the Roman soldiers took him in accordance with the Jewish desire.[99] His argument rests on three points: (1) that historically, Romans did the crucifying, thus the evangelist's "to them" would not be misunderstood; (2) that pronominal antecedents are hardly reliable: that audiences do not follow them consistently and authors make mistakes; and (3) that Luke shows elsewhere in Acts that he understood the Romans to be involved with the crucifixion. The first point is an uncertain basis for argument, since Luke and John may well have been wanting to make a point that ran contrary to historical understanding. A narrative has a world of its own, and it is not always in accordance with history. The second point, concerning antecedents of pronouns, is well taken, but given the general thrust of the anti-Jewish rhetoric in Luke's revision of the Passion narrative, this feature of Pilate's turning Jesus over to their (=Jews) will hardly seems to be an accident. Moreover, Luke's editorial adaptation of Mark in the Passion narrative has not yet been seen to be haphazard. Brown's third point, that Acts includes the Romans as being responsible for Jesus' death, would be

---

[98] Dibelius, "Herodes und Pilatus," 120; Conzelman, 141, n.1; Fitzmyer, *Luke* (X–XXIV), 1496; I. Howard Marshall, *The Gospel of Luke* (Grand Rapids, MI: William B. Eerdmans, 1978), 861.

[99] Brown, *Death*, 857-58.

pertinent if it were correct or complete.¹⁰⁰ But the very Acts passage that Brown quotes (Acts 4:25–28) includes the Jewish people as equally as culpable as Pilate and the Gentiles. And the passage's interpretation of Psalm 2 is very general, not speaking specifically of the crucifixion. Overlooked by Brown, however, is a clearer statement in Acts that the Jews did crucify Jesus: in Peter's speech at Pentecost, he says, speaking to a Jewish crowd "This man ... you crucified and killed by the hands of those outside the law" (Acts 2:23). It appears to be more likely that Luke did mean to suggest that the Jews were given charge of the crucifixion. Schneider concludes, more correctly, that the two features of no scourging and delivering Jesus to "their will" are related; by omitting the scourging, which would have been by Roman soldiers, Luke was emphasizing that the Jews crucified Jesus.¹⁰¹

Of these two significant differences between Luke and Mark, both represent commonalities between Luke and John. John also has no knowledge of a scourging at the sentencing—it has already occurred in some fashion during the hearing (John 19:1). And John also has Pilate handing Jesus over to the Jews for crucifixion (παρέδωκεν αὐτόν αὐτοῖς).¹⁰² Previously, Jesus seems to predict that he would be handed over to the Jews (John 18:36), a narrative foreshadowing of the subsequent event. Later on, John indicates that the soldiers actually crucified Jesus (John 19:23), but the activity of the

---

¹⁰⁰ It is surprising that he makes this point here. In his commentary on John, he notes, "We find the theme that *the Jews* crucified Jesus in Acts ii 36, iii 15, x 39; and it is continued in Justin, *Apology* I.xxxv.6; PG 6:384B. We are told by Tertullian, *Apology* xxi 18; CSEL 69:57, that the Jews extorted from Pilate a sentence giving Jesus 'up to *them* to be crucified'." Brown, *John* (XIII–XXI), 884. And previous to his assertion in *The Death of the Messiah* that Acts shows the Romans involved, he has clearly acknowledged these Acts texts (*Death*, 856). Thus Brown knows that Acts and other early interpreters (using Luke or John?) understood Pilate to have turned Jesus over to the Jews.

¹⁰¹ Schneider, *Passion*, 104.

¹⁰² Bailey, 76, fn. 4. αὐτοῖς is clearly referring to the Jews. Brown, *John* (XIII–XXI), 884; which he later modifies in *The Death of the Messiah*, 856, to suggest that John is guilty of careless narrative structuring.

chief priests in objecting to the title over the cross still suggests their oversight of the crucifixion.[103]

Here again, then, Luke's account appears to be a conflation of two differing accounts, those of Mark and John. The initial narrative Luke took from Mark, with some modifications that accord with Luke's understanding of the importance and pervasiveness of Pilate's judgment of innocence (e.g. the suppression of Pilate's pronouncing the sentence of crucifixion). But the conclusion of the narrative Luke modified in accordance with John's understanding that a scourging was not a part of the crucifixion and that the Jewish people were actively involved in the crucifixion. Luke did not closely follow the *language* of either Mark or John. But he wove together the contents of the two different versions of the Pilate trial.

SUMMARY

In Luke 23:13–25, then, there is clear pattern of Luke's interweaving of Mark and John, a process under the creative direction of Luke's own sense of the narrative flow. Most commentators have noted that at least in verses 18–25, Luke was following the Markan pattern. Although there is often not a lot of direct use of Markan language, the flow of the narrative appears to derive from Mark. Based on the lack of clear Markan language, Taylor argues, "The origin of 18–25 is more speculative. It appears to be derived from a non-Markan source to which verse 25 may have been added when the Third Gospel was composed."[104] But a more reasonable assessment is offered by Green:

> Verses 13–25 present a mixed picture as regards Luke's redactional activity. The three-fold pronouncement of contact with the Johannine tradition, the unparalleled vv. 13-16, the absence of v. 17—

---

[103] Grant argues that precisely this tension between Pilate's turning Jesus over to the Jews here, and the later indication that the soldiers actually crucified him points toward an oral source (299).

[104] Taylor, 89.

these factors are among the more prominent pointing to a non-Markan, pre-Lukan source. At other points, however, there is no need to posit an alternative source, for Luke's text can be explained easily enough with appeal to his editing of the Markan trial narrative and to his own creative hand. We conclude on the basis of this inquiry that Luke did know another account of the Roman trial of Jesus which overlapped with the Markan, and that in relating this phase of Jesus' trial he has conflated his two sources while including a few phrases of his own invention.[105]

Luke's general use of Mark as the foundation, with which he combined elements of John, is seen especially in the following areas. First, the order of events, especially beginning in verse 18 with the demand for the release of Barabbas, the call to crucify Jesus, the question by Pilate what wrong Jesus had done, the second call to crucify, the sentence, and finally the handing over of Jesus: this macro-order is virtually identical in Luke and Mark and must show Luke's reliance on Mark. Second, the language usage, especially the description of Barabbas' crimes (Luke 23:19, 25) and Pilate's question as to what Jesus had done (Luke 23:22): the direct usage is clear and likewise must show Luke's reliance on Mark.

In addition to Luke's use of Mark, Luke's careful construction of the entire Pilate trial is evident. His effort is most apparent in the transitional passage, Luke 23:13–16, where he picks up themes from the first appearance before Pilate and the Herod trial and anticipates themes from the subsequent appearance before Pilate. Luke's careful construction is also evident in the use of the threefold declaration of innocence, which is used to divide the trial into three separate sections, as well as the threefold desire to release Jesus. The two threefold features come together in the final comment by Pilate, so that each emphasizes the other.

But there is also strong evidence for another source, John, which Luke combined with Mark to create a unique account of the trial of

---

[105] Green, *Death*, 86.

Jesus. The major elements that show Luke's use of John are, in descending order of importance, as follows:

1. The order of events relative to the crowd's call for Barabbas' release. Luke varies from Mark in a sudden unexpected call for Barabbas' release, followed by a description of who Barabbas is. This order of the narrative is common to Luke and John.

2. The strong feature of the threefold declaration of innocence by Pilate. This pattern is used in a sophisticated fashion by Luke and suggests his further development of a theme that he read in John. Indeed, Luke appears to have constructed the entire trial narrative around this threefold pattern.

3. Pilate's desire to release Jesus. This feature occurs three times in Luke and only once in John. Luke again seems to have seized upon a feature from John that he could use in his literary construction to his advantage.

4. The surprising feature of the doubling in the crowd's call for Jesus to be crucified. The doubling of the imperative is more naturally a Johannine feature (cf. his double call for Jesus to be taken away); it appears to have been echoed by Luke.

5. The turning over of Jesus to the Jews for crucifixion.

6. The absence of a scourging in Luke, where the idea of scourging is always associated with Jesus' release. John has scourging as an alternative punishment to crucifixion. Luke appears to have utilized this theme, dropping the event of the scourging altogether.

A few other less decisive features support these major items.

7. The direct address form of the cry to release Barabbas. This may be Luke's echo of John, over against Mark's indirect address.

8. Certain lexical features. Luke uses some lexical features that may also be echoes of John: the use of αἶρε and ἀνακράζω would seem to be in this category.

In summary, then, Luke 23:13–25 is a strong witness to Luke's use of both Mark and John in the construction of his unique narrative.

Road To Golgotha. Luke 23:26–32

²⁶ Καὶ ὡς <u>ἀπήγαγον</u> αὐτόν, ἐπιλαβόμενοι <u>Σίμωνά</u> τινα <u>Κυρηναῖον ἐρχόμενον ἀπ' ἀγροῦ</u> ἐπέθηκαν αὐτῷ <u>τὸν σταυρὸν</u> φέρειν ὄπισθεν τοῦ Ἰησοῦ. ²⁷ Ἠκολούθει δὲ αὐτῷ πολὺ πλῆθος τοῦ λαοῦ καὶ γυναικῶν αἳ ἐκόπτοντο καὶ ἐθρήνουν αὐτόν. ²⁸ στραφεὶς δὲ πρὸς αὐτὰς ὁ Ἰησοῦς εἶπεν, Θυγατέρες Ἰερουσαλήμ, μὴ κλαίετε ἐπ' ἐμέ· πλὴν ἐφ' ἑαυτὰς κλαίετε καὶ ἐπὶ τὰ τέκνα ὑμῶν, ²⁹ ὅτι ἰδοὺ ἔρχονται ἡμέραι ἐν αἷς ἐροῦσιν, Μακάριαι αἱ στεῖραι καὶ αἱ κοιλίαι αἳ οὐκ ἐγέννησαν καὶ μαστοὶ οἳ οὐκ ἔθρεψαν. ³⁰ τότε ἄρξονται λέγειν τοῖς ὄρεσιν, Πέσετε ἐφ' ἡμᾶς, καὶ τοῖς βουνοῖς, Καλύψατε ἡμᾶς· ³¹ ὅτι εἰ ἐν τῷ ὑγρῷ ξύλῳ ταῦτα ποιοῦσιν, ἐν τῷ ξηρῷ τί γένηται; ³² Ἤγοντο δὲ καὶ ἕτεροι κακοῦργοι <u>δύο</u> <u>σὺν αὐτῷ</u> ἀναιρεθῆναι.

The opening verse of this pericope about the road to Golgotha, Luke 23:26, is reliant on Mark.[106] The sequence of leading Jesus out, the naming of Simon of Cyrene, and the further identification of Simon as one coming from the country is striking and is clearly derivative of Mark.

The following unit, verses 27–31, is unique to Luke. In this section, the setting appears to be very compatible with Luke: a crowd (πολὺ πλῆθος τοῦ λαοῦ),[107] as well as a group of women, follows Jesus on the way to the cross. Within this setting, Jesus delivers what appears to be an eschatological address to the women. The question is whether Luke created this scene or based it on a source. While there is significant Lukan redaction, the possibility that Luke composed it without reference to any tradition, as Goulder suggests, seems remote.[108] Fitzmyer argues for a source, L. Likewise, Taylor notes that despite the extensive Lukan style, a large number of words are non-Lukan, and the

---

[106] Fitzmyer, *Luke* (X–XXIV), 1494; Taylor, *Passion*, 90. In "Narrative of the Crucifixion," *NTS* 8 (1961–62): 333–34, Taylor calls this verse a Markan insertion to explain its closeness to Mark.

[107] Which is clearly redactional. Jeremias, *Sprache*, 305.

[108] Goulder, 762–63; but cf. Jerome Neyrey, "Jesus' Address to the Women of Jerusalem," *NTS* 29 (1983): 74–86.

scene is likely to have been pre-Lukan in origin.[109] Soards, in a detailed analysis of the passage, makes a convincing argument that Luke combined Markan features (vv. 26, 32), traditional material (vv. 29, 31), the Septuagint (v. 30), and his own compositional style to create this unit. This method of combining elements from disparate sources and weaving them into a coherent whole marks Luke's strategy in the Passion narrative, as we have seen in his combination of Mark, John, and traditional material in previous passages.[110] It appears that Luke here took over a traditional saying with strong similarity to the Gospel of Thomas (Gos. Thom. 79), a reading from Hosea 9, and composed or redacted it with his own emphases.[111] There are no echoes of John in Luke 23:27–31.

Verse 32 is very similar in content to Mark, Matthew, and John. The common terms δύο, σύν, and αὐτῷ point to a possible memory of Mark by Luke. Certainly, he was aware of the basic Markan story being told at this point. But Luke's statement here is different from the other Gospels in that Luke alone describes the movement of the criminals along with Jesus to Golgotha. He more closely follows the other Gospels in a description of the criminals on the cross in verse 33. Verse 32 is, then, an anticipatory passage that undoubtedly signals Luke's own desire to emphasize that Jesus was crucified with the criminals. It is Lukan composition, a foretelling of 22:33.[112] There are no echoes of John in Luke 23:32.

---

[109] Taylor, *Passion*, 90. Cf. Jeremias, *Sprache*, 305.

[110] Marion Soards, "Tradition, Composition, and Theology in Jesus' Speech to the 'Daughters of Jerusalem' (Luke 23,26–32)," *Bib* 68 (1987): 221–44.

[111] Brown, *Death*, 929. Cf. Soards, "Tradition...Daughters." who argues Luke 23:36–42 is Luke's composition. He based verses 26 and 32 on Mark; verses 29 and 31 on an early tradition which also informed Gospel of Thomas; and verse 30 on Hosea, which he probably quotes from memory.

[112] Brown, *Death*, p. 927.

CRUCIFIXION. LUKE 23: 33–38

³³ καὶ ὅτε <u>ἦλθον ἐπὶ τὸν τόπον</u> τὸν καλούμενον <u>Κρανίον</u>, ἐκεῖ ἐσταύρωσαν αὐτὸν καὶ τοὺς κακούργους, ὃν μὲν <u>ἐκ δεξιῶν</u> ὃν δὲ ἐξ ἀριστερῶν. ³⁴ <u>διαμεριζόμενοι δὲ τὰ ἱμάτια αὐτοῦ</u> ἔβαλον <u>κλῆρον</u>. ³⁵ καὶ εἱστήκει ὁ λαὸς θεωρῶν. ἐξεμυκτήριζον δὲ καὶ οἱ ἄρχοντες λέγοντες, Ἄλλους ἔσωσεν, <u>σωςάτω ἑαυτόν, εἰ οὗτός ἐστιν ὁ Χριστὸς τοῦ θεοῦ ὁ ἐκλεκτός</u>. ³⁶ <u>ἐνέπαιξαν</u> δὲ αὐτῷ καὶ οἱ στρατιῶται προσερχόμενοι, <u>ὄξος</u> προσφέροντες αὐτῷ ³⁷ καὶ λέγοντες, Εἰ σὺ εἶ ὁ βασιλεὺς τῶν Ἰουδαίων, σῶσον σεαυτόν. ³⁸ <u>ἦν</u> δὲ <u>καὶ ἐπιγραφὴ ἐπ'</u> αὐτῷ, Ὁ <u>βασιλεὺς τῶν Ἰουδαίων</u> **οὗτος**.

In terms of its basic elements, this passage is clearly derived from Mark. Taylor looks at the large passage 23:33–49 and argues that only 28 percent of Luke's language is found in Mark. But Taylor's figure understates the level of reliance in the pericope under consideration here since it includes verses 39–43, which are unique to Luke, as well as the textually dubious verse 34a. Luke does have significant unique material here, and he has put his own stamp upon all of it, but the main structure of Luke 23:33–38 is Mark's. Some sections of text are highly reliant on Mark's language, as, for instance, 23:34b, which Taylor has termed a Markan insertion.[113]

The initial scene of Jesus' crucifixion between the criminals is found in both Mark and John. The language of being on the right and the left appears to be Mark's, although Luke uses ἀριστερῶν instead of εὐωνύμων. The term for the two criminals, κακοῦργος, is Luke's, but the scene is Mark's. The textual variant of verse 34a (And Jesus said, "Father, forgive them; for they know not what they do") is very unlikely to be original to Luke, despite the Lukan theme of forgiveness, so it can be excluded from consideration.[114]

---

[113] Taylor, "Crucifixion" 333–34.
[114] Metzger, *Textual Commentary*, 180. As has been noted in Fitzmyer, *Luke* (X–XXIV), this variant is strikingly similar to Stephen's comment in Acts 7:60b, which is certainly Lukan (1503). But the manuscript evidence shows the

Luke varies from Mark, however, in important features, especially in the order of certain events.[115]

Mark 15:22–32	Luke 23:33–38
1. Jesus brought to Golgotha (v.22).	1. Jesus brought to the Skull (v.33).
2. Wine and Myrrh are offered (v.23).	
3. "They crucified him" (v.24).	3. "They crucified him" (v.33).
	7. Criminals are on right and left (v.33).
4. Lots are cast to divide his garments (v.34).	4. Lots are cast to divide his garments (v.24)
5. It is the third hour (v.25)	
6. Inscription is placed over him (v.26).	
7. Criminals are on right and left (v.27)	
8. People come by and scoff (vv.29–30)	8. People stand by (v.35).
9. Chief priests mock: "He saved others, let him save himself" (vv.31–32)	9. Rulers scoff: "He saved others, let him save himself" (v.35).
	10. Soldiers mock. Vinegar is offered (vv.36–37).
	6. Inscription is placed over him (v. 38).

The significant differences can be readily seen in the absence of the offer of wine and myrrh, the reference to the criminals *immediately*

---

absence in many older manuscripts, both Alexandrian and Western (P^{75}, B, D*, ℵ^c, W, Θ, 0124, 579, 1241). It is hard to imagine why it would have been deleted from an original text, but one can imagine an attempt to soften the criticism of the Jewish leaders, perhaps in harmonization with Mark/Matthew. Eldon Epp, "Ignorance Motif in Acts and Anti-Judaic Tendencies in Codex Bezae," *HTR* 55 (1962): 51–62, notes that the Western text often modifies the text as part of an anti-Jewish polemic. So this might explain the deletion of the text in certain manuscripts. This variant could be an example of that, but is it a Western variant that has crept into P^{75} and B? For an opposing opinion on the originality of the text, see Goulder, 765.

[115] For another comparison, with the conclusion that Luke was relying on a separate source, see J. Jeremias, "Perikopen-Umstellungen bei Lukas?" *NTS* 4 (1957–58): 115–19.

after the statement that he was crucified, and the transference of the comment about the inscription to the end of the unit. The first part of the passage in Luke (23:33) follows the same order as John: movement to Golgotha, statement that they crucified him, and reference to the two criminals on either side. But John then mentions the inscription, followed by the casting of lots and the reference to the people (Jesus' mother and two Marys) standing by. It is possible that Luke's order shows some influence from John, but that is not clear. The completely different order of the inscription suggests Luke's own attempt to produce a more dramatic rendition of the event.

It is also noteworthy that Luke deleted the reference to wine and myrrh, choosing only to relate the offer of vinegar, which is also found in Mark later, after Jesus' cry of dereliction on the cross (Mark 15:36). The absence of the wine and myrrh in Luke removes a doublet found in Mark and Matthew that might appear to be unhistorical: first wine, later vinegar.[116] But it is difficult to imagine that John and Luke would have independently deleted such a feature. Did Luke, then, choose only the one drink, following John, who also has only the one?[117] Finally, Luke also expanded the mocking on the cross to form a doublet: first the Jewish leaders mock Jesus, and then the soldiers also mock him in similar language. By adding the second taunt, which exhorts Jesus to save himself, Luke created a series of three, which is completed by a similar statement from the thief on the cross (Luke 23:39). Following the triple desire to release Jesus, which is built around the triple judgment of innocence, this threefold series of taunts suggests Luke's creative hand.[118]

There is, of course, a textual variant at Luke 23:38, that further describes the inscription on the cross, which would be a significant similarity between Luke and John. In certain manuscripts, with a num-

---

[116] Schniewind, 77.

[117] Bailey also sees this as unlikely to be accidental, but understands John to have used Luke. Bailey, 82.

[118] Büchele, 68; see previous footnote on p. 355 ; Fitzmyer, *Luke* (X–XXIV), 1501; Brown, *Death*, 930–31.

ber of variations, Luke reads γεγραμμένη ἐπ᾽ αὐτῷ γράμμασιν ἑλληνικοῖς καὶ ῥωμαικῖς καὶ ἑβραικοῖς. This agrees substantially with John 19:20, although it is not exactly the same.[119] The longer form, though, is almost certainly secondary and therefore represents a later harmonization of the text.[120]

While it is clear that Luke was following Mark in this pericope, there are some differences that probably suggest some influence from John. It is probable that John influenced Luke in his deletion of the wine and myrrh offered to Jesus, as well as in his the placement of the statement about the criminals early in the pericope. Other differences between Luke and Mark probably arose from Luke's own editorial agenda.

Two Criminals. Luke 23: 39–43

[39] Εἷς δὲ τῶν κρεμασθέντων κακούργων ἐβλασφήμει αὐτὸν λέγων, Οὐχὶ σὺ εἶ ὁ Χριστός; σῶσον σεαυτὸν καὶ ἡμᾶς. [40] ἀποκριθεὶς δὲ ὁ ἕτερος ἐπιτιμῶν αὐτῷ ἔφη, Οὐδὲ φοβῇ σὺ τὸν θεόν, ὅτι ἐν τῷ αὐτῷ κρίματι εἶ; [41] καὶ ἡμεῖς μὲν δικαίως, ἄξια γὰρ ὧν ἐπράξαμεν ἀπολαμβάνομεν· οὗτος δὲ οὐδὲν ἄτοπον ἔπραξεν. [42] καὶ ἔλεγεν, Ἰησοῦ, μνήσθητί μου ὅταν ἔλθῃς ἐν τῇ βασιλείᾳ σου. [43] καὶ εἶπεν αὐτῷ, Ἀμήν σοι λέγω, σήμερον μετ᾽ ἐμοῦ ἔσῃ ἐν τῷ παραδείσῳ.

The story of the exchange between Jesus and the two criminals on the cross is unique to Luke. It is parallel to a brief mention in Mark that the other crucified individuals reviled him (Mark 15:32b). Predictably, Goulder argues that this is Lukan redaction of Matthew (rather than Mark!), but he has little substance to offer to the discussion.[121]

---

[119] John reads: γεραμμένον Ἑβραιστι, Ῥωμαιστι, Ἑλληνιστι.

[120] Metzger, *Textual Commentary*, 180; cf. Schniewind, 83. The primary witnesses to the long reading are ℵ*,c, A, C³, D, W, Θ, 0250, f¹,¹³, Majority text, lat, sy^p,h and some bo. The evidence for the long form is for primarily in Western and Byzantine texts. Moreover, there is little reason for omitting the inscription, but the harmonizing tendency would explain its addition.

[121] Goulder, 766–69.

Some tend to see this as a special Lukan tradition (L) with little redaction.[122] Taylor obviously sees it as part of his special Passion source, but he agrees with Creed in seeing a core tradition that has been edited by Luke.[123] Jeremias finds a significant amount of non-Lukan language in this unit of text; its quantity would tend to argue for the use of a pre-Lukan tradition here.[124] It appears that Luke was drawing on a unique tradition, one that shares a minor point with Mark in the comment that the criminals reviled Jesus, so that Luke included it here in the crucifixion story.

There is no connection in this pericope with the Gospel of John. Luke relied on his own separate traditions for this pericope, weaving them together according to Mark's order of the narrative.

DEATH OF JESUS. LUKE 23: 44–49

⁴⁴ Καὶ ἦν ἤδη ὡσεὶ ὥρα ἕκτη καὶ σκότος ἐγένετο ἐφ᾽ ὅλην τὴν γῆν ἕως ὥρας ἐνάτης ⁴⁵ τοῦ ἡλίου ἐκλιπόντος, ἐσχίσθη δὲ τὸ καταπέτασμα τοῦ ναοῦ μέσον. ⁴⁶ καὶ φωνήσας φωνῇ μεγάλῃ ὁ Ἰησοῦς εἶπεν, Πάτερ, εἰς χεῖράς σου παρατίθεμαι τὸ πνεῦμά μου· τοῦτο δὲ εἰπὼν ἐξέπνευσεν. ⁴⁷ Ἰδὼν δὲ ὁ ἑκατοντάρχης τὸ γενόμενον ἐδόξαζεν τὸν θεὸν λέγων, Ὄντως ὁ ἄνθρωπος οὗτος δίκαιος ἦν. ⁴⁸ καὶ πάντες οἱ συμπαραγενόμενοι ὄχλοι ἐπὶ τὴν θεωρίαν ταύτην, θεωρήσαντες τὰ γενόμενα, τύπτοντες τὰ στήθη ὑπέστρεφον. ⁴⁹ εἱστήκεισαν δὲ πάντες οἱ γνωστοὶ αὐτῷ ἀπὸ μακρόθεν, καὶ γυναῖκες αἱ συνακολουθοῦσαι αὐτῷ ἀπὸ τῆς Γαλιλαίας, ὁρῶσαι ταῦτα.

The account of Jesus' death in Luke is drawn primarily from Mark, but with significant modifications.[125] The initial marker of time and the reference to the darkness over the whole land is from Mark

---

[122] Fitzmyer, *Luke* (X–XXIV), 1507.
[123] Taylor, *Passion*, 95; Creed, 285; Marshall, *Luke*, 871.
[124] Jeremias, *Sprache*, 306–7.
[125] Taylor, *Passion* (98), finds almost no indications of pre-Lukan language. He sees this pericope as having arisen from Luke's embellishment of sources, Mark, and a special source.

almost verbatim.[126] Schniewind discusses Spitta's theory that Luke's time reference here is actually to the hour of the crucifixion.[127] In that case, Luke's chronology would be closer to John. But such a case is unlikely. John has few specific time markers in his narrative, and the simple reading of Luke yields an agreement with Mark's version. Luke next records the temple curtain being torn—before Jesus' death. The language of Mark in this reference is retained, but the placement of the reference within the pericope is significantly changed, perhaps to emphasize by their close proximity two signs of God's judgment: the darkness and the rending of the temple veil.[128]

Unlike Mark (15:34), Luke has no reference to Jesus' cry of dereliction from the cross. Instead at this point, he has Jesus utter his final statement, a triumphant "Father, into your hands I commit my spirit." Luke has Jesus die willingly, with no sense of despair. The final phrase of the death of Jesus, ἐξέπνευσεν, returns to Mark's version.

Immediately following the death of Jesus, Luke has Mark's account of the centurion speaking, but with a modified statement that supports Pilate's verdict: Jesus was innocent (righteous).[129] This is

---

[126] Once again, Taylor, "Crucifixion," has suggested that 23:44 was a Markan insertion into a pre-Lukan source, thus pointing to the extensive nature of the similarity with Mark.

[127] Schniewind, 81. There is no previous reference in Luke to the third hour, as in Mark 15:25. So this first-time reference could refer to the entire pericope from Luke 23:33 to 23:49.

[128] Brown, *Death*, 1038.

[129] Robert Karris, "Luke 23:47 and the Lukan View of Jesus' Death," in *Reimaging the Death of the Lukan Jesus*, ed. Dennis D. Sylva (Frankfurt am Main: Anton Hain, 1990), 68, argues against considering this declaration of the centurion as (merely) another instance of the Romans' verdict of innocence. It should be "righteous," with its broad theological implications. But even given the broader theological meaning of "righteous," this statement by the centurion resonates with Pilate's previous "secular" declarations of Jesus' innocence and indicates Luke's recurring interests in this theme. Cf. Joel Green, "The Death of Jesus, God's Servant" in *Reimaging the Death of the Lukan Jesus*, 19–21.

Luke Chapter 23   371

certainly a Lukan editorial modification.[130]

Luke also adds a note that the people who observed the crucifixion returned home beating their breasts. This has been interpreted as an indication that Luke viewed the people positively (as opposed to the leaders; note the distinction in Luke 23:35).[131] It is true that in the crucifixion scene Luke moves to reframe the response of the people as distinct from the leaders: the people do not mock Jesus on the cross; the leaders do. Jesus addresses a prophetic oracle of warning to the people who follow him to the cross in an attitude of mourning; and here they leave Golgotha in traditional mourning postures. While Luke constructed the people as equally at fault in the prosecution of Jesus, it appears that here he wanted to soften his previous condemnation of the Jewish people, or at least to leave open the possibility that some would respond (as they do in Acts).[132] Perhaps the broad Lukan themes of forgiveness and of openness to the Jewish people for the future reception of the Gospel were being woven into the narrative by Luke.[133]. Given the similar feature in Gospel of Peter, which interprets the people as expressing pity on themselves, perhaps Luke was reflecting and expanding a tradition.[134] At any rate, this feature is a Lukan addition to Mark's account that heightens the tragedy of Jesus' death.

As in Mark and Matthew, Luke's scene concludes with a reference to the women who observed the crucifixion. Much of the language in Luke 23:49 is Markan.[135] Unlike the other Synoptics,

---

[130] Green, *Death*, 99.

[131] So cf. Marshall, *Luke* (877), who suggests the breast beating as a sign of repentance. Fitzmyer, *Luke* (X–XXIV), who argues that it could indicate the people's acknowledgement of their guilt (1520).

[132] Charles Giblin, *The Destruction of Jerusalem According to Luke's Gospel* (Rome: Biblical Institute Press, 1985), 96–7.

[133] Brown, *Death*, 989.

[134] Gos. Pet. 7:25. Cf. Green, *Death*, 100.

[135] Taylor, "Crucifixion" (333–34), "possibly" considers this verse also to be a Markan insertion into his pre-Lukan source. But he brackets the verse, indicating that he is aware of the combination of Markan and non-Markan elements.

though, Luke makes an additional reference to all Jesus' acquaintances (πάντες οἱ γνωστοί), who also were present and observed the crucifixion. In Mark, of course, the disciples have all fled; there, it is reasonable that only the women are present. Luke, in contrast, presents a different understanding of the observers of Jesus' death.

Of the differences from Mark noted above, two are significant for the relationship with John. The first is the absence of Jesus' cry of dereliction and the presence of his final, triumphant statement. John reports a similar feature at Jesus' death: Jesus says τετέλεσται, and bowing his head, he gives up his spirit. The contrast between this view of Jesus' death and the Mark/Matthew view is significant. Jesus is in control of his death and faces it with resoluteness and confidence.[136] It appears that Luke here wove together the Markan and Johannine stories. Knowing that Jesus cried out on the cross from Mark, he deletedk's ἐβόησεν and the Psalm 22 reference from Mark 15:34, but in Luke 23:46 retained the feature of Jesus' cry: Mark's ἀφεὶς φωνὴν μεγάλην (Mark 15:37) was changed to φωνήσας φωνῇ μεγάλῃ (Luke 23:46), which is typical of Lukan style.[137] But the *content* of the cry was drawn from John: Jesus gives up his spirit in a conscious act. Here the handing over of his spirit (παρατίθεμαι τὸ πνεῦμα) echoes John's παρέδωκεν τὸ πνεῦμα (John 19:30). Matthew also reports that Jesus gave up his spirit (ἀφῆκεν τὸ πνεῦμα), which Goulder thinks shows Luke's reliance on Matthew at this point.[138] But the yielding of the spirit in Matthew lacks the sense of intentionality found in John and Luke. Matthew also reports Jesus' cry of dereliction on the cross, which makes his "giving up the spirit" simply another term for dying, not an intentional act. The similarity in emphasis of Luke and John could point to a common use of tradition,[139] but in light of the pattern

---

[136] Fitzmyer, *Luke* (X–XXIV), 1519.

[137] Luke likes the use of cognate words. See Jeremias, *Sprache*, 307; Green, *Death*, 97.

[138] Goulder, 770.

[139] Green, *Death*, 97.

already found between Luke and John, this similarity more likely reflects Luke's echoing of John's understanding of the death of Jesus. The second difference in which Luke has similarity to John is the reference to the bystanders at the crucifixion. The reference to Jesus' acquaintances (male plural) indicates that Luke understood some of the disciples (perhaps including others besides the Twelve) to be present as well.[140] Since this reference is clearly at odds with Mark, what could have been its source? John's reference to the beloved disciple at the cross (John 19:26–27) might very well have provided the idea for this reference in Luke.[141]

Luke's account of the death of Jesus, then, follows Mark, but with very significant modifications that are in agreement with John, There is no indication of use of John's language. But the portrayal of the death of Jesus in John appears to have influenced Luke's construction of the event.

BURIAL OF JESUS. LUKE 23: 50–56

⁵⁰ Καὶ ἰδοὺ ἀνὴρ ὀνόματι Ἰωσὴφ βουλευτὴς ὑπάρχων καὶ ἀνὴρ ἀγαθὸς καὶ δίκαιος ⁵¹ οὗτος οὐκ ἦν συγκατατεθειμένος τῇ βουλῇ καὶ τῇ πράξει αὐτῶν-- ἀπὸ Ἀριμαθαίας πόλεως τῶν Ἰουδαίων, ὃς προσεδέχετο τὴν βασιλείαν τοῦ θεοῦ, ⁵² **οὗτος προς** ελθὼν τῷ Πιλάτῳ ᾐτήσατο τὸ σῶμα τοῦ Ἰησοῦ, ⁵³ καὶ καθελὼν **ἐνετύλιξεν αὐτὸ** σινδόνι, καὶ ἔθηκεν αὐτὸ ἐν μνήματι λαξευτῷ οὗ οὐκ ἦν **οὐδεὶς οὔπω** κείμενος. ⁵⁴ καὶ ἡμέρα ἦν **παρασκευῆς**, καὶ σάββατον ἐπέφωσκεν. ⁵⁵ Κατακολουθήσασαι δὲ αἱ γυναῖκες, αἵτινες ἦσαν συνεληλυθυῖαι ἐκ τῆς Γαλιλαίας αὐτῷ, ἐθεάσαντο τὸ μνημεῖον καὶ ὡς ἐτέθη τὸ σῶμα αὐτοῦ, ⁵⁶ ὑποστρέψασαι δὲ ἡτοίμασαν ἀρώματα καὶ μύρα. Καὶ τὸ μὲν σάββατον ἡσύχασαν κατὰ τὴν ἐντολήν.

The burial of Jesus in Luke, as with the previous pericopes, follows Mark in its general construction. The elements of the introduction of Joseph of Arimathea followed by his asking Pilate for the body of

---

[140] Brown, *Death*, 1172–73.
[141] Schniewind, 80.

Jesus, the removal of the body from the cross, and the preparation of the body for burial and placement in the tomb all agree in sequence with both Mark and John. But a number of grammatical features make it clear that Luke was following Mark:

1. The description of Joseph in Luke 23:51 as seeking the kingdom of God is the same.

2. The phrase used in Joseph's request to Pilate (ᾐτήσατο τὸ σῶμα τοῦ Ἰησοῦ) is identical in Mark and Luke.[142]

3. The reference to Joseph's taking down the body (καθελὼν) is the same.[143]

4. The language used for the preparation, particularly the linen shroud and the placing (ἔθηκεν) of the body in the tomb, is very similar.

But while following Mark, Luke has some differences that must be noted.

1. Unlike Mark, Luke expands on the description of Joseph, especially noting that Joseph, although a member of the council, had not consented to the "purpose and the deed" (Luke 23:51).

2. While expanding the description, Luke omits a passage from Mark that has Pilate making sure that Jesus was dead before turning over the body to Joseph (Mark 15:44–45).

3. At the burial of Jesus, Luke has a number of minor variants with respect to Mark: the tomb is described as having never before been used, there is no reference to a stone's being used to close the tomb, and there is no reference to its being the Preparation day for the sabbath.

The first two major variations from the Markan account are clearly the result of Luke's persistent attempt both to place the responsibility for the crucifixion on the Jewish leaders and people and to exonerate Pilate. The deletion of Pilate's inquiry into the death of Jesus

---

[142] But some of this verse is closer to Matthew (cf. Matt 27:58) than to Mark. Cf. Goulder, 771.

[143] As in the request for the body, there is a strong connection with Matthew here also in the phrase ἐνετύλιξεν αὐτό σινδόνι (Matt 27:59).

is entirely understandable as an attempt to reduce Pilate's personal responsibility in the death of Jesus. Similarly, since Luke has painted the Jewish council as culpable, he must especially explain Joseph's desire to remove the body with a reference to his character.[144] Both of the these modifications have obvious redactional interest. There is little contact with John on these variations.[145]

The three minor variations from Mark, however, do not give evidence for a clear redactional purpose. Moreover, these three points of departure from Mark also show connections with the Gospel of John. The points need to be considered independently.

1. It is striking that both Luke and John refer to Jesus' being placed in a tomb that has never been used. The language used in each Gospel is different; Luke has ἦν οὐδεὶς οὔπω κείμενος, while John reads ἐν ᾧ οὐδέπω οὐδεὶς ἦν τεθειμένος. There is no clear evidence of literary dependence. At the same time, Matthew reports a related idea, that the tomb in which Jesus was laid was new (καινός).[146] But the ideas are not the same, and Luke and John bear a striking similarity to one another. It appears that Luke at least was aware of this description of the tomb from John.[147]

2. Luke follows the description of the burial with the comment that it was the Preparation day, and the Sabbath was beginning. The time marker supplies a reason for the women to immediately prepare spices before the sabbath, for later use on Jesus. Mark also calls the day the Preparation day, but he does so at the beginning of the pericope, with no additional comment. John, like Luke, also follows

---

[144] Green, *Death*, 101; Brown, *Death*, 1227-28.

[145] Schniewind (82-83) makes the observation that in the reference to Joseph is an intriguing, although obscure, similarity with John — that is, that both Gospels portray a member of the Jewish council as a friend of Jesus: Joseph in Luke, Nicodemus in John (cf. John 3:1-15; 7:50-52). Moreover, in this passage on the burial of Jesus, John mentions both Joseph and Nicodemus. Is it possible that Luke conflated the two, imbuing the character of Joseph with some of the attributes of Nicodemus from John?

[146] And so Goulder argues for Luke's use of Matthew (771).

[147] Schniewind, 80.

the burial with a comment about it being the Preparation day, and therefore the body is laid in a new tomb because of time constraints. Luke and John, then, have in common both the reference to it being the Preparation day immediately *after* the burial, together with a reference that it was the end of the day, so as to cut off other possibilities (preparing spices, burial elsewhere).[148] The two accounts are very similar and should be attributed to literary knowledge one of the other. Given the pattern of similarities seen already in this study, the likely direction of that knowledge is Luke's reliance on John.

3. A third feature of commonality between Luke and John in the burial scene is the absence of the stone used to close the tomb.[149] This commonality is not a substantive agreement: both Luke and John later report that the stone was rolled away from the tomb (Luke 24:2, John 20:1). The absence of the first reference to the stone over the opening could simply be an attempt to remove unnecessary duplication in the narrative.

The burial of Jesus in Luke essentially follows Mark, but in the description of the tomb and the time reference there are signs of Luke's knowledge of John.

CONCLUSIONS

My analysis of Luke chapter 23, indicates that Luke used Mark as his major source for the Pilate trial, crucifixion, and burial scenes. But in addition to Mark, Luke used other sources and/or traditions. In particular, there are a number of instances where Luke's treatment of Mark has been significantly altered under the influence of another narrative. Most frequently, this narrative can be understood to be some form of the Gospel of John. My results can be summarized as follows:

    23:1–5.   Lukan redaction of Mark, heavily influenced by John, particularly in verses 2, 4–5.

    23:6–12. Lukan composition based on Mark and an indepen-

---

[148] Brown, *Death*, 1256.
[149] Schniewind, 82.

dent source, with echoes of John.
23:13–25. Lukan composition (verses 13–16) and redaction of Mark (verses 18–25), heavily influenced by John.
23:26–32. Lukan redaction of Mark.
23:33–38. Close reliance on Mark, with some influence by John.
23:39–43. Lukan composition or redaction based on an independent tradition.
23:44–49. Lukan redaction of Mark, heavily influenced by John.
23:50–56. Lukan redaction of Mark, somewhat influenced by John.

Chapter 8

LUKE CHAPTER 24

Luke chapter 24 presents a situation completely different from the previous chapters. Except for the very first pericope, in which the women go the tomb on Sunday morning, Mark does not have material similar to Luke's final chapter. There are, therefore, few instances in which Luke's reliance on Mark as a source can even be considered. Matthew does have a post-Resurrection appearance, but it is not similar to Luke's (e.g., the women's meeting Jesus in Matt 28:9–10 has no relationship to any appearance in Luke, and the commission in Matt 28:16–20 has a completely different setting and emphasis than Luke's), and even if there were a relationship between Matthew 28:16–20 and Luke 24, it would only account for a small portion of Luke's material.

In addition, and peculiar to Luke, the post-Resurrection appearances and the Ascension of Jesus function as a transition between the Gospel of Luke and Acts. No other Gospel is part of a two-volume work, and that very feature creates dynamics at the end of the first volume that have implications for this study. It is important, therefore, to be open to the possibility that Luke chapter 24 rehearses themes developed earlier in the Gospel or, more importantly, anticipates themes that will be developed later in Acts.

Furthermore, the issue of textual problems presents itself; there are a great number of textual variants in Luke 24, and many of them have a striking similarity to John. The variants have already been discussed in chapter 4, but as a complicating factor in the analysis of the current chapter, they must be acknowledged again. I concluded in chapter 4 that the longer non-Western text should be considered original in most instances. In this chapter, I will base my discussion on the text established in chapter 4, but I will also explore the strengths and weaknesses of each claim as it relates to Luke's use of Johannine material.

The unique situation in Luke 24 demands some adjustments in the procedure of this examination. Aside from Luke verses 1–7, there are no Markan parallels, since Mark 16:8 cuts off the narrative of the Resurrection appearance. (Were there any, they would be in Galilee, unlike Luke's). In the first pericope, then, Luke's use of Mark and Matthew will be considered, as above. After the first pericope, however, the active question will be primarily whether Luke has actively composed material or is echoing a tradition or a source, and then whether the material deemed traditional is based on John. Over a number of distinct narrative units, one would expect Luke's composition and redaction to develop some consistent perspectives. The use of a non-Lukan tradition, as opposed to Lukan composition, might then be found in unusual unique features that do not fit exactly the Lukan pattern.

For those pericopes after Luke 24:1–12, examples of Lukan composition or redaction will be signified in the Greek text by underlining (as opposed to underlining's previous denotation of Markan language); Johannine similarities will still be signified by bold italics, and Matthean similarities will be highlighted. And, as always, careful attention will be given to those places where Luke's narrative has special links with the Fourth Gospel.

The Empty Tomb. Luke 23:56b–24:12

⁵⁶ᵇ Καὶ τὸ μὲν σάββατον ἡσύχασαν κατὰ τὴν ἐντολήν, ¹ τῇ δὲ μιᾷ τῶν σαββάτων ὄρθρου βαθέως ἐπὶ τὸ μνῆμα ἦλθον φέρουσαι ἃ ἡτοίμασαν ἀρώματα. ² εὗρον δὲ τὸν λίθον ἀποκεκυλισμένον ἀπὸ τοῦ μνημείου, ³ εἰσελθοῦσαι δὲ οὐχ εὗρον τὸ σῶμα τοῦ κυρίου Ἰησοῦ. ⁴ καὶ ἐγένετο ἐν τῷ ἀπορεῖσθαι αὐτὰς περὶ τούτου καὶ ἰδοὺ ἄνδρες *δύο* ἐπέστησαν αὐταῖς ἐν ἐσθῆτι **ἀστραπ**τούσῃ. ⁵ ἐμ**φόβων** δὲ γενομένων αὐτῶν καὶ κλινουσῶν τὰ πρόσωπα εἰς τὴν γῆν εἶπαν πρὸς αὐτάς· Τί ζητεῖτε τὸν ζῶντα μετὰ τῶν νεκρῶν; ⁶ [οὐκ ἔστιν ὧδε, ἀλλὰ ἠγέρθη]. μνήσθητε ὡς ἐλάλησεν ὑμῖν ἔτι ὢν ἐν τῇ Γαλιλαίᾳ, ⁷ λέγων τὸν υἱὸν τοῦ ἀνθρώπου ὅτι δεῖ παραδοθῆναι εἰς χεῖρας ἀνθρώπων ἁμαρτωλῶν καὶ σταυρωθῆναι καὶ τῇ τρίτῃ ἡμέρᾳ *ἀναστῆναι*. ⁸ καὶ ἐμνήσθησαν τῶν ῥημάτων αὐτοῦ. ⁹ καὶ ὑποστρέψασαι ἀπὸ τοῦ μνημείου **ἀπήγγειλαν** ταῦτα πάντα τοῖς ἕνδεκα καὶ πᾶσιν τοῖς λοιποῖς. ¹⁰ ἦσαν δὲ ἡ Μαγδαληνὴ Μαρία καὶ Ἰωάννα καὶ Μαρία ἡ Ἰακώβου· καὶ αἱ λοιπαὶ σὺν αὐταῖς ἔλεγον πρὸς τοὺς ἀποστόλους ταῦτα. ¹¹ καὶ ἐφάνησαν ἐνώπιον αὐτῶν ὡσεὶ λῆρος τὰ ῥήματα ταῦτα, καὶ ἠπίστουν αὐταῖς. ¹² Ὁ δὲ Πέτρος ἀναστὰς *ἔδραμεν* ἐπὶ *τὸ μνημεῖον, καὶ παρακύψας βλέπει τὰ ὀθόνια* μόνα· καὶ *ἀπῆλθεν πρὸς* ἑαυτὸν θαυμάζων τὸ γεγονός.

In terms of the basic structure of the story of the women's witness to the empty tomb, it is clear that Luke and Mark share very strong similarities. In both of them, the basic narrative outline is presented in the same order:

a. The women go to the tomb early on the first day of the week.
b. They go with spices to anoint Jesus.
c. Upon arrival at the tomb, they find the stone rolled away.
d. They enter the tomb.
e. In the tomb they are met by "angelic" visitor(s), called a man or men, in bright clothing.
f. The angelic visitor(s) announce(s) that Jesus is raised / alive.
g. The women depart from the tomb.

Based on simply the structural similarities of the narrative, it is very likely that Luke was relying on Mark for his telling of the story.[1] Despite the similar structure, however, there is very little verbatim similarity between Luke and Mark. It is difficult to assess the degree of similarity in this text unit, in part because of the number of textual variants. Based on our previous analysis of the variants, the text οὐκ ἔστιν ὧδε ἀλλὰ ἠγέρθη (Luke 24:6a) will not be considered part of the original text of Luke, but τοῦ κυρίου Ἰησοῦ (24:3b) and ἀπὸ τοῦ μνημείου (24:9a) will be considered original, as well as Luke 24:12, the story of Peter's return to the tomb.[2] Using the text established in chapter 4, the number of verbatim contacts is only thirty words, or 16.7 per cent. As a result of this low statistical count, Taylor has argued that Luke was relying on a separate source for his material.[3]

In addition to the low count of verbatim contacts, there are a number of significant differences between Luke's narrative and Mark's:

1. In Luke, the women do not discuss the problem of rolling the stone back as in Mark (Mark 16:3).

2. The women in Luke notice the absence of the body of Jesus without any prompting (Luke 24:3 vs. Mark 16:6).

3. There are two "men/angels" in Luke, not one as in Mark (Luke 24:4 v. Mark 16:5). The description of the clothing of the men differs somewhat, but there is a striking similarity in that the clothing is mentioned in both.

4. The women are given totally different messages: although each message is said to be based on Jesus' own words, Luke's women are given a proof of the Resurrection (Luke 24:6–8), whereas Mark's women are instructed to tell the disciples to go to Galilee (Mark 16:7).

---

[1] Richard J. Dillon, *From Eye-Witnesses to Ministers of the Word* (Rome: Biblical Institute Press, 1978), 4 f, provides a helpful overview of scholarly opinion about the matter.

[2] See chapter 4 above.

[3] Vincent Taylor, *The Passion Narrative of St. Luke* (Cambridge: University Press, 1972), 104. Taylor counts slightly differently; excluding all textual variants (which we do not), he arrives at verbatim contacts of 19.7 percent.

In both cases the angels/men announce Jesus' Resurrection, but in very different words (Luke 24:5 vs. Mark 16:6).[4]

5. In Luke, the women announce what they have seen to the rest of the disciples (Luke 24:9), while in Mark they run away and tell no one (Mark 16:8).

6. Luke tells of Peter's visit to the tomb (Luke 24:12), while Mark has no other mention of the tomb.

In addition to these major differences, there are other, less significant differences that do not present any significant difficulties to seeing Luke's use of Mark. But the major differences cited above raise the possibility of Luke's having relied on an additional source or sources in the construction of the empty tomb story. Although Mark appears to have provided the framework of the story, Luke clearly departed from that account, especially at the end: the women's return to the disciples with the announcement and the subsequent visit by Peter bear no relationship to Mark's tensive ending. While noting the possibility of a hypothetical proto-Luke narrative upon which Luke could have relied in addition to Mark,[5] one must note the points of definite similarity that Luke shares with both Matthew and John.

Luke shares with Matthew the following points of similarity:

1. Like Mark, and unlike Luke, Matthew only tells of one angel (clearly an angel) who rolls the stone away. But the description of the angel in Matthew 28:3 as having the appearance of ἀστραπή is suggestive of the men's (angels') clothing in Luke, i.e. it is dazzling apparel, ἀστραπτούσῃ. Goulder has suggested that Luke has taken one angel (at the entrance) from Matthew and one angel in the tomb from Mark and combined them, conflating the descriptions.[6] Although possible, that would be an odd conflation since both Matthew and Mark speak of white clothing; it is the angel's countenance in Matthew that is lightening-like.

---

[4] When the short form of the text is used.
[5] Taylor, *Passion*, 113.
[6] M. D. Goulder, *Luke: A New Paradigm* (Sheffield: JSOT Press, 1989), 774.

2. In Luke, the women's reaction to the men at the tomb is fear, not amazement as in Mark. A reaction of fear at the presence of the angel is also found in Matthew, although there it is the guards, not the women, who are afraid. The angel in Matthew then also tells the women *not* to fear, which according to Goulder would explain the account of the women's fearful reaction in Luke.[7] Mark reports only that the women were amazed.

3. In both Luke and Matthew, the angelic announcement of the Resurrection refers back to Jesus' words. In Matthew, this comes as a brief explanation of the Resurrection: "He is not here, he is risen, just as he said (καθὼς εἶπεν)." In Luke, the women are called on to remember Jesus' predictions (ὡς ἐλάλησεν ὑμῖν) while still in Galilee, that he would be delivered to sinful men, be crucified, and on the third day be raised. While Mark also refers to Jesus' words, those words concern not the fact of the Resurrection, but Jesus' assurance that he would meet the disciples in Galilee after the Resurrection.

4. In both Luke and Matthew, the women return (ἀπελθοῦσαι in Matt, ὑποστρέψασαι in Luke) from the tomb to tell the disciples. In both cases, moreover, the announcement of the discovery to the disciples is said to be effected with the verb ἀπαγγέλω (although in Matthew this is only anticipated; it is never actually narrated). This is the most striking agreement between Luke and Matthew—an agreement that is suggestive, but not sufficient as the basis of a strong theory of Luke's reliance.[8] As will be discussed below, this occurrence is also related in John 20:2 (ἔρχεται πρός).

5. The whole disputed passage of verse 6a exhibits almost verbatim agreement with Matthew. In particular we note that the order of the clauses in the passage, in which ἠγέρθη follows οὐκ ἔστιν ὧδε, is common to Luke and Matthew, contra Mark. This textual variant is undoubtedly a harmonizing corruption based on Matthew.

At the same time, and more significantly, there are striking features that link Luke with John:

---

[7] Goulder, *Luke*, 775.
[8] Goulder, *Luke*, 775–76.

1. In Luke, the women go to the tomb very early and immediately see the tomb already opened, without any reference to the need for the stone to be rolled back. This immediate statement about the stone's removal is very similar to John. In contrast, Mark has the women discussing the problem, and Matthew recounts the earthquake and the angel's rolling back of the stone.

2. In Luke, the women report the empty tomb to the disciples. In John, also, Mary immediately runs back to the disciples and tells them of the empty tomb. In one respect this feature is present in Matthew also, that is, that the women return for the purpose of telling the disciples, but Matthew never narrates their actual announcement to the disciples. The scene where the women actually relate what they have seen is present only in Luke and John.

3. In both Luke and John, there are two angels who ask a question ("Why do you seek the living with the dead?" in Luke 24:5; "Why are you weeping?" in John 20:13). But the exchange in John between Mary and the angels takes place after the disciples inspect the empty tomb, and is very different from the Synoptic account.

4. In Luke, the disciples' response to the women's report is disbelief (ἠπίστουν) in their account. Peter's dash to the tomb (v. 12) is then apparently a doubtful response to their report of the empty tomb. In John, when the "other disciple" steps into the tomb, he is said to believe (John 20:8). But believe what? The passage is ambiguous because immediately after this statement it says they did not yet know the scripture that Jesus would rise from the dead. Presumably, the other disciple is showing exemplary faith without any basis. The personae are different, and the object of the belief (the women's report versus the [unanticipated] Resurrection) is different. The sole similarity is the feature of believing or disbelieving.

5. In Luke, Peter responds to the women's report by rushing (ἔδραμεν) to the tomb, stooping (παρακύψας) and entering, and seeing (βλέπει) the burial clothes (τὰ ὀθόνια). This account is very similar to John's, in which two disciples, Peter and the one whom Jesus loved,

run (ἔτρεχον/προέδραμεν) to the tomb and the other disciple stoops (παρακύψας) and sees (βλέπει) the burial clothes (τὰ ὀθόνια). Despite these striking similarities in the basic story and certain key words, John's account is much longer and more nuanced. In John, two disciples run. One arrives first; the other is the first to enter. The burial clothes are described in some detail as being divided in two piles on the floor. And, as noted above, one of the disciples believes because of the empty tomb.

What, then, do we have in Luke 24:1–12? The pericope is marked by a basic structural similarity to Mark, but with fewer verbatim connections than are found in many instances where Luke relied on Mark. At the same time, there are significant differences between Mark and Luke. Moreover, there are a number of instances where Luke seems to have a relationship with John, and some additional ones that might point to a connection with Matthew. What is striking is that Luke at the beginning of the pericope is fairly closely to Mark, yet at the end, very close to John. Aside from verse 10, which in its list of names is similar to material in Mark 16:1 and appears to be placed later in Luke for emphasis, the similarities with Mark are primarily in verses 1–3, corresponding to Mark 16:2–5. The latter part of Luke's empty tomb narrative, then, draws on another account that replaces Mark's negative report of the women's fear and flight.

A closer look at the passage is needed to understand Luke's relationship with the other Gospels.

LUKE 23:56b, 24:1–3

Luke, like Mark, makes the transition from the burial of Jesus to the empty tomb scene with an interest in the Sabbath observance. In both instances, the preparation of the spices has to be arranged around the Sabbath. In Luke's case, the women prepare the spices and ointment before the Sabbath, very specifically avoiding work on the Sabbath, while Mark has the women buying spices early on the first day of the week, after the Sabbath has ended (Mark 16:1).

Luke Chapter 24

The difference in preparation for the anointing seems to be integrally related to a change in the time of day that the women arrive at the tomb.[9] Luke reports that the women arrive at the tomb in the early dawn (ὄρθρου βαθέως), while Mark has the women arrive after the sun has risen (ἀνατείλαντος τοῦ ἡλίου). Both of these accounts are

---

[9]The other difference from Mark found in Luke, that the women bring ointment as well as spices, points to Luke's thoroughgoing redaction of the burial-anointing scenes. One will recall that Luke does not have an anointing at Bethany before entering Jerusalem, which in Mark and Matthew is perceived as a pre-burial anointing (Mark 14:3–9; Matt 26:6–13; cf. John 12:1–8 which has the same anointing, but does not cast it as a pre-burial anointing). Instead, Luke records an anointing of Jesus' feet by a sinful woman (Luke 7:36–50) just before he lists the women who follow Jesus (Luke 8:1–3)—women who are also linked to Luke 24:1–11! (see the discussion of this in Dillon, 11 f.) As will be pointed out below, the reference to the women "remembering" is a very specific intertextual link back to Luke 8:2 and 9:22 that provides the narrative basis for recalling the prophecy of Jesus' death.

Luke's mention in 23:56 that the women prepare their μύρα as well as ἀρώματα seems to be a conscious awareness (1) that the women have not yet anointed Jesus, (contra Mark and Matthew) and (2) that the women mentioned in Luke 24:10 and 8:2–3 probably include the woman in 7:36–50. Or, to put it more succinctly, Luke may have transferred the anointing story to Luke 7:36–50 because of this linkage between the women at the tomb and those at Luke 8:2–3. If the anointing of Jesus was not preparatory for burial, then perhaps its displacement from the passion narrative and attachment to the story of the women who follow Jesus and hear his words would make more sense. According to John, the anointing by Mary (interpreted by Luke as Mary Magdalene, named at Luke 8:2–3 and 24:10?) was not for Jesus' burial; she was to keep some ointment for that later purpose. The striking feature in both Luke and John, that the woman (Mary) anointed Jesus' feet with her hair, already suggests some literary relationship between the two accounts. Luke, then, reinterpreted the anointing by Mary that is found in John and moved it to Luke 7:36 to help establish the role of the women who follow Jesus as disciples, anticipating the later connection where the same women come to anoint Jesus after his burial. In other words, it appears that Luke's mention of ointment in the Resurrection story points us toward understanding Luke's method as a complex interweaving of references to the women, including the anointing story. Luke clearly seems to have been aware of John's anointing story and its reference to a post-burial (not pre-burial) occurrence. Is it not likely that the "confusion" of the church (cf. Raymond E. Brown, *The Gospel According to John* [X–XXI] AB 29A [Garden City, NY: Doubleday, 1970] 452) in which the figures of the sinner woman, Mary Magdalene, and Mary of Bethany are intertwined and become a unity was first created by Luke in his own reading of John?

coherent, but they are significantly different from each other.[10] In Luke, the women have prepared the spices and ointment before the Sabbath (Luke 23:56a); thus they go directly to the tomb in the deepest dawn. In Mark, the women apparently must go to market early to buy spices; by the time they arrive at the tomb, the sun has risen.

Luke's editorial hand appears to be at work in these modifications to the Markan account. Certain features seem to point to Luke's particular style, showing that he has reworked the material at this point: ὑποστρέφω (used in v. 56a with the pre-Sabbath preparation of the spices) and ἡσυχάζω are almost uniquely Lukan words, as well as ὄρθρου as an alternative for πρωί.[11] Luke, then, rewrote his Markan source, especially imposing his own interpretation of the timing of the visit.

What could have prompted this fundamental change in timing? Unlike Mark, both Matthew and John lack the description of the spices, and their accounts of the visit to the tomb emphasize the early period of the dawn: Matthew uses the term τῇ ἐπιφωσκούσῃ; John indicates that it was still dark, πρωί σκοτίας ἔτι οὔσης. Goulder points out that the only other example of the word ἐπιφωσκέω occurs in Luke 23:54 and suggests that Luke was recording here a memory of Matthew's time notation.[12] But Luke uses the word in a very different way, referring instead to the onset of the Sabbath itself at the burial of Jesus; that is, it is the Sabbath (evening!) that is coming near, rather than the dawning of a day. With the stark difference in its use, this word is too slender a string to connect Matthew with Luke. Matthew's time, while seeming to emphasize early dawn, still suggests the onset of daylight;

---

[10] The difference is perhaps "historically" trivial, as I. Howard Marshall, *The Gospel of Luke* (Grand Rapids: Wm. B. Eerdmans, 1978), 885 suggests, but it is not trivial in a narrative sense. Luke must have deliberately modified Mark's account, necessitating substantial adjustments to both the preparation and the empty tomb accounts.

[11] J. Jeremias, *Die Sprache des Lukasevangeliums* (Göttingen: Vandenhoeck & Ruprecht, 1980), 310, 63, 236, 283–4.

[12] M. D. Goulder, "Mark xvi.1–8 and Parallels," *NTS* 24 (1997–98): 237.

the Sabbath has passed, and the early light of morning has arrived.[13] In contrast to both Mark and Matthew, John's time emphasizes darkness, making the period very early. Luke's time notation is much closer to John's than it is to either Matthew's or Mark's.[14] It appears that Luke was influenced by John's concept of the time of the women's visit to the tomb and that he thus modified the story to accommodate this feature. Since the women in John go very early, they cannot possibly go to the market to buy spices first; they must have prepared them before the Sabbath.

Unlike either Matthew or Mark, Luke records no concern for how the stone might be removed (Mark), or any mention of an angel's moving it (Matthew).[15] In Luke, as in John, the story moves directly from the early trip to the tomb to the discovery that the stone has already been removed. This similarity, along with the abruptness of the announcement of the stone's having been removed, is all the more striking because neither Luke nor John notes previously that a stone was rolled in front of the tomb, a feature that both Mark and Matthew do report (Mark 15:46 and Matt 27:60). Rather than following Mark's account of the women's concern about the stone, Luke follows the more sparse account of John, in which the stone is simply found to be removed.

Luke's language for the discovery of the stone's removal, εὗρον δὲ, is Lukan, especially as it replaces Mark's θεωρέω,[16] and it seems particularly to have been used to parallel the discovery of the missing body.[17] Not only do the women find the stone rolled back, they find the

---

[13] So cf. F. C. Burkitt, "ἘΠΙΦΩΣΚΕΙΝ," *JTS* 14 (1913): 538–46; P. Gardner-Smith, "ἘΠΙΦΩΣΚΕΙΝ," *JTS* 27 (1926): 179–81; contra C. H. Turner, "Note on 'επιφωσκειν," *JTS* 14 (1913): 188–90.

[14] Julius Schniewind, *Die Parallelperikopen bei Lukas und Johannes* (Hildesheim: Georg Olms Verlagsbuchhandlung, 1958), 86.

[15] The striking feature of this absence was disturbing to some early scribes, who harmonized with Mark at this point ἐλογίζοντο δὲ ἐν ἑαυταῖς, Τίς ἄρα ἀποκυλίσει τὸν λίθον. ἐλθοῦσαι δὲ εὗρον... (D 0124 it^c).

[16] Jeremias, *Sprache*, 81, n. 7.

[17] Dillon, 18.

body missing as well. While showing strong evidence of Luke's interests and wording, the sentence in many ways echoes both Mark's and John's account at this point. Following Mark, Luke uses the pluperfect form of the verb ἀποκυλίω to describe the state of the stone. But following John the stone is said to have been rolled back "from the tomb" (ἀπὸ τοῦ μνημείου, only slightly different from John's ἐκ τοῦ μνημείου[18]), a term that is missing in Mark's account of the stone.

The climax of the women's arrival at the tomb in Luke is their discovery that the body of Jesus is gone. Differently from Mark or Matthew, this discovery is not mediated by the men in the tomb. In Mark and Matthew, the man/angel announces to the women that Jesus is not here, having risen, and demonstrates that fact by pointing to the (empty) place where Jesus was laid. The man/angel announces the absence and draws the women's attention to it. In Luke, the women simply find the *body* gone, but this "body" language serves to emphasize the physicality of the death of Jesus. So the discovery of the empty tomb is phrased by Luke in a more anti-docetic manner, which appears to be one of his redactional emphases.[19] The lack of angelic mediation in the discovery and its attendant suddenness in the narrative serve to place the focus on the missing body. The comment by Luke in 24:4 that the women were confused by the empty tomb, which appears to be a modification of Mark's suggestion that the women were con-

---

[18] Luke in general preferred ἀπό to ἐκ, modifying, for instance, a number of places where Mark chose the latter. ἐκ, on the other hand, is far more common in John.

[19] This coheres with other elements of Luke that emphasize the physicality of the dead and subsequently resurrected Jesus, namely that the women see the body of Jesus placed in the tomb (23:55), and that the resurrected Jesus has flesh and bones (Luke 24:39) and can eat and drink with the disciples (Luke 24:30, 42–43; Acts 1:4; Acts 10:41); cf. Charles Talbert, *Luke and The Gnostics* (Nashville: Abingdon Press, 1966), 29–32, and Luke Timothy Johnson, "Luke 24:1–11," *Int* 46 (1992): 58. These observations also have implications favoring the originality of the non-Western readings. If the longer forms of the readings tend to be anti-docetic, as Ehrman has argued, their originality ought not be surprising given Luke's anti-docetic tendencies.

fused about how to open the tomb, serves also to further focus attention on the emptiness of the tomb.[20]

As if to signal that the missing body is indeed a sign of something significant, Luke adds here the title κύριος; Jesus can now be referred to as the Lord Jesus.[21] For Luke, the title "Lord" is theologically weighted and is to be understood as a sign of Jesus' exaltation, not just polite address; this theological thrust is suggested more explicitly in Acts 2:36, where Luke understands that by the Resurrection, and more completely the Ascension, God has established Jesus as Lord.[22] In general, Luke in his Gospel uses κύριος either as a reference to God or as a respectful title, although occasionally as an anachronistic or anticipatory reference to Jesus' exalted status.[23] But in Acts it becomes a common title for Jesus, often in this form, κυρίου Ἰησοῦ. Not only here, but also in Luke 24:34, Luke uses the term in its titular fashion, "the Lord has risen indeed." Luke 24, then, seems to be a transition to the subsequent view of Jesus as risen Lord.

It is noteworthy that Matthew and Mark make no use of the term κύριος in the Resurrection stories. But like Luke, John does use the term in the Resurrection accounts. In John, the use of the term as a title occurs very rarely in the first 19 chapters, then becomes frequent in chapters 20 and 21.[24] It would appear that in John, as in Luke, the

---

[20] Grant Osborne, *The Resurrection Narratives* (Grand Rapids: Baker Book House, 1984), p. 105–6.

[21] This discussion assumes the longer reading of "the body *of the Lord Jesus*" in Luke 24:3, a Western non-interpolation. See the discussion in chapter 4, p. 189.

[22] Ferdinand Hahn, *The Titles of Jesus in Christology* (New York: World Publishing Co., 1969) notes Luke's use of the term as being particularly rooted in the Easter event, 112–14.

[23] There are some references that appear to be narrational anticipations of Jesus' exaltation: Luke 1:43 (Elizabeth's reference to the unborn Jesus as Lord), 2:11 (the angelic announcement of Jesus as Lord and Savior); 7:13, 19; 10:1, 39, 41; 11:39; 13:15; 17:5, 6; 18:6 (narrator's references to Jesus as "the Lord"). All of these references are either to unique Lukan material (L) or to Matthew/Luke material (Q) in which Matthew does not use the term. They are, then, clear indications of Luke's use.

[24] Hahn, 112.

Resurrection initiates a change in title, so that Jesus becomes in this last chapter "the Lord." Indeed, the first report of the missing body of Jesus in John is "they have taken the Lord out of the tomb..." (John 20:2). And the significance of this term in John is equally as clear as it is for Luke in Acts 2:36: in the Fourth Gospel, Thomas, upon touching Jesus, declares that he is ὁ κύριός μου καὶ ὁ θεός μου (John 20:28). While this is perhaps not a decisive point of similarity, it is certainly suggestive that Luke was modifying Mark's account of the empty tomb story under the influence of John.

LUKE 24:4–5

In response to the empty tomb, the women in Luke are puzzled (ἀπορέω) about the absence of the body. In Mark's account, the women only learn of the absent body from the "young man," so this feature does not come from Mark. Luke appears to have added it to the story as a seam introducing the arrival of the men in bright clothing. While the word used here is only slightly better attested in Luke than in the rest of the New Testament (2 times in Luke-Acts, 4 times elsewhere), the word group of -πορειν is strongly Lukan.[25] Moreover, other features in this sentence strongly point to Luke's hand: the periphrastic καὶ ἐγένετο ἐν τῷ plus an infinitive, transitional καὶ ἰδού, and ἐσθής are all well-attested elements of Luke's style.[26]

As with all the Gospels, the women meet "angelic" visitors at the tomb. But there is wide diversity about the visitors' description, their number, and the timing of their appearance. In Mark and Matthew, there is only one visitor. In Matthew, it is an angel (ἄγγελος) of the Lord who also has rolled back the stone; in Mark, it is a young man (νεανίσκος) who meets the women inside the tomb. In both cases, the visitor is dressed in white, but in Mark's case this seems to be simply normal clothing, while Matthew the whiteness is amplified (white as

---

[25] Jeremias, *Sprache*, 310.

[26] John Hawkins, *Horae Synopticae* (Oxford: Clarendon Press, 1909), 37, 40; Jeremias, *Sprache*, 310.

snow!) and is parallel to the visitor's lightning-like appearance. The sum total is that Mark's visitor appears to be human, while Matthew's is heavenly. Mark's visitor is found inside the tomb; Matthew's remains outside, yet beckons the women inside to see the empty tomb. John also has angelic visitors at the tomb, not at Mary's initial arrival, but rather after Peter and the other disciple's visit. Only at that point does Mary Magdalene return to the tomb (John 20:12) and see two angels in white inside the tomb.

Luke's account seems to have similarities to each of the various accounts. Like Mark, the initial description of the visitors is that they are men (ἄνδρες) whom the women meet upon entering the tomb. But in a later account, Luke (put in the words of recollection of one of the disciples on the road to Emmaus) understands these men to be angels (Luke 24:23). Unlike Mark and Matthew, but like John, Luke knows of two men/angels in the tomb. But unlike all of them, the angels are not dressed in white; the clothing is brilliant (ἀστραπτούσῃ), which is related to the word used to describe the angel's appearance in Matthew.

Luke begins his account more or less using Mark's narrative structure, that is, the angels at the tomb are described as men, perhaps in order to retain the narrative suspense at the tomb. But Luke's narrative introduces elements not found in Mark, elements that seem to have a relationship to the Johannine account. The question is, In which account do these features originate? It appears that Luke was influenced in these features by John. This is more likely than John's having taken them from Luke, since there is little evidence of other Lukan elements in John—the meeting between the angels and Mary is completely different in John; the announcement that Jesus was alive is not even present. But Luke does follow in a general way the Mark/Matthew narrative. How, then, did some of the variations from that account arise? If Luke knew the different Johannine version, then it is reasonable that John would have exerted an influence on the narrative similar to what we see in Luke; functions somewhat as a middle term. Thus, he knew that the men were really angels, and that knowledge found its way into the later recapitulation of the story. He also knew that there were two angels, not one. The latter feature is significant since it represents a clear modification of Mark under the influence of John.[27] Luke's variations from Mark can be explained almost entirely as echoes of another account—John's—that found their way into the Third Evangelist's portrayal.

A striking similarity between Luke and Matthew is the word ἀστραπτούσῃ to describe the angel/men. Did Luke derive the description for the clothing from Matthew's description of the angel's appearance?[28] The similarity of the word is striking. But Matthew, like Mark, describes the clothing as white (as does John); in Matthew, it is the angel's appearance (face?) that has the lightening-like visage. Rather than having come from Matthew, the description seems more likely to have simply derived from Luke's own usage: the word and its cognates are more common in Luke than in Matthew, being used in uniquely Lukan pericopes (cf. Luke 10:18) and Lukan redaction (Luke 17:24 with Matthew, Luke 11:36 different from Matthew, cf. cognate ἐξαστράπτων, Luke 9:29 par. Mark 9:2, Matt 17:2) for heavenly signs.[29] Indeed, the use of ἀστραπτ- stem words points to the likely source for Luke's description of the men at the tomb. Rather than drawing on an outside source, Luke seems to have been developing his own internal narrational links. This reference to two men who are clothed in brilliant apparel strongly echoes another reference to two

---

[27] Goulder, *Luke* (774), notes, correctly, that Luke would hardly have added the feature of the second angel without having had some support in his sources. But Goulder's argument that Luke found the two angels by combining Mark and Matthew is hardly convincing. Dillon (21) also argues that in much of this verse the semitizing style should be seen as a sign of Luke's redaction, and yet he admits that this may well suggest some non-Lukan source.

[28] See p. 383 above.

[29] The use of this word is the strongest basis for Goulder's argument that Luke relied on Matthew, and it is striking. But note that far more frequent and substantive points of commonality exist between Luke and John than between Luke and Matthew.

"men" who appear in glory at the Transfiguration.[30] Note especially that at the Transfiguration, Jesus' clothes also become dazzling white (λευκός ἐξαστράπτων). The narrative seems to equate Jesus' changed image and his dazzling white clothes with Moses' and Elijah's appearance ἐν δόξῃ! Therefore, the two men who appear at the grave are described in a way that the reader has previously encountered, one that suggests heavenly beings in glorious array. In other words, here, as with the list of women in verse 10, Luke is strongly linking Luke 24:4 with a previous narrative—in this case Luke 9:29–30. But Luke 24:4 not only refers *back* to Luke 9:29–30, with its two men in bright clothing, it also links *forward* to Acts 1:10, in which two men in white clothing interpret for the disciples the Ascension of Jesus. Thus this feature of bright clothes on angelic witnesses is an indication of Luke's frequent intertextual references.[31]

The women's response to the angels in Luke is fear and obeisance; they bow to the ground. Again, Luke seems to have been creating his own version by freely editing Mark. Mark—at least in the initial confrontation with the young man—says that the women were amazed (ἐκθαμβέομαι), not that they feared. Matthew says that the guards were afraid, not the women. Yet Mark does report that the final response of the women was fear, and perhaps that was a sufficient reference to suggest to Luke that the women would have been afraid at the angels, since the proper response to divine messengers is fear. Luke, therefore, interpreted Mark's account; although his narrative does not explicitly say that the two men were angels, the women nonetheless react to them with an appropriate response that is only suggested in Mark. Luke, then, reframed the story to underline both the women's appropriate response and the significance of the angels' appearance.

As in the first part of Luke 24:5, Luke continued the verse with a free editing of Mark in his construction of the angels' response to the women. Rather than pointing out the empty tomb, the discovery of

---

[30] Johnson, 59.
[31] Dillon, 22–23.

which, as noted above, Luke had already highlighted in order to emphasize the absent body of Jesus, the Third Evangelist placed a rhetorical question on their lips: "Why do you seek the living among the dead?" As Johnson points out, Luke's replacement of the announcement in Mark/Matthew that Jesus was risen from the dead with this question was more than simple phraseology, it was crucial to his reinterpretation of the event.[32] This question, like others in Luke-Acts, was actually a rebuke of the women's misinterpretation.[33] The women should have known what the empty tomb meant—that Jesus was alive because he had risen—as the subsequent reference to Jesus' previous words makes clear. But despite the distinctive emphasis that Luke gave to the account by means of the rhetorical question, his overall narrative still follows Mark quite closely. The men/angels announce that Jesus is alive/risen. Verse 5, then, is Luke's redaction of Mark's account of the empty tomb.

LUKE 24:6-8

Luke's emphasis on recalling the words of Jesus finds its genesis in Mark's narrative. Mark's young man tells the women that the disciples should go and meet Jesus in Galilee, *as he told you*. Luke deliberately deleted Mark's call for the disciples to go to Galilee, but the structural emphasis of Mark's narrative is nonetheless maintained: after the angels announce that Jesus is risen, they point the women back to the words of Jesus for support of their statements. In the case of Luke, the central issue in the recollection is proof of the Resurrection based on Jesus' words; in the case of Mark, it is instruction about how the disciples should act (i.e., go to Galilee) in order to meet Jesus again. Luke seems to have been following the basic structure of Mark even as he develops a very different view of the early disciples' response to the empty tomb.

---

[32] Johnson, 60.
[33] Cf. Luke 2:49; Acts 1:11.

Luke did not completely strike the reference to Galilee, however. He, too, connected the risen Jesus with the Galilee traditions, but not by making Galilee the locus of the post-Resurrection appearances. Instead, he connected both the teaching of Jesus and the women's hearing with Galilee. The reference "remember how he told you" was not merely a general reference, but appears to have been a specific reference to Luke 9:22, the setting of which is Galilee.[34] The cross-reference has some difficulties, though, prompting some scholars to suggest that Luke was instead referring at this point to a pre-Lukan source or narrative.[35] The Passion prediction given in Luke 9:22, while located in Galilee, does not specifically mention women in the audience; it is addressed only to the disciples. And a subsequent Passion prediction in Luke 9:44 is addressed to a broader audience, but it does not mention the Resurrection. Still, in Luke, the term disciples is an inclusive term and would seem to include women;[36] the audience in Luke 9:22 would seem to include the group of women listed in Luke 8:2. As further evidence of the intertextual link between chapters 8–9 and chapter 24, Luke is seen to have modified the list of women at the tomb (Luke 24:10) to agree in part with this cross-reference. Like Mark, Luke included Mary Magdalene and Mary the mother of James;

---

[34] So Paul Schubert, "The Structure and Significance of Luke 24," in *Neutestamentliche Studien für Rudolf Bultmann* (Berlin: Alfred Töpelmann, 1954), 165–86, argues that this proof from prophecy is the central theme and unifying feature of all of Luke 24.

[35] See R. H. Fuller, *The Formation of the Resurrection Narratives* (Philadelphia: Fortress Press, 1980), 98.

[36] In Luke, the term disciples is clearly more inclusive than the Twelve. The Twelve are called from out of the larger group of disciples (Luke 6:13), and the larger group continues to follow him even after the selection of this inner circle (so 6:17, a great crowd of disciples). The contrast is seen in chapter 8, where Luke mentions the Twelve (8:1) and the women who followed (8:2), and then the disciples (8:9), which seems to be inclusive (although it could be understood as restricted). The vast majority of the references to disciples in Luke find Jesus addressing them as a group and could include twelve or many more. In chapter 9, Luke seems to have been acutely aware of the distinction between the Twelve and the disciples: Jesus sends the Twelve out to proclaim the kingdom; when they return, they are called apostles. Thus disciples, in Luke, appears to be a broad term

these two seem to have been strongly connected with the empty tomb (compare Matthew, who lists these, but omits Salome). But Luke changed Salome to Joanna, who is mentioned at Luke 8:3, and added "other women" as if to echo the reference in Luke 8:3, "and many others." This generic "other women" is broad enough to include Susanna also, who is listed in Luke 8:3 but not mentioned in Luke 24:10. Exact correlation between Luke 8:3 and 24:10 is not possible, but it seems clear by virtue of the specific names listed and the reference to "as you have heard while still in Galilee," as well as the imagery of the two men in white, that Luke wanted to refer the reader back to the Galilean unit of Luke 8:2 through 9:22 (or even through 9:36 or 9:50) as the context by which to interpret the men's message to the women.

Luke's changed emphasis with respect to Jesus' words is not, however, based simply on a recollection of different elements from his previous teaching. It is based on a crucial difference from Mark and Matthew in his perspective of post-Resurrection activity. For Luke, Jesus would not appear to the disciples in Galilee; instead, Jerusalem alone was to be the locus of the post-Resurrection appearances and the formation of the church (Luke 24:36–53, Acts 1–7). The thoroughgoing nature of Luke's change is illustrated by his earlier deletion of Mark's prediction that after the Resurrection, Jesus would go before the disciples to Galilee (Mark 14:28; cf. Matt 26:32). With respect to the importance of Jerusalem in post-Resurrection appearances, John also stands apart from Mark and Matthew. Not only are the disciples not directed to Galilee, but Jesus' appearances to them occur in Jerusalem.[37] It must be noted that Luke's emphasis on Jerusalem is even stronger than John's. But it is certainly possible that Luke took

---

within which exists a smaller subset called the Twelve.

[37] John chapter 21 does have Jesus meeting the disciples at the Sea of Tiberius some time later. But John 21 presents special problems; most scholars consider it a later addition to John, and thus this chapter can be bracketed for our purposes here. See Raymond E. Brown, *The Gospel According to John* (X–XXI), AB 29A (Garden City, NY: Doubleday, 1970), 1077–82; C. K. Barrett, *The Gospel According to St. John*, 2nd ed. (Philadelphia: Westminster, 1978), 479–80.

John's account that Jesus appeared to the disciples in Jerusalem and developed that idea in Luke and Acts as a fundamental theological perspective; that is, that beginning with Jesus' appearance to the disciples and the giving of the Spirit, the church spread from Jerusalem out to all the world. Given the importance of the Jerusalem church and her leaders in the nascent period of the Christian movement, if Luke was working with Mark and John as his primary sources it is easy to imagine his having been attracted to John's Jerusalem appearances and thus having modified his basic Markan narrative under the influence of John.

LUKE 24:9–11

Luke's account of the women's reaction to the empty tomb and to the angels' announcement is a radical departure from Mark's account. In Mark, the women say nothing to anyone, out of fear, and so ends the Second Gospel. Matthew records the women's intention to tell the disciples but then has them interrupted by Jesus himself. And after the women meet Jesus, Matthew does not record them actually telling anything to the disciples, although some such announcement is presumed by the subsequent narrative. Luke, in contrast, has the women return immediately and in fact tell the disciples—a group made up of the inner circle of the Eleven together with the others that followed Jesus—what has happened. Somewhat similar to, but still quite different from, Luke, John has Mary immediately run and tell certain of the disciples—specifically, Peter and the beloved disciple. Each of the four Gospels is distinctively different at this point, with the closest similarities occurring between Luke and John.

In lexical and stylistic features, Luke's narrative in 24:9–11 shows extensive signs of his own construction. The use of ὑποστρέφω in the framing participle is clearly Lukan; virtually all the uses of ὑποστρέφω in the New Testament are Luke's (Mark 1 time, Luke 21 times, Acts 12 times, others 3 times).[38] Similarly, the use of ἀπαγγέλλω

---

[38] Jeremias, *Sprache*, 63.

is a sign of Luke's style.[39] And the precise designation of the inner circle of the disciples as "the Eleven," a self-conscious modification of the earlier designation of the core disciples as "the Twelve," is Lukan (cf. Luke 24:33, Acts 2:14; also Acts 1:26, Matt 28:16), together with the reference to the broader group of disciples present at the announcement: τοῖς ἕνδεκα καὶ πᾶσιν τοῖς λοιποῖς.[40] And, as has already been discussed, the listing of the women in verse 10 is based on Mark 16:1, yet the modification of Mark shows Luke's mindfulness of his previous list of women in Luke 8:2. The addition to the list of women at the end of the verse and the subsequent recapitulation of their address to the apostles are Lukan in style:[41] the generalizing addition of unnamed others in αἱ λοιπαὶ σὺν αὐταῖς,[42] the use of λέγω πρὸς and accusative,[43] and the use of the word apostles for the Twelve.[44] All these features suggest that the modifications to the list of women in v. 10, and the placement late in the empty tomb narrative result from Luke's redaction. The conclusion to the women's report—that the gathered disciples did not believe it—also appears strongly Lukan in style. In addition, Luke's use of ἀπιστέω in a nonreligious sense, that is, to be convinced of a fact, is Lukan.[45] So the entire unit of Luke

---

[39] Jeremias, *Sprache*, 311–12.

[40] Joseph Plevnik, "'The Eleven and Those with Them' According to Luke," *CBQ* 40 (1978): 205–11. Compare, for instance, the similar language in Luke 24:33 τοὺς ἕδεκα καὶ τοὺς σὺν αὐτοῖς.

[41] The syntax of this verse is notoriously difficult. I take it that the sentence goes something like this: "They (the women that returned) were Mary Magdalene, and Joanna, and Mary the mother (wife?) of James, and the rest of the women who were with them. They (i.e., the women just named) were saying these things to the apostles and ..." In other words, I take it that that the unstated subject of ἔλεγον is understood to be all the women listed previously, not just "the rest of the women."

[42] Jeremias, *Sprache*, 111, 312.

[43] Joseph A. Fitzmyer, *The Gospel According to Luke*, I–IX, AB 28 (Garden City, NY: Doubleday, 1981), 116; Jeremias, *Sprache*, 33. Jeremias notes that the use of πρός with the accusative after verbs of speaking is overwhelmingly Lukan (Luke 100 times, Acts 49 times, Mark 0 times, Matthew 0 times, John 14 times, Hebrews 6 times).

[44] Matthew 1 time, Mark 2 times, John 1 time, Luke 6 times, Acts 28 times.

[45] Jeremias, *Sprache*, 312.

24:9–11 is thoroughly Lukan: only the list of women in verse 10 shows traces of Markan origination, and it has been modified under Luke's hand.

But why did Luke compose this story of the women's return to the disciples, and the disciples' subsequent failure to believe their report? The disciples' reaction to the risen Jesus is absent in Mark, where they never hear the news. Matthew and John have stories in which some disciples doubt (Matt 28:17; John 20:25, 27) but in both cases the doubt or disbelief is that the figure in their midst is indeed Jesus. Here, Luke's doubt is simply a disbelief in the report of the women. Rather than reflecting either Matthew's or John's report of the disciples' doubt about Jesus, Luke seems to have constructed the story in order to set the stage for Peter's own trip to the tomb (Luke 24:12). In other words, Luke's construction of verses 9–11 reflects the need to accomodate his narrative to verse 12, in which one of the disciples runs to inspect the tomb to verify the story. Up to verse 9, Luke was working with a Markan narrative, modifying it in places to accommodate certain Johannine features, as well as Luke's own emphases. But verse 12 represents a completely non-Markan feature, with a different story line, Peter's dash to the empty tomb, that presumes the women's announcement to the disciples. In order for Peter to run to the empty tomb and find the burial clothes, the women must first return to the disciples and tell the story of the empty tomb. By moving the list of women and adding the note that the disciples disbelieved, Luke created a viable segue between the two disparate stories.

LUKE 24:12

Verse 12 presents two related problems: the text is missing in the Western manuscripts, and the verse sounds very much like John 20:3–10. Stylistic and transcriptional reasons for considering the verse to be part of the original text of the Third Gospel have been addressed in chapter 4 above, but the contours of the problem should be briefly revisited.[46]

A Johannine origination is suggested by its extensive non-Lukan material. In particular, βλέπει as a historical present,[47] ὀθόνια, παρακύψας and ἀπῆλθεν with πρὸς are all non-Lukan in style; furthermore, they strongly echo language found in John. Most of these "intrusive" stylistic features can be considered marks of John's style. The historical present is a common feature in John. The word ὀθόνιον occurs only in John outside of this passage; In John, it is used in both chapters 19 and 20. The use of ἀπέρχομαι with πρός occurs only here in Luke-Acts, but is a clear sign of Johannine style.[48] So also παρακύπτω, although found in the Gospels only in the empty tomb stories of Luke and John, can be said to have better Johannine attestation, since there it is found in the Mary Magdalene story (John 20:11), as well as that of Peter and the other's disciple's visit to the tomb (20:5). In addition to these relatively non-Lukan, but Johannine, features in Luke 24:12, there is a striking agreement in the order of common words and events between verse 12 and John 20:3–10.[49] This agreement in order makes a literary relationship with John all but certain.

But while the large number and the striking nature of the similarities between Luke and John—from extensive Johannine vocabulary to the common order of features—indicate a literary relationship, very distinctive differences from John argue for Luke's active incorporation of Johannine material rather than a later scribe's simple insertion of such material into Luke's text.[50] A brief review of stylistic features will help show Luke's active redaction of the material. Three features in particular point to Luke's style in this passage: the use of

---

[46] See chapter 4, p. 189.

[47] Jeremias, *Sprache*, 313.

[48] Gilbert van Belle, *The Signs Source in the Fourth Gospel* (Leuven: University Press, 1994), 406.

[49] See the chart in Chapter 4, p. 192.

[50] Dillon, 61, n. 174.

the pleonastic ἀναστὰς, the use of θαυμάζω, and the substantival use of τὸ γεγονός.[51] These are very strong instances of Lukan style, certain minor peculiarities notwithstanding.[52] The use of the phrase ἐπὶ τὸ μνημεῖον is also very Lukan. While Mark and John use the term μνημεῖον extensively, Luke tends to describe travel to the tomb as ἐπὶ τὸ μνημεῖον (Luke 24:9, 22, 24; cf. Mark 16:1). This phrase stands in contrast to John, who always has travel to the tomb expressed in terms of going εἰς μνημεῖον, in which εἰς clearly does not necessarily mean "to enter" the tomb.[53] Thus the passage bears many stylistic indications of Luke's active editing. But the substantive modification of the story is also telling. The avoidance of the "disciple whom Jesus loved," the absence of the motif of belief at the empty tomb, and the contraction of the various burial clothes (ὀθόνια and σουδάριον), and their relationship to the burial custom to the terse reference to the ὀθόνια μόνα all point to a careful and gifted restructuring of the disciples' visit.[54] Such modification can hardly be attributed simply to scribal insertion.

If Luke was combining Mark and John in the story of the empty tomb, why did he omit certain of John's elements? Specifically, why is the "other disciple" absent from the account of Peter's trip to the tomb, and why is Mary's encounter with Jesus (John 20:11–17) missing? The simple answer might be that Luke had some question as to their accuracy. But given Luke's overall thrust in the Resurrection narrative,

---

[51] See above, chapter 4, p. 189, and Jeremias, *Sprache*, 312.

[52] As in the word order of the participle and subject; cf. my discussion in Chapter 4, p. 190.

[53] See for instance John 20:1, where Mary seems to simply arrive at the tomb. NRSV translates ἔρχεται ... εἰς μνημεῖον as "Mary Magdalene came *to* the tomb." Or similarily John 20:3 where the two disciples run to the tomb. NRSV translates ἤρχοντο εἰς τὸ μνημεῖον as "went toward the tomb"; not until 20:5 does Peter finally stoop and peer in.

[54] Frans Neirynck, "John and the Synoptics: The Empty Tomb Stories." *NTS* 30 (1984): 176, argues that the use of μόνα here and the fact that there are two kinds of burial clothes mentioned in John (versus one in Luke) show John's secondary nature. He asserts that since μόνα can mean "by themselves" (i.e., separated, apart), as well as "only," John has taken the former meaning and expanded the account to explain the term by showing two kinds of burial clothes, separated from one another.

a more specific rationale can be offered that makes the absence of these features coherent. Two features about John's account of the race to the tomb would have proved difficult for Luke to use. First, the "other disciple" is never named in John (throughout he is the ὁ ἄλλος μαθητής, though in 20:2 he is identified in an equally elliptical way as the "one whom Jesus loved"). To have included him at this point would have meant either using John's cumbersome terminology or inventing a name. The Beloved Disciple is after all a distinctly Johannine character with a unique role. It would have proved easier just to delete the other disciple and allow the narrative to be much shorter and more directed to the essential point of verifying the empty tomb; for this, Peter would do very nicely. Second, the "other disciple" believes because of the empty tomb (John 20:8). But for Luke the crucial issue in the Resurrection narratives was not abstract belief based on the empty tomb, but rather whether the disciples are witnesses to the risen Lord (cf. Luke 24:48; Acts 1:8; 2:32). While the women's testimony to others about the empty tomb begins this process, it is only fully realized after the disciples *see the risen Lord* and testify to others.[55] Indeed, the exact opposite inclination from John's "belief at the empty tomb" seems better to represent Luke's understanding of the events. The empty tomb experiences by the women suggest that a full understanding of the mystery of Jesus' death will be given only by Jesus' own appearance.[56]

---

[55] It is worth noting the importance of testimony about the risen Jesus in the latter part of Luke and in Acts: the women report the empty tomb, but they are doubted (Lk 24:11); Cleopas and his companion report their encounter with Jesus (Luke 24:35) and are told that Simon has seen Jesus also and declared that Jesus is risen indeed (Luke 24:34); the disciples meet Jesus and are told that they are witnesses to the death and resurrection of Jesus (Luke 24:48); the disciples in Acts are told that they will receive power from the Holy Spirit in order to be witnesses to the Resurrection (Acts 1:8); at Pentecost the larger group of disciples are all witnesses that Jesus was raised up (Acts 2:32).

[56] Dillon is correct in asserting that Luke has carefully constructed a *Leidengeheimnis*, the understanding of which the disciples do not gain until they see Jesus risen (23–26). Thus the mystery of Jesus' Passion begins with Jesus' predictions of his death (9:22), and the subsequent recollection of his predictions by

With the story of the disciples' visit pared down to only Peter's peering into the tomb, elements that might distract from the central focus could be eliminated: the race to the tomb, the pause by the other disciple, the description of both burial clothes and a face cloth, belief based on the absence of the body. But even with this paring down of John's account, a further trace of Luke's knowledge of that account is still found in Luke 24:24, where the subsequent report speaks of disciples (plural) who went to the tomb to verify the story.

John's story of Mary's second visit to the tomb also presents some difficulties for Luke's use. The first is the chronological and geographical displacement. If Mary has returned to tell the disciples of the empty tomb, how is it that she is back at the tomb after Peter leaves? To accommodate this surprising shift in locale would have taken some work by Luke. And since Luke was still following the broad outline of Mark's empty tomb account, such a re-working would have been difficult and perhaps, therefore, rejected in favor of Mark's order. But perhaps more importantly, the Johannine story ends with Mary's reporting back to the disciples that she has seen the risen Lord. For Luke, based on his use of another tradition, this first vision was reserved for Peter (Luke 24:34).[57] So John's report of the appearance to Mary could not be used as it stands. But perhaps Luke did not entirely discarded this epiphany. One is struck by several Johannine features that appear to be echoed in Luke: (1) two angels appear to Mary, a feature which seems to have crept into Luke 24:4, 23; (2) Jesus is not recognized at first, a feature that appears in Luke's Emmaus episode; and (3) Jesus speaks of not yet having ascended, the only reference to the Ascension outside of Luke. Thus certain features in John 20:11–18 resonate with Luke's continued Resurrection narratives but are left out of his empty tomb account.

---

the women ("they remembered") does nothing to alter the fact that they still do not understand. So also, then, Peter himself goes to the tomb, but nothing is said of his understanding. That awaits Jesus' appearance to him.

[57] It appears that Luke knew of the tradition recorded also in 1 Cor 15:5, that Cephas (Peter) saw Jesus first.

Of course the Lukan origination of verse 12 need not point to Luke's use of John. Two other alternatives to explain the text of verse 12 have commonly been suggested; these should be examined as alternatives to the proposal that Luke drew on John. The first is that Luke and John were using common traditional material, which explains the series of striking similarities between their stories of the disciple(s)' trip to the empty tomb.[58] The second is that verse 12 represents Luke's creative adaptation of Mark, upon which John further expanded to create the account found in John 20:3–10.[59]

While it is certainly possible that Luke was relying on an independent piece of tradition for Luke 24:12, it does not appear to be most likely, because there is no evidence to support such a claim. In this view, the original story would have contained the following information: (1) Peter ran to the grave, (2) he stooped in and saw the burial clothes lying alone, and (3) he left by himself.[60]

Luke, then, would have added his own peculiar language: ἀνάστας, θαυμάζω, τὸ γέγονος. John would have taken the same story and added the additional material relative to the second disciple, the race to the tomb with the delay by the other disciple, the description of the additional burial clothes. But one must explain why Luke has the historical present; it must have existed in the common tradition.

---

[58] This approach comes closest to representing a scholarly consensus on the status of verse 12. See, for example, Joseph Fitzmyer, *The Gospel According to Luke* (X-XXIV), AB 28A (Garden City, NY: Doubleday, 1985), 1542; Dillon, 62; Marshall, *Luke*, 888; Darrell Bock, *Luke* (Grand Rapids: Baker Book House, 1996), 1900; Gerd Luedemann, *The Resurrection of Jesus* (Minneapolis: Fortress Press, 1994), 138–39, 156. In earlier treatments see Robert Leaney, "The Resurrection Narratives in Luke (xxiv. 12-53)," *NTS* 2 (1955–56): 112; M.-É. Boismard and P. Benoit, *Synopse des Quatre Évangiles*, Tome 2 (Paris: Les Éditions deu Cerf, 1972), 445–46; Schniewind, 89.

[59] Frans Neirynck in a number of articles: "The Uncorrected Historic Present in Lk xxiv.12," *ETL* 48 (1972): 548–53; "Once More Luke 24,12," *ETL* 70 (1994): 319–40; "ΠΑΡΑΚΥΨΑΣ ΒΛΕΠΕΙ. Lc 24,12 et Jn 20,5," *ETL* 53 (1977): 113–52; "ΑΠΗΛΘΕΝ ΠΡΟΣ ΕΑΥΤΟΝ. Lc 24,12 et Jn 20,10," *ETL* 54 (1978): 104–18; "A Supplementary Note on Lk 24,12," *ETL* 72 (1996): 425–30; "John and the Synoptics: The Empty Tomb Stories," 161–87.

[60] Boismard, 446.

Furthermore, one must explain the use of the Johannine word for burial clothes, ὀθόνια, since Luke previously followed Mark's use of σίνδων; it, too, must have existed in the common tradition. One is left, then, with a source that must have contained certain features of "Johannine" style.

What this view does not adequately account for is the plural reference in Luke 24:24 καὶ ἀπῆλθόν τινες τῶν σὺν ἡμῖν ἐπὶ τὸ μνημεῖον. If the common source had two disciples running to the tomb,[61] which would thus explain the plural reference in Luke 24:24, then that hypothetical source would be almost identical with John's account. But if it were identical with John's account, why would one posit a separate hypothetical source? With no evidence of a common tradition, it is preferable to suggest that Luke in this passage relied on John.

Frans Neirynck has argued regularly and frequently that Luke 24:12 was Luke's creation based upon Mark and that John was literarily dependent upon Luke. It is important to note that, for Neirynck, establishing Luke 24:12 as an editorial composition is a foundation stone in his edifice since, in his view, "John's dependence on Luke will be an unavoidable consequence."[62] In his discussions about the literary relationship between Luke and John, Neirynck follows closely the major points that have been discussed in this examination, especially the emphasis on the order of similarities. He is less than convincing, however, when he not only denies that certain Johannine features in Luke 24:12 came from John (as discussed above: the historical present, ὀθόνια, and the pattern of ἀπέρχομαι plus πρός), but sees them as Luke's creation based exclusively on Mark. Neirynck argues that all of Luke's empty tomb story is a retelling of Mark's (Mark 16:1–8). Of particular interest for the present discussion of verse 12, Neirynck finds that the Lukan story of Peter's visit to the tomb follows along the same lines as the women's earlier journey in Mark: they go to the tomb, they look up and see the empty tomb, and they return. The most

---

[61] Leaney, 111, 114.

[62] Neirynck, "John and the Synoptics: The Empty Tomb Stories," 175.

important element in Neirynck's understanding is the identification of Luke's παρακύψας βλέπει with Mark's ἀναβλέψασαι θεωροῦσιν (Mark 16:4), the point where the women arrive at the tomb to find the stone rolled away. Neirynck is correct in asserting that Luke could certainly accommodate certain features, such as the historical present with *verbum videndi* as in Luke 16:23 (ἐπάρας τοὺς ὀφθαλμοὺς αὐτοῦ ... ὁρᾷ, cf. Acts 10:11).[63] But how exactly did Luke create verse 12? According to Neirynck, Luke first followed Mark 16:1–8 in the construction of the women's trip to the tomb (=Luke 24:1–9), and he then constructs a doublet of Peter's going to the tomb (Luke 24:12) based on the very same narrative pattern from Mark. Thus, Peter's dash to the tomb would correspond to the women's going to the tomb (ἔρχονται ἐπὶ τὸ μνημεῖον); his peering into the tomb to the women's finding the tomb open (ἀναβλέψασαι θεωροῦσιν);[64] the mention of only the burial clothes corresponds to the women seeing the empty spot where Jesus' body had been; and Peter's departure, marveling, to the women's return, where ἀπῆλθεν πρὸς ἑαυτόν is understood to mean "he went home."[65] How likely is this reconstruction of the relationship between Luke and Mark? In the first place, it does not easily fit with Luke's general avoidance of doublets. Rather than creating such doublets,

---

[63] Neirynck, "John and the Synoptics: Empty Tomb Stories," 175.

[64] Neirynck, "ΠΑΡΑΚΥΨΑΣ ΒΛΕΠΕΙ," especially 149–62. Note that Neirynck argues that the Gospel of Peter follows a similar pattern, using the phrase "stooped down and saw" to describe the sight upon entering the tomb before meeting the young man, instead of Mark's "looked up and beheld." For Neirynck, that pattern demonstrates the interchangeability of the terms. But more likely, the Gospel of Peter represents a conflation of John and Mark, not an independent witness to a pattern of redaction. See Raymond E. Brown, "The Gospel of Peter and Canonical Gospel Priority," *NTS* 33 (1987): 321–43; Alan Kirk, "Examining Priorities: Another Look at the Gospel of Peter's Relationship to the New Testament Gospels," *NTS* 40 (1994): 572–95; Frans Neirynck, "The Apocryphal Gospels and the Gospel of Mark," in *The New Testament in Early Christianity* (Leuven: University Press, 1989), 123–75.

[65] Neirynck, "ΑΠΗΛΘΟΝ ΠΡΟΣ ΕΑΥΤΟΝ," 104–18.

Luke tended to remove them in his editing of sources.[66] But more importantly, how likely is this method of Luke's having worked with Mark? Nowhere else did Luke repeat his Markan material with major modifications. It seems to be simply an imaginative leap to try to attribute Luke's account in verse 12 to a Markan base.

If one simply allows for the possibility that John's version existed prior to Luke's, however, the solution is very simple. First of all, one can agree, with Neirynck, that Luke 24:12 is indeed part of the original text of Luke. Moreover, one can affirm, with others, that Luke has significant and critical points in common with John. In this view of Luke's using John as one of his sources, along with Mark, the agreements with John as well as the Lukan editing (including the residual historical present) are sufficiently well explained. In agreement with Neirynck's appeal to Occam's razor, one need not turn to a hypothetical source to explain Luke's divergence from Mark. Mark alone is not sufficient to explain Luke 24:12; John is required as well.

SUMMARY

In the empty tomb narrative, one can see Luke's use of various sources as well as his own thoroughgoing editorial style. It is clear that Luke developed the skeleton of his empty tomb narrative from Mark. The "backbone" is the account of the women, three of whom are named, who return to the tomb after the Sabbath to finish the burial duties and find Jesus' body missing. At the tomb, they meet an angelic messenger who affirms that Jesus is alive. But Luke modified the Markan account significantly, drawing especially on John. From John, Luke drew the following features: the timing of the visit to the tomb, the unexplained note that the stone had been rolled away, the number of angels (two) at the tomb, the importance of Jerusalem as the locus of

---

[66] See Fitzmyer, *Luke* (I–IX), 81–82. Cf. also, H. Schürmann, "Die Dubletten im Lukasevangelium," in *Traditionsgeschichtliche Untersuchungen zu den Synoptischen Evangelien* (Düsseldorf: Patmos-Verlag, 1968), 272–78, in which he argues that the few doublets that Luke did allow arose from oversight that was due to the highly schematic nature of his construction.

post-Resurrection activity, the return of the women to the disciples, and the subsequent trip of Peter to the grave. And finally, it has become apparent that Luke has a redactional pattern that is uniquely Lukan. The Third Gospel exhibits an interest in linking the women at the empty tomb with the previous Galileen mission, a tendency to formalize representations of angelic epiphanies, and a theological interest in maintaining the misunderstanding of the Passion until the disciples actually see Jesus. Under Luke's control, the story still anticipates the subsequent epiphanies; Peter's empty tomb experience leaves him wondering, just like the women who earlier were perplexed.[67]

THE EMMAUS NARRATIVE. LUKE 24:13–35.

[13] Καὶ ἰδοὺ δύο ἐξ αὐτῶν ἐν αὐτῇ τῇ ἡμέρᾳ ἦσαν πορευόμενοι εἰς κώμην ἀπέχουσαν σταδίους ἑξήκοντα ἀπὸ Ἰερουσαλήμ, ᾗ ὄνομα Ἐμμαοῦς, [14] καὶ αὐτοὶ ὡμίλουν πρὸς ἀλλήλους περὶ πάντων τῶν συμβεβηκότων τούτων. [15] καὶ ἐγένετο ἐν τῷ ὁμιλεῖν αὐτοὺς καὶ συζητεῖν καὶ αὐτὸς Ἰησοῦς ἐγγίσας συνεπορεύετο αὐτοῖς, [16] οἱ δὲ ὀφθαλμοὶ αὐτῶν ἐκρατοῦντο τοῦ μὴ ἐπιγνῶναι αὐτόν. [17] εἶπεν δὲ πρὸς αὐτούς, Τίνες οἱ λόγοι οὗτοι οὓς ἀντιβάλλετε πρὸς ἀλλήλους περιπατοῦντες; καὶ ἐστάθησαν σκυθρωποί. [18] ἀποκριθεὶς δὲ εἷς ἐξ αὐτῶν ὀνόματι Κλεοπᾶς εἶπεν πρὸς αὐτόν, Σὺ μόνος παροικεῖς Ἰερουσαλὴμ καὶ οὐκ ἔγνως τὰ γενόμενα ἐν αὐτῇ ἐν ταῖς ἡμέραις ταύταις; [19] καὶ εἶπεν αὐτοῖς, Ποῖα; οἱ δὲ εἶπαν αὐτῷ, Τὰ περὶ Ἰησοῦ τοῦ Ναζαρηνοῦ, ὃς ἐγένετο ἀνὴρ προφήτης δυνατὸς ἐν ἔργῳ καὶ λόγῳ ἐναντίον τοῦ θεοῦ καὶ παντὸς τοῦ λαοῦ, [20] ὅπως τε παρέδωκαν αὐτὸν οἱ ἀρχιερεῖς καὶ οἱ ἄρχοντες ἡμῶν εἰς κρίμα θανάτου καὶ ἐσταύρωσαν αὐτόν. [21] ἡμεῖς δὲ ἠλπίζομεν ὅτι αὐτός ἐστιν ὁ μέλλων λυτροῦσθαι τὸν Ἰσραήλ· ἀλλά γε καὶ σὺν πᾶσιν τούτοις τρίτην ταύτην ἡμέραν ἄγει ἀφ' οὗ ταῦτα ἐγένετο. [22] ἀλλὰ καὶ γυναῖκές τινες ἐξ ἡμῶν ἐξέστησαν ἡμᾶς· γενόμεναι ὀρθριναὶ ἐπὶ τὸ μνημεῖον [23] καὶ μὴ εὑροῦσαι τὸ σῶμα αὐτοῦ ἦλθον λέγουσαι καὶ ὀπτασίαν ἀγγέλων ἑωρακέναι, οἳ λέγουσιν αὐτὸν

---

[67] Dillon, 66.

ζῆν. ²⁴ καὶ ἀπῆλθόν τινες τῶν σὺν ἡμῖν ἐπὶ τὸ μνημεῖον, καὶ εὗρον οὕτως καθὼς καὶ αἱ γυναῖκες εἶπον, αὐτὸν δὲ οὐκ εἶδον. ²⁵ καὶ αὐτὸς εἶπεν πρὸς αὐτούς, Ὦ ἀνόητοι καὶ βραδεῖς τῇ καρδίᾳ τοῦ πιστεύειν ἐπὶ πᾶσιν οἷς ἐλάλησαν οἱ προφῆται· ²⁶ οὐχὶ ταῦτα ἔδει παθεῖν τὸν Χριστὸν καὶ εἰσελθεῖν εἰς τὴν δόξαν αὐτοῦ; ²⁷ καὶ ἀρξάμενος ἀπὸ Μωϋσέως καὶ ἀπὸ πάντων τῶν προφητῶν διερμήνευσεν αὐτοῖς ἐν πάσαις ταῖς γραφαῖς τὰ περὶ ἑαυτοῦ. ²⁸ Καὶ ἤγγισαν εἰς τὴν κώμην οὗ ἐπορεύοντο, καὶ αὐτὸς προσεποιήσατο πορρώτερον πορεύεσθαι. ²⁹ καὶ παρεβιάσαντο αὐτὸν λέγοντες, Μεῖνον μεθ᾽ ἡμῶν, ὅτι πρὸς ἑσπέραν ἐστὶν καὶ κέκλικεν ἤδη ἡ ἡμέρα. καὶ εἰσῆλθεν τοῦ μεῖναι σὺν αὐτοῖς. ³⁰ καὶ ἐγένετο ἐν τῷ κατακλιθῆναι αὐτὸν μετ᾽ αὐτῶν λαβὼν τὸν ἄρτον εὐλόγησεν καὶ κλάσας ἐπεδίδου αὐτοῖς· ³¹ αὐτῶν δὲ διηνοίχθησαν οἱ ὀφθαλμοὶ καὶ ἐπέγνωσαν αὐτόν· καὶ αὐτὸς ἄφαντος ἐγένετο ἀπ᾽ αὐτῶν. ³² καὶ εἶπαν πρὸς ἀλλήλους, Οὐχὶ ἡ καρδία ἡμῶν καιομένη ἦν ἐν ἡμῖν ὡς ἐλάλει ἡμῖν ἐν τῇ ὁδῷ, ὡς διήνοιγεν ἡμῖν τὰς γραφάς; ³³ καὶ ἀναστάντες αὐτῇ τῇ ὥρᾳ ὑπέστρεψαν εἰς Ἰερουσαλήμ, καὶ εὗρον ἠθροισμένους τοὺς ἕνδεκα καὶ τοὺς σὺν αὐτοῖς, ³⁴ λέγοντας ὅτι ὄντως ἠγέρθη ὁ κύριος καὶ ὤφθη Σίμωνι. ³⁵ καὶ αὐτοὶ ἐξηγοῦντο τὰ ἐν τῇ ὁδῷ καὶ ὡς ἐγνώσθη αὐτοῖς ἐν τῇ κλάσει τοῦ ἄρτου.

NOTE: In this passage, and in the subsequent ones, indications of Lukan style are signified with underlining.

Luke's Emmaus story is one of the unique elements in Luke's Gospel, and it shows both the narrative mastery and the fidelity to key concerns that are hallmarks of the Third Evangelist. It is generally agreed that the Emmaus narrative is primarily the result of Luke's composition,[68] although some traditional elements appear to have been woven into the story. Given the overwhelming evidence for Luke's composition, a key question of this examination will be how much of the material in 24:13–35 could be attributable to a source or tradition.

---

[68] John Creed, *The Gospel According to St. Luke* (London: Macmillan, 1930), 290; Fitzmyer, *Luke* (X–XXIV), 1554–60; Dillon, 155; Joachim Wanke, *Die Emmauserzählung* (Leipzig: St. Benno-Verlag, 1973), 109–21.

LUKAN STYLE

One can certainly identify Lukan redaction or composition throughout the pericope. The following features of Luke's style can be readily identified:

1. καὶ ἰδού (24:13). This term has been frequently recognized as Lukan. ἰδού occurs most frequently in Luke and Acts, often in uniquely Lukan narratives.[69]

2. ἐν αὐτῇ τῇ ἡμέρᾳ/ὥρᾳ (24:13, 33). Luke commonly has the intensive use of the pronoun with time expressions.[70]

3. ἦσαν πορευόμενοι (24:13) This phrase points to Luke's hand on two grounds: the verb πορεύομαι is predominately Luke's choice,[71] and the use of the periphrastic participle is Lukan.[72] On the periphrastic use of the participle, see also καιομένη ἦν (v. 32).

4. Ἰερουσαλήμ (24:13, 18, 33). This spelling of Jerusalem is found predominately in Luke-Acts (26 times in Luke, 39 times in Acts, 1 time in Matthew, 11 times in the rest of the New Testament). The other spelling, Ἱεροσόλυμα, is also found in Luke and Acts, as well as most of the Gospels; the existence of Ἰερουσαλήμ is usually a good sign of Luke's redaction.[73]

5. ᾗ ὄνομα Ἐμμαοῦς (24:13). Luke used ὄνομα more frequently than other writers, but this particular use especially points to Luke's hand. The use of the place name in the construction dative plus ὄνομα

---

[69] Fitzmyer, *Luke* (I–IX), 121; Dillon, 83; although Jeremias, *Sprache*, 313 lists this as an indication of the use of tradition.

[70] For ὥρα see Luke 2:38; 10:21; 12:12; 13:31; 20:19; 24:33. For ἡμέρα see Luke 23:12; 24:13. A related term is ἐν αὐτῷ τῷ καιρῷ, Luke 13:1. See note in Fitzmyer, *Luke* (I–IX), 117–118; Dillon, 84, n. 42; Jeremias, *Sprache*, 313.

[71] 50 times in Luke, 39 times in Acts, versus 28 times in Matthew, 1 time in Mark, 13 times in John, and 16 times in the rest of the New Testament. See also Dillon, 89; Jeremias, *Sprache*, 56.

[72] Fitzmyer, *Luke* (I–IX), 122; Jeremias, *Sprache*, 42–43.

[73] Jeremias, *Sprache*, 91.

plus name is uniquely Lukan in the Gospels.[74] The use of ὀνόματι plus name (v. 18) is also Lukan.[75]

6. τινες (24:17, 22, 24). Fitzmyer points out that the use of τινες is predominately Lukan.[76]

7. πρὸς with words of speaking (24:14, 17, 18, 25, 32). This use is Lukan.[77]

8. πρὸς ἀλλήλους (24:14, 17, 32). The reflexive "one another" as the object of a verb of speaking is almost exclusively Lukan.[78]

9. ἐγένετο with an infinitive (24:15, 30). The periphrastic use of ἐγένετο, a Septuagintism, is a very common construction in Luke's writings.[79]

10. ἐν τῷ with an infinitive (24:15, 30). This construction, a Septuagintism as well, is a sign of Luke's composition or redaction.[80] This use of the infinitive is frequently coupled with the periphrastic use of ἐγένετο (see above).

11. τοῦ plus the infinitive (24:16, 25, 29). While not exclusively Lukan, this use is comfortably part of his style.[81]

12. ἀποκριθεὶς εἶπεν (24:18). Another Septuagintism, this phrase is one of the features of Luke's style.[82]

13. ἐν ταῖς ἡμέραις ταύταις (24:18). This is a purely Lukan term.[83]

---

[74] Luke 1:26; 1:27; 2:25; 24:13. Hawkins, 44; Jeremias, *Sprache*, 46.

[75] Hawkins, 44.

[76] Fitzmyer, *Luke* (X–XXIV), 1556; *Luke* (I–IX), 111. Cf. Hawkins, 47; Jeremias, *Sprache*, 15.

[77] Fitzmyer, *Luke* (I–IX), 116; Jeremias, *Sprache*, 33–34; Hawkins, 45–46.

[78] Jeremias, *Sprache*, 84.

[79] Hawkins, 37–38; Jeremias, *Sprache*, 25–26.

[80] Jeremias, *Sprache*, 26–29; Hawkins, 40.

[81] Hawkins, 48; Jeremias, *Sprache*, 27–29; Fitzmyer, *Luke* (I–IX), 108.

[82] Fitzmyer, *Luke* (I–IX), 114.

[83] Jeremias, *Sprache*, 55.

14. τὰ περὶ (24:19, 27). This term, while occurring only here in Luke, is more frequent in Acts (10 times), so that it is a good indication of Lukan redaction.[84]

15. ἀνὴρ προφήτης, (24:19). The word ἀνήρ here seems to be little more than a specifying addition, that is, a prophet (a prophet-man?). A similar pattern of the use of ἀνήρ can be seen in Luke 5:8; 11:32; Acts 1:11, 16.[85]

16. σύν (24:21, 24, 29, 33). This preposition is extremely common in Luke (23 times), and relatively uncommon in the other Gospels.[86] In particular, the use of σύν in expressions such as τῶν σὺν ὑμῖν or τοὺς σὺν αὐτοῖς is Lukan.[87]

17. ὀρθριναί (24:22). The use of the word group ὀρθρ- is, as Jeremias notes, almost exclusively Lukan in the New Testament.[88]

18. ἀρξάμενος ἀπὸ (24:27).[89]

19. διανοίγειν (24:31, 32). This verb is almost uniquely Lukan: Luke 2:23; 24:31, 32, 45; Acts 7:56; 16:14; 17:13. The only other use in the New Testament is at Matt 7:34. The concept of the minds of the disciples being opened at the appearances is part of Luke's special emphasis in the Resurrection stories.[90]

20. ἀναστάντες (24:33). As has been noted above, the pleonastic use of ἀνίστημι is a clear sign of Luke's redaction.[91]

---

[84] Fitzmyer, *Luke* (X–XXIV), 1556; Jeremias, *Sprache*, 315; Hawkins, 47–48.

[85] cf. also Acts. 2:14, 22, 29, 37; 3:12, 14; 5:35; 7:2, 26; 8:2; 10:28; 11:20; 13:16, 26, 38; 15:7, 13; 16:9; 17:22; 19:35; 21:28; 22:1, 3; 23:1, 6. Jeremias, *Sprache*, 134–35.

[86] Matthew, 4 times; Mark, 6 times; John 3 times; Acts, 52 times. Cf. Jeremias, *Sprache*, 63.

[87] Jeremias, *Sprache*, 316, 319.

[88] Jeremias, *Sprache*, 284; Wanke, 71.

[89] Jeremias, *Sprache*, 317.

[90] Jeremias, *Sprache*, 318–19.

[91] See chapter 4, p. 189 above. Also Jeremias, *Sprache*, 55; Hawkins, 35–36.

21. ὑπέστρεψαν (24:33). As has been noted above, the use of ὑποστρέφω is Lukan.[92]

22. τοὺς ἕνδεκα (24:33). As noted above, Luke's use of τοὺς ἕνδεκα is part of his own editing style.[93]

23. ὄντως (24:34). Although this term is not used extensively by Luke, Dillon observes that its use at critical junctures in the narrative (here and at 23:47) strongly implies Luke's editorial hand. The use of the word "truly" is meant to sum up and respond to disbelief and incredulity, first at the cross, and now at the Resurrection.[94]

24. ἐν τῇ κλάσει τοῦ ἄρτου (24:35). The term only occurs in Luke-Acts; this occurrence appears to be Luke's special use.[95]

On the basis of this list of stylistic features, which is not exhaustive but rather suggestive of common agreement, it is relatively certain that Luke's compositional efforts have been heavily imposed on the Emmaus narrative; Luke's style seems to be well dispersed throughout the pericope. The evidence of Lukan features is somewhat greater at the beginning and end of the unit of text, but one can conclude that Luke had a strong influence, if not complete compositional control, over the entire narrative unit.[96]

TRADITION

Such a recognition of Luke's pervasive editorial efforts does not eliminate the possibility that there is traditional material in the

---

[92] See p. 402 above. Cf. Jeremias, *Sprache*, 63.

[93] See p. 402 above. Cf. Jeremias, *Sprache*, 311.

[94] Dillon, 99–103. Cf. also Wanke, 44–45. Although note that Jeremias, *Sprache*, 319 classifies it as tradition since it is, in his opinion, a pre-Pauline Easter cry of jubilation.

[95] Jeremias, *Sprache*, 320; Fitzmyer, *Luke* (X–XXIV), 1556.

[96] Taylor, *Passion*, (111) summarized the situation well: "The evidence supplied by the vocabulary, syntax, and style strongly suggests that the evangelist has composed the narrative. The possibility, however, that he has embellished existing tradition is not excluded, although signs of an older source are few." Cf. Wanke, 109–14.

pericope that has been adapted and shaped around Luke's purpose. It appears that Luke worked over whatever traditions were available to him to produce a coherent single narrative.

Schubert identified three areas of text that he felt contained such traditional material: (1) 24:13, in which the Emmaus story is initially framed, (2) 24:15b–16, which relates Jesus' coming to the disciples and their inability to recognize him, and (3) 24:28–31, the meal scene in which Jesus is revealed in the breaking of the bread.[97] The rest, according to Schubert, is Lukan composition. It is difficult to assess Schubert's proposal since he does not document how he distinguished tradition material from Lukan composition. But there is a certain intuitive reasonableness to his proposal: the "traditional material" is that which in the shortest compass tells the story of the Emmaus disciples. Everything else must be expansion and commentary on that core story.

Bailey has a completely different perspective on the differentiation between tradition and composition. For Bailey, the large bulk of the Emmaus narrative must have already been available in written form; otherwise, Luke would not have allowed the tension between 24:11 and 24:24. Furthermore, he understands 24:34 to be, of necessity, traditional as well, since the disciples' reaction in 24:37 is inexplicable if Jesus had already appeared to Peter.[98] Bailey's observations are colored by his rejection of Luke 24:12, a rejection that reduces, but does not eliminate, the tension between 24:1–12 and 24:24. Given the predominance of Lukan style in the passage (as noted above), and the pervasiveness of certain Lukan theological interests in the chapter as a whole,[99] Bailey's argument that Luke took over the

---

[97] Schubert, 174–75.

[98] J. A. Bailey, *The Traditions Common to the Gospels of Luke and John* (Leiden: E. J. Brill, 1963), 88.

[99] Schubert notes: "[W]e concluded that Luke's proof from prophecy theology is the heart of his concern in chapter 24" (176). That "proof from scripture" is central to the Emmaus narrative as well. See especially vv. 25–27 and v. 32. Moreover, the unit further develops the central connection that the risen Christ is the same person as the Jesus who had been crucified. The narrative progression from the mysterious absence of the body to the presence of the living risen Christ is

Emmaus narrative as a pre-formed unit seems untenable. But Bailey's perceived conflict between 24:34 and 24:37 does raise the problem of how to identify traditional material or sources in a thoroughly redacted text.

Given the pervasiveness of the Lukan composition, identifying traditional material that Luke might have used in constructing the narrative is difficult. The existence of discontinuities with other elements in Luke's account or of certain liturgical language might be evidence of embedded tradition. There are three sub-units of text that seem to point beyond the narrative and suggest some kind of traditional source with which Luke may have been working.

1. Verses 22–24 seem to point back to the earlier Lukan account of the empty tomb—and possibly to John's account as well—and thus may represent a unit of traditional material that Luke has used. The question is whether Luke constructed this passage or relied directly on another source or tradition.

The passage presents a short but accurate recapitulation of Luke 24:1–12. The women (unnamed) go to the tomb early (ὀρθριναὶ; cf. ὄρθρου, 24:1). They do not find the body (μὴ εὑροῦσαι τὸ σῶμα; cf. οὐχ εὗρον τὸ σῶμα, 24:3) but instead behold a vision of angels (cf. the appearance of men in dazzling clothes, 24:4). These angels announce that Jesus is alive (cf. "why do you seek the living among the dead?" 24:5). The women return and relate the story, and certain disciples go to the tomb and find the situation as the women reported (cf. Peter's running to the tomb and no mention of the body, 24:12). The order of events is the same, and even the special language of Luke 24:1–12 is echoed at a number of points in the recapitulation (ὀρθριναί, μὴ εὑροῦσαι τὸ σῶμα).[100] As noted above, the entire passage contains

---

first confronted in the Emmaus narrative. (Cf. Dillon, 193–97.) These Lukan interpretations imbedded in the Emmaus narrative give further support that Luke thoroughly shaped and edited the unit.

[100] Wanke, 74.

evidence of Luke's style; it appears, therefore, that Luke has written verses 22–24 to summarize the essence of verses 1–12.[101]

But despite the essential unity of content between the two passages, there are some distinctive differences that must be noted. First, here Luke reports that the women saw "angels," while in verses 1–12 he says that they met men. Luke's tendency to use men in bright clothing to indicate angelic visitors has already been noted, so there is really no conflict between these statements.[102] But perhaps the direct reference to angels in verse 23 should alert us to the possible influence of another source or tradition. Second, here Luke reports that "some of those who were with us" returned to the tomb, while in verses 1–12 he says that only Peter returned. This plural could possibly be a generalizing plural, one that is still based only on the single individual Peter in verses 1–12.[103] But it seems more likely that the plural τινες here refers to a tradition that knows of more than one disciple who went to the tomb. If such is in fact the case, then it appears that the "tradition" is actually John 20:3, in which Peter and the other disciple race to the tomb. Similarly, the basis for the "angels" in verse 23 appears to be John's terminology in 20:12 that two angels met Mary at the tomb.

What can be said about the reference back to the empty tomb story is that the Emmaus narrative records an account, in recapitulation, that is essentially the same as that found in Luke 24:1–12; this determination seems to confirm again the long reading of verse 12. If Luke created this recapitulation himself, as my study of the Emmaus narrative suggests, then he must have had verse 12 to work with. Still, the second telling of the story was corrected with certain "facts" from John that were not included in the first telling. The presence of angels and of more than one visitor to the tomb suggests that Luke created this recapitulation with a knowledge of the fuller narrative of John 20:1–18 in mind.

---

[101] Wanke calls it a "schriftsellerischer Nachtrag" (82).

[102] See p. 394 above.

[103] Luedemann, 141.

2. Verses 28–31 have the ring, in some measure, of a eucharistic meal, which suggests the possible use of an independent tradition. Jeremias notes within the textual unit of 24:28–31 the two most significant instances of "traditional material" in the Emmaus narrative. He cites the conjunction of μεῖνον μεθ' ἡμῶν and μεῖναι σὺν αὐτοῖς in verse 29 as an indication that Luke used tradition.[104] And, more importantly, he identifies the blessing of the bread, λαβὼν τὸν ἄρτον εὐλόγησεν καὶ κλάσας ἐπεδίδου αὐτοῖς, in verse 30, as unmistakably based on the Eucharist.[105]

But is verse 30 really eucharistic? While breaking the bread and blessing it can be likened to the Last Supper (Luke 22:19–20), there are actually more similarities to the feeding of the five thousand (Lk 9:13–17): (a) the blessing over the bread is εὐλόγησεν, not εὐχαριστέω; (b) the verb to give is in the imperfect tense, not perfect; and (c) there is no wine as part of the meal. Moreover, the setting of the meal at Emmaus has other ties to the feeding of the five thousand: in both, the time of day is late, that is, the day "reclined" (κλίνειν); in both, Jesus reclines κατακλίνειν vs. ἀναπίπτω in the Last Supper).[106] It appears that Luke's Emmaus narrative has echoes of the feeding of the five thousand, not the Last Supper! But, on the other hand, the feeding of the five thousand itself may anticipate the Last Supper. And this breaking of the bread in the Emmaus narrative seems to anticipate the (eucharistic) meals of the early church in Acts. So while echoing and anticipating a eucharistic meal, it appears that verse 30 is less an example of tradition than another example of Luke's intertextual linkages.

But perhaps behind the Emmaus narrative is a tradition of a post-Resurrection meal, one that is closer to the miraculous feeding than to the Eucharist. Some support for this might be found in the post-

---

[104] Jeremias, *Sprache*, 318, 63.

[105] Jeremias, *Sprache*, 318. See also Fitzmyer, *Luke* (X–XXIV), 1559. Thus, the conclusion to the episode, expressed in terms of the meal, "how he had been made known in the breaking of the bread" (24:35), establishes the "breaking of the bread" as the mark of the gathered church (cf. Acts 2:42), a meal that is understood to be the Eucharist.

[106] Dillon, 149–50.

Resurrection meal in John 21. In John 21, the risen Jesus, after helping Peter and other disciples catch a large group of fish, shares with them a meal of bread and roasted fish. While it is tempting to try to draw parallels between the John 21 account and Luke,[107] that account in its present form provides little basis for any organic link. There is virtually no point of commonality other than the fact that both passages record a post-Resurrection meal. In John 21 the emphasis is on the fish, not on the bread. And Jesus does not speak any words of blessing over the food, nor does he utter any words that might relate to Luke 24:30.[108] Moreover, Jesus is not revealed in the meal; he is already known by the miraculous catch.

There is some evidence, then, that verse 30 is built upon a tradition of Jesus at the miraculous feeding. But it is just as possible that Luke, as in other places in the Resurrection narratives, deliberately created an intertextual echo to the miraculous feeding in order to amplify the meaning of the passage.

3. Verse 34 points to an event that has not been related within the narrative world of Luke and may thus be evidence of a tradition that is embedded in the text. The announcement to the disciples who have just returned from Emmaus that the risen Jesus has been seen by Peter seems to take the punch out of the entire Emmaus narrative. Instead of building up to the announcement of Jesus' meal with them, this announcement becomes almost anti-climactic after word of Jesus' appearance to Peter. This anti-climax, together with the conflict noted by Bailey between verse 34 and the disciples' reaction in verse 37, suggests that verse 34 was inserted into Luke's narrative at some point late in the composition. The relationship with 1 Cor 15:5 adds further sup-

---

[107] As Dillon does (150–52), arguing that John 21 presents a meal patterned closely on the miracle story of the feeding of the five thousand (the miraculous catch, with its emphasis on the size of the catch, is in his mind an unmistakeable allusion to the miracle of multiplication in John 6). Thus, at the very least, Dillon argues for a tradition of post-Resurrection meals that are based largely on the model of the miraculous feeding.

[108] It is not called, for instance, "breaking bread." The meal is a breakfast or a midday meal, not a supper.

port that this is an early tradition that was added to Luke's narrative after it was already shaped.[109] Luedemann suggests that Luke added here a Jerusalem perspective in order to correct the Emmaus narrative: Peter was the first to see Jesus, even if that story is not related in Luke.[110] Since Peter is not said to have left Jerusalem, the implication indeed seems to be that Jesus appears to Peter in Jerusalem, not in Galilee. But it hardly seems to function as a clear corrective to the Emmaus story. Rather, the tensive relationship of verse 34 in the context of verses 13–35 argues for its origination as an independent tradition.

SUMMARY

Close analysis of the Emmaus narrative has shown it to be Luke's composition. In constructing this episode, Luke used material from his previous narratives, as well as some traditions. Most particularly, the reference to the vision by Peter in verse 34 appears to stem from a tradition which was inserted into the Emmaus narrative. The other possible cases of tradition might be more properly called intertextual references. The eucharistic language in verse 30 is probably Luke's way of recalling previous feeding episodes, especially the feeding of the five thousand. And the empty tomb account in verses 22–24 seems to be Luke's own recapitulation of the story from verses 1–12. I have argued previously that verses 1–12 are based in large part on John 20:1–18. In this recapitulation, Luke seems still to have been relying on the story in John 20; certain elements of the story have been modified in accordance with John, not with the previous account in Luke 24:1–12.

---

[109] Fuller, 112–13.
[110] Luedemann, 143.

Appearance Before The Disciples. Luke 24:36-43.

³⁶ Ταῦτα δὲ αὐτῶν λαλούντων αὐτὸς ἔστη ἐν μέσῳ αὐτῶν καὶ λέγει αὐτοῖς, Εἰρήνη ὑμῖν. ³⁷ πτοηθέντες δὲ καὶ ἔμφοβοι γενόμενοι ἐδόκουν πνεῦμα θεωρεῖν. ³⁸ καὶ εἶπεν αὐτοῖς, Τί τεταραγμένοι ἐστέ, καὶ διὰ τί διαλογισμοὶ ἀναβαίνουσιν ἐν τῇ καρδίᾳ ὑμῶν; ³⁹ ἴδετε τὰς χεῖράς μου καὶ τοὺς πόδας μου ὅτι ἐγώ εἰμι αὐτός· ψηλαφήσατέ με καὶ ἴδετε, ὅτι πνεῦμα σάρκα καὶ ὀστέα οὐκ ἔχει καθὼς ἐμὲ θεωρεῖτε ἔχοντα. ⁴⁰ *καὶ τοῦτο εἰπὼν ἔδειξεν αὐτοῖς τὰς χεῖρας καὶ* τοὺς πόδας. ⁴¹ ἔτι δὲ ἀπιστούντων αὐτῶν ἀπὸ τῆς χαρᾶς καὶ θαυμαζόντων εἶπεν αὐτοῖς, Ἔχετέ τι βρώσιμον ἐνθάδε; ⁴² οἱ δὲ ἐπέδωκαν αὐτῷ ἰχθύος ὀπτοῦ μέρος· ⁴³ καὶ λαβὼν ἐνώπιον αὐτῶν ἔφαγεν.

NOTE: In this passage, as in the previous one, indications of Lukan style are signified by underlining.

There are no Markan or Matthean accounts that can serve as points of contact with this appearance story in Luke. Unlike in Matthew and Mark, in which are reported predictions that Jesus would appear to his disciples in Galilee, Luke reports that appearance took place in Jerusalem. In terms of the basic structure of the story, Luke has some significant elements of similarity with John's account. These similarities occur in the same order:

1. Jesus' appearance to the disciples takes place in Jerusalem, not Galilee.
2. Jesus appears suddenly in the disciples' midst.
3. Jesus shows his body (hands and side/feet).
4. The disciples react with joy to the appearance.

These features, in themselves, provide a strong connection between Luke and John. But as in Luke 24:12, there are textual variants that significantly affect the degree to which one finds close verbal similarities between the two. In chapter 4, it was argued that the longer readings of 24:36 and 24:40 should be considered original, in part because the addition of the non-Western text does not substantially increase the anti-docetic nature of the passage (which is already present), and in part because the variants' quite Johannine style would have met with suspicion of tampering by those in the early church who were opposed to the Fourth Gospel.[111] Both longer texts yield readings that are verbatim, or nearly verbatim, echoes of John:

5. Immediately after appearing to the disciples, Jesus speaks to them with identical words: καὶ λέγει αὐτοῖς, Εἰρήνη ὑμῖν.[112]

6. At the appearance, Jesus presents his body as a verification that he indeed is risen. The wording is remarkably similar to καὶ τοῦτο εἰπὼν ἔδειξεν τὰς χεῖρας καὶ τὴν πλευρὰν αὐτοῖς (John 20:20). The first part of the sentence in the two Gospels is essentially the same, only the placement of αὐτοῖς varies. The conclusion of the sentence, however, containes significant difference: the other part of the body shown to the disciples is Jesus' feet (πόδας) in Luke, as opposed to Jesus' side (πλευρὰν) in John.

There are two additional similarities in the content of these passages that might further suggest a literary relationship, although along with these points of similarity are marked differences:

7. In both Gospels, the disciples are said to be in fear, but the fear is quite different. John has the disciples meeting behind closed doors for fear of the Jews. Luke, on the other hand, records fear after the disciples meet the risen Christ, thinking him a spirit.[113] That is what we would expect if Luke had used John; Luke would have eliminated the feature of the "fear of the Jews." Perhaps the reference to the disciples' fear at meeting Jesus is a post-redactional remnant of this Johannine story, although it is hard to say.

---

[111] See chapter 4 p. 209 and 212 above.

[112] It is striking that both use the historical present: λέγει. The peace blessing is particularly Johannine-sounding, occurring in precisely this form three times in John 20 and with variations on the statement, twice in John 14:27 and once in 16:33.

[113] Anton Dauer, *Johannes und Lukas: Untersuchungen zu den johanneisch-lukanischen Parallelperikopen Joh 4,46-54/Lk 7,1-10 — Joh 12,1-8/Lk 7,36-50; 10,38-42 — Joh 20,19-29/Lk 24,36-49* (Würzburg: Echter Verlag, 1984), 208, 217.

8. In both Gospels, the disciple(s) exhibit disbelief. John records disbelief in the parallel appearance of Jesus to Thomas (John 20:25, 27), who will not believe until he sees the wounds of Jesus' crucifixion. Luke presents disbelief in two contexts. At the initial appearance of Jesus, the disciples are troubled and they question (τεταρααγμένοι ... διαλογισμοὶ ἀναβαίνουσιν ἐν τῇ καρδίᾳ ὑμῶν). And after Jesus shows his hands and feet, the disciples do not believe for joy (i.e., they are so overjoyed they can not believe it is really happening?).

SIGNS OF JOHANNINE STYLE

The passages that are strikingly similar in Luke and John show strong indications of Johannine style. The entire clause in Luke 24:36b is Johannine in style. The use of the historical present, in this case λέγει, is a very common element of John's narrative style.[114] In addition, the salutation εἰρήνη ὑμῖν occurs elsewhere in John in this exact form, as well as in other variations, so that it is comfortably Johannine.[115] Precisely because the wording is almost self-evidently Johannine, many would see v. 36b as a textual corruption. But if one is open to the possibility of Luke's having drawn on John as a source, the similarities are understandable. Rather than try to explain with great difficulty how John might have used Luke, when simultaneously trying to explain how Luke had Johannine language, it is simpler and neater to simply see Luke relying on John.

It is more difficult to assess the style of verse 36a. The first part of the clause, ταῦτα δὲ αὐτῶν λαλούντων, is comfortably Lukan. The use of the genitive absolute and the verb λαλέω fits well with Luke's style, although neither use is unique to Luke.[116] The second half of the

---

[114] Nigel Turner, *Style*, vol. 4 of *A Grammar of New Testament Greek*, ed. James Hope Moulton (Edinburgh: T&T Clark, 1976), 70. The historic present occurs in John 164 times, more even than Mark (where it occurs 151 times).

[115] Also John 20:21, 26; cf. also John 14:27; Barnabas Lindars, "The Composition of John xx," *NTS* 7 (1960–61): 145.

[116] Dauer, *Johannes und Lukas*, 260.

clause, however, is more problematic. Dauer argues that it is Lukan, based on the use of ἐν μέσῳ and the use of ἵστημι.[117] Such use is comfortably Lukan, to be sure, but John's wording, ἔστη εἰς τὸ μέσον, is likewise comfortably Johannine.[118] In particular, John uses the same term at John 20:26 in the story about Thomas, which might well indicate that the term came from John's own hand. One could easily see either evangelist's having derived the text from the other or from a common source. The clause certainly does not have strikingly Lukan features, and Luke could well have drawn on John's form, making stylistic changes.[119]

Similarly in verse 40, certain features of the language tend toward John's use. The opening clause, καὶ τοῦτο εἰπὼν ἔδειξεν [αὐτοῖς] τὰς χεῖρας..., begins with a Johannine phrase. While Dauer argues that this construction is a sign of Lukan redaction,[120] pointing out six instances in Luke-Acts of such a pattern (ταῦτα or τοῦτο plus the participle for εἶπεν [εἰπών or εἰποῦσα] followed by a finite verb that resumes the narrative), it is actually far more common in John. The construction occurs ten times in John, excluding John chapter 21, and it occurs twice more in John 21.[121] One finds a similar case with δείκνυμι, which Dauer cites as a possible sign of Lukan redaction,[122]

---

[117] Dauer, *Johannes und Lukas*, p. 261.

[118] ἵστημι is very common in John, and μέσος, though not as common, occurs in other Johannine situations. Compare especially John 1:26, μέσος ὑμῶν ἔστηκεν ὃν ὑμεῖς οὐκ οἴδατε, in which both ἵστημι and μέσος are used together.

[119] Fitzmyer, *Luke* (X–XXIV), "See John 20:19 which may preserve the original formulation since *en meso auton* is used elsewhere by Luke" (1575).

[120] Dauer, *Johannes und Lukas*, 269. Dauer argues that v. 40, contrary to the rest of vv. 37–40, is Luke's own creation; "Manche Beobachtungen sprechen dafür, daß Lukas ihn delbst gebildet hat" (268); and "Rückblickend läßt sich zu vv. 37–40 mit *Leaney* sagen: Lukas folgt hier — außer in v. 40, seiner eigenen Bildung — im wesentlichen dem Bericht siner Quelle." (269–70). Contra Dauer, it appears that precisely at v. 40 Luke was relying even more strongly on his source (John), although there is evidence that he followed a source in the construction of the rest of the pericope as well.

[121] John 7:9; 9:6; 11:28; 11:43; 13:21; 18:1, 38; 20:14, 20, 22. And also in John 21:19 (2 times).

[122] Dauer, *Johannes und Lukas*, 269.

despite there being only one instance in Luke of its positive use in preference to a Markan word—and that, an instance that has a Matthean parallel.[123] In contrast, the instances of its use in John are more numerous and are always in very Johannine contexts.[124] Finally, Dauer cites the absence of the personal pronoun in connection with Jesus' hands and feet—yet another feature that is also in agreement with John. Although, as Dauer notes, there are a number of instances where Luke omits the personal pronoun, the same is also true for John.[125] The overall assessment of the verse, which coheres with the bulk of the Resurrection narrative, is that John's account is thoroughly Johannine and shows little sign of using a source.[126] So Luke, verse 40 would appear to be Johannine in style also, not Lukan.

LUKE'S EDITING

While verses 36 and 40 show evidence of Johannine style, there are few indications of non-Lukan tradition elsewhere in this story. Jeremias argues only that traditional (i.e., non-Lukan) material occurs in verse 38, and he cites three instances: καὶ εἶπεν αὐτοῖς, διαλογισμοί, and ἀναβαίνουσιν ἐν τῇ καρδίᾳ.[127] The first of these is arguable, since the occurrence of both καὶ εἶπεν and εἶπεν plus the dative are well attested in Luke.[128] Jeremias' identification of διαλογισμός as non-

---

[123] Luke 20:24 par. Mark 12:15 and Matt 22:19. Luke used δείξατε in preference to Mark's φέρετε, but Matthew has ἐπιδείξατε. Other instances of Luke's use of δείκνυμι are in 4:5; 5:14; 22:12; and 24:20. In Acts the word occurs in 7:3, which is a quote from Genesis 12:1, and in 10:28.

[124] John 2:8; 5:20 (2 times); 10:32; 14:8, 9; 20:20.

[125] Cf. John 11:32, 44; 13:9, 10; and 20:12 with πούς; and 7:30, 44; 13:3; 20:20 with χείρ.

[126] Lindars, 142–47.

[127] Jeremias, *Sprache*, 320.

[128] Jeremias, *Sprache*, 39, argues that Luke always preferred εἶπεν δέ. While εἶπεν δέ is more common in Luke, instances of καὶ εἶπεν are very common. Moreover, many of them occur either in material that is primarily Lukan in origination (2:10; 2:49; 3:14; 4:23), or in passages where Luke has redacted Mark (5:10; 5:27; 8:45; 9:3; 9:48). Luke's ability to use both is perhaps best seen in 8:45 and

Luke Chapter 24 427

Lukan is quite surprising, since, of the entire New Testament, the term and its verbal cognate are most commonly attested in Luke. Moreover, Luke used the term in uniquely Lukan material, in his own modification of Markan material, and when he took Mark's use of the term with little or no modification.[129] Finally, Jeremias claims that the term ἀναβαίνω plus ἐν τῇ καρδίᾳ is non-Lukan, since the Lukan form would be ἐπὶ τὴν καρδίαν, following Acts 7:23. But the use of ἐν τῇ καρδίᾳ or ἐν ταῖς καρδίαις in Luke is very common—both in special Lukan material and in Lukan redaction—particularly, with διαλογίζομαι, which is also found in this passage.[130] The evidence for a pre-Lukan tradition outside of the material common to John (i.e., verses 36, 39, and 40) is not, then, compelling. It appears, rather, that Luke used a source similar to, if not exactly like, John, and composed an appearance scene around it.

46, where Luke has first one then the other and both appear to derive from Luke's editorial hand.

Not only does Jeremias list εἶπεν plus the dative as an indication of non-Lukan or pre-Lukan material, so does Rehkopf (105). As with the previous example, however, Luke does occasionally have εἶπεν with a dative object, even though πρός plus accusative is more frequent. Again, it is helpful to see Luke's ability to use both in close proximity, and in instances where Luke's composition or editing are apparent: Luke 1:19, cf. 1:18; 7:48, cf. 7:50; 9:58, cf. 9:59; 11:2, cf. 11:5. Nonetheless, εἶπεν plus the dative is not common in Luke. But that construction *is* common in John. Might the construction in this section be an element of John's style that has bled over into Luke's own redaction? It seems likely that Luke heard John's style, as well as his words, in this section and left traces of that style in his own composition.

[129] See, for instance, διαλογισμός at Luke 5:22; 6:8; 9:46, 47, all of which show Luke having actively modified Mark with some use of the noun. Similarly, Luke used the verb in making modifications at 3:15; 5:21; 20:14. 3:15 and 5:21–22 are particularly interesting, since in both cases Luke actively worked with his material, and in both cases the "being troubled" is completed with the prepositional phrase ἐν ταῖς καρδίαις. Dauer, *Johannes und Lukas*, 264 notes also that the term διὰ τί is not uncommon in Luke (4 times in Luke, 1 time in Acts). And he questions whether διαλογισμός is a pre-Lukan word, noting Luke's use especially of the noun form.

[130] Cf. Luke 1:66; 2:19; 2:51; 3:15; 5:22; 21:14; Acts 5:4. Interestingly, Taylor cites this as a sign of characteristic Lukan style (*Passion*, 112).

Not only are non-Lukan features absent from this account, except in those passages that are similar to John, there is evidence that Luke carefully formed it as part of his unfolding theological program. The evidence of Luke's composition is extensive. In particular, certain words in the account tend to be predominately or exclusively Lukan: πτόεσθαι, ἐνθάδε, ἔμφοβος, ἐνώπιον, and ἐπιδίδωμι.[131] In addition, some grammatical usages are characteristically Lukan: δοκέω with the infinitive is primarily found in Luke (5 times in Luke, 2 times in Acts, 1 time in Mark, 2 times in John); ἀπιστέω is clearly Lukan (only in Luke in the Gospels), and it is used together with θαυμάζω twice in Luke;[132] and εἰμί plus a perfect participle (ἐστὲ τεταραγμένοι) is frequent in Luke-Acts but unusual in the other Gospels (24 times in Luke, 21 times in Acts, 10 times Matthew, 6 in Mark).[133] These Lukan features, scattered throughout the account except in the remarkably Johannine sections (verses 36, 39, 40), suggest that Luke was fitting his source material into a thoroughly Lukan composition.[134]

There is some question about the Lukan origination of verse 39. Dauer claims that none of it is Lukan, while also arguing that all of verse 40 is from Luke's hand. This conclusion seems to be exactly backward. I already argued above that verse 40 seems to be very Johannine in style; what about verse 39? Part of the problem is that verse 39 and verse 40 share much of the same language. The description of the hands and feet and the presenting of them to the disciples suggest that the two verses are somehow linked. Was one developed in order to explain or elucidate the other? Dauer makes much of the fact

---

[131] Jeremias, *Sprache*, 320–21; Taylor, *Passion*, 114; Dauer, *Johannes und Lukas*, 262–75.

[132] Jeremias, *Sprache*, 321.

[133] Jeremias, *Sprache*, 24.

[134] Bailey argues that verses 41–43 show evidence of being pre-Lukan because Jesus eats but the disciples do not. This poses a conflict, he asserts, with Acts 10:41 (that the witnesses to the Resurrection had eaten and drunk with Jesus) and thus indicates a pre-Lukan source (p. 89). While it is certainly possible that Luke had other sources, one of which contained this meal, one wonders if this disparity is real. Is not the natural conclusion of the appearance here in 24:26–43 that the disciples did eat with Jesus?

Luke Chapter 24

that a number of words in verse 39 are rarely used in Luke: ψηλαφήσατε, ὀστέα, and σάρκα.[135] Dauer considers such an emphasis on flesh and bones by Luke to be "wenig warscheinlich"; he bases that judgment, it would seem, on the unusual language and imagery, which he concludes is "jüdischer Anschaung."[136] But these words are rare in the other Gospels as well, and their use here seems to be directly related to the concern for verification that Jesus is really resurrected. In addition, as has been previously argued, the references to flesh and bones and to touching the body cohere particularly well with Luke's emphasis on the physicality of the Resurrection.[137] Luke 24:39 is, in my judgment, Luke's composition that is based on the Johannine material in 24:40.

IGNATIUS' TESTIMONY

If in fact, in 24:36–43, Luke composed his own narrative around Johannine-sounding material, how likely is it that he used John, as opposed to a pre-Johannine tradition? It has especially been argued that in this pericope, Luke and John were drawing on an independent tradition. A passage in Ignatius' letter to the Smyrneans has been adduced in support of this view. At Ignatius Smyr 3:1–3:

Ἐγὼ γὰρ καὶ μετὰ τὴν ἀνάστασιν ἐν σαρκὶ αὐτὸν οἶδα· καὶ ὅτε πρὸς τοὺς περὶ Πέτρον ἦλθεν ἔφη αὐτοῖς· Λάβετε, ψηλαφήσατέ με καὶ ἴδετε ὅτι οὐκ εἰμὶ δαιμόνιον ἀσώματον. καὶ εὐθὺς αὐτοῦ ἥψαντο καὶ ἐπίστευσαν κραθέντες τῇ σαρκὶ αὐτοῦ καὶ τῷ αἵματι. διὰ τοῦτο καὶ θανάτου κατεφρόνησαν ηὑρέθησαν δὲ ὑπὲρ θάνατον. Μετὰ δὲ τὴν ἀνάστασιν συνέφαγεν αὐτοῖς καὶ συνέπιεν ὡς σαρκικός, καίπερ πνευματικῶς ἡνωμένος τῷ πατρί.[138]

---

[135] Dauer, *Johannes und Lukas,* 267–68.
[136] Dauer, *Johannes und Lukas,* 267–68.
[137] See above p. 390, n. 19; Talbert, p. 30.
[138] Ignatius, "Ignatius to the Smyrnaeans" in *Apostolic Fathers* (Cambridge: Harvard University Press, 1949), 254. "For I know and believe that also after the Resurrection he was truly in the flesh. And when he came to those around Peter, he

The passage has many strong echoes of Luke's account, as a number of features suggest: the post-Resurrection appearance to the disciples (those around Peter), the invitation to touch, and the meal with the disciples. Koester has argued that Ignatius was drawing on an independent tradition, not Luke.[139] If Ignatius was quoting from an independent tradition or source, that source could well account for the common material in Luke and John. But others have argued, more convincingly, that Ignatius was quoting freely the Luke passage, with some rhetorical modifications.[140]

There are three primary arguments for an independent tradition: (1) the actual wording of the passage bears little direct similarity to Luke, (2) there is no other evidence that Ignatius knew or used Luke, and (3) the term "a bodiless demon" is foreign to Luke, and represents a different stream of thought.[141] In assessing the case for an independent tradition, it seems that the major crux is the wording οὐκ εἰμὶ δαιμόνιον ἀσώματον, which not only is not found in Luke, but also was found by various church fathers in other, now lost, sources.[142] But is this term completely foreign to Luke? It is possible that it represents

---

said to them, 'Take, touch me, and see that I am not a disembodied daimon (spirit).' And immediately they touched him, and they believed, being mixed both with his flesh and blood. Because of this, they despised death and were found to be above death. And after the Resurrection he also ate and drank with them as an enfleshed being, although in spirit he was united with the Father" (My translation).

[139] Helmut Koester, *Synoptische Überlieferung bei den Apostolischen Vätern* (Berlin: Akademie-Verlag, 1975), 45-56.

[140] P. Vielhauer, "Jewish Christian Gospels" in *New Testament Apocrypha* (Philadelphia: Westminster, 1963), 129–30; Frans Neirynck, "Lc 24, 36–43. Un récit lucanien," in *A Cause de l' Évangile* (Cerf: Publications de Saint-André, 1985), 672–77.

[141] Cf. also William Schroedel, *Ignatius of Antioch* (Philadelphia: Fortress Press, 1985), 226–27.

[142] Origin, *De Principiis*, preface to book 1, said it was in the *Doctrina Petri*; Jerome, *Commentary on Isaiah*, said it came from the Gospel of the Hebrews; Eusebius, *Ecclesiastical History*, 3.36.11, claims not to know where it came from.

Luke Chapter 24 431

an early textual variant of Luke.¹⁴³ But it is far more likely that Ignatius was simply quoting loosely from Luke. The evidence of Ignatius' use of scripture is not clear, because there are few direct citations.¹⁴⁴ Maurer, in his study of Ignatius' relationship to the Fourth Gospel, shows a clear affinity between them, and argues convincingly that Ignatius freely drew on John in his writings.¹⁴⁵ Given this pattern of Ignatius' use of John, then, it is very likely that he also drew on Luke for his reference.¹⁴⁶

The conjunction of such features as the post-Resurrection appearance to the disciples, the reference to touching Jesus, and the meal suggests Luke 24:36–43 as the source behind the Smyr. 3:1–3 passage in Ignatius. Moreover, the troubling reference to δαιμόνιον

---

¹⁴³ William Petersen, "What Text Can New Testament Textual Criticism Ultimately Reach?" in *New Testament Textual Criticism, Exegesis and Church History* (Kampen: Kok Pharos, 1994), 144–45, suggests that the existence of this terminology in Ignatius, attested as well by Jerome and Origen, represents the earliest form the text of Luke. That is, the word πνεῦμα in Luke 24:40 may have originally read, at least in some manuscripts, δαιμόνιον ἀσώματον. In support of this, Petersen also points to the known variant in Lk 24:37, where D (and Tertullian) attest to the reading φάντασμα instead of πνεῦμα.

¹⁴⁴ Schroedel notes that a strong case for Ignatius' use of the New Testament can only be made for Matthew and Paul (9–10). The relationship with other writings (John, 1 John, 1 Clement) is explained by him as only traditional material. Perhaps, though, Ignatius made free references with little concern for exact quotation.

¹⁴⁵ Christian Maurer, *Ignatius von Antiochen und das Johannesevangelium* (Zürich: Zwingli-Verlag, 1949). An important element in his argument is the evidence he gives that other Apostolic Fathers used the same freedom in drawing on the New Testament. He shows (16–21) that in I Clement, and particularly in Polycarp, references from the New Testament are often loosely quoted and indeed often show conflations of more than one verse. Furthermore, he shows that Ignatius' own comments in Eph 18:1 clearly echo Paul's in 1 Cor 1:18–31, but exact word correspondence is difficult to precisely identify. As a result, Maurer shows convincingly that Ignatius has relied on John in Phld 7:1 (drawing on John 3:8 and possibly 8:14), 9:1 (drawing on John 10 and 14), and Rom 7:3 and Smyr 7:1 (drawing on John 6). Based on this pattern, Ignatius' variation from Luke in Smyr 3:1 is not at all unusual.

¹⁴⁶ So also Robert Grant, "Scripture and Tradition in St. Ignatius of Antioch," *CBQ* 25 (1963): 327; cf. also Neirynck, "Lc 24, 36–43. Un Récit Lucanien," 672–77.

ἀσώματον can be understood as having been based on Luke's text. Luke himself indicated that Jesus' appearance was misunderstood as a spirit (v. 37) and that the touching of the body was meant to demonstrate that he was truly flesh and bones, not spirit.[147] The addition of the word ἀσώματον to πνεῦμα in verse 37 or verse 39 would only serve to clarify Luke's point, and Ignatius' word δαιμόνιον perhaps better represents common Greek usage for dead spirits. But more tellingly, Ignatius' own polemical purpose in Smyrneaens—to counteract the docetists—would have led him to modify and strengthen Luke's language. That this is the case is clear when one considers the framework of Ignatius' argument. At Smyr 2:1, Ignatius laid out the polemical argument against the docetists:

> "For he suffered all things for our sakes that we might be saved. And he truly suffered, as he also truly raised himself, not as some unbelievers say, that he only appeared to suffer, since they are the ones who only appear to exist. And just as they think, so it shall happen to them; they shall be bodiless and phantasmal (ἀσωμάτοις καὶ δαιμονικοῖς)."[148]

It appears that Ignatius linked Luke's verse with his own rather pointed reference to the docetists. The phrase δαιμόνιον ἀσώματον seems to be a polemical interpretation, not an indication of an independent tradition.

Indeed, Ignatius' use of Luke and John is suggestive for understanding Luke's use of the Fourth Gospel. Ignatius's use was rarely a verbatim quotation or reliance. Instead, the author shows that he is aware of the traditions, with language which echoes the original text, but reinterpreted and recast for a new rhetorical situation. Ignatius seems to have known John and Luke but not, perhaps, to have considered them "authoritative." In the same way, it is not difficult to see

---

[147] As the textual variant φάντασμα also understood the main thrust to be.

[148] *Ignatius to the Smyrnaeans* 2. In Apostolic Fathers, 252–54, my translation.

that Luke could have known John and, while influenced by the Fourth Gospel's version of events, not considered it authoritative.

SUMMARY

What is seen, then, in Luke 24:36–43 is a Lukan story that is built around two striking references to John. It appears that the Johannine account served as the core of Luke's version. From the Fourth Gospel, Luke derived a basic structure and the remarkable features of the appearance story: Jesus' appearing in the disciples' midst, his giving a blessing of peace, and his showing his body as a demonstration that he was indeed risen from the dead. Around those basic elements, Luke then constructed his own version.

While Luke knew and generally approved of John's account, he also operated with his own theological program in which several motifs continually assert themselves: (1) an emphasis on the disciples' being witnesses to the bodily Resurrection, a preparation for the subsequent kerygma of the church; (2) an anti-docetic interest, in which the body of Jesus is continually emphasized, (3) the tendency to present post-Resurrection meals, perhaps as part of the anti-docetic interest, but perhaps also as an anticipation of the eucharistic and communitarian importance that meals would have in the early church, and (4) the importance that proof from scripture played in understanding the significance of the Resurrection. These motifs are found in varying degrees in the empty tomb story; the Emmaus narrative; the early chapters of Acts; and in particularly close interconnection, in this appearance to the disciples.

Thus, around the core of John's account of Jesus' appearance to the disciples, Luke first added verses 37 and 38 as an interpretation of the disciples' response. The initial disbelief and the thought that this was a ghost are important narrative elements that underline the significance of both the physical features of the appearance (touching, eating) and Jesus' proof from scripture, which follows this scene.

Indeed, it appears that the disciples' touching of Jesus's body and Jesus' own eating only serve to set the stage for Jesus' enabling the disciples to understand the Resurrection on the basis of the law and the prophets in verses 44–49. Disbelief when Jesus appears and disbelief even after touching him (v. 41) seem to drive the story forward to the proof from scripture.[149]

Next, Luke added verse 39 as both a narrative anticipation and an interpretation of verse 40. In the Johannine account, in contrast, Jesus' presentation of his hands and side is quite surprising. Why does Jesus show them his hands and side? Viewed in the context of the subsequent Thomas story, the presentation of hands and side becomes more understandable, but it is nevertheless abrupt and enigmatic. Luke's addition of verse 39 interprets Jesus' presentation of his body in a way that emphasizes the anti-docetic interest.

Finally, Luke added verses 41 and 42, in which Jesus eats in the disciples' presence. This last feature echoes the earlier post-Resurrection meal at 24:29–31, an account that is certainly a Lukan construction. Jesus' eating, again, emphasizes the physicality of the risen Jesus.

In sum, then, a quite reasonable case can be made that Luke used John's basic appearance story and interwove a number of recurring motifs from the post-Resurrection narratives. This passage appears to be an excellent example of Luke's redaction of the Gospel of John.

LUKE'S GREAT COMMISSION. LUKE 24:44–49

⁴⁴ Εἶπεν δὲ πρὸς αὐτούς, Οὗτοι οἱ λόγοι μου οὓς ἐλάλησα πρὸς ὑμᾶς ἔτι ὢν σὺν ὑμῖν, ὅτι δεῖ πληρωθῆναι πάντα τὰ γεγραμμένα ἐν τῷ νόμῳ Μωϋσέως καὶ τοῖς προφήταις καὶ ψαλμοῖς περὶ ἐμοῦ. ⁴⁵ τότε διήνοιξεν αὐτῶν τὸν νοῦν τοῦ συνιέναι τὰς γραφάς. ⁴⁶ καὶ εἶπεν αὐτοῖς ὅτι Οὕτως γέγραπται παθεῖν τὸν Χριστὸν καὶ ἀναστῆναι ἐκ νεκρῶν τῇ τρίτῃ ἡμέρᾳ, ⁴⁷ καὶ κηρυχθῆναι ἐπὶ τῷ ὀνόματι αὐτοῦ μετάνοιαν καὶ ἄφεσιν ἁμαρτιῶν εἰς πάντα τὰ ἔθνη-- ἀρξάμενοι ἀπὸ Ἰερουσαλήμ· ⁴⁸ ὑμεῖς

---
[149] Schubert, 176–77.

μάρτυρες τούτων. ⁴⁹ καὶ ἰδοὺ ἐγὼ ἀποστέλλω <u>τὴν ἐπαγγελίαν τοῦ πατρός μου</u> ἐφ᾽ ὑμᾶς· ὑμεῖς δὲ <u>καθίσατε</u> ἐν τῇ πόλει <u>ἕως οὗ</u> ἐνδύσησθε ἐξ ὕψους δύναμιν.

NOTE: In this passage, as in the previous ones, indications of Lukan style are signified by underlining.

At Luke 24:44, the narrative moves into a unique pattern. While Matthew also relates a commissioning scene in which Jesus gives final admonitions, there seems to be no relationship between the two Gospels in this pericope.[150] The scene in Luke reiterates a number of themes that Luke has already developed: (1) the proof from Scripture motif, which has been woven throughout the final scenes of Luke, (2) the central role that Jerusalem plays in the unfolding of the church's actions, (3) the role of the disciples as witnesses to the Resurrection, and (4) the anticipation, still future, of the reception of the Holy Spirit. These are consistent Lukan themes, and at least initially indicate that the pericope is Luke's own composition.

The style is thoroughly Lukan.[151] Evidence of Luke's redaction can be seen in the long list of Lukan traits: εἶπεν and ἐλάλησα with πρός, the use of σύν, πάντα τὰ γεγραμμένα, ἐν τῷ νόμῳ Μωυσέως, the use of the διάνοιγειν, the articular infinitive with τοῦ, παθεῖν, μετάνοιαν εἰς ἄφεσιν ἁμαρτιῶν, ἀρξάμενοι ἀπὸ Ἰερουσαλήμ, μάρτυρες, τὴν ἐπαγγελίαν τοῦ πατρός μου, καθίσατε, ἕως οὗ.[152] In addition to this list, one should add δεῖ πληρωθῆναι.[153] Jeremias lists

---

[150] Although Goulder, *Luke* (792) tries to find points of similarity, aside from the fact that both gospels relate a final scene with Jesus, and that in both scenes Jesus declares the scope of the message goes as far as πάντα τὰ ἔθνη (Luke 24:47, Matt 28:19), there are no points of contact.

[151] Dauer, *Johannes und Lukas*, 275.

[152] Jeremias, *Sprache*, 321–22; Fitzmyer, *Luke* (X–XXIV), 1580–81.

[153] Jeremias, *Sprache* (321) argues that this is from tradition. But δεῖ is used by Luke more than other New Testament writers. Moreover, it fits with Luke's emphasis on the fulfillment of scripture. See Dillon, 205.

some items that he believes point to tradition, not Lukan composition, but they are scattered and not definitive.[154] There are no points of contact with John. The entire passage shows signs of active Lukan composition.

THE ASCENSION. LUKE 24:50-53.

⁵⁰ Ἐξήγαγεν δὲ αὐτοὺς ἕως πρὸς Βηθανίαν, καὶ ἐπάρας τὰς χεῖρας αὐτοῦ εὐλόγησεν αὐτούς. ⁵¹ καὶ ἐγένετο ἐν τῷ εὐλογεῖν αὐτὸν αὐτοὺς διέστη ἀπ' αὐτῶν καὶ ἀνεφέρετο εἰς τὸν οὐρανόν. ⁵² καὶ αὐτοὶ προσκυνήσαντες αὐτὸν ὑπέστρεψαν εἰς Ἰερουσαλὴμ μετὰ χαρᾶς μεγάλης, ⁵³ καὶ ἦσαν διὰ παντὸς ἐν τῷ ἱερῷ εὐλογοῦντες τὸν θεόν.

NOTE: In this passage, as in the previous ones, indications of Lukan style are signified by underlining.

The concluding story of Luke's post-Resurrection narratives is a grand finale of sorts: Jesus leaves his disciples by ascending to heaven, in response to which the disciples worship and praise God at the temple. This conclusion has the feel of a constructed literary unit; indeed, the language in this short unit is extensively Lukan. The following list of secure Lukan traits from this story includes many that have already been seen in the analyses above: ὑποστρέφω, ἐπαίρω, καὶ αὐτοί, Ἰερουσαλήμ, ἐξάγω, ἐγένετο with an infinitive, διΐστημι, χαρὰ μεγάλη, εὐλογοῦντες τὸν θεόν, διὰ παντός.[155] I agree with Dillon's assessment that "the case for pre-Lucan tradition is too meagre to argue successfully."[156] In other words, Luke constructed his own liter-

---

[154] So, for instance, εἰς ἄφεσιν ἁμαρτιῶν in 24:47 is listed as tradition, yet the longer phrase μετάνοιαν εἰς ἄφεσιν ἁμαρτιῶν is considered redaction. It seems that Jeremias is marking out formulas that he thinks sound traditional. See also ὑμεῖς μάρτυρες τούτων (Luke 24:48) and τοῦ πατρός μου (Luke 24:49). In each of these instances, Jeremias also lists the key member as a sign of Luke's redaction.

[155] Hawkins, 37–51; Jeremias, *Sprache*, 323, 63; Taylor, *Passion*, 115.

[156] Dillon, 220.

ary conclusion, drawing on whatever non-recoverable traditions that might have been available to him.

The Ascension narrative in Luke ends in an open manner, anticipating the subsequent narrative in Acts. Thus the reactions of the disciples to the Ascension, namely, worship, remaining in Jerusalem, and blessing God in the temple, are hallmarks of the early church's activity in Acts.[157] The conclusion to Luke, then, is a brief prospectus on the second book.

It is interesting that only Luke records an Ascension narrative. There seems to be an awareness of the Ascension in John 20:17: "Do not hold on to me, because I have not yet ascended to the Father. But go to my brothers and say to them, 'I am ascending to my Father and your Father, to my God and your God.'" But this awareness is not translated into a narrative account, as in Luke. Such a slight connection does not offer a sufficient basis to suggest that Luke was aware of John's comment, let alone that he built a narrative based on it. But even here, the unique relationship between Luke and John is suggestive.

What one must conclude, however, is that Luke's Ascension narrative is unique among the Gospels, and it shows strong evidence of having been composed by the Third Evangelist.

CONCLUSIONS

Once again, I have found that Luke used a mixture of sources. In the opening pericope, he followed Mark, but with strong influence from the Fourth Gospel. After the empty tomb story (Luke 24:12), of course, there is no longer a Markan narrative to follow. From that point Luke composed units of material, many of which show some evidence of influence from John. The Johannine influence is particularly important in the appearance narrative (Luke 24:36–43), but also present in the Emmaus narrative (24:13–35).

---

[157] I have previously discussed the relationship between Luke 24:50–53 and Acts 1 in chapter 4, p. 215 above.

We can summarize the results of our investigation of Luke's use of sources in chapter 24 as follows:

24:1–12. Lukan redaction of Mark, interwoven with material from John 20:1-10.

24:13–35. Lukan composition, but with some further influence from John 20:1–10 and 20:12.

24:36–43. Lukan composition, built around the narrative from John 20:19–20.

24:44–49. Lukan composition.

24:50–53. Lukan composition.

Chapter 9

CONCLUSIONS

The special relationship between Luke and John is extensive and complex. It does not admit of simple or simplistic characterizations. What I have attempted in this study is, in a systematic way, to re-examine that relationship with a new perspective on Luke's role as a composer and editor. My approach to the question of the relationship between Luke and John is influenced by two understandings that derive from modern rhetorical and literary theory: (1) that Luke constructed his Gospel in order to bring his readers to certain conclusions that were not present in the Gospels then extant, (2) that Luke, in using other written sources, engaged in a dialogue with them (as he states in 1:1). Thus, if Luke did not just blindly accept previous formulations of the Gospel, but was, instead, in dialogue with various differing narrative accounts of Jesus, then this situation might explain both the extensive points of contact between Luke and John, as well as some of the puzzling features of Luke—in particular the difference between Luke and the other Synoptics in the Passion narrative.

PRELIMINARY ASPECTS OF THE STUDY

The preliminary aspects of the study addressed the scope of the problem and its treatment heretofore. I began the preliminary examinations in chapter 2 with a survey of the scholarship on the Luke-John relationship. With very few exceptions (notably F. Lamar Cribbs and Barbara Shellard), previous studies, despite a variety of approaches, have begun with a preconception that John was the last Gospel written. As a result, the question posed to the relationship has been "Is it likely that John used Luke?" The difficulty of answering that question in the affirmative for more than a handful of pericopes has suggested the need for a new approach. Aware of the difficulty of reading John as reliant on Luke with respect to those points of contact, a number of scholars have attempted to explain the relationship by recourse to various oral traditions or a complex interplay of text and tradition (e.g., Schniewind, Dauer)—and yet the simpler approach of Luke's use of John has remained unexplored. Since many studies have already called into question the reasons supporting John's posteriority, the presupposition itself seemed worth setting aside— at least for this study.

The second preliminary examination, in chapter 3, was a survey of the scope and nature of the relationship between Luke and John. In that examination, I pulled together the various points of contact between Luke and John that have been noted in the literature. I also grouped them under broad rubrics that would highlight the diversity of the points of contact. Some points of contact, verbatim and almost verbatim similarities, are very precise. Together with common ordering and common omissions, these seemed most helpful in clarifying the relationship. But there are more subtle points, less easily explained in terms of standard source criticism, that might well suggest a very long and thoughtful dialogue between the two texts. Such aspects as common geography and shared theological perspectives are suggestive of a mature reflection on the gospel tradition and other Gospels.

A final preliminary examination sought to explore the authenticity of a number of textual variants in Luke chapter 24: the problem of the Western non-interpolations was engaged. These textual variants have often been excluded from the discussion of the Luke-John relationship because the long form of the text was questioned by

Conclusion 441

Westcott and Hort. The issue is particularly important because some of the textual variants in that group, if authentic, demonstrate strong points of contact with John. In a re-examination of the matter, I concluded that most of the variants, especially the ones with strong points of contact with John, were indeed part of the original text of Luke and should be part of any subsequent studies. The important readings that should be considered original are found in Luke 24:12, 24:36, and 24:40.

THE ANALYSIS OF TEXTS

Having painted the background of the canvas, so to speak, with the preliminary examinations of the scope of the relationship and its interpretation, I turned to the main work: the examination of the Luke-John relationship from the standpoint of Luke. The survey of the various points that Luke and John hold in common showed the majority of them to be found in the Passion and Resurrection narratives. The detailed study, then, was limited to those narratives, specifically, Luke chapters 22–24.

Because the approach of this study was to examine the Luke-John relationship from the perspective of Luke, a brief review of the approaches to redaction critical study of Luke, especially Luke's Passion narrative, was necessary. Luke's Passion narrative deviates rather extensively from the other synoptic Gospels, and a variety of approaches has been used to explain Luke's compositional and redactional method. I found that, in general, the various approaches fell into three groups. The first group emphasized linguistic patterns, and tended to see Luke pasting together fragments from sources based on detailed analysis of the linguistic pattern in the Third Gospel. This first group concluded that Luke relied on some hypothetical source or sources as the primary basis for the Passion narrative. The second group emphasized Luke's creativity as an author, and it concluded that Luke relied solely on Mark and Matthew and the Old Testament. And the third group emphasized thought content over linguistic analysis (especially the study by Marion Soards). This third group concluded that Luke primarily relied on Mark with the occasional influence of various other sources. I found the approach of Soards to be, for the most part, more sound; I therefore concluded that linguistic analysis should be complementary to thought content and order in detecting Luke's use of sources.

In the final three chapters, I undertook a careful examination of Luke's Passion and Resurrection narratives. In each case, I began by considering Luke's reliance on Mark. I concluded, like Soards, that Luke did indeed use Mark as his primary source in the Passion narrative. But the divergences from Mark are many and varied. I compared those divergences with Luke's own redactional tendencies and theological pattern; with Matthew; and especially, given the extensive number of points of contact, with John. Luke seems to have composed some material; certain pericopes show extensive Lukan style and features with no known Gospel source as a point of contact. And at least some of those pericopes seem to be intertextually related to other units in Luke's own writings, often alluding to previous gospel stories or anticipating the Acts. I found few instances in the Passion and Resurrection narratives in which Luke is dramatically similar to Matthew. But the extent of the contact with John is particularly impressive, and especially so since the Johannine features are often strongest where Luke varies the most from agreement with Mark.

A variety of connections between Luke and John was noted in the detailed analysis; those connections can be summarized here under a few major headings. First, there are not many close verbal agreements, but there are some striking similarities (e.g., Luke 22:34; 22:67; 24:12; 24:36). Second, and more importantly, Luke modified the generally Markan order of his presentation at a number of points, and those re-orderings often agree with the order of events in John. A number of examples might be offered here, but 22:31–34, 22:67–68, and 23:2–4 demonstrate the agreement well. Third, a related issue, the matter of common omission of Markan material, is also worthy of note. Luke often seems to have left out aspects of his Mark-derived narrative. And at those points, I found that John often did not present that same material (e.g., in Luke 22:31–34 and 23:44–45). While the omissions need to be treated carefully, they can be thought of as similar to modifications to the order, where the order in question involves the absence of features. And finally, in a number of instances, Luke's narrative seems to follow Mark but at points is different from Mark and, at the same time, has Johannine features (e.g., Luke 22:47–53). In those instances Luke's narrative seems to function as a middle term between Mark and John, such that Luke's narrative stands midway between the two other narratives, with elements of both intertwined.

Luke as a middle term, of course, does not prove that it is dependent on Mark and John. In the synoptic problem the fact that Mark is often middle term can equally point to it being first or last, as the opposing use of this feature in both the two-source and two-gospel theories illustrates. Points where Luke stands midway between Mark and John have often been used to argue for a trajectory from Mark to Luke to John. But it is certainly possible, and indeed probable in the case of Luke and John, that the very feature of being a middle term point to Luke being reliant on both Luke and John.

No one connection is sufficient to demonstrate a literary relationship. Certainly not the mere occasional verbatim agreement, which has been shown to be relatively unusual. As was noted before, however, when a number of connections occur, then the likelihood of a literary relationship is greater. The cumulative weight of the variety of connections, especially the common departure from Mark's order together with similar or verbatim material, is more important than any single striking similarity. What has been shown in this study is an extensive pattern of similarities between Luke and John that lend credence to a literary relationship.

These observations, of course, are nothing new; they reflect observations that have been made in previous studies. But my aim in this study was to examine the relationship from the standpoint of Luke. Does it make sense that Luke had John as a source? Would Luke's use of John serve, at least in part, as a reasonable explanation both for Luke's deviation from Mark and for the presence of features in the Third Gospel common also to John? The answer, in general, is yes. But that answer must be qualified in the sense that while Luke had John as a source, he only rarely (outside of chapter 24, where there is no Markan parallel) used John directly; instead, Luke engaged in a dialogue with John, and often only echoed John's account. Given Luke's known editorial practice, the introduction of features that agree with John occurs in places where Luke might well have been influenced by another reading. Moreover, there seems to be discernible distinction between passages that are closely linked to Mark, passages that were probably composed by Luke, and passages that seem to be drawing on John. In the case last named, it does not appear that Luke created the pericopes that have elements in common with John, but rather that Luke adjusted his Markan account with features from another narrative. It seems reasonable to suggest that that other narrative was John.

There is, of course, no way to *prove* that Luke used John. There does seem to be a literary relationship of some kind between Luke and John in the Passion narrative. In each case one might argue the direction of reliance; it is possible that Luke created the narratives and John used them. But, as I have previously discussed, that approach causes some problems. Why are there not more indications of Luke's style or thought in the Fourth Gospel? Why is there no clear representation of L material in John? Why do the points of contact seem to occur in Markan-derived narratives, but where Luke has departed from Mark's narrative? But our reading of Luke has not presented any significant difficulties. If Luke used John, that use took place alongside his use of Mark, and the result was an admixture of sources together with Lukan shaping and modification. In short, my assessment of the relationship, based on a careful analysis of the text, is that it is very reasonable to read Luke as having used John in addition to Mark.

Luke's Work as Author

How, then, might one conceive of Luke's work as an author and editor in the Passion narrative? As I have indicated a number of times, I do not see Luke functioning in a cut-and-paste mode; the resultant text shows no evidence of such a stilted editorial process. It appears that for the Passion narrative, as with the rest of the Gospel, Luke relied on Mark as his primary source. I would imagine that he had a codex[1] or scroll of Mark available as he wrote the Third Gospel. But he also had available another Gospel, one that was very similar to John. That second Gospel was consulted, in the Passion narrative at least, on a regular basis, although no consistent effort was made to reconcile it at every point to Mark. It appears that Luke adjudged certain items in the Johannine Gospel reliable, and modified his Markan text based on that assessment: sometimes he modified the order of events; sometimes he incorporated certain Johannine language into the text; sometimes he worked to combine or reconcile the two accounts. The picture one gets is of Luke as a historian, working with multiple versions, weighing them against one another and generally considering Mark the most reliable, but, at some points giving credence to John's account. Luke also knew some other traditions which he introduced at places, and he shaped and connected the narratives in any case using his own style and perspective. But Luke's use of John as a major source in the narrative is consistent with his approach in the Third Gospel, and coheres at each point with his method of writing.

This new understanding of Luke's use of sources fits particularly well with Luke's own statement of his authorial method in Luke 1:1. That is to say, Luke indicated that many (πολλοί) had undertaken to

---

[1] The possibility that the earliest Christian writings were codices, not scrolls, makes the conception of Luke's process of writing as the intermixing of two Gospel narratives more reasonable. The idea of Luke's working with two scrolls simultaneously is far more difficult than that of his working with two open codices. See the discussion in Harry Gamble, *Books and Readers in the Early Church* (New Haven: Yale University Press, 1995), 49–66.

write narratives (διήγησις), and that Luke wrote his gospel on the basis of those previous narratives.[2] The understanding argued in this dissertation, then, takes seriously Luke's own statement of method: Luke indeed used another narrative along with Mark, that is the gospel of John (or an early Johannine narrative).

FUTURE RESEARCH

The results of this study—which conclude that the reading of Luke as having used the Gospel of John is reasonable and likely—opens the door to a number of further studies that would expand and confirm Luke's use of the Fourth Gospel.

This study focused on the Luke-John relationship in Luke's Passion and Resurrection narratives, Luke chapters 22–24. But, as was suggested in the various tables of the Luke-John relationship in chapter 3, the connections between Luke and John are not limited to the Passion and Resurrection accounts. Further study of Luke's composition with an eye to his use of John is needed in the rest of the Gospel. In particular, study of Luke's editorial work in chapters 3, 5, and 7 would be profitable. Does this approach to Luke's composition explain why Luke's call of the disciples in chapter 5, for instance, is so different from the Markan call and, at the same time, so similar to John chapter 21? Similar questions can be posed in the John the Baptist material, the anointing pericope, and the story of the centurion from Capernaum. While the Passion narrative is particularly significant and provocative, especially given the large number of contacts and the similar scope of the Passion narratives in Luke and John, those other points of contact could confirm, expand, or modify this new understanding of Luke's use of John.

A major question which I have not resolved, however, is whether Luke actually had the Gospel of John or, rather, some document similar and perhaps antecedent to it. When one examines the portions of John that Luke seems to have used, one notes that virtually

---

[2] The hypothetical source Q, of course, is not a narrative at all.

none of the revelation discourse material (e.g., John 10:1–18; chapters 14–17) found its way into Luke.[3] The Luke-John relationship seems to be based primarily on the narrative portion of the Fourth Gospel. Given certain source and multiple-stage theories of John's composition, this differentiation is curious at the very least.[4] Might Luke have used a version of John that did not contain the revelation discourses? A brief comparison of the points of contact in chapter 3 with a basic reconstruction of the early narrative of John yields suggestive results. When the points of contact were compared with Robert Fortna's reconstructed Signs Gospel, a very high majority of the contacts were found.[5] That, together with the absence of material from the prologue and revelation discourse chapters, might suggest that Luke used an early form of John, not our final John. That suggestion, if proved accurate, might provide external confirmation of the source theories presented by Fortna and others.[6]

On the other hand, one could argue that Luke has the Fourth Gospel, but was influenced only by his narrative, because his presentation is so different from the Johannine discourses' presentation. The Gospel of John seems to be on a trajectory that leads to the Gospel of

---

[3] The term is from Rudolf Bultmann, *The Gospel of John: A Commentary* (Philadelphia: Westminster, 1971), who proposed that one of John's major sources was a collection of revelation discourses (7).

[4] On the source and multiple-stage theories, see Raymond E. Brown, *The Gospel According to John (I–XII)*, AB 29, (Garden City, NY: Doubleday, 1966), xxvii–xxxix.

[5] Robert Fortna, *The Gospel of Signs* (Cambridge: University Press, 1970), 235–45.

[6] In addition to Fortna, various early narrative versions of John that emphasize the signs material have been proposed by W. Nicol, *The Semeia in the Fourth Gospel: Tradition and Redaction* (Leiden: E. J. Brill, 1972); Hans-Peter Heekeren, *Die Zeichen-Quelle der johanneischen Redaktion* (Stuttgart: Verlag Katholisches Bibelwerk, 1984); U. C. von Wahlde, *The Earliest Version of John's Gospel* (Wilmington, DE: Michael Glazier, 1989); and R. Bultmann, *The Gospel of John*. See the discussion also in Gilbert van Belle, *The Signs Source in the Fourth Gospel* (Leuven: University Press, 1994).

Truth and other similar documents. And one might question whether, once a Christology as high as John's was presented, a Synoptic type of Gospel would have been subsequently written. But is that valid? John, after all, certainly faced opposition in the second century church.[7] And we now realize that early Christian thought did not develop on a single line, but rather along several. Luke seems to use John's narrative, but not his discourses. Why only the narrative? If one takes Luke's own statement of historiographical purpose seriously, then one can see Luke attempting carefully to assess and examine his sources, in this case Mark and John. Luke primarily uses Mark, yet he knows John and at times prefers John. And indeed John also claims to be a reliable witness. Luke then takes John into account where he can without defeating his basic reliance on Mark and Matthew/Q.

If Luke relied on some form of John—and this study suggests that that is likely—then we have a new tool to help us understand Luke's theology. An analysis of Luke's theology that takes into account his knowledge and use, as well as his avoidance and modification, of John would be productive. Such a study of Luke's theology would also help to further clarify Luke's authorial method, particularly his tendency in using sources and tradition, an element touched on in this and previous studies, but which is still not fully understood.

---

[7] See chapter 4 above, p. 200.

BIBLIOGRAPHY

Aland, Barbara. "Proclus." *Encyclopedia of the Early Church*, 713. New York: Oxford University Press, 1992.

Aland, Kurt. "Die Bedeutung des P-75 für den Text des Neuen Testament. Ein Beitrag zur Frage der "Western noninterpolation." In *Studien zur Überlieferung des Neuen Testamentes und seines Textes*, 155–72. (ANTT 2) Berlin: Walter de Gruyter, 1967.

———. "Neue Testamentliche Papyri II." *New Testament Studies* 12 (1965–66): 193–210.

Aland, Kurt & Barbara. *The Text of the New Testament*. Translated by Erroll F. Rhodes. Leiden: E. J. Brill, 1989.

American and British Committees of the International Greek New Testament Project. *The Gospel According to St. Luke.* Oxford: Clarendon Press, 1984.

Arndt, William and F. Wilbur Gingrich. *A Greek-English Lexicon of the New Testament.* Second edition. Chicago: University Press, 1957.

Ashton, John. *Understanding the Fourth Gospel.* Oxford: Clarendon Press, 1991.

———. "The Identity and Function of the Ἰουδαῖοι in the Fourth Gospel." *Novum Testamentum* 27 (1985): 40–75.

Bacon, B. W. *The Fourth Gospel in Research and Debate.* New Haven: Yale University Press, 1918.

Bakhtin, Mikhail. *The Dialogic Imagination.* Austin: University of Texas Press, 1981.

———. *Rabelais and His World.* Cambridge, MA: M. I. T. Press, 1968.

Bailey, John Amedee. *The Traditions Common to the Gospels of Luke and John.* Supplements to Novum Testamentum 7. Leiden: E. J. Brill, 1963.

Barrett, C. K. *The Gospel According to St. John.* Second edition. Philadelphia: Westminster Press, 1978.

Bauckham, Richard. "For Whom Were Gospels Written?" In *The Gospels for All Christians: Rethinking Gospel Audiences*, 9–48. Edited by Richard Bauckham. Grand Rapids: Wm. B. Eerdmans, 1998.

Baum-Bodenbender, Rosel. *Hoheit in Niedrigkeit: Johanneische Christologie im Prozess Jesu vor Pilatus (Joh 18,28-19, 16a).* Forschung zur Bibel 49. Würzburg: Echter Verlag, 1984.

Baur, F.C. *Kritische Untersuchungen über die kanonischen Evangelien.* Tübingen: Verlag und Druck von Ludw. Fr. Fues, 1847.

Becker, Jürgen. *Das Evangelium nach Johannes.* Gerd Mohn: Gütersloher Verlagshaus. 1981.

van Belle, Gilbert. *The Signs Source in the Fourth Gospel.* Leuven: University Press, 1994.

Birdsall, J. Neville. "The Western Text in the Second Century." In *Gospel Traditions in the Second Century*, 3-18. Edited by William L. Petersen. Notre Dame: University of Notre Dame Press, 1989.

Blackman, E. C. *Marcion and His Influence*. London: S. P. C. K., 1948.

Bleickert, G. "Ostern und Pfingsten. Lukanische und johanneische Schau." *Wort und Antwort* 17 (1975): 33-37.

Blinzler, Josef. *Johannes und die Synoptiker. Ein Forschungsbericht*. Stuttgarter Bibelstudien 5. Stuttgart: Verlag Katholisches Bibelwerk, 1965.

———. *The Trial of Jesus*. Translated by Isabel and Florence McHugh. Westminster, MD: The Newman Press, 1959.

Bludau, August. *Die ersten Gegner der Johannesschriften*. Freiburg: Herder, 1925.

Bock, Darrell L. *Luke*. Volume 2: 9:51-24:53. Grand Rapids: Baker Books, 1996.

Boismard, M.-É. "Saint Luc et la rédaction du quatrième évangile (Jn. 4.46-54)." *Revue Biblique* 69 (1962): 185:211.

———. "Le Chapitre XXI de Saint Jean." *Revue Biblique* 54 (1947): 473-501.

———. "Un procédé rédactionnel dans le quatrième évangile: la 'Wiederaufnahme'." In *L'Évangile de Jean*. Edited by M. de Jonge. Leuven: University Press, 1976.

Boismard, M.-É. and P. Benoit. *Synopse de Quatre Evangiles*. Volume II. Les Editions du Cerf, 1977.

Boismard, M.-É. and A. Lamouilee. *L'Évangile de Jean.* Volume III of *Synopse de Quatre Evangiles.* Les Editions du Cerf, 1977.

Bovon, François. *Luke the Theologian: Thirty-three Years of Research (1950-1983).* Princeton Theological Monograph Series. Allison Park, PA: Pickwick, 1987.

Brandon, S.G.F. *The Trial of Jesus of Nazareth.* London: B. T. Batsford, 1968.

Brawley, Robert L. "The Pharisees in Luke-Acts." Ph.D. Dissertation. Princeton, 1978.

Brodie, Thomas L. "Greco-Roman Imitation of Texts as a Partial Guide to Luke's Use of Sources." In *Luke-Acts.* Edited by Charles Talbert. New York: Crossroad, 1984.

Brown, Raymond. *The Gospel According to John.* I–IX. The Anchor Bible, Volume 29. Garden City, NY: Doubleday and Co., 1966.

———. *The Gospel According to John.* X–XXI. The Anchor Bible, volume 29A. Garden City, NY: Doubleday and Co., 1970.

———. *The Death of the Messiah.* Garden City, NY: Doubleday, 1994.

———. "The Gospel of Peter and Canonical Gospel Priority." *New Testament Studies* 33 (1987): 321–343.

———. *The Birth of the Messiah.* Garden City, NY: Image Books, 1979.

Büchele, Anton. *Der Tod Jesu im Lukasevangelium.* Frankfurt am Main: Josef Knecht, 1978.

Buck, Erwin. "The Function of the Pericope 'Jesus before Herod' in the Passion Narrative of Luke." In *Wort in Der Zeit*, 165–78. Edited by Wilfrid Haubeck and Michael Bachmann. Leiden: E. J. Brill, 1980.

Bultmann, Rudolf. *The Gospel of John. A Commentary*. Translated by G. R. Beasley-Murray. Oxford: Basil Blackwell, 1971.

Burke, Kenneth. *A Rhetoric of Motives*. Berkeley: University of California Press, 1969.

Burkitt, F. C. "ΕΠΙΦΩΣΚΕΙΝ." *Journal of Theological Studies* 14 (1913): 538–46.

Cadbury, Henry J. *The Style and Literary Method of Luke*. Harvard Theological Studies 6. Cambridge: Harvard University Press, 1919.

———. *The Making of Luke-Acts*. London: S.P.C.K., 1968.

———. "Four Features of Lukan Style." In *Studies in Luke-Acts*, 87–102. Edited by Leander Keck and J. Louis Martyn. Philadelphia: Fortress Press, 1980.

von Campenhausen, Hans. *The Formation of the Christian Bible*. Translated by J. A. Baker. Philadelphia: Fortress Press, 1972.

Carroll, John T. "Luke's Crucifixion Scene." In *Reimaging the Death of the Lukan Jesus*, 108–24. Edited by Dennis Sylva. Bonner Biblische Beitrage, Band 73. Frankfurt am Main: Anton Hain, 1990.

———. *Response to the End of History. Eschatology and Situation in Luke-Acts*. SBL Dissertation Series 92. Atlanta: Scholars Press, 1988.

Casey, R. P. "Professor Goodenough and the Fourth Gospel." *Journal of Biblical Literature* 64 (1945): 535–42.

Catchpole, David R. *The Trial of Jesus.* Leiden: E. J. Brill, 1971.

Chance, J. Bradley. *Jerusalem, the Temple, and the New Age in Luke-Acts.* Macon, GA: Mercer University Press, 1988.

Chevallier, M.-A. "'Pentecôtes' lucaniennes et 'Pentecôtes' johanniques." *Recherches de Science Religieuse* 69 (1981): 301–313.

———. "Apparentements entre Luc et Jean en matière de pneumatologie." In *A cause de l'Evangile.* Festschrift J. Dupont. Paris: 1985.

Coakley, J. T. "The Anointing at Bethany and the Priority of John." *Journal of Biblical Literature* 107 (1988): 241–256.

Conzelmann, Hans. *The Theology of Luke.* London: Faber and Faber, 1960.

Cope, Lamar. "The Earliest Gospel was the 'Signs Gospel.'" In *Jesus, the Gospels and the Church,* 17–24. Edited by E. P. Sanders. Macon, GA: Mercer University Press, 1987.

Craig, William L. "The Disciples' Inspection of the Empty Tomb (Lk 24,12.24; Jn 20,2–10). In *John and the Synoptics,* 614–619. Edited by Adelbert Denaux. Leuven: University Press, 1992.

Creed, John M. "The Supposed Proto-Luke Narrative of the Trial before Pilate." *Expository Times* 46 (1934): 378–79.

———. *The Gospel According to St. Luke.* London: Macmillan and Co., 1930.

Cribbs, Lamar. "Study of the Contacts that Exist Between St. Luke and St. John." *SBL 1973 Seminar Papers*, 1–93. Edited by George McCrae. Cambridge, MA: Society of Biblical Literature, 1973.

———. "St. Luke and the Johannine Tradition." *Journal of Biblical Literature* 90 (1971):422–50.

———. "Agreements Between John and Acts. In *Perspectives on Luke-Acts*, 40-61. Edited by Charles Talbert. Danville, VA: Association of Baptist Professors of Religion, 1978.

———. "The Agreements That Exist Between Luke and John." *SBL 1979 Seminar Papers*, 215–51. Edited by Paul Achtemeier. Missoula Montana: Scholars Press, 1979.

———. "A Reassessment of the Date of Origin and the Destination of the Gospel of John." *Journal of Biblical Literature* 89 (1970): 38–55.

Crossan, John Dominic. *The Cross that Spoke*. San Francisco: Harper and Row, 1988.

———. *The Historical Jesus*. San Francisco: Harper Books, 1991.

Curtis, K. Peter G. "Luke xxiv.12 and John xx.3–10." *Journal of Theological Studies* (NS) 22 (1971): 512–15.

———. "Linguistic Support for Three Western Readings in Luke 24." *Expository Times* 83 (1972): 344–45.

Daniélou, Jean. *The Theology of Jewish Christianity*. Translated and edited by John Baker. London: Darton, Longman & Todd, 1964.

Dauer, Anton. *Johannes und Lukas: Untersuchungen zu den johanneisch-lukanischen Parallelperikopen Joh 4,46-54/Lk 7,1-10—Joh 12,1-8/Lk 7,36-50; 10,38-42—Joh 20,19-29/Lk 24,36-49*. Forschung zur Bibel 50. Würzburg: Echter Verlag, 1984.

———. *Die Passiongeschichte im Johannesevangelium: eine traditions-geschichtliche und theologische Untersuchung zu Joh. 18, 1-19, 30.* Studien zum Alten und Neuen Testament 30, Munich: Kosel, 1972.

———. "Spuren der (synoptischen) Synedriumsverhandlung im 4. Evangelium - Das Verhältnis zu den Synoptikern." In *John and the Synoptics*, pages 307–340. Edited by Adelbert Denaux. Leuven: University Press, 1992.

———. *Beobachtungen zur literarischen Arbeitstechnik des Lukas.* Bonner Biblische Beitrage 79. Frankfurt am Main: Verlag Anton Hain, 1990.

———. "'Ergänzungen' und 'Variationen' in den Reden der apostelgeschichte gegenübervorausgegangenen Erzählungen. Beobachtungen zur literarischen Arbeitsweise des Lukas." In *Von Urchristentum zu Jesus.* Festschrift Joachim Gnilka. Freiburg: Herder, 1989.

———. "Lk 24,12 — ein Produkt lukanischer Redaction?" In *The Four Gospels 1992.* Festschrift Frans Neirynck. Leuven: University Press, 1992.

———. "Zur Authentizität von Lk 24,12." *Ephemerides Theologicae Lovanienses* 70 (1994): 294–318.

Dawsey, James. *The Lukan Voice.* Macon, GA: Mercer University Press, 1986.

Dibelius, Martin. "Herodes und Pilatus." *Zeitschrift für den neutestamentliche Wissenschaft* 16 (1915): 113–26.

Dillon, Richard J. *From Eye-Witnesses to Ministers of the Word: Tradition and Composition in Luke 24.* Rome: Biblical Institute Press, 1978.

Dodd, C. H. *Historical Tradition in the Fourth Gospel.* Cambridge: University Press, 1963.

———. *The Interpretation of the Fourth Gospel.* Cambridge: University Press, 1953.

———. *The Apostolic Preaching and Its Development.* London: Hodden and Stoughten, 1936.

Donahue, John R. *Are You the Christ? The Trial Narrative in the Gospel of Mark.* Missoula, MT: Society of Biblical Literature, 1973.

Drury, John. *Tradition and Design in Luke's Gospel.* London: Darton, Longman & Todd, 1976.

Egelkraut, Helmuth L. *Jesus' Mission to Jerusalem: A Redaction Critical Study of the Travel Narrative in the Gospel of Luke, Lk. 9:51–19:48.* Europäische Hochschulschriften 80. Frankfurt: Peter Lang, 1976.

Ehrman, Bart. *The Orthodox Corruption of Scripture.* New York: Oxford University Press, 1993.

———. "Jesus' Trial before Pilate: John 18:28-19:16." *Biblical Theology Bulletin* 13 (1983): 124–31.

Ehrman, Bart and Mark Plunkett. "The Angel and the Agony: The Textual Problem of Luke 22:43–44." *Catholic Biblical Quarterly* 45 (1983): 401-16.

Elliott, J. K. "The United Bible Societies' Textual Commentary Evaluation." *Novum Testamentum* 17 (1975): 130–50.

Engelbrecht, J. "The empty tomb (Lk 24:1–12) in historical perspective." *Neotestamentica* 23 (1989): 235–49.

Epiphanius of Salamis. *The Panarion of St. Epiphanius, Bishop of Salamis*. Translated and edited by Philip R. Amidon. Oxford: Oxford University Press, 1990.

Epp, Eldon Jay. *The Theological Tendency of Codex Bezae Cantabrigiensis in Acts*. Cambridge: University Press, 1966.

———. "The Ignorance Motif in Acts and Anti-Judaic Tendencies in Codex Bezae." *Harvard Theological Review* 55 (1962): 51–62.

———. "The Ascension in the Textual Tradition of Luke-Acts." In *New Testament Textual Criticism: Its Significance for Exegesis*, 131–46. Edited by Eldon Jay Epp and Gordon D. Fee. Oxford: Clarendon Press, 1981.

———. "Eclectic Method in New Testament Textual Criticism: Solution or Symptom?" *Harvard Theological Review* 69 (1976): 211–57.

Eusebius Pamphili. *Eccesiastical History*. Translated by Roy J. Deferrari. New York: Fathers of the Church,1953.

Evans, Craig. *St. Luke*. Philadelphia: Trinity Press, 1990.

———. "Peter Warming Himself: The Problem of an Editorial Seam." *Journal of Biblical Literature* 101 (1982): 245–249.

Farmer, William R. *The Synoptic Problem: A Critical Analysis*. New York: MacMillan, 1964.

Farrer, A. M. "On Dispensing with Q." In *Studies in the Gospels: Essays in Memory of R. H. Lightfoot*, 55-88. Edited by D. E. Nineham. Oxford: Blackwell, 1955.

Fee, Gordon D. "Rigorous or Reasoned Eclectecisim — Which?" in *Studies in New Testament Language and Text*, pages 174–197. Edited by J. K. Elliott. Leiden: E. J. Brill, 1976.

———. "Codex Sinaiticus in the Gospel of John: A Contribution to Methodology in Establishing Textual Relationships." *New Testament Studies* 15 (1968–69): 23–44.

Fearghail, Fearghus. *Introduction to Luke-Acts.* Rome: Editrice Pontifico Istituto Biblico, 1991.

Feine, Paul. *Eine vorkanonische Überlieferung des Lukas.* Gotha: Friedrich Andreas Perthes, 1891.

Feuillet. A. *Jesus and His Mother according to the Lucan Infancy Narratives, and according to St. John.* Still River, MA: St. Bede's Publications, 1984.

———. "Les deux onctions faites sur Jésus, et Marie-Madeleine. Contribution à l'étude des rapports entre les Synoptiques et le quatrième évangile." *Revue Thomiste* 75 (1975):357–394.

Finegan, Jack. *The Archaeology of the New Testament.* Princeton: University Press, 1969.

Fitzmyer, Joseph A. *The Gospel According to Luke.* The Anchor Bible, Volume 28. Garden City, NY: Doubleday and Company, Inc, 1981.

———. *The Gospel According to Luke.* The Anchor Bible, Volume 28A. Garden City, NY: Doubleday and Company, Inc, 1985.

———. "Papyrus Bodmer XIV: Some Features of Our Oldest Text of Luke. *Catholic Biblical Quarterly* 24 (1962).

———. *Luke the Theologian.* New York: Paulist Press, 1989.

Fortna, Robert T. *The Gospel of Signs.* SNTS Monograph Series 11. Cambridge: University Press, 1970.

———. *The Fourth Gospel and its Predecessor.* Philadelphia: Fortress Press, 1988.

———. "Jesus and Peter at the High Priest's House: A Test Case for the Question of the Relation between Mark's and John's Gospels." *New Testament Studies* 24 (1977/78): 371–83.

Franklin, Eric. *Luke: Interpreter of Paul, Critic of Matthew.* JSNTS 92. Sheffield: JSOT Press, 1994.

Freed, Edwin D. and Russell B. Hunt. "Fortna's Signs-Source in John." *Journal of Biblical Literature* 94 (1975): 563–579.

Fuller, Reginald H. *The Formation of the Resurrection Narratives.* Philadelphia: Fortress Press, 1980.

Gamble, Harry. *Books and Readers in the Early Church.* New Haven: Yale Univerity Press, 1995.

Gardner-Smith, P. *St. John and the Synoptic Gospels.* Cambridge: University Press, 1938.

———. "'ΕΠΙΦΩΣΚΕΙΝ." *Journal of Theological Studies* 27 (1926): 179–81.

Garrett, Susan. *The Demise of the Devil: Magic and the Demonic in Luke's Writings.* Minneapolis: Fortress Press, 1989.

Giblin, Charles H. *The Destruction of Jerusalem According to Luke's Gospel.* Rome: Biblical Institute Press, 1985.

Goodacre, Mark S. *Goulder and the Gospels.* JSNTS 133. Sheffield: Sheffield Academic Press, 1996.

Goodenough, E. R. "John: A Primitive Gospel." *Journal of Biblical Literature* 64 (1945): 145–82.

———. "A Reply." *Journal of Biblical Literature* 64 (1945): 543–44.

Goulder, M. D. "From Ministry to Passion in John and Luke." *New Testament Studies* 29 (1983): 561–68.

———. *Luke: A New Paradigm.* 2 volumes. JSNTS Supplement 20. Sheffield: JSOT Press, 1989.

———. "Mark xvi.1–8 and Parallels." *New Testament Studies* 24 (1977–78): 235-240.

———. *Midrash and Lection in Matthew.* London: S. P. C. K., 1974.

———. "On Putting Q to the Test." *New Testament Studies* 24 (1977–78): 218-24.

———. "Farrer on Q." *Theology* 83 (1980): 190–95.

Grant, F. C. "Was the Author of John Dependent upon the Gospel of Luke?" *Journal of Biblical Literature* 56 (1937): 285–307.

Grant, Robert. "The Origin of the Fourth Gospel." *Journal of Biblical Literature* 69 (1950): 305–22.

———. "Scripture and Tradition in St. Ignatius of Antioch." *Catholic Biblical Quarterly* 25 (1963): 322–335.

Green, Joel. *The Death of Jesus: Tradition and Interpretation in the Passion Narrative.* Wissenschaftliche Untersuchungen zum Neuen Testament 33. Tübingen: J. C. B. Mohr (Paul Siebeck), 1988.

———. "The Death of Jesus, God's Servant." In *Reimaging the Death of the Lukan Jesus*, 29–56. Edited by Dennis Sylva. Bonner Biblische Beitrage, Band 73. Frankfurt am Main: Anton Hain, 1990.

Grundmann, W. "κραζω." In *Theological Dictionary of the New Testament*, Volume III, 898–903. Grand Rapids, MI: Wm. B. Eerdmans, 1965.

Guillet, J. "Luc 22,29. Une formule johannique dans l'évangile de Luc?" *Recherches de Science Religieuse* 69 (1981): 113–22.

Haenchen, Ernst. *The Acts of the Apostles.* Philadelphia: Westminster Press, 1971.

Hahn, Ferdinand. *The Titles of Jesus in Christology.* Translated by Harold Knight and George Ogg. New York: World Publishing Company, 1969.

von Harnack, Adolf. *History of Dogma.* Translated by Neil Buchanan. New York: Dover Publications, 1961.

———. *Marcion: Das Evangelium vom fremden Gott.* Texte und Untersuchungen zur Geschichte der altchristlichen Literatur, 45 Band. Leipzig: J.C. Hinrichs'schen Buchhandlung, 1924.

Harris, Rendall. *Study of Codex Bezae.* Cambridge: University Press, 1891.

Hatch, William Henry P. *The 'Western' Text of the Gospels.* Evanston, Illinois: Seabury-Western Theological Seminary, 1937.

Hawkins, John. *Horae Synopticae.* Oxford: Clarendon Press, 1909.

———. "Three Limitations to St. Luke's Use of St. Mark's Gospel." In *Studies in the Synoptic Problem*, 29–94. Edited by W. Sanday. Oxford: Clarendon Press, 1911.

Heekerens, Hans-Peter. *Die Zeichen-Quelle der johanneischen Redaktion.* Stuttgarter Bibelstudien 113. Stuttgart: Verlag Katholisches Bibelwerk GmbH, 1984.

Hippolytus. *Refutatio Omnium Haeresium.* Edited by Miroslav Marcovich. Berlin: Walter de Gruyter, 1986.

Hoehner, Harold W. "Why did Pilate hand Jesus over to Antipas?" In *The Trial of Jesus*, 84–90. Edited by Ernst Bammel. Studies in Biblical Theology, Number 13, Second Series. London: SCM Press, 1970.

———. *Herod Antipas*. SNTSMS 17. Cambridge: University Press, 1972.

Hollander, J. *The Figure of an Echo: Modes of Allusion in Milton and After.* Berkeley: University of California Press, 1981.

Holtzmann, H. J. "Die schriftstellerische Verhältniss des Johannes zu den Synoptikern." *Zeitschrift für wissenschaftliche Theologie*, 62–84, 155–77, 446–56. Leipzig: Fues's Verlag, 1869.

———. *Evangelium des Johannes*. Zweite Auflage. Tübingen: J. C. B. Mohr (Paul Siebeck), 1893.

Holtzmann, Oskar. *Das Johannesevangelium*. Darmstadt: Verlag von Johannes Waitz, 1887.

Hoskyns, Edwyn. *The Fourth Gospel*. London: Faber & Faber, Ltd., 1947.

Ignatius of Antioch. "To the Smyrnaeans." In *Apostolic Fathers*, pages 251–67. Translated by Kirsopp Lake. Loeb Classical Library. Cambridge, MA: Harvard University Press, 1949.

Ireneaus. *Against Heresies*. In The Anti-Nicene Fathers, Volume 1. Edited by Alexander Roberts and James Donaldson. Grand Rapids, MI: Wm. B. Eerdmans Co, 1981.

Jeremias, Joachim. *Die Sprache des Lukasevangeliums*. Göttingen: Vandenhoeck & Ruprecht, 1980.

———. *The Eucharistic Words of Jesus*. Translated by Norman Perrin. Philadelphia: Trinity Press, 1990 (1960).

———. "Perikopen-Umstellungen bei Lukas?" *New Testament Studies* 4 (1957–58): 115–19.

Johnson, Luke Timothy. "Luke 24:1–11." *Interpretation* 46 (1992): 57–61.

———. *The Gospel of Luke*. Collegeville, MN: Michael Glazier, 1991.

Judge, P. J. "Luke 7,1–10: Sources and Redaction." In *L'Evangile de Luc*, 473–89. Edited by F. Neirynck. Leuven: University Press, 1989.

Karris, Robert. "Luke 23:47 and the Lucan View of Jesus' Death." In *Reimaging the Death of the Lukan Jesus*, 68–78. Edited by Dennis Sylva. Bonner Biblische Beitrage, Band 73. Frankfurt am Main: Anton Hain, 1990.

Kearney, Suzanne M. "A Study of Principal Compositional Techniques in Luke-Acts based on Lk. 4:16–30 in Conjunction with Lk. 7:18–23." Ph.D. Dissertation. Boston University, 1978.

Kelber, Werner. "Conclusion: From Passion Narrative to Gospel." In *The Passion in Mark*, 153–80. Edited by Werner Kelber. Philadelphia: Fortress Press, 1976.

Kirk, Alan. "Examining Priorities: Another Look at the Gospel of Peter's Relationship to the New Testament Gospels." *New Testament Studies* 40 (1994): 572–95.

Kittlaus, Lloyd R. "The Author of John and the Gospel of Mark." Ph.D. Dissertation. University of Chicago, 1988.

Klassen, William. *Judas. Betrayer or Friend of Jesus?* Minneapolis: Fortress Press, 1996.

Klein, Hans. "Die Lukanish-johanneische Passiontradition." *Zeitschrift für die neutestamentliche Wissenschaft* 67 (1976):155–87.

———. "Die Verleugnung des Petrus: Eine traditionsgeschichtliche Untersuchung." *Zeitschrift für Theologie und Kirche* 58 (1961): 285-328.

Klijn, A. F. J. *Survey of Researches into the Western Text of the Gospels,* Parts I & II. Leiden: Brill, 1969.

Koester, Helmut. *Synoptische Überlieferung bein den Apostolischen Vätern.* Berlin: Akademie-Verlag, 1975.

Kremer, J. "Der arme Lazarus. Lazarus, der Freund Jesu. Beobachtung zur Beziehung zwischen Lk 16,19–31 und Joh 11,1–46." In *A cause de l'Evangile.* Festschrift J. Dupont. Paris: 1985.

Kümmel, Werner. *Introduction to the New Testament.* Translated by Howard Clark Kee. Nashville: Abingdon Press, 1973.

———. *The New Testament: The History of the Investigation of its Problems.* Translated by S. McLean Gilmour and Howard C. Kee. Nashville: Abingdon Press, 1972.

Kysar, Robert. *The Fourth Evangelist and His Gospel.* Minneapolis: Augsburg Publishing House, 1975.

———. *John.* Minneapolis: Augsburg Publishing House, 1986.

———. "The Fourth Gospel. A Report on Recent Research." In *Aufstieg und Niedergang der römischen Welt*, Principat 25.3, 2389–480. Berlin: Walter de Gruyter, 1985.

Landis, Stephan. *Das Verhältnis des Johannesevangeliums zu den Synoptikern. Am Beispiel von Mt 8,5-13; Lk 7,1-10; Joh 4,46-54.* BZNT 74. Berlin: Walter de Gruyter, 1994.

Leaney, Robert. "The Resurrection Narratives in Luke (xxiv. 12–53)." *New Testament Studies* 2 (1955–56): 110–14.

Liddell, Henry G. and Robert Scott. *A Greek-English Lexicon*. Ninth edition. Oxford: Clarendon Press, 1968.

Lightfoot, Robert Henry. *History and Interpretation in the Gospels*. London: Hodder and Stoughton, 1935.

Lindars, Barnabas. "John and the Synoptic Gospels. A Test Case." *New Testament Studies* 27 (1981): 287–94.

———. "Traditions Behind the Fourth Gospel." In *L'Évangile de Jean*. Edited by M. de Jonge. Leuven: University Press, 1976.

———. *The Gospel of John*. Grand Rapids: Wm. B. Eerdmans Co., 1972.

———. "The Composition of John xx." *New Testament Studies* 7 (1960–61): 142–47.

Lohfink, Gerhard. *Die Himmelfahrt Jesu*. München: Kösel-Verlag, 1971.

Luedemann, Gerd. *The Resurrection of Jesus*. Minneapolis: Fortress Press, 1994.

Maddox, Robert. *The Purpose of Luke-Acts*. Edinburgh: T&T Clark, 1982.

Mahoney, Robert. *The Two Disciples at the Tomb*. Bern: Herbert Lang, 1974.

Marshall, I. Howard. *Luke: Historian and Theologian*. Exeter: Paternoster Press, 1974.

———. *The Gospel of Luke*. Grand Rapids: William B. Eerdmans, 1978.

Martyn, J. Louis. *History and Theology in the Fourth Gospel*. Revised and Enlarged Edition. Nashville: Abingdon Press, 1979.

Matera, Frank J. "Jesus before the Presbuterion." In *L'Evangile de Luc*, 517–33. Edited by F. Neirynck. Leuven: University Press, 1989.

———. "Jesus before Pilate, Herod, and Israel." In *L'Evangile de Luc*, 535–51. Edited by F. Neirynck. Leuven: University Press, 1989.

Matson, Mark A. "The Contribution to the Temple Cleansing by the Fourth Gospel." In *SBL 1992 Seminar Papers*, 489–506. Edited by Eugene Lovering, Jr. Atlanta: Scholars Press, 1992.

Maurer, Christian. "The Gospel of Peter." In *New Testament Apocrypha*, 179–87. Edited by E. Hennecke, W. Schneemelcher and R. McL. Wilson. Philadelphia: Westminster, 1963.

McCant, Jerry Walter. "The Gospel of Peter: The Docetic Question Re-Examined." Ph.D. Dissertation, Emory University, 1978.

Metzger, Bruce. *The Text of the New Testament*. Third edition. Oxford: Oxford University Press, 1992.

———. *A Textual Commentary on the Greek New Testament*. Second Edition. Stuttgart: United Bible Societies, 1994.

Moore, Stephen D. *Literary Criticism and the Gospels*. New Haven: Yale University Press, 1989.

Muddiman, J. "A Note on Reading Luke xxiv.12." *Ephemerides Theologicae Lovanienses* 48 (1972): 542–48.

Myllykoski, Matti. "The Material Common to Luke and John. A Sketch." In *Luke-Acts: Scandinavian Perspectives*. Edited by Petri Luomanen. Finnish Exegetical Society Number 54. Göttingen: Vandenhoek and Ruprecht, 1991.

Neirynck. Frans. "ΑΠΗΛΘΟΝ ΠΡΟΣ ΕΑΥΤΟΝ. Lc 24,12 et Jn 20,5." *Ephemerides Theologicae Lovanienses* 54 (1978): 104–18.

———. "ΠΑΡΑΚΥΨΑΣ ΒΛΕΠΕΙ. Lc 24,12 et Jn 20,5." *Ephemerides Theologicae Lovanienses* 53 (1977): 113–52.

———. "The Uncorrected Present in Lk. xxxiv.12" *Ephemerides Theologicae Lovanienses* 48 (1972): 548–55.

———. "Lc. 24,36–43. Un récit lucanien." In *À Cause de L'Évangile*. Mélanges offerts à Dom Jacques Dupont. Cerf: Publications de Saint-André, 1985, pages 655–680.

———. "John and the Synoptics." In *L'Évangile de Jean*. Edited by M. de Jonge. Leuven: University Press, 1976.

———, in collaboration with Joël Delobel et. al. *Jean et les Synoptiques: Examen critique de l'exégèse de M.-É. Boismard*. Louvain: University Press, 1979.

———. "John and the Synoptics: The Empty Tomb Stories." *New Testament Studies* 30 (1984): 161–87.

———. "John and the Synoptics: 1975–1990." In *John and the Synoptics*. Colloquium Biblicum Lovaniense, 1990, pages 3–62. Edited by A. Denaux. Leuven: Leuven University Press, 1992.

———. "John and the Synoptics. Response to P. Borgen." In *Interrelations of the Gospels*, 438–50. Leuven: University Press, 1990.

———. "Lc xxiv.12. Les témoins du texte occidental." In *Evangelica*, pages 313–28. Leuven: University Press, 1982.

———. "Once More Luke 24,12." *Ephemerides Theologicae Lovanienses* 70 (1994): 319–340.

———. "A Supplementary Note on Lk 24,12." *Ephemerides Theologicae Lovanienses.* 72 (1996): 425–30.

———. "The Apocryphal Gospels and the Gospel of Mark." In *The New Testament in Early Christianity.* Edited by Jean-Marie Sevrin. Leuven: University Press, 1989.

Neyrey, Jerome. "Jesus' Address to the Women of Jerusalem." *New Testament Studies* 29 (1983): 74–86.

Nicol, W. *The Semeia in the Fourth Gospel.* Supplement Novum Testamentum. Leiden: E. J. Brill, 1972.

Osborne, Grant R. "Redactional Trajectories in the Crucifixion Narrative." *Evangelical Quarterly* 51 (1979): 80–96

———. *The Resurrection Narratives.* Grand Rapids, MI: Baker Book House, 1984.

Osty, E. "Les points de contact entre le récit de la passion dans saint Luc et dans saint Jean." In *Mélanges Jules Lebreton I*, 146–54. Récherches de Science Religiuse 39. Paris, 1951.

Oube, Antonio. "Irenaeus." In *Encyclopedia of the Early Church*, 413. New York: Oxford University Press, 1992.

Page, Allen F. "Proto-Luke Reconsidered: A Study of Literary Method and Theology in the Gospel of Luke." Ph.D. Dissertation. Duke University, 1968.

Pagels, Elaine. *The Johannine Gospel in Gnostic Exegesis: Heracleon's Commentary on John.* Nashville: Abingdon Press, 1973.

Parker, D. C. *Codex Bezae. An Early Christian Manuscript and its Text.* Cambridge: University Press, 1992.

———. *The Living Text of the Gospels*. Cambridge: University Press, 1997.

Parker, Pierson. "Luke and the Fourth Evangelist." *New Testament Studies* 9 (1963): 317–36.

———. "The Kinship of John and Acts." In *Christianity, Judaism and Other Greco-Roman Cults*. Edited by Jacob Neusner. Leiden: E. J. Brill, 1975.

———. "Herod Antipas and the Death of Jesus." In *Jesus, the Gospels, and the Church*, pages 197–208. Edited by E. P. Sanders. Macon, GA: Mercer University Press, 1987.

Parsons, Mikeal. *The Departure of Jesus in Luke-Acts*. JSNT Supplement Series 21. Sheffield: JSOT Press, 1987.

Pearce, K. "The Lucan Origins of the Raising of Lazarus." *Expository Times* 96 (1984): 359–361.

Perrin, Norman. *What is Redaction Criticism?* Philadelphia: Fortress Press, 1969.

Perry, Alfred. *The Sources of Luke's Passion-Narrative*. Chicago: University of Chicago Press, 1920.

Pesch, Rudolf. *Der reiche Fischfang*. Düsseldorf: Patmos-Verlag, 1969.

———. "La rédaction lucanienne du logion des pêcheurs d'hommes (Lc., V, 10c)." In *L'Évangile de Luc,* 135–54. Edited by Frans Neirynck. Leuven: University Press, 1989.

Petersen, William L. "What Text Can New Testament Textual Criticism Ultimately Reach?" In *New Testament Textual Criticism, Exegesis, and Early Church History*, 136–152. Edited by Barbara Aland and Joël Delobel, Kampen: Kok Pharos, 1994.

Petzer, J. H. "Luke 22:19b–20 and the Structure of the Passage." *Novum Testamentum* 26 (1984): 249–52.

Petzer, Kobus. "Style and Text in the Lucan Narrative of the Institution of the Lord's Supper (Luke 22.19b–20)." *New Testament Studies* 37 (1991): 113–29.

Petzke, Gerd. *Das Sondergut des Evangeliums nach Lukas*. Zürich: Theologischer Verlag, 1990.

Plevnik, Joseph. "'The Eleven and Those with Them' According to Luke." *Catholic Biblical Quarterly* 40 (1978):205–11.

Plummer, Alred. *The Gospel According to St. Luke*. ICC. New York: Charles Scribner's Sons, 1902.

Rehkopf, Friedrich. *Die lukanische Sonderquelle*. Tübingen: J.C.B. Mohr (Paul Siebeck), 1959.

Rengstorf, K. H. "ληστης." In *Theological Dictionary of the New Testament*, Volume IV, 257–62. Grand Rapids: Wm. B. Eerdmans, 1967.

Rice, George. "Western Non-Interpolations: A Defense of the Apostolate." In *Luke-Acts*. Edited by Charles H. Talbert. New York: Crossroad, 1984.

Richard, Earl ,ed. *New Views on Luke and Acts*. Collegeville, MN: The Liturgical Press, 1990.

Robinson, John. A. T. *The Priority of John.* Oak Park, Ill.: Meyer-Stone Books, 1987.

Robinson, William C. Jr. *Der Weg des Herrn.* Hamburg: Herbert Reich Evangelisher Verlag, 1964.

Ross, John M. "The Genuineness of Luke 24:12." *Expository Times* 98 (1987): 107–08.

Ruckstuhl, Eugen. *Die literarische Einheit des Johannesevangeliums.* Freiburg: Paulusverlag, 1951.

———. "Johannine Language and Style. The Question of Their Unity." In *L'Évangile de Jean.* Edited by M. de Jonge Leuven: University Press, 1976.

Sabbe, M. "The Arrest of Jesus in John 18:1–11 and its Relation to the Synoptic Gospels. A Critical Evaluation of A. Dauer's Hypothesis." In *L'Évangile de Jean.* Leuven: University Press, 1977.

Sanders, E. P. *Tendencies of the Synoptic Tradition.* Cambridge: University Press, 1969.

———. *The Historical Figure of Jesus.* London: Penguin Books, 1993.

Sanders, E. P. and Margaret Davies. *Studying the Synoptic Gospels.* Philadelphia: Trinity Press, 1989

Sanders, J. N. *The Fourth Gospel in the Early Church.* Cambridge: University Press, 1943.

———. "Those Whom Jesus Loved." *New Testament Studies* 1 (1954–55): 29–41.

Schleiermacher, Friedrich. *The Life of Jesus.* Edited by Jack C. Verheyden. Translated by S. Maclean Gilmour. Philadelphia: Fortress Press, 1975.

———. *A Critical Essay on the Gospel of Luke.* London: John Taylor, 1825.

Schmidt, K. L. *Der Rahmen der Geschichte Jesu.* Berlin: Trowitzsch & Sohn, 1919.

Schnackenburg, Rudolf. *The Gospel According to St. John.* 3 volumes. New York: Crossroad, 1980-82.

Schneider, Gerhard. *Verleugnung, Verspottung und Verhör Jesu Nach Lukas 22, 54–71.* München: Kösel-Verlag, 1969.

———. *Lukas, Theologie der Heilsgeschichte. Aufsätze zum lukanischen Doppelwerk.* Bonn: Peter Hanstein Verlag, 1985.

———. "The Political Charge Against Jesus." In *Jesus and the Politics of His Day*, 403–14. Edited by Ernst Bammel and C. F. D. Moule. Cambridge: University Press, 1984.

———. *Die Passion Jesu nach den drei älteren Evangelien.* München: Kösel-Verlag, 1973.

Schniewind, Julius. *Die Parallelperikopen bei Lukas und Johannes.* 2. Auflage. Hildesheim: Georg Olms Verlagsbuchhandlung, 1958 (1914).

Schoedel, William R. *Ignatius of Antioch.* Hermeneia Commentary. Philadelphia: Fortress Press, 1985.

Schramm, Tim. *Der Markus-Stoff Bei Lukas.* Cambridge: University Press, 1971.

Schubert, Paul. "The Structure and Significance of Luke 24." In *Neutestamentliche Studien für Rudolf Bultmann*, 165-86. Berlin: Alfred Töpelmann, 1954.

Schürmann, Heinz. *Traditionsgeschichtliche Untersuchungen zu den Synoptischen Evangelien*. Düsseldorf: Patmos-Verlag, 1968.

———. "Der Paschalmahlbericht. Lk 22,(7–14)15–18. I Teil Einer Quellenkritischen Untersuchung des lukanischen Abendmahlberichtes." *Neutetstamentliche Abhandlungen* 19 Band, 5 Heft. Münster: Aschendorffsche Verlagsbuchhandlung, 1953.

———. "Jesu Abschiedsrede. Lk 22,19–20. II Teil Einer Quellenkritischen Untersuchungdes lukanischen Abendmahlberichtes." *Neutestamentliche Abhandlungen* 20 Band, 4 Heft. Münster: Aschendorffsche Verlagsbuchhandlung, 1955.

———. "Der Einsetzungsbericht. Lk 22,21–38. III Teil Einer Quellenkritischen Untersuchung des lukanischen Abendmahlberichtes." *Neutestamentliche Abhandlungen* 20 Band, 5 Heft. Münster: Aschendorffsche Verlagsbuchhandlung, 1957.

Schweizer, Eduard. *Ego Eimi*. Göttingen: Vandenhoek & Ruprecht, 1939.

———. "Zur Frage der Quellenbenutzung durch Lukas: I. Sprachliche und sachliche Beobachtungen, II. Analyse lukanischer Perikopen." In *Neues Testament und Christologie im Werden*. Göttingen: Vandenhoek & Ruprecht, 1982.

Shellard, Barbara. "The Relationship of Luke and John: A Fresh Look at an Old Problem." *The Journal of Theological Studies*. 46 (1995, New Series): 71–98.

———. "Luke as the Fourth Gospel: Its Purpose, Sources and Literary Context." M. Phil. Thesis. University of Oxford, 1994.

Sloyan, Gerard S. *Jesus on Trial*. Philadelphia: Fortress Press, 1973.

———. "The Gnostic Adoption of John's Gospel and Its Canonization by the Church Catholic." *Biblical Theology Bulletin* 26 (Fall 1996):125–32.

de Solages, Mgr. *Jean et les Synoptiques*. Leiden: E. J. Brill, 1979.

Smith, D. Moody. *John Among the Gospels*. Minneapolis: Fortress Press, 1992.

———. *Johannine Christianity*. Columbia, SC: University of South Carolina Press, 1984.

———. *The Composition and Order of the Fourth Gospel: Bultmann's Literary Theory*. New Haven: Yale University Press, 1965.

———. "John and the Synoptics and the Question of Gospel Genre." In *The Four Gospels 1992*, 1783–98. Festschrift Frans Neirynck. Edited by F. Van Segbroeck, C. M. Tuckett, G. Van Belle, and J. Verheyden. Leuven: University Press, 1992.

Smith, Joseph Daniel. "Gaius and the Controversy over the Johannine Literature." Ph.D. Dissertation. Yale University, 1979.

Snodgrass, Klyne. "'Western Non-Interpolations.'" *Journal of Biblical Literature* 91 (1972): 369–79.

Soards, Marion L. *The Passion According to Luke*. JSNTS Supplement Series, 14. Sheffield: JSOT Press, 1987.

———. "A Literary Analysis of the Origin and Purpose of Luke's Account of the Mockery of Jesus." In *New Views on Luke and Acts*, 86–93. Edited by Earl Richards. Collegeville, Minnesota: Michael Glazier, 1990.

———. "Tradition, Composition, and Theology in Luke's Account of Jesus Before Herod Antipas." *Biblica* 66 (1985): 344–63.

———. "Tradition, Composition and Theology in Jesus' Speech to the 'Daughters of Jerusalem' (Luke 23:26–32)." *Biblica* 68 (1987): 221-44.

Spitta, Friedrich. *Das Johannes-Evangelium als Quelle der Geschichte Jesu.* Göttingen: Vandenhoeck & Ruprecht, 1910.

Stagg, Frank. "Textual Criticism for Luke-Acts." *Perspectives in Religious Studies* 5 (1978):152–65.

Stanton, Graham. "The Fourfold Gospel." *New Testament Studies* 43 (1997):317–346.

Stein, Robert. *The Synoptic Problem.* Grand Rapids: Baker Book House, 1987

Stonehouse, Ned B. *The Apocalypse in the Ancient Church.* Goes (Holland): Oosterbaan & Le Cointre, 1929.

Streeter, B. H. *The Four Gospels.* London: MacMillan and Co., 1951.

Talbert, Charles H. *Luke and the Gnostics.* Nashville: Abingdon Press, 1966.

Tannehill, Robert. "The Disciples in Mark: The Function of a Narrative Role." *Journal of Religion* 57 (1977): 386–405.

———. *The Narrative Unity of Luke-Acts. A Literary Interpretation.* Volume 1: Luke. Philadelphia: Fortress Press, 1986.

Taylor, Vincent. *The Passion Narrative of St. Luke.* A Critical And Historical Investigation. Edited by Owen E. Evans. Cambridge: University Press, 1972.

———. *Behind the Third Gospel.* Oxford: Clarendon Press, 1911.

Teeple, Howard M. *The Literary Origin of the Gospel of John.* Evanston: Religion and Ethics Institute, Inc., 1974.

Thyen, Hartwig. "Aus der Literature zum Johannesevangelium." *Theologishes Rundshau.* various dates.

Todorov, T. *Mikhail Bakhtin: The Dialogical Principle.* Minneapolis: University of Minnesota Press, 1984.

Tolbert, Mary Ann. *Sowing the Gospel.* Minneapolis: Fortress Press, 1989.

Trites, Allison. "The Prayer Motif in Luke-Acts." In *Perspectives in Luke-Acts*, 168-86. Edited by Charles Talbert. Danville: Association of Baptist Professors of Religion, 1978.

Turner, C. H. "Note on ἐπιφωσκειν." *Journal of Theological Studies* 14 (1913): 188–90.

Turner, Nigel. *A Grammar of New Testament Greek.* Edited by James Hope Moulton. Volume IV, *Style.* Edinburgh: T&T Clark, 1976.

Tyson, Joseph. *The Death of Jesus in Luke-Acts.* Columbia: University of South Carolina Press, 1986.

———. "The Lukan Version of the Trial of Jesus." *Novum Testamentum* 3 (1959): 249–58.

Vielhauer, Philipp. "Jewish-Christian Gospels." In *New Testament Apocrypha*, 117–139. Edited by E. Hennecke, W. Schneemelcher and R. McL. Wilson, Philadelphia: Westminster, 1963.

Vogels, Heinrich Joseph. *Die Harmonistik im Evangelientext des Codex Cantabrigiensis.* Leipzig: J. C. Hinrich'sche Buchhandlung, 1910.

Vorster, Williem. "Intertextuality and Redaktionsgeschichte." In *Intertextuality in Biblical Writings*, 15–26. Edited by Sipke Draisma. Kampen: Uitgeversmaatschappij J. H. Kok, 1989.

von Wahlde, Urban C. *The Earliest Version of John's Gospel.* Wilmington, DE: Michael Glazier, 1989.

———. "The Johannine Jews: A Critical Survey." In *New Testament Studies* 28 (1982): 33–60.

Walasky, Paul W. "The Trial and Death of Jesus in the Gospel of Luke." *Journal of Biblical Literature* 94 (1975): 81–93.

Wanke, Joachim. *Die Emmauserzählung.* Leipzig: St. Benno-Verlag, 1973.

Weiβ, Bernhard. *Die Quellen des Lukasevangeliums.* Stuttgart und Berlin: J.G. Cotta'sche Buchhandlung Nachfolger, 1907.

Westcort, B. F. and F. J. A. Hort. *The New Testament in the Original Greek.* Two volumes. New York: MacMillan Co., 1929

Wickes, Dean Rockwell. *The Sources of Luke's Perean Section.* Chicago: University of Chicago Press, 1912.

Williams, C. S. C. *Alterations to the Text of the Synoptic Gospels and Acts.* Oxford: Basil Blackwell, 1951.

Windisch, Hans. *Johannes und die Synoptiker.* Leipzig: J.C. Hinrichs'sche Buchhandlung, 1926.

Winter, P. *On the Trial of Jesus.* Second edition. Studia Judaica 1. Berlin: de Gruyter, 1974.

Wright, Benjamin G., III. "Cerinthus apud Hippolytus: An Inquiry into the Traditions about Cerinthus's Provenance." *Second Century* 4 (1984): 103–15.

Zahn, Theodor. *Das Evangelium des Johannes.* Kommentar zum Neuen Testament. Leipzig: A. Deichertsche Verlagsbuchhandlung, 1921.

———. *Das Evangelium des Lucas.* Kommentar zum Neuen Testament. Leipzig: A. Deichertsche Verlagsbuchhandlung, 1920.

———. *Geschichte des Neutestamentlichen Kanons.* Erlangen: Verlag von Andreas Deichert, 1888.

Zehnle, Richard. "The Salvific Character of Jesus' Death in Lucan Soteriology." *Theological Studies* 30 (1969): 420–44.

Zurhellen, Otto. "Die Heimat des vierten Evangeliums." in *Theologische Arbeiten aus dem Rheinischen Wissenschaftlichen Prediger-Verein.* Volume 11: 33–92. Tübingen: J.C.B. Mohr (Paul Siebech), 1909.

Zwiep, A. W. "The Text of the Ascension Narratives (Luke 24:50–3; Acts 1:1–2, 9–11)." *New Testament Studies* 42 (1996): 219–44.

DATE DUE